Aleister Ros

The Life and Times of
William Shakespeare

also by Peter Levi

Poetry
The Gravel Ponds
Water, Rock and Sand
The Shearwaters
Fresh Water, Sea Water
Ruined Abbeys
Pancakes for the Queen of Babylon
Life is a Platform
Death is a Pulpit
Collected Poems
Five Ages
Private Ground
The Echoing Green

Prose
Beaumont
Mr Seferis' Tone of Voice
The Lightgarden of the Angel King
The English Bible (1534–1859)
In Memory of David Jones
John Clare and Thomas Hardy
The Noise made by Poems
The Hill of Kronos
Atlas of the Greek World
The Flutes of Autumn
A History of Greek Literature
The Frontiers of Paradise

Thrillers
The Head in the Soup
Grave Witness
Knit One, Drop One

Translations
Yevtushenko
Pausanias
Pavlopoulos, The Cellar
The Psalms
Marko the Prince (Serbo-Croat heroic verse)
Papadiamantis, The Murderess
The Holy Gospel of John: A New Translation

The Life and Times of
William Shakespeare

PETER LEVI

MACMILLAN
LONDON

First published 1988 by
MACMILLAN LONDON LIMITED
4 Little Essex Street London WC2R 3LF
and Basingstoke

Associated companies in Auckland, Delhi, Dublin, Gaborone,
Hamburg, Harare, Hong Kong, Johannesburg, Kuala Lumpur,
Lagos, Manzini, Melbourne, Mexico City, Nairobi, New York,
Singapore and Tokyo

Reprinted 1989

British Library Cataloguing in Publication Data
Levi, Peter
The life & times of William Shakespeare.
1. Shakespeare, William—Biography
2. Dramatists, English—Early modern,
1500–1700—Biography
I. Title
822.3'3   PR2894
ISBN 0–333–43584–2

Designed by Robert Updegraff
Typeset by Wyvern Typesetting Ltd, Bristol
Printed and bound in Great Britain by
Butler & Tanner Limited
Frome and London

Contents

FOR DEIRDRE

*To whom this book belongs
more than any other*

In paradisum
deducant te angeli,
in tuo adventu
suscipiant te martyres
et perducant te
in civitatem sanctam Jerusalem,
ut cum Lazaro quondam paupere
aeternam habeas requiem.

List of Illustrations

Map of Warwickshire from Michael Drayton's *Polyolbion*, with the 'Illustrations' or notes by John Selden, 1612   *endpapers*

Family trees   xiii–xv

Between pages   168–169

The Shakespeare coat of arms.

Shakespeare's Warwickshire: Saxton's map of 1576.

The Cotswold Games: frontispiece to *Annalia Dubrensia*.

William Shakespeare: the Chandos portrait.

The Droeshout portrait of Shakespeare.

An Elizabethan masque.

The Swan Theatre.

The Globe Theatre.

Titus Andronicus in performance, 1594.

A scene from *Antony and Cleopatra* in the First Folio, marked by the proofreader.

The First Folio list of leading actors in Shakespeare's plays.

Richard Tarlton.

Robert Armin.

Will Kemp.

Richard Burbage.

William Sly.

Michael Drayton.

Ben Jonson.

Henry Wriothesley, 3rd Earl of Southampton.

Queen Elizabeth I.

The Southampton monument.

The tomb of Alice, Countess of Derby.

Shakespeare's monument, Stratford-upon-Avon.

Pedigree of Shakespeare and Arden

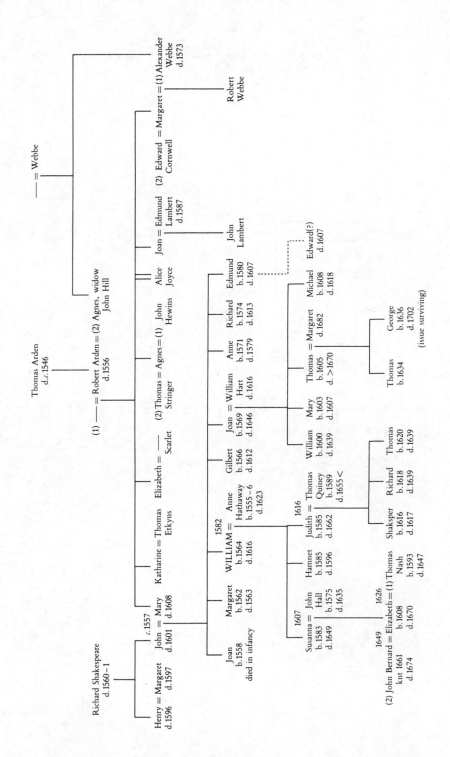

The Shakespeare – Quiney – Bushell – Greville – Winter –
Arden – Sheldon – Russell – Catesby – Tresham Connection

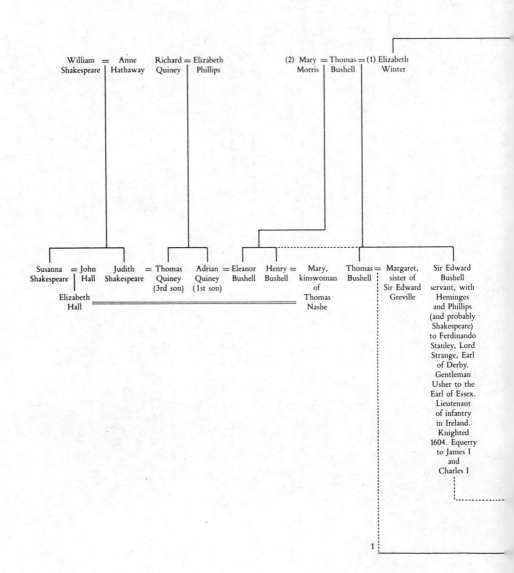

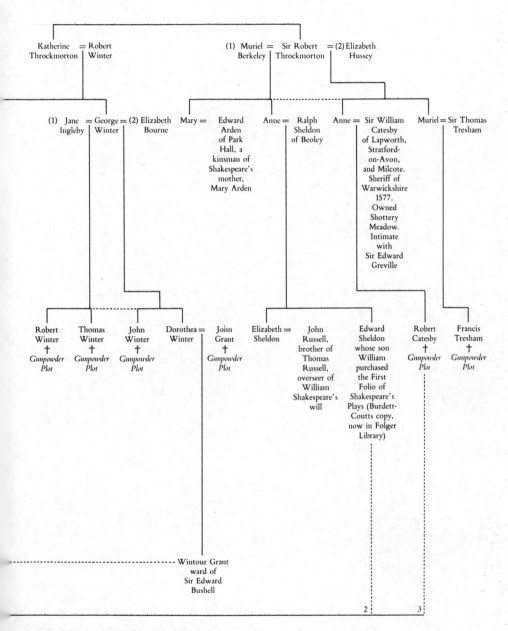

Katherine = Robert   (1) Muriel = Sir Robert = (2) Elizabeth
Throckmorton | Winter   Berkeley | Throckmorton Hussey

(1) Jane = George = (2) Elizabeth Mary = Edward   Anne = Ralph   Anne = Sir William   Muriel = Sir Thomas
Ingleby | Winter | Bourne   Arden   Sheldon   Catesby   Tresham
                                      of Park   of Beoley   of Lapworth,
                                      Hall, a   Stratford-
                                      kinsman of   on-Avon,
                                      Shakespeare's   and Milcote.
                                      mother,   Sheriff of
                                      Mary Arden   Warwickshire
                                                       1577.
                                                        Owned
                                                        Shottery
                                                       Meadow.
                                                        Intimate
                                                        with
                                                        Sir Edward
                                                        Greville

Robert   Thomas   John   Dorothea = John   Elizabeth = John   Edward   Robert   Francis
Winter   Winter   Winter   Winter   Grant   Sheldon   Russell,   Sheldon   Catesby   Tresham
†   †   †   †   brother of whose son †   †
Gunpowder *Gunpowder* *Gunpowder*   *Gunpowder*   Thomas   William   *Gunpowder* *Gunpowder*
Plot   *Plot*   *Plot*   *Plot*   Russell,   purchased   *Plot*   *Plot*
                                              overseer of the First
                                            William   Folio of
                                            Shakespeare's Shakespeare's
                                            will   Plays (Burdett-
                                                    Coutts copy,
                                                    now in Folger
                                                    Library)

Wintour Grant
ward of
Sir Edward
Bushell

2   3

Greville, Sheldon, and Catesby were also second cousins,
through their grandmothers, the three sisters Willington

Introduction

It is tempting to write about Shakespeare because he is not only the greatest but also the most interesting of the English poets. He has the most contradictions and the most to say. Admittedly, those who call for the biographies and local backgrounds of poets rather than for the pure liquor of their verses are a bit like the old His Master's Voice dog, peering in stupefaction down the horn of the gramophone. But history and family connection do as much to throw light on Shakespeare as a poet as academic criticism has done, and maybe more. The problem is that England and Stratford and the Elizabethan age are all somehow part of his great mystery, and all three are potently mythical. Every generation has to make its own attempt to get at the truth, and we shall not succeed unless we allow for the enormous differences that separate Shakespeare from our own world. Even the theatre, in which he seems to communicate so immediately, is ours and not his, and therefore a barrier as well as a link. We read Shakespeare in our own voices.

I want to put Shakespeare's poetry in the context of his life and times. It is some years since the last full-scale and critical biography of Shakespeare, and so much knowledge has now become available that bears on him, some of it even while I have been working on this book, that a new attempt to relate his life history to his work is obviously worth making. It is an axiom of method that the facts of his life, including the dates of his plays and poems, must be established as firmly as possible and without wishful thinking, before those facts can be related to his writings. One must not make up fantasies about the bank where the wild thyme blew. Many inspiring and misleading writers about Shakespeare impart to his characters and passages of his plays an experience of life they merely imagine, building conjecture on conjecture and cobweb on cobweb. Between severe critics and enthusiastic and conjectural biographers there is now a great gulf fixed. You cannot get at Shakespeare's life through fragments of cloudy glass chipped from his plays. His life and background must be studied separately, and only then will the relationship of his life and his work become clear. All the same, a great deal about both is knowable, and it is time to bring this mass of dispersed material together, as Dante says of the universe, *legato con amore in un volume*. This can no longer be done in terms of an academic treatise: there is simply too much material. But it can be done for the ordinary reader. In this book I have decided not to give detailed proofs, or to dispute any point needlessly, where the proofs are already easily available in the fifty or a hundred standard works of specialized scholarship on which all Shakespeare scholars rely. I have listed most of those at the end of the book, and have specially noted standard works in passing only where I differ from them.

But my experience has been that almost every writer about Shakespeare has at least a few grains to add to the general stock of knowledge. It is unlikely that anyone will ever again read all of them, there are so many. The last general study of all Shakespeare's critics, A. J. Ralli's *History of Shakespeare Criticism* (1932), was an extremely useful reference book, though a little too enthusiastic about Professor W. Raleigh, whose admittedly thrilling *Shakespeare* was written under the pressure of patriotic feeling, and of sympathy for a self-made man. That appeared in 1907. Since then books have proliferated, and fundamental views have slowly altered. I have tried to mention by name the writers I found helpful (sometimes to my surprise), and to avoid the pitfalls that every generation digs for itself. It appears to me that the greatest mistake is to ignore the intervening ages between us and Shakespeare, from every one of which we have received an influence, and to attempt a direct relationship with the Elizabethans. Something similar is true of the ancient Greeks and their poetry. There is no eternal England or eternal Greece, and however we pride ourselves on historical insight, the Victorians were closer to Shakespeare than we are: not as historians, but in their life, particularly in remote villages and small provincial towns. *The Dillen*, the dictated memoirs of a Victorian Stratford slum-dweller, throws some valuable light on Shakespeare. The eighteenth century was closer still. The possibilities of confusion without a serious study of history are so great that I believe there can be no standard critical biography of Shakespeare. Every attempt will be personal, but the more solidly it is based on historical fact the more useful it will be.

You will not really get to the bottom of *Hamlet* just by reading the text or by seeing it in the theatre. The text has a history, and one of the most thriving branches of the Shakespeare industry, and recently the most rewarding, has been the study of printers, printings and textual transmission. And the play has a context among other plays, and it prompts questions about Shakespeare's attitude to old plays and traditional styles. It is often thought to have some special relation to his private life. It raises the old and too much belaboured problem of Shakespeare's religion. Polonius is supposed by some critics to satirize a real person. What is to be said about the element of comedy in *Hamlet*? Has the play a political meaning? What are the sexual mores it takes for granted? Why is it so long? There are answers to all these questions I think. History throws more light on some plays than on others, and the same may be said of the light shed by Shakespeare's biography. It is almost more important to exclude false inferences from the life to the works than it is to bring the two into relation, but when one does relate them over the course of his lifetime, light begins to appear even where one had scarcely expected any.

Here is an example of the sort of inference one must exclude. Edgar Fripp, the indefatigable ransacker of Stratford records, discovered that in Shakespeare's boyhood a girl called Kathleen Hamlet was drowned in the river. She seems to have been fetching water for cattle and to have fallen in. But suicide was apparently not ruled out, though the inquest, which was long delayed, permitted Christian burial. Fripp thinks of Ophelia, and as he claims (for no good reason) that Shakespeare was employed in a local lawyer's office at the time, he is able to have young Shakespeare much affected. One might go further, which Edgar Fripp was too respectable to do. Suicide is in fact quite likely, and until modern times the usual reason for a young girl taking that course was pregnancy. Shakespeare was sixteen; we know that within a matter of months he got Ann Hathaway pregnant and had to marry her. Later he named his own son Hamnet, a form of the name Hamlet. When that son died, he wrote the play, in which the sexual relation between Hamlet and Ophelia is an unexplained theme, and sexual guilt a dominant theme. Game, set and match? But these conjectures will not do. The story of Hamlet is old, there were already revenge tragedies based on it, and the Ophelia character occurs in the early sources. Hamnet Shakespeare was named after Hamnet Sadler, his god-father, Shakespeare's friend. Of course the poet knew about the girl's death, but the name is common, and drownings were not uncommon in the untamed rivers of the past. The published biographies of Shakespeare are full of hasty attempts to build on conjecture of this kind, and I have tried to avoid them.

What about the Dark Lady of the Sonnets? I am not quite sure that Shakespeare wrote them about a real individual, and if he did so, he was careful she should not be easily identifiable. The sonnets are not a work of fiction as *A Lover's Complaint* is, because they do not have a coherent plot: what happened is always presupposed. It is possible that they are artificial variations on set themes; indeed it is certain that among other things they are that. But I am swayed by the simple consideration that Shakespeare is so much more exciting than the numerous other writers of English sonnets in his time just because he means what he says. If there really was a Dark Lady then A. L. Rowse is surely right about her. His candidate – Emilia Lanier – touches Shakespeare's life in London at more than one point; she was no better than she should be, and if her name had been recorded in some scrap of contemporary gossip about Shakespeare no one would have doubted the identification for a moment. Nonetheless, the right attitude to this interesting conjecture must rest on tactful and careful literary judgement about what kind of poems these sonnets are. It is clear enough that Shakespeare meant to keep the uninstructed reader guessing.

I have given these two examples as a foretaste of the kind of problem that every critical biographer of Shakespeare must confront. Scholars have come to favour a reductionist attitude, a minimal life of Shakespeare from which all rubbish, all romantic gossip and all mere conjecture is excluded. The most recent, most distinguished and severest example of this school is the careful but genially written *William Shakespeare: A Documentary Life* by Samuel Schoenbaum (1975, the *Compact Documentary Life*, 1977, being a revised and even more readable version). Still, there are things Schoenbaum leaves out and subjects he maltreats; his work is the most useful, but it is not perfect. An earlier attempt of the same kind survives in Tucker Brooke's *Shakespeare of Stratford* (1926), which is part of the Yale Shakespeare. Its motive is that one wants students to have all the ascertainable facts and nothing but the facts, but in reality facts and arguments overlap, and definitions of safe and unsafe areas in Shakespeare studies are not as clear as they look.

The short and late book by E. K. Chambers, *Sources for a Biography of William Shakespeare* (1946), is the thinnest of the three: he had already written a fully documented but incomplete biography subtitled *A Study of Facts and Problems* (1930), supplanting the essentially Victorian *Life* by Sir Sidney Lee (deputy editor of the *Dictionary of National Biography*), published in 1898 though not much altered in its third edition in 1922. Chambers in his lifework spans the change from accumulative to reductive scholarship. Modern science is said to depend often on Victorian accumulation, but there can be no science of Shakespeare. The subject still demands a process of accumulation and sorting, but it also demands rigorous reasoning. My feeling is that there is slightly more to be said than the scholarly establishment is at present saying, though the utterances of the rather vocal lunatic fringe are scarcely worth discussion.

It is implicit in this book that Mr William Shakespeare of Stratford wrote more or less the works normally attributed to him, though there is some margin for argument about a few cases. His works were not written by Bacon or Lord Oxford or any other contender. His contemporaries knew him as poet and as dramatist; he was not an obscure rustic genius, though his sense of country realities is much sharper than that of any of his contemporaries. His circle of friends extended into the nobility and country gentry, and the more research that is done, the further that circle is discovered to extend. No doubt there is always something mysterious about a poet, particularly a great poet, of whose juvenilia we have almost nothing. If we had, it would probably not be recognizable as Shakespeare's. There are special reasons for this which I shall discuss. But the argument for his genuine authorship of his own works is multiple and overwhelming, and every day's work I have spent in preparing to write about him has confirmed it.

I was brought up with an unusual view of the Elizabethans. Christopher Devlin was a master at Beaumont when I was a boy there, and later became a writer in a Jesuit house of studies where I lived in my early twenties. He was an enchanting man, and I find the memory of him now almost more inspiring than I found him then. It was he who directed me to Norman Ault's *Elizabethan Lyrics* (1949) and *Seventeenth Century Lyrics* (1950), and gave me the courage to write my first published article, which was in that area. But we saw the Elizabethans through Jesuit eyes. We wanted Robert Southwell, whose biography Christopher was writing, to be even greater than the great poet he was. Evelyn Waugh's *Edmund Campion* (1935) inspired us.

I had become a Jesuit partly under the influence of John Gerard's account of his sufferings in the Tower and his escape in 1597. A number of Jesuit scholars in those days were engaged in unravelling the labyrinthine plots and counterplots by which Lord Burghley and his son Robert Cecil sought to implicate and discredit Catholics. Admittedly, in my own small circle it was felt that the unravellers had become as crazy as the plots they unravelled; we were as cynical about Father Robert Persons as we were about the Cecils. But we were certainly unwilling to accept the established, establishment view of Elizabethan England. So far as Shakespeare is concerned, I think this background has been gain rather than loss to me. There is some virtue in an outsider's attitude to Elizabethan politics, so long as the outsider sees the insiders' points of view. The image of Shakespeare as an honorary insider, the national poet of a golden or heroic age of English history, is overdue for demolition.

The views I shall express about history, economic history, theatrical and social history are taken from standard works, which are mostly up to date, except, inevitably, for the Victoria County Histories, in some ways the most useful pillaging place of all. For Queen Elizabeth and many minor characters I found the *Dictionary of National Biography* helpful and suggestive. I have not reread any Jesuit books except Christopher Devlin's *Robert Southwell* (1956), and his *Hamlet's Divinity* (1963), an uneven but fascinating collection of essays. I have come to admire the Queen and to feel compassion for her, though I still feel bleakly about the Cecils, for all their ruthless wisdom and near genius at politics. It may be a legacy of youth, but I simply cannot help preferring losers, as Shakespeare perhaps did. 'The secrets of princes', wrote William Camden the historian (1551–1623), 'are an inextricable labyrinth. . . . Who can dive into the secret meanings of princes? Wise men do keep their thoughts locked up within the closets of their breasts.' That goes for Shakespeare. The fact that he lived in an age of violent vengeances, panic fears and appalling risks, when it was out of the question to say anything serious about religion or the state, an age of constant suppression, goes far towards explaining why it is that whatever he did express emerged with such energy, like water breaking out of a rock. I think it is relevant that a student at Cambridge with Christopher Marlowe might have lived to see in his old age the King's head taken off at Whitehall: the only Stuart masque in which something really happened.

No doubt every age gets the Shakespeare it deserves or secretly desires. The Elizabethans knew of his 'sugared sonnets for his private friends', they knew he was a personal poet and they sang his songs. In the theatre they had an entire artillery barrage of great plays, and constant changes of style, incomparable verse and inexhaustible energy. They had the assurance that he was on their side, as progressives used to think of Bertrand Russell and melancholy intellectuals of T. S. Eliot. The Stuart audiences still enjoyed a startling fireworks display. We have from Dryden the evidence of John Hales (speaking about 1635) that 'the Age wherein he liv'd, which had contemporaries with him *Fletcher* and *Jonson*, never equall'd them to him in their esteem: And in the last King's Court when *Ben's* reputation was at its highest, *Sir John Suckling*, and with him the greater part of the Courtiers, set our *Shakespeare* far above him.' For Dryden he was the ultimate English classic, the poet one must strive to revive, 'the *Homer*, or Father of our Dramatick Poets.' The Civil War was an abyss the depth of which it is hard to exaggerate. It made Shakespeare seem a distant and a haloed figure. The eighteenth century got the Shakespeare Pope and Lord Bathurst imagined for the monument in Westminster Abbey. The romantic cult of Shakespeare at Stratford began then. The gap between his genuineness on the page, slowly established by two hundred years of scholars until now, and his falseness in production after the Civil War, has narrowed only slowly. I have sometimes feared it was beginning to widen again, but in the theatre the taking of liberties is the price of life.

Every age gets the version not only of Shakespeare but of Shakespeare's England that it deserves. The Shakespeare's England of the two large volumes with that title, inspired by Professor Raleigh and published in 1917, errs on the heroic side. It contains many crumbs of information, but it is really too Merry Englandish. Today historians are divided. Hugh Trevor-Roper's common-sense minimal case for the Elizabethan establishment seems to me convincing, and I have been stirred, entertained and delighted by A. L. Rowse on the subject of Puritans. But the populist historians, who are usually to some degree Marxist, have telling points to make about enclosures, about the wilder fringes of religion, and about what went wrong. England was a suppressed ferment, and if suffering could be quantified the human cost of the Queen's reign would be seen to be high. Leaving aside the torture of individuals, the burnings and guttings and hangings and the rest of it, the plight of the ordinary poor and the aged was serious enough. England had seen two big changes of religion under Henry VIII, if one includes his conservative period at the end of his life, then another with Edward VI, another more violent still with Mary, and a significant change of policy in midstream under Elizabeth. Small wonder that the reformers were out of control. Small wonder that when the Elizabethan curate of Henley in Arden heard that a French marriage might be imminent, bringing yet another change of rules, he shaved off his beard to be ready for it. The problem of enclosures of common land is even more important, but I can deal with it only locally, as it arises. There is fundamental research still to be done on this subject: what holds for one parish does not necessarily hold for another. It all has a bearing on the life of Shakespeare.

The history of English poetry in the given period is an easier matter, partly because of the largely magisterial study by C. S. Lewis in his *English Literature in the Sixteenth Century Excluding Drama* (1954), but also because of the swarm of scholars that Shakespeare's greatness attracts to every subject in his vicinity. In the course of preparing this book I have come to admire Saintsbury's *History of Elizabethan Literature* (1887) for its delicacy of intuition and certainty of touch. I expected little from it, but I would now put it high on the list of treatments of this subject. Another advantage that Elizabethan poetry has is that most of it is so easy to read and so easily available in libraries. How strange it is to think that no town can have been so combed over for survivals as Stratford, no records so much consulted, no individual so stalked and hunted from archive to archive as Shakespeare, and yet simply by reading Elizabethan writers one can throw constant light on him, and even make one's own small but fresh discoveries and analogies. Shakespeare wrote a lot for one man, though all in little more than twenty years. Today there are probably more leads for a student of his work to follow, and more resources of research to master, than one person's lifetime can encompass.

St Catherine's College, Oxford
14 March 1988

The Background

In the April of 1565 Pierre Ronsard was the greatest living poet in any language, and the polar star of the French renaissance, on which the later English renaissance depends. He was forty years old. As a boy he had been page to the Dauphin, and then to the Princess Madeleine, who in 1537 became Queen of Scotland; his name is to be found in the accounts of the Lord Treasurer to James V. This adventure did not last long, and just before his fourteenth birthday he was back in France, though he revisited Scotland that same December. As a young man, he met Rabelais. Later in life he wrote poems for Mary Stuart when she was Queen of France. In 1565 he dedicated his *Elegies Mascardes et Bergeries* to Elizabeth, the Queen of England. It was to celebrate a peace between the two countries attained at last by two queens which so many kings and wars had failed to attain: a charming and a diplomatic thought, but only loosely related to the realities of politics.

Part One of Ronsard's *Bocage Royal*, in the collected works which he put together in 1584, the year before his death, contains a 'Discours' to Queen Elizabeth, followed by another (to the same) on a prophecy of Merlin. The date of these two poems is uncertain, but if the first was written in or before 1564, as seems likely, it contains a remarkable prophecy. The 'Discours' opens with a compliment to Elizabeth's beauty, which if it is like that of Mary Queen of Scots entails two suns in one island; then comes a charming fantasy about Britain having been a floating island like Delos, sometimes gambolling off like a lamb to play on the Breton coast, sometimes wandering among the Orkneys. Proteus the prophet begs it from Neptune, who chops off a piece of France to make it an anchor. Proteus then prophesies in a long speech about the virtues of the island.

Topographic poetry was not uncommon in the sixteenth century, and this is not quite the first about England, but it is certainly better than the 'Song of the Swan' by Leland, the official antiquary to Henry VIII – 699 hendecasyllables in Latin giving a swan's-eye view of the Thames from Oxford to the sea, fortunately published with a commentary on the place-names, which occur in the text in Latinized imaginary Anglo-Saxon forms of fiendish obscurity. Ronsard is too wily to use English place-names on any scale, so one is not always certain whereabouts one is in his poem, but it has a magical enchantment. I think his swans on the Thames at Windsor might be Leland's swans remodelled.

Only Bacchus is unfriendly: the English will never grow grapes, but Ceres grants the gift of a new drink:

> Non corrosif, ny violent, ny fort,
> Trouble-cerveau, ministre de la mort,
> Mais innocent à la province Angloise,
> Et de Ceres sera nommé Cervoise,
> Qui se pourra si gracieux trouver
> Que tes voisins s'en voudront abreuver.

From beer he moves to mines of gold, of silver and of tin refined by the nymphs underground, then to strong horses and flocks of sheep, 'as white as milk, whose fleece the Moon covets'. But the astonishing prophecy comes at the end.

> Soon the proud Thames shall see
> A flock of white swans nesting on his grass,
> his holy guests, they mount to the heavens
> in circles over those delightful banks
> uttering song, which is the certain sign
> that many a Poet, and the heavenly troop
> of sister Muses quitting Parnassus
> shall take it for their gracious dwelling place,
> to tell the famous praise of England's Kings
> unto the crowded nations of the world.

On 26 April 1564 William Shakespeare, the son of John and Mary Shakespeare, was baptized in the parish church of Stratford-upon-Avon, Warwickshire. Children were normally baptized on the third day after birth, so he was born on St George's Day, 23 April; and he died on the same day of the month in 1616. It is worth delaying a little longer over the England, the Stratford and the moment of history in which he was born.

When Elizabeth came to the throne in November 1558 at the age of twenty-five, she was forced to tread extremely delicately. The year 1485 had brought the dynastic wars to an end, but in the sixteenth century the succession to the throne remained uneasy. There were plots, beheadings and rebellions. The old nobility still had great prestige and some power, but it was terribly thinned out at the top. Three dukes had been beheaded in the early 1550s; only one was left alive – the Duke of Norfolk, whom Elizabeth beheaded in 1572 because he was named as a possible new husband for Mary, Queen of Scots. There were no dukes at all from that moment until the creation of the Duke of Buckingham in the next century.

Nine bishoprics were vacant at Elizabeth's accession, and within a month three more. Cardinal Pole, who was not only papist but of royal blood as well, had also died, so at least the slate was cleaner than it might have been. Still, no bishop would crown her but the Bishop of Carlisle. She had the matter debated, and only Llandaff submitted; she put the rest of them into the Tower, whence they emerged crestfallen.

Her nearest relatives were Henry Carey, Lord Hunsdon, her harmless first cousin through Ann Boleyn; and Mary Stuart, the Queen of Scots, nine years her junior and her likeliest heir. Every marriage proposed to her was politically dangerous: Philip of Spain, the Duke of Alençon, the Earl of Leicester and so on. She settled uneasily for a succession of youthful gallants whom she kept at a distance, saying 'This shall be for me sufficient, that a marble stone shall declare that a Queen, having reigned such a time, died a virgin.' She could trust no one at all but Lord Burghley, on whom she came to rely more heavily while he slowly removed his rivals one by one, and she discredited every policy that he opposed. There is no doubt at all that Burghley was a Machiavellian politician, the centre of a vast private spy service, a faker of evidence and a manipulator of *agents provocateurs*, but he was a kind of genius, and he served the Queen well.

The first year of Elizabeth's reign was the first since Henry VIII without massacre or rebellion or disaster. The hostile bishops were deposed, English services took the place of Latin, and peace with France was negotiated. All the same, by 1 November tapers and a silver crucifix had reappeared in the Queen's private chapel. When she was offered temporary control of Dieppe and Le Havre she wanted to keep them, but in 1563 peace with France was confirmed, and for a time she tried to keep that peace. She never travelled beyond Bristol and the southern Midlands. She had no ambition, virtually no foreign policy, and she hated war because it was expensive. Both before and after her time England played at the top table of European politics, but under Elizabeth the English situation was one of defiant piracy and despair. The cultural renaissance scarcely took hold until the 1590s. The first English *virtuoso*, a fellow of New College, Oxford, published his book in 1598. When Burghley or any other nobleman drew up instructions for young kinsmen travelling abroad, they suggested observation of agriculture, industry and government, with no mention of art or architecture. Yet in 1561 Lady Catherine Grey went to the Tower for her clandestine marriage to Lord Hertford, and Lady Lennox for practising magic.

The Queen was a reluctant murderess, but her Court was full of dark corners and deadly rumours, and a kind of paranoia possessed Court and country alike. 'All men are evil,' said Walter Ralegh, 'and will declare themselves to be so when occasion is offered.' 'Depart from your enemies,' said the Bible, 'yea, and beware of your friends.' A conspiracy theory of social relations reinforced a conspiracy theory of politics. The success of the Jesuit mission to England, the fear at Court of the wild and enraged Catholics who might be lurking in the countryside, the threat from Spain, from the Pope and from Mary Stuart as presumptive heir to the Crown, made it imperative to end the uneasy tolerance of her first years and to try to wipe out the diehard Catholics, to make life impossible for their priests, and at the same time to control anti-episcopal Puritans, who were the first blast of the trumpet against all authority, monarchy included. The first missionary priest was caught in 1577, thirteen more entered England illegally in 1578, twenty-one in 1579 and twenty-nine in 1580, with the Jesuits Robert Persons and Edmund Campion, formerly fellows of Balliol and St John's respectively. Campion was a transparently innocent man, quite without any taint of treason. He was caught in the machinery of the Elizabethan state, and in him one of the greatest English writers of that or any age, one of its most sparkling characters and a saint, perished by hanging, drawing and quartering in the early winter of 1581. Catholics at that time were officially disarmed, and yet a Warwickshire gentleman like Ralph Sheldon of the famous tapestries bought gunpowder by the barrel and had his rapier regularly sharpened.

In the 1580s the persons commissioned to question prisoners under torture were Richard Topcliffe – whose zeal for hunting out recusants gave the word 'topcliffizare' to Court language – Richard Young and the young Francis Bacon. When Robert Southwell refused to crack in Topcliffe's hands, Robert Cecil went along out of curiosity to see him being tortured. The famous scholar John Selden remarks in his *Table Talk*, probably in 1628, 'The rack is used nowhere as in England ... here in England, they take a man and rack him I do not know why, nor when, not in time of Judicature, but when somebody bids.' In the case of the assassin Felton, tried in that year, the judges answered that 'No such punishment is known or allowed by our law.' We have no need therefore to discuss the whipping of the mad or the baiting of bears or any other of the commonplace barbarities of the day to establish that Elizabethan life had a side darker than we allow ourselves to imagine. Topcliffe and Bacon were determined to succeed in that world, and they did so.

It was a world in which those who were frantic to rise high, the 'new men' one might call them, did so by alliance, by treachery, by intrigue and by financial corruption on an extraordinary scale. In this last the Queen and her courtiers took part with enthusiasm. Elizabeth gave away about 200 pieces of plate a year, which was precisely weighed and easily valued. Among other presents, she was given in 1577 'a tooth and ear pick being a dolphin enamelled', and in 1579 'a toothpick of gold made gun-fashioned'. In the year 1605 James I spent £2530 at two jewellers. Their system was a parody or corrupted version of a society bonded by loyalty and patronage, in which honour, with public display and the exchange of presents, was the greatest good, and shame, including obscurity, the worst disaster: in a sense a premonetary society which social upheavals had shaken and money values colonized.

An older world survived in nooks and corners of the provinces, for instance in the Forest of Arden. In the Middle Ages Coventry had been an important town with a royal mint, but it paid half its dues to the King in honey; even in 1500 the town's proudest treasure was the relic of a prehistoric boar of huge size. There were still maypoles, games and country dances, with music of many kinds. Philip Sidney heard a blind ballad-singer from Northamptonshire sing 'Chevy Chase' at Chipping Norton. As a boy at Polesworth, further north, the poet Michael Drayton heard a Welsh harper called Hew. He dedicated his own ballad *The Bataille of Agincourt* (1627) to Welsh harpers.

In Shakespeare's youth chimneys were only beginning to be added to the old hall houses, so that they could be subdivided into upper storeys and three downstairs rooms – a parlour, a cool dairy and a kitchen. Until that happened, and no doubt for long afterwards, halls were places of substantial hospitality and popular entertainment. A little later the gentry heard stringed instruments in the chamber, or withdrawing chamber (hence 'drawing room'), while the village people danced in the great hall to the music of bagpipes. Robert Armin, who was Shakespeare's fool after 1600, writes of such a house. In smaller halls everyone came together with no worries about social class. Their accent was the same: Walter Ralegh spoke broad Devonshire and Shakespeare's accent was much like Dr Johnson's, only broader.

Farms overlapped into houses and the households overlapped into the air outside. Men and boys spent most of their time out of doors or working. The roads were miry and the rivers ungoverned. Everyone could ride, everyone had an eye for a horse or a hawk. Everyone was familiar with freezing cold, with physical hard work, and at least with the sight of all the operations of agriculture: milking, shearing, ploughing, harvest and so on.

Big houses had their fools – usually not professional jesters but village naturals on first-name terms with their masters. As late as the seventeenth century the Countess of Arundel, the first English subject to be painted by Rubens, was painted with her fool and her dog. Dogberry the Constable and Justice Shallow in his orchard are drawn from life. The Vicar of Temple Grafton, near Stratford, of whose ramshackle church a photograph hangs on the west wall of the spruce Victorian edifice which has replaced it, was famous for his ability to cure sick birds – hawks, perhaps. As late as the Civil War, a squire with a pack of hounds rode straight between the lines of two armies drawn up for battle. The armies restrained themselves until the fox, the hounds and the squire had got clear, and then the battle started.

John Selden remarked over dinner, 'There was never a merry world since the fairies left dancing, and the parson left conjuring. The opinion of the latter kept thieves in awe, and did as much good in a country as a Justice of Peace.' There was indeed a *douceur de vivre* that survived in the country: the pastoral nostalgia of the Elizabethans was not without a genuine basis. Izaak Walton was conscious of it, and one can sense it in the lives of Richard Hooker and George Herbert, who set up an altar in his church at Bemerton instead of a table, and a maypole at the church door.

For all this however, country life was not without violence, and it was infested with economic troubles of several kinds. A bankrupt estate where nothing had altered for a hundred years might then change hands six times in thirty-five years. Falling profits, unemployment and high prices were bound to have disastrous social effects. Much has been written recently about the evil of enclosures, which directly affect our interpretation of Shakespeare's attitudes; but as the economic historian Joan Thirsk has wisely pointed out, 'It seems that enclosures were scapegoats for other more immediate ills.' Warwickshire was not a prosperous county: it had sixteen markets, whereas poor Oxfordshire had only thirteen and frozen Derbyshire only ten, but Kent and Suffolk had thirty-three each and Lincolnshire (still undrained) had thirty-seven.

Nonetheless, class mobility was swifter in the sixteenth century than it later became. Old Spencer, the direct ancestor of today's Princess of Wales, was a shepherd who began buying land in Warwickshire in 1506; his principal asset was that he knew where the best grazing lay. As he bought land so he bred sheep. Sir John Spencer in Shakespeare's lifetime had fourteen thousand head; his son married into one of the richest families in Northamptonshire, and his descendant into the family of the Earl of Southampton, Shakespeare's patron. Southampton's looks and a certain trick of the eyes are recognizable in the Princess of Wales.

The biggest step towards class mobility however was the withering away of serfdom, which in 1549 was still a lively enough issue for Robert Kett and his sixteen thousand fellow rebels to blockade Norwich, demanding 'that all bond men may be made free, for God made all free with his precious blood shedding'. As late as 1575 the Queen granted compulsory liberation to two hundred Crown bondsmen, and then to another hundred; these men were the serflike equivalent of tenant farmers and had to pay a third of the value of their lands and goods. Sir Thomas Smith, in his study of the Tudor constitution *De republica Anglorum* (posthumously published, 1583), wrote of slaves that there were none, and of bondsmen that 'so few there be that it is not almost worth the speaking'. The system that replaced bondage was tenantry by copyhold, which could at times be precarious – particularly in Warwickshire, it appears. When bondage ceased, economic forces took over; it was the end of bondage that made the Poor Laws necessary.

And yet consider the good yeoman's happy life in Sir Thomas Overbury's *Characters* (1614):

He never sits up late but when he hunts the badger, the vowed foe of his lambs; nor uses he any cruelty but when he hunts the hare; nor subtlety but when he setteth snares for the snipes and pitfalls for the blackbird; nor oppression but when, in the month of July, he goes to the next river and shears his sheep. He allows of honest pastime, and thinks not the bones of the dead anything bruised or the worse for it though the country lasses dance in the churchyard after Evensong. His good news is a hawk's nest on his own ground or a colt foaled from a good strain.

Sir Thomas was a Warwickshireman, born in 1581 in Compton-Scorpion. Shakespeare probably knew the Overbury family; his aunt had lived in their village. He certainly knew this kind of farmer.

One of Shakespeare's most obvious attractions is that no other poet has given us so fresh, so lyrical and so sharp a sense of the English countryside in all weathers. He was born in a sleepy country town just round the corner from the cattle market (called Rothermarket). Many of the houses were thatched and had no chimneys, only a hole in the roof. The town was so full of elm trees that it must have looked and sounded like a woodland settlement. For example, Mr Gibbs's house on Rothermarket had twelve elms in the garden and six in front of the door. Thomas Attford in Ely Street had another twelve. The town boundaries were marked by elms or groups of elms, the last of which survives as the name of a public house. The Rothermarket was on the edge of town because that is where cattle had to be slaughtered. The smell must have been disgusting and the noise amazing. The council had trouble with dungheaps in the street and pigs loose in the alleys. As late as the nineteenth century you could tell the height of the river by the smell as you came from the opposite direction.

The River Avon was an important social boundary. North of it lay Arden, and south of it Fielden. Arden means 'the woods', so Forest of Arden says the same thing twice. Arden and Fielden divide Warwickshire, and Stratford is one of the most important bridges. The first stone bridge was built by Sir Hugh Clopton of Clopton Manor, a mile from Stratford, who was Lord Mayor of London in 1491, a rich and childless man. He also built in 1483 the grand house called New Hall which Shakespeare later bought and died in. It continued to be thought of as a grand house: the Queen stayed there when the royalists held Stratford in the Civil War. Nothing is now left of New Hall apart from some foundations in a garden, but the bridge is too useful to be allowed to fall down. It had to be repaired in Shakespeare's lifetime, and again in the Civil War when the parliamentary army broke down one of its arches. In the days of trams it was called the tram bridge. Today it carries some of the most terrifying traffic in the Midlands; it is better to go round by Bidford or Welford, where bridges that Shakespeare knew were recorded by 1572. Given these bridges, the social difference between Arden and Fielden may seem surprising, yet it was great. Arden in Shakespeare's day still had to import food from Fielden. Fielden was rich, Arden poor; Fielden was Protestant and Arden a lurking place of mad squires of extreme conservatism, the seed-ground of the Gunpowder Plot.

Arden is still hilly and wooded, though many of its villages are now superior suburbs for the managing class of the great Midland industries. Only the ghost of its charm remains, because that belongs to the landscape. The woodwork in the church at Aston Cantlow, and in Holy Trinity, Stratford, itself, and the great beams of Snitterfield church, bear witness to a forest culture. The King's House in Rothermarket, once presumably used by the King's officials, was a tavern in Shakespeare's time, and a contemporary inventory shows that it still used wooden platters. Arden was so conservative that at the end of the seventeenth century it formed an association of gentry called the Bowmen of Arden, which to this day plays matches with the Queen's Bodyguard in Scotland. People still belong to it by hereditary right.

The Shakespeares came from Arden. When John Shakespeare, the poet's father, moved to Stratford, he lived, and his son was born, on the edge of town in Henley Street, the road that led to Henley in Arden. There he dealt (illegally) in wool, close to the Rothermarket. He must certainly have known the Spencers.

Shakespeare's Arden connection explains the conundrum of a rhyme about the local villages traditionally attributed to him. Rhymes of this kind are numerous in many languages, and comic or satirical proverbs about neighbouring villages are commoner still.

> Piping Pebworth, Dancing Marston,
> Haunted Hilborough, Hungry Grafton,
> Dodging Exhall, Papist Wixford,
> Beggarly Broom and Drunken Bidford.

The insults are not uninteresting: haunted, hungry, dodging, papist, beggarly and drunken. They offer a coherent view at least. But Pebworth and Marston are complimented – they sound jollier places. A look at the map reveals that Pebworth and Marston are in Fielden, and the other six villages are in the woods, north of the river, in Arden. So the rhyme was probably written by a Marston man (Pebworth gets in for alliteration), certainly by a Fielden man, certainly not by Shakespeare.

Stratford-upon-Avon was not only a bridge town and a market town but a meeting of important roads. As its name suggests, the main road was once Roman, and the river was fordable when it was not in flood. From Stratford there are two simple roads to London across the Cotswolds, one by Edgehill and Banbury and perhaps Tring, the other by Oxford. Local taxi drivers are in no doubt that the Banbury route, which passes Long Grendon where Dogberry was the local constable, is the shortest, but Shakespeare seems often to have used the Oxford route, probably because at Oxford there were books. North of Stratford the roads fan out through Arden. Crossing the Avon northwards, in Shakespeare's time and long after, one entered a more innocent and traditional England: Dr Johnson's Lichfield was not far away, nor were the favourite fishing waters of Izaac Walton and Charles Cotton. When Falstaff marches to the Battle of Shrewsbury in *Henry IV, Part 1* he takes the main Roman road northwards from London as far as Daventry, then cuts west across wilder country that avoids the Cotswolds, passing through villages which are now part of Birmingham. Shakespeare knew this route perfectly well, because Welsh drovers used it.

The Avon has tributaries north of Coventry; it runs down through Stratford and Evesham to the western sea. Very few miles away from Kenilworth, which sits on a tributary of the Avon just above Stratford, a fantail of streams runs northwards together, into the Trent and so to the eastern sea. Warwickshire really is the heart of England, as Michael Drayton said.

In 1612, in the thirteenth book of his topographic epic poem *Poly-Olbion*, Drayton published his description of Warwickshire. It is worth a glance, because people sometimes imagine that Shakespeare, as a lyric poet, exaggerated the natural qualities of the place. I doubt whether Drayton wrote under his influence, being a Warwickshire man himself and having all England to cover. His central mythical figure is Guy of Warwick, the great knight who became a hermit in the woods. It was the most famous local myth and had a deep influence on Shakespeare, among others:

> Upon the Mid-lands now th'industrious Muse doth fall;
> That Shire which we the Heart of *England* well may call . . .
> Muse, first of *Arden* tell, whose footsteps yet are found
> In her rough wood-lands more than any other ground:
> That mighty Arden held even in her height of pride,
> Her one hand touching *Trent*, the other *Severne's* side.

The very sounds of these names wake the wood nymphs, and the Forest makes a speech about herself. Drayton is more awkward than Ronsard, but he is fully of shaggy, warm-hearted feelings:

> We equally partake with woodland as with plain,
> Alike with hill and dale; and every day maintain
> The sundry kinds of beasts upon our copious wastes,
> That men for profit bread, as well as those of chase.
> Here *Arden* of herself ceased any more to show;
> And with her sylvan joys the Muse along doth go.
> When Phoebus lifts his head out of the Winter's wave,
> No sooner doth the Earth her flowery bosom brave,

> At such time as the year brings on the pleasant Spring,
> But Hunts-up to the Morn the feather'd *Sylvans* sing:
> And in the lower grove, as on the rising knole,
> Upon the highest spray of every mounting pole,
> Those Quiristers are perched with many a speckled breast.

The verses about birdsong that follow are as clear and loud as the birds themselves. We must realize that it was ordinary for Drayton and Shakespeare to hear a dawn chorus of many hundreds of birds at once, and ordinary in summer to hear nightingales. Those were numerous in the elm avenues of Christ Church Meadow even in the late nineteenth century; as a young man thirty years ago I have heard a deafening dawn chorus in the wooded Chilterns, on Shakespeare's road to London. Drayton's birds are not scientifically but they are observantly noted, and they are very pleasing. On the word *Merle* he notes, 'Of all Birds, only the *Blackbird* whistleth.'

> The *Throstell*, with shrill sharps, as purposely he sang
> T' wake the listless Sun; or chiding, that so long
> He was in coming forth, that should the thickets thrill;
> The *Woosell* near at hand, that hath a golden bill. . . .
> Upon his dulcet-pipe, the *Merle* doth only play
> When in the lower brake, the *Nightingale* hard-by,
> In such lamenting strains the joyful hours doth ply,
> As though the other birds she to her tunes would draw. . . .

He goes on to Linnet, Woodlark, Reedsparrow, Nope, Redbreast and Wren, Yellowpate, Goldfinch, Tydie, Hecco and Jay. (The Hecco I take to be a cuckoo, the Nope and Tydie are the bullfinch and some unknown small bird with 'notes as delicate' as a finch.) The verse bounds happily along through a discourse on wild deer, a description of a hunt, the hermit gathering herbs and their uses for medicine.

> But from our Hermit here the Muse we must inforce,
> And zealously proceed in our intended course.

Warwickshire contained a lot of monastic land. By 1558 the Southamptons had bought twenty per cent of the old monastic manors, and paid in cash for half of them. The father of Shakespeare's Lord Southampton was lord of the manor of Snitterfield where John Shakespeare was born. But in the poet's lifetime the dominant influence at Stratford was that of the Greville and the Lucy families.

The lord of the manor of Stratford, a rapacious individual much hated by the town council, was Sir Edward Greville, who lived nearby at Milcote. Clopton influence was waning, because the Cloptons were Catholic. Fulke Greville the poet (later Lord Brooke) boasted once that Shakespeare had been his servant, though he probably meant only that Shakespeare had acted in his house, which is likelier in London than in the country. The Grevilles had more than one house: Fulke Greville was heir to Beauchamp Place, a very grand house, which his father had acquired by marriage.

The Lucy house is Charlecote, which survives. One must think away Capability Brown's waterworks and the classic bridge, and realize that there was no deer park; then it was a house in a warren, a preserve of rabbits and other small animals, with trees growing close to the house. It still has rabbits, but whatever few wild deer it may have known in Shakespeare's time, the park with its wonderful-looking animals came later.

The kind of community Stratford was in the sixteenth century appears more easily from nineteenth-century photographs than it does from the carefully preserved or deliberately restored buildings the visitor mostly goes to see today. A hundred years ago it still had a tannery, and children ran to see a dancing bear (they learned to 'dance' by standing on hot iron). There were migrant, seasonal workers and an annual Mop fair, when an ox was roasted in Rothermarket. 'Old is poor and poor is starving' ran a proverb. People would remember an especially bad winter or a flood of the Avon all their lives. They believed in ghosts – or more than half believed – and they were superstitious. 'It's a queer plant, parsley: sow on Good Friday, seven times down to Hell before it chits.' 'These two growed lovely parsley, it went to show, folks said, what a God-fearing old couple they was.' This is the Dillen talking. He goes on to record that one night out eel-fishing he met a great swarm of eels migrating across a field. He was amazed, and sickened by the slaughter that ensued. At Yarnton near Oxford twenty years ago they knew all about that night, which comes once a year. They wait for it, for the annual ambush.

In Shakespeare's time the majestic progress of the seasons would have been even more strongly punctuated by such events, and by holy days and summonings of bells. Holy Trinity, the parish church, is said to have had bells taken from Hales Abbey not far to the south. Later surveys carefully recorded the weight of bell-metal. A hundred years ago or so, Stratford still had a morning work-bell at six and a curfew bell at eight, muffled mourning bells, service bells and fire bells; all these were rung at the Guild Chapel, the medieval centre of Stratford and its physical centre.

The importance of the Guild Chapel is that the Guild became the corporation of Stratford. It built the grammar school which King Edward VI only formally refounded, it hired and fired, and it regulated the town's affairs. Its council chamber is still to be seen in the grammar school building, with the painted crucifixion whitewashed over once but now just hazily to be seen on the wall. The Guild Chapel had a vigorous and blood-curdling Doomsday painting, scrubbed off and painted over by orders from on high in John Shakespeare's time as a small town official. Shakespeare never saw it, of course, and his father, as Chamberlain, will not have been

11

proud of the whitewashing. Great black wooden angels like human birds were removed at the same time, I suppose. In the museum where they now live they are extremely unexpected: like migrant angels from Suffolk.

John Shakespeare's official life centred on the Guildhall. His private life centred on the two houses side by side which he owned in Henley Street. No one knows which of the two he bought first. One was demolished long ago, so the surviving one was picked on for restoration and is conventionally accepted (though it might as easily have been the other) as the house where Shakespeare was born.

Still, there is a lot to be learned from the houses in Stratford associated with Shakespeare; what survives gives quite a clear idea of the kind of place Stratford was, and the kind of houses the Shakespeares had – the relative size of things, the crooked upper floors and the flagstones polished by feet. Providing one is not too literal-minded, and if one retains one's good humour about the Shakespearean Disneyland aspect of Stratford, one can sense the bones of the old place and observe what remains of its former life. Beyond what used to be the Hilton Hotel, in a loop or backwater of the canal, one gets a clear view of the country across some rough, marshy ground which is a sanctuary for wild swans. The view of Stratford church at sunset from the fields near Clifford Chambers is thrilling. Drayton used to spend the summer there with the Rainsfords; he wrote an elegy on Sir Henry Rainsford in 1621 or 1622, and was still visiting the house ten years later: to Drummond of Hawthornden, a charming and grossly underestimated poet with a face like an Elizabethan mouse that has smelt cheese, Drayton wrote from Clifford Chambers in 1631 of 'a Knight's house in Gloucestershire to which Place I yearly use to come, in the Summer Time, to recreate myself, and to spend some two or three months in the country'. Sir Henry Rainsford married Anne Goodere, the heroine of Drayton's early verse, only in 1595. Her family were lords of the manor near the village where Drayton was born, on the far north-eastern edge of Warwickshire. Shakespeare undoubtedly knew the Rainsfords, and knew that walk to Clifford Chambers from boyhood. He knew the vast rectory, a more impressive half-timbered house than what survives in Stratford in some ways. Sir Henry and Lady Rainsford's monument in Clifford Chambers church is unforgettable, though it is only on the same scale as Shakespeare's own. The Rainsfords took the King's side in the Civil War, as Shakespeare's daughter did, but they had more to lose, and lost it.

The Shakespeares were not gentry, and the word 'burgesses' applied to them by Victorian writers makes little sense in Stratford terms. What happened is quite clear. They were originally tenant farmers around Snitterfield in Arden, on the hills above Stratford. One may get some idea of what the early Shakespeares looked like by observing the stone heads carved around the Snitterfield font, in which John Shakespeare was baptized. His brothers lie under the heaving turf of the churchyard outside, in unmarked graves.

Genealogists have tracked down a formidable number of early Shakespeares, and it seems they may all be related, all the descendants of one man whose nickname it was. In the Middle Ages a Shakespeare was hanged, and another avoided the gallows by disappearing. They came from further north than Warwickshire, where they multiplied perhaps in the early fifteenth century. Adam Shakespeare was a tenant by military service – that is, a man at arms allowed the use of land – at Baddesly Clinton in Warwickshire in 1389. When John Shakespeare applied for his coat of arms in 1596, he mentioned that his grandfather had been granted land in Warwickshire in 1485 by Henry VII in recognition of his service in the Wars of the Roses. The moment itself is symbolic, even if the story may not be true. It almost certainly is true, but no one has yet discovered where in north Warwickshire the land was.

The Shakespeares were long confined to a few parishes. We hear, for example, of a Richard Shakespeare, who may be Adam's great-grandson, with a partner called Woodhall taking out a twenty-five-year lease on some land from the Prior of Wroxall in the 1520s, with the condition that he must clear the brambles from it. Anyone who has attempted such a task armed only with a billhook will realize that it was a sentence to some years of hard labour. In 1534 Richard was bailiff of Wroxall Manor.

The first Shakespeare of Snitterfield, six miles or so from Wroxall, is recorded in 1535; he was another Richard. His landlord was Robert Arden of Wilmcote; the Snitterfield house lay on the High Street and extended to the brook. Richard Shakespeare of Snitterfield died late in 1560, leaving property valued at £35 17s; he had not been a wealthy man. His sons were John, Henry and probably the Thomas who held a lot of Snitterfield land from 1563 to 1583. John administered the will, so perhaps he was the eldest son.

John Shakespeare moved down to Stratford nearly ten years before his father's death, though the record of Richard's will describes him as *Johannem Shakere de Snytterfyld agricolam*. This may well be a simple mistake, not an uncommon phenomenon in the Worcester diocesan records. The last time John can be traced to Snitterfield local records is 1561, when he was fined for a failure to make hedges. His father had been fined the year before for having his swine unringed, which means they were free to excavate without inhibition.

John had his first house in Henley Street in 1552, and the next-door house and another in Greenhill Street with a garden and a cottage by 1556. He was a glove-maker, and since he was also a wool-dealer and a whittawer (a fine skin-curer) we know he prepared his own skins as well. In John Aubrey's time he was remembered as a butcher. He dealt in any market where he saw an opportunity, as most Stratford dealers did, and in any commodity where he saw a profit, including corn and malt. Sir John Mennes, an admiral and poet under Charles I, told Archdeacon Plume (who wrote it down about 1656) that he remembered John Shakespeare in his shop: 'a merry cheeked old man that said, Will was a good honest fellow, but he durst have cracked a jest with him at any time'. Sir John was only two when John Shakespeare died in 1601, and the words do not sound like a father talking about a son, so there is some confusion about this anecdote. Sir John does say that old Shakespeare was a glover, which is true, and probably the anecdote, though mangled in transmission, does go back to someone who knew him. John Shakespeare took root slowly in Stratford; until his father's death in 1560 documents called him a husbandman of Snitterfield, as if in Stratford he was only an agent for the family business. That is probably not far from the truth: Snitterfield certainly used the Rothermarket.

Stratford got its charter in 1553, and John Shakespeare entered local politics and public life, rising year by year in the hierarchy of the council, from ale-taster in 1557, which gave him control of the quality of ale and bread, to one of the four constables in 1558 and 1559, assessor of fines in 1559 and 1561, and Chamberlain or accountant, a two-year office which he held twice, from 1561 to 1564.

He married Mary, the youngest of seven daughters of Robert Arden, all but two of whom Arden had contrived to marry off. The Ardens had bought Snitterfield in 1501, and it was not their only estate. When Robert died in 1556 he left a big farm at Wilmcote and two tenant farms; he was Catholic, like all Ardens, and Mary Tudor was on the throne. His youngest daughters, Alice and Mary, were his executors. Mary inherited the house and fifty acres; she also had an interest in Snitterfield. The inventory of the farm she inherited with 'The crop upon the ground sown and tilled as it is', an important part of agricultural dealings to this day, happens to have survived. The farm, which was called Asbyes, had a house decorated with numerous painted tapestries, a barn of wheat and barley, oxen, bullocks, colts, swine and weaning calves, bees, poultry, wood in the yard and bacon in the roof – the hall roof, one assumes. The house at Wilmcote now called Mary Arden's house, however, is certainly not hers or Robert's: it is a wealthier house, and the farm with its magnificent barns is more substantial; the cider press added by the Shakespeare Trust could cope with a great many apple trees. All the same, the general atmosphere it conveys is right.

John Shakespeare was doing well in Stratford by 1556; he and Mary married about a year after her father's death, probably at Aston Cantlow. Neither the date nor the place is quite certain, but this would be normal. The ceremony would have been a Catholic one, beginning at the door of the church where her father was buried, with the wedding procession travelling several miles from the hilltop at Wilmcote down to the church at Aston Cantlow, among the green meadows of a small river. It used to be claimed that Shakespeare's father and mother must have had their wedding breakfast at the King's Head, the tavern still in use beside the church. It was a long walk or a long ride home otherwise, but the Ardens were used to that journey: they must have done it every Sunday, because Wilmcote had no church. Personally I would have settled for the King's Head, but in John Shakespeare's days it is much likelier that they had their feast at the farm. It would have been more like one of those French country wedding feasts which gather in such crowds of clansmen and go on for such an amazingly long time.

Mary Arden's first daughter Joan was born in September 1558 and baptized in Stratford church on the 11th. Queen Mary died on 17 November. The next year, with Queen Elizabeth on the throne, came the change of religion. The Stratford corporation, on which John Shakespeare sat, got rid of their Catholic curate Roger Dyos, who had baptized Joan, by the clever expedient of not paying him. He withdrew to Wiltshire, but seventeen years later he sued the bailiff of Stratford for his salary, and got it awarded with damages. In 1561 Stratford appointed a new vicar called John Bretchgirdle, a Christ Church man from Witton, Northwick. Bretchgirdle was unmarried, but his sister or sisters kept house for him. Half the value of his estate was in books, including Tyndale's New Testament and some Latin classics. On 2 December 1562 he baptized the Shakespeares' second daughter Margaret, and a few months later he buried her. On 26 April 1564 he baptized William Shakespeare.

Stratford church was not in good condition. The small building that stuck out like a monstrous Gothic growth from the north side of the east end had once been a choir school, but now it was a charnel-house. It has been suggested that this place terrified young William. That seems unlikely: neither death nor sex is news to a country boy, and Stratford was only a small country town of two thousand souls, 'well builded, with wooden houses' Leland says – hardly more than a village. St Paul's in London had an enormous charnel-house which was a place of public resort, pulled down in the end to be used as building stone for Somerset House. At Stratford the chancel was boarded off from the church because of its papist atmosphere, which is how it became a burial place on such a scale. In the body of the church people had their appointed pews, bailiff and councillors and the New Place family were to the fore. Its owner William Clopton was in 1580 the only esquire in Stratford, but his pew was probably empty, since he died still a Catholic in 1592. Communion was taken in pews, seated, eight or ten quarts of claret at a sitting. Old people from the almshouses sat at the back. The body of the church is magnificent; the stone angels still smile enigmatically from below the tall windows, and the wooden figures on the misericords of the choir still beam with medieval zest. In 1617 the bells were out of order; it was the Guild Chapel bell that must have tolled for the dead. Some fragments of ancient glass have survived from the porch: a winged figure with a scythe and a book, with the Latin word *Scrutamini*, and bits of a reference to Psalm 15, with *oliva . . . victa terra . . . udo Dei*.

Suddenly the career of John Shakespeare suffered a series of setbacks that amount to catastrophe. This is an important fact about the poet's boyhood and about his future, which might have been otherwise. Was the source of the trouble John Shakespeare's religion? This matter has been argued over by scholars who want to rescue Shakespeare for Catholicism or to stress Catholic influence on his work, and at least as vehemently by those determined to suffer no such thing. I believe that the problem has a simple solution which has been neglected, and that if we first enquire into the Stratford community and then observe outside influences, this solution will fall easily into place.

Stratford was a small town, with a suppressed division of feeling and loyalty which might flare up; and in the wider context of Elizabethan history changes took place under the surface. We know from county records that over the forty-five years of her reign Elizabeth was very largely successful in eliminating Catholicism, though her policy had its ups and downs and moments of excitement.

In 1565 Alderman William Bott was thrown off the council for failing to answer charges of abuse against council and bailiff, and that was how John Shakespeare became alderman in his place. He wore a black gown faced with fur and a thumb ring: he was definitely somebody. In 1567 he stood for bailiff and in 1568 he was elected by majority vote of his colleagues. In 1571 he was chief alderman and deputy to the bailiff, Adrian Quiney, a Henley Street mercer.

What went wrong? From 1576 onwards he scarcely ever attended a council meeting. His colleagues kept him on the list, they reduced his tax in a levy for equipping soldiers, they let him off a fine in 1578 and let him off an alderman's tax of fourpence a week poor relief. In September 1586 they let him and another alderman go, 'for that Mr Wheler doth desire to be put out of the company, and Mr Shaxspere doth not come to the halls when they be warned, nor hath not done of long time'. In 1589 he was recorded as having no goods that could be seized for debt, but when he died in 1600 he left £169 10s in goods and standing corn, including eight oxen and twelve cattle. There is no doubt about the money trouble. In November 1578 he mortgaged a house and fifty-six acres at Wilmcote for £40 to Edmund Lambert of Barton on the Heath, husband of his wife's sister Joan. He was already in debt to Lambert; he owed £5 to Roger Sadler, a baker in the High Street, which was guaranteed by Edmund and Mary Arden's stepfather Edward Cornwell. The £40 mortgage fell due at Michaelmas 1580, and John Shakespeare was still unable to pay it, so that Lambert died possessing the Wilmcote land. Two London law cases followed, with the

Shakespeares claiming that the Lambert heir John had promised another £20 if they gave him the property outright, and then that they really had offered the £40 to his father and had been spurned because they owed the other money. The rights and wrongs are a matter of guesswork, but it is painfully clear that John Shakespeare had his back to the wall.

In 1580 he was fined £20 for failing to appear in the court of the Queen's Bench in London to find security for keeping the Queen's peace, and a further £20 as surety for a hatmaker of Nottingham who had also failed to appear. One hundred and forty of these fines were imposed at once, varying from £10 to £200; the victims came from all over England. All the cases were interwoven by sureties in the same way. It is clear enough that John Shakespeare was on a list of some kind, and that his enemies were not in Stratford. The only evidence of trouble close to home was that in summer 1582 he himself petitioned for securities of the peace against Ralph Cawdrey, William Russell, Thomas Logginge and Robert Young 'for fear of death and mutilation of his limbs'. This was a common formula, and petitions and counter-petitions in cases of quarrel do not necessarily have a straightforward meaning. Fighting and bloodshed, duelling, revenge and murder were very common. In the case of Cawdrey, a butcher in Bridge Street who was bailiff at this time, the quarrel seems to have been private and may possibly have blown over, since John Shakespeare attended the meeting to elect a new bailiff on 5 September of that year. But other interpretations remain open, and may be likelier. He was in deep water.

There is no doubt that John Shakespeare was inclined towards Catholicism, though we have no particular reason to think him an obstinately enthusiastic Catholic. He had been in public life, as other Catholics had. He was not suspected in Stratford of harbouring a priest. In or around 1580 he got from Edmund Campion, possibly at the Catesby house, possibly through his wife's family, a Catholic form of Last Will and Testament, framed originally by St Charles Borromeo, Archbishop of Milan, and in England secretly distributed by the Jesuits. John Shakespeare's 'Spiritual Testament' was discovered hidden in the roof of New Hall when Thomas Hart (buried in the churchyard in 1793) had the tiles rehung. Edmond Malone (1741–1812), the first great Shakespearean scholar, examined it, by now missing its first page, and published it in 1790. In 1923 a Jesuit rootling in the British Museum found the same form in a Spanish version printed in Mexico City in 1661. There is therefore no doubt whatsoever about the genuineness of this document. But it does not reveal why Shakespeare's father had it or kept it or hid it, or what his wife thought. My own view is that in 1580 the shades were darkening for him personally. The moment of deep division in the nation had come, and his Catholic identity was at least at that time important to him. We shall be able to cast more light on this.

The penal laws against Catholics became more severe as time went on. A list of recusants – that is, persons who failed to attend church once a month – was required from Stratford in 1592. The churchwardens, or whoever it was, added a list of nine persons whom 'we suspect . . . absent themselves for fear of processes', and John Shakespeare was on it. Later in the year a further enquiry by commissioners under Sir Thomas Lucy got the same result. The unlikely excuse was apparently hard to get round. But his allies and enemies do not precisely correspond to religious divisions. The Cawdreys, for example, were Catholic and so the quarrel with them must have another explanation. Similarly, none of the nine Stratford men in fear of legal process appear on the recusant list of 1593.

Schoenbaum puts John Shakespeare's troubles down to general economic depression in the Midlands, but his difficulties are too particular. They began in the 1570s. Documents recently discovered show that Shappere alias Shakespeare of Stratford upon Haven was prosecuted in 1570 for lending money to John Musshem of Walton D'Eiville, probably a sheep farmer who died in 1588. He seems to have lent £80 and £100, at £20 interest in each case. The entire country was held together by such transactions, however illegal, and Shakespeare and Musshem were partners; they were sued together for a debt by a certain Henry Higford.

Two years later John Shakespeare was attacked for illegal wool dealing, a monopoly of the Merchants of the Staple. He was supposed to have bought two and a half tons in Westminster, and half that again in Snitterfield. His operations were evidently on a considerable scale, and the prosecution was most damaging to him. The offences had both been in 1571 and he had paid £210 for three and three-quarter tons. It is significant that he was fined forty shillings in one of the usury cases – though the others ended inconclusively – and that all three cases were brought by a notorious professional informer called James Langrake. Langrake had been in prison for blackmailing those he informed against, and had been accused of raping his own servant. Later he was fined and banned from informing for a year.

How did this unsavoury person come to batten on John Shakespeare? I think that he was hired to do so. I think John Shakespeare's loyalty in the 1570s was Arden loyalty: he was not persecuted as a Catholic, but as an Arden kinsman and ally. When he applied to the College of Heralds for a grant of arms about 1576, his two claims were his bailiffship of Stratford and his marriage into the Arden family. It was a proper claim, not proceeded with presumably because of the fees; his son William pursued the matter successfully in 1596, and it is from that occasion that documents have survived. It was even suggested that Shakespeare should impale the arms of Arden. The Ardens had been gentry and sheriffs since Edward the Confessor, and showed documentary evidence of their ancient family grandeur to Dugdale, a good witness. They bitterly resented the new power of the Earl of Leicester and his family: religion was only one element in that dispute of an older world against a new one.

The life of Stratford as I construe it indicates that a quarrel like the one between Edward Arden, High Sheriff in 1575, and the Earl of Leicester had ramifications across the county. Thomas Lucy of Charlecote was a creature of Leicester's. It was Leicester who sent extreme Protestant preachers to Stratford. Probably at the time of the Queen's visit to Kenilworth in July 1575 Edward Arden contemptuously refused to wear Leicester's livery; I cannot imagine any other occasion when he could have been asked to wear it. He called Leicester an upstart and an adulterer. The remark was reported, and it was the more painful for being true. It was particularly dangerous because Leicester seems to have been sleeping with a lady-in-waiting while the Queen, whose devoted suitor he was supposed and required to be, was actually in his house. Leicester set out to crush Edward Arden, and succeeded in doing so in 1583. There is no doubt that he sought equally to crush any Arden faction that existed in Warwickshire, and John Shakespeare certainly belonged to it. The quarrel of Arden and Leicester was a mask or an excuse for political in-fighting of a dirty kind, for solidly material rewards. Leicester was a treacherous, immoral and boundlessly ambitious figure, but Edward Arden and his class were born losers.

Arden was a Catholic who kept a chaplain, formally disguised as his gardener but well known to be a priest called Father Hall, an elderly man of unblemished and obvious innocence; it is quite likely that William Shakespeare as a boy may have known him. It is even more likely that there was wild talk in Edward Arden's house against the Queen, though Campion if he ever went there would not have liked or encouraged it. Fate played into the hands of Arden's enemies. A crazy son-in-law of his called John Somerville with a mania for the Queen of Scots is said to have set off for London on a personal mission to assassinate the Queen. This idiotic scheme was far too hare-brained to have been concocted by Edward Arden. The young man sat about in London taverns, apparently declaring his intention to anyone who would listen. He was arrested, and under torture said that he was in Edward Arden's commission and that Father Hall had dreamed up the plot. The young man was then declared to have strangled himself in prison, so his evidence could not be withdrawn. Father Hall was arrested and then simply set free without trial; but Edward Arden was hanged, drawn and quartered, and his head stuck on a spike on London Bridge with the two or three dozen others already festering there. They are clearly visible in Claes Jansz Visscher's 1616 engraving of London.

John Shakespeare was not an impassioned Catholic, but a conservative and an Ardenite and proud of it. Father and son suffered the consequences. In William's infancy his father was a powerful and active man within the somewhat crumbling market town of Stratford and in the surrounding countryside; by the time William was ten or eleven his father was in serious trouble; and when William was nineteen his cousin Edward Arden's head was stuck on London Bridge. The decision to crush the

Ardens was probably taken in 1575, the year Edward Arden was High Sheriff and the Queen came to Kenilworth. John Shakespeare's recorded troubles started in 1576. At the time of his Catholic 'Spiritual Testament' they were reaching their height. Persecution of him seems to have relaxed after the Earl of Leicester's death in 1588. Leicester's brother 'the good Lord Warwick' survived longer, dying in the end in 1590 of an old war wound. He was politically less active and perhaps had little to do with all this.

William Shakespeare was not brought up Catholic in any normal sense of the word. He went to school and church with the other Stratford boys, prayed for the Queen, heard sermons and took communion when the time came. Not only the official Bible (never the Rhemes-Doway Catholic version) but the homilies appointed to be read in the Church of England (now alas neglected) have left discernible traces in his writing. Both the quarrel and its consequences were chiefly political, social and economic. In religion the boy went the way of his generation.

He does betray some sympathy with the old Church here and there, but that is not abnormal. Even Robert Armin was still swearing 'By the Mass' in the seventeenth century. Shakespeare shows the sharpest indignation against torture and against tyranny, and particularly against corruption, and has a lot of sympathy with old-fashioned characters, as well as with outsiders of every kind. He was to some degree a political but hardly a religious dissident. His personal religion, so far as his plays reveal it – which is not very far – seems to have been something like Montaigne's with a touch of neo-platonism. I think he was perhaps a Socinian: the heresy of the Sozzini, father and son, which became the dominant ideology of liberals in the 1630s (Lord Falkland and his circle) and which orthodoxy later overtook and more or less absorbed. The belief that connects it with Shakespeare is that God is omnipotent and that man is quite free, but at the same time impotent. That sounds like what Shakespeare believed, at least with one side of his mind. But his mind had many sides, and he was not, thank God, a theologian, except in the more serious sense in which a poet must be.

· 2 ·

Shakespeare's Youth

William Shakespeare's first friends outside the family will have been the children of his father's friends. The same names crop up again and again in his life: his was a world in which alliances of blood and kinship were paramount, and the local loyalty of one's own region, even if one moved into the greater world of London, worked as an extension of kinship. But John Shakespeare's intimate circle must have narrowed a little in the year his son was born, because the plague, which infested London more intensely than usual in 1563, broke out in Stratford, in Lichfield and in Leicester in 1564, and in Stratford one in seven persons died of it. The Shakespeares escaped the plague, but no Elizabethan family could escape infant mortality. Five children out of their eight lived beyond childhood: the first Joan (1558) and Margaret (1562) died as small children, so William (1564) was not only eldest son but eldest surviving child. His brother Gilbert (1566) and the second Joan (1569) lived, but Ann (1571) died at the age of eight when William was fifteen. That must have been a painful loss. Richard (1573/4) and Edmund (1580) lived. Richard was named after his grandfather, and Edmund after his uncle, Edmund Lambert.

William's grandmother, old Mrs Arden, died just after Christmas in 1580. She had lived long enough for him to know the old-fashioned farm at Wilmcote, as well as those tough old farmers his uncles at Snitterfield. Admittedly the sort of record we have underlines this kind of thing, but his Uncle Henry gets fined for fighting a constable in 1574, in a dispute over tithes in 1580, for wearing a hat to church in 1583, and for neglecting a ditch and failing to bring a team to repair the highways in 1596. As we have seen, William's father was fined for his dung heap in Henley Street, but he was not alone in that: anyone who reads through the records will see that the putting down of illegal dung heaps in streets leading from the Rothermarket was an obsession of the council. Uncle Henry's children Lettice (1582) and James (1585, d.1589) were baptized at Hampton Lucy, where the Shakespeares rented land from the Cloptons. I have a particular affection for this obstreperous old man. He had several disputes over money, the amounts being £10 and less; in 1591 and 1596 he went to prison

21

in Stratford, and two oxen for which he failed to pay were removed from his farm. Yet he died in his own house, with money in coffers and corn and hay in his barns 'amounting to a great value'. He was buried four days after Christmas 1596, and his widow followed him early in February.

No one knows exactly how all the Shakespeares around Stratford were related: they were cousins of some kind. Thomas, Anthony (who was a billman in the military muster of 1569 and brother to John of Clifford Chambers, who gave that village its strong wooden hearse, still kept under the church tower) and William Shakespeare of Snitterfield (maybe the poet's godfather) might any or all of them have been John Shakespeare's brothers. About the precise interrelations of the numerous Warwickshire Ardens and Ardernes we can discover even less, though genealogists believe them to be another of the rare cases where everyone of that name is related by family. Since Robert Arden, who died in 1636, had documents that proved the ancestry of the Park Hall Ardens beyond Sir Henry (knighted in 1375), who held his manors from the Earl of Warwick at the rent of a red rose, as far back as Alwin, Sheriff of Warwickshire under Edward the Confessor, the branches are numerous.

Within so small a rustic world, the interrelationships were multiple and intertangled; they are not always easy to unravel. The constable whom Henry fought in 1574, for instance, was Edward Cornwell, who married Margaret Arden, widow of Alexander Webbe, and thus became Mary Arden's stepfather. Webbe died the year before this affray, and John Shakespeare was his executor and Henry a witness of his will. In 1579, the John Shakespeares sold their interest in a house, a cottage and a hundred acres at Snitterfield to Mrs Shakespeare's kinsman Robert Webbe. In 1582 Uncle Henry and John Shakespeare were both examined as witnesses for this same Robert Webbe in a property case. There were other, interlocking village relationships.

Relationships of kinship and alliance might of course go sour, particularly where money was at stake. That is what happened between John Shakespeare and Edmund Lambert of Barton on the Heath over the mortgaged land at Wilmcote. In this case the physical distance went beyond Stratford, but John Shakespeare will not have thought it very great. He had been to London as bailiff, and his wool-trade connections certainly extended all over the Cotswolds and as far as London. Local ties were crucial, even in London: Robert Greene makes that plain in *the Art of Coney-Catching* (1591–2), where the London villain approaches an innocent countryman. 'Why, sir, saith the setter, guessing by his tongue what country man he is, are you not such a country man?' If he answers no, 'In good sooth sir I know you by your face and have been in your company before . . . let me crave your name, and the place of your abode . . . who be his neighbours, and what Gentlemen dwell about him.' If this fails to make friendship, a second villain informed by the first will accost the victim. 'What goodman Barton, how fare all our friends about you? . . . You are welcome to town . . . Have you forgot me? Why I am such a man's kinsman, your neighbour not far off: how doth this or that good gentleman my friend?' In thieves' slang, the poor countryman is called 'the cousin ', hence presumably the word 'couzenage': 'A notable discovery of coosnage' as Greene calls it.

William Shakespeare knew intimately, and from childhood onwards, the variations and progressions of human relationships. His dramatic power to express relationships and their consequences was rooted in his experience of life. Chaucer's *Canterbury Tales* offer a sketch of an entire society, but Shakespeare cuts deeper and more sharply, and his range in the end is greater. A cattle market is not a bad place to learn human nature, but his father's connections extended further.

The bridge was Stratford's most important asset, though in 1588 it flooded so swiftly that three men were caught in the middle, unable to go forwards or back. On the Stratford side stood two inns, the Swan and the Bear. The Swan was a substantial place, where Sir Thomas Lucy and the Grevilles and even the Earl of Warwick stayed. Thomas Dixon also called Waterman, who kept it, was a fellow glover and an alderman, and his wife came from Snitterfield. Since John Shakespeare became an alderman in virtue of belonging to the glovers' guild, Thomas Dixon was almost certainly his patron; Edgar Fripp, who edited the Stratford archives, thinks he was Dixon's apprentice.

When Dixon's inventory was taken, the Swan had £13 worth of claret, £34 worth of sack and six barrels of beer worth £3, which of course would not keep so well or sell for so much. Dixon owned ten shirts, a woollen gown furred with fox, and a brown robe, blue lined with lamb, which was worth £5. His son took over the Swan, and was an alderman in his turn until 1590, when he quarrelled with the council. His third wife was the widow of John Sadler, the miller downstream of the church, who died in 1583. Old John Sadler was a wealthy miller and the owner of the Bear; John Shakespeare came out of his bolt-hole to vote for him as bailiff in 1582. Sadler's son John the second was three years older than the poet; his son Thomas inherited the Bear; his daughter Margaret married William Persons; his grandson John the third was born in 1587, and in that generation a daughter married a Quiney. The first John Sadler's nephew was Hamnet Sadler, whose wife was called Judith, and Hamnet and Judith are therefore certain to be the godparents of William Shakespeare's twin children, Hamnet and Judith, who were born in 1585.

The Bear was kept for a time by Thomas Barber, three times bailiff, and perhaps only kept from a fourth term of office by the Catholicism of his second wife, Joan. Barber died in August 1614, four days after her funeral. The church records call him Gentleman. As bailiff, Barber fought strenuous battles against the Grevilles and against a rich, well-connected family called Combe, the first Combe having once been Lord Warwick's bailiff or agent in Stratford. William Shakespeare grew up knowing the Combes, and yet in September of 1615 he was making urgent plans to protect 'Master Barber's interest' against them. We will treat that matter in its place; here it serves only to indicate the network of relationships of various kinds within Stratford. Clearly innkeepers were diplomats and important citizens, and to some degree rivals. Lucy and the Grevilles and Lord Warwick favoured the Dixons and the Swan and the Combes.

The Combes seem to have been rich and unpopular. Their money came from monastic land, and by Shakespeare's time they had been around Stratford for several generations. John Combe of Astley married Katharine Quiney as his second wife in 1534. She was the widow of Adrian Quiney's grandfather, which makes her great-grandmother of the Thomas Quiney who married Judith Shakespeare, the poet's daughter.

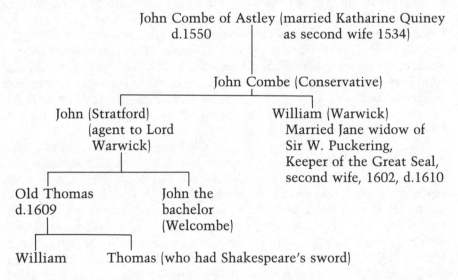

John Combe of Astley (married Katharine Quiney
d.1550   as second wife 1534)

John Combe (Conservative)

John (Stratford)   William (Warwick)
(agent to Lord   Married Jane widow of
Warwick)   Sir W. Puckering,
                                        Keeper of the Great Seal,
                                        second wife, 1602, d.1610

Old Thomas   John the
d.1609   bachelor
                    (Welcombe)

William   Thomas (who had Shakespeare's sword)

Thomas Combe lived in the College or College House, a former priest's house, the only stone house in Stratford. His household was of fourteen persons, the biggest recorded Stratford household being of twenty-two — that of Hugh Reynolds, to whose son William, born in 1575, Shakespeare left a ring. Thomas took a lease of College House only in 1596, just a few months before Shakespeare bought New Place fifty yards away. The suggestion of close friendship and alliance is at least inviting.

Thomas was godfather to Sir Henry Rainsford's son, and in 1608 Rainsford and his stepfather William Barnes became overseers of Thomas Combe's will. Thomas's younger brother John was a bachelor and was considered to be a miser, since he lent money at interest and was constantly going to law to recover it. He and his uncle William at Warwick owned property which Shakespeare bought in 1602. John Combe died in 1614, leaving Shakespeare and Rainsford, his overseer, £5 each, and Lady Rainsford forty shillings to buy a ring in his memory. Old Thomas Combe had left his wealth to his eldest son, William; brother John left his to Thomas, the younger son of Old Thomas. When Shakespeare died in 1616 he left this young Thomas Combe his sword, something which a man normally left to his own son. He had known Combe since childhood.

A rude rhyme about John Combe was persistently attributed to Shakespeare, although Sir Sidney Lee proved long ago that it was simply a traditional epigram about a usurer, directed to John Combe of Stratford by a report of 1618, in which it was said to be 'fastened upon a Tombe that he had caused to be built in his Life Time'. But John Combe left £60 for his tomb in his will: it was not built in his lifetime. The rumour does seem to have come from Stratford, and the name John-a-Combe is more or less right, but Shakespeare's authorship is wildly unlikely and there is no evidence that the verses were ever stuck up on John Combe's monument. Still, the gossip existed by the 1630s, which makes it venerable if not reliable, so these silly verses had better be recorded here. I choose Rowe's version rather than Aubrey's:

> Ten-in-the-hundred lies here ingrav'd.
> Tis a hundred to ten his soul is not sav'd.
> If any man ask, who lies in this tomb?
> Oh ho! quoth the devil, 'tis my John-a-Combe.

This is a joke which, to judge by the variety of its versions, must have been thought witty in taverns, and suffercd much transformation by drunken word of mouth.

The Combe family were not only rich and well connected, but clever as well. Old Thomas translated from the French and published in 1593 *The Theatre of Fine Devices, An Hundred Moral Emblems*, a charming and ingenious book. It was entered in the Stationers' Register on 9 May, just three weeks after *Venus and Adonis*. Both these somewhat dandy publications were produced by Richard Field, a London printer from Stratford-upon-Avon just two and a half years senior to William Shakespeare. Field was apprentice to Thomas Vautrollier, and their business was as enterprising as that of any printer in London; in 1588 Field married his master's widow and took control.

The one copy of Combe's book that survives was printed not in 1593 but in 1614. Combe added to his translation an appeal 'To the Reader', hoping that 'if the verse be anything obscure, the Impreses or pictures make it more lively'. More lively is what the woodcuts do make this book, but without the rather lucid verses they would be incomprehensible illustrations, mostly of strange or fabulous narratives.

Combe's verses are quasi-sonnets of eight lines each, rhyming a b a b a b, c c. They are moralizing, but they have a dull elegance, as in 'By which is shown, as we may plain perceive,/That wine and women wisest folk deceive', or in 'He that presumes to shave the Lion's skin/Full little knows what danger he is in' – a remark more or less echoed by Henry V to the French herald at Agincourt. Many of the examples are homely: the flies in the milk pan, and 'One bird in hand is better far/Than three which in the hedges are'. The illustration to that is a tennis match and 'the ball's uncertain bound'. The sixth emblem declares the dangers of masks and masking. Pythagoras warns readers of the dangers of melancholy. Rome warns against civil war:

> Where equity maintained without sleights,
> And justice was the Monarch's looking glass,
> Till avarice possessed their conceits:
> Then civil discord set their hearts at war,
> And caused each man his own good to mar.

It would be hard to encapsulate Shakespeare's doctrine of the state more neatly: it is proverbial wisdom of course, and as easy to find in Stratford or in Paris as in the *Mirror for Magistrates*, a long and tedious poem which critics insist Shakespeare had read. The same may be said of Combe's verses on choosing friends carefully and on youth and age:

> Youth is too hot, and void of care and dread;
> The aged cold, and full of doubts and fears. . . .

The poet distrusts those who soar too high 'with piercing insearch of things most divine', and thinks the donkeys so happy in Thessaly, 'fair, plumb, smooth, fat and full', that scholars should go play. He has a severe view of the proper role of women, and shows particular enthusiasm about eel-fishing. In fact he is a normal, provincial Elizabethan. It is for this reason, for the closeness of his mentality and background to Shakespeare's, that Thomas Combe is important. Yet he is neglected: at present one is lucky to find a facsimile of his book, and that only in a great library. *The Theatre of Fine Devices* ought to be reprinted. In *Pericles* Shakespeare probably drew on Paradin's *Dévises Heroiques*, but he must also have known Thomas Combe's *Fine Devices*.

More is known about the Combes' dates of death than of their dates of birth, but it is likely that Shakespeare encountered them as a schoolboy. The Elizabethan grammar school was an extremely important leveller and an easy instrument for those who were going to climb intellectually or socially in a society both intellectually and socially more mobile than ours. That was how Lord Burghley began to climb.

Another of Shakespeare's schoolfellows was William Tyler, son of John

Shakespeare's fellow chamberlain Richard; William was not quite two and a half years younger than the poet. He volunteered at the Armada muster in 1588, but that summer he got a girl pregnant. She was about sixteen, eldest daughter of Richard Woodward of Shottery Manor, and William married her secretly. Her family was furious and her grandfather, Robert Perrott of Nether Quinton, the brewer and landlord of the King's House or King's Hall on Rothermarket, cut her out of his will, with thunderous warnings to her sisters. Perrott was a Puritan and it was thought an eccentric reaction; Shakespeare had been a married man since 1582 after doing much the same. Tyler served on the council like his father before him; he was called 'Gentleman', and Shakespeare left him money for a ring.

In a society that divides differently in six or seven ways, social division is ambivalent. Barnhurst and Badger of Sheep Street were a Protestant and a Catholic wooldraper. Badger was fined, imprisoned, deprived of his alderman's gown, found in possession of 'massing relics' from Clopton House at the time of the Gunpowder Plot, and had his house searched by candlelight ten years later, at a cost of twopence for candles noted by the borough chamberlain. Barnhurst called him a knave and a rascal in the council but had to apologize, and in the end was thrown out of the council for abusing everybody present. They were rival wooldrapers and Barnhurst had an explosive temperament.

Adrian Quiney, the Henley Street mercer, had two sons: Richard, and Thomas who married Shakespeare's daughter. Thomas Badger, father of the recusant Badger whom Barnhurst hated, was godfather to Richard Quiney; but Abraham Sturley, a Cambridge man and a strong Puritan who admired the Warwick preacher Thomas Cartwright, exchanged a charming series of letters in Latin with the little boy. At eleven, Richard could compose as well as most Oxford undergraduates can today.

There is no doubt that William Shakespeare grew up knowing more than one side in more than one quarrel. Ralph Cawdrey the butcher had a son who was a Jesuit. Can that have been the occasion of his quarrel with John Shakespeare? George Whately the wooldraper, who endowed an elementary school at Henley in Arden in 1586, had two brothers who were Catholic priests on the run in that area. Yet he was twice bailiff, and for many years was warden of Clopton Bridge.

It has been suggested that William Shakespeare was a rustic who could scarcely have aspired to study at Oxford, and counter-suggested that recusants avoided the oath-taking necessary for a degree. The more likely explanation is money. We must thank God anyway that his hungry talents were not canalized by academic study at that level. He was admirably self-taught, owing to his father's misfortunes and near disgrace. But universities were locally as well as nationally rooted in those days. The son of Philip Rogers, the Stratford apothecary, went to Oxford and was licensed as a surgeon; William Chandler, stepson of Shakespeare's cousin Thomas Greene, had a son there; William Persons, who married Margaret Sadler, sent his son John to Balliol in 1597.

It was socially, and might have been financially, possible for William to study in Oxford and then at the Inns of Court. His friend John Davies, son of a tenant farmer on a Magdalen College farm, was later deprived of the title of gentleman by a heraldic visitation at Wotton under Edge (1623), but he went to Oxford with gentlemen's sons whom both he and Shakespeare knew well: Thomas Russell, for example, of Broad Campden and Alderminster. It is not always easy to know when Shakespeare met those of his later friends who lived outside Stratford. From the early 1590s all doors were open, and he was resented only by graduate writers whose own position was insecure: his success was what they minded.

I doubt whether he knew his most interesting friends as a schoolboy, except for Thomas Combe. One day a Quiney was to marry a Bushell; Thomas Russell was to be overseer of Shakespeare's will, Henry Willoughby of West Knoyle was to write a very funny poem about Shakespeare as an unsuccessful lover, but we need not suppose he knew any of these people until the 1590s. All the same, John Davies was his contemporary, and Marston and Alderminster and Broad Campden are close enough to Stratford for it to be certain that he knew the places. John Combe the bachelor was a kinsman by marriage of John Davies, held land from him and left him money. The connection is tantalizing, but I fear impossible to date with certainty to Shakespeare's boyhood.

I am sure, however, that Shakespeare knew Robert Dover, who founded the Cotswold Olympic Games early in the reign of James I. Dover was born in Barton on the Heath about 1575, where Shakespeare's aunt Joan lived. When Robert grew up he had many friends in common with Shakespeare, including Drayton, Ben Jonson, Thomas Russell and Endymion Porter.

I think the greyhound at Windsor in *The Merry Wives of Windsor* which was 'outrun upon Cotsall' must have been run in the unreformed version of the Cotswold Whitsun meeting, not far from Stanway, and that Shakespeare knew those country sports. Robert Dover must have known them in boyhood too, but we have no clinching proof that Shakespeare had met him before he was seventeen, by which time Shakespeare was in London. All the same, we do know that Robert Dover lived at Winchcombe, where he was a lawyer specializing in keeping cases out of court, and that he died in his house at Stanway in 1644 and was buried in that village. No one has ever understood what Falstaff was doing at Winchcombe, in Justice Shallow's orchard; or, to transpose the question, what Shakespeare was doing there. The key that fits this closed door is Robert Dover. Shakespeare knew him as a boy from Barton in the Heath, and probably later as a young lawyer at the Inns of Court. What they had in common was the Cotswolds. Sir John Mennes, the old man who claimed (wrongly, it seems) to have known Shakespeare's father in his shop, was another friend of the Dovers, but only eighteen when Shakespeare died. Those who contributed poems in celebration of the Dover Games, *Annalia Dubrensia* (1636), include a Dover nephew from Winchcombe, a Willersey man, an Alcester man, someone from Weston sub Edge, and William Basse, who also wrote an epitaph on Shakespeare.

The local scale of the Cotswold Olympics is easy enough to imagine. The sports included backsword, wrestling, coursing of hares, javelin and hammer throwing, feasting and dancing, and barrages of gunfire, jumping in bags, and 'an infinite number of Ancient Pastimes . . . the whole being calculated to create Mirth and Jollity'. They were abolished in the nineteenth century after the growth of Birmingham and the addition of horse-races. Similar games continued at the scouring of the White Horse in Berkshire until 1875, and long enough at Much Wenlock in Shropshire to draw the attention of a visiting King of Greece, making him receptive to the revival of the Olympic Games at Athens. In the Cotswolds Robert Dover presided in a dashing suit of clothes belonging to King James I, procured for the Cotswold Olympics by Endymion Porter.

Young Shakespeare went to the free school at Stratford. The new generation of English poets all went to grammar schools of this kind, though some of them went to universities as well from about the age of fifteen. The English grammar schools of the day were formidable, and English literary culture was from that time until yesterday a product of the traditional grammar school curriculum. In this I include what are now called public schools, where the teaching would have been much the same. It was based on Latin, and it was remarkable. Children learned to read and write from the age of four and five, and to learn by heart. Discipline was sometimes rough, and conditions hard. The only surviving school desk from Stratford is a standing desk, and we hear elsewhere of a schoolmaster who fought off the winter morning frosts by beating all his boys first thing to warm himself up. On the other hand, the only authentic drawing of an Elizabethan schoolroom I have ever seen has a huge dog lolling in the foreground chewing a bone. Shakespeare makes several jokes about Ovid of a particularly schoolboy kind in his plays. But his farcical scenes of schoolboys under instruction are based on French farces, in spite of echoing his own schoolbooks. That tradition goes back to Aristophanes.

It was possible to learn a great deal in an Elizabethan grammar school, both about verse and about prose. Shakespeare shows a particular knowledge of the first two or three poems of Ovid's *Heroides*, which suggests that the rhetorical artifice of his Sonnets is an adaptation of Ovid's passionate rhetoric. Ovid is intensely musical and halfway to being dramatic, because the seeds of ancient dramatic poetry are still germinating in his verse, and so is his rhetorical education, the pleading of cases out of mythology. A handbook of rhetoric by Aphthonius was used in schools: its examples include Venus and Adonis, and Pyramus and Thisbe. The specially cultivated language called 'euphuism', based on the sheep-bell tinkling of harmonious rhetoric in John Lyly's *Euphues* (1578–80), though it is best appreciated in other works by Lyly (?1554–1606), had its roots in schoolroom Latin. It was an ongoing joke about its own elegance, and enjoyed a powerful vogue among upper-class women as well as men in exactly the years of Shakespeare's first flowering. All the same, Chaucer meant more to him.

The influence of Latin plays on the English theatre is another matter. Seneca's tragedies were not meant to be acted, though the Elizabethans did adapt and translate them, and their metre had an important effect on the adoption of iambic pentameter for the English stage. But Shakespeare had no real mission to be an English Plautus, or even an English Terence, a writer to whom he comes a little closer. The theatre was already in the hands of professionals, and he did not learn its skills in the classroom.

Stratford was not a learned community. The old curate and archivist and clockwinder, whom everyone seems to have liked, wrote his notes in very peculiar Latin. But the schoolmaster had £20 a year and a house, where his equivalent at Eton had only £10 a year. Mr Bretchgirdle the Vicar installed his ex-pupil John Brownsword, who published his own Latin verses and probably taught Latin verse composition in Stratford. T. W. Baldwin, the great authority on Shakespeare's Little Latin and Less Greek, has discovered that Brownsword was remembered with high praises as a teacher as late as 1612 in a book called *The Grammar School*. But he is hardly relevant to Shakespeare, since he was gone by 1568, and his successor had also left by 1569 when Shakespeare was five. The new master was a Lancashire clergyman from Corpus Christi, Oxford, called Walter Roche, who ran a parish at Droitwich at the same time. He gave up the school in 1571 to practise as a lawyer, in which capacity he sometimes represented Robert Webbe of Snitterfield, the poet's cousin. He sounds a person of lively intelligence, but this swift succession of schoolmasters does not create confidence in the school.

Simon Hunt (b.1551) might be of greater interest, since he seems to have gone abroad and become a Jesuit in 1578, dying in Rome in 1585. If one does not wish to credit this, then there was an obscure Hunt about whom almost nothing is known except that he died in Stratford about 1598, leaving £100. The two could have been kinsmen of course. In 1575 Shakespeare was only ten, so Hunt matters rather little to him; but Hunt's successor Thomas Jenkins is more interesting still. I am not concerned with his religion but with his prose style.

Jenkins as the son of an old servant of the founder went to St John's College, Oxford, and was a fellow there from 1557 to 1572. St John's had been founded in 1555 by Sir Thomas White in imitation of Trinity College nearby, founded by Sir Thomas Pope. In 1557 Edmund Campion and

Gregory Martin went to St John's, remaining there together for thirteen years. In 1569 Campion ceased to be Proctor, and not long afterwards he became a Jesuit. Gregory Martin became a tutor in the Duke of Norfolk's family, and later the principal translator of the Doway Bible. They were the best writers in Oxford in their day. This high estimate of Campion in particular is not eccentric: it must be the only opinion ever shared by Lord Burghley, the Earl of Leicester and Evelyn Waugh. If as seems likely enough Jenkins in 1566 felt the influence of these literary comets, then he transmitted it to Shakespeare. Modern experience is that when one leaves university to teach in a school, the best one transmits is an electrical charge that one has just received. But if nothing else this fascinating coincidence about Jenkins shows what a small world Shakespeare's was.

In 1579 Jenkins resigned and Stratford got (through him) another Catholic, John Cotton. Did all these Catholics or crypto-Catholics recommend each other in turn? But Jenkins may well have been a Protestant, so the succession may be coincidence. Perhaps the life of a schoolmaster looked to Catholics like a quiet niche. Cotton's younger brother was arrested and tried as a missionary priest with Edmund Campion; he was gruesomely executed in 1582. In 1581 when Shakespeare was sixteen Cotton withdrew to Lancashire, lived on his father's land which he inherited, paid his fines and died a Catholic recusant. Shakespeare had certainly left school by then, and Cotton probably never taught him.

For the next schoolmaster Alexander Aspinall Shakespeare is supposed to have written a rhyme to accompany the present of a pair of gloves:

The gift is small: the will is all: Alexander Aspinall.

This is recorded and attributed to Shakespeare by Sir Francis Fane, who was not born until 1611. Aspinall was a widower who married a widow in 1594, but the verses might date from any time after 1581; he may have been an amorous or a flirtatious widower. What makes the story likelier is the fact that John Shakespeare was a glover, and that Aspinall married the widow Shaw of Henley Street. When Ralph Shaw died, John Shakespeare was one of the appraisers – that is, valuers and itemizers – of his goods; and Ralph Shaw's son July was in turn a witness to William Shakespeare's will.

It may be considered in addition that we are utterly lacking in any apprentice verses of Shakespeare. He emerges at twenty-seven years old as a perfect poet. These verses are traditional in style, theme and feeling; almost anyone could have written them, and there is no reason why this 'anyone' should not have been the young Shakespeare. They are talented, elegant, and almost a parody. I think he wrote them at about the age of seventeen. They are like verses on a ring or on the blade of a knife. The metre is highly traditional. For instance, when the devil appeared to the Bishop of Winchester in a chronicle, he said 'Gileberte Foliot, qui meditaris tot et tot, Deus tuus est Astharoth.' The Bishop replied, 'Non

non sed Deus Sabaoth.' That is not the kind of verse technique that Shakespeare learned at school. He never forgot his Latin learning, but luckily for us he left school early. His roots as a poet stretch into more than one language, but his taproot is traditional English. He liked Chaucer and Skelton and Gower, none of whom he would have read at school.

He may well have seen Mystery Plays, and he certainly heard all about them. Until 1573, when he was nine, the Mysteries based on the quasi-epic of the Bible and the life of Christ were played every year at Coventry by the Cappers' Company. They are powerful plays, and affected their hearers powerfully. The Smiths' Company were still acting them in 1577 and 1578, about the time the poet left school. 'Paid to Fawston for coc-croying four pence'. Fawston must have done a particularly good cock-crow for St Peter's betrayal of Christ; they paid no more to Cocken for the bagpipes in 1584. In that year the Smiths' Company put on *The Destruction of Jerusalem* by Mr John Smith of St John's College, Oxford, which had a chorus and rehearsals, but that was a new type of play; the Mysteries were Catholic, and in Coventry they were suppressed by about 1580. In 1586 the Smiths sold their pageant huts and props, in 1587 the Weavers did the same; only the Cappers hung on to theirs, hoping for a revival. In 1591 in Coventry all the maypoles were taken down.

But the Mysteries lingered, and Shakespeare may well have seen them just about anywhere in some debased form, none the less dramatic for being debased. As late as 1644 the Rev. John Shaw was doing duty at Cartmel in Lancashire, where he met an old man who knew nothing about Christianity, not even how many gods there were or how his soul was going to be saved, which he thought was an even harder question. When the Vicar instructed him he remembered having seen the story in a Mystery Play at Kendal. An early-seventeenth-century manuscript of Mystery Plays of some kind exists at Stonyhurst. Willis, in his *Mount Tabor, or Private Exercises of a Penitent Sinner*, written in 1639 at the age of seventy-five, describes a Morality Play he saw at Gloucester as a little boy on his father's shoulder. He was exactly Shakespeare's age. All the same, the Mysteries are more dramatic and better poetry than the Moralities (with a few great exceptions like *Everyman* and John Skelton's *Magnyfycence*), and Coventry was not beyond the orbit of Stratford.

None of Shakespeare's exact contemporaries at school went on to Oxford or Cambridge; at least none has been traced. One boy went to Winchester and Oxford, and ended up as a country schoolmaster in Norfolk. There was a rumour later of another boy who was Shakespeare's friend and just as brilliant as he was, who died young. There is no reason why it should not be true. Aubrey records the story and says the boy was 'another butcher's son'; Schoenbaum suggests Adrian Tyler. Shakespeare is certainly very sensitive to the friendships of children and those of young men, but it is hard to distinguish the attractiveness of characters played by pre-sexual child actors from their basis in the experience of life. The romantic attachments of pairs of young men, bound up with ideas of honour and of love, did in real life reach a hectic degree.

As little boys of ten, Fulke Greville and Philip Sidney entered Shrewsbury School on the same day, and after Sidney's death in 1586 their friendship strayed beyond hero-worship into some degree of falsity. Lucius Carey, Lord Falkland, had an inseparable friend whom Ben Jonson commemorated and whose sister Lord Falkland married. These relationships were not directly, physically sexual: the less was done the more was felt. The drama of suppressed feelings was an exciting dance, but not a mating dance. There seems no doubt at all from Shakespeare's later writings that he was imaginatively bisexual, but he grew up in a provincial world of innocent manners and severe conventions, enchanted by music.

The liberation of mind that came like a blast of wind in Shakespeare's generation, and was most intensely experienced by the best of them, is hard for us to grasp. The renaissance is essentially a fifteenth-century Italian event that had its climax in the lifetime of Henry V. It hardly touched England beyond the royal Court, and such great men as Wolsey and their patronage. In Shakespeare's day it had entered a refined and sunset phase in Italy; Monteverdi was his contemporary. In Italian poetry it was paying diminishing returns. But it had done its work in Europe, by reviving and transmitting the ancient, secular classics, and a philosophized religion based ultimately on Plato, which in encoded forms colonized the intellectual furniture of Christianity like a beneficent infestation of woodworm. Giordano Bruno visited England and knew Sidney; he published in this country a little treatise on how to encode neo-platonic eros or divine love in poetry, and he inspired Sidney and Spenser. Livy, Tacitus and Plutarch offered a pre-Christian analysis of history. The intoxicating poetry of Ronsard and Du Bellay created the 'golden' style, which C. S. Lewis contrasts with the 'drab' earlier style of English poetry. One may agree with him that the drab style is undervalued, but the golden style is invaluable. In the year that Shakespeare was fourteen, St John of the Cross, doubly intoxicated by the mystical contemplation of God and by the possibilities of renaissance metre in Spanish, heard from prison a boy singing in the street, and began to write his own greatest poetry. While Shakespeare was still a young man, Florio was translating Montaigne.

The special English tradition of Protestantism has included a sturdy independence of mind, and a certain refusal to be easily misled by logical systems, Calvinist, Thomist or any other. The special tradition in politics has perhaps been the same. England in Shakespeare's youth was still shaken by the memory and the fear of dynastic civil wars, but far more shaken by religious impositions and alterations. An intelligent boy was not therefore likely to take established wisdom lying down.

Christopher Marlowe went, as Shakespeare did, to grammar school, but then to Cambridge, which was in a state of scarcely suppressed excitement. Years after his death (in 1593) the Bishop of London burned his English verse translation of Ovid's *Amores*. Shakespeare admired those brilliant poems, as we shall see. It is easy to forget that these two poets were born within a year of each other and read much the same books at school. What Cambridge added was time and books and the opportunity of self-confidence. I associate Marlowe's verse translations with his Cambridge years, and I believe that in them he reinvented English poetry and taught himself the otherwise incredible skills of his dramatic verse. Shakespeare first appears in London riding on Marlowe's style like the wren on the eagle's shoulder. But he began to read Ovid at school, and the *Amores* or *Amours* in one way, and the *Metamorphoses* or *Transfigurations* in another are poems that would have amazed an intelligent sixteenth-century schoolboy.

The stray fragments of school learning that can be traced in Shakespeare's plays are a much lesser matter: they are the merest allusions to a common classroom culture. He read Virgil, Juvenal and Caesar. He knew Mantuan, a popular renaissance Latin poet of deadly tedium, valued for his Protestant tendency. In Plautus and Terence he encountered the division of plays into five acts, which has a basis in Latin grammarians though it was not a universal rule for the Greeks. It was imposed, though not unjustifiably, by scholars on the texts they edited. I have the impression that Shakespeare never understood it until late in life, and that he left the playhouse or the printers to amalgamate his scenes into acts as they chose. He may have read some dialogue of Erasmus, whose views on happiness I have sometimes fancied that he repeats: but he could as easily have known those from Marot's French translation.

He learned no French at school, but he did learn it. Even at Oxford it was an unofficial study, though the number of foreign-language books in the inventories of goods left by students dying in Oxford in his time is surprisingly high. Almost everyone possessed them. The one certain thing we know about Shakespeare's youthful occupations is that he read a great deal – he was an omnivorous reader. Where and when he learned, and in what order, we have no way of knowing, but at some point he read a lot more Latin, learned French well, and I think some Italian later, attempted a study of law, and in general devoured whatever came to his hand. He liked Gower and Lydgate – dull, nourishing writers whom he respected because they were poets. He does not seem to have read much Horace, though I take it that the lyric about 'plumpy Bacchus' in *Antony and Cleopatra* is a parody of Horace, perhaps at a remove or two. He knew virtually no Greek. Much the same may be said of most professional scholars of the subject in the Elizabethan age.

*   *   *

34

Shakespeare is supposed to have been apprenticed to a butcher, perhaps his father, and Aubrey tells a tale that 'when he killed a calf, he woud do it in a *high style*, and make a speech.' His father was not a butcher, and the law forbade that a leather-dealer should be one. Still, he was certainly present at the slaughter of beasts, and Shakespeare is most likely, almost certain in the circumstances, to have worked at some related trade under his father. The story about making a speech to a calf is the kind of thing often said about poets in their boyhood, and likely enough to be true. Robert Burton puts the matter succinctly: 'All poets are mad.'

What is much less likely is the tale that Shakespeare stole a deer from Sir Thomas Lucy at Charlecote, and therefore had to leave the district. Sir Thomas paid two keepers, and he may have had some stray deer in his warren, though he had no licence for an enclosed park in those days. All the same, the Sheldon tapestry (1588) does show Charlecote with a deer park. Anyway, the crime was serious. Though the law under Elizabeth was lighter than it later became, Sir Sidney Lee gives the penalty as three months in prison and triple damages. The story about Shakespeare's deer is a bit of Robin Hood sentiment, possibly based on *As You Like It*. It is not impossible that the speech to the calf has some relation to the same play or to *Henry VI, Part 2*, but I doubt that. Shakespeare is often sorry for animals.

Sir Thomas Lucy was not popular; what great landlord and state official was? The story of a ballad written against him and pinned up on his gates has been attached to Shakespeare, but the ballad is lost, and the record of an odd verse or two dates only from an old man of ninety who died in 1703. Edmond Malone records a version of two verses of the Lucy Ballad collected by one of the few great English classical scholars, Joshua Barnes, at Stratford between 1687 and 1690. Barnes stopped overnight at an inn and heard an old woman singing it. He gave her a new gown for the two stanzas which were all she remembered:

> Sir Thomas was so covetous
>   To covet so much deer,
> When horns enough upon his head
>   Most plainly did appear.
>
> Had not his worship one deer left?
>   What then? He had a wife
> Took pains enough to find him horns
>   Should last him during life.

In the mid-eighteenth century that fascinating old antiquary William Oldys recorded another Stratford version, and told its first stanza to the Shakespeare scholar George Steevens.

> A Parliament member, a justice of peace,
>   At home a poor scarecrow, at London an ass,

If lousy is Lucy as some folk miscall it
Then Lucy is lousy whatever befall it:
   He thinks himself great,
   Yet an ass in his state,
We allow by his ears but with asses to mate.
   If Lucy is lousy as some folk miscall it,
   Sing lousy Lucy, whatever befall it.

These ballads are not by Shakespeare I imagine, but they bear witness to a level of humour and to a rich tradition of popular entertainment with which he was familiar. It nourished him in some ways, though in later life he despised London ballad-making at least with one side of his head: and was impatient to break free of the shackles of such raggle-taggle metres into the Elysian fields of Virgil and Ovid and Spenser and Chaucer and Marlowe. Shakespeare does make an anti-Lucy joke about three louses rampant in the arms of Justice Shallow, and a dozen white louses on his old coat. He derided the family and held it in scant respect. There is plenty of reason for that without any poaching incident.

Archdeacon Davies the late seventeenth-century Vicar of Sapperton noted in a manuscript now at Corpus Christi, Oxford, that Shakespeare 'was much given to all unluckiness in stealing venison and rabbits, particularly from Sir Thomas Lucy, who had oft whipt, and sometimes imprisoned, and at last made him fly his native county to his great advancement'. It is the same Archdeacon who records that Shakespeare 'died a Papist'. It seems to me that his informant was a Lucy. Shakespeare was an enemy, a scum of the earth, a poaching scoundrel, whom Sir Thomas used to have whipped, and what a joke, look what came of it. The same Lucy would be highly likely to mutter the dark rumour that Shakespeare lived and died a papist. The two accusations confirm one another. By the time of the Archdeacon, the Lucy family did have a deer park of which they were proud. I do not suppose Shakespeare had been more or less of a poacher than anyone else. He may well have written a ballad, and I wish it survived. We know already why he thought as he did of the Lucy family, and the ballads confirm that others thought the same.

Shakespeare seems to have been a wild and innocent young man. In 1582, when he was eighteen, he got the orphan Anne Hathaway pregnant. She was twenty-six, the eldest of three daughters of the late Richard Hathaway of Shottery, a short walk from Stratford through the fields. The Hathaway house survives, heavily restored but bigger and prettier than Shakespeare's birthplace can ever have been. The pleasantest part of it is the old railway carriages that have come to rest in a remote corner of the back gardens, along with a few ducks or hens. The orchard at the rear gives on to open wheatfields and must be enchanting by moonlight. Hathaway farmers were still living there in the late nineteenth century.

Anne's father appears to have married twice, with two sets of children, for he also had four sons. Her grandfather was an archer in muster rolls, a beadle, a constable, and one of the Twelve Men of Old Stratford who presided on one day of the year at the Law Day there (Shottery and Welcombe had their own Twelve Men); in 1550 his goods were valued at £10. Richard continued the farm, on three holdings amounting to less than a hundred acres altogether. He and John Shakespeare were already friends in 1566, when John Shakespeare paid debts for him as his surety. The Hathaways had a shepherd called Thomas Whittington, so this may be a wool-trade connection. In his will Richard pays £4 6s 8d to Whittington, and in 1601 Whittington leaves forty shillings, 'that is in the hand of Anne Shaxspere, wife unto Mr Wyllyam Shaxspere, and is due debt unto me', to the poor of Stratford.

Anne's pregnancy seems to have happened in late September, because the child, Susanna, was born about 23 May and baptized on the 26th, Trinity Sunday. William Shakespeare was a minor, and the last opportunity for calling the banns before Advent had been missed, so on 27 November 1582 two friends of the bride's family rode to the Bishop's court at Worcester to negotiate a special licence. The Bishop was the formidable John Whitgift, Archbishop of Canterbury from 1583 to 1604, but his consistory court was run by a chancellor, Richard Cosin, and a registrar called Robert Warmstry. Ninety-eight licences of this kind were granted at Worcester in 1582, so they were not uncommon. But they involved letters from consenting parents, and no doubt William had gone through some difficult moments, though it is possible that the sudden urgency of the marriage arose only in quite late November and that the couple then told their families at once. The Hathaways were probably pleased that Anne should be married off.

The licence was granted on 28 November, and the two friends had to give surety of £40 that no impediment to the marriage would later come to light. They were Fulke Sandells of Stratford and John Rychardson of Stratford, farmers. Sandells was a supervisor or trustee, and Rychardson was a witness of the will of Richard Hathaway, which he made during his illness on 1 September 1581. We know nothing about any marriage settlement beyond the terms of this will, under which Anne (called Agnes) was left £6 13s 4d (ten marks) to be paid on her wedding day.

The clerk of the Worcester court had entered the marriage licence on his register on the 27th; presumably it took another day to draw up the document in full. The clerk was a nincompoop: he wrote Baker for Barbar in his register, and Darby for Bradeley, and Edgock for Elcock, and Anne Whateley for Anne Hathaway. A lot of ingenious ink has been spilt over this error, but it is surely a simple one: the name Whateley occurs in a tithe appeal by a vicar on the same page of the register; the clerk could not follow his own notes, or he was distracted. He also wrote Temple Grafton and not Shottery. The question of Temple Grafton is much more interesting. The Vicar of Temple Grafton had been in trouble with the Bishop in 1580 about his irregular marriage procedures. Temple Grafton is a close and obvious walk from Shottery, just far enough from the neighbours to be private, and we have no other explanation of how it got into the register, unless Anne Hathaway intended to be married there.

The Vicar of Temple Grafton, John Frith, is one of my favourite characters in the whole ramifying story of Shakespeare's life. In 1586 a survey of the clergy of Warwickshire with a strong Protestant or Puritan bias says John Frith of Temple Grafton was 'an old priest and unsound in religion; he can neither preach nor read well, his chiefest trade is to cure birds that are either hurt or diseased, for which purpose many do usually repair to him.' A hawk could be worth £30 or £40, so his trade may have been profitable. The village was small, and the few traces of it as it was in his day are still charming, but it was not wealthy. Frith sounds much like Friar Lawrence in *Romeo and Juliet*: a gatherer of herbs and a hawk-doctor, an old Catholic priest from the reign of Queen Mary who lived out his life in Arden, in the backwoods. Shottery is really part of Stratford parish, but as an outlying village it could easily think of itself as belonging to Temple Grafton, which is the nearest parish church by the obvious road from Shottery, the Roman road leading west.

We are not quite certain where Shakespeare was actually married, because local registers have not survived. However in 1862 Mrs Dyke of Luddington near Shottery on the Avon, and to that degree likely, reported that an old lady had been told as a child that Shakespeare was married there, and 'had seen the ancient tome in which it was registered. This indeed we found on visiting the neighbouring cottages, was remembered by persons still living, when it was in the possession of a Mrs Pickering, who had been housekeeper to Mr Coles the last curate; and one cold day had burnt the register to boil her kettle.' Mr Flower the Victorian brewer told someone that Luddington was generally accepted in the early nineteenth century to be the place where Shakespeare was married. I think this Luddington story may well be a mirage, since no reliable witness ever examined the register. Malone, Halliwell-Phillipps, and many other scholars would have gone a long way to do so. It is possible however that there were other Shakespeares who might have been married at Luddington. Luddington lies across the river from Shottery.

In the year of his marriage, Shakespeare was still at work in Stratford, with an income of some kind. Edgar Fripp has made the effective point that the poet knows a great deal about leather, the technical terms of the leather trade, cheveril (kidskin) and its properties, and the skins of calf, sheep, lamb, fox, dog and deer. This reinforces the likelihood that he worked with his father. As his children were being born, he must have continued to do so; but the suspicion remains attractive that at some time, maybe not for long, he was a schoolmaster, probably in a small gentleman's family since he had no degree, and certainly learning as much as he taught. He appeared in London ten years after his marriage knowing very much more than a schoolboy, and the country schoolmaster story derives from one of his fellow actors – a reliable source. His experience of life goes without saying, but he got book-learning as well, and disposed of it with the authority of a self-taught man.

On 2 February 1585, Richard Barton of Coventry christened Hamnet and Judith Shakespeare, twin children of William and Anne, at Stratford, the godparents being Hamnet and Judith Sadler, who in 1598 named their own son William. The Sadlers lived on the corner of Sheep Street and High Street; the Shakespeares were still in Henley Street in John's house. In 1586 William was a party with his father and mother in an attempt to raise a further £20 on the property at Wilmcote, which was mortgaged to Edmund Lambert, in return for letting it go altogether. The attempt failed.

It is important to stress the intimacy and durability of this family link, because writers have over-emphasized what they call Shakespeare's lost years – the years between now and his arrival in London – in which they imagine that he virtually deserted his family. Yet there is no evidence whatever that he left home while his three children were so extremely young. The view of love that he constantly expressed emphasizes faithfulness in love as the greatest good. My impression is that Shakespeare thought of human love with the same mystical intensity as John of the Cross thought of the love of God. Germaine Greer has made this point very well, and it is certainly consonant with my own reading of Shakespeare, and with the weight one should put on his greatest lyric, 'The Phoenix and the Turtle'. Still, in 1586 all that was to come. First he emerges as an Ovidian and multiple poet, and faultless, which must mean practised in verbal and metrical technique, ice-cool in control, extremely funny and sharply sensuous. That was surely the mood of the moment in 1582, but Shakespeare went beyond other poets, perhaps because he was provincial and meant more by what he said.

It is an important point that Shakespeare was already a poet before he undertook plays: first probably to patch them, then to adapt them. He was indeed a constant adapter, a renewer and cannibalizer of his own forms, as restless and multifarious and fertile as Picasso (or Ovid). His works are not a single monument but a mountain range. The only play he ever wrote without adapting any known story or stories is the *Tempest*, which draws on Montaigne, on a recent report of a sea voyage and on the Italian Comedy players, the adapters and remakers of plots *par excellence*. The verses on the gloves for Mr Aspinall tell us very little, and the rumours of the ballad on Sir Thomas Lucy tell us even less. When he arrived in London he knew the work of Spenser and, I think, of Ronsard, of whose style we have a fascinating parody in Richard Tarlton's *Newes out of Purgatorie* (1590), probably by Robert Armin. Shakespeare's own eye as a poet was on the relatively short long poem, the amusing, thrilling, ornamental narrative with dialogue, in the style that derives from episodes in Ovid's *Metamorphoses*. He was amorous, light-hearted and sharp.

It is just possible that his Sonnets contain very early work. Sonnet 145, 'Those lips that Love's own hands did make', with its awful pun about Hathaway, if the pun is really intended, would have to be early.

> 'I hate' she altered with an end
> that followed it as gentle day
> doth follow night. . . .
> 'I hate' from hate away she threw,
> and saved my life, saying 'not you'.

I would be pleased to disregard the pun, but the Sonnets do seem to contain other naming puns, all jejune to my mind. It was a game the Elizabethans liked to play. The unusual and light metre of this sonnet, combined with its trivial theme, might sway a reasonable critic to believe that the poem is early and the pun intended. The latest editor of the Sonnets, John Kerrigan, calls it 'a pretty trifle which has been much abused'. This odd sonnet uses 'you' where the others about the Dark Lady use 'thou'. (God forbid that some lunatic should suggest Anne Hathaway was the Dark Lady.) Yet, as Kerrigan points out, sonnet 145 does fit very neatly between its neighbours in the collection. The suggestion that it is meant to do so was made by Andrew Gurr in *Essays in Criticism* in 1971 and must stand until it is demolished, which it has not yet been. I find it almost too tasteless to credit, but not quite. Yet how very odd of Shakespeare to have kept this and only this from his early verse. If this one is a genuine relic of his juvenilia, are there perhaps others among the Sonnets?

Shakespeare was not isolated from the theatre by living in the remoter shires. Actors travelled whenever there was plague in London, going as far as economic necessity might drive them. The roads were crowded with wanderers of many kinds, most of them poor and miserable and some of them villains, perhaps driven to villainy by necessity. Players were whipped as sturdy beggars and parasites unless they were a nobleman's servants or had letters from two justices of the peace. Robert Greene, in *The Art of Coney-Catching*, makes it plain that a famous patron was help in trouble: one had only to name him. The recognized companies of players would wear his badge or livery. In the 1590s Shakespeare wore that of the Lord Chamberlain, the Queen's cousin Lord Hunsdon – a rampant swan still to be seen stamped in gold on the books Lord Hunsdon gave to the Bodleian Library.

The first actors' company licensed under the new reign were Lord Leicester's Men in 1574. In 1582 the Earls of Sussex, Leicester and Oxford, perhaps Derby and Lord Hunsdon all had companies, though until the 1590s their actors and their precise activities are very hard to trace. The Lord Mayor of London hated them, and the Privy Council growled about them. One company would take men from another, and one might rise as another declined.

In England the players acted in tavern yards and provincial town halls, alternating with fencers and acrobats. When there was a riot in the audience, the tougher actors joined in. The company of the Queen's Men, picked by the Master of the Rolls in 1583, broke up into small groups for lack of effective patronage and disintegrated. In 1589, they were at Maidstone in January, Canterbury in February, Dover, Winchester and Gloucester in April, Leicester, Ipswich and Aldeburgh in May, Norwich in June, then Lancashire, Carlisle, Scotland, Coventry, Oxford, Reading and Nottingham. They were recorded more than once at Stratford-upon-Avon, and at small places like Marlborough.

The first Stratford visit is not precisely dated, but the substantial fact remains that Shakespeare was drawn to London by the theatre. He started as an employee. The story that he simply set out to seek his fortune makes no sense, and if there is any truth in Sir William Davenant's anecdote about his holding the heads of people's horses so successfully that he was noticed, it lies only in the tiny detail that the boys who held horses were called 'Shakespeare's boys'. Shakespeare employed them of course, but he was not a boy himself. The tale that he was call-boy or prompter's assistant might be true, particularly if he was a patcher-up of plays, but the theatrical tradition about this cited by Malone is terribly late. (It is a pity about the heads of the horses, because J. O. Halliwell-Phillipps did some of his most brilliant research on the subject. He proved that the Earl of Rutland owned a horse-washing pond in Shoreditch, where Shakespeare could have conveniently done some washing and grooming. He also discovered that the Mayor complained of horse-thieves at the playhouse, thus creating employment for the young Shakespeare.)

People did go to London to seek their fortunes, but the difference is great. John Sadler of Stratford 'joined himself to the carter' in order to get there, and sold his horse at Smithfield for £10. An anecdote from the *Holy Life of Mrs Elizabeth Walker* (1690) tells us that he found it extremely difficult to get himself apprenticed to any master for so little, but at last he was taken on trial by a Mr Brokesbank, a grocer, and then bound as apprentice at Bucklesbury for eight years.

The Strolling Player in *Ratsey's Ghost* (Part 2) (1606) says 'I have heard indeed of some that have gone to London very meanly, and have come in time to be exceeding wealthy,' but Shakespeare lacked the motive for such a desperate move. Unless he had had something obvious to offer the theatre, he would not have been taken on in the first place. That something included charm and confidence, as well as a very good memory and power of poetry. He was a poet before he was an actor, but it was surely acting that taught him Kyd's style, and Marlowe's different style, both of which he mastered at once. From the time he first smelt it, he was essentially a man of the theatre.

Peter Milward and others have elaborated the view that Shakespeare went from Stratford into Lancashire through a Catholic network, perhaps as a tutor, then as one of a little troop of players in a gentleman's house, where he appears as Shakeshaft, ending up in the players' company of Ferdinando Lord Strange, the shortlived Catholic Earl of Derby. E. A. J. Honigman recently restated the case in *Shakespeare: The Lost Years*. I have tried to convince myself that he is right, but I have failed to do so. There is really no evidence for the belief at all, unless you are prepared to stretch conjecture into evidence. The conjecture is seductive, but it relies on some degree of the conspiracy explanation of history and there is really no ground for it. In the Elizabethan period that is often tempting; I am convinced, for instance, that Lord Strange was the victim of a conspiracy devised by Burghley, and that he was poisoned because he saw through it and went straight to the Queen. That particular plot was unearthed by Christopher Devlin in *Hamlet's Divinity*. But Ferdinando was a credible Catholic claimant to the Crown of England. *Circa regna tonat*, wrote Wyatt of his own imprisonment. Thunder growls around the Crown.

I do not believe that Shakespeare drifted shiftlessly into a troop of ragged players, or that he took private service in obscure Lancashire. His talent was enormous and obvious. I think he went to London following actors he met in the provinces. James Burbage was one of Leicester's players in the 1570s, and there were Burbages in Stratford (one was bailiff in 1555); that might easily have been Shakespeare's connection. The most likely date for his move to London is 1589. By 1591 he was an effective and brilliant dramatic writer, and that can scarcely have taken less than two years. In 1589 the twins were five; Shakespeare was twenty-five and seven years married. The absolute earliest he can have gone to the capital is 1587, the year of Thomas Kyd's *Spanish Tragedy* and Marlowe's *Tamburlaine*, the greatest prevailing influences in his early work, but I reckon he was at home for the Armada scare of 1588. The goings-on at Stratford at that time, the issue of elderly weapons to untrained men, and the quantities of sack consumed by the gentry who supervised the muster (with even less bread to go with it than Falstaff had) must have been memorable. The Stratford records of the event have been edited by Fripp with a lively commentary. When the army got to Gravesend the Armada had already been dispersed by bad weather, with some annoyance from volunteers and pirates, who appeared on the heels of the great ships from places like the Helford river and the Fowey. The Queen made her famous speech to men who had marched all day, and arrived to find no camp, no bread and no beer. The Jesuit Pedro de Ribadeneyra made an even better speech when the Armada set out from Spain – but anyway, our side won, which was a relief to the people of places like Stratford.

· 3 ·

Early Shakespeare

The first great success of the English verse theatre is a phenomenon of the 1590s, coinciding rather exactly with Shakespeare's own success. It is worth pausing to trace at least the outlines of what had happened, though I shall not offer the reader the very full details to be found in the works of E. K. Chambers and others.

Nicholas Udall's *Ralph Roister Doister* dates from about 1550, when Peele and Spenser and Lyly were not yet born. It was an adaptation from Plautus of more interest than merit. In the early 1560s Seneca's tragedies were translated into English. In 1561 *Gorboduc* by Thomas Norton and Thomas Sackville (later Lord Buckhurst) was played at the Inner Temple before the Queen. Its blank verse is said to owe something to Surrey's translation of part of the *Aeneid*, but *Gorboduc* is not very good. In the later 1560s the variety and dexterity of dramatists increased, but nothing exciting occurred in English poetry or dramatic art until the 1570s. In 1576, the year that Spenser left Cambridge having already written some remarkable blank verse sonnets, James Burbage built the Theatre at Shoreditch, and the Curtain Theatre there followed at once. The fifty-two popular plays presented to Queen Elizabeth between 1568 and 1580 were all written in rhymed verses. As late as 1578, in his preface to *Promos and Cassandra*, George Whetstone is pleading for a new kind of play which is neither popularly low nor academically severe. He uses a mixture of couplets, rhymes, ballad metre and blank verse: mixtures of almost this kind look normal to Shakespeare, at least in comedy.

The pull of the new tide was felt in 1579, with Spenser's *Shepheardes Calender* and Lyly's *Euphues*. I have come to admire Lyly greatly, though not so much *Euphues*, but it must be pointed out that most of his dramatic work is in prose and lyric verse, only his early *The Woman in the Moon* being in blank verse. He wrote his comedies for child actors: they were elite entertainments. But the state of the adult profession of acting was deplorable, however lively. The old Royal Interlude Players who dated from Henry VII and Henry VIII having died out, the Privy Council commissioned the Master of the Rolls in 1581 'to order and reform, authorize and put down' plays, players, playmakers and their playing-places. The City made a long series of moves to suppress them on disciplinary and puritanical grounds, which is why the Theatre and the Curtain were built in Shoreditch, outside the City limits. In order to stop plays there in time of plague, the City authorities had to negotiate with the Under-Sheriff of Middlesex. When one of the Queen's players, Richard Tarlton the clown, died in Armada year, the best company of the day soon fell to pieces. His place was taken a little later by Will Kemp, clown, acrobat and morris dancer, who danced his way from London to Norwich and wrote a book about it; he was Shakespeare's clown. Several people now had a financial interest in organizing the theatre in London, but plays and tumblers still went together, even at Court, and in 1589 a political crisis arose which ruined whatever company structure existed.

This surfaced as a war of pamphlets, the first by 'Martin Marprelate', which fiercely and gleefully attacked the authority of bishops. The players' companies suffered from the clamp-down that resulted, and those that survived were watched for subversive plays until the end of the reign or later. After Marprelate came the plague, and the players were forced to travel because theatres shut. Or 'they broke', says Henslowe the theatre manager, 'and went into the country to play'. That was not an easy life. 'Our company is great, and thereby our charge intolerable, in travelling the country, and the continuance thereof will be a means to bring us to division and separation.'

The separations make it hard at times to follow the fortunes of individual companies. If Shakespeare started as an actor and nothing else, which I doubt, since he was certainly a talented writer and never became a famous actor, then it is not quite certain to which of the wandering groups he attached himself. Consider the case of the Turk, for example. We hear around 1590 of 'the Turkey Tumblers', then 'the Turk went upon ropes', then at Coventry 'the Queen's players and the Turk'. At Shrewsbury he turns out to be a Hungarian. At Gloucester a few years later we hear the last of him: 'a waggon in the pageant for the Turk'.

The London theatres were built because the City's moral and political hostility to plays and players drove the managers to build them; otherwise the lives of players and the production of plays had an intolerably slipshod economic basis. At last when the plague was over in 1594 the entire profession was reorganized under the Lord Chamberlain. His company took the best established players and writers it could get, including William Shakespeare. They played at Court when the Queen chose, mostly around Christmas, and at other times they performed for money in playhouses. Threepence, then sixpence, was the minimum entry fee, and it was up to a shilling by the end of the reign. You paid more for a seat. Suddenly the profession of acting became steadier and more lucrative, particularly for the 'sharers' in the company, its fellows or managers who had a financial stake in it. They died rich men. Shakespeare had attained that status when he was thirty.

More important still from our point of view, he was a retained writer. He could write as much as he liked and his audience was assured. The normal way of getting a play commissioned was to submit a plot, then perhaps an act or two. More often than not the management commissioned several writers at once to work on different sections of a plot, because writers had their specialities, and anyway the management were always in a hurry for a new play. Shakespeare certainly adapted old material, and I think he occasionally fleshed out the bones of plots that someone handed him. A camel is a horse designed by a committee, and some of his early plots have camel-like qualities. But in principle he wrote his own plays, at least from the time he was a sharer. Revisions and interpolations happened later. It was an actors' theatre and the writer dealt directly with the actors, which made it an ideal writers' theatre. There was no producer or director other than the actors, which made it a golden age of a kind.

Clowns did much as they liked. Kemp used to put in jokes of his own, and even where the poet wrote them they followed traditional themes of the clown's repertory. The scene of Lancelot Gobbo and his father in *The Merchant of Venice*, which had me in ecstasies of laughter as a little boy when Donald Wolfit played Shylock (with a memorable spitting range in one scene), turns up in Armin's *Fool upon Fool, or A Nest of Ninnies* as an anecdote about the Court jester to Henry VIII and his country uncle. The gravediggers' scene in *Hamlet* appears from the same source to have origins that are just as old. Shakespeare mingles comedy and tragedy because they were not traditionally distinct, except perhaps in academic plays. Edmund Campion has a preposterous comic scene in a Latin play of heroic high seriousness, which he wrote for the Jesuit college in Prague. The English play *Horestes*, based on an Italian adaptation of a Latin version of Euripides, begins 'Enter Rusticus and Hodge, upon the battlements of Mycenae'. The English popular theatre was only beginning to be classicized in Shakespeare's lifetime, and the process was never quite completed, though there are not many jokes in *Julius Caesar*. Shakespeare was extremely free in how he wrote, so long as the audience was entertained, the Church and state and social order presupposed and not too openly mocked, and the Queen prayed for at the end – a custom formalized until yesterday by the singing of 'God Save the Queen'. The theatre was a new force, and all he had to do was play on it: an empty shell, and all he had to do was fill it.

His greatest opportunity of all was musical. England was crazy about music, not just private gentlemen's performances, but every barber had a lute lying about in his shop for customers to play while they waited. The Italian influence on English music taught the English in the late 1580s and the 1590s a new lyric poetry, a mastery of lyric form and a sharper sense of

47

the sound-value of language, the effect of metre on syllables, than we have ever had again since the profound social changes of the Civil War. The lyric poem was fresh to Shakespeare and it fascinated him. If any works by him lurk unrecognized, they are probably among the Elizabethan lyrics we call anonymous. Robert Graves argued that he wrote the classic version of the traditional mad beggars' song called Tom o' Bedlam's song. The song in *Robin Good-fellow, Part 2* (1628) beginning 'And can the physician make sick men well?' sounds thirty years earlier than the play, which puts it well within Shakespeare's working lifetime. But in lyric poetry, though less so in dramatic poetry, an entire generation came forward together, among which one could be forgiven for feeling that almost anyone could have written almost any of these lyrics. They were certainly more different from all other poets than they were from one another. Even so, Shakespeare used music more often and more effectively – more variously – than any other dramatic writer. He was born at the perfect moment, and he seized this opportunity as he did the others.

The occasion of his success was the breakdown of Thomas Kyd (1558–94) and the death of Christopher Marlowe in a tavern brawl in June 1593. It is clear enough that Burghley had intended to use Marlowe to implicate Walter Ralegh in a charge of atheism and heaven knows what else. Marlowe himself was implicated by some papers found in lodgings he shared with Kyd, who broke under torture and was never the same again. The evidence at Marlowe's inquest suggests that he was assassinated, and if so the patron behind the hired killers is likely to have been Ralegh, or some nobleman as powerful as Ralegh, acting in fear of Burghley's spider's web. But this dramatic story is not, alas, unusual; Marlowe had previously been charged with a knifing: and spying, intrigues and crimes of violence were common among players. Ben Jonson among others went to prison for a killing. When he went there again for seditious writing and came out unscathed, his mother boasted at the celebration dinner, in the presence of Camden the historian and Selden the scholar, that if he had been condemned to have his ears hacked off she would have smuggled him poison into the prison. Shakespeare was first the imitator, then swiftly the successor of Kyd and of Marlowe.

The London into which Shakespeare arrived was a thin, densely populated forest of buildings strung along the banks of the Thames; it extended in depth not much further than Roman London, the walled town between St Paul's and the Tower, though to the west it reached Westminster and to the east perhaps a mile downriver. The fringe of buildings along the Surrey shore was very much thinner, a mere waterside screen, and extended less far, though it included the Bishop of Winchester's Palace, and St Mary Overy, which is now Southwark Cathedral. Not far east of London Bridge, the Clink prison and the Marshalsea prison faced the marshes downriver.

Cardinal Wolsey's ambitious and extensive palace, which had extended from Westminster nearly to Trafalgar Square (as it now is) had become the Palace of Westminster, but it was still a jumble of separate structures. Henry VIII had taken in St James's Park, and Elizabeth had built a vast, timber banqueting hall near her private apartments, on the site now called Whitehall after its white paint. This was the centre of Court life, and Shakespeare will have acted there. In 1606 it was rebuilt in stone and brick; in 1619 it was burned down and replaced under Inigo Jones by the present magnificent hall. But in Shakespeare's early days it was a great hall differing only in size and grandeur from houses he already knew all over the countryside. Edward Arden's head was still stuck on Tower Bridge like a rotten apple. The playhouses on the south bank as they arose had the same names as the brothels there. London swarmed like a rabbit warren, but its great expansion had scarcely begun. Its principal highway was the Thames, and its only great houses were noblemen's houses. Its population was socially and racially extremely mixed. High above everything else towered Gothic St Paul's like a black crow, and the Tower like some ominous cliffs.

The noise, the crowds, the animals and their droppings, the glimpses of grandeur and the amazing squalor of the poor, were beyond modern imagination. When the plague came, it spread like a field fire. But London was alive as it had never been. Crazy astrology, superstitious medicine and genuine science flourished in the same courtyards and under the same roofs. Conspiracy and the rumours of conspiracy were in this tavern or the next. Fortunes were made by wholesalers, merchants and adventurers. Courtiers spent money on a fantastic scale. In the printing of books, in the arts of luxury and decoration, London was at last a renaissance city. The Queen ordered public lectures in the use of globes and maps. Roman or italic type was driving out blockletter, Gothic type. The crudest and the finest amusements were available within yards of each other. The Master of the Rolls had his office practically in the stews, and the bagpipes were as common as the lute. This intense, crowded place was so small that there was no part of London from which it took more than ten minutes to escape on to the river, which still had salmon in it, or into the fields, which were full of wild flowers.

London Bridge was a long series of four-storey buildings like the Ponte Vecchio at Florence, except that its buildings were taller and grimmer, and the road across the bridge passed continually through narrow archways and gloomy courtyards. It was a stone bridge standing on huge islands of elmwood, which is rot-proof, sunk into the bed of the river. Beyond the gardens on the south bank lay meadows and marshes. State barges of Venetian design, but on less than Venetian scale, and a swarm of ferry boats moved on the water. A daily barge service connected London with Dagenham, far away down the huge windings of the Thames. Upstream as far as Hampton Court a clock built for Henry VIII by the son of a central European immigrant recorded the southing of the moon, to show the time of high tide at London Bridge. To the north the green hills of Harrow and Hampstead were visible far away across the fields, and the air was crowded with windmills. The cattle that fed London came from as far away as the Welsh and Scottish mountains. There were far more churches in London than have survived. The houses of great noblemen were scarcely distinguishable from fortresses.

It is hard to know quite how far the explosion of London had extended in a given year. When Shakespeare was born it had scarcely begun, but by 1600 it was at full blast. Stow's Survey (1598) already observes 'in place of elm trees many small tenements raised' at Shadwell, which was owned by the Dean of Paul's, and the houses of shipwrights and cottages of sailors from Radcliffe 'almost to Poplar and so to Blackwall'. On the road east from Aldgate, 'both the sides of the street be pestered with cottages, even up to Whitechapel Church, and half a mile beyond it, into the common field', leaving no room for a carriage and a herd of sheep to pass, and no dry ground for pedestrians. The cross that once stood at Shoreditch was now a smith's forge, and at Aldermanbury 'a fair well with two buckets' was 'of late years converted to a pump'. There are pastoral touches to the street names of Cripplegate to this day: Wood Street, Lad Lane, Maiden Lane, Milk Street, Monkswell Street and Gayspur Lane. But these streets were swarming with flatcaps (apprentices) and with business of every kind, even though the boundaries of Cripplegate were still defined by a cowhouse. The stews on the south bank had existed by privilege since the reign of Henry II. Monarchs shut them down now and then. Henry VIII did so 'by sound of trumpet' and royal proclamation. But they always came back, and the antiquary John Stow records the signs painted on their walls: the Boar's Head, the Swan, the Bell, the Cardinal's Arms, and the Gun. Murder was common and fighting was casual. Everyone carried a weapon. The whole of the vast trade of London depended on patronage.

Poetry flourished under patronage like everything else. I do not know when Shakespeare started to write sonnets, but what he produced was a sequence, deliberately linked and subdivided, with the traditional ironic longer poem added at the end: *A Lover's Complaint*. He did not put all the work together until he had become a close friend of the young Earl of Southampton, probably near to the time of *The Rape of Lucrece*. I will deal with all the sonnets together later, though as I reckon that *A Lover's Complaint* is an early poem I will deal with it here. It has the humour, the sharpness, the structural absurdity and the dandy quality of an early work. It is full of parody and self-parody and high spirits, yet it is definitely not as good as *Venus and Adonis*. Shakespeare was getting better all the time, and any exception requires close scrutiny. *A Lover's Complaint* first appeared with the full sonnet sequence in 1609, and recent scholarship has suggested a date for it of about 1600 or so; but I am unable to credit that late date on the arguments advanced for it, which depend on the quasi-computerized measurement of Shakespeare's style from year to year. I think that not only most of the Sonnets, as everyone agrees, but also *A Lover's Complaint* were hanging around for a long time before they were leaked to the press in 1609.

I thought I had never doubted the authorship of this brilliant and amusing poem, but find that my old notes reveal many rereadings and increasing certainty; Shakespeare's authorship used to be doubted in the early 1900s – the Victorians disliked its subject matter – and critics have neglected the poem, though Swinburne saw its point; indeed, I cannot imagine a poet unable to do so. It is written in rhyme royal, which Shakespeare perhaps learned from Spenser; it is 329 lines long: *Venus and Adonis* is 1194 lines. *A Lover's Complaint* begins with surrealist vividness and rushes straight into the middle of its subject, like *Venus and Adonis*.

> From off a hill whose concave womb reworded
> A plaintful story from a sist'ring vale,
> My spirits t'attend this double voice accorded,
> And down I laid to list the sad-tun'd tale;
> Ere long espied a fickle maid full pale,
> Tearing of papers, breaking rings a-twain. . . .

Shakespeare begins with self-echoing noises like those of Virgil's first Eclogue, *'Tityre tu . . .'*, with the poet listening to a self-echoing pastoral love-lament, and by line 6 he is laughing. He is pleasant about the girl's straw hat, only mildly sentimental about her age – 'Time had not scythed all that youth begun' – and humorously compassionate – 'Some beauty peep'd through lattice of sear'd age'. These twelve lines are full of the grit and gravel of poetry, detailed observation and uninhibited thought and feeling. They are both swift and ornamental. The maid weeps into her handkerchief, 'Laund'ring the silken figures in the brine'; she sits by a river, 'Like usury, applying wet to wet'. The parody rant, the parody of 'putting on the agony, putting on the style', as they sang in the 1960s, is extremely funny. Shakespeare can impersonate and parody at the same time. But there must be a confidant, an interaction, a conversation observed. 'A reverend man that graz'd his cattle nigh' provides it. He is a man of the world retired from the world; a real peasant would not do.

> So slides he down upon his grained bat,
> And comely distant sits he by her side. . . .

She tells him how she fell in love too young. '"Small show of man was yet upon his chin"', but never was an Elizabethan youth so attractively painted in words. Shakespeare can see him better in the girl's eyes than he sees the girl in his own; but as the girl proceeds, one sympathizes and identifies with her, poor thing. The boy addresses her at eloquent length, making a number of points that Shakespeare likes to make, about jewels and 'deep-brained sonnets', and blushes. He seems to speak of emblems.

> 'O, then, advance of yours that phraseless hand
> Whose white weighs down the airy scale of praise;
> Take all these similes to your own command,
> Hallowed with sighs. . . .'

> 'Lo, this device was sent me from a nun,
> Or sister sanctified, of holiest note,
> Which late her noble suit in court did shun,
> Whose rarest havings made the blossoms dote;
> For she was sought by spirits of richest coat,
> But kept cold distance, and did thence remove
> To spend her living in eternal love. . . .'

> 'My parts had pow'r to charm a sacred nun. . . .'

The flickering play of paradoxes and ironies is pleasing but almost too swift, too intellectual. One has to pause at certain lines for them to sink in, as at 'Whose rarest havings made the blossoms dote'. One feels that Shakespeare is using up quarryloads of gems, the material for twenty poems. One almost longs for the jog-trot of the drab style or the monotonous beauty of ballads about which everyone thinks and feels the same. This is young man's poetry, and like all successful pastoral it is essentially urban: the young lover is a sophisticated, self-loving deceiver, and the old man knows a thing or two, as does the poet.

> 'O father, what a hell of witchcraft lies
> In the small orb of one particular tear! . . .'

> When he most burn'd in heart-wish'd luxury,
> He preach'd pure maid and prais'd cold chastity. . . .

> 'Ay me! I fell; and yet do question make
> What I should do again for such a sake. . . .'

She longs that his wicked attractions, the 'infected moisture of his eye' and all the rest,

> Would yet again betray the fore-betray'd,
> And new pervert a reconciled maid!

And the poem is over, as suddenly as it began. We hear no more of the reverend man, nothing of the girl's fate, no comment from the poet. The last words are her wish that it would happen all over again. The tone is light, the poem cuts somewhat deep, and that is all. *A Lover's Complaint* is just a joking lyric set as a narrative. Conventional thoughts and feelings are rhetorically exploited in such a way that they are freshened and mocked. It is a brisk and cheering poem, and we can see at once that we have on our hands a poet who will be enjoyable for a hundred years – perhaps a great poet, if all the fireworks can lead to development: human deepening seems too much to hope for, but he has got a long way beyond Alexander Aspinall's gloves.

Venus and Adonis was written in 1592 or early 1593, when the theatres were shut. Just as the girl in *A Lover's Complaint* is older than her lover, and is left lamenting, so Venus in the later poem is older than Adonis. It would be absurd to say that Shakespeare fails to relish these girls; I think that, in an indirect way, they are a tribute to his wife, who taught him some degree of humorous tenderness towards women which one would not learn from Ovid or even from Chaucer.

Shakespeare made his living among players. The dates of his early plays are difficult to fix with perfect precision, but several of them were written before 1594 and some before 1592, and the order in which they were written is more or less detectable. We are helped in deciphering it by the records of two men, Francis Meres and Philip Henslowe, who moved in Shakespeare's milieu and became acquainted with his work in one way or another.

Meres and Henslowe are two sides of the coin of Elizabethan culture. Meres came to London about 1594. He wrote *Gods Arithmeticke* (1597), translated *Devotion* by Luis of Granada (1598) and became Rector of Wing in Rutlandshire. His Spanish translation shows original and admirable taste. In 1598 he also published *Palladis Tamia and Wit's Treasury*, a derivative but amusing commonplace book of the kind that underlies Montaigne's *Essays*, like a Latin or Greek *Gnomologium*. It includes comparisons of Elizabethan with Latin and Greek writers. Meres's hero is Shakespeare, the English Ovid and Plautus and Seneca in one – one of the six immortals (the others are Sidney, Spenser, Drayton, Samuel Daniel and William Warner) and our answer to the Greeks in tragedy, in comedy and in poetry about 'the perplexities of love'. He says that 'the Muses would speak with Shakespeare's fine filed tongue if they would speak English.' In a similar but much odder comparison of ancient and modern in 1595 or 1596, Richard Carew said that Roger Ascham was the English Cicero, Daniel the English Ovid, Chaucer the English Varro(!), Spenser the English Lucan, and Shakespeare the English Catullus.

Meres refers to the Sonnets in particular and gives a list of plays, which is of invaluable help in dating them. He mentions only one that seems to be lost: *Loves Labour Won*, unless we have it under an alternative title. He also discusses English painters and musicians; his editor D. C. Allen (facsimile 1938) thinks he had some connection with the Chapel Royal. Thomas Combe rates a mention as one of the three English emblem poets.

Tarlton the clown gets very high praise; it sounds as if he could extemporize in verse. So does 'young Charles Fitz-Jeffrey, that high-touring falcon' for his life of Drake.

Philip Henslowe was a head gamekeeper's son from Sussex, who worked for the bailiff of some great estates. He lived in Southwark in the Liberty of the Clink, and married his master's widow in 1577. He was a dyer, a dealer, a pawnbroker, a brothel and tavern owner, a dock·owner and a moneylender. He was also an early theatre owner. He bought the Little Rose on the south bank in 1584 or 1585 and began to rebuild in 1586. In 1592 his stepdaughter Joan married the actor Edward Alleyn, and from that time Alleyn and Henslowe were business partners. From February 1592 we have detailed accounts of his theatrical ventures. He hired out not only theatres but plays and props. Dekker, Drayton, George Chapman, Henry Chettle and others sold plays directly to him. He liked to have a financial hold on writers. In 1594 he controlled the theatre out at Newington Butts, and had an interest in Paris Gardens on the south bank. In 1603 he lost his lease of the Rose, which he then threatened to pull down. In 1604 he bought from its holder what in 1598 he had tried and failed to acquire: the office of Master of the King's Game of bulls, bears, mastiffs and lions. His dock sheltered the King's barges under James I. He was an unpleasant customer in many ways. He died in the same year as Shakespeare, leaving his wealth to his wife because he admitted to having treated her unkindly; the will was vainly disputed by a nephew. In Shakespeare's earliest London days, it was impossible for him not to deal with Henslowe.

The first of Shakespeare's plays is surely the most lamentable Roman tragedy of *Titus Andronicus*, an adaptation of Kyd's style with some touches of Marlowe, an interesting exercise with signs of great talent for playmaking. Henslowe's diary calls it 'ne', meaning new, in January 1594, but that would mean only that it had not been played in London before then. Ben Jonson in 1614 assumed it was very old and classed it with Kyd's *Hieronimo*. 'He that will swear, *Hieronimo* or *Andronicos* are the best plays yet, shall pass unexcepted at here, as a man whose judgement shows it is constant, and hath stood still these five and twenty or thirty years . . . such a one the author knows where to find him.' He made the same *Hieronimo* joke in 1600 but without giving the timespan. Jonson was paid by Henslowe for improvements to *Hieronimo* in September 1601 and June 1602, but if he wrote any they are lost; the ones printed in 1602 are not by him. It appears then that the old ranting, bloodstained style was popular for some time.

Someone called Danter registered a ballad on the subject of *Titus* in February 1594, which, if it is the pitiful piece that survives, has little relation to Shakespeare, but he also printed a quarto text of the play in that same year, 'as played by Derby's Men, Pembroke's Men, and Sussex's Men'. Chambers thought this might be the same play that Henslowe recorded as *Titus and Vespasian* in 1592, revamped. George Peele (1556–96) has been suggested as the original author, on no evidence. In 1687 Edward Ravenscroft assured the world that Shakespeare 'only gave some master-touches to one or two of the principal parts', but that is surely because the style and plot revolted Ravenscroft. It is authentic Shakespeare all the same, and was known as his in 1598 to Francis Meres, and was included in the posthumous folio edition of his works called the First Folio, a most reliable criterion.

An interesting drawing by Henry Peacham of what looks like a perform- ance of *Titus Andronicus* has survived at Longleat, dated 1594. It stands at the head of a combined text of two passages from the play, joined by an otherwise unknown line. Infinite variations of subtlety can be and have been expended on the history of the play; revision is always a strong card to play in these matters, and W. W. Greg suggested that there were two plays of the same name, one played by Pembroke's Men and possibly revised by Shakespeare, the other by Sussex's Men and printed in the first quarto. Pembroke's Men's version gets burned at the Globe in 1613 so the King's Men use a quarto of 1611 (the third quarto). Since act 3, scene i, first appeared in the Folio of 1623, Greg is forced to suppose that Shakespeare's fellow actors added that from memory. This is all far from likely, and I record it only as an example of the sort of argument textual scholars of Shakespeare have to face: I will not burden the reader with more of them than I can help in this book. The play reads and acts very well as it is. My reason for refusing to date it in late 1593 is that in *Henry VI* Shakespeare was throwing off this style, and I do not see how that play can possibly be later than 1591. Therefore I think *Titus Andronicus* in its first form dates from 1589 or 1590.

I am not able to disentangle the history of its revisions, though we are lucky enough to have an edition by the acutest of textual editors, J. C. Maxwell. The only surviving copy of the first quarto was found in Sweden in 1904. Maxwell is fairly certain that its printer worked from the author's manuscript, 'not always finally tidied up for the stage'. The Folio was based on the 1611 quarto; each of them added new corruptions to the text as well as making new corrections, including the new scene Greg noticed, added from manuscript of course. This scene has some very good bits of Shakespeare in it, including the grotesquely dramatic killing of the fly, yet it hardly furthers the action and its loss would not be noticed.

> To bid Aeneas tell the tale twice o'er
> How Troy was burnt and he made miserable?
>
> ... How if that fly had a father and mother?
> How would he hang his slender gilded wings
> And buzz lamenting doings in the air!
> Poor harmless fly,

That with his pretty buzzing melody
Came here to make us merry! And thou hast kill'd him.

I'll to thy closet, and go read with thee
Sad stories chanced in the times of old.
Come, boy, and go with me; thy sight is young,
And thou shalt read when mine begin to dazzle.

It is best to make up one's mind how good Shakespeare is, with all his warts, and what kind of poet he is, with his gritty details, his drifting phrases of music, which so often have a Latin origin, and his essentially dramatic quality. The sad stories, and the tale Aeneas told to Dido that brings them to his mind, are Virgilian. The dramatic quality lies not only in the power of rhetorical speeches, but in interruption, in variety of sentence and change of mood, and in the fact that these characters are not talking to an audience but to each other, so that we see them, including the business of the fly and of the spectacles, differently from how they know or express themselves. The poet is absent, as he mostly was in *A Lover's Complaint*, and the characters do not know they are being observed. And yet one can see precisely how and why Shakespeare wrote in the incident of the fly. The word 'doings' is unexpected, yet one has only to try substituting another word to catch how right 'doings' is. It is not poetic invention but a kind of recorded, characterized speech, an observation of life.

In *Titus Andronicus* the English have got in among the Romans in numerous details. The Elizabethan stage Romans are a convention, and Shakespeare was expected to 'bring them home to men's business and bosoms' as he did. Terence Spencer says in a discussion of this play what is so often true of Shakespeare as a young man, that he 'seems anxious not to get it all right, but to get it all in'. The play has startling structural weaknesses, yet as a drama it is still beyond the powers of any other writer of the day, with the single exception of Kyd. I suppose it remains possible that Kyd chose the setting and wrote the plot before he was arrested, and that to finish it was Shakespeare's first commission, but the play we have shows no trace of Kyd's actual writing, and I think its date must be too early for it to be a leftover fragment of Kyd's career as a writer.

The play's Roman world is a kind of grotesque wonderland, and its momentum is hellish. Its language is civilized, but the heart of it is the despairing barbarity of Seneca and Ovid. One should not underestimate the nastiness of the Romans. Elsewhere on the Elizabethan stage, the grotesque is meant to be funny: the devils in *Doctor Faustus* and the ghost jokes in *Hamlet* offer another view of solemn themes, and Aaron in *Titus Andronicus* has a black humour that alienates his audience. The play is intended to be deadly serious, to disgust, horrify, terrify and sadden, because that is what Shakespeare in 1589 thought tragedy was for.

All the same, he is unable to restrain his lyrical tones altogether, even at a moment of tense horror.

> Did ever raven sing so like a lark
> That gives sweet tidings of the sun's uprise?

Nor can he restrain himself from emblems, from exciting pleasure even where he intends gloom, or from puns 'my suit, sweet, pardon what is past' or 'Mark, Marcus, mark'. Something akin to cheerfulness keeps breaking in: something akin to provincial sanity.

> A barren detested vale you see it is:
> The trees, though summer, yet forlorn and lean,
> Overcome with moss and baleful mistletoe;
> Here never shines the sun; here nothing breeds,
> Unless the nightly owl. . . .

It is obvious that Shakespeare is not really frightened of this dank and chilly place. He likes moss and mistletoe and owls: the horrid pit is just bad grazing, infertile, and full of snakes. Even in *Macbeth*, when the dark bird 'makes wing to th' rooky wood', one is thrilled partly because one has so often heard and seen them do it, and with unfailing pleasure. There is something homely and comforting about this level of evil in Shakespeare, perhaps because it derives from folktales and ghost stories. Still, one can see the characters being frightened of snakes, even if one feels otherwise oneself.

The play has an odd plot. It begins with the Emperor's son Saturninus and his brother Bassianus making Roman election speeches, but suddenly Titus Andronicus returns to Rome with prisoners, a coffin and his sons. The prisoners include Aaron the Moor, Tamora, Queen of the Goths, and her children. Andronicus buries his dead and decides to slaughter a son of Tamora at the family tomb. She protests. His daughter Lavinia and brother Marcus arrive, and Titus is elected Emperor. The Romans quarrel over Titus' daughter; they fight and Titus kills his son Mutius, observed by Tamora and the Moor. Saturninus adopts Tamora as his bride, and Titus sees his son buried. Tamora reconciles the quarrelling Romans.

In the second act, Aaron's sons quarrel over Lavinia, but Aaron offers them a stratagem.

> The Emperor's court is like the house of Fame,
> The palace full of tongues, of eyes, and ears;
> The woods are ruthless, dreadful, deaf, and dull.
> There speak and strike, brave boys, and take your turns. . . .

The hunting scene is brisk and cheerful, but Aaron and Tamora plot together. Aaron's sons murder Bassianus and rape Lavinia, and Aaron throws the blame for Bassianus' murder on two sons of Titus. The girl has her hands cut off and tongue cut out.

In the third act Titus pleads in vain for his sons, and laments furiously over his handless daughter.

> What fool hath added water to the sea,
> Or brought a fagot to bright-burning Troy?
> My grief was at the height before thou cam'st,
> And now like Nilus it disdaineth bounds.

Titus Andronicus agrees to have his hand cut off by Aaron to ransom his sons: but he has been tricked, and a messenger arrives with their dead heads and Titus' detached hand. The young Shakespeare was pleased with stage props like these. The sad scene with the killing of the fly follows and closes the act.

In act 4 Lavinia reveals what was done to her by pointing to Ovid's story of Philomela and Tereus, and writing names in the dust. Andronicus sends Aaron and his sons an emblematic present of weapons wrapped in a verse. Tamora bears a black baby by Aaron. 'Here is the babe, as loathsome as a toad,' says the nurse, whom Aaron kills to keep her quiet; but he keeps his baby – 'Wheeke, wheeke! So cries a pig prepared to the spit.' He switches two babies. Titus is going mad; he conveys hints and strange messages through a clown, who is hanged for delivering them. Another Gothic war breaks out, with the last surviving son of Andronicus leading the Goths, who in act 5 arrive and by chance capture Aaron and his baby. Under threat of death, Aaron triumphantly confesses to utter wickedness:

> Yet, for I know thou art religious
> And hast a thing within thee called conscience,
> With twenty popish tricks and ceremonies
> Which I have seen thee careful to observe,
> Therefore I urge thy oath. . . .

The baby is to live: that is the oath. Tamora goes to Andronicus saying she is Revenge and her sons are Rape and Murder. He appears to accept this, but then cuts the throats of the sons.

> Hark, villains! I will grind your bones to dust,
> And with your blood and it I'll make a paste;
> And of the paste a coffin I will rear,
> And make two pasties of your shameful heads;
> And bid that strumpet, your unhallowed dam,
> Like to the earth, swallow her own increase.

Andronicus kills his daughter to release her from the shame of her rape, serves the pie ('coffin' is a pun) to Tamora and kills her and is killed, and his killer is killed. Aaron is condemned to be buried to the neck and starved to death, and Tamora's dead body to be thrown to the birds and animals.

This amazing rigmarole is warmed by intimate family feeling and chilled by the story's disgustingness. The structure of scenes does not go beyond contrast and variation, and the act divisions are negligible. And yet it works. The machinery of horror operates at a majestic pace. This is a better play than Kyd's *Hieronimo*, and in many ways more restrained. Its source seems to be a miserable prose fiction, a chap-book. But Shakespeare sets up his situation with deliberate slowness, and his verse holds the hideous action and the obscurities of motivation in suspense, so that the violence is almost unexpected. The same may be said for violence of words, which breaks shockingly through the tapestries of rant and rhetoric: the 'Wheeke, wheeke!', for instance. Shakespeare has put too much into this play, but many of its types of scene and its speeches are wonderfully reworked in later plays: in *Hamlet* and *King Lear* and *Richard II* and *Cymbeline*. The sacrifice of the Gothic prince in act 1 seems to be invented by Shakespeare, and may indicate a revision by Shakespeare to make some sense of the motives of characters, creating a further complexity of revenges. This prince has no speaking part, and in Dutch and German adaptations of Shakespeare in the next century he fails to appear.

The plot of *Titus* is so peculiar that it needs discussion. It is, after all, the first dramatic enterprise to engage Shakespeare's powers as a poet. Its momentum when enacted is that of a poem rather than that of its idiotic story. Verse theatre is a bastard form, but to Shakespeare it appears natural, and he is quite content, indeed delighted, to let the words serve the action, and the eye be entertained and held before the mind. A play is swiftly enacted and many of its lines are hardly noticed. Poetry is essentially memorable, but in the theatre it was the actors who were meant to remember it, and to find it dramatic. Only moments and phrases would linger in the memories of the audiences. There would be another play next week.

Nor did Shakespeare himself agonize over writing his verse plays. Like Menander, he took care with his fundamental plots, and with the characters that the plots demanded or suggested (more care with some characters, less with others), and then, when it was organized, he cast the whole thing quite swiftly into verse. Does that mean that the best passages of poetry are a gratuitous bonus? Sometimes yes, sometimes no, as we shall see. But it is extremely important that he was a poet before he was a dramatist; in the plays, it is always a poet who is writing: a poet who has no inhibition or snobbery about extending his talent in any direction and into any material that offers. As for the form of the play itself, he spent his life constantly and restlessly reshaping that. He was never satisfied with it, he was always exploiting it in new ways, because the theatre is competitive, and consumes freshness as a dog drinks water.

Titus Andronicus reflects London life and, in the hunt scene, country life. Dead people's heads are gruesome but commonplace horrors; the sexual violation of innocence is much more horrible. Lines like 'If there were reason for these miseries' and 'There greet in silence, as the dead are wont' and 'This monument five hundred years hath stood' have a ring of truth and of the experience of life. Seneca's Latin, invoked by Titus in act 4, scene i, is not just literature; it has a contemporary resonance: 'Lord of the great planet are you so slow to hear, so slow to see wickedness done?' Is it Rome or London that 'is but a wilderness of tigers'? In his Roman world, Shakespeare is free to embody utter wickedness and to express absolute despair. That side of his mind was as real as the Arcadian side. Yet in the same play he associates sunrise and hunting with the extreme of pleasure, and his imagination, like ours, was formed by his childhood. One would give a lot to know whether his own mother had read him 'sweet poetry, and Tully's Offices'; her influence on him is one of the great unknowns of this biography.

A few more scraps may tempt readers towards this absurd but often wonderful play.

> . . . our cheeks
> How they are stain'd, like meadows yet not dry
> With miry slime left on them by a flood?

> As who should say 'Old lad, I am thine own.'

> I'll make you feed on berries and on roots,
> And feed on curds and whey, and suck the goat,
> And cabin in a cave, and bring you up
> To be a warrior and command a camp.

That is Aaron to his baby. I think that by striving to understand characters like Aaron and Shylock and Othello, who are not real, of course, but fictions (Aaron being an inherited wicked character of a type dreamed up by Marlowe), Shakespeare taught himself a great deal about human suffering. The key to the conventions of revenge both on the stage and in real life is suffering, as he saw. The suffering that underlies revenge was a literary problem with a far-reaching moral solution which it was his lifework to unravel.

He was an Ovidian poet, a poet of situations. Dramatic enactment is full of incident, and situations as well as characters are transfigured in its course. Schoenbaum has written that he has sometimes toyed with the idea that in Elizabethan drama all roads lead to *King Lear*. This viewpoint is beguiling but, even though Shakespeare's development was swift and in more directions than one, at the time of his first play such a masterpiece as *Lear* was far beyond his horizon.

*   *   *

Titus Andronicus is largely a Senecan tragedy on a theme from Ovid; at least those are its ingredients, but it had already come a long way from the kind of play with similar ingredients that the Queen saw on her Oxford and Cambridge visits in the 1560s. In the first thirty years of her reign, the universities, fed by King Edward's grammar schools, had bred a drama that had outsoared its nest, and poets who did the same – in particular, Christopher Marlowe. Shakespeare knew Marlowe, and was spellbound by him. He was in London in the years of Marlowe's personal tragedy, and London was a small place then and the theatre a smaller place still. It is extremely likely that he acted in Marlowe's plays, and developed much of his own power by learning Marlowe by heart. They were the same age, but I do not believe that they ever co-operated: Marlowe was a mature poet and Shakespeare was not.

We do not know where Shakespeare lived first in London. Probably on the south bank, in one of Henslowe's inns or lodging houses. There is no doubt that he was acquainted with low life – not just with a bohemian circle but with criminal riff-raff too. He seems to see them *de haut en bas*; it is a world into which he adventures, but he knows it rather intimately. That experience probably belongs to his first London years. The location of the Boar's Head in *Henry IV* is interesting, because he puts it north of the river; but Henslowe owned a Boar's Head south of it, and the lively murder play *Arden of Feversham*, which was printed in 1592, before *Henry IV* was written, seems to me to satirize Shakespeare personally and to connect him with the south bank.

No one knows who wrote *Arden of Feversham*. It has two comic or at least low and bungling murderers called Black Will and Shakebag, and another villain called Greene. The verse wallows in blood as if it were written by Kyd, but it was not. It describes a murder that really happened, in February 1550/1. The play is full of thrilling wickedness: of a painter, for instance, 'for he can temper poison with his oil', so that you die by seeing the painting. But it also has some charming Marlovian lines:

> Sweet love thou knowst that we two Ovidlike
> Have oft chid morning when it gan to peep
> And often wish'd that dark Night's purblind steeds
> Would pull her by the purple mantle back.

Arden of Feversham is not good enough to be by Shakespeare, even at his earliest, though the play was attributed to him in 1770 and Swinburne accepted the attribution. At times it reads like a parody:

> . . . some ayrie spirit
> Would in the shape and likeness of a horse
> Gallop with Arden cross the Ocean. . . .

The lines that connect Shakespeare (Shakebag and Black Will) with the south bank occur in the last act:

> In Southwark dwells a bonny northern lass
> The widow Chambly: I'll to her house now. . . .

Shakebag is hoping to be hidden by this very fat widowed landlady, but he pushes her downstairs in the end 'and cut her tapster's throat' and flings them into the Thames. Black Will says of someone, 'I robbed him and his man once at Gad's Hill.' We seem to be in Falstaff's world, and the writer of *Arden* seems to associate Shakebag and Black Will with it. In the Epilogue we hear the fate of Shakebag and Black Will (Greene is hanged):

> The one took sanctuary and being sent out
> Was murthered in Southwark as he past
> To Greenwich where the Lord Protector lay.
> Black Will was burnt in Flushing on a stage.

The allusions to Shakespeare in this play are irresistibly funny and convincing, at least as much so as many more famous allusions to him. It is even possible that the name Arden gave rise to this vigorous mockery, Shakespeare being a backwoodsman from Arden, though that goes beyond what I wish to argue. One ought to be able to solve the problem of authorship by such clues as trisyllabic pronunciations of Ocean and Jelious ('Yet pardon me, for love is Jelious'), but the first is common, and the second too eccentric. Nonetheless, the connection of *Arden of Feversham* with Shakespeare is at least as obvious as that of Sir Thomas Lucy with Justice Shallow, and the date of the play (1590–1?) is precisely right: Shakespeare is young enough and junior enough in London to be mocked, and the coincidence with material in *Henry IV* seems beyond coincidence.

This is not to say that Shakespeare never worked on the north bank in these years, at the Theatre or the Curtain in Shoreditch, or that he never trod the road out from the City that went beside a stream which was also a common sewer. He knew the stews of Clerkenwell, where the Master of the Revels had a rehearsing room in the monastic ruins and a greenroom for props. He knew Black Luce by sight, though she was not the Dark Lady of the sonnets. And, as Halliwell-Phillipps pointed out, he knew the fields which lapped the limits of London like a green sea. In 1597 John Gerard, in his *Herball*, recorded a special double-flowered crowsfoot 'in a field next unto the Theatre by London', and pennyroyal growing in a crevice above the door by Chaucer's tomb in Westminster Abbey. Shakespeare knew the London apprentices, whose attendance at plays the City fathers particularly deprecated, and felt a cheerful contempt for them. They rioted once at least in his day, and the so-called ringleaders were hanged. The social atmosphere of the theatres where he worked is nicely registered by a letter written to Lord Burghley in June of 1584:

That night I returned to London and found all the wards full of watches; the cause thereof was for that very near the Theatre or Curtain, at the time of the plays, there lay a prentice sleeping upon the grass, and one Challes alias Grostock did turn upon the toe upon the belly of the same prentice, whereupon the apprentice start up, and after words they fell to plain blows.

The theatres emptied and the immediate result was a general affray, a running battle through the streets. In the same month we hear 'By reason no plays were the same day, all the City was quiet.' In 1580 the Lord Mayor wrote to the Privy Council that 'the players of plays which are used at the theatre and other such places, and tumblers and such like, are a very superfluous sort of men, and of such faculty as the laws have disallowed, and their exercise of those plays is a great hinderance [sic] to the service of God.' One can see everyone's point of view only too clearly. In 1592 the City tried to have plays restricted to private performances: the Archbishop told them that all they had to do to accomplish this purpose was to bribe the Master of the Revels, but they were too mean to do so. The opportunity lapsed, and no doubt England has been out of hand ever since, thank God.

Shakespeare's work at this time is not always easy to date accurately. We do not even know how many plays he could write in a year. But the three parts of *Henry VI* can be dated between 1591 and 1593, and *Richard III* follows as a sequel. In 1592–3 the London theatres shut, and Shakespeare wrote *Venus and Adonis*, then *The Rape of Lucrece*. The Adonis sonnets printed later in *The Passionate Pilgrim* (1599) look like the relics of a game among friends dating from the time when he wrote *Venus and Adonis*. Between 1591 and 1594, or a little later, he composed his great series of Sonnets. Meanwhile he wrote *The Comedy of Errors* before December 1594 (maybe long before), *The Taming of the Shrew* probably earlier still, *Love's Labour's Lost* and *The Two Gentlemen of Verona*. *Love's Labour* may belong close to *Venus and Adonis* and the Sonnets (1592 or maybe 1593); it is tempting to see as its occasion the Queen's visit to Lord Southampton at Titchfield on the Hamble river in September 1591. *The Two Gentlemen* belongs between *Love's Labour* and *A Midsummer-Night's Dream*, at the end of this fertile period.

In the course of these years Shakespeare became extremely well known, found a great patron, and was made a sharer in the new company of the Lord Chamberlain's Men, the foundation of his wealth and security. He was attacked by Robert Greene in *Groats-Worth of Witte* (1592), mocked by Henry Willoughby in *Willobie his Avisa* (1594) and playfully aimed at as a wicked sonneteer in the play *Edward III* (1594–5) by George Peele or perhaps Henry Chettle.

By 1600 a play could be printed with Shakespeare's name on the cover, though he certainly had no hand in it. (It was *Sir John Oldcastle*, which we know from Henslowe's diary was by Munday, Drayton, Wilson and Hathway.) The Stationers' Register and the publication it announced credited him with *A Yorkshire Tragedy* (1608); and *The Two Noble Kinsmen*, 'written by the memorable worthies of their time, Mr John Fletcher, and Mr William Shakespeare, Gentlemen'. This last has over-awed a number of scholars, but Shakespeare did not write it. The false attributions increased in print and still more wildly in manuscript. These things are only the graph of his fame and success, which were achieved early. But the issue must be mentioned now because, although we know what to expect from the writer of *Lear* and the writer of the *Tempest*, it is harder in principle to rule out his collaboration with other writers, or his finishing their plays or their finishing his, in his earliest years in the theatre.

In the Elizabethan theatre there were adaptations of re-adaptations, and there were dirty deals. Greene sold his *Orlando Furioso* to the Admiral's Men for twenty nobles, and then again to another company while the Admiral's Men were out of London. It is hard to exclude the possibility that Shakespeare took part in some messy transactions; the signs are that he did. But his style is recognizable from the beginning, from *Titus Andronicus* onwards. He is really better than the others, good as the others often are. He adapted and reused old material, quite certainly, but he stamped it with his own style, which is inimitable and easy to identify; the same is true of Aeschylus. In this matter of Shakespeare's supremacy, I have been convinced by reading that Saintsbury was right: his genuine writings are recognizable by their merit. I am not stating this as a dogma – at least about the work of the late 1580s and very early 1590s – but as my own conclusion, because it indicates clearly the line I am going to take.

Henry VI, Part 1 follows easily on *Titus Andronicus*, and I do not think the first comedies are quite so early, since they seem to depend on upper-class patronage. Shakespeare's best comic vein is in his history plays, in the rough, popular theatre, at least at the beginning of his career. We can argue the date of *Henry VI* closely, because the first quarto of *Part 3* records the names of actors in place of those of characters in its stage directions: Gabriel (Spencer), Sinklo (John Sincler), Humfrey (Jeffes); *Part 2* has Bevis and John Holland.

The quarto title-page of *Henry VI, Part 3* tells us that it was acted by Lord Pembroke's Men, a company which broke up in 1593. Holland and Sincler were in Part 2 of *Seven Deadly Sins* about 1590, of which the plot – that is, the bill posted up behind scenes which regulated performances – has been preserved at Dulwich. Lord Strange's Men played this in the early 1590s. Sincler joined the Chamberlain's Men in 1594, though Spencer and Jeffes were still with Pembroke's Men in 1597, and then with the Lord Admiral's

Men. So it looks as if Pembroke's Men played *Henry VI* in 1590 or so, and as if the quarto publication was printed when they scattered in 1593. Henslowe's accounts record 'Strange's men, Harey the VI, ne 3 March 1592'. *Part 2* appeared in print in 1594, and the complete series in 1595. The Chamberlain's Men revived these plays at the time of *Henry V* (1599) and no doubt they were revised then. But Robert Greene parodied *Part 3* in his *Groats-Worth of Witte*, and he died on 3 September 1592, when the theatres had been shut since midsummer, in which case the right date must be 1591–2.

Robert Greene was a Cambridge MA, born in 1558. He was a talented and at times a delicate writer, and a brilliant polemical pamphleteer, but his life veered wildly between the coarsest squalor and grovelling repentance. He was the son of a saddler from Norwich. Kett was burned for heresy at Norwich in Shakespeare's adult lifetime: he was a crazy revivalist from Christopher Marlowe's Cambridge college. One must not think of the universities as all sweetness and light, still less the provinces. Cambridge was not to blame for Kett, however, whose father before him had been hanged in chains at Norwich.

Robert Greene's *Groats-Worth of Witte*, his final barrage, was printed with his *Repentance* soon after his death. It tells how he was lured away to the stage, like Pinocchio, by a finely dressed actor who found him sighing Latin verses behind a hedge. He warns his three 'fellow scholars about this city', Marlowe, Thomas Nashe (1567–1601) and Peele, of a betrayal. Shakespeare was breaking their virtual monopoly of dramatic poetry, or that was what Greene thought:

> Yes, trust them not: for there is an upstart crow, beautified with our feathers, that with his tiger's heart wrapped in a player's hide, supposes he is as well able to bombast out a blank verse as the best of you, and being an absolute Johannes Factotum, is in his own conceit the only Shake-scene in a country.

The image of the tiger's heart comes from York's speech as a prisoner in *Henry VI, Part 3*. There appears to be an implied charge of plagiarism, or of taking the bread out of the writers' mouths, lurking in these wild mutterings. The likeliest reason is that Greene felt the original plot of *Henry VI* was his. It is true that all the faults there are in the plays are faults of plot, and I do not myself believe the plot of *Part 1* is by Shakespeare.

Part 1 also contains some strange historical errors, though Shakespeare is usually extremely careful over history, which fascinates him. Sir Sidney Lee saw this obvious point about adapted plots many years ago, but not all scholars have recognized it since. They seem to feel it is below Shakespeare to co-operate or merely adapt, and the suspicion that he did so is too untidy for them. In the quarto text of *Part 2*, there are lines that seem to derive directly from Marlowe's *Edward II*, but *The Massacre at Paris* has lines that seem to derive from *Henry VI*, and A. L. Rowse thinks even that *Edward II* shows an influence of *Henry VI*.

This deeper question of an influence of early Shakespeare on late Marlowe, which Rowse and Dover Wilson raise, is fascinating, but I am unable to answer it. The influence is not really surprising if the dates can be made to fit. My own view is that in a closely competitive theatre, where actors' memories can influence the transmission of plays, these cases of one or two lines are to be expected. We do know that Pembroke's Men acted *Edward II*. Such transmissions occur in quarto texts of other plays. In the quarto of *Henry VI* Cade has more jokes, some of them obscene: surely the actor wrote them, just as an actor might transfer lines from one play to another. But I am as certain as Dr Johnson that 'the diction, the versification, and the figures are Shakespeare's' and that the *Henry VI* plays were written in chronological order; they get better as they go on.

Nonetheless, the opening scene of *Part 1* is Marlovian and it lacks intimacy. It begins with a snowstorm of classical allusions, many of them explained by the first two poems of Ovid's *Heroides*, which I guess that Shakespeare had attempted to translate or knew by heart. The allusions come early in the poems, so he may have learned them at school and half forgotten them. In any case, Shakespeare is challenging the university poets at their own game. He was not, of course, the first to write dramatic history. George Peele's *Edward I* appeared at just this time; so did Marlowe's *Edward II*. At his best, Peele is an excellent poet, but at other moments he is a clodhopper. He was a Christ's Hospital and Christ Church man, a contemporary of John Lyly, Thomas Lodge and Fulke Greville, and a fellow student at Christ Church of Sir Philip Sidney, Richard Hakluyt and the great historian William Camden; also of some Latin dramatists higher in academic reputation in their own day than they are now. The text that survives of Peele's *Edward I* is an ungodly jumble, but it is worth citing some lines to show what his dramatic verse sounded like. His plot included Robin Hood-like rebel outlaws, a friar and his wench, and some rustic romps. The noble parts are overgrand:

> Illustrious England, auncient seat of kings
> Whose chivalry hath royalized thy fame;
> That sounding bravely through terrestrial vale
> Proclaiming conquests, spoils and victories,
> Rings glorious Echoes through the farthest world.
> . . . I tell thee Joan, what time our highness sits
> Under our royal canopy of state,
> Glistering with pendants of the purest gold,
> Like as our seat were spangled all with stars,
> The world shall wonder at our majesty:
> As if the daughter of eternal *Ops*

> Turned to the likeness of vermilion fumes,
> Where from her cloudy womb the *Centaurs* leapt,
> Were in her royal seat inthronized.

In spite of the liveliness of these verses they are mechanical: having once learned the trick, one could pour them out. They are pastiche Marlowe, like Maurice Baring's pastiche Shakespeare, 'all clinquant, riding on an elephant'. But something quite close to automatic writing of this kind is an essential precondition of dramatic poetry. A dramatic poet is like an epic poet of the oral tradition: he learns by hearing and repeating and adapting. Memory and imagination come very close together in that process.

The plan of the prolonged dramatic epic of the Wars of the Roses, and its political message, had already been laid down in prose sources that the players knew well enough. Edward Hall's *Union of the two Noble and Illustre families of Lancastre and York*, composed in the 1540s, had a particular influence. But within the general pattern of the evils of civil war and the glory of the Crown, as time went on Shakespeare began to take a line of his own.

In the first and second scenes of *Part 1*, act 1, the strong sinews of his poetry are already apparent: in 'A nourish of salt tears', in 'They want their porridge and their fat bull-beeves', and above all in 'their arms are set, like clocks, still to strike on'. His treatment of Joan of Arc is interesting: she gets extremely good lines; indeed at first she looks like the heroine:

> Glory is like a circle in the water,
> Which never ceaseth to enlarge itself
> Till by broad spreading it disperse to nought.
> With Henry's death the English circle ends;
> Dispersed are the glories it included. . . .

Since the poet knows the end of a history before he writes the beginning, this image has some importance. Shakespeare's view is tragic. In his day the British Empire (as it were) had been lost: it was in France. The fall of Calais was within living memory. In considering the structure of dramatic history, Shakespeare has gone rather deeply into the question of prophecy. In Sophoclean tragedy the fulfilment of prophecy is the fundamental skeleton of plays, but Shakespeare uses prophecies only for colouring, and false prophecies almost as often. The first evidence of this interest of his comes at the end of scene ii, and then in act 3, 'that fatal prophecy', and 'a comet of revenge,/A prophet to the fall of all our foes!'

Prophecies and omens were already present in the chronicles he used. Aubrey's *Omens and Apparitions* is a safe guide to popular belief; Shakespeare is more intelligent and much less credulous – he knew some of Aubrey's stories that he never used, but there are others that he might well have used had he known them, and one in particular:

In one of the great fields at Warminster in Wiltshire, in the harvest, at the very time of the fight at Bosworth field, between King Richard III and Henry VII, there was one of the parish took two sheaves, crying (with some intervals) now for Richard, now for Henry; at last lets fall the sheaf that did represent Richard; and cried, now for King Henry Richard is slain. This action did agree with the very time, day and hour. When I was a schoolboy I have heard this confidently delivered by tradition, by some old men of our country.

The Wars of the Roses were not a distant age to Shakespeare's generation, but they were already hoary with mythology. John Stow (d.1605) the antiquary, historian of London and editor of Chaucer, had known a man who remembered Richard III, and I think it likely that Shakespeare knew Stow and used his vast collection of books and manuscripts, about which Stow was very generous. (I cannot otherwise explain how Shakespeare had access at this time to all the books and the unprinted manuscripts he is known to have used.) A more rigorous kind of history did not emerge in England until late in the life of William Camden (1551–1623). Shakespeare rationalizes history, but it is mythological history.

Vignettes which are really of contemporary life engage his sympathies. The Mayor, like all mayors in Shakespeare, is a buffoon. Shakespeare likes the heroic, older generation of Salisbury, Mortimer and poor old Bedford, who has to be carried in a chair. He takes Talbot's titles from his tomb at Rouen (Stow probably supplied them), and counters them at once with 'Stinking and fly-blown'. He hates high-talking lords and wicked ecclesiastics: there are very few bishops and only the fewest most patriotic noblemen that Shakespeare does not despise. He has a sympathy for poor soldiers, but no illusions about them at all. By contrast, they define the great men:

> Sergeant, you shall. Thus are poor servitors,
> When others sleep upon their quiet beds,
> Constrain'd to watch in darkness, rain, and cold.
> ... I'll be so bold to take what they have left.
> The cry of Talbot serves me for a sword;
> For I have loaden me with many spoils,
> Using no other weapon but his name.

Henry VI, Part 1 has scenes that are more successful and more mysterious than any in *Titus Andronicus*: Mortimer as an old man dying in prison; the quarrel among the roses; Warwick's expertise in hawks, dogs, swords, horses and girls; the rhyming scene of Talbot and his son in battle, which is so chivalrous and convincing in its artifice of rhymes. The play also has bare-looking lines which are wonderfully ominous: 'Here dies the dusky torch of Mortimer'; 'This quarrel will drink blood another day'; 'As fest'red members rot but by degree'. Shakespeare is learning restraint. He shortens Joan of Arc's tortures, and deals so sketchily with her denial of her father, with her false pregnancy and her devils, that these things scarcely affect her character at all. Yet at the same time her eloquent curses are all to come true. In a way she goes beyond Aaron, though she is a cardboard figure cut from a myth, and less real than Aaron is. She is a brilliant sketch of what Shakespeare might do if he were free.

Like other early plays, this one introduces lasting or recurring themes in some profusion. Also, like all early Shakespeare, it has some touches of Warwickshire – Arden of course, not Fielden – which are the more attractive for being unexpected: swans and hunting, and the comic shepherd. He knows the stag at bay, and the choice of hounds for their voice. It was north of the Avon that hounds of different quality and voice were deliberately mingled to run in stiff, half-wooded country, as late as the eighteenth century. Shakespeare knows the beautiful harmony of a well-selected pack, of which families like the Grevilles were proud.

He has also observed young noblemen, with a beady and unflattering eye, probably in the Inns of Court. The chivalrous side of the nobility is to him Chaucerian, antique and hazed with the past: he sets it in rhymed verse. He enters with almost keener relish into villainy such as Suffolk's; to this he gives a very modern ring. But Shakespeare is fond of Henry VI, and more interested in the King as a saint than the King as a disaster, so he leaves a certain void and sadness at the centre of the play.

Part 1 and *Part 2* are so closely linked that act 5 of *Part 1* belongs almost properly with *Part 2*. One small-looking matter is worth attention before making the jump. In *Part 1*, speaking of spirits, Shakespeare uses the odd technical word 'periapt'. He got it, as for many years he got many other strange bits and pieces, from Scot's *Discoverie of Witchcraft* (1584). This book turns out to be of less specialized interest than it sounds. It has detailed and very amusing instructions about how tricks are performed: how to produce one's own head on a dish, for example, with a fringe of dough kneaded with blood. Shakespeare's reading it has nothing to do with any murky interest in the dark side of superstition; this treatise was a God-given how-to-do-it book for a young actor, and must have been much used by actors on the road and behind the scenes of theatres. Its advice is highly relevant to the theatrical use of decapitated heads. It deserves reprinting, and so do its sometimes hilarious illustrations. The copy in the Bodleian Library comes from an early gift of books by Lord Hunsdon, Shakespeare's employer, all stamped with his rampant swan, which on this reduced scale alas looks rather like an infuriated duck.

There really was a witch-hunting craze under Elizabeth all the same, and it has some influence on the way Shakespeare is forced to treat Joan of Arc, who had indeed been burned as a witch. Five hundred and thirty-five cases were brought under the Queen, and at least eighty-two poor women were executed. Almost all these cases were in Essex (303 and 53 executions) and

Middlesex (17 and at least 3 executions). They came under the horrible Bishop of London, Edmund Grindal, and when he moved to Canterbury there were more cases there. He had learned the mania as a Protestant exile among the witch-hunting Calvinists of Strasbourg, Speier and Frankfurt. When he applied to Cecil in 1561 for an exemplary punishment which the Church had no power to inflict, Cecil noticed that the latest precedent for the trial of a witch in England had been in 1371.

The Elizabethan statute against witches was passed in 1563; the Commons had promoted it in 1559, but Parliament was dissolved too soon. The mania was imported by men like Grindal and John Jewel, Bishop of Salisbury, and associated by them with the secret wicked powers of the papists, as Grindal wrote to Cecil. That is the colouring of Joan of Arc's case in *Henry VI*; by 1591 it had become an unchallengeable orthodoxy. From 1558 to 1567 the Home Circuit tried 24 and hanged 4; from 1568 to 1577 it tried 88 and hanged 16; from 1578 to 1587 it tried 147 and hanged 19; and from 1588 to 1597 it tried 156 and hanged 18. It is significant that the number of executions steadied at one or two a month, but the clamour for execution continued to increase.

Unexplained illness had something to do with it. 'This kind of people', wrote Jewel to Elizabeth, '(I mean witches and sorcerers) within the last few years are marvellously increased within your grace's realm. These eyes have seen the most evident and manifest marks of their wickedness. Your grace's subjects pine away even unto death, their colour fadeth, their flesh rotteth, their speech is benumbed, their senses are bereft.'

Jewel died in 1571, but his works lived after him. The great witch-scare began after the Armada. It was promoted in Huntingdonshire, for example, after a big local case at Warboys in 1589 and three executions, by an endowed annual sermon on the subject that was not stopped until 1814, and all over England by pamphlets and ballads. The Calvinist judge Sir Edmund Anderson addressed a jury in 1602: 'The land is full of witches, they abound in all places, I have hanged five or six and twenty of them. . . . Few of them would confess it, some of them did. . . . They have on their bodies divers strange marks, at which the Devil sucks their blood. . . . The Devil is a spirit of darkness, he deals closely and cunningly, you shall hardly find direct proofs in such a case. . . .' The Scots were worse than the English: they burned 8000 in the forty years before they flooded England under James I, proud author of *Daemonologie* (1597).

Part 2 of *Henry VI* continues the themes of murders, treasons and captivities, ominous dreams and dead heads. The Duchess of Gloucester brings it first to life with the subplot of witch and conjuror, treated with scornful glee by the dramatist. But in this play the handling of popular distress and insurrection is quite different. Shakespeare takes it more seriously, or engages with it more seriously than with the nobly worded quarrels of the peers or their sulphurous treasons. Peasant petitioners appear in act 1, scene iii. The petition against Suffolk 'for enclosing the commons of Melford' is just a traditional complaint, since the enclosures there seem to be old abbey enclosures: the contemporary resonance was merely general. Cloptons lived at Kentwell Hall in Long Melford, and there are verses by Lydgate on the church wall. Lord Strange's Men were nearby in 1593, and actors knew the road from Sudbury to Bury St Edmund's where Long Melford lies. But I think Shakespeare chose the name at random, for the irony of the petition being presented to Suffolk himself. What he shows in this scene is how the division in the kingdom presses on poor men and quarrel breeds quarrel. The armourer has a quarrel with his apprentice and the witch raises a spirit that prophesies tricky and ominous truths. In the second act we get a false miracle at St Alban's in which one is sorry for the rogue and his wife: 'Alas, sir, we did it for pure need!' The nobles are harsh, they laugh at the terrifying sentence of whipping 'through every market town till they come to Berwick, from whence they came'. Seeing them laugh, we lose any inclination to laugh.

The poor rogues are comic figures though, which is why we like them. The armourer's apprentice and his friends are comic too: 'Be merry, Peter, and fear not thy master: fight for credit of the prentices.' Peter wins his duel and the King rewards him, yet he remains comic and highly sympathetic. It may be thought that these are slight episodes set against the political drama (always in these plays the drama of a fall, of fall after fall from power), but they are small statements of a theme to come. The bigger matters of York's treason, Gloucester's murder, Suffolk's death, and Cardinal Beaufort's haunted, Faustus-like death – a story recorded by historians – swell the play towards its climax. The murder of Suffolk is a splendidly deadly scene, but the play so far has been too full of incident, and perhaps of long, lordly rants.

> *Lieutenant* Poole!
> *Suffolk* Poole?
> *Lieutenant*   Ay, kennel, puddle, sink, whose filth and dirt
> Troubles the silver spring where England drinks. . . .

Suffolk dies with a garbled but metrical quotation from Lucan on his lips: the same scene contains references to Bargulus the Illyrian pirate (from Cicero), Bezonians (a word Nashe uses), Sylla (from Marlowe's *Lucan*?) and in the quarto text Abradas (a Macedonian pirate twice named by Greene). Shakespeare seems to have fits or fevers of this kind of language, but they become shorter and less violent before he is thirty.

It is in the next scene, the second of act 4, that the popular revolution under Jack Cade is presented. John Holland is a very sleepy sort of revolutionary, cynical of government and of change, gloomily resigned to the world: 'Well, I say it was never merry world in England since gentlemen came up.' These small tradesmen or peasants, with their topsyturvey proverbial wisdom and their local roots in places like Wingham in Kent (had Shakespeare been there on the road as an actor, or did he know people who had?) are mildly clownish but quite unsinister. At their very worst Cade's rebels are a parody of the great lords, and Cade's pretensions only a parody of the English state itself. I believe many in the audience would have been sharp enough to see this. It is a line of thought that goes back to Thomas More and Erasmus, and in popular thinking back to the peasant revolutions of the Middle Ages. We have a clothier, a tanner, a weaver, a sawyer and so on, *'with infinite numbers'*. The vagueness of this stage direction suggests Shakespeare wrote it: prompt books have to be more precise.

The comic crowd is patriotic in its way; the peasants remember Henry V with affection, hate the French, and hate betrayal. They are doomed, of course, if only by the real course of history from which Shakespeare will not depart too far, but he likes this stage army, and enjoys writing about them.

> All scholars, lawyers, courtiers, gentlemen,
> They call false caterpillars and intend their death.

Shakespeare knows about gardening, and in numerous mentions seems to be fiercely opposed to caterpillars, so the phrase may not be quite as comical as we imagine, but comical it surely is.

The King retires to Killingworth, which means Kenilworth – not the only case in which a London scribe or actor or printer has mangled a place name more familiar to the poet than to him. Most of this fourth act is Cade's rebellion. In the end Cade gets caught stealing herbs in the garden of Alexander Iden, a Horatian country squire in Kent. He dies well enough: they both behave decently. There are certain exact prophecies here: the garden withers and becomes a burial ground, and Iden will have his sword hung up over his own monument when he dies. I assume it all happened, and that Shakespeare knew the place, which was not in Kent but near Heathfield in Sussex. It looks to me as if he goes out of his way to compliment Iden's family: Iden was Sheriff of Kent, but I have not discovered where he was buried. His last speech is fierce, but then Cade is already dead, and this short speech is only a formal closure and a sop to the received view of rebels. For me at least, Cade's rebellion is the most surprising feature of the entire play, and no one but Shakespeare could have carried it off. It is a minor theme that insists on behaving like a major one.

The last act is brief: its central scene is the battle of St Alban's. Stage battles are managed with economy and variety from this play onwards. Action is swift and movement swifter; it is the words that make the enactment dramatic and terrible, though it must be said that in this battle

Clifford, quoting his own heraldic motto as Suffolk did his before he died, is a little stiff in his heroism. York who kills him is suppler, even in words. Young Clifford with his father's dead body rants perhaps, but brilliantly. This is a set-piece in the tradition established by Marlowe, just as the battle scenes must I assume have been heraldic set-pieces. Shakespeare had seen the Queen's annual jousting matches, and he knew old, crippled soldiers, but he had never seen a battle except in a painting. Still, the heroic poetry that goes with battles has in this act outsoared anything that Marlowe ever wrote. Since Marlowe (or in a lesser compass Ralegh) is possibly the greatest of all English poets after Shakespeare, this is a very high claim to make. Marlowe's talent was as prodigious as his influence; Peele fainted under the burden of his style. *Tamburlaine* was printed only in 1590, yet in 1591 the verses to the reader of *The Troublesome Raigne of John King of England* (attributed in 1611 to W. Sh. and in 1622 to Shakespeare, though wrongly I suspect) begin:

> You that with friendly grace of smoothed brow
> Have entertain'd the Scythian Tamburlaine. . . .

One ought not therefore to be surprised to find Marlowe's influence in the theatre so overwhelming, but it was an influence that Shakespeare had now mastered. If *The Tragedie of Dido, Queene of Carthage*, which Marlowe wrote with Nashe or which Nashe finished, shows a falling off from Marlowe's greatest plays, it is still fine, but not as fine as Shakespeare. It was published in 1594, in the same year as *Edward II* and *Henry VI*; Marlowe had then been dead since the previous summer.

The third part of *Henry VI* is the dynastic war itself, which really broke out only in act 5 of *Part 2*. There is a sense in which these history plays are revenge plays, because they are about dynastic feuding. But this play has other elements: its characters and their pathos have more power, and what happens to England itself is more clearly realized, sometimes in images that appeared in the earlier parts: blood, dew, growth, wilderness, tempest and the rest. It is wrong to think Shakespeare carefully or ingeniously devised the images and then applied them with tweezers. He feels through them and thinks through them; whether they are original or not, he senses the world through them. The pauses and formalities and rhetoric of this play are pieces of theatrical artifice. They have a special interest because he is learning to manage speed and momentum, and to set free individual character more effectively than before. Shakespeare seems to have been influenced by Kyd's *Spanish Tragedy* and by the sixteenth-century play called *Soliman and Perseda*, but orally, not through a written text. He still draws on Ovid but less than before. The idea that he used some particular scholarly commentary and must therefore have been a schoolmaster is too flimsy to be taken seriously.

The play begins with unblushing goriness and the brandishing of a head, with verse of a metallic quality and business about the royal chair of state. The lords are like playing cards, scarcely characterized at all except by the feud; the air is brisk with threats of vengeance. The first act comes to life with Richard of York's treacherous and seductive speech over the crown itself:

> An oath is of no moment. . . .
>   . . . And, father, do but think
> How sweet a thing it is to wear a crown,
> Within whose circuit is Elysium
> And all that poets feign of bliss and joy.

Does Shakespeare feel like this? Certainly not: the crown is to him a magical thing, enchanted or enchanting, and we are going to see just how little of Elysium lies within its circuit. York is taken by the termagant Queen and given a handkerchief dipped in his son's blood. He is stood on a mole-hill, crowned with a paper crown, and mocked at length; the scene really occurred, but it has an ancient resonance in English folklore, and from this time on Shakespeare plays constantly with the idea of mock kings and mocked kings. York and the Queen are a match for one another, and one hates them both. She kills him, of course.

> What, weeping-ripe, my Lord Northumberland?
> Think but upon the wrong he did us all,
> And that will quickly dry thy melting tears.

Unfortunately the sorrow and grandeur of York's dying, which is perhaps out of tune with the powerful figure of wickedness he was in life, exist only as the foundation for more vengeance. The images of hawking and of bear-baiting in this play are vivid and appropriate; those of tears and fire are equally so.

Having enacted York's death in one act, Shakespeare recounts it in a messenger speech in the next, setting it in a context of grief. This scene proceeds to a battle that lives only in words, in Warwick's description of it, and to violence and weariness of violence that live only in a metaphor:

> Their weapons like to lightning came and went:
> Our soldiers, like the night-owl's lazy flight
> Or like an idle thresher with a flail,
> Fell gently down, as if they struck their friends.

These lines are both visually and tactually strong: one can feel the despairing and tired arms of the soldiers, and the underlying metaphor, with its suggestion of a more innocent world and more natural, earthly actions, is by the abuse of it in tension between natural and unnatural. The lines are thrilling and appalling: 'Fell gently down' goes not only for the weapons but for the dead. It is both their appropriateness and shocking inappropriateness that make the words so powerful. The alteration of tone and pace by the unexpected carry-over of rhythm into the fourth line contributes to the arresting effect: the words 'lazy' and 'idle' take another turn in 'gently down'. The effect of natural images on battle scenes is to formalize and to still them:

> A thousand men have broke their fasts to-day
> That ne'er shall dine. . . .

> That stain'd their fetlocks in his smoking blood. . . .

> The common people swarm like summer flies;
> And whither fly the gnats but to the sun?

The King is a saint and an eloquent one, but almost hysterically weak in his extraordinary monologue scene (act 2, scene v). His fate is to see a son kill his father and a father kill his son, and to know himself to blame. Shakespeare's plays have been thought to be often about the breakdown of nature and its restoration. That is true of this play and this scene, which is a long one as formal as a Mystery or Morality, and I think it is a central truth.

As the play ends, the rise of Richard to be Duke of Gloucester and in the end Richard III begins. Shakespeare has said what he has to say about civil war by the end of act 2. Henry is imprisoned by two gamekeepers in a kind of pastoral interlude, and the horrible King Edward has a wooing scene intended to provoke disgust on many levels. As Richard's career proceeds, the complexity of his character develops. Halfway through this play his laconic nastiness and wit have already provided the sketch of a highly original character, but with his long and startling monologues in act 3, scene ii, he becomes overpowering, and the play of *Richard III* heaves into sight.

Richard's monologue is like Aaron's in *Titus Andronicus* – another analysis of evil in terms of suffering, but more full-blooded, stranger in its details, deeply convincing as a portrait of an individual. People used to overstress the sublimities of Shakespeare's characterization: it is not sublime but an art of telling detail, like Roman late Republican or fifteenth-century Italian head sculpture. It has its importance in his work, and the character often seems to overweigh the play: all the same, the play is a formal dance, and the character has its being only within that dance. One must mark Richard's career as well as his suffering:

> Well, say there is no kingdom then for Richard;
> What other pleasure can the world afford?
> I'll make my heaven in a lady's lap. . . .
> Why, love forswore me in my mother's womb. . . .

This carefully written set-piece has a musing drama of its own; it formalizes the moment of Richard's decision ('I'll set the murderous Machiavel to school') and towers over much of the rest of the play. The treacheries and reversals and deaths take on a ritual quality, like musical closures. Only Henry in the tower has an integrity of his own, 'Like to his island girt in with the Ocean', because evil cannot touch him. The lords are doomed by their ancestry.

> I will not ruinate my father's house,
> Who gave his blood to lime the stones together. . . .

There is a nice ambivalence about this gruesome metaphor. It is spoken by George of Clarence, a doomed prince. Warwick the Kingmaker has a fine, stoical speech before he dies in act 5, but his main characteristic has been power, and the speech is hollow at the core, unlike Richard's monologue. The climax of the play is between Richard and Henry: wit has full play in it, but so has passion; the rhythms and their voices are in contrast. Richard drives Henry to taunt him and Henry drives Richard to murder him. He makes him the thing he is by naming it, and Richard having killed the King becomes pure evil.

This is not a cheerful view of English politics: indeed it expresses passionate detestation. The only gleam of light is Henry prophesying over young Henry Tudor, but that is a brief moment, a passing flicker and not in a position of climax. The play ends with Edward on his throne, and Richard ready to strike: it ends in suspense.

> And now what rests but that we spend the time
> With stately triumphs, mirthful comic shows,
> Such as befits the pleasure of the court?

It is worth underlining the savage irony of these lines: it is the irony, not the lines themselves, that reveals Shakespeare's view of the Court, and of stately triumphs, mirthful comic shows. He loathes these people, and in his plays he dooms them.

· 4 ·

Comedy and Poetry

Shakespeare began to write comedy early enough in his career for the dates to be uncertain, the textual tradition confused, and the acting company, like other companies of the day, rather obscure. Three of his first comedies, *The Taming of the Shrew, The Two Gentlemen of Verona* and *The Comedy of Errors*, are all in the same Italian and classic mould, but *Love's Labour's Lost* is more courtly than the others, denser in poetry, denser in comic complexity, and more private, more for the real aristocracy. I take that play to be a masterpiece, of the period of the Sonnets.

The *Shrew* is earlier work and probably the first comedy. Scholarly discussion of its date is particularly bedevilled, but the date of 1591 given by Brian Morris in the Arden edition is not far wrong: Shakespeare quotes the introduction to Kyd's *Spanish Tragedy*, which was written by 1590, and Lord Strange's Men acted the *Shrew* for Henslowe on 23 February 1592. A similar play was printed in 1594, which might be, indeed must be, a badly transmitted version of our play. Our modern text was first printed after Shakespeare's death, in the 1623 Folio. Francis Meres in 1598 had never heard of it. Its plot was inherited, and the play was therefore probably a commissioned work. It has merits all the same, and it was played at Court as late as 1633. The 1594 version was played by Pembroke's Men as *Henry VI* was: it featured Sly and Petruchio and Kate and her sister; Sly was less developed than he is in the Folio text, where one prefers him to the central characters, but for some reason the Folio text leaves him more in mid-air. No doubt the play got mutilated in the process of production and revival.

It was a bold attempt for a young countryman to compose an Italian comedy. He must have used *Supposes*, Gascoigne's prose version of Ariosto's play *I Suppositi*. Tranio comes from the *Mostellaria* of Plautus, and Shakespeare had probably seen Italian plays. But this enterprising comedy reeks of the accomplishments of the Inns of Court, where the young upper middle class learned public business, and so do its style of humour – very funny but on the sharp side – and its attitude to women. The particular touches of Warwickshire colouring might suit a fellow countryman at the Inns of Court, of whom there were many.

77

Brian Morris thinks the actor William Sly played Sly, and the actor Alexander Cooke played Sander, but I think the evidence for Sander is doubtful. They were both members of Pembroke's Men who later joined the Chamberlain's Men, as Shakespeare did. The character Sly is a Warwickshire man, and the name was common there, though it was common in London as well: but this actor knew the Warwickshire accent. We know from the token books recording communions at St Saviour's parish church that the actor William Sly lived on Bankside, south of the river, in Norman's Rents, as early as 1588, and in 1593 at Horseshoe Court, where three other actors also lived; he was witness to one of their wills. In 1594 he bought 'a jewel of gold set with a white sapphire' from Henslowe for eight shillings, to be paid in instalments, but he never paid above six and sixpence. Still, he prospered in the Chamberlain's Men and lived to become a sharer in the Globe. In 1606 he was living in Shoreditch among other actors – there must have been a hundred or two hundred actors in London, practising or intending, most of them obscure – and had a bastard son there who lived for less than two weeks. He died in August 1608 and was buried as William Sly, Gentleman.

In *The Taming of the Shrew*, Sly's part and Sly's world are only a sketch of a play to frame the play itself. This odd device was not original; other writers used it, but in Shakespeare's hands it has a peculiar freshness. Sly is a country drunk discovered by a lord, and tricked, or at least much bemused first by mocking actors, and then by the acting of a play which he sees. This joke or device is not very funny, though it may well have been funnier once and its humour lost in later productions, the Warwickshire setting having been meant for particular patrons: otherwise it is hard to see why Shakespeare ever thought he needed it, since the main play stands on its own feet. But Kyd and Peele both used these frames, called 'inductions', and for Shakespeare as a very young man perhaps that was reason enough.

Sly has only two short scenes, for part of which he is dead drunk, but these scenes are vivid:

> What, would you make me mad? Am not I Christopher Sly, old Sly's son of Burton heath; by birth a pedlar, by education a cardmaker, by transmutation a bear-herd, and now by present profession a tinker? Ask Marian Hacket, the fat ale-wife of Wincot, if she knows me not. . . .

> *Second Servant* Dost thou love pictures? We will fetch thee straight
> Adonis painted by a running brook,
> And Cytherea all in sedges hid,
> Which seem to move and wanton with her breath
> Even as the waving sedges play wi' th' wind.

The smooth verses about the classic erotic scenes – 'Io as she was a maid' and 'Daphne roaming through a thorny wood Scratching her legs, that one shall swear she bleeds' – are fine poetry no doubt, but there is a crude, deep poetry in Sly himself. The surface texture of the erotic pictures is overfine, and they are false in more ways than one: it is fascinating that Shakespeare, who can spin such wonderful verses as long as his breath lasts, is aware of this so early: it is a theme of his Sonnets, and ought to affect the way we read *Venus and Adonis*. Crude old Sly is beguiled as Bottom was beguiled, but Shakespeare is not taken in by the magic of his own poetry. He is even more conscious than Ovid that he might at any moment take a different tone; the division of scenes in the English theatre encouraged him to sense this. Spenser fails to spot the irony of Ariosto, but Shakespeare sees it at once. Sonnet writers are to be found puffing and panting with sincerity, but Shakespeare knows that sonnets can be false, and the knowledge sets him free to be deadly serious or to take a dozen moods just as he chooses.

The local allusions in this induction are probably of more interest to a biographer than to a literary critic, but as a general colouring they concern both. Burton Heath is obviously Barton on the Heath, just off the road from Stratford to Oxford and so to London. Greece may be a farm called Greet, not far from Winchcombe, which still exists. Marian Hacket sounds real: there were Hackets in Quinton parish where John Davies farmed, and Wincot was a hamlet four miles south of Stratford, lying half in Quinton and half in Clifford Chambers. In 1581 Sir William Catesby, High Sheriff of Warwickshire in 1577, was called before the Star Chamber, where he refused to swear that he had not been harbouring and entertaining Edmund Campion at 'Willycote adjoining Wincot in Quinton'. I would not go so far as to say that 'old John Naps of Greece, and Peter Turph, and Henry Pimpernell, and twenty more such names and men as these' are real people: the point is only that they are meant to sound real; and so they do, as Marian Hacket does, though in my heart of hearts I do not believe she was real either.

Sly's career sounds likely. His father was a small village pedlar, lucky to have a cottage. He was brought up to set the iron teeth in wooden wool-combs, useful in a cottage industry and saleable by his father. But he took to the road and led a bear, such as visited Stratford regularly less than a hundred years ago; he probably had bagpipes as well. He lost his bear, and now he is a tinker. He is known all over the Fielden part of Warwickshire, in every pub from Stratford to the Cotswolds. He has never seen a fine painting or an Italian play, or ever drunk sack in his life. He has only the clothes he stands up in. The lady they offer him is a page dressed up: not very like his wife maybe.

> . . . What must I call her?
> Madam.
> Al'ce madam, or Joan madam?

As for the real play, 'let them play it. Is not a comonty a Christmas gambold or a tumbling-trick?' Shakespeare is a little in love with his own sophistication.

The first sentence of the comedy is easy-moving and crisply syntactic and nine lines long. Italian phrases are sprinkled here and there in this play, but almost all of them are in the first act. Nothing shows that the poet ever went to Italy, but he knew a lot about it. He knew Italians and had seen Italian comedy: the Commedia dell'arte players who improvised their plays on given plots between traditional characters who were always the same. Some of them turn up here.

The story is as the title says. The Shrew is tamed by marriage, by a husband who breaks her self-will and her whims by pretending to worse whims of his own. In the course of this prolonged tease, which has its cruel side, as Feste's teasing does in *Twelfth Night* and as so many real Elizabethan practical jokes did, we get some glimpses of an idea of Italy and of the world:

> . . . and that part of philosophy
> Will I apply that treats of happiness
> By virtue specially to be achiev'd.

Shakespeare has hit off something central about the renaissance. Perhaps he got it from the smooth moral writings of Erasmus, who uses similar words in a dialogue Shakespeare may well have read at school. Quite long bits of Shakespearean comedy sometimes sound like the dialogues of Erasmus, but the influence may be indirect, or a memory of real conversations, since the Latin of Erasmus comes close to normal, educated speech. All the same, this comic verse can contain robust phrases, such as 'To comb your noddle with a three-legg'd stool'. The prose, when characters break into prose, is as careful as the verse, with controlled rhythms that derive from Lyly, whose style had become such a fashion that it infected the air. It was prevalent among upper-class women, and therefore among young gallants. Here it helps to characterize educated Italians. The lord in the induction took his style from Marlowe, but he was less suave. This is an educated kind of play: you are expected to recall Virgil, to know who Agenor's daughter was, and to smile when someone says 'our cake's dough on both sides', or 'there's small choice in rotten apples'. The first two of Ovid's *Heroides* recur, as does the adder's painted skin.

Still, the play has good scenes, and some memorable lines: 'Such wind as scatters young men through the world', and 'It shall be what o'clock I say it is'; and of the sea, 'Rage like an angry boar chafed with sweat', and 'though she chide as loud As thunder when the clouds in autumn crack'. Shakespeare's weather poetry seems to me better than his poetry of country pleasures. Part of his skill is a traditional country incision of speech: 'carv'd like an apple-tart' for example, and these dismissive words:

And do you tell me of a woman's tongue,
That gives not half so great a blow to hear
As will a chestnut in a farmer's fire?

These details are a crucial element of dramatic poetry, and perhaps of all poetry. Shakespeare's wording is sharper than thoroughly educated wording, though he has learned every trick available to him, and more than are available to us.

How say you to a fat tripe finely broil'd?

What say you to a piece of beef and mustard?

These lines are set in a series of questions and answers of a Mozartian formality, ending in bursts of passionate rhetoric and action. Feelings are eloquently and consciously expressed, more so than they could be in any more realistic medium, and yet the play convinces. Katharina's conversion speech is as eloquent as any speech of the kind in Terence or Menander, but only as convincing as they are. What is most telling in this play is the alterations of tone.

Why, there's a wench! Come on, and kiss me, Kate.
Well, go thy ways, old lad, for thou shalt ha't.

In the 1594 version Sly is always longing for the fool. 'Sim, when will the fool come again?' 'Look Sim, the fool is come again now.' He hates the idea of prison: 'I tell thee Sim we'll have no sending to prison, that's flat.' He wakes up at the end where he was first found, 'Just underneath the alehouse side below', prepared to face his wife as dawn breaks, because he now knows how to tame a shrew. Nature is somehow restored.

The Sonnets come so close to *Venus and Adonis* and *The Rape of Lucrece*, and appear to be so closely bound up with Lord Southampton's marriage problem, which can be dated to 1590–4 or so, when he was between the ages of seventeen and twenty-one, that one is strongly inclined to put lesser plays which scarcely display the powers of the Sonnets at an earlier date than all these poems. No doubt this is too schematic, and poetry and plays overlapped. But I will treat *The Comedy of Errors* as if it were written earlier, if only for the sake of leaving an open field to treat the poems together, as if every single one of them was written in the same period. *The Two Gentlemen of Verona* seems to me a public not a private play, and later therefore than *Love's Labour's Lost*, which I think was a private entertainment while the plague raged and the theatres were closed. I think it was written for Lord Southampton at Titchfield, and that Southampton plucked Shakespeare out of plague-stricken London and retained him for a time in the country as his poet. That period altered Shakespeare's life; Southampton gave him money, tranquillity and the opportunity to develop as a poet, just at the critical moment. Of course it is still possible that *Love's Labour* was performed for the Queen at Titchfield as early as 1591, but that is a conjecture and would push back the date of Shakespeare's other early work into years which are already sufficiently crowded with his writings.

The Comedy of Errors is an adaptation from the *Menaechmi* of Plautus, though the double set of the long-lost twin brothers who are masters of long-lost twin-brother slaves comes more likely from the plots of Italian impromptu comedians. They could derive from the *Amphitruo* of Plautus, which is where the Italian comedy actors got them, but that is less likely. For a text of Plautus, Shakespeare used the 1576 Lambinus edition, with its emphasis on error, and William Warner's lively prose version 'for the use and delight of his private friends', which was not printed until 1595.

At any rate Plautus, who was himself an adapter with a strong contemporary and local flavour to spice his Greek originals, would have been delighted with the contrivances and the spirited detail of Shakespeare's drama. This was Shakespeare's first thoroughly and carefully constructed play, or do we have that feeling because Plautus lies behind it? An older play, called *A History of Error*, apparently based on Plautine mistaken identity, was performed at Court by Sussex's Men in 1583, and scholars have suggested Shakespeare revised a revision of that. Nothing is impossible in the Elizabethan theatre, but our play reads to me like pure Shakespeare, and its magisterial control of varied metres seems Shakespearean.

The Comedy of Errors was played at the Inns of Court in 1594, and what we have may be only a version adapted for that occasion. Meres knew it in 1598, but it was not printed until 1623. A reference to civil war in France and a parody of Marlowe's *Edward II* suggest the date 1591 or 1592, but no conclusive evidence exists. It plays very well indeed in the theatre, and it has its own crispness and balance. The way in which Shakespeare adapted and adopted from Plautus and from Warner, and his own alterations of plot and emphasis, can be studied in detail by anyone, and they are worth the study, because they reveal a theatrical master. His Ephesus is a more exotic place than Epidamnum was to Plautus, and marriage and courtship interest him more than the Roman commonplace of prostitution, which I think shocked him. The suggestion of witchcraft at Ephesus may derive from St Paul, but I take it to be comic. Even Shakespeare's slaves are more like servants. He knew nothing about Roman beating: the Dromio brothers are beaten like boys, not like slaves.

The funniest character is the fat cook Dowsibel, the 'mountain of mad flesh', who alas never appears. The Duke is kindly and lofty but not quite real, and the same may be said of the Abbess. There are characters like her in Plautus, the priestess in the *Rudens* for instance. The only really low characters are the two comic slaves, but they invade the normal world of the play, the essential world of the plot, less than Jack Cade's rebels do in *Henry VI*. This is the shortest and the least complex of the comedies, and the only one to call for no music; there is something slightly academic about it, or neo-classic, as if Shakespeare set out to prove his mastery of the form.

In the first scene of the fifth act he touches on melancholy and madness. His treatment is analytic here, and more allusive in later plays, so that one does well to pay attention, this being one of the fundamental themes of all his writing.

> This week he hath been heavy, sour, sad . . .
> Hath he not lost much wealth by wreck of sea?
> Buried some dear friend? Hath not else his eye
> Stray'd his affection in unlawful love. . . . ?

Love turns out to be the trouble, and constant reproach has failed to cure it, hardly surprisingly.

> And thereof came it that the man was mad.
> The venom clamours of a jealous woman
> Poisons more deadly than a mad dog's tooth.
> It seems his sleeps were hinder'd by thy railing,
> And thereof comes it that his head is light.
>
> Sweet recreation barr'd, what doth ensue
> But moody and dull melancholy. . . .
>
>   . . . I will not let him stir
> Till I have us'd the approved means I have,
> With wholesome syrups, drugs, and holy prayers,
> To make of him a formal man again.

To analyse the plot would be picking the wings off a butterfly. It is a farce, of course, and moves swiftly, but it has a deeper resonance, in cure of madness, abolition of delusion, saving from death, and a certain charity. Blank verse and high sentiment rub shoulders with knockabout scenes. It has zestful phrases ('The capon burns, the pig falls from the spit'), pungent language like 'sinking-ripe', and in the second act Shakespeare's heavenly women, unLatin, unItalian and unobscene. In a rage they are deadly serious and almost too moral. But the human passion of the women in this play is the beginning of one of the most remarkable ways in which Shakespeare differs from other writers. The *Comedy* has many of the lines we begin to think of as his stock in trade, though they too are inimitable.

> Before the always wind-obeying deep. . . .
>
> Usurping ivy, brier, or idle moss. . . .
>
> Spread o'er the silver waves thy golden hairs.

And as a bed I'll take them, and there lie. . . .

This is the fairy land. . . .

His verbal texture is deliberately varied, and he is not above throwing in a few odd lines of doggerel to achieve this effect. Too much metrical brilliance would be as monotonous as footprints in the snow. His characters are allowed to speak, to be dramatic and to express quite momentary feelings as clearly as possible.

The Gray's Inn performance of 1594 is of some special interest. On 28 December a 'Comedy of Errors, like to Plautus his *Menechmus*' was presented by professional players, but before the play the students rioted against an invasion of members of the Inner Temple. The next day they blamed their behaviour on 'a Play of Errors and Confusions . . . vain Representations and shows . . . Sorceries and Enchantments' and so on. This of course is a joke. Shakespeare's company was paid for the play, and one must assume he played in it; the company had been performing the two previous nights at Greenwich before the Queen. The laboriously jokey records of the Gray's Inn production refer to the Chamberlain's Men as 'a Company of base and common fellows', 'And this was the end of our Law-sports, concerning the Night of Errors.' One detects the voice of the youthful Justice Shallow.

Venus and Adonis is very good Shakespeare indeed, above all for its freshness. It combines the charms of an idyllic anecdote, a poem both funny and erotic, and a genuine and lyrical poem about the real country: I will not call it pastoral. I first found it at about nineteen and could hardly believe my eyes or ears, nor have I ever reread it without the keenest pleasure since that time. It is a more dashing, better sustained performance than anything in the early comedies; in *Venus and Adonis* Shakespeare deliberately set out to make a great reputation, a bid for supremacy in English poetry. It was registered in April 1593 – the same year as Marlowe's *Hero and Leander* – and printed that year and again the next by Richard Field, who came from Stratford. John Shakespeare had appraised his father's goods the year before.

The poem was dedicated to the Earl of Southampton.

I know not how I shall offend in dedicating my unpolished lines to your lordship, nor how the world will censure me for choosing so strong a prop to support so weak a burden; only if your Honour seem but pleased, I account myself highly praised, and vow to take advantage of all idle hours, till I have honoured you with some graver labour. But if the first heir of my invention prove deformed, I shall be sorry it had so noble a godfather; and never after ear so barren a land, for fear it yield me still so bad a harvest. I leave it to your honourable survey, and your Honour to your heart's content; which I wish may always answer your own wish, and the world's hopeful expectation. Your Honour's in all duty, William Shakespeare.

Are these polite and playful words to be taken seriously? In tone they suggest some degree of familiarity, but that might be an effect of Lyly's style, the courtly style of the comic theatre. The quotation from Ovid's *Amores* (1, 15, 35–8) on the title page looks even more formal – a Latin tag and no more. But if one considers Marlowe's version of this same poem, more appears. Ovid defends the calling of poets even though envy may dismiss their works as 'fruits of an idle quill'. He has refused 'War's dusty honours' and the study of law:

> Thy scope is mortal, mine eternal fame,
> That all the world may ever chant my name.

His examples are Homer, Hesiod and so on through the ages.

> While bondmen cheat, fathers be hard, bawds whorish,
> And strumpets flatter, shall Menander flourish.
> Rude Ennius, and Plautus full of wit,
> Are both in fame's eternal legend writ. . . .
> Verse is immortal, and shall ne'er decay.
> To verse let kings give place, and kingly shows,
> And banks o'er which gold-bearing Tagus flows.
> Let base-conceited wits admire vile things,
> Fair Phoebus lead me to the Muses' springs,
> About my head be quivering myrtle wound,
> And in sad lovers' head let me be found. . . .
> Then though death rakes my bones in funeral fire,
> I'll live, and as he pulls me down, mount higher.
>
> (*trans.* MARLOWE)

Shakespeare found these lines inspiring: they resounded in his mind throughout the period of the Sonnets, and they imply the same boast about the Muses that Francis Meres made about him. Ovid says Homer lives while Tenedos and Mount Ida stand 'Or into sea swift Simois doth slide'; Hesiod lives 'while grapes with new wine swell, Or men with crooked sickles corn down fell'. It may be that this kind of identification played a part in Shakespeare's determination to identify his own poetry with the English countryside he knew best, which I think is deliberate in *Venus and Adonis*.

The poem is Ovidian in several ways, but its sources in Ovid are multiple: Adonis in Book X of the *Metamorphoses*; Salmacis, a sardonic and very funny erotic interlude in Book IV; the boar in Book VIII, with a touch of real life added; and maybe Narcissus in Book III. Shakespeare used Golding's version of *Metamorphoses* as well as the Latin, and echoed

Thomas Lodge's Ovidian verse fable *Scilla*. He admired Lodge and used him again for *As You Like It*. The idea of scornful Adonis had already been exploited by Marlowe in *Hero and Leander*, by Spenser in *The Faerie Queene*, and by Greene. The stanza form was popular and Shakespeare used it in early comedies.

It is unchivalrous to suppose that Venus is Anne Hathaway, but the poem is uninhibitedly erotic; its country freshness is just a foil to set off erotic freshness, and the love scenes are based to some degree on the experience of life: the poem is an artifice, but it is not a parlour game. Erwin Panofsky was the first to observe the possible influence of a particular painting by Titian, now in the Prado, though about this I remain stubbornly uncertain, since a common source may well exist for these treatments of the same subject, even if no one has yet spotted it. But there is no doubt Shakespeare did think of Venus and Adonis in terms of an erotic painting, since he says so in the induction to the *Shrew*, quoted earlier. The Elizabethans were much excited by erotic paintings of mythology: the Jesuit John Gerard talks of them as a vicious taste. If I remember rightly, he destroyed a painting of Mars and Venus on glass. *Venus and Adonis* is a tease. It excites appetite and frustrates it as Ovid does, and transmutes the sharper physical passions and sensations into an appetite for poetry, which the poetry can and does satisfy. With its 1194 lines, of which 623 are direct speech, it is an extraordinary tour de force.

The surreal vividness of the poem's opening lines nails it to the influence of Marlowe:

> Even as the sun with purple-colour'd face
> Had ta'en his last leave of the weeping morn,
> Rose-cheek'd Adonis hied him to the chase;
> Hunting he lov'd, but love he laugh'd to scorn.
> Sick-thoughted Venus makes amain unto him,
> And like a bold-fac'd suitor gins to woo him.

In Marlowe's *Hero and Leander* (2, 87f.):

> Now had the Morn espied her lover's steeds,
> Whereat she starts, puts on her purple weeds,
> And red for anger that he stayed so long,
> All headlong throws herself the clouds among.
> And now Leander, fearing to be missed,
> Embraced her suddenly, took leave, and kissed. . . .

It appears to be a convention peculiar to Marlowe that the sun is the dawn's or morn's lover, and that she weeps to see him go. Ovid, in the *Amores* (1,13), in the famous poem that gave Marlowe's Faustus his *Lente, lente currite, noctis equi*, begins:

> Now o'er the sea from her old love comes she
> That draws the day from heaven's cold axle-tree,

but her lover is Cephalus or Tithon, 'Thou leav'st his bed because he's faint through age.' So far as I recollect, her lover is never the sun: Shakespeare has copied this mythological mistake from Marlowe, who made it in his early and free adaptation of Musaeus, but would not have made it after translating Ovid's *Amores* a little later. Shakespeare had grabbed the image from *Hero and Leander* without remembering the *Amores*, which he had already read. The mistake is wholly unimportant, but the link with Marlowe and the urge to outdo him is fascinating. Shakespeare's image is clear and definite, and he sprinkles his colours accurately, while Marlowe's image is confused and his colours are intermingled.

Shakespeare is swift as well as ornamental, and the urgency of Venus dictates an amused urgency in the verse:

> The studded bridle on a ragged bough
> Nimbly she fastens – Oh, how quick is love!

> So soon was she along as he was down. . . .

> Upon this promise did he raise his chin,
> Like a dive-dapper peering through a wave,
> Who, being look'd on, ducks as quickly in;
> So offers he to give what she did crave;
>   But when her lips were ready for his pay,
>   He winks, and turns his lips another way.
> Never did passenger in summer's heat
> More thirst for drink than she for this good turn. . . .

The poem is full of pretty lines about delicate and pretty things – blue-veined violets, for instance, nymph on the sand, fairy on the green, sappy plants, primrose bank: but they do not cloy, because they are tempered by cool, rather sour wit and an enthusiastic realism.

> These blue-vein'd violets whereon we lean
> Never can blab, nor know not what we mean.

Shakespeare draws on a wider reading and more intense experience of poetry than most scholars can command. It is pleasing that Edmond Malone noticed the origin of 'Leading him prisoner in a red-rose chain', which Venus says of Mars, in an ode of Ronsard, where the Muses do the same to Love. Shakespeare is as hungry for words as he is for images, 'the stillitory of thy face', for example. English increased its vocabulary enormously in his generation; every stream of the new language flows into him and he can control it. He likes country and dialect words, new Latinate and foreign words, archaic words and technical words of every kind: in *Venus and Adonis* he invents and adapts his own special verbal devices in such abundance that they often reappear later: a choir of echoes 'like shrill-tongu'd tapsters answering every call,/Soothing the humour of fantastic wits' – a scene played out with the tapster Francis in *Henry IV*; or a tranquil and majestic dawn quite unlike the opening, 'the gentle lark, weary of rest,/From his moist cabinet mounts up on high'; or an unforgettable snail, 'backward in his shelly cave with pain'; or 'poor Wat' the hunted hare on the hillside; or an Ovidian theory of the origins of earthquakes, 'As when the wind, imprison'd in the ground . . . earth's foundation shakes'.

The death of Adonis is intimately shocking:

> And nuzzling in his flank, the loving swine
> Sheath'd unaware the tusk in his soft groin.

Venus curses love for the future and makes it tragic for ever. Ovid's Salmacis was a boy out swimming who melted into the nymph that raped him and became Hermaphroditus. Adonis has a memorial flower that springs from his blood: a fritillary I assume, 'A purple flow'r . . . check'red with white' with 'Green dropping sap' if you pick it. Weary of the world, Venus flies away to Paphos, where she 'Means to immure herself and not be seen'. A verbal echo of the rhythm of this final stanza occurs later, of all places in *Henry V*: 'Holding their course to Paphos', 'Holding due course to Harfleur'. These self-echoes do happen to poets, but I do not suppose Shakespeare was conscious of them. The experience of writing *Venus and Adonis* was so intense that both conscious and unconscious memories of it broke surface again and again.

Venus and Adonis was carefully printed and often reprinted. In his dedication, Shakespeare was already promising Southampton a more substantial work, 'some graver labour': *The Rape of Lucrece*, which was registered with the Stationers on 9 May 1594, about a year later. It will not have taken a year to write, but he was also writing sonnets, one of which (26) so echoes the *Rape*'s dedication to Southampton that it helps to date the series. But I will deal first with *The Rape of Lucrece* – a nasty story out of Livy and Ovid, welcomed into English by Chaucer, Gower, Lydgate and others. The set-piece about the picture of the fall of Troy (ll.1366ff.) owes something to the temple paintings in Book I of the *Aeneid*, or perhaps to a renaissance tapestry based on Virgil's description – a tapestry of the Fall of Troy hung at Westminster.

Shakespeare's poem is a sombre, indoor study of the defiling of innocence and beauty, the breakdown of society at its heart, and the betrayal of kinship and honour. Not surprisingly, it turned out to be less popular than *Venus and Adonis*. It was certainly an ambitious and seriously intended work, though its purposes may seem to us contradictory and working against one another. Christopher Devlin suggested that through Southampton Shakespeare must have encountered Robert Southwell and felt his stern influence to become a graver poet, but that is not certain: to be grave is a natural element in the ambition of any poet who seeks to increase his range, as Shakespeare did constantly throughout his working life.

The *Rape* is a formal poem of 1855 lines, treating just one episode of its moralizing, anti-tyrannical prose argument. The anti-tyrannical colouring has nothing to do with the Elizabethan Court but may derive from Florence. To the Elizabethans it was an exotic and classic tale in familiar, dignified metre; they could be shocked and pleased at once. Today one notices with particular pleasure that the prose narrative – one of the few pieces of formal narrative prose by Shakespeare that we have, and I think the only plot analysis by him that mediates between his sources and his finished work – is crisply classical, lucid and well organized. 'Which done . . .' and 'Collatinus the victory, and his wife the Fame' are phrases that deliberately recall Livy's style. He hovers closely over Livy's Latin, but he adapts, reorganizes and abbreviates his original. He omits *conclamat vir paterque* and introduces the word Actor. The suggestion that Shakespeare's brilliant and laconic prose version is at least halfway towards a theatrical *Plot* is irresistible. The woman's bedchamber scene did become part of Shakespeare's repertory. The themes of rape, seduction and mutilation go back to *Titus Andronicus* and *A Lover's Complaint*, and figure largely in his early work. But the fact that he can so easily throw off a prose pastiche of Livy is enthralling, and has many implications.

Shakespeare begins his poem with 'lightless fire . . . pale embers . . . embracing flames'. The verse technique is interesting: the stanza endings are like still photographs held at the end of a film sequence, or like morals at the end of a story. His long verse analysis of behaviour, exploiting every Ovidian paradox he can elicit, which in his dramatic work is equally but only implicitly present, and the infallible dexterity of his phrasing are very impressive. In this last matter if in no other, I think the *Rape* is an advance even on *Venus and Adonis*: 'This silent war of lilies and of roses', 'And in her vaulty prison stows the Day', 'And moody Pluto winks while Orpheus plays', 'Tears harden lust, though marble wear with raining'.

The motif of the midnight rapist, which occurs more than once in Shakespeare, had a resonance in life if only from Pierre de Chastelhard, who was discovered on a February night in 1563, hiding under the bed of Mary Queen of Scots. He was tried and beheaded. He had been sent by French Huguenots deliberately to create a sexual scandal, to prevent the Queen from marrying the son of Philip of Spain.

The interior decor of the poem is palatial and authentic; evidently by now Shakespeare knows something about grand houses and luxurious taste. The green bedspread under which Lucrece lies merits particular attention, since this (ll.386ff.) is the only bit of Shakespeare for which we have a rejected draft. Sir John Suckling, a courtly poet of the next generation, found it as an unfinished fragment after Shakespeare's death and, not knowing where it fitted, finished it himself. The version Shakespeare adopted and Richard Field printed in 1594 is a great improvement on the draft version. What is more, the draft is written in the six-line stanza form of *Venus and Adonis*, whereas the *Rape* as we have it is in heavier seven-line stanzas. Suckling has:

> Out of the bed the other fair hand was
> On a green satin quilt, whose perfect white
> Looked like a daisy in a field of grass [so far Shakespeare]
> And showed like unmelt snow unto the sight. . . .

Shakespeare has:

> Without the bed her other fair hand was,
> On the green coverlet; whose perfect white
> Show'd like an April daisy on the grass,
> With pearly sweat, resembling dew of night.
> Her eyes, like marigolds, had sheath'd their light,
> And canopied in darkness sweetly lay,
> Till they might open to adorn the day.

Suckling's version was posthumously printed in his *Fragmenta Aurea* (1646), and entitled 'A Supplement of an imperfect Copy of Verses of Mr. Wil. Shakespeare'. One would like to know the history of that stray bit of paper. If Suckling got it from his friend William Davenant of Oxford, with whose father Shakespeare often stayed, then we would have the interesting likelihood that Shakespeare was at work on the poem in Oxford, where he left a scrap of it lying around. But that of course is a conjecture. This may have been a stray leaf from a notebook, or a scribble on the back of a tavern bill. Whatever the case, the difference between the final Shakespeare version and Suckling's supplement is overwhelming; but the improvement over the first draft is almost as impressive. It is a matter of sound (*Without* for *Out of*), taste (*April daisy* is less surreal, and *coverlet* better textured) and sensuousness (the sweat). I do not think it is a matter of crispness of definition, but rather of enrichment; indeed, some parts of *The Rape of Lucrece* are to my own taste over-rich, admirable as they are. The colours are subtle and often light, but there are sometimes too many of them: azure, alabaster, coral and snow in two lines (419–20). The excitement is somehow more in the metaphors than in any erotic momentum ('Rude ram to batter such an ivory wall!'), and suggests that Shakespeare was personally more innocent than his subject matter in this poem.

All the same, *The Rape of Lucrece* has moments of brilliance as well as moments of failure. Among the failures I count 'She wakes her heart by beating on her breast', and among the brilliant moments 'In thy weak hive a wand'ring wasp hath crept', and the end of the stanzas on Night:

> ... yet ere he go to bed,
> Knit poisonous clouds about his golden head.

> With rotten damps ravish the morning air;
> Let their exhal'd unwholesome breaths make sick
> The life of purity, the supreme fair,
> Ere he arrive his weary noontide prick;
> And let thy musty vapours march so thick
>   That in their smoky ranks his smoth'red light
>   May set at noon and make perpetual night.

The eye glides from stanza to stanza, and is delighted, but the texture of the whole is too elaborate and too forced to hold normal attention: the poem smells of the lamp. All the same, it should interest a scholar of the plays, since among the numerous interwoven or scarcely interwoven set-pieces of which it consists there lurk some interesting mad or hysterical poetry: 'Distress likes dumps ...'; and an invitation to Philomel, 'Make thy sad grove in my dishevell'd hair ...'; and verses on the frighted deer, on body and soul, and on tears, which have their echoes in his dramatic poetry. The poem uses his view that women are waxen, impressionable, and nicer, morally stronger than men:

> In men, as in a rough-grown grove, remain
> Cave-keeping evils that obscurely sleep.

There are touches of Marlowe in the poem ('cloud-kissing Ilion') and of the classical world of intrigues and 'deep policy'. But the voice is Shakespeare's own, and unmistakable by now.

> For sorrow, like a heavy-hanging bell,
> Once set on ringing, with his own weight goes. ...

Even in his weakest conceits, he has by now attained his own nature. No English writer has ever used so vast a vocabulary as Shakespeare, yet his word-plays as a poet are never out of control. (Comedy is another thing.) This was a matter partly of generation and partly of the theatre, but it also denotes an appetite and an ambition to extend the art of English poetry itself. At his most mannered he is at his most direct: 'A lily prison'd in a gaol of snow' and 'Her two blue windows faintly she upheaveth.' In these phrases he has something in common with the Spanish poet Góngora. But his exotic and Propertian rhetoric of set-pieces is always transmuted into the plainest English:

> Once more the ruby-colour'd portal open'd,
> Which to his speech did honey passage yield;
> Like a red morn, that ever yet betoken'd
> Wreck to the seaman, tempest to the field,
>   Sorrow to shepherds, woe unto the birds,
>   Gusts and foul flaws to herdsmen and to herds.

This ill presage advisedly she marketh.
Even as the wind is hush'd before it raineth,
Or as the wolf doth grin before he barketh,
Or as the berry breaks before it staineth,
  Or like the deadly bullet of a gun,
  His meaning struck her ere his words begun.

The poem includes some references of an agreeably extravagant kind to pestilence:

... To drive infection from the dangerous year!
That the star-gazers, having writ on death,
May say the plague is banish'd by thy breath.

As burning fevers, agues pale and faint,
Life-poisoning pestilence, and frenzies wood,
The marrow-eating sickness, whose attaint
Disorder breeds by heating of the blood,
  Surfeits, imposthumes, grief, and damn'd despair. ...

Here and there he introduces themes that appear in the Sonnets, 'Love-lacking vestals, and self-loving nuns', 'as one on shore ... a late-embarked friend', 'What is thy body but a swallowing grave,/Seeming to bury that posterity'. His intention is to astonish and to delight, as it was in *Venus and Adonis*. *The Rape of Lucrece* is a poem of wonderful moments, rather than one that repays solid, continuous reading, but the moments are numerous, and the dramatic variations extraordinary.

... Whose words, like wildfire, burnt the shining glory
Of rich-built Ilion, that the skies were sorry,
  And little stars shot from their fixed places,
  When their glass fell wherein they view'd their faces.

The moment of suicide itself is an awkward one, stiffer and more laborious than anything in the Sonnets, and yet strong enough on an intellectual level to sustain this meditative poem.

The Rape of Lucrece quotes the Southampton family motto (1.144), and the book was dedicated 'To the Right Honourable Henry Wriothesly, Earl of Southampton, and Baron of Titchfield', as *Venus and Adonis* had been, but in more intimate terms:

The love I dedicate to your Lordship is without end: whereof this Pamphlet without beginning is but a superfluous Moity. The warrant I have of your Honourable disposition, not the worth of my untutord Lines makes it assured of acceptance. What I have done is yours, what I have to doe is yours, being part in all I have, devoted yours. Were my worth greater my duety would show greater, meane time, as it is, it is bound to your Lordship; To whom I wish long life still lengthned with all happinesse. Your Lordships in all duty. William Shakespeare.

The relationship of Shakespeare and Southampton is of great importance for the poet's life since, according to Davenant, Southampton 'gave him a thousand pounds to go through with a purchase which he heard he had a mind to', and that was a huge and most unlikely amount of money. The Queen gave the entire plum estate of Breamore in Hampshire to her early favourite Sir Christopher Hatton, and a thousand pounds is what he sold it for, so we are talking of a large sum. Elizabethan patrons were expected, as A. L. Rowse remarks, to dig into their pockets. The likely year would be 1594, when Southampton came into his fortune. But Davenant was a wild fantasizer, who claimed that the King owed him a thousand pounds, and who, when he produced the play, altered the witches in *Macbeth* to a ballet on broomsticks in mid-air. What surely lies behind this story, which first reached print in Rowe's edition of the plays (1709), is that Southampton bought Shakespeare his 'share' in the Chamberlain's Men, which he joined as a sharer in 1594: it is hard to see how else Shakespeare could have found the money, since the theatres had been shut for some time. His career as a sharer was worth 'a thousand' to him.

I do not think that the Sonnets furnish any unambiguous true story about Shakespeare and Southampton. They are the most thrilling and intimately deep poems in our language; they are often passionate, but they are like a record that leaves out most of the facts, and all the names and dates. William Empson rightly points out that their dedication is deliberately ambiguous, and I think that the same goes for some of the poems themselves. It is not absolutely impossible that they are the first and best novel ever written, but they do at least start from real life, and my own view is that Shakespeare is so much better and more powerful than other writers of sonnets precisely because he means what he says. There are tones that are impossible to fake: that of Villon, that of Archilochos, that of Catullus. After infinite qualifications, one must admit that this is so. The extraordinary thing about the Sonnets is that the simple reader, according to his or her capacity, can understand them and enter into their feeling at once. The trouble starts when one tries to unload and translate and deconstruct.

Before going through the Sonnets themselves it is as well to establish whatever facts history offers us. The first problems are those of date and dedication. The printer in 1609 dedicated them to Mr W.H., 'the only begetter of these ensuing sonnets'. I will not recite the dismal catalogue of all the impossible candidates for these initials, except the amusing idea that they might mean Master Wriothesly Henry, and the recent crazy suggestion that they mean William Hathaway, Anne's brother (whose very existence is pure conjecture).

One further W.H. ought to be recorded, though I do not believe he is the right one: William Hole, who was appointed in 1618 'Head Sculptor of the iron for money in the Tower and Elsewhere for life', which is the office of Cuneater or Engraver. He died in office in 1624, as 'Chief Graver of the Mint, and Graver of the King's Seals, Ensigns and Arms'. He was the first English engraver of music and almost certainly knew Shakespeare, since he made engravings of Drayton, Florio, Chapman and Thomas Egerton, and some maps for Camden. The poet Hugh Holland, another friend of Shakespeare's, wrote Hole a poem in 'Parthenia, or the Maydenhead of the first musicke that ever was printed for the Virginalls' (1611), 'Ingraven by William Hole for Dorothie Evans'. He headed the poem 'Mr Hugh Holland On his worthy friend W.H. and his Triumviri of Musicke'. Those were William Byrd, John Bull and Orlando Gibbons. But Hole's known works can be dated between 1607 and 1619, and if the Sonnets are as early as I think, they could not have been written for him. If, on the other hand, 'begetter' means the getter or procurer of the manuscript, as Lee in his *Life of William Shakespeare* shows with a quotation from Dekker that it certainly could, then William Hole might have got them through a musical friend, since a few were set to music, and those were the ones copied in stray manuscripts that survive. He would at least be a more likely 'only begetter' than the undistinguished theological publisher William Hall proposed by Lee.

I am, however, disinclined to accept that 'begetter' means getter or procurer. The begetter is not the author, who was named, so it must mean either the person idealized or the person who got hold of the Sonnets. The first of these two meanings is much commoner and likelier, so it seems clear enough, as A. L. Rowse has argued, that William Harvey is intended, that the manuscript the printer used had been in his possession, and that the printer supposed the poems might be about him. They were not, but Sir William Harvey had been married to Southampton's mother, as her third husband. She died in 1607, and in 1608 he married again. The 1609 dedication is therefore perfectly fitting: 'To the only begetter of these ensuing sonnets, Mr W.H., all happiness and that eternity promised by our ever-living poet wisheth the well-wishing adventurer in setting forth. T.T. [the printer Thomas Thorpe].'

The 1609 edition of the Sonnets was not reprinted for a long time; no contemporary discusses it as a book except that a young friend and fan of Shakespeare's, Leonard Digges, refers to it on the flyleaf of some Lope de Vega poems (Madrid 1613) now in Balliol College library. The 1609 edition of the Sonnets survives in extremely few copies, and the text it prints was certainly not supervised, nor I believe authorized by Shakespeare: it is even possible or probable that Southampton or else Shakespeare had the edition suppressed. Robert Burton of Christ Church had *Venus and Adonis* and the *Rape*, but no copy of the Sonnets, though he admired Shakespeare and even met Southampton at a London bookseller's.

A few sonnets crept into print before 1609 in *The Passionate Pilgrim*, printed by William Jaggard without registration in 1599: they are spicy enough but not seriously compromising. I will discuss that puzzling volume on its own. Thomas Heywood complained in *An Apology for Actors* (1612) that two of his own poems were printed there as Shakespeare's, and 'the author I know much offended with Mr. Jaggard that (altogether unknown to him) presumed to make so bold with his name'. The Stationers' Register records in 1600 the advance registration of 'A book called Amours by J.D. with certain [other?] sonnets by W.S.', but no copy of that has survived and it may never have been printed. The authors sound tantalizingly like John Donne and Shakespeare, who almost certainly knew one another when Donne was local Master of the Revels at his Inn of Court; no other writers with the same initials are so likely, but some exist, so the existence of an earlier suppressed edition than that of 1609 must remain a conjecture.

The Sonnets as we have them are arranged more carefully than at first appears, though they need not have been written in the order of this arrangement. They are a series of 125 with an *envoi* or closing poem, followed by another 25 of which the second last (151) is surely obscene. The last two sonnets (153 and 154) are translations from a Greek original in the Palatine Anthology, perhaps by way of a Latin version. The original is very beautiful. This arrangement, including *A Lover's Complaint* at the end of the book, was conventional.

The first few sonnets of the entire collection, certainly sixteen and perhaps many more, are clearly written to Lord Southampton, whose marriage problem, whose recorded looks and whose youthful vanity (no Elizabethan nobleman was so often painted) they mirror. Southampton was presented at Court at seventeen, when he left Cambridge. His father died when he was six and he was a ward of Lord Burghley: an arrangement of financial profit to that peer, who had a number of such wards. Burghley tried to marry Southampton to his own grandchild – an honourable, profitable and convenient alliance, as he must have thought. Southampton's mother agreed, but the boy refused, and the crisis lasted from the summer of 1590 when he was seventeen until at least 1594.

In that year he came into his money, and commissioned the great monumental tomb at Titchfield for his father and his grandfather and also his mother, for which money had been left by his father's will. He had himself carved with his sister kneeling on the side of the tomb, which is elaborately heraldic, two of his ancestors having been Garter Kings of Arms. He and his sister share the same painted arms, but his are impaled (as would happen on marriage) with blank unpainted stone. He could scarcely have made a more obvious point of his refusal to name his bride or his reservation of the right to choose her for himself. Scholars have not looked carefully at this remarkable monument, which surely confirms the date of the Sonnets.

In what seem to be the earliest ones addressed to Southampton, Shakespeare is attempting on behalf of his family and friends to persuade Southampton to take a wife: not a particular wife, but any wife. I doubt whether they met in 1590, but in 1591 Burghley's secretary John Clapham wrote Southampton an insulting Latin poem called *Narcissus*, wishing him 'increase of manliness'. Shakespeare wrote much more nicely, probably on behalf of the young man's mother.

In 1592, after a riot in June followed by the plague, the theatres shut. Shakespeare was Southampton's poet by the end of that year. In 1594 Burghley fined Southampton £5000 no less, for refusing to marry his granddaughter, quite apart from substantial inheritance fees payable to the Crown. Burghley married this granddaughter to Lord Derby in 1595. The sonnets to Southampton were apparently finished by September 1595, and I think a year earlier, when Shakespeare went back to work full time in the theatre. In that September 'My Lord of Southampton doth with too much familiarity court the fair Mistress Vernon.' Elizabeth Vernon was a Maid of Honour, but in 1598 Southampton married her secretly because she was pregnant, and the Queen sent them both to prison. All this leaves us with some problems.

How did Southampton and Shakespeare meet? Probably in 1591 or 1592, perhaps over the Sonnets, which were commissioned poems; they are a counterblast to Clapham's *Narcissus*. They may have met through John Florio, Southampton's Italian and French tutor, installed by Burghley as a spy in his household. The sonnet signed 'Phaeton', printed as a compliment in front of Florio's *Second Frutes* (1591), is surely by Shakespeare: he certainly knew Florio, though we don't know when they met, and almost no other poet in 1591 could have written the sonnet. Since it is not usually printed among Shakespeare's works I will give the text without much argument, and readers can judge for themselves. If I am right, it follows that Shakespeare did meet Southampton through Florio, and that his sonnets to Southampton followed on the Phaeton sonnet. Shakespeare certainly owed to Florio his well-nourished curiosity about all things Italian, and his knowledge of Montaigne, whom Florio translated. Florio's father came to England as a Protestant exile, and Shakespeare had other connections with such people, who greatly enriched the somewhat provincial hawking and hunting culture of the English.

Phaeton to his friend Florio
Sweet friend, whose name agrees with thy increase,
How fit a rival art thou of the spring!

For when each branch hath left his flourishing,
And green-locked summer's shady pleasures cease,
She makes the winter's storms repose in peace,
And spends her franchise on each living thing:
The daisies sprout, the little birds so sing,
Herbs, gums, and plants do vaunt of their release.
So when that all our English wits lay dead
(Except the laurel that is evergreen),
Thou with thy fruits our barrenness o'erspread
And set thy flowery pleasance to be seen.
Such fruits, such flowerets of morality,
Were ne'er before brought out of Italy.

Why 'Phaeton'? Because he borrowed the sun's horses and drove them badly and fell from heaven: Phaeton is a symbol of too much daring, and therefore a modest name, though it scarcely conceals great ambition. The story is in Ovid, and the name perfectly fits the young Shakespeare, and fits the title quotation of *Venus and Adonis*. No other writer of sonnets is as good as this except Spenser, but Spenser would have signed it. The humour is Shakespeare's, and so is the movement of thought, so is the seasonal colouring. This is not Shakespeare's greatest sonnet, though not his worst either; it fits its place well as one of his earliest, perhaps the very first.

Who really was Southampton, and what was he like outside the Sonnets? The family name was Writh, which one of the heraldic members of it altered to Wriothesly. They were at least fourth-generation courtiers and old nobility, extremely rich from the monastic spoils under Henry VIII. Shakespeare's young man grew up in the shadow of his fellow ward the Earl of Essex, who was a crucial four years older. Leicester was dead and Essex was a star. Elizabeth Vernon, Lady Southampton, was Essex's first cousin, and the Southamptons named their daughter Penelope after Essex's sister.

Elizabeth Vernon had no dowry. In 1593 Southampton had been refused the Garter, and in 1595 after signs of favour while Essex was away, 'My Lord of Southampton offering to help the Queen to her horse, was refused, and is gone from Court.' In 1596 he was refused permission to sail under Essex against Cadiz, but in 1597 he commanded Garland in Essex's unsuccessful Azores expedition, on which he sank a Spanish frigate. His finances were rickety, and he applied through Robert Cecil for permission to live in France for a time. He may well have felt by then that he was too deeply involved with Elizabeth Vernon.

Southampton got into a silly scrape. The Queen had gone to bed and he was left in the Presence chamber playing cards for money with someone called Parker and Sir Walter Ralegh (who had just done time in prison for seducing Elizabeth Throckmorton, another Maid of Honour), when the Squire in Attendance ordered them to leave. They ignored this man until he threatened to call in the guard, at which Ralegh 'put up his money and went his ways'. Southampton encountered the same Squire 'between the tennis-court wall and the garden' and hit him, so the Squire pulled out some of Southampton's long and sweeping hair. When the Queen heard the story next day she thanked the Squire 'and told him he had done better if he had sent him to the porter's lodge, to see who durst have fetched him out'. Southampton was rusticated from Court for a month. Meanwhile Robert Cecil prepared an embassy for France. Southampton arranged an entertainment with plays and banquets before he left, using Shakespeare's company, and at the last minute was allowed to go with Cecil and reside abroad for two years, taking ten servants, six horses and £200. He was not going to cut a very fine figure.

'His fair mistress doth wash her fairest face with many tears' we are told. That was in February 1598. He returned secretly in August and married her, went back to France, was summoned home, and joined her in prison only about a week before their daughter was born. This whole saga reveals a character, and one is not surprised a little later that Southampton joined Essex's idiotic rebellion, if only from loyalty to Essex. It is an important point that it was Burghley who saved England from the likes of Leicester and Essex, and from more wars of the roses, of ambition, of religion, of heaven knows what. But this later generation (Leicester was more formidable and more treacherous) behaved like spoilt, unruly children, and Burghley and the Queen must bear some psychological responsibility for that. Southampton, even at the time of his calamitous treason, when he avoided execution by a whisker, was not yet thirty. He settled down under James I and became what passed in that world for a model citizen. He even presented his old college (St John's, Cambridge) with a large collection of theological books, which he had bought on request from an impoverished scholar. He never lost his love of the theatre though.

Wise men agree that sonnet 107 must be about the death of the Queen ('The mortal Moon hath her eclipse endured'), the arrival of James I ('this most balmy time') and Southampton's emergence from prison, but I do not agree with them. The sonnet is about omens in nature; there was an olive tree in the church glass at Stratford, and 'My love looks fresh' is not a likely compliment to a thirty-year-old prisoner after three years in the Tower. The reference to 'tyrants' crests and tombs of brass' has nothing to do with Elizabeth; such an insult would be unthinkable. The olive and the balm are scriptural but not necessarily royal. Balm heals: 'Is there no balm in Gilead? Is there no physician there?' We can therefore reject the dating of this sonnet to 1603. Sonnets of Shakespeare's were circulating by 1598 and Francis Meres knew them, though they were for 'his private friends'. I do not see any reason why the entire series of Sonnets should not have been largely complete by 1594 or 1595; the closeness with which they are woven together suggests that is what happened; exceptions and revisions may exist, but I find no substantial trace of either. The story at which they hint is coherent and intended although allusive.

The sonnet sequence was a very popular form, and the stray sonnet of compliment an idle, almost a casual composition. Southampton got one in 1594 from Barnabe Barnes, another from Gervase Markham in 1595, and several attentions from Nashe. Years later, Thomas Heywood chose in verses on the King's death (1625) to add Southampton's name, 'in duty bound, because his servant once'. It was from this circle that *The Passionate Pilgrim* was put together. Barnes called Southampton's eyes 'Those heavenly lamps which give the Muses light'. Markham said 'thy blessed tongue stills music in the spheres', and Nashe called him 'fairest bud the red rose ever bare' in the dedication sonnet of an obscene poem called 'The Choice of Valentines' (1595). In an epilogue to that poem, Nashe makes a claim that throws some light on Shakespeare:

> Yet Ovid's wanton muse did not offend.
> He is the fountain whence my streams do flow. . . .

In the prologue he says:

> Complaints and praises, everyone can write,
> And passion out their pangs in stately rhymes;
> But of love's pleasures none did ever write
> That have succeeded in these latter times. . . .

The ambition was common, only Shakespeare was more restrained than Nashe, and deeper. Sir Sidney Lee accumulated a long list of compliments to Southampton by poets and musicians, including the memorial verses of *Tears of the Isle of Wight* (1624), printed when their subject was already buried in honey like his father and his grandfather, under the same monument at Titchfield. He has no monument of his own, though his daughter Mary, who died in 1615 at four years old, has the finest that any English child can ever have had, by Epiphanius Evesham.

Another of Lee's useful accumulations is in his fifteen pages on 'The Vogue of the Elizabethan Sonnet' (1591–7), the final section of his *Life of William Shakespeare*. Sonnet sequences are amazingly numerous, and the French influence on them, which is nowadays sometimes forgotten, is very strong. It extends to the concluding ode or longer poem, in Shakespeare's case *A Lover's Complaint*. The sonnet sequence is essentially a set of variations on a theme of love, and the patron may be addressed in lovers' terms. A manageable and well-judged discussion of the form sequences take is easily available in John Kerrigan's Penguin edition of Shakespeare's Sonnets (1986): I will not repeat its arguments, but take them for granted. Sidney's *Astrophel and Stella* sonnets were published in 1591, Samuel Daniel's *Delia* in 1592, Lodge's *Phillis* in 1593 and Drayton's *Ideas Mirrour: Amours in Quatorzains* in 1594. In his plays Shakespeare did not restrict the word 'sonnet' to a specific fourteen-line scheme or schemes, and some of his own sonnets (126, for example) are irregular. 'A proper sonnet (to any pleasant tune)' in *A Handful of Pleasant Delights* is in four-line stanzas. Sonnets occur in romances and in the course of plays. They were a trick everyone thought they could perform.

Sonnets were often set as songs – Samuel Daniel's by his brother John, for example – or adapted as stanza songs, and these share some of their attitudes and materials with songs like John Morley's. They are Ovidian variations, and they overlap and run counter to one another. The best of Shakespeare's have the stamp of clarity, and their movement, their rhythmic momentum, which is never quite the same in any two sonnets, runs continuously from beginning to end of the poem. The effect is startling and includes an amazing sense of the freedom and reality of feeling. Their images and their resonance give great pleasure and seem to wrench at the heart, and yet they are swift: much more so than the stanzas in *The Rape of Lucrece*.

Because of their privacy, the Sonnets are passionately direct, and every nail is hit on the head as if Shakespeare knew very well what he had to say. He deals with matters of great importance to him. Yet he can be humorous, various and playfully ornamental. One has the impression that his whole self is speaking. If the truth and the best of his poetry were pouring into these Sonnets, small wonder that *The Rape of Lucrece* was a gilded husk if he was writing it at the same time. The best of his Sonnets are among the most perfect poems ever written in any language, and when he died one might think it was time for English to go to bed – yet the Sonnets were written almost at the beginning of his life's work, probably before he was thirty. He was in love with Southampton, in love with love, in love with poetry and in love with life. Yet in his plays he takes the view that sonnets are false, love-verse is false, poets are false, and that the truth cannot be said: it is beyond expression. In his late plays the most important moments are silent or have very few words.

Since this is a biography, I am bound to say what I think happened. Shakespeare and Southampton were not complete lovers, and the Sonnets are not about buggery. They move between extravagance of compliment and intimate jokes; the tone is subtle and the note of passion comes and goes. They were not intended for our eyes, and yet they contain wild outpourings about eternal fame. Perhaps Shakespeare might not have admitted his knowledge of his own everlasting fame and honour, or his appetite for it, so directly in less private poems. The private circulation of the poems occurred at once, and the two translations (a common enough feature in sonnet sequences), with the final *Lover's Complaint*, suggest that Shakespeare did intend them for a book, though not necessarily a book that would ever be printed. I believe it was this privacy that set him free to express what he most deeply felt, leaving other poets to flounder on the published surface of life. When he saw how far his Sonnets went beyond his two long formal poems, he wrote no more long formal poems. The theatre supplied his appetite for fame, which was sated well before the end of his life. He was secure of fame. And love? I think he loved his wife and his children.

The Sonnets begin playfully and intimately, but with the extraordinary beauty that only Shakespeare has mastered:

> ... Thou that art now the world's fresh ornament
> And only herald to the gaudy spring. ...

Southampton is warned of waste and of old age, and of self-love – not so rude an accusation then as it is today: the song 'Away with these self-loving lads/Whom Cupid's arrow never glads' more or less catches the flavour. In these opening sonnets it is mostly stray lines that are wonderful, like the straying music of stringed instruments. Some are simple ('For never-resting time leads summer on') and some witty ('Then were not summer's distillation left/A liquid prisoner pent in walls of glass . . .') and every poem is charming. The seventh sonnet has the continuous momentum, the sustained, single rhythm that later becomes a vehicle of passion, but here the tone is still light. By the time the entire sequence had been put together this had come to seem deliberate, but it also probably reflects chronology. Shakespeare is writing a polite, intimate set of verses from the point of view of Southampton's mother and his friends, almost as an elder brother at times. The family motto gets noticed, accusations fly: of fear, of lack of love, of self-hatred even. The best of this first sub-series of poems is the twelfth, 'When I do count the clock . . .', but even that is reduced a little by its closure; the repeated advice to breed has become a kind of refrain, and a little tiresome. All the same, sonnet 12 is an almost perfect poem, and from this point onwards the tone of the sequence begins to deepen. By sonnet 14, 'Not from the stars do I my judgement pluck', somehow the entire universe has been called into play, so that one scarcely notices the daringness, or what would in other hands be the jejuneness of the conceit.

In sonnet 15, this same sense of the rhythms and momentum of the whole world increases:

> When I consider . . .
> That this huge stage presenteth nought but shows
> Whereon the stars in secret influence comment. . . .

Now Shakespeare is claiming to save the young man from time and decay ('As he takes from you, I engraft you new'), and it is no longer perfectly clear that his only remedy is marriage; it may be the immortality of poetry. In sonnet 16, he goes back to urging 'With means more blessed than my barren rhyme'; when the Sonnets discard their refrain, as they have now done, they become freer and more thrilling. Sonnet 17 mingles freshness and age with enchanting effect, and rhetorically and syntactically it shows great freedom and energy. It is the last one to mention the child:

> But were some child of yours alive that time,
> You should live twice – in it, and in my rhyme.

Sonnet 18 is a new beginning, the first full statement of the immortality of poetry, and the first perfect sonnet: 'Shall I compare thee to a summer's day?' Shakespeare is drawn on by the logic of his belief in immortal verse to the immortality of love when verse records it, and to the immortality of his own love. Poem after poem deepens this theme: 'My love shall in my verse ever live young' (sonnet 19). Shakespeare is infallibly drawn into his own poems as a lover.

> A woman's face, with Nature's own hand painted,
> Hast thou, the Master/Mistress of my passion. . . .

> And for a woman wert thou first created;
> Till Nature, as she wrought thee, fell a-doting,
> And by addition me of thee defeated
> By adding one thing to my purpose nothing.
> But since she prick'd thee out for women's pleasure,
> Mine be thy love, and thy love's use their treasure.

This twentieth sonnet is emancipated, frank and very clearly stated. There is a mysteriousness about the Sonnets which no commentary will ever disperse, but there is no mystery about what this one says or what it implies. The rules of conduct that Shakespeare takes for granted are not those of our world, and it is hard for us to imagine this particular mixture of fearless frankness and absolute taboo. The Salmacis episode in the *Metamorphoses* of Ovid on which Shakespeare drew in *Venus and Adonis* lurks behind this poem too. We have not yet arrived among the sonnets of the experience of love, or else they begin here, but these are still very innocent poems. Nonetheless, I do find Shakespeare very innocent in love and astoundingly deep. He is already troubled in sonnet 21 by the vanity and falseness of verse:

> O, let me, true in love, but truly write,
> And then believe me, my love is as fair
> As any mother's child, though not so bright
> As those gold candles fix'd in heaven's air. . . .

From sonnet 22 he worries about the disparity of age, and the first hint of the possibility of unfaithfulness. Can this be real? Did he really delude himself that the Earl of Southampton would love him alone for ever, or was it all a brilliant game, the entire sequence just a box of pretty tricks? I think the seriousness, like the passion, comes and goes, and that conceits like the exchange of hearts do attract exaggeration.

Shakespeare was more in love with poetry than he was with his young nobleman, who was crazy about poetry too. To the extent that it was all a game, it was a game very seriously played, as Shakespeare's expression of panic and stage-fright indicate. 'Oh, let my looks be then the eloquence. . . . O, learn to read what silent love hath writ!' (sonnet 23). He knows he can never have a nobleman's or a great soldier's glory, and his luck in love amazes him. The twenty-sixth sonnet, 'Lord of my love, to whom in vassalage . . .', is a simple literary dedication, and yet a perfect poem. I do not differ in any important way from the received view of which of Shakespeare's Sonnets are best. I like the lines about night and dreams and stars ('When sparkling stars twire not thou gild'st the even' – sonnet 28), but the most powerful sonnets are so good they hardly seem to linger on a line: sonnets 29, 30 and 33 for instance.

From a biographical point of view, we should note that Shakespeare in the thirtieth sonnet weeps:

> For precious friends hid in death's dateless night,
> And weep afresh love's long since cancell'd woe. . . .

This poem hints at and subtly introduces a new theme of the present sorrows of love, which as with earlier themes is fully stated a few poems later, in sonnet 33: 'But out, alack! he was but one hour mine.' This brings us to poems of sorrow and forgiveness, 'Excusing thy sins more than thy sins are;/For to thy sensual fault I bring in sense . . .' (sonnet 35). At this point the Sonnets begin to have a submerged plot: they are more intimate, very scrupulous, slightly claustrophobic. They are either the records of an enclosed Elizabethan house or of a relationship that has something of the same quality as such a house. In sonnet 38 one begins to sense the approach of rivals, and in sonnet 39 the necessity of separations; in sonnet 40 reproaches begin to surface ('I do forgive thy robbery, gentle thief'). It looks as if Southampton has stolen Shakespeare's girlfriend; this triple relationship is better and more neatly sketched here than by any other writer until Turgenev, and corresponds all too painfully to the experience of life. I do not think Shakespeare can have invented it to improve his flow of variations: he is as sensitive as the snail in *Venus and Adonis* and at a deeper level as melancholy as the hare. He is in everything and everywhere an outsider: he is not at home in the world. Yet these poems are as playful as they are painful.

Poems of dreams and distance may be about a projected or an imagined, dreamtime separation, but it looks as if some separation really happened. Anyone who reads the Sonnets through continuously will feel battered by the reiteration of love; that is as Shakespeare intended. But they have phases of variation, and the suggested or submerged plot is not easy to fit in with what we must assume about real life. We seem to know Shakespeare best in his most perfect poems, and to know him there with complete immediacy. Sonnet 53, 'What is your substance, whereof are you made./ That millions of strange shadows on you tend?', is an extraordinary and revealing moment. Southampton is Adonis, he is Helen, 'But you like none, none you, for constant heart'.

This is only the first of an entire handful of powerful poems, answering and extending and arguing with one another. Of course they are a one-sided conversation, so there is something solipsistic and extreme about them just as there is about Southampton. Sonnet 60, 'Like as the waves make towards the pebbled shore', is the melancholic side of survival only through immortal verse, and is one of my oldest favourites. I like the gloomy Shakespeare of the poems that follow it too, 'Beated and chopt with tann'd antiquity' (sonnet 62) and brooding like a French theologian on the nature of his own self-love. In sonnet 64 he admits the truth that threatens him – 'That Time will come and take my love away' – and despair follows. Shakespeare in love is fresh and infectious, but Shakespeare in grief is more impressive still; it is his December, not his April and May, that utterly convinces and subdues. The list of his despairs in sonnet 66 lies at the root of all his later work: beggary, broken faith, defiled virginity, art tongue-tied by authority, truth called simplicity, 'And captive good attending captain ill'.

Rage follows despair: the grieving invective of sonnet 69 – 'But why thy odour matcheth not thy show,/The soil is this – that thou dost common grow' – and the sorrow of those that follow it must have been hard to take if they were delivered as they were written, but I doubt that. I think the Sonnets were always intended to be read in groups, perhaps first the early seventeen, then maybe the first 126 together, or if not that then about a dozen at a time, so the remedy was written with the stinging rebuke. The rebuke is clearly one to a younger man, and Shakespeare is as much his father as his lover.

The magnificent mortality sonnet 73, 'That time of year thou mayst in me behold', follows immediately. Elaboration runs to fantasy in sonnet 74, where Shakespeare sees himself as 'The coward conquest of a wretch's knife', having in mind perhaps Marlowe. In sonnet 76 he worries about the sameness of his own style, 'dressing old words new,/Spending again what is already spent'. He gives Southampton a notebook in sonnet 77 – 'The vacant leaves thy mind's imprint will bear'. (Sonnet 122 is about a similar gift, a written notebook: the theme was conventional.)

In sonnets 78 and 79 the rival poet appears in person, though he is not named. But sonnet 86, which concludes this little episode, makes his identity clear enough: 'Was it the proud full sail of his great verse,/Bound for the prize of all-too-precious you'. A reference to spirits as 'his compeers by night' who taught him poetry 'Above a mortal pitch' has been used to prove that he was Chapman, and an entire school of nocturnal, spirit-raising poets has been sniffed out by scholars. Real cabbalists and alchemists and mystical charlatans certainly existed in London, and Shakespeare knew them: the allusions in sonnet 86 are a joke at their expense, and possibly at the expense of Faustus, because the poet is not Chapman: he is Marlowe. 'The proud full sail of his great verse' seems to me, as to A. L. Rowse, unmistakable.

As for Chapman and his mystical School of Night, there never really was one. Chapman often makes excellent reading, and he was a mildly crazed neo-platonist, but no rival to Shakespeare. Rowse goes so far as to think *Hero and Leander* was intended to rival *Venus and Adonis*. I am unable to follow him there, since I feel sure that *Hero and Leander* is not very late Marlowe, and I see it as an influence on Shakespeare. But at the end of Marlowe's life they were racing neck and neck, and there was no other rival who could have left Shakespeare as he says, tongue-tied at his 'polish'd form of well-refined pen' (sonnet 85), unless he means Spenser, who had notoriously failed to offer any compliment to Southampton. Marlowe never finished *Hero and Leander*; Chapman finished and printed it in the year of Marlowe's death (Stationers' Register, 28 September 1593). It was dedicated by Edward Blount to Sir Thomas Walsingham, in whose house Marlowe had been arrested on 18 May. It was much more likely to have been an old translation Marlowe abandoned (*desunt nonnulla* it says) than a new one unfinished.

The section of the sequence following the sonnets about the rival poet begins with the technically and in all ways fascinating sonnet 87, which ends 'Thus have I had thee, as a dream doth flatter:/In sleep a king, but waking no such matter'. Its feminine endings in '-ing' work remarkably and I think quite unpredictably well. Other poems of rejection, self-loathing and suspicion follow. One of the best (sonnet 94) ends with the line 'Lilies that fester smell far worse than weeds', with which Shakespeare is taunted in the play *Edward III*. *Edward III* has some merit; its authorship remains obscure, but it was clearly by a rival poet of some kind, particularly scornful about sonnets yet well able to write them.

Absence becomes more concrete in sonnet 97, 'How like a winter hath my absence been': Shakespeare has spent the summer away. If one chooses to stretch out the Sonnets over a longer period, it might have been the summer of the Azores expedition, 1597. But elsewhere he speaks of three years of friendship: an average of a sonnet a week for three years would be enough to produce the entire sequence, but I think he worked faster and less regularly. In the next sonnet it is absence in the spring, which makes a famous and irresistible poem:

> From you have I been absent in the spring,
> When proud-pied April, dress'd in all his trim,

Hath put a spirit of youth in every thing,
That heavy Saturn laugh'd and leap'd with him.

No other poet given the first three lines could have supplied the fourth. In sonnet 104, the two have known each other only three years: this is one of the best and last of the small group of seasonal poems about absence and presence – 'To me, fair friend, you never can be old,/For as you were when first your eye I ey'd,/Such seems your beauty still.'

Sonnet 106 is of some interest as a new version of the old theme of beauties of the past, 'And beauty making beautiful old rhyme,/In praise of ladies dead and lovely knights . . .'. It shows Shakespeare's affection for romantic chroniclers, and for old verse. He had a little more than the normal antiquarian taste of intelligent people in his time. He felt the chill of monastic ruins, and the tragedy of broken castles and vandalized tombs; when he came to a new town he went to see its buildings and monuments; he liked even the names of old writers, including the dullest poets. He could read black letter and had an eye for old pictures. Hard-nosed as some of his poetry may be, he was fascinated by antiquity of every kind.

Given that sonnet 107 is not about the Queen's death or any such subject, but private like the other sonnets, the question arises what it is about. It treats the extent of love to which no omen, no augury and no fear can set a limit. The Moon survives eclipse, the augurs are proved wrong, things uncertain become certain, 'And peace proclaims olives of endless age.' The 'drops of this most balmy time' probably mean the plague is over. The next extraordinary sonnet is 116, 'Let me not to the marriage of true minds . . .'. Here again, love is triumphant and invincible. The sequence is moving into its final phase. Quarrels are in the past and understood, and forgiveness is exchanged: 'That you were once unkind befriends me now' (sonnet 120). Sonnet 124 is a tour de force of complexity and powerful scorn: 'If my dear love were but the child of state/. . . No, it was builded far from accident/. . . It fears not Policy. . . .' This sonnet shows Shakespeare's rather final dismissal of politics and politicians (to translate him perhaps insecurely into modern terms). The meaning of the poem is that his love does not alter as the opinions and actions of the politic, the fools of time, alter. Love is his creed. For the dying Hotspur life itself was time's fool. The *envoi* which stands as sonnet 126 is a poem in couplets about time and nature.

With sonnet 127 we come across the Dark Lady. I have no ideas about her better than Rowse's suggestion that she was Emilia Lanier, *née* Bassano, a mistress of Lord Hunsdon the Chamberlain, who made her pregnant and married her off in 1592 to Captain Alfonso Lanier, a Court musician. The Bassano family were musicians too, originally it seems Jewish–Italian silk merchants. Emilia was five years younger than Shakespeare. If coherence and coincidence of detail could make a proof, Rowse's case would be proved. If the Dark Lady really did exist, one must hope she never saw some of the poems addressed to her, but it is possible to believe that she did not exist, and that the Sonnets tail off into fantasy, into jokes and variations (some in bad taste), that each small group of sonnets keeps tailing off like this, that the form is centrifugal. Yet Shakespeare keeps returning to the dead centre of his soul or his poem or his amour, until all three coincide. The Dark Lady sonnets might still contain fantasy, intended only for the entertainment of Southampton, since Elizabethan poetry admits of voyeurism. I do not think the Dark Lady is necessarily the same girl whom Shakespeare says Southampton stole from him, but she might be an elaboration of that theme.

At least sonnet 129 is real enough: it is the suffering of this sequence that makes it real and not its mildly sparkling eros. Sonnet 129 is 'Th' expense of spirit in a waste of shame'; I do not think a better or a more terrible poem about lust has ever been written. It is neither Catholic nor Protestant (religion furnishes only a metaphor); it is about the experience of life, and can be properly tested only against experience. Technically it is a forceful poetic machine, a torrent of words icily controlled and cumulatively convincing. Shakespeare is coarser about women in the Sonnets than about men: 'the breath that from my mistress reeks' (sonnet 130) could not have been said about an Earl of Southampton by a poet. He is physically and brutally, but less spiritually, intimate with the woman than the man. Sonnets that engage her in dialogue are poetic contrivances, not real conversations. His most convincing feelings are about himself, not about her: she is really little more than an object of mixed feelings. Her portrait is for Southampton's eye.

Some of these later sonnets are full of puns, others are fragile and rhetorical. In sonnet 142 ('Love is my sin, and thy dear virtue hate') the phrase 'scarlet ornaments' to describe lips is another link with *Edward III* – a weak link on its own, but enough to strengthen the well-founded surmise that the author of that play knew these sonnets and despised them. He may, of course, never have known the best ones. (What if the Dark Lady wrote *Edward III*?) Some of the series are haunting all the same: 'Two loves I have, of comfort and despair' (sonnet 144) is a more intricate and deeper-cutting poem than Drayton or Daniel or Warner at their best, and 'Poor soul, the centre of my sinful earth' (sonnet 146), with its scriptural last line, is surely the principal inspiration of Donne's 'Divine Sonnets'. This is not to underestimate Donne, but his brilliant and thrilling poems are only his apprenticeship, his masterpieces are his sermons as Dean of St Paul's.

The remaining few sonnets are in a way impersonal and might have been written about anybody, though not quite about nobody. That goes for the obscene sonnet 151 with its enchanting opening:

> Love is too young to know what conscience is,
> Yet who knows not conscience is born of love?

I do not find the obscenity very obscene; there are worse things in Chaucer that shock nobody. If just one of all this ragbag of a second series of sonnets were removed, we would have sonnet 125 and an *envoi*, then twenty-five more, with this jeu d'esprit as their *envoi*, and finally the two translations. But I fear the sonnets after 126 are just an *omnium gatherum* in which some of them (145, for instance, with its 'hate away' pun) hardly earn their place. Sonnet 152 stands where it does for its outspokenness: 'In act thy bed-vow broke'. The translations are variations on fifth-century AD Greek verses by Marianos, both based on the same poem. Giles Fletcher translated it as a sonnet in his *Licia* (1593), and that is possibly where Shakespeare got it, though it already existed in Latin and in foreign languages.

John Kerrigan speaks of 'pervasive, sterile bawdry' in these translations: 'they are very knowing'. He thinks the bath that boils because love's torch was quenched in it alludes to 'the sweating tubs used to cure the pox in Jacobethan London'. Shakespeare's innuendo, if any, is very much lighter than this piece of salacious pedantry, which I fear is a case of the critics he cites being more knowing than their poet. They think Cupid's torch is 'obviously phallic' as well. But what Kerrigan has to say about the conventional position of poems like this in a sonnet sequence to separate the true love sonnets from the final lover's complaint is well founded and illuminating. The stage was set for insights of this kind by K. Duncan-Jones in the *Review of English Studies* in 1983.

Shakespeare's sequence deliberately performs over an extended range, because it was conventional to do so: one ought not to be surprised to see how far the range extended. As he wrote, reality took over poem after poem. The playful naughtiness at the end of the collection was as expected as the dance at the end of a play, tragedy as well as comedy. This Elizabethan appetite for many elements in art is a key to Shakespeare's whole lifework.

I have left for final consideration the fascinating personal lines about the dyer's dirty hand, or in Shakespeare's case the poet's, in sonnet 111, 'O, for my sake do you with Fortune chide'. He accuses Fortune as 'guilty goddess of my harmful deeds,/That did not better for my life provide', because he has no money and is a poet, or perhaps he means an actor:

> Thence comes it that my name receives a brand,
> And almost thence my nature is subdu'd
> To what it works in, like the dyer's hand.
> Pity me, then, and wish I were renew'd. . . .

Again in the next poem, Southampton's love and pity will cure the wound 'Which vulgar scandal stamp'd upon my brow'. It looks as if Shakespeare was ashamed of himself in several ways, as client, as poet and as an actor condemned to a social world of spies, whores and riff-raff. Even Thomas Thorpe, who printed the Sonnets, was a spy (for Burghley against English Catholics in Spain). He died in the royal almshouses at Ewelme built by the Earl of Suffolk. John Florio was a spy. But Shakespeare was not: he behaved for all his scruples with rocklike integrity. The climax of his sequence to Southampton (sonnets 124 and 125) is the consciousness of that integrity:

> Hence, thou suborn'd informer! A true soul,
> When most impeach'd, stands least in thy control.

These scraps at least are personal, and directly autobiographical. What about his taste for the master–mistress, the boy–girl? Shakespeare's girls in the theatre are boys dressed up, of course, and he makes jokes about that: a boy dressed as a girl disguises as a boy and then pretends to be a girl. Sexuality is a Chinese box, no doubt. At least in French, Shakespeare could find an old example of a poet writing sonnets to his patron as if the patron were a lover: Jodelle did it, whom Francis Meres calls a French Marlowe. C. S. Lewis says that in all Elizabethan literature he can find no example to match Shakespeare for extremity of love-language between men, but Shakespeare might have found that too in French. He was not scrupulous about picking phrases or conceits from other writers.

The fate of the Sonnets has left some traces in a manuscript tradition which, according to Gary Taylor, preserves early versions of a few sonnets, the 1609 text being a revision. These stray sonnet manuscripts give Latin titles to two poems, 'Spes Altera' (sonnet 2), and 'In Laudem Musicae et opprobrium contemptoris eiusdem' (sonnet 8). I cannot imagine the titles are original, but the text is not uninteresting: it is certainly inferior, and might easily result from someone writing down a poem he thought he knew by heart, and getting it wrong. Yet the case of Suckling's fragment of Shakespeare bids one pause. Probably the few widely circulated sonnets were all thought of as songs: one was set by Henry Lawes. The great mass of the Sonnets left no trace in manuscripts that have survived; Alleyn the actor certainly had no manuscript copy, because he bought a printed copy for sixpence in the June of 1609.

· 5 ·

Fame

At this point I would like to recapitulate my argument. In the years 1592–4 there was plague in London and Shakespeare was suddenly on close terms with the young Earl, who was mad on the theatre, a patron of poets, and whose character and appearance we know. *Venus and Adonis* and *The Rape of Lucrece* are dedicated to him. A beautiful young nobleman is urged to marry and get an heir in a series of sonnets which precisely mirror Southampton's marriage problem. If they are not about Southampton they are about someone else of the same nature and circumstances, but no one like that exists. His mother was perhaps at the back of this commission; we know from contemporary letters that she favoured the marriage, and she later married Mr W.H., who is surely therefore the 'only begetter'. The relationship appears to last three years: a sonnet a week for three years is not hard work. Somebody buys Shakespeare into the Chamberlain's Men: Southampton is rumoured to be that someone. The patron did less for Thomas Nashe, because Nashe did less for him: the big difference is the Sonnets.

The Sonnets did not circulate widely. It is a nice point whether Shakespeare achieved his supreme fame among the poets of his day while the theatres were shut or from the moment they reopened with Marlowe dead, the Chamberlain's Men formed, and his new plays in the theatres. Francis Meres in 1598 is applauding when the games are over and Shakespeare has been victorious in the three categories of comedy, tragedy and the poetry of personal love. There were earlier signs of his triumph. In the aftermath of Greene's criticism in 1592, Greene's editor Henry Chettle felt the need to placate and compliment Shakespeare, who seems to have behaved like a perfect gentleman. It may also be important that he now enjoyed Southampton's patronage. The mockery of the pair of them in the delightful and amusing trifle, *Willobie his Avisa* (1594), marked recognition of another kind (see p. 117). But to be sharer and principal poet for the Chamberlain's Men was the greatest honour and the most important opportunity Shakespeare ever had.

Henry Chettle was a London dyer's son, apprenticed to a stationer in

1577. As soon as Greene died in 1592, Chettle edited the red-hot pamphlet of repentance and invective that Greene left behind him, his *Groats-Worth of Witte*. (In the next ten years pamphlets went up from fivepence to sixpence, but theatre entrance money doubled from sixpence to a shilling.) The response to this publication from its victims was furious: Chettle himself was thought to have written or added to it, and Thomas Nashe to have had a hand in it. Immediately, at the very end of 1592, Chettle registered his own *Kind Harts Dreame* with the Stationers, and printed it early in 1593. Chettle was apparently a printer himself, perhaps as an apprentice; a little later he signed a communication to Nashe as 'your old compositor'.

Kind Harts Dreame is set 'not far from Finsbury, in a Taphouse of Antiquity', and consists of 'the remembrance of sundry of my deceased friends, personages not altogether obscure. . . .' They are named as 'old Antony Now now', Richard Tarlton the famous clown, 'William Cockoe, better known than lov'd', Dr Burcot, and Robert Greene 'of face amiable, of body well proportioned, his attire after the habit of a scholarlike Gentleman, only his hair was somewhat long. . . . the only Comedian of a vulgar writer in this country'. The tone of the entire pamphlet is that of relatively gentle satiric ribaldry – too gentle for Nashe to have had a hand in it.

Chettle's pamphlet begins with an address 'To the Gentlemen Readers':

> To come in print is not to seek praise, but to crave pardon. . . . About three months since died M. Robert Greene, leaving many papers in sundry Booksellers hands, among other his Groatsworth of Wit, in which a letter written to divers playmakers is offensively by one or two of them taken. . . . With neither of them that take offence was I acquainted, and with one of them I care not if I never be [he means Marlowe]. The other, whom at that time I did not so much spare as since I wish I had. . . . I am sorry, as if the original fault had been my fault, because myself have seen his demeanour no less civil than he excellent in the quality he professes: Besides, divers of worship have reported his uprightness of dealing, which argues his honesty, and his facetious grace in writing, that approves his art [this undoubtedly refers to Shakespeare].

Chettle had some difficult wriggling to do in this preface. It is worth noticing that the few months between Greene's death and the appearance of *Kind Harts Dreame* are probably the moment of Shakespeare's apotheosis as poet to Southampton. I count myself fortunate in this biography in not having to enter deeply into the tangled history of Elizabethan pamphlets by minor writers: they are a can of worms, and their warfare was as vigorous as it was ill directed. But we cannot leave out minor writers altogether. Chettle's ambitions were those of a writer. His *Piers Plainnes seauen yeares Prenticeship* (1595) is a good, freakish read; it takes one to Thrace and to Crete. By 1598 he was known to Meres as a writer of comedy, and from 1597 to 1603 he was a hack working for Henslowe, the bloodsucking theatrical manager, in co-operation with numerous other writers. In 1598, for example, he and Drayton presented Henslowe with 'A book wherein is a part for a Welshman', but this is not the only case of a play title forgotten or misremembered by Henslowe, who recorded only what to him was essential about the play.

In 1598 Chettle went to prison for debt for about a year. In 1602 he landed a contract to write exclusively for the Earl of Nottingham. When the Queen died, Chettle mentioned Shakespeare again, in *Englands Mourning Garment* (1603), as the 'silver-tongued Mellicert', adjuring him to 'remember our Elizabeth,/And sing her rape done by that Tarquin death'. For an example of maladroit bad taste that would be hard to better; anyway, Shakespeare was already working for James I. He does remember Elizabeth all the same, at the end of the last play he ever wrote. In 1607 Henry Chettle was dead, in the limbo of the poets in Dekker's *A Knight's Conjuring*.

Thomas Nashe lived at the same time as Chettle and Shakespeare (1567–1601), though he was younger and died before them. He was a curate's son from Lowestoft and a St John's, Cambridge, graduate, though a certain smell of brimstone hangs over his departure from that beautiful and chilly place. He suffered all his life from lack of success; he was a proud man, a snarling satirist and of all Elizabethan writers the one who most obviously failed to fulfil an enviable talent. His path and Shakespeare's cross several times, particularly in the plague years. Richard Tarlton, as an established comedian and wit, was good to Nashe when he first came to London, where he arrived at the age of twenty-one in 1588 or earlier, so Nashe is sometimes credited with Tarlton's *Newes out of Purgatorie* (1590), although that is more probably by Tarlton's fellow clown Robert Armin. Nashe's first publication was a critical introduction to Greene's *Menaphon* in 1589. He found a patron at about the same time as Shakespeare did. In 1593 he dedicated *Christs Teares* to the wife of Sir George Carey, son of Lord Hunsdon and his successor as Chamberlain, who inherited the Chamberlain's Men as one might inherit other servants. In 1594 he dedicated *The Terrors of the Night* to Sir George's daughter. That is a fascinating, musing work about superstition, like Sir Thomas Browne on the same subject, though with more fireworks and less cold reason.

In 1594 Nashe had already tasted in his 'forsaken extremities' what he called 'the full spring' of Southampton's generosity, and visited him as Governor of the Isle of Wight, where Carey was his deputy: perhaps at Carisbrooke Castle on the island, though Southampton also owned Beaulieu in the New Forest and Titchfield on the Hamble river. A few years later it was to Southampton that Nashe dedicated his Rabelaisian proto-novel, his *Unfortunate Traveller*, with the picaresque adventures of the earlier poet Lord Surrey. It was his masterwork in prose. He also wrote his naughty *Choice of Valentines* for Southampton.

The skills Nashe mastered and those he never mastered make a fascinating contrast to Shakespeare's. In 1589 he praised 'divine Spenser', Peele and Warner, but despised the bombast of (it seems) Kyd. Later he praised Spenser, Surrey, Sidney and Watson. One of his early mistakes in London was an edition of Sidney that annoyed other poets, whose work he added without permission, so that the edition had to be replaced. He was hyperactive as an anti-Puritan pamphleteer; he scourged the priggish Cambridge don Gabriel Harvey with particular and ceaseless vigour. Given the target, one sympathizes with him, but it was a terrible waste of time for a poet, and the kind of trap into which Shakespeare never fell.

The reason for my own high estimate of Nashe is *Summers Last Will and Testament*, a masque or secular mystery, or dramatic and lyrical entertainment, that he wrote for private performance either at the Archbishop's country house at Croydon in 1593, or at the Carey house nearby, at just about the time Shakespeare was writing *Love's Labour's Lost* under similar conditions for the Earl of Southampton. At this point Shakespeare's blazing and rising star crosses the downward trail of Nashe, whose later history in the theatre was unhappy. In 1594 he completed Marlowe's unfinished *Dido*, but his own dramatic verse was flatter than Marlowe's. In 1597 *The Isle of Dogs*, of which he was co-author, was thought so critical of the state establishment that Henslowe lost his theatre licence for a time, and Nashe spent a far longer time than that keeping out of London, fearing the Fleet prison where the young poet Ben Jonson was actually committed for the same offence. Gabriel Harvey published a cartoon of Nashe in chains. It is a sad thought that if only Nashe had lived a few more years he might have been the greatest poet of the Jacobean masque. He was better than Jonson in that field.

Summers Last Will and Testament is an extraordinary piece of work. It contains some of the best lyrics ever written in English in that or any other age. Nashe calls it 'A Pleasant Comedy', and the induction or preprologue is spoken by Will Summers, Court jester to Henry VIII. 'And I, fool by nature and by art, do speak to you in the person of the idiot our playmaker.' His prologue is distinctly satiric, and too long; Nashe could never suppress his canine growl, nor had he been schooled in the commercial theatre. 'Why, he hath made a Prologue longer than his play! Nay, 'tis no play neither, 'tis a show. . . . What can be made of Summer's last Will and Testament? Such another thing as Gillian Bransford's will, where she bequeathed a score of farts among her friends. Forsooth, because the plague reigns in most places in this latter end of summer, Summer must come in sick. . . .' Summer and Spring get songs to celebrate them, and Summer's long but static blank verse explanation of his plight has a poignancy in

114

strong contrast to the prose jokes. Nashe's dramatic prose is less gracious and less crisp than Shakespeare's; but there is no doubt about the pathos of the theme and design of this play, which are the progress and fading of the seasons, or about its conclusion. The quarrel of seasons is a medieval theme, but here more subtly treated, and interwoven with a genuine and haunting sorrow. Some of the good lines are Autumn's against Christmas, who

> Delighteth in no game or fellowship,
> And loveth no good deeds and hateth talk,
> But sitteth in a corner turning crabs
> Or coughing o'er a warmed pot of ale. . . .

There is an allegorized Winter painted on glass in the Bodleian Library which might have been made for an illustration of that speech. In his later seasonal poetry, Shakespeare several times betrays consciousness of this play. The refrain of the spring song, 'Cuckoo, jug, jug, pu we, to witta woo!', is a more elaborate set of bird noises than any earlier example I recall in English. I wonder whether someone has been reading Aristophanes' *Birds* with their extraordinary noises: the '*tio tio tinx*' and so on. Or was this a foreign musical tradition? At any rate Shakespeare adopted it gleefully. In French *turelure* was a bagpipe but *turlut* was a skylark, and English larks in seventeenth-century poems sing 'tirra lirra': 'Tirry-tirry leerers upward fly'. The most elaborate French example is by Du Bartas:

> La gentile Alouette avec son tyre-lire
> Tire l'yre à l'iré, et tiri-lyrant vire
> Vers la voute du ciel, puis son vol vers ce lieu
> Vire, et desire dire, adieu Dieu, adieu Dieu.

As *Summers Testament* closes, it settles to a more solemn tone to which everything in it has led up:

> Sing me some doleful ditty to the lute,
> That may complain my near-approaching death.

The song that follows, with the refrain 'I am sick, I must die: Lord have mercy on us', is as memorable as any lyric that Shakespeare ever wrote, and its style and metre affected him deeply, though he never wrote anything exactly like it: it comes from an older tradition than those on which Shakespeare seems to draw. All the other lyrics in Nashe's play, thrilling as they are, come below Shakespeare's abilities; this alone, in its simple gravity, goes beyond them, if anything in English can be said to do so.

> . . . All things to end are made,
> The plague full swift goes by;
> I am sick I must die:
> Lord have mercy on us.

> Beauty is but a flower
> Which wrinkles will devour,
> Brightness falls from the air,
> Queens have died young and fair,
> Dust hath closed Helen's eye.
>   I am sick, I must die:
>   Lord have mercy on us.

> . . . Haste therefore each degree
> To welcome destiny:
> Heaven is our heritage,
> Earth but a player's stage,
> Mount we unto the sky.
>   I am sick, I must die:
>   Lord have mercy on us.

Nashe's poem is a kind of litany I suppose. The stage metaphor comes from Seneca, it was a commonplace, displayed for example on the banner of the Globe theatre. The very last lyric of the play is on the theme 'Gone is our sport', and its refrain is 'From winter, plague and pestilence, good Lord deliver us.' Will Summers concludes: 'How is't, how is't? You that be of the graver sort, do you think these youths worthy of a *Plaudite* for praying for the Queen and singing of the Litany?' The performance may have been by the Archbishop's choir, trained singing men. It had certainly absorbed some of its atmosphere from house and audience and circumstances, as *Love's Labour's Lost* did from Southampton's circle. Summer's parting speech is like the valediction of an age:

> . . . Item I give my wither'd flowers and herbs
> Unto dead corses, for to deck them with,
> My fruits to Autumn, my adopted heir,
> My murmuring springs, musicians of sweet sleep,
> To murmuring malcontents, whose well-tuned cares
> Channel'd in a sweet-falling quaterzaine,
> Do lull their ears asleep, listening themselves.

> Farewell my friends; Summer bids you farewell,
> Archers and bowlers, all my followers,
> Adieu, and dwell in desolation,
> Silence must be your master's mansion. . . .

A 'quaterzaine' (quatorzaine) is a sonnet. This play is impregnated with music, which is why it continues to be haunting; the same may be said of much of the verse of this period, because music has distilled itself into the roots of poetic style, a style not only dominant but universally victorious for ten or twenty years or more, until music itself had altered. The history

116

of poetry in the 1590s is essentially musical, though the musical culture on which it draws is more various than we imagine: it includes jigs and children's rhymes, dances, street cries, ballads and popular songs fifty years old, as well as the music of the Church, which was gradually replaced and has gone on getting worse ever since.

It was not hard for Nashe to be a stunning lyric poet, because in his day you were that if you had any ear at all. He was never an effective dramatic poet for longer than five or six lines together, because dramatic poetry was a special skill, acquired or invented by just one generation, and transmitted only to the immediate apprentices of that generation. What remained of it perished with the Civil War. But the example of Nashe is crucial as a background to Shakespeare and as a contrast, and because Nashe ran level with Shakespeare in the early 1590s in the desperate endeavour to secure a great patron.

Willobie his Avisa was printed in 1594. It is an amusing, mocking poem, a sort of mock epic, of seventy-four songs and a few other poems, in which Avisa, an innkeeper's wife, has her chastity tested by scheming lovers and repels them all. The hardest hit is H.W., who turns to 'his familiar friend W.S. who not long before had tried the courtesy of the like passion'. W.S. took a hand: 'in viewing afar off the course of this loving Comedy, he determined to see whether it would sort to a happier end for this new actor than it did for the old player.' The name *Avisa* is Latin for Avis or Avice, a real name; there is an 'Avice's Cottage' on the Isle of Portland.

Someone signing some complimentary verses in this volume with the name 'Vigilantius Dormitanus' refers to Shakespeare's newly published *Rape of Lucrece*, and to 'Sweete Wylloby', who occurs in the poem as Willobego. Common sense confirmed by many lesser arguments suggests that W.S. and H.W., in a spirited joke of this kind and in this year, are William Shakespeare the poet and Henry Willoughby. The writer and his circle know Shakespeare's poetry, including I think the Sonnets and *A Lover's Complaint*. *Willobie his Avisa* reveals a lot about Shakespeare's relationships outside poetry, though it furnishes no reliable information for a gossip columnist. None of it need ever have really happened: it is far more interesting to know who wrote it.

The poem is set in the West Country and Leslie Hotson has left no doubt that its author is Henry Willoughby of West Knoyle on the edge of the Blackmore Vale. At Bruton Abbey, which is less than fifteen miles away but in Somerset, Shakespeare's friend Thomas Russell was brought up by Sir Henry Berkeley, who was his stepfather – a comically quarrelsome and robust squire who fought strenuous campaigns against Lord Pembroke for the control of the local forest. Russells and Willoughbys were closely related by marriage, and Sir Henry Berkeley and old man Willoughby were close confederates. Thomas Russell held the manor of Alderminster just south of Stratford, administered in his minority by Berkeley; Throck-morton, whose sister was married to Sir Walter Ralegh not far away at Sherborne, used to call and collect the rent for Alderminster from Bruton Abbey. Thomas Russell also owned Broad Campden on the edge of the Cotswolds. He was five years younger than Shakespeare, and overseer of Shakespeare's will. We shall have more to say about him, because these connections lead in many directions. In 1594 Thomas Russell was twenty-four and married, while Henry Willoughby was nineteen and at St John's College, Oxford.

The verses signed 'Vigilantius Dormitanus' may well be by two Balliol undergraduates of the same year as Henry Willoughby, though younger: Robert Wakeman, a parson's son from Worcestershire, and Edward Napper of Holywell, Oxford, a gentleman's son. Napper later married Wakeman's sister, and Napper's father-in-law was a steward to Lord Mountjoy, a cousin of Sir Henry Berkeley and a friend of Thomas Russell. Wakeman's mother was a Gloucestershire Hathaway and therefore some kind of cousin of Shakespeare's wife. It was a small world; multiple connections were the rule, and people were conscious of them. But notice that Shakespeare was famous: Wakeman at eighteen and Napper at sixteen knew *The Rape of Lucrece* almost before the printer's ink was dry on it. Henry Willoughby took his degree the next February; the same year he was recognized in William Covell's *Polymanteia*, in a note to the sentence 'Oxford, thou hast many, and they are able to sing sweetly when it please thee.' We know almost nothing more about him except that he was dead before he was thirty. His *Avisa* was a victim of the purge of disturbing or satirical books in 1599, and its second edition, which was due then, appeared only in 1635.

Shakespeare does not do much in *Willobie his Avisa*. The innkeeper's wife was born 'At wester side of Albions Isle,/Where Austin pitcht his monkish tent,/Where shepherds sang, where Muses smile . . .'. This was once thought to mean Sherborne, but Bruton near West Knoyle had an abbey, though all that remains of it now is some heavings of the turf. Avisa's first trial is by a nobleman before her marriage. 'Hands off my Lord, this will not serve,' she says. 'Your golden Angels I repel,/Your lawless lust I here defie. . . .' The nobleman answers her nastily (Canto 12). The second temptation comes from 'Ruffians, Roysters, young Gentlemen, and lusty Captains, which all she quickly cuts off'. The third trial is D.B., a comic Frenchman of bombastic eloquence. Avisa quotes Catullus at him (Canto 30) and they exchange letters of wildly farfetched learning. Dydimus Harco, an Anglo-German, is the next, with the tide of comic learning by no means abated. She sees him off and he swears to be chastely loving for ever, with more Catullus (Canto 42).

Henrico Willobego, an Italian–Spaniard, then tells in prose how he fell for the same girl and pined for love, and 'bewrayeth the secrecy of his disease unto his familiar friend W.S.'. W.S. then leads Willoughby by the nose, pretending the affair to be easy. 'But at length this comedy was like to have grown to a Tragedy. . . . In all which discourse is lively represented the unruly rage of unbridled fancy, having the reins to rove at liberty, with the divers and sundry changes of affections and temptations, which Will, let loose from reason, can devise.' (*Will* is a pun.) The verses pursue the leitmotif of familiar friendship between H.W. and W.S.

Avisa's inn is called the George. Her exchanges with H.W. are perhaps more ambitiously written than the rest, but therefore less light and less successful, unless one chooses to admire their deepening tone and varied metres. Shakespeare occurs in person only as the adviser who played a trick on Henry Willoughby. Since I believe that brief sketch to be taken from the life, I value it highly. Beyond it, one constantly senses an admirer of Shakespeare in the verse, but that may be illusion. If it is not, it looks as if Willoughby was Shakespeare's first disciple. I do think him to have been a most promising poet and regret his death.

Willoughby's friend W.S. is connected with Shakespeare by numerous strong links: references to actors, comedy, tragedy, the gratuitous 'Will', and to *Lucrece*, likenesses to his verse, and links with places and persons he knew. But in Shakespeare studies conjecture is rightly discredited: let me show why. Scholars have said the H.W. of *Avisa* must be Henry Wriothesly, that the George must be a pub in Sherborne and that Walter Ralegh must have commissioned the poem to mock Southampton. They have even suggested that Avisa is the Queen and that the sign of St George means Greenwich. They have argued that Lord S., to whom 'A Choice of Valentines' was dedicated by Nashe, must be Ferdinando Strange, a devout and severe Roman Catholic, and a candidate for this dedication about as likely as Archbishop Whitgift. They have applied the same sonnet of Shakespeare's to the Queen's death in 1603 and to the Armada in 1588. Yet if one cuts away romantic or perverse conjecture and uses common sense, a clear and a coherent picture of Shakespeare slowly emerges. I think it has more positive colouring than scholars expect, because we know much more about Shakespeare than we realize. Doubts and obscurities remain, but no insuperable enigma. The young man from the small town on the edge of the woods and the sheep country was now fully grown. He was courteous, witty, well read, socially successful, and the finest poet in Europe.

Love's Labour's Lost brings this argument together. We have seen Shakespeare on intimate terms with his nobleman, and on close terms with young Willoughby. We have learned to expect a touch of humour in him, and we know that he knew how to value himself. He was master of his art, in comedy as in poetry. In *Love's Labour's Lost* he shows just such a coterie as he knew, and the sense this play conveys in performance of parody of persons and of jokes lurking behind jokes is the reason for supposing it was first written for a private production among people who knew one another. That is an impression and may be mistaken, but even if Shakespeare always intended it for the theatre, it remains a rather personal play, an intimate portrait of a small group, full of mockery. Its low figures come from Italian comedy. The Earl of Southampton revived it for the King at his own house in 1605, and may very likely have commissioned it originally.

The first quarto, 'A pleasantly conceited comedy called Love's Labour's Lost', was not printed until 1598 'as played at Court last Christmas', and the Folio of 1623 follows that. It is supposed to have been 'newly corrected and augmented' by Shakespeare; the text is muddled and mangled, yet without act or scene division, so its textual history remains mysterious. Some of its sonnets appear in *The Passionate Pilgrim* collection in 1599, another pointer to Southampton's circle. It uses numerous verse forms, intended for virtuoso variations, including the *Venus and Adonis* stanza, yet it has a kind of *basso continuo* of formality, the better to show off its elegant caperings. *Love's Labour's Lost* is a very good play indeed: the flower of early Shakespeare. The French background seems to be built on the Court of Navarre in 1591, and the parody of affected language in act 4, scene ii suggests Gabriel Harvey. Shakespeare closely echoes Harvey's war of pamphlets with Nashe in 1592–3. A. L. Rowse thinks the character Armado is a parody of the Spanish ex-Secretary of State and rhetorician Antionio Perez, who was hanging around Essex House from April 1593 to July 1595. He dates the play to 1593, and I am sure he is right.

The Russian disguise in act 5, scene ii with attendant 'blackamoors' sounds very like the Gray's Inn masque of Christmas 1594, the year of the riot over *The Comedy of Errors* in that Inn. It is much likelier that the young lawyers adapted *Love's Labour* than vice versa. Giles Fletcher's *Of the Russe Commonwealth* (1591) is an influence in common. References to the plague in act 5, scene ii, including the phrase 'Lord have mercy on us', do not derive from Nashe: those were the words painted on the doors of plague-infected houses when they were sealed up. The London plague was worse than anything we imagine. The poor who fled downriver from their infested dens were never seen in London again: they were murdered at Gravesend as they came ashore, for fear they might be plague-spreaders. Thomas Dekker gives the atmosphere with full details, in a pamphlet that marks a new age in English prose: *The Wonderfull yeare* (1603). The sense of an enclosed world of briskness and light in *Love's Labour's Lost* is intended to keep out the Gothic horrors of Elizabethan London, to dream away London altogether, at Carisbrooke Castle or somewhere similar in the Christmas season of 1593.

The play's humour is really too exuberant: its characters are sparkling with quirks, and by being so individual become harder to play than the less eccentric characters of maturer Shakespeare, though high spirits can carry off everything, and make the silliest and sometimes the oldest jokes seem best. Shakespeare thumbs his nose at Florio, who wrote in *Second Frutes* (1591) that English plays were 'neither right comedies nor right tragedies . . . mere representations of histories without any decorum', yet he learns Florio's lesson. *Love's Labour's Lost* has an indecorous decorum of its own. The school scenes, which everyone insists are a memory of Shakespeare's own schooldays, are an adaptation from French farce. Shakespeare may never have travelled abroad, but plenty of experience of foreign theatres was available to him through the actors among whom he lived: many of them had roamed the Continent, where English actors were famous. His own plays were swiftly adapted into German.

The men of the French Court are going to live encloistered as 'fellows' for three years to study philosophy, though fame and honour are the supreme motive here as much as in *Henry VI*. There are constant images of light and frost and sharp sensory details; 'Of the sea-water green, sir'. It is notable from the beginning that the fool Costard makes sense but that the lords do not. The King is less omnipotent than the Duke in *The Comedy of Errors*, and the haggling and the lawyers in act 2 are more like Stratford than a royal Court. One might think the motto of the play was 'Good wits will be jangling', and indeed the verbal humour, and the verbal humours, present a dazzling surface, wittier than Lyly and more memorable. But the deeper patterns of the plot go to the root of love-comedy. One is struck by Shakespeare's healthy, all but naive relish, as if he were as hungry for philosophy as for the spring, and as hungry to mock it, as Berowne does in the first scene, as to indulge in it:

> Study is like the heaven's glorious sun,
> That will not be deep-search'd with saucy looks;
> Small have continual plodders ever won,
> Save base authority from others' books.
> These earthly godfathers of heaven's lights
> That give a name to every fixed star
> Have no more profit of their shining nights. . . .

How well he's read, to reason against reading!

It is not by chance that so many stray phrases of this play linger in the mind: 'Sweet smoke of rhetoric', for example, and 'A woman, that is like a German clock'. That joke is original here. Later it was copied by Jonson, Webster, Middleton, Dekker and others. Shakespeare's version is funniest, because he brings to bear his mastery of metre and rhythm on the timing of his joke. Berowne's speeches and the pedant scenes are opportunities for virtuoso comic performance in quite different styles. He parodies verse style even more full-bloodedly than Willoughby's Frenchman in the *Avisa*: 'The preyful Princess pierc'd and prick'd a pretty pleasing pricket. . . .' He can use even the most appalling parody jog-trot verse as a timing mechanism for a joke:

> He hath not eat paper, as it were; he hath not drunk ink; his intellect is
> not replenished; he is only an animal, only sensible in the duller parts;
> And such barren plants are set before us that we thankful should be –
> Which we of taste and feeling are – for those parts that do fructify in
> us more than he.

The sonnets in this play are all perjured, because they all break the oath to live cloistered; but they are not precisely false, and Shakespeare likes love to triumph (think of the nun wooed from her cloister in *A Lover's Complaint*). The jokes about Ovid and Mantuan are mere glitter, and the schoolmaster Holofernes, who almost is Gabriel Harvey, is a minor character. It is the love poetry that draws on deeper reserves. 'Sweet leaves, shade folly' is verbally mocking, but when it is played in the theatre it rings true: it has an inelegant over-elegance made awkward by being real. Shakespeare plays two tunes in descant to one another. Berowne will forswear rhyme, affectation and ostentation, 'Nor woo in rhyme, like a blind harper's song'. In the spoiled masque, one prefers the masquers to the mockers. The Queen's progresses commonly included a rustic entertainment, often put on by a local schoolmaster, which the Queen and her retinue took a ritual pleasure in mocking. Here again I think Shakespeare is on both sides, just as much as he is when the lovers are condemned each to woo the wrong girl when the girls change masks: as common a theme of his as the rustic entertainment. But on the nature of love he is perfectly wholehearted:

> Love's feeling is more soft and sensible
> Than are the tender horns of cockled snails;
> Love's tongue proves dainty Bacchus gross in taste.
> For valour, is not Love a Hercules,
> Still climbing trees in the Hesperides?
> Subtle as Sphinx; as sweet and musical
> As bright Apollo's lute, strung with his hair.
> And when Love speaks, the voice of all the gods
> Make heaven drowsy with the harmony.
> Never durst poet touch a pen to write
> Until his ink were temper'd with Love's sighs. . . .

We have two versions of this speech, one after the other, rammed together as if one was not cancelled when the other was substituted (act 4, scene iii, lines 285ff.). The second, longer version is an all but incredible improvement on the first. Something similar happens at act 5, scene ii, line 809, but less strikingly. It is extremely odd and interesting that a similar expansion and improvement took place in a somewhat similar speech to the one about 'love's feeling' that Theseus makes at the beginning of act 5 of *A Midsummer-Night's Dream*. One might suppose that Shakespeare could write like this whenever he chose, from the time of the Sonnets onwards, but he kept himself on a tight rein for dramatic reasons, and added this thrilling love poetry only where he saw on reflection that it might work, or only when the temptation became overwhelming.

Shakespeare was surely in love with love in these years, and Berowne's praise of love (can he possibly have read the *Symposium* of Plato?) is one of the great set-pieces in the whole of Shakespeare's works. It is not a love speech but the praise of love:

> O, we have made a vow to study, lords,
> And in that vow we have forsworn our books.
> For when would you, my liege, or you, or you,
> In leaden contemplation have found out
> Such fiery numbers as the prompting eyes
> Of beauty's tutors have enrich'd you with?

I think Shakespeare feels that he is revealing the nature and true purpose of poetry, and the fact that he frames it in the developing scenes of a comedy has more effect on the substance of his comedy than the theatre has on the poetry. All the same there is a sour-sweet quality about the conclusion. This play might have ended with act 4 and been purest comedy. As it is, in the greatly improved fuller version of act 5 that coexists with a shorter version, Berowne must visit the sick and dying every day for a year to purge himself of mockery, 'To weed this wormwood from your fruitful brain'.

> Our wooing doth not end like an old play:
> Jack hath not Jill. These ladies' courtesy
> Might well have made our sport a comedy.

In *Love's Labour's Lost*, Shakespeare not only changes horses in midstream, and reverses the nature of his comedy in its last act, but improves it and makes it humanly more touching by rewriting and expanding certain lines. He successfully mingles comedy of different types, and sets one world against another: curate, pedant, school, rustics, love-intrigue like a formal dance, and so on. I am left with the impression that from beginning to end of this process his true hero is Costard. This play is particularly suitable even today to be played by intelligent amateurs who are already on intimate terms. It is warmer and less prickly than might appear on first readings, and has deep crevices of humour. It is not only the sour aftertaste that raises it to the rank of masterpiece, but the constant dramatic interplay from beginning to end, which by leaving relationships alive and in the air makes the final reversal possible. In 1604, Burbage told the Lord Chamberlain that it would please exceedingly for mirth and wit, which is true enough but superficial. In comedy as in tragedy Shakespeare is exploring pain among other things.

In the last fifty lines of *Love's Labour's Lost*, the order of nature is as it were restored. Armado, like Berowne, becomes 'A votary: I have vow'd to Jaquenetta to hold the plough for her sweet love three year.' He is permitted to introduce the songs of the owl and the cuckoo, with its bird-noises like Nashe's, and its dialogue like his but in miniature, between Winter and Spring. These songs are fresh and real: spring pretty and fresh and real, and winter biting and fresh and very real. Scholars believe Shakespeare got his flowers from Gerard's *Herball* (1597), but the date is wrong. Shakespeare did use that book, but not before it was printed. The 'lady-smocks all silver-white/And cuckoo-buds of yellow hue' grew in the suburban fields near the theatre, and by 1595 Shakespeare lived nearby. His cuckoo buds sound like kingcups or crowsfoot or buttercups: the recorded regional names of English flowers are exceedingly numerous, and in Shakespeare's generation they were only beginning to be written down. The stanzas answer one another like the sweet and then bitter of the play.

> When icicles hang by the wall,
> And Dick the shepherd blows his nail,
> And Tom bears logs into the hall,
> And milk comes frozen home in pail. . . .
> And coughing drowns the parson's saw,
> And birds sit brooding in the snow,
> And Marian's nose looks red and raw,
> When roasted crabs hiss in the bowl,
> Then nightly sings the staring owl:
>   'Tu-who;
>   Tu-whit, To-who' – A merry note,
> While greasy Joan doth keel the pot.

That is Shakespeare's England. It is not London, but the world of his childhood, of winters that you never forgot. It sounds more like Wilmcote or Snitterfield than Stratford, but it might be anywhere in England; Nashe knew all about the roasted crab-apples, and so did Milton, who speaks in a Latin poem of the hiss of roasting pears. The last sentence of the play is bitter and sweet again: 'The words of Mercury are harsh after the songs of Apollo. You that way: we this way.' It may be that an epilogue has got lost.

The Two Gentlemen of Verona was, I think, written just after *Love's Labour*, part of the difference between them being that it is a public play from its first conception. It is a clever piece of playmaking, since the plot is multiple and yet symmetrical. It was not printed until the Folio, the collected works, where it takes second place after *The Tempest*; but that is not a reliable argument for its being the first play or the first comedy Shakespeare wrote, nor is 'style' a perfectly safe criterion, since that is either subjectively apprehended or mechanically (even more unreliably) computed. Meres knew it in 1598, and it comes first in his list of Shakespeare's plays. The text refers twice to Marlowe's *Hero and Leander*, uses the idea of 'love's labour lost', and draws twice on Ovid's *Heroides*. I think I am bold in dating it as late as 1594, but it certainly comes close to *Love's Labour* one way or the other.

The plot has little in my view to do with Shakespeare's biography, though A. L. Rowse is surely right to underline the relevance of its triangular shape (two boys in love with one another and the same girl) to the plot of Shakespeare's Sonnets, and certain echoes of detail between the Sonnets and the play. Of the two, the play appears to be later, so I do not think my dating is far off target. Modern critics want to put it extremely early, discern two versions of it, dislike bits of its verse technique, compare a few lines with Kyd, and in general display ungrateful horror at the confusion of its text. Their mistake is one of method. One can clean up the text to get an excellent play, and so dissolve these problems.

The basic plot combines betrayal of friendship and of love. Its conclusion has shocked some heavyweight critics, but MacEdward Leach, who edited the late-thirteenth-century *Amis and Amiloun* for the Early English Text Society in 1937, collected eighty-six examples of these 'two brethren' stories, and every single one had the same conclusion. Plays about betrayed girls wandering about disguised as boys were common enough in England from the 1570s onwards; Greene wrote one. Shakespeare used Chaucer's *Knight's Tale* and some derivative version of the Portuguese poet Montemayor's beautiful and civilized *Diana* (?1559), and took a few details from Arthur Brooke's awful poem *Romeus and Juliet* (1562). This is not the only occasion when one can spot, in a book that Shakespeare is using, the seed of a later, more important play.

Launce is the first genuinely and hilariously funny character Shakespeare has ever dreamed up. One can see how earlier comic figures have prefigured and led up to him. He is a more precise social study than Costard. Launce's dog Crab is an extension of his master's personality: the scenes seem to be written for Kemp the clown. It is quite possible that the confusion about time and place and about names in the play, which seem to have been matters of indifference to Shakespeare, arise from swift composition, at the moment when the theatres reopened and new plays were suddenly in demand. Later, Shakespeare becomes noticeably conscious of time and its problems, so he may have been criticized for this play.

Act 1 opens with an idea Shakespeare found stirring in several early comedies: 'To see the wonders of the world abroad' rather than sitting at home dull and sluggish 'Wear out thy youth with shapeless idleness.' This setting out and parting of friends is charming: the wit is courtly with a literary flavour, and love has been introduced within the first twenty lines: 'And on a love-book pray for my success?'

> Yet writers say, as in the sweetest bud
> The eating canker dwells, so eating love
> Inhabits in the finest wits of all.

The story begins gently. The verse is beautiful enough but not incisive: it has 'The uncertain glory of an April day' of which it speaks. Nor are the characters deeply engaged in anything: they are figures from a romance, and carry with them something of a romance's nullity and sweetness. 'He after honour hunts, I after love.' In scene iii comes the classic statement of renaissance youth, which even Shakespeare never bettered: it is a rephrasing of the theme of setting out:

> He wonder'd that your lordship
> Would suffer him to spend his youth at home,
> While other men, of slender reputation,
> Put forth their sons to seek preferment out:
> Some to the wars, to try their fortune there;
> Some to discover islands far away;
> Some to the studious universities. . . .

The youth will go to Court, 'practise tilts and tournaments,/Hear sweet discourse, converse with noblemen . . .'. It is important to realize that unless a young man left home he would never in Shakespeare's day 'Hear sweet discourse' or learn to talk or write in the fashionable style of Lyly; his wits might atrophy. It was an open secret until the other day that upper-class children in England seldom saw their parents; they were largely brought up by grooms, hence their passion for country sports, and their charming awkwardness in civilized society when they first encountered it. A number of Shakespeare's comedies are about the initiation of young men. In other and deadlier terms the history plays are just as full of almost ritual initiations. The youth begins immature, but the girl is born cool and self-possessed. Visual art in Shakespeare's day sometimes gives the same impression.

The servant Launce – with his smelly dog that 'thrusts me himself into the company of three or four gentlemen-like dogs under the Duke's table; he had not been there, bless the mark, a pissing while but all the chamber smelt him' – makes a nice contrast to this situation, but clowns are heroes and Launce takes the blame, saying he made the smell himself. Launce mocks love and love-language too, but the play continues in spite of him, and the serious characters go on using it; 'revenge of my contempt of love' is a serious issue. Still, Launce remains as real as the lovers and the lords. 'I think Crab my dog be the sourest-natured dog that lives: my mother weeping, my father wailing, my sister crying, our maid howling, our cat wringing her hands, and all our house in a great perplexity; yet did not this cruel-hearted cur shed one tear.'

The love verses are rich and fluid, but less particular than Launce's dog Crab, for all their fine phrases.

> . . . Why man, she is mine own;
> And I as rich in having such a jewel
> As twenty seas, if all their sand were pearl,
> The water nectar, and the rocks pure gold.

The images are delicious enough for Ralegh, but the idea was common, and although Ralegh may well have seen this play he was a fine enough poet to pick his own exotic images. When he had to entertain a French embassy he took them to the bearpit, which they greatly enjoyed, but not to the theatre. Perhaps the fluidity of the verse and the young manner of the lovers is meant to be ominous: one knows it will not last.

> . . . for now my love is thaw'd;
> Which like a waxen image 'gainst a fire
> Bears no impression of the thing it was. . . .

> . . . O! but I love his lady too too much. . . .

The girls are more spirited; their verse is as particular as Launce's prose, and far more sinewy. Their images are fire and ice, but they can make jokes between themselves about codpieces. Their setting out scene is braver and sadder than the boys. Its image is a river flowing to the sea (act 2, scene vii):

> I'll be as patient as a gentle stream,
> And make a pastime of each weary step,
> Till the last step have brought me to my love;
> And there I'll rest as after much turmoil
> A blessed soul doth in Elysium.

In the third act Valentine has become coarse and intolerable. It is all part of growing up, no doubt. He assures the Duke in couplets that exaggerate his lack of taste how easily women fall: any man can win any woman. That is more or less Ovid's opinion I am sorry to say, but what follows shows it is not Shakespeare's. The ups and downs of the intrigue are fast enough to be amusing. Launce is in love with a milkmaid: 'She hath more qualities than a water-spaniel – which is much in a bare Christian.' At the end of the scene 'I'll have her; an if it be a match, as nothing is impossible'. Proteus instructs the Duke in lovemaking, in incandescent lines close to Berowne's speech, and therefore a dying echo of it:

> For Orpheus' lute was strung with poets' sinews,
> Whose golden touch could soften steel and stones,
> Make tigers tame, and huge leviathans
> Forsake unsounded deeps to dance on sands.
> After your dire-lamenting elegies,

> Visit by night your lady's chamber window
> With some sweet consort; to their instruments
> Tune a deploring dump – the night's dead silence
> Will well become such sweet-complaining grievance. . . .

The fourth act enters the world of outlaws, where Valentine becomes their king. 'By the bare scalp of Robin Hood's fat friar' sets the atmosphere clearly enough. Henry Chettle and Anthony Munday wrote a play in two parts about Robin Hood in 1598; Shakespeare never wrote one, but he takes up the motif of outlaws in the green forest both here and in *As You Like It*, with the atmosphere and moral system of Robin Hood. It is strange how universal these themes were. Ben Jonson's last, unfinished play *The Sad Shepherd* was about Robin Hood. The lover singing under the balcony occurs at the other end of Europe in the Cretan poem *Erotokritos*: 'His hand was sugar and his sword was death,' and the lute song was followed by a sword fight. Outlaws in a forest, with a captain of their band and a green uniform, occur in a Serbian ballad or epic fragment at just the same time. No doubt art copies life just as life copies art, but these romantic themes travelled mysteriously swiftly.

There is a deliberate artificiality about this play less vigorous than *Love's Labour's Lost*: Shakespeare has set out to give pleasure, and does little more. The song 'Who is Sylvia?' is false in more ways than one, and deliberately so. The romantic trappings include Friar Patrick's Cell 'Where I intend holy confession'; plays at Pentecost (act 4, scene iv); sunset – 'The sun begins to gild the western sky . . .'; Friar Laurence 'As he in penance wander'd through the forest'; and a lion.

> This shadowy desert, unfrequented woods,
> I better brook than flourishing peopled towns.
> Here can I sit alone, unseen of any,
> And to the nightingale's complaining notes
> Tune my distresses. . . .

Proteus has gone a long way downhill. He is very unkind to Launce about the dog Crab, and threatens and begins a rape. Still, he repents and the plot whizzes to its conclusion. He is outwitted and humiliated, but this is a tale where everyone gets their girl:

> Come, Proteus, 'tis your penance but to hear
> The story of your loves discovered.
> That done, our day of marriage shall be yours;
> One feast, one house, one mutual happiness!

These words are not the true end of the play, because the action of such a play dissolved into a dance, and the dance rather than any words was the true solution of the plot. Kemp was a famous dancer, and it will have included him. *The Two Gentlemen of Verona* is Shakespeare's first attempt at formal Italian love comedy of this dance-like kind; the experience went on being useful to him for years.

It will be seen by now that Shakespeare is an uneven writer, restless at formal innovation, but slow to relinquish his entangled themes. Launce never reappears after Proteus sends him slinking off to find an expensive lost lapdog, but the Launce view of life persists in other plays; so do those dance-like, casually composed love-intrigues, to which the clown is always an outsider. Launce's taking a whipping to save his dog from one is the most generous action in the entire play: the gentry are mere playing cards by comparison, and the two worlds hardly meet. For a full interplay of relationship by which Shakespeare can better express what he deeply feels about society, we shall have to wait for *Twelfth Night*, saddest of comedies. In *The Two Gentlemen of Verona*, Launce's and the page Speed's scenes look detachable, but they are momentous because they suggest a real world in contrast to the two-dimensional one of Courtly romance.

The date of Shakespeare's first masterpiece of revenge history *Richard III* is a vexed question, but so long as we can limit the area of dispute, as fortunately we can, it makes little difference to the poet's biography: I incline to a late date only because the play is so extremely good and so mature emotionally that it might almost presuppose the Sonnets, and because I can scarcely find time for Shakespeare to have written it before the theatres shut in 1592. It was certainly already planned while Shakespeare was finishing *Henry VI*; it belongs as an achievement in that series which it completes, and technically it stands on the shoulders of the three *Henry VI* plays. I suppose that Shakespeare wrote it as soon as he was commissioned to do so, almost certainly for the Chamberlain's Men.

The foundation of that company when the plague was over was meant to regularize and reform the whole intolerably disorganized theatrical profession under royal patronage. Shakespeare was one of their principal members by Christmas 1594. The Treasurer's accounts for 15 March 1595 record a payment 'To William Kempe, William Shakespeare, and Richard Burbage, servants to the Lord Chamberlain . . . for two several comedies or interludes showed by them before her Majesty in Christmas time last past.' We are speaking of the season of the Night of Errors at Gray's Inn. They got £13 6s 8d, which is forty marks, 'and by way of her Majesty's reward' another few pounds to make up a round twenty.

Richard III became famous: it was reprinted seven times in quarto, starting in 1597; Meres knew it; it was quoted and often imitated. The Folio text is extremely long: at 3619 lines it is second only to *Hamlet* with 3929. The usual question of cut versions, acting or touring versions and corrupt versions arises, but need not detain a mere biographer beyond the remark that the length of *Richard III* suggests a conscious, deliberate attempt to produce the great play Shakespeare did produce; it also creates the suspicion of a special audience that might be willing to sit longer than a normal theatre audience. The jack that jumps out of the jack-in-the-box of the Wars of the Roses is the complex and terrifying character of Shakespeare's Richard III.

The visiting Italian Polydore Vergil laid down the structure of nemesis and revenge for the saga of York and Lancaster in his *Anglicae Historiae* (1534–55), chronicles gave detail, and Holinshed drawing on Thomas More, suggested the character; but between one play and the next Shakespeare's Richard develops. The subject was alive. Polydore Vergil was popular enough to be read by a shepherd keeping his sheep on the Cotswolds under Henry VIII: he annotated the flyleaf of the book. John Stow, the London antiquary to whose library I think Shakespeare had access, and whose advice and conversation one must invoke to explain Shakespeare's historical knowledge and variety of sources, found somebody alive who remembered Richard III. Since it was the Tudors who defeated that unpleasant monarch, he offered the unique opportunity of portraying a really villainous king. Shakespeare as usual gets so interested in his villain and the suffering behind the villainy that the horror one feels is not unmixed. His characters are stock characters, adapted from books or older plays, but his secret is to ask himself what such a character would really be like, and always fully to imagine the suffering behind a motive.

Behind the security of the opening speech the audience reads a more ominous future between the lines. 'Now is the winter of our discontent Made glorious summer by this sun of York' introduces an unstable season, and the painted sun on the royal arms is a piece of arrogance that will not hold back the weather. It recalls the mock King with the paper crown in *Henry VI, Part 3*, the King of shadows. Is it War or the King who 'capers nimbly in a lady's chamber To the lascivious pleasing of a lute'? Richard's sexual frustration and physical deformity are the mainspring of his motives: he despises what he cannot have – 'I am determined to prove a villain.' In the theatre it is the sexual undertone of this play that gives it such power and makes it so shocking.

> . . . I, in this weak piping time of peace,
> Have no delight to pass away the time,
> Unless to spy my shadow in the sun
> And descant on mine own deformity.

The play begins fullbloodedly. When Richard's monologue, recapitulating his speeches in *Henry VI* but with more emphasis on sexual rage, is over, his brother the Duke of Clarence passes on his way to the Tower: the King is brooding over 'prophecies and dreams' and the family is already breaking up, the Queen is distrusted, the King has a mistress, the scene buzzes with rumour, sarcasm and intrigue.

The second scene is a piece of theatre to dwarf the first. '*Enter the corpse of King Henry the Sixth, with Halberds to guard it; Lady Anne being the mourner.*' This is not a state funeral like the heraldic pageant that was staged for Philip Sidney's funeral in 1586 to distract London from the murder of the Queen of Scots. The point of it as a spectacle is its loneliness and the grimness of the halberdiers: the same no doubt who have just taken Clarence to the Tower. Anne's monologue is an opposite to Richard's in scene i, a lamentation with curses: 'Poor key-cold figure of a holy King . . .'. The explosive dialogue that follows, in which Richard halts the guards and offers love to Anne over the King's corpse, is almost a play in itself. It is astonishingly real, far more so in the theatre than on paper. Richard as a hypocritical lover is both sickening and credible:

> . . . Your beauty that did haunt me in my sleep
> To undertake the death of all the world
> So I might live one hour in your sweet bosom.

The scene has subtle undercurrents, because there really is an electric attraction between them. He is a horrible wooer, but with just enough honesty to win her over, and having done that he is so delighted with himself that he really does fall nearly half in love. His capering vanity at this thought makes him of course all the more repulsive. Act 1, scene ii of *Richard III* is made of starkly simple ingredients, yet it marks the maturity of the Elizabethan theatre. It is one of the best scenes that even Shakespeare ever wote.

Richard has demonic energy throughout the play. His third scene, another contrast, is a quarrel at Court carried through with antiphonal hatred, both male and female:

> Why strew'st thou sugar on that bottled spider
> Whose deadly web ensnareth thee about?

> Look when he fawns, he bites; and when he bites,
> His venom tooth will rankle to the death . . .

The hatred is open, but Richard is so devious that he must have monologues to explain his Machiavellian manoeuvres. Was it only from the chronicles that Shakespeare drew this poison, or by matching a tragic villain with a wicked King, or does *Richard III* rely to any degree on the experience of life? Ralegh's outbursts against corruption in his time suggest that it just might. Shakespeare's furious and vulnerable women are almost more interesting from this point of view than the hunchback. He knew plenty about hypocrisy, which Marlowe in a similar passage in *Edward II* calls Puritan. The spiderish Henslowe after all was a church-warden, and hypocrisy in that society was in plentiful supply. Where religion is compulsory, the suspicion of hypocrisy will be as rank as the thing itself.

> And thus I clothe my naked villainy
> With odd old ends stol'n forth of holy writ,
> And seem a saint when most I play the devil.

The act ends with Clarence's murder: the murderers are low figures on the edge of being comic, but eloquent enough, and more intellectual than most Shakespearean murderers. One repents and refuses his fee. 'How fain, like Pilate, would I wash my hands. . . .'

The second act opens with the King's sentimental piety, and with reconciliations that will not last: the news of Clarence's death turns him to passionate remorse, and Clarence, who was noble in his murder scene, gets a noble lamentation from his brother. The King staggers away to die. His mother and Clarence's children hear of his death from the widowed Queen: the lamentation of women is important in *Richard III*, even more so than in *Henry VI*. The anxious discussion of succession, always a real issue to the Elizabethans, is followed by a sudden scene of even more worried citizens. They read the signs of the times as they might read the weather, with gloomy accuracy and great insight, and in doing so reveal how far a political conversation might go in Shakespeare's London between citizens, the extent to which thoughts would be expressed or half-expressed or conveyed in proverbs or in metaphors.

> All may be well; but, if God sort it so,
> 'Tis more than we deserve or I expect.

The act ends with the first growls of political thunder, and somehow in these few scenes the whole of England is involved: Ludlow, Northampton and Stony Stratford, and Pomfret Castle as much as London. The menace hanging over the heads of royal children has also become palpable. In act 3 the Prince goes to the Tower.

> I do not like the Tower, of any place.
> Did Julius Caesar build that place, my lord?

> But say, my lord, it were not regist'red,
> Methinks the truth should live from age to age,
> As 'twere retail'd to all posterity,
> Even to the general all-ending day.

> Death makes no conquest of this conqueror. . . .

The Prince will die in the Tower, though he intends to rival Caesar and reconquer France. The purpose of the passage is a little more than pathetic contrast; it is to bring home to Londoners the reality of history. The Tower both was and looked extremely sinister, and Tower Hill was a place of public execution. The antiquarian question was real, and sounds as if Stowe had been consulted; the foundation of the Tower by Caesar is not of course recorded, but the Tower is in fact built on a Roman fort.

Shakespeare's language here recalls that of the Sonnets: the antiquity of
the monuments attracts his poetry as a steeple attracts lightning. The
Tower is a solid presence in this act, almost a character in the play; so to a
lesser extent is the bloodstained castle of Pomfret.

In scene iv Richard accuses his victims of witchcraft: this monstrously
false accusation is exactly in line with Puritan thinking and practice, as
Shakespeare must have known. It is also worth noting that the Mayor of
London, like virtually all Shakespeare's mayors, is an ass. Richard's
hypocrisy as he takes the crown makes little impression on the sullen
citizens: all they say is 'Amen'. It is not Elysium to be a King, and the
crown brings no joy. Anne wishes

> ... that the inclusive verge
> Of golden metal that must round my brow
> Were red-hot steel, to sear me to the brains!
> Anointed let me be with deadly venom. ...

The fourth act opens with another scene of unhappy women. Richard is
crowned, but no time is lost in compliment or ceremony. He sends for a
'discontented gentleman Whose humble means match not his haughty
spirit', to murder the Princes in the Tower. At the same time Richmond's
rebellion begins to take shape. All these themes are intricately woven
together, so that the play is as full of actions and events as its scenes are of
contrasting atmosphere. Prophecies about Richmond are mulled over,
including one by 'a bard of Ireland', and by the end of act 4, scene ii, Richard
is doomed and knows it. Yet his energies increase. 'Then fiery expedition
be my wing. ...' The wronged women are his Furies, and in scene iv the
widowed queens and his own and the late King's mother come together
again to curse him. The confrontation is prolonged, formal, and convincing. He proposes marriage again.

> *Queen Elizabeth* Yet thou didst kill my children.
> *King Richard* But in your daughter's womb I bury them;
>   Where, in that nest of spicery, they will breed
>   Selves of themselves, to your recomforture.

The fourth act ends with this matter unconcluded and the rebellion
rampant, messengers of bad news swiftly multiplying. The next opens
with the execution of the King's last friend, Buckingham. The battle of
Bosworth follows.

> *Richmond* The weary sun hath made a golden set,
>   And by the bright tract of his fiery car
>   Gives token of a goodly day to-morrow. ...

The ancestors of the Tudor aristocracy are named, in a glorious-sound-
ing rollcall, a device Shakespeare repeats and improves on in *Henry V*, and

one which throws light on the episodes enacted and those not enacted in his selective play about Henry VIII. The Earl of Derby gets special attention, because he changed sides and so altered the course of battle when he came over to Richmond. This piece of ordinary treachery is carefully explained away and the Earl appears in a heroic light, probably not because Shakespeare had dealings with Strange's (Lord Derby's) company of actors, but because his own great-grandfather had served, probably at Bosworth under Derby, and been rewarded by Henry VII with land in Warwickshire.

For a moment Richard falters. 'Give me a bowl of wine. I have not that alacrity of spirit Nor cheer of mind that I was wont to have.' When he sleeps, the ghosts of those he murdered visit him. This is another of Shakespeare's famous set-pieces. The dead men are like and unlike the raging women, but the scene has the same mixture of formality and realism, and so has the texture of the verse. Their refrain is 'despair and die'. Such a scene may be thought a throwback to older revenge plays or to Seneca, but psychological penetration and powerful poetry make it thrilling. Its function in the play is heightened by contrast with Richmond's cheerful evening, his brief prayers and quiet dreams. Richard wakes to his last long monologue, a disturbed self-wrestling that owes something perhaps to *Faustus*, but only a general conception:

> ... conscience hath a thousand several tongues,
> And every tongue brings in a several tale,
> And every tale condemns me for a villain.

Burbage must have been pleased with his part: what Burbage demanded as his stature increased as an actor was an incalculably great influence on Shakespeare's writing.

The battle itself is a series of alternating scenes of the two armies that succeed one another with increasing speed and urgency, always in sharp contrast, until Richard meets Richmond in a wordless swordfight on foot, and dies with no last words. The play ends with a prayer for peace and a prayer against traitors, 'That would reduce these bloody days again/And make poor England weep in streams of blood!' One must never forget in reading Shakespeare that traitors and discontented gentlemen existed, and that we owe it only to Burghley and the Queen that their plots were brought to nothing by government counterplots, and that England did not see another civil war in Shakespeare's lifetime. It was not only mad squires or religious fanatics like the gunpowder plotters who were dangerous men. Leicester was as treacherous as any theatrical courtier, Essex and Ralegh died on the block, Southampton was lucky to be let live, and if Sir Philip Sidney had not died he might well have been as dangerous as they were. were part and parcel of the make-up of these fiery gallants, and Shakespeare understood their tragedy. Tragedy happens when some heroic figure goes beyond bounds. *Richard III* is more a saga than a tragedy, but to make Richard's character Shakespeare has taken ingredients from the philosophy of his day, and from life.

It is not true, as one might suppose, that the two houses of York and Lancaster had exterminated one another: their annihilation was completed slowly by the Tudors. The son of Richard III, whom Shakespeare never mentions, as his existence would alter one of his father's characteristics, died in 1484, a year before Bosworth. Richard then adopted a nephew, John de la Pole, who died in the rebellion at Stoke in 1487. The next male heir was Clarence's son the Earl of Warwick, executed in 1499, and so on to the reign of Elizabeth, when it was still perilous to have royal blood: as the Duke of Norfolk and the Earl of Derby discovered. The play *Richard III*, with Richard's cynicism as a lover and all the ghastly nemesis of civil war, teaches fundamental lessons about Elizabethan life. And yet *A Midsummer-Night's Dream* is a projection or a wish-fulfilment fantasy of that same world in nearly the same year. The same audience saw them both, and they use the same rules of rhetoric.

The *Dream* was not printed until 1600, though Meres knew it by 1598, and the amazing bad weather it refers to looks like 1594. It is about love and mistakes in love, so it ends in marriage, but it refers nowhere to any marriage outside itself. Scholars have tried to hitch it to the wedding celebrations of likely patrons, and imagined that it had two endings, but wrongly in my view. It was a public play, using a number of boy actors and a lot of music, and the wedding theme was natural to May. It is set in May, in the woods, and the title refers to the common custom of divining by midsummer dreams and flowers who one's lover was or whether one's lover was faithful: that is, the title refers directly to the plot. Sir Thomas Heneage married the dowager Lady Southampton on 2 May 1594, which gives him a better chance than the others of a first performance which would be on Mayday that year. But May 1594 is too early for the bad weather of that summer, so I am inclined to ignore Heneage and say that the *Dream* was written in the winter of 1594–5. I do not really believe it was commissioned by a nobleman; Shakespeare was now working for the Chamberlain, and extremely busy.

In 1595, Shakespeare's friend Richard Field printed a new edition of Plutarch's *Lives*, and in this play Shakespeare uses Plutarch for the first time. His reference to a lion that might frighten the ladies is not necessarily linked to the baptism of Prince Henry of Scotland in August 1594, since Henslowe had lions, but it may be; Shakespeare is likely to have frequented Field's printing-house, and an account of Court celebrations in Scotland, as described in this public Court bulletin, is just what he would have read: 'This chariot should have been drawn in by a lion, but because his presence might have brought some fear to the nearest, or that the sights of the lights and the torches might have commoved his tameness, it was thought meet that the Moor should supply that room.' He was still using Reginald Scot's *Discoverie of Witchcraft* (1584) too; it has a lot about Robin Goodfellow, and the donkey's-head trick comes from Scot. The love-juice comes from Chaucer's *Merchant's Tale*. The prestige of Chaucer was very great: John Gerard in the *Herball* speaks of his tomb as a place of pilgrimage, one of the sights of London, and Thomas Wilson in his *Arte of Rhetorique* (1553; 1560) says Chaucer's style is the way a gentleman should speak. I am sure that a thorough search would discover more of Chaucer in Shakespeare than has yet been noticed, since his language can be traditional when it seems most original: the word 'key-cold' in *Richard III*, for example, which Thomas More uses, and 'We owe God a death.' Spenser's *Epithalamion* was registered in November 1594 and printed early in 1595: I think that Shakespeare got hold of that in some form while he was actually writing this play, the balance of which Spenser's inspiring verse has altered.

I used to be amazed by Shakespeare's carelessness about act and scene division, and about names, and to attend to those scholars who divined a play behind the play and other such perplexed histories, but I have come to see that one must accept that Shakespeare cared more about some things than others. The Folio (at act 5, scene i, line 125) prints Tawyer for a character: he was an apprentice or employee of Heminges the actor, a member of the Chamberlain's Men. In *Love's Labour* Armado is sometimes *Braggart*, Nathaniel *Curate*, and so on. In this play Bottom appears as *Clown*, Quince as *Peter*, and Robin Goodfellow as *Puck*, for example. Robin Goodfellow has become known as Puck through Shakespeare, but 'a puck' or 'the puck' is a general word, like 'an elf', not a proper name, and that is how Shakespeare is using it, just as in the *Epithalamion* Spenser speaks of 'the Pouke', a wicked imp. There are some small contradictions about time as well, but I do not think Shakespeare cared twopence about them, and nor shall we.

The weather is another matter: dramatic bad weather is something English country people never forget. In our village they still talk about a winter twenty-five years ago, and a summer ten years ago; the older people remember the snow and the floods of forty-five years ago, and so do I. Shakespeare would not have made a mistake about the weather. When James I saw the play on New Year's Day of 1604, I am certain that the weather of 1594 was still precisely remembered.

Saintsbury calls the *Dream* 'an *olio* of metres', and so it is. The play is deliberately lyrical. Lyly's private theatre with boy actors had been closed down, and Shakespeare's company seized the opportunity to exploit its most popular features, including I imagine some of its boys. Without boys the *Dream* could not be acted; the full blast of lyricism is essential to it. Some of the mixed metre is parody – Pyramus' lament comes from

Lamphedon and Clarisia in *Common Conditions* (1514–23) and follows its metre – but most is lyrical. The boys' theatre has brought its special atmosphere with it, and its own tricks. It is a curious fact that the last play ever played in Long Chamber at Eton, which was in 1844, and viewed from an amphitheatre of piled-up beds, was a comedy called *Pyramus and Thisbe*.

Shakespeare knew Welshmen in Stratford and used a Welsh boy actor in *Henry VI*, so it is not surprising, merely curious, that his fairies are more like Welsh fairies than any other kind – a fact of some further interest in connection with Shakespeare's other fairy play, *The Merry Wives of Windsor*. Educated Elizabethans thought fairies were a kind of terrestrial devil; a 1628 woodcut of Robin Goodfellow is distinctly alarming and sexually potent; Robert Burton's *Anatomy of Melancholy* puts them all in the sixth rank of sublunary devils. Uneducated Elizabethans believed fairies existed: John and Alice West, for instance, were tried in June 1613 for going about claiming to be special friends of the King and Queen of the Fairies, and offering for money fairy information about life and death and lost property. Literary fairies were more obscenely tricky than Shakespeare permitted. *The Maid's Metamorphosis*, played by the Children of St Paul's for whom Lyly wrote, and printed in 1600, had fairies called Penny, Cricket and 'little, little Prick':

> When I feel a girl asleep
> Underneath her frock I peep,
> There to sport, and there I play,
> Then I bite her like a flea
> And about I skip.

Shakespeare has no room for this revolting little monster, though the Puck is mischievous enough, and Falstaff in the *Merry Wives* gets pinched black and blue. The fairies in the *Dream* belong to the kind of polite lyrical comedy that Lyly wrote. They are innocent, like the ones George Waldron recorded in the Isle of Man in 1726: 'They live in wilds and forests, and on mountains, and shun great cities because of the wickedness acted therein.' Shakespeare has transformed the enchanted wood, which usually has a darker aspect; he has made it a fit place for innocent music.

Walter de la Mare noticed that the lovers are boring compared to the lyrical parts of the play, and encouraged John Dover Wilson to use that as a criterion for distinguishing an inferior 'early' play from the one we have. Shakespeare did revise, but wholesale theories like this never hold water. The point about the lovers is that upper-class persons in Shakespeare under the rank of duke are generally made of cardboard: they were figures from stories, and he seldom put his heart into them as he did into clowns and pages. Also Walter de la Mare, who like his contemporary and fellow poet John Masefield is an unexpectedly good critic of Shakespeare, exaggerates the woodenness of these lovers. Some of their verse is splendid (act 1, scene i, lines 209–17). They are better in the theatre than they are on the page.

The lovers are caught up in a blind dance of illusion, of which passion is only the beginning. Theseus and Hippolyta are much more real, but then they are outside the web. Theseus' speech in act 5 about the imagination of poets, added or extended like Berowne's in praise of love in *Love's Labour*, is a full statement of the theme of illusion. Like *What You Will*, the secondary title of *Twelfth Night*, which Marston stole some years later for a play of his own, the *Dream* focuses on illusion in love rather sharply; it should be taken as a comment on midsummer nights' divinations of lovers. The wood where Oberon is king is one where all travellers get lost, and love is a wood where all travellers get lost, though it may have a happy ending.

Oberon, king of the magic wood, was known to Shakespeare from the translation *Huon of Burdeux* by Lord Berners, printed by Wynkyn de Worde in 1534. The marriage comes from Chaucer's *Knight's Tale*, and so does the May setting. The verse parodies were suggested by Chaucer's parody of Sir Topas I imagine. Shakespeare borrowed his hunting scene from Seneca and some names and mythology from Ovid. It appears that his ambition as a poet at this time drew him to read extremely widely, and to ransack as he read. He certainly learned all Lyly could teach him. Lyly is a wonderful writer, but given only his writings one could not imagine a Shakespeare, not even a Shakespeare confined to comedy. Shakespeare is merrier, less inhibited, a far better poet, and his bitter streak and his philosophic streak go beyond Lyly. Over years, I have regretfully put aside several arguments by Frances Yates about Elizabethan intellectuals, but I am sure she was right about the depth to which Shakespeare imbibed ideas. He is a philosophized poet.

The play opens with enchanting verses about moonlight; but so much of the verse in this play is irresistibly quotable, and the play itself is so well known, that I must treat it with restraint. The name of Theseus' Master of Revels, 'Philostrate', pronounced like 'illustrate', is not just a proof that Shakespeare knew no Greek but is a medieval English form, a piece of deliberate, Chaucerian colouring: Shakespeare's Greece is still Chaucerian:

> Go, Philostrate,
> Stir up the Athenian youth to merriments;
> Awake the pert and nimble spirit of mirth. . . .

One might feel that this 'pert and nimble spirit' foreshadowed the Puck. The business of the forced marriage puts an end to this cheerfulness; Egeus, Hermia's father, is lucid though longwinded, because to be tedious is part of his character, yet he is not quite tedious enough to be boring. He is a fearful spoilsport, but his accusations are worth watching, because

coming from him they reveal a new aspect of Shakespeare's view of true
and false in love and in poetry:

> Thou, thou, Lysander, thou hast given her rhymes,
> And interchang'd love-tokens with my child;
> Thou hast by moonlight at her window sung,
> With feigning voice, verses of feigning love. . . .

The falseness of singing adds a new dimension to that of versifying. The
girl is threatened with death or a nunnery, the nun's life being so magically
described that Shakespeare only just manages to make wedded happiness
more attractive.

The lovers flee to the woods, and an audience tiring of their emotions
settles down to the carpenter Quince, the joiner Snug, the weaver Bottom,
the bellows-mender Flute, the tinker Snout and the tailor Starveling.
These names are almost too admirable: one laughs before the jokes have
started. They are Jack Cade's mob in a happier setting. Can there really
have been bellows-menders? One of the things one likes most about
Shakespeare is that he so enjoys his own jokes. These craftsmen will put on
a play and be mocked, like the one in *Love's Labour*. Bottom parodies a
verse translation of Seneca; one likes to think of Shakespeare splitting
himself with laughter over Seneca, in whose works the average reader will
not find very many laughs per hundred pages.

Act 2 introduces the Fairy and the Puck, then Oberon and Titania. This
is not exactly a romantic world, nor exactly an exotic one, nor a pantomime transformation scene, though it has elements of all these, but it is
grounded in real folklore and country jokes as well as being dipped in
literary moonlight. If all poetry had to do were to be beautiful, this poetry
would be perfect, but there is something claustrophobic about the purely
beautiful, partly a sense of illusion, partly a sense of missing truths.
Shakespeare counters that problem, which in Lyly's plays often arises, by
the earthly roots of his poetry. If he learned to do so from Chaucer, that was
an important lesson, but I think it was instinctive in him. His pastorals
have a realism unlike Spenser's, but his verse technique when Oberon
stole away,

> And in the shape of Corin sat all day,
> Playing on pipes of corn, and versing love
> To amorous Phillida . . .

has the genuine Virgilian cadence, and Corin merges into the Virgilian
Corydon more easily than any of Spenser's shepherds. Such a moment will
never last too long, and the bad weather which follows is even more
exciting than the good:

> The seasons alter: hoary-headed frosts
> Fall in the fresh lap of the crimson rose;

> And on old Hiems' thin and icy crown
> An odorous chaplet of sweet summer buds
> Is, as in mockery, set. . . .

Country people complain bitterly when that happens, they long for their childhood, when summer really was summer and winter really was winter. Shakespeare is attracted by the poetry of it, but the reality and consequence for agriculture frighten him. Oberon sends Puck to find the love-juice; for continuous lyric impetus without loss of dramatic momentum this first scene of act 2 is invincible even among Shakespeare's comedies. The fairy song – 'You spotted snakes with double tongue' – in scene ii is charming, but more gratuitous. Still, it leads well into the spell and the intrigue of the lovers found asleep and enchanted by mistake.

The trouble with the illusions and cross-purposes is that they make the lovers unreal in their passions, as if only Oberon and the Puck were adults in this wood. In act 3 the Athenian clowns offer the relief of a rougher humour, and Bottom gets his donkey's head and is loved by the Queen of the fairies. There is something Falstaffian about Bottom: he is a much funnier version of Sly in the opening scenes of the *Shrew*, and here as there one most loves him when invited to mock him. My favourite character in the whole of Shakespeare is Caliban, but Bottom is leading up to him, and not far behind.

His song about the 'ousel cock, so black of hue, With orange-tawny bill' (with which he wakes Titania) is oddly moving. Bird men say Shakespeare confused a blackbird with a ring-ousel. He confused certain flower names as well, but we know too little about the regional names for things, which varied and which often owe more to resemblance than to science, to complain. The name may be wrong but the observation is sharp. 'Orange-tawny' incidentally occurs in an inventory of coloured cloth sold by a draper in Henley Street, Stratford; later in this play Shakespeare uses it of a wig. He has colours on his mind for some reason, bright or plain. I am inclined to think he felt the very word 'orange-tawny' was funny. One remembers the 'plain-song cuckoo grey' and the 'russet-pated choughs' (jackdaws) 'Rising and cawing at the gun's report'.

The intrigues work themselves out with extraordinary self-mocking poetry. Titania in love with Bottom is fantastically set free to be funny, beautiful and touching all at the same time:

> Come, sit thee down upon this flow'ry bed,
> While I thy amiable cheeks do coy,
> And stick musk-roses in thy sleek smooth head,
> And kiss thy fair large ears, my gentle joy.

Why do the last three words make it so funny? The answer has to do with rhyming and timing, but also with convention and inappropriateness. Dawn drives away the fairies and brings out Theseus and Hippolyta to hunt 'And mark the musical confusion Of hounds and echo in conjunc-tion'. The hounds may come in detail from Seneca, but the verse improves him unbelievably. The echo of hounds in full cry rebounding from a wood is a sound I have heard and remembered for more than thirty years: to him it was familiar. The lovers are found asleep, and woken with the huntsmen's horns; their problems are over. Bottom when he wakes goes back to his friends, and *Pyramus and Thisbe* is imminent.

The speech Theseus makes at the opening of act 5 is a direct discussion of poetry, expanded from a simpler version perhaps at the time it was first written. Theseus hardly knows what to make of the stories he must by now have been told:

> Lovers and madmen have such seething brains . . .
> The lunatic, the lover, and the poet,
> Are of imagination all compact . . .
> The poet's eye, in a fine frenzy rolling,
> Doth glance from heaven to earth, from earth to heaven;
> And as imagination bodies forth
> The forms of things unknown, the poet's pen
> Turns them to shapes, and gives to airy nothing
> A local habitation and a name. . . .

Theseus takes a mature man's cynical view: poetry is an illusion like madness or lovemadness. The lover, the madman and the poet are deluded, what they see is not there, and what they say is false. That is why at the end of Shakespeare's life Prospero is going to drown his book: 'How easy is a bush suppos'd a bear!' I think it was David Gascoyne who asked God for the grace to tell the truth as purely in his poetry as he tried to tell it when not writing poetry. The problem is a real one, and I doubt whether any poet could be important to the rest of us who had not felt it in some form. Shakespeare was obsessed by it. On the other hand, in terms of this play Theseus is wrong. We have seen the things happen which he dismisses.

The end of the play dissolves into dancing, but when the Bergomask is over the fairies bless the house. Oberon has his dark side but this is a masque of blessing and dancing, and very pretty it must have been. 'Through the house give glimmering light,' 'To each word a warbling note'. It is a great pity we have lost the song.

If the fairies have no dance they have no climax: they were merely decorative, part of Bottom's dream. Oberon and Titania and the Puck would have melted away in the fourth act leaving no conclusion but Bottom's comedy. But the triple marriage is essential: it is what the entire play intends. So how would that be dealt with after Bottom's play is over? It seems then that the magic blessing of house, bed and marriage is essential. Shakespeare has trouble combining elements, combining worlds. Bottom can meet Theseus only as a clown meets a prince, and the play which is mocked is a traditional way of doing this. The same thing happens in Anthony Munday's *John a Kent and John a Cumber*, which as Nevill Coghill pointed out may well have given Shakespeare his plot. But fairies will not mix with real people unless by enchanting them.

Shakespeare has enjoyed writing about them and by happy mischance made them so real that they cannot simply dissolve away, leaving the fifth act to humans on their own. Bottom's actors have their Bergomask because all plays end with a dance, and funny as his epilogue might be, we do not want an epilogue by Bottom so close to the real epilogue. The Bergomask is charming, and bridges the gap between Bottom's friends and the wedding. All the humans must then leave the stage for the fairies to appear and give their blessing. All these gaps have been skilfully bridged over, and the sequence of scenes carefully worked out. It is less disjointed in the theatre than it appears when analysed: I am always disappointed if the Bergomask is left out. The view of recent editors that we have two alternative endings to the *Dream* is therefore mistaken.

The Chamberlain's Men used the Theatre; Henslowe had Alleyn and the Admiral's Men south of the river, but no dramatic poet of any merit. His solution to this problem has a kind of idiotic cunning: he went in for multiple authorship. Some did the drama and some did the poetry. Munday did plots, Drayton and Chapman were good poets, Chettle and Heywood had talent, and London contained as many intending authors as it did horse-traders. From 1594 to 1610 or later, London had dramatic mania. One of these multiple plays is called *Sir Thomas More*, an incoherently revised manuscript in five hands. Some respectable scholars used to believe a bit of it was by Shakespeare. I think that was originally owing to the temptation to produce a crushing argument against Baconians and other people with bees in their bonnets, whose Victorian argument was that a country lad like Shakespeare could not have written great poetry about great persons. His handwriting in a dramatic manuscript would settle the matter. Later on Thomas More's stern, conservative views in the play became another motive. (I deal seriously with the arguments in Appendix 5.) A recent study of the manuscript by G. Melchiori in *Shakespeare Survey* fixes the revision as not later than 1593–4.

Sir Thomas More had been rejected by the censor, the Master of the Revels, Sir Edmund Tilney. It was then revised piecemeal in its various handwritings, but never played and never printed. We have only this messy manuscript of a revised version. Henslowe must have been desperate to employ such a gang: it is impossible that Shakespeare was one of them, since by this time he was working full time for the rival company, nor is it conceivable at any time since his earliest days, let us say since 1592, that he would take on a botching job of this kind. What the play *Sir Thomas More* does show though is the lower depths of the profession of dramatic poet, and Henslowe with his back to the wall. Not that he failed to survive. He did so by wheeling and dealing, by the profits of his bearpit and his brothels and inns, and by treating poets with a cynical meanness unparalleled until modern times. Between 1594 and 1596 the Admiral's Men lost their position at Court. In 1594 they ran level with the Chamberlain's Men for number of Court performances, but they fell behind in 1595 and dropped out in 1596. In 1595 Francis Langley built the Swan in Paris Garden, a quarter of a mile west of Henslowe's Rose. Henslowe spent a hundred pounds on painting and repairs to the Rose, but the Swan was now the biggest and grandest theatre in London. A sketch of a scene at the Swan made from memory by a Dutchman soon after it opened has survived.

When the plague was over, Shakespeare lived in the parish of St Helen's, Bishopsgate, inside London but close to the Shoreditch Theatre. He turns up there in some tax documents for November 1597, owing five shillings, his goods being assessed at £5. Since this is a record of defaulters, he probably paid his first instalment of £7 or £8 in 1595 or 1596, but in November 1597 he was among those 'dead, departed, or gone out of the said ward, or their goods . . . conveyed out of the same'. Throughout his lifetime the expansion of London into industrial suburbs from Clerkenwell to Whitechapel was taking place, and a tax defaulter might be hard to find. Anything outside the precise limits and direct jurisdiction of the City was beyond the reach of its authorities. The buzzing of the great hive of London closed around him.

In 1595 Shakespeare's son Hamnet was ten years old. He had one more year to live.

· 6 ·

Troubled Years

In 1594 part of Stratford was burned down. Since later on we hear of a new Stratford regulation that thatched cottages ought to have stone or brick chimneys instead of letting firesmoke escape through a hole in the roof, it is surprising that the catastrophe had not happened earlier. Nearly the whole of Henley Street was gutted, but the Shakespeare houses survived, probably by being close to a brook that ran by the smithy almost next door. Gilbert Bradley's house beyond it was lost. The western Shakespeare house, being nearest to the fire, was severely damaged: John Shakespeare sold part of it as a toft (or building site) to Mr Badger, whose house was burned, and leased whatever was left to another victim, Mr Johnson, to use as a barn. The western house seems to have emerged without the tall gable that it probably once had. Disasters like that were common. In 1583 Nantwich burned for twenty days: only a single fifteenth-century hall, one town house and the church survived. This Stratford fire was commonplace by comparison.

The next year, 1595, Stratford suffered another, even worse fire. Hamnet and Judith Sadler's house at the corner of Sheep Street, and those of a number of others of Shakespeare's family friends were destroyed and had to be rebuilt, including that of Rogers the butcher and bailiff, now called Harvard House after his grandson John Harvard, an otherwise undistinguished clergyman who was the first benefactor of the first university college in America, now Harvard University. That house was restored with much pomp by Marie Corelli in the 1890s. Many of the fine rebuilt 1595 houses now to be seen at Stratford had the plain but innocent nineteenth-century stucco ripped from their faces at about the same time. The changes that rebuilding in the 1590s entailed are noteworthy, because it appears that everyone wanted to improve their property. The Shrive's House, for example, from which the Sergeant of the Mace would issue forth to arrest or to distrain, in his leather suit and large boots (five shillings in the town accounts), was rebuilt on a larger scale to include a tavern where he distilled his own *aqua vitae*. He also sold ale and a drink made of aniseed and liquorice. The wooden ornamental carving on these houses

145

gives the strong impression of agricultural prosperity; it can be matched on German houses of a similar date in the Harz mountains.

At this time, in probably the three busiest years of Shakespeare's life, his writings have little to do with the country ways and small-town concerns of Stratford, yet the strings that tied him there were strong as we shall see. He must by now have intended what he later accomplished, in securing his father's coat of arms as a gentleman, and buying New Place. He did what he could for his brother Edmund as an actor in London, and he answered appeals from Stratford for money or advice; he seems never to have wanted anything so much as to go back there for good.

All this raises the problem of his relations with his wife. We are not able to prove the date of almost any visit he made to Stratford, and writers have often assumed either that he was constantly there, or that he remained in London, living like a bohemian. The hints of this bohemian life of his are either found in his own plays, which we shall discuss as we come to them, or from the different, rather younger and more bohemian circle of poets around Ben Jonson: they are extremely fragile fantasies. After 1592, Shakespeare was too successful to need to live in taverns, or as a bohemian parasite, as Jonson was forced to live. We have an Inns of Court joke, more or less contemporary but by no means first hand, that Burbage and Shakespeare wanted the same girl; Burbage said tell her King Richard is here, but Shakespeare had got there first and sent a message that William the Conqueror came before King Richard. This bit of repartee is certainly a contemporary joke, but nothing at all follows from it. The truth is that we know nothing certain of that kind about Shakespeare, and that no evidence exists that he was ever untrue to his wife. We do know that he hated jealousy, and had an almost mystical belief in fidelity. We have noticed in him also a certain distrust of poetry.

There is a family tradition that later on, after Hamnet's death, Hamnet's twin Judith was painted by Richard Burbage, son of James. Should that be true, either Shakespeare entertained Burbage at New Place, which is not impossible, or Judith came to London, as I think is more probable. If Judith came to London, it is almost certain that her mother came, but in either case the link between Shakespeare's friends in the theatre and his life at home with his family would be strengthened by the existence of this portrait. I fear I do not believe in it.

Mrs Shakespeare was not the only Elizabethan lady to bring up her children at home while her husband was attached to the Court. How often then would he be free to go home to Stratford? Certainly once a year, when the gentry all went home to look after their harvest and their rents. Once a year even the goldsmiths and great merchants travelled out of London to the Stourbridge Fair in September, which was a London in miniature that stood for three weeks. Aubrey was told that Shakespeare was wont to go to his native country once a year, and that is surely what he did. In 1594 and 1595 the Chamberlain's Men were still doing summer tours, but Shakespeare is not likely to have been in the touring company, since he was writing. In 1594 'the Lord Chamberlain's players' were paid 2s 8d by the Mayor at Marlborough, and in 1595 forty shillings at Ipswich and forty shillings at Cambridge. One faint possible trace of Shakespeare emerges in a lawsuit at Stratford between two widows, Field the printer's sister and Mrs Perrott, about some misappropriated property. Mention is made of 'Mr. Shaxpier's book', but it is hard to be sure what that means.

Shakespeare's life was based on London because the public theatres were there, as well as the Court for much of the year. In July 1596 there was a crisis when Lord Hunsdon died. His son inherited the players with his father's title and money, but William Brooke, Lord Cobham, became Lord Chamberlain, and that was a disaster. The pressure against public plays intensified. The inns where the players had been used to perform in winter were now shut to them. In November Lord Hunsdon's players moved south of the river to the Swan, about which the Lord Mayor of London had written to Burghley, 'I understand that one Francis Langley intendeth to erect a new stage or theater (as they call it) for the exercising of plays upon the Bankside . . . nothing else but unchaste fables, lascivious devices, shifts of cozenage, and matters of like sort . . .' which attracted 'thieves, horse-stealers, whoremongers, cozeners, coneycatching persons, practicers of treason, and such other like', to the detriment of religion. Meanwhile the lease of the old Theatre was running out: it was due to be renewed in 1597, but the ground landlord wanted to double its rent. So in 1596 Burbage bought part of the habitable ruins of Blackfriars Priory not far away, where the Children of the Chapel Royal used to play, and built a private theatre there. Citizens petitioned against it on grounds of noise and plague, and Cobham refused to let it open.

In February 1597 old Burbage died, and his sons Cuthbert and Richard, Shakespeare's friend the actor, inherited. In March of that year Lord Cobham conferred on British history an incalculable benefit by dying, and Lord Hunsdon became Lord Chamberlain. The worst public pressure was over, but its existence for eight months and the uncertainties of the time must be borne in mind as the background of the plays Shakespeare was now writing: that is why I have run a little ahead of my account in order to explain them. There is a further matter somehow entangled with the theatre crisis, and best dealt with as part of it. At the end of November 1596 one William Waite sought securities against a breach of the peace, for fear of death and mutilation of his limbs, from William Shakespeare, Francis Langley, Dorothy Soer wife of John Soer, and Anne Lee. Langley, the builder of the Swan, was a goldsmith with interests in the wool trade; as an official inspector of woollen cloth in London he was later sued for violence and extortion, but legal battles of these kinds were normal and one must look behind them. The suit against Shakespeare turns out to be only a countersuit against a similar suit brought by Langley alone against William Gardiner and William Waite, and an earlier suit in the series (1591) refers to Waite as 'wholly under the rule of the said Gardiner'.

Gardiner was a justice of the peace of Surrey; he later had the happiness of shutting down Langley's Swan over the Isle of Dogs scandal in 1597. In autumn of 1596 Gardiner had been suing Langley for slander committed that May, and demanding colossal damages of £1000 each for two occasions and £200 for a lesser case; Langley had called him 'a false perjured knave', and now proved it by referring to legal records of Gardiner's perjury: the suits for security against breach of the peace followed, because Gardiner was not a meek man. The theatre therefore was simply sucked into an existing feud, and Shakespeare with it. Gardiner was an appalling villain, usurer, perjurer, rackrenter, a violent and bloody man, an oppressor of the poor, and the defrauder of his wife, his stepson and his son-in-law.

Leslie Hotson, who discovered this cockroach and discussed him in *Shakespeare versus Shallow*, traces an appalling tale of his misdoings. Not untypically, he became High Sheriff of Surrey and Sussex (1594–5). He died at sixty-six in 1597, leaving £10 to buy church plate for St Mary Magdalen's, Bermondsey: a cup which survives. In his lifetime he was variously accused of atheism, immoralism, perjury, violence, witchcraft, sorcery and the keeping of two toads. He persecuted papists and play-actors with equal and perhaps equally meaningless ferocity, his understanding of Calvinism being limited to a cynical reliance on predestination. He was a nasty piece of work; but he had been useful to the authorities, and Camden as herald saw to the ceremony of his burial.

In the middle of these disturbances, in early August 1596, Hamnet Shakespeare died. He was buried on the 11th. What it must have meant to his father and his mother or worst of all to his twin sister, one shudders to imagine. The twins were eleven and a half years old. August is the likeliest time in the year for Shakespeare to have been at home, so it is not unreasonable to suppose that he was there. It is not certain who buried the child, because in that year Stratford lost John Bramhall, a vicar who had announced that the fires of 1594 and 1595 had both been sent by God as punishments for sabbath-breaking, which cannot have made him popular. The new Vicar Richard Byfield may have been worse, since he was a professor of theology whose two sons became famous Puritan preachers. He can have been little consolation, and I have wondered sometimes whether Shakespeare's famous horror of death and dead bones may have had something to do with the committal of that small body to the damp green earth beside the river, in the knowledge that it must be dug up and jumbled among other bones.

How strange it is at first sight that William Shakespeare chose this moment to renew and carry through his father's application for a grant of arms, the official sign of the status of a gentleman. In 1596 John Shakespeare had no other living grandson than Hamnet so far as the records show, but he had other male children, and of course he had daughters and so had the poet. Anne Hathaway was forty and the twins had been her last children, but William's brother Richard was only twenty-two, and his brother Edmund only sixteen. Gilbert was thirty. Genealogists have paid close attention to the later ramifications of the Shakespeare family, but records are sometimes defective or simply lacking: it seems to me nearly certain that one of these brothers married and had children. It was not Edmund, who died a bachelor in London and was buried by his brother in St Saviour's, Southwark, on the last day of 1607, and the great bell tolled for him. His only child was illegitimate. I therefore believe that Richard, who stayed in Stratford and inherited his father's business, or else his brother Gilbert was a married man and had children. Whatever the truth may be about the future history of the family, the renewed application for the coat of arms was an act of family solidarity and a righting of the old man's wrongs. John Shakespeare was sixty, Leicester and Warwick were dead, Sir Thomas Lucy was an elderly widower, and William Shakespeare had powerful friends and patrons and was beginning to be rich.

Two rough drafts of the grant of arms were drawn up on 20 October 1596 by Garter King of Arms, Sir William Dethick, with the note that a preliminary sketch of these proposed arms had been submitted twenty years ago in the hand of Clarenceux, who was Robert Cook. (Clarenceux is the title of an heraldic officer; York Herald and Garter are others.) Cook is the last of the five heralds in Thomas Lant's *Funeral Roll* of the burial of Sir Philip Sidney, bearing the *insignia et ornamenta equestris dignitatis*. The draft of the grant records that John Shakespeare's grandfather was rewarded 'for valiant service' by Henry VII, a story on which the poet had clearly been brought up; that John Shakespeare had married a daughter and one of the heirs of Robert Arden of Wilmcote, Esquire; that fifteen or sixteen (twenty-six) years ago he was a justice of the peace, bailiff and Queen's officer, and had 'lands and tenants of good wealth and substance worth £500'. The crest was a falcon with a spear and the shield was gold with a silver spear on a black band. The motto seems to have been Non Sans Droict, but it was never used. Three years later John Shakespeare applied to impale his arms with those of Arden. The heralds considered permitting the arms of Arden of Park Hall, which derived from the Beauchamps as Earls of Warwick, but in the end they settled on a form of the arms of the entire Arden clan. The Shakespeares must have found this unacceptable, because they never did impale the arms of Arden.

William Dethick was a stormy petrel, who is recorded as having hit his father, stabbed his brother, assaulted the minister at Sir Henry Sidney's funeral, and berated and battered the lesser heralds. He is supposed as a young man to have granted a slightly different version of the royal arms of England to a plasterer called Dawkins. York Herald, who was Peter Brooke, drew up a list of grants of arms by Dethick and Camden that he thought improper, and 'Shakespeare the player' was number four, but Garter and Clarenceux answered York in 1602 with a well-reasoned and low-toned series of arguments, and that was the end of the matter. The Shakespeares were not the only family in Stratford to have a coat of arms: the Quineys for example had one, which appears on the seal of a letter to William Shakespeare. Nor was Shakespeare the only actor to get one: Heminges had a grant of arms. Social mobility was swifter then than it became later. The only person thought to have mocked Shakespeare for pretension is Ben Jonson in one or two obscure jokes in his plays: one a general sneer about common players, and the other a motto 'not without mustard'. They seem harmless enough jibes, but one can sense the difference between snarling London and ceremonious, provincial Stratford.

In 1595 a very old-fashioned kind of play was printed called *The Lamentable Tragedy of Locrine, the eldest son of King Brutus, discoursing the Wars of the Britons and Huns, with their discomfiture . . . No less pleasant than profitable. Newly set forth, overseen and corrected, by W.S.*, printed by Thomas Creede, who printed a number of plays by Shakespeare, including *Henry VI* and *Romeo and Juliet*. The revision was up to the minute, as the epilogue shows with its prayer for the Queen:

> Lo here the end of lawless treachery
> Of usurpation and ambitious pride,
> And they that for their private amours dare
> Turmoil our land, and set their broils abroach
> Let them be warned by these premisses.
> And as a woman was the only cause
> That civil discord was then stirred up,
> So let us pray for that renowned maid
> That eight and thirty years the sceptre swayed,
> In quiet peace and sweet felicity;
> And every wight that seeks her Grace's smart,
> Would that his sword were pierced in his heart!

It appears to me probable that Shakespeare, not any other W.S. but the only famous one, revised or tidied up this play for the press. He seems to have relished its archaisms and been amused by it, though I greatly doubt its being his own early work: it must have been written by some minor university wit after an overdose of Seneca. The prologues to acts are spoken by a hellish wench called Atey (the *Ate* of the Greeks, the spirit of the curse), with a burning torch in one hand and a bloody sword in the other. But it has some good lines dotted throughout it, some of which I would be happy to attribute to Shakespeare: about Cerberus for instance, who 'scarreth the ghoasts with high resounding noise', and this:

> When golden Hebe, daughter to great Jove,
> Covered my manly cheeks with youthful down. . . .

But only the slightest touches or phrases recall Shakespeare, the archaisms are extraordinary, the rhetoric and affectation awful and the syntax incompetent. The comic bits are better and the pastoral verses charming. For what it is worth, the play has Welsh fairies 'Close by the boisterous Iscan's silver streams Where lightfoot fairies skip from bank to bank'. The play has been thought an early work of Greene, which is a shrewd guess, but it may have had several authors, or no known author. The other plays attributed to 'W.S.', or even 'W. Sh.', by printers in the 1600s have nothing to do with it, or with Shakespeare, but the theatre was hungry for new plays, few poets were any good, and Shakespeare may easily have spent a few days tuning up this veteran dramatic machine. He will have enjoyed the cobblers' song:

> . . . The can stands full of nappy ale;
>   Dan, dan, dan, dan:
> In our shop still withouten fail:
>   Dan diddle dan.
> This is our meat, this is our food:
>   Dan , dan, dan, dan:
> This brings us to a merry mood:
>   Dan diddle dan.

One hardly needs to stress how far below Shakespeare's accomplishment *Locrine* falls. If he did cast an eye over it and adjust it a little, one might fear that this exception to his normal habit would open the floodgates to every partial and conjectural attribution to him in Elizabethan literary history. I do not think that is so, because the mass of *Locrine* is so obviously not by him, and the touches that he might have put to an old manuscript are so tiny. The only lines in *Locrine* which I feel must be his are the second and third of the prayer for the Queen quoted above. Still, I advance this attribution without confidence.

At just about the same time Shakespeare was writing *Romeo and Juliet*, not his first Italian play but so far as I know the first tragedy in English about private, personal love: the first love tragedy without a classical setting. The feud is not a civil war, and privacy and personality overshadow it. Shakespeare knew plenty about feuds: that of the Danvers and the Longs for example, which happened in 1594. Young Henry Danvers killed young Henry Long, and the Danvers brothers got to France by way of Southampton's house at Titchfield, with some help from Florio. John

Aubrey tells their story. They served out their exile under Henry IV, and when they came home at last, one built the Apothecaries' Garden at Chelsea, and the other the Botanic Garden at Oxford, on the site of the old Jewish cemetery. But *Romeo and Juliet* is not a play about feuding, it is a tragedy of two lovers in which murder is only one of the dramatic factors that separate them. In a way it is a more serious version of Pyramus and Thisbe. *Romeo and Juliet* is one of Shakespeare's greatest masterpieces, as alive now as when it was written.

The play was printed in 1597 'as it hath been often played by Lord Hunsdon's men', and again by a different printer and publisher 'newly corrected, augmented and amended' in 1599. Francis Meres knew it. The Italian story was *The Tragicall Historye of Romeus and Juliet* from Arthur Brooke's poem (1562) and the prose *Romeus and Juliet* by William Painter (1567). Shakespeare had discovered Brooke when he was writing *The Two Gentlemen of Verona*, and the two plays have a few features in common. *Romeo and Juliet* has a chorus: a sonnet in drab style for act 1, and another in golden style for act 2. I think they are meant to mark a tragedy, and to pinpoint Verona, a city of prickly gallants where London social rules need not apply. Shakespeare is telling us what kind of a play this is, because its originality makes that necessary. It will be about a feud, and about a pair of star-crossed lovers, who will reconcile the feud by their deaths. The truth is, of course, that they as much transcend it as Hamlet transcends the wars that frame his play, but Shakespeare feels the need to reveal his structure from the beginning, because a tragedy of pure love is not quite acceptable on the stage. Love belonged to comedy: it could be a theme in history or tragedy, but not as central as it is here.

Brooke's poem was reprinted in 1582 and 1587. Possibly a play already lay behind the structure of his story: he says so, but no one knows in what language it was, and no trace of it has ever been discovered. Shakespeare used Italian stories of broken nuptials and reconciliations in a number of plays from now on, but his interest in them seems to precede their exploitation on the stage. They give, as Brian Gibbons pointed out in the Arden edition, 'a feeling of modernity, through detailed setting and characterization, to tales which have their origins deep in folklore'. He was conscious of those deeper patterns. Their antiquity and simplicity underlie the strength of his dramatic treatments, as the *Romeo* sonnets suggest and the play itself wonderfully confirms. He not only does not mind elements of melodramatic unrealism, he delights in them because they make the quasi-magical depths of drama transparent to his audience.

In this play there are moments of silence that one can experience only in the theatre. The alterations of pace and tone are as exact as if the whole play were a piece of music. It uses some of the techniques of a sonnet sequence. Shakespeare may have thought that the story really happened. It was legendary of course, but an Italian writer in 1530 gave it a real historical setting, and in 1594 it was mentioned in a history of Verona.

The first scene is a brilliant construction: a quarrel between comic and obscene servants draws in their masters, citizens break up the fight, old Capulet and old Montague make to join in, and the Prince's entry creates a silence. In the ensuing explanations the main characters are introduced. Romeo is in the woods melancholy with love in the freshness of the early morning which sets a tone for many images, though the bud is as usual 'bit with an envious worm' by line 149. Romeo speaks in sonnet-like couplets which have a certain falsity, and yet some hints of truth. One can see how the real thing is going to devastate him.

> Love is a smoke rais'd with the fume of sighs;
> Being purg'd, a fire sparkling in lovers' eyes;
> Being vex'd, a sea nourish'd with loving tears.
> What is it else?

The next scene makes it plain that Juliet is not quite fourteen, Shakespeare having reduced her age from eighteen in his original to intensify her freshness and her innocence. She is new, no one knows her yet, she is about Judith's age, and Shakespeare uses a boy of about that age to play her.

> At my poor house look to behold this night
> Earth-treading stars that make dark heaven light.
> Such comfort as do lusty young men feel
> When well-apparell'd April on the heel
> Of limping winter treads, even such delight
> Among fresh female buds shall you this night
> Inherit at my house. . . .

That is old Capulet: Romeo re-enters and shows his range of personality by talking prose, but when love comes into question he and Benvolio exchange sestets of sonnets and leave with a formal couplet. The third scene gives us the most original character in the play, and one of its most memorable speeches: the traditional Nurse of Italian comedies transformed into an old English countrywoman, much more moving and more interesting than a clown, though she may have been played by one. The wonder-working ingredient is her not being exactly a low character but speaking in verse, in which her vernacular rhythms in descant with the verse lines create a completely new kind of poetry:

> 'Tis since the earthquake now eleven years;
> And she was wean'd – I never shall forget it –
> Of all the days of the year, upon that day;
> For I had then laid wormwood to my dug,
> Sitting in the sun under the dove-house wall;
> My lord and you were then at Mantua.

> Nay, I do bear a brain. But, as I said,
> When it did taste the wormwood on the nipple
> Of my dug, and felt it bitter, pretty fool,
> To see it tetchy, and fall out with the dug!

Romeo gets into the feast as a masquer, but in the next scene we meet Mercutio and a second new kind of poetry, focusing on minute detail. It recalls the fairy scenes of the *Dream*, but being a monologue its description can go beyond them. Mercutio's Queen Mab speech is immensely spirited and densely full of images both delicate and comic, as if Mercutio had pepper in his veins. He deals with lovers' illusions:

> She is the fairies' midwife, and she comes
> In shape no bigger than an agate stone
> On the fore-finger of an alderman,
> Drawn with a team of little atomies
> Athwart men's noses as they lie asleep. . . .

We are only in scene iv of act 1, but in it Romeo already sees or surmises his fate. The feast scene, like the fight scene, begins with servants, all the hustle and bustle of a great house, before it concentrates on old Capulet and his guests, on hot-blooded Tybalt and the masquers. Romeo and Juliet at once fall in love among these dangerous circumstances.

The immediacy of love puzzled the Elizabethans like any other phenomenon of nature. Aubrey, in his *Miscellanies*, places love at first sight between ecstasy and second sight, in a chapter called 'Glances of Love and Malice': '*Amor ex oculo*: Love is from the eye: but (as the Lord Bacon saith) more by glances, than by full gazings; and so for envy and malice. . . .' He quotes a stanza from Fletcher's *Cupid's Revenge*. ''Tis something divine and inexplicable. It is strange, that as one walks the street sometimes one shall meet with an aspect (of male or female) that pleases our souls; and whose natural sweetness of nature we could boldly rely upon. . . . Gaze not on a maid, saith Ecclus. 9.5.' These flashes of recognition or of love have special importance in the theatre: they are the most intense illusion of a world which is all illusion. *Romeo and Juliet* is an extremely convincing play.

> Now old desire doth in his death-bed lie,
> And young affection gapes to be his heir. . . .

In the first scene of act 2 Mercutio makes the sexual implications very plain, but he withdraws, leaving Romeo and Juliet alone for their balcony scene, and all the more innocently and intensely in love by contrast with Mercutio's delicately sharp bawdy. The language of the lovers is both cosmic and intimate:

> . . . wert thou as far
> As that vast shore wash'd with the farthest sea,
> I should adventure. . . .

> . . . by yonder blessed moon I vow,
> That tips with silver all these fruit-tree tops. . . .

They are allowed a lyrical beauty that is new to tragedy and not to be found in Shakespeare before the *Dream*. The scene takes on tension because they are bound to be interrupted, and are so, 'And fleckel'd darkness like a drunkard reels From forth day's path.' I find it hard not to think in this famous scene of the Hathaway orchard at Shottery, and in the next of the old priest of Temple Grafton, the curer of sick hawks, but these are temerarious ruminations, and I only admit to entertaining them because I am sure they occur to other readers. The friar gathering herbs in the forest is a stock character in literature as in life; so is his sententious speech, and so, of course, is the moonlight on the fruit trees. The friar's powers are both religious and in a way magical, through his closeness to natural magic:

> Within the infant rind of this weak flower
> Poison hath residence, and medicine power. . . .

Mercutio and Benvolio meet in prose: Mercutio's is as remarkable as his verse. He is as voluble as a clown, but perfectly controlled, as extravagant as Greene or Nashe but sharper: he flickers, he glimmers, his words are a swordplay. His mannered conversation is lithe and full of energy. This longish prose scene might have strayed from comedy, though Romeo, the Nurse and Mercutio all take part in it. Juliet in the next sticks to her verse, though the Nurse has one prose outburst, but her verse when she speaks it is better than ever.

The third act opens with the duel scene, with Mercutio mostly in prose, which permits fantastical wit and his usual touch of hot spice and humour. 'I am peppered, I warrant, for this world. A plague a both your houses! Zounds, a dog, a rat, a mouse, a cat, to scratch a man to death! A braggart, a rogue, a villain, that fights by the book of arithmetic! Why the devil came you between us? I was hurt under your arm.' He is given just four verse lines as his closure, which are sad but antiheroic in tone.

Juliet, in scene ii, almost incredibly but in the context of the last scene effectively, speaks lines that recall Marlowe's *Edward II*, and the tragedy of Phaeton from Ovid. She is mature at a blow, and the tragedy which is now to run its course begins to be audible in her verse, though the plot has not yet really predetermined it. Love already has the aspect of death, but one must not exaggerate that aspect.

> Spread thy close curtain, love-performing night,
> That runaways' eyes may wink, and Romeo
> Leap to these arms, untalk'd of and unseen.
> Lovers can see to do their amorous rites
> By their own beauties; or if love be blind,

> It best agrees with night. Come, civil night,
> Thou sober-suited matron, all in black,
> And learn me how to lose a winning match,
> Play'd for a pair of stainless maidenhoods;
> Hood my unmann'd blood, bating in my cheeks,
> With thy black mantle, till strange love grows bold,
> Think true love acted simple modesty.

I have quoted this at some length because it is yet a third completely original kind of poetry. It can exist only on the lips of a young woman passionately longing for her first complete encounter. It could not have been written in any other way, because Shakespearean men are less modest and more knowing, as Mercutio was. It is not just a character study, but love poetry of a radically new kind: a poetry of full-blooded, innocent desire. It is not voyeuristic like Nashe, and indeed Ovid, nor has it any touch of coyness or comedy, like certain Elizabethan lyrics, nor of course is it obscene, as innocence observed so often is in Italian renaissance comedies. Marlowe's *Hero and Leander* is very beautiful but, typically of its Greek origins, voyeuristic and elegantly knowing: Juliet is something new.

As the play enters deeper into tragedy it continues to astound. The fifth scene of act 3 with its larks and nightingales is an unlooked-for transmutation of the earlier balcony scene. The old Capulets are very incisively sketched, and it is possible that Shakespeare, who played old men's parts, may have played old Capulet. The Friar's description of his potion in act 4 is blood-chilling: one knows it will go wrong, and all the scenes to do with it create anxiety, which at this stage, the lovers being parted, carries the play. Juliet's potion monologue is gruesome and of course prophetic, but above all it is exciting: one is desperate to know what happens next, as one is in the horror scenes of *Macbeth*. Shakespeare is writing a new kind of play that has no rules yet. It is not a melodrama, and a million miles from *Arden of Feversham*, which is earlier, or John Webster, who is later. Its strength is to combine elements that did not look as if they could combine. The Capulet preparations for a wedding feast are like those for the earlier feast, and make the point that throughout domestic tragedies the lives of great houses simply go on. The Nurse's memoirs expressed that same stability:

> I have a head, sir, that will find out logs,
> And never trouble Peter for the matter.

It is the Nurse who finds Juliet 'dead'. The formal lamentation that follows moves so swiftly from tone to tone that it looks like parody; the more ridiculous grief is, the more one thinks it may be real, but I do think Paris is meant to be funny, one is meant to despise him, and the musicians are pure farce. I find this scene in very strange taste, and can only feebly note that in the theatre it works. At the end of act 4 one does not know what to think or what to feel, except fear for the future.

Act 5 begins with Romeo in exile, and his thrilling description of the apothecary's shop. The verse recalls the style of Mercutio's Queen Mab speech, being equally crammed with strange and fresh details. I take the alligator to be for love potions, which is how South American tribesmen still use it. I do not know what other use it would have. The Shakespeare scholar Steevens saw one in an apothecary's shop in Limehouse in the eighteenth century, and Nashe refers to 'an apothecary's crocodile, or dried alligator'. If they are not American then they are Egyptian; Shakespeare is interested in exotic things from Egypt, but this is just something in a London shop, at the time when apothecaries were persecuted by licensed doctors for exceeding their permitted limits. It is one of the oddest vignettes of Shakespeare's London we possess.

> I do remember an apothecary,
> And hereabouts a dwells, which late I noted
> In tatt'red weeds, with overwhelming brows,
> Culling of simples. Meagre were his looks;
> Sharp misery had worn him to the bones;
> And in his needy shop a tortoise hung,
> An alligator stuff'd, and other skins
> Of ill-shap'd fishes; and about his shelves
> A beggarly account of empty boxes,
> Green earthen pots, bladders, and musty seeds,
> Remnants of packthread, and old cakes of roses
> Were thinly scatter'd, to make up a show.

He is an antitype of Friar Laurence, some lesser Doctor Dee, blushing unseen, someone who might observe the effect of snow in delaying the putrefaction of a dead chicken. Bacon died doing that. Romeo thinks him sinister, but Shakespeare relishes him. The apothecary has a meagre part, the description is all, one's curiosity remains unsatisfied.

The end of *Romeo* is rather swift; its core is the wild scene of the opening of the tomb. It concludes with skilfully brief explanations. The Friar is not punished because 'We still have known thee for a holy man'. The families are reconciled in the last few lines, as if somehow the natural magic had worked after all. If you count love as natural magic, so it had. Romeo and Juliet might just as easily have lived to be old until almost the last moment of the play, but it is their tragedy that defines their love, and their death that defines the intensity of their emotion.

Shakespeare at his busiest not only mingled the forms of various kinds of plays in his constant wrestle for new variations, but he alternated between kinds, not probably because he chose to do so but by demand. His *Richard*

II was utterly unlike his *Richard III*, being intended for the first of a new series, another four histories from a similar period, linking up at the end with those he had already written. He begins with a weak king, as in *Henry VI* he began with a child king, but this time the dynastic wars have a different colouring, and the climax is not the diabolical hunchback but heroic Henry V, the only perfect king Shakespeare ever portrayed, and perhaps the only king he ever admired. He wrote these four new plays in chronological series over several years as before, and paused before writing the climax as before.

Richard II has no prose, no jokes, plenty of rhyme, and blank verse of high quality. It admits no commoners at all except royal servants. We are back in a world of kings and nobles with its own decorum and impetus, but the King around whom it centres is a green reed of weakness and of poetry. The King's deposition scene was never printed until 1608, the fourth quarto edition, and not fully until the Folio in 1623. Shakespeare thought no good had come of that abdication, and Richard II ends very ominously. Henry feels it as much as Richard does: Cirencester burns, and civil war and pestilence are clearly to follow.

Richard II may possibly be meant to follow on an obscurer play called *Thomas of Woodstock*; Richard had murdered Thomas, but this historical connection does not necessarily imply a literary link, though a verbal echo of the phrase 'pelting farm' (paltry farm) is suggestive. The subject of historical tragedy was a fraught one for the Elizabethans, and political philosophers interpreted its essence in more ways than one. Fulke Greville had to suppress a tragedy for political reasons, so he says. Under Henry VIII a shepherd near Chipping Camden read Polydore Vergil on the nemesis of fifteenth-century kings. I do not think that *Richard II* at least is the vengeance of God on tyrants, but it is a play about nemesis, and the nemesis extends beyond it, to be purged only with the death of Henry IV.

The play was widely discussed and very popular. On the eve of Essex's crazy rebellion, one of his followers had it revived in the public theatre. When old William Lambarde, the Canute expert who was antiquary to the Queen, brought some documents from the archives in the Tower to show her at Greenwich, she cried out, 'Do you not know that *I* am Richard II?' She complained this play had been 'shown forty times in open streets and houses'. Yet Richard was proverbial before Shakespeare's treatment of him. In 1578 Sir Francis Knollys, treasurer of the royal household, wrote to the Queen he would not 'play the parts of Richard II's men', would not flatter. Lord Hunsdon wrote something similar in the 1580s. Ralegh wrote to Robert Cecil in July 1597, 'I acquainted my Lord General [Essex] with your letter to me and your kind acceptance of your entertainment, he was also wonderfully merry at the conceit of Richard II. I hope it shall never alter, and whereof I shall be most glad of, as the true way to all our good, quiet and advancement, and most of all for her sake whose affairs shall thereby find better progression.'

Shakespeare's play was published soon after that letter. One of the charges against Essex at his trial in 1600 was his connection with John Hayward's prose history *King Henry IV (part one)*, of which Essex had had the dedication to him suppressed when it appeared the year before. Hayward went to prison. A note of evidence to be used against Essex records 'the Earl himself being so often present at the playing thereof, and with great applause giving countenance and liking to the same'. Essex was descended from Thomas of Woodstock. The preachers in 1601 claimed his treason went back six or seven years, which confirms a date for the first vogue of the new play in 1595–6. The second editions of *Richard II* and *Richard III* (1597) and the *Love's Labour's Lost* of 1598 are the first plays printed with Shakespeare's name on them.

Shakespeare used Holinshed and other chronicles for his play, but he added a good deal: the gardener, the mirror, the groom, Gaunt's death scene, Aumerle's scene with York, and Henry's lament over Richard for example. Some of his sources were French. Although the common people have no part in the action, England does: it is almost the hero, 'such dear souls'. The people have more and more part in the later plays of the series, culminating in *Henry V*, which is Shakespeare's final and classic statement on the English people.

Critics have sneered at Richard as being like 'a poet' or 'a bad poet'. This is certainly nonsense; Richard's slightly hysterical edge is not only part of his character, but it permits him to speak in more haunting and more penetrating poetry. Shakespeare has already explored this avenue of expression in *Henry VI* and *Richard III*, and of course in his love plays. Heightened emotion, always in contrast with other speakers, and sometimes verging on madness, had been a fundamental instrument in the theatre since Marlowe and Kyd, but Shakespeare had now refined it into a devastating stillness.

The formal quarrel of Bolingbroke and Mowbray is touched from the beginning by the King's language: they are 'In rage, deaf as the sea, hasty as fire'. Such noblemen did not seem unreal at the time – the prudent Robert Cecil at forty and Lord Hertford at over seventy tried to fight a duel in the August of 1609 – but the King's words formalize, and their own words formalize and freeze their conflict, until it seems a phenomenon of nature. They are formidable, and their encounter is going to be awe-inspiring, its causes almost mythic in stature:

> . . . Sluic'd out his innocent soul through streams of blood;
> Which blood, like sacrificing Abel's, cries,
> Even from the tongueless caverns of the earth,
> To me for justice and rough chastisement. . . .

Kingship is to be mythologized as well as vengeance, in the language of John of Gaunt's wife which separates the first two scenes and two stages of Bolingbroke's quarrel:

> Edward's seven sons, whereof thyself art one,
> Were as seven vials of his sacred blood,
> Or seven fair branches springing from one root.

Gaunt, with his age and dignity, has dominated the stage from the opening of scene i by force of his mere name, then scene by scene established his authority until one is more interested in the father's grief than his son's exile. In the third scene he has couplets to speak where others have almost none. Mowbray and Bolingbroke use them for closures of resignation, Gaunt for a more deep-seated and expressive sadness. When it comes to parting advice, he drops the couplets to speak more vigorously; the scene ends with famous lines about the weakness of self-delusion which have a resonance throughout the play: they are the first crack of thunder of the storm to come. The last scene of the act establishes the awfulness and nastiness of Richard's Court, and the machinery of his fall through the Irish war. Aumerle is a minor Mercutio. Richard's most shocking offence is the climax of the act: he wishes John of Gaunt were poisoned.

> Now put it, God, in the physician's mind
> To help him to his grave immediately!
> The lining of his coffers shall make coats
> To deck our soldiers for these Irish wars.

Gaunt's death scene is a prophecy of powerful poetry, sonnet-like in structure. The influence of the sonnet sequence in *Romeo* persists in *Richard II*, but with a lighter touch, with fainter hints to the audience of what verse structure he is using. In the theatre one is hardly conscious of what devices he uses, though at one's desk it becomes obvious. Part of Gaunt's power is his proverbial quality of speech: it has roots that make it sound genuine.

> His rash fierce blaze of riot cannot last,
> For violent fires soon burn out themselves;
> Small showers last long, but sudden storms are short. . . .

From these proverbs he bursts into his eloquent praises of England, which are only one part of a furious lament for the harm done by Richard II. The substance of his argument is that England of the glorious kings, impregnable and sea-defended, famous in the Crusades, 'Is now leas'd out . . . Like to a tenement or pelting farm'. England that was bounded by the sea is now 'bound in with shame, With inky blots and rotten parchment bonds'. Is this passionate denunciation without a contemporary relevance for Shakespeare's audience? It seems to me the very voice of

Warwickshire in the 1590s, wildly libertarian and distinctly reproachful to the monarchy. The speech is left vague because if Gaunt's complaints were more closely defined the play could not be presented. To whom is England leased out, and what are the rotten parchment bonds? I do not think Shakespeare's feelings are realistic, but they are deeply felt, like all farmers' feelings about modern times. To pluck out only the lines about 'This precious stone set in the silver sea' (a piece of his old, surreal vividness) is to lose sight of one of the most important speeches in his history plays. The scene proceeds to the reversal of nature in its many forms: 'Seen how his son's son should destroy his sons', and so forth. Richard is told a thousand flatterers sit within his crown: later he will realize that death sits there.

Gaunt is dying of course: 'The ripest fruit first falls, and so doth he,' but it will not be the last, and by the end of this first scene of act 2 the rebellion has already broken out. The play so far, fine as it is and without a boring moment (unlike early histories), has only set up the machinery that is now in motion. In the second scene the Queen feels the future, as Juliet suddenly felt it, and the bad news and the ineffective measures begin: obvious devices that never fail. In scene iii Bolingbroke's invading army appears: they are lost in the wilds of Gloucestershire, 'These high wild hills and rough uneven ways'. The Cotswolds are called 'Cotshall', just as Evesham was 'Easam' to Robert Armin. Shakespeare knew the country near Berkeley Castle, but it is surprising to see what he thought about it. One must think away roads and good weather and the extent of modern cultivation and the size of modern villages. As late as the eighteenth century Gilbert White of Selborne referred to the Downs as high mountains.

This scene introduces Harry Percy, the budding Hotspur. Shakespeare has invented the encounter, which adds to the gallantry of the episode and the accumulating power of Bolingbroke. The Duke of York's tetchy phrase 'Tut, tut! Grace me no grace, nor uncle me no uncle' is based on a similar bit of tetchiness by old Capulet. His argument with the invader is an excuse to show what fragments of right are on his side.

The last scene of the act is brief, and meant only to show the desertion of Richard's allies. His absence in Ireland is useful, since in his absence he can no longer be his offensive self, and by the time we see him again we have begun to pity him. Yet this tiny scene has wonderful lines, prophetic like Gaunt's, but in another vein.

> The bay trees in our country are all wither'd,
> And meteors fright the fixed stars of heaven;
> The pale-fac'd moon looks bloody on the earth,
> And lean-look'd prophets whisper fearful change . . .
> These signs forerun the death or fall of kings.

The third act shows the capture of Bushy and Greene, Richard at Barkloughly (*Hertlowli*, meaning *Harlech*, but the mistake is in Holinshed) and his collapse. 'Let's talk of graves, of worms, and epitaphs; Make dust our paper, and with rainy eyes Write sorrow. . . .' There is something narcissistic about his exquisiteness of speech, so that one knows he is going to suffer a disaster. It is akin to the false poetry of lovers who are not going to be faithful (Romeo and Rosalind for example), and yet true at the same time. 'Not all the water in the rough rude sea Can wash the balm off from an anointed king. . . . Weak men must fall; for heaven still guards the right.' Blood can wash it off, and the right is not on his side. Richard's magic begins with his softness and self-pity. He is like Christ in a mystery play, he is not a tyrant like Herod, but a born loser, a king of shadows meditating on the death of kings. His fall is unlike any earlier tragedy; it is more like the fall of leaves. 'A king, woe's slave, shall kingly woe obey.' Against such weakness, Bolingbroke's trumpets sound too harsh a blast:

> Go to the rude ribs of that ancient castle;
> Through brazen trumpet send the breath of parley
> Into his ruin'd ears. . . .

The King's submission is ironic and exaggerated, but none of his verse is merely virtuoso, like Mercutio on Mab and Romeo on the apothecary; it has a deadly dramatic force, even at its most fantastical, because the increasing fear of death affects it. The moralizing gardener and his man among the 'dangling apricocks' mirror Richard's fall in the imagery of nature and of popular wisdom until it seems impersonal. 'He that hath suffer'd this disorder'd spring Hath now himself met with the fall of leaf.' One event has a luxuriant multiplicity of images, but everything is enacted as well as said.

The fourth act is the single scene in which Richard is deposed, Henry IV crowned and Richard indicted. In the last act Henry IV has his first troubles, Richard is murdered, and Henry grieves:

> Lords, I protest my soul is full of woe
> That blood should sprinkle me to make me grow. . . .
> I'll make a voyage to the Holy Land,
> To wash this blood off from my guilty hand.
> March sadly after; grace my mournings here
> In weeping after this untimely bier.

Shakespeare broke this series of histories in order to write *King John*. Perhaps he was asked to revise an old play. I date it with reluctance and diffidence to just after Hamnet's death. It is streaked with violence and horror of death, but the equation of life with literature is certainly not a proper criterion for dating the play. One must use whatever other criteria are available, and seek no more certainty than the nature of the evidence permits. *King John* is similar to *Richard II* in some ways, but less exquisite. It is just possible that it had a strong political resonance, in the analogy of Hubert's fate with that of the Queen's secretary William Davison, sent to the Tower as scapegoat for the murder of Mary Queen of Scots (but royal murderers often become scapegoats, as Exton does in *Richard II*), and of Arthur's claim to the throne with Mary's (too dangerous to be likely). Shakespeare apparently intended only the lightest allusion, but he does manipulate the historical facts of John's reign to make them fit the Queen's: suspicion of bastardy, excommunication, defiance of the Pope, imprisonment of a rival, foreign invasion and a wrecked fleet, and England unified against foreign threats. Here as usual it is not precise allusions to contemporary characters and events, but the tidal flow and massive momentum of English history that make sense of the play. I do not think Essex is the Messianic Bastard, but Shakespeare knew the type, and so did other writers of the day.

The religious polemics of the older anonymous play, *The Troublesome Raigne of John, King of England* (1591), and the Bastard's bombast in it, make it unlikely to be an early work of Shakespeare, but Shakespeare's *King John* does use it. *The Troublesome Raigne* will scarcely (to my mind) pass muster even as a bad or corrupt version of an earlier Shakespeare sketch of this subject. He may well have acted in it as a young man, but the plot is not his. He abolishes Peter's prophecy from it, which entailed five moons on stage, and the Abbey looting, and the scurrility, and developed the Bastard in a line of character that leads from Mercutio to Hotspur, and the theme of commodity and its corruption which begins in John of Gaunt's dying prophecy. But dramatic tension is less in *King John* than in *Richard II*, lyrical impetus is exhausted: this play is less perfect in conception. On the other hand, all this being said I think it underestimated by most critics and have always thought so: Masefield felt the same. Nor is it careless; Shakespeare and not *The Troublesome Raigne* writer has ransacked chronicles, including manuscript ones. We must assume he knew Stowe and later Camden, and probably Lambarde; his copy of Lambarde's *Archaeonomia* is in the Folger Library.

Act 1 is tough, hard and sensuous. John is Holinshed's John, but the other royal characters are Shakespeare's. He hates these people and their story; their world is as alien to him as ancient Rome, and as cold-blooded. He finds the torture horrifying, and the people following their mad prophet lamentable. To increase pathos and express suffering he transforms Arthur from a soldier to a young boy speaking in simple words. The scolding match of Eleanor and Constance is meant to appal; it is often cut in modern productions. The Bastard has the star part, and his monologue near the end of act 1 has a Mercutian taste of gunpowder and of detail. His verse rhythms are the liveliest yet of their kind. His satiric tone is sour and vigorous. He brings to mind the anonymous madrigal set by Thomas Weelkes about this time and published in 1600:

> The Andalusian merchant, that returns
> Laden with cochineal and china dishes
> Reports in Spain how strangely Fogo burns
> Amidst an ocean full of flying fishes. . . .

The year 1596 saw the death of Drake, twenty years after his journey round the world: the Bastard's interest has to be limited to Europe, but it expresses the same hungry curiosity and the same underlying rapacity as inspired Drake's generation.

The use of stanza form and couplets in the first two acts have dwindled to mere touches. Lewis of France in act 2 is sonnet-like, and gets a mocking stanza from the Bastard. Arthur in act 2 is a boy star: good, lyrical and doomed; but his mother is an *Ate* from Seneca, a word the Folio misspells as Ace. The English volunteers are Leicester's men or Essex's men, an appalling rabble:

> Rash, inconsiderate, fiery voluntaries,
> With ladies' faces and fierce dragons' spleens. . . .
> In brief, a braver choice of dauntless spirits
> Than now the English bottoms have waft o'er
> Did never float upon the swelling tide
> To do offence and scathe in Christendom.

Undertones of patriotism persist in contrast with realism and roughness, down to 'that pale, that white-fac'd shore, Whose foot spurns back the ocean's roaring tides', which recalls John of Gaunt's speech. The white cliffs Shakespeare knew best were those of the Isle of Wight; it is a pity he never had cause to mention Alum Bay. His local settings are firm and deliberate in these history plays; topography and antiquity went together. In *Richard II* Coventry was real, and St Lambert's Day which was celebrated there was real; in this play it is Northampton and St Edmundsbury and Swinstead. 'The mutines of Jerusalem', mutineers out of the Jewish *Antiquities* of Josephus, may perhaps take us back to Coventry, because Strange's Men had a play about them, and one was acted at Coventry in 1584 and again in 1591. The images in *King John* are the more sinister for being homely, like those of Aeschylus – blooding at a foxhunt for example:

> Their armours that march'd hence so silver-bright
> Hither return all gilt with Frenchmen's blood . . .
> And like a jolly troop of huntsmen come
> Our lusty English, all with purpled hands,
> Dy'd in the dying slaughter of their foes.

Death goes mousing, Time is a clock setter, an old bald sexton, 'Preach some philosophy to make me mad', the imprisoned child will look hollow, dim, meagre, 'And so he'll die,' and his mother will not know him in heaven.

The Bastard's tone is victorious; he becomes a hero in act 5. His monologues end every act of the play except the third, and mark his transformation, the seed of Prince Henry's into Henry V. All the same, his bragging in the second scene of the act may be splendid, but we have had enough of it, and Shakespeare's heart is not in it. Yet the King dying of poison in the monastic orchard is written in fire. It is briefer than other royal deaths, and more terrible, more telling. His lament comes before he is carried on to the stage:

> I am the cygnet to this pale faint swan
> Who chants a doleful hymn to his own death,
> And from the organ-pipe of frailty sings. . . .

The King's words express the physical agony of the poison. This last scene of the play is the best thing in it, and makes a climax so powerful that one scarcely has ears for the Bastard's heroic epilogue.

King John foreshadows a blacker kind of tragedy that is coming soon. It would be tempting to say all its poetry comes from *Richard II* and earlier works – castles have 'flinty ribs' and so on; but in fact it raises the question of two unexpected influences on Shakespeare: that of Henry VIII's laureate John Skelton, because it refers to Skelton's poem 'Philip Sparrow', and that of Ronsard. Shakespeare would be bound to appreciate such a free and hilariously funny poet as Skelton, and there are a number of points of contact. Skelton was edited in 1588, Angel Day in his letter-writing manual *The English Secretary* added a few lines to the canon in 1586, Burton collected him, and the 1588 excellent anonymous translation of six idylls by the Greek bucolic poet Theocritus imitates a stanza form of his, so it is not strange that Shakespeare should have read him. The Ronsard connection is the image of Britain as a floating island which Neptune might remove and plant somewhere else (act 5, scene ii, lines 33f.), which I am sure must come from his poem to Queen Elizabeth. If Shakespeare really read Ronsard's poem, as he must have done, then he knew Ronsard's prophecy of his own birth. And through Ronsard he knew Pindar.

The Merchant of Venice continued Shakespeare's miscellaneous Italian series. It was registered, presumably to prevent piracy, in July 1598, and Meres knew it then, but it was not printed until 1600. In this play Shylock is a towering tragic figure who scarcely fits into a world of comedy and reconciled love. He disorients its form worse than King John disorients the form of history. When his frightful vengeance is foiled, he is made to be a 'Christian' like those London Jews that Shakespeare knew. W. H. Auden in *The Dyer's Hand* treats the problem with more than his usual brilliant subtlety and wide reading, and his distinction between the Arcadian Belmont and urban Venice is surely right, but he does not solve the problem of Shylock, because he is really more interested in Christianity as a universal reconciliation, and Antonio as a homosexual lover excluded from paradise. Shylock is etched in darkness and his suffering is overwhelming. His rage for revenge must in the terms of the theatre be punished: in a tragedy it would have ended in mutual slaughter, and the comedy of reconciliation is inadequate because he belongs in a tragedy. Hence the length and the cosmic imagery of the end of the play: but no comic framework can really be constructed which will contain Shylock.

Bassanio may well take his name from Emilia Bassano, as A. L. Rowse pointed out: it is somehow satisfying that the connection with Court music recurs in a later generation, since a direct linear descendant of Bassano played a trombone at the wedding of the Prince of Wales. Shakespeare certainly knew Bassano. But I do not think Shylock is based on poor Lopez, the Elizabethan Jew; he is just the Jew from the Italian story *Il Pecorone* and the *Ballad of Gernutus*. His name is like Mr Bones the Butcher, or Falstaff (Fall-staff) the drunken lecher, from his being a miser. Shakespeare makes him a densely complex character: comic, savage, crafty, profoundly suffering, all within only five scenes of *The Merchant of Venice*. The play itself is complex because of him, and one hears the tempest singing in the wind in more tones than one in its opening scene.

The *Andrew*, the great ship run aground in the first thirty lines, was taken at Cadiz in 1596, and the play probably written soon afterwards. In 1597 Essex asked the Queen's permission to anchor 'under the Isle of Wight' because of the danger of the Goodwin Sands 'this ill-time of the year, especially the St. Andrew'. Had Shakespeare seen her there?

> But I should think of shallows and of flats,
> And see my wealthy Andrew dock'd in sand,
> Vailing her high top lower than her ribs
> To kiss her burial. Should I go to church
> And see the holy edifice of stone,
> And not bethink me straight of dangerous rocks,
> Which, touching but my gentle vessel's side,
> Would scatter all her spices on the stream,
> Enrobe the roaring waters with my silks. . . .

Salerio is suggesting that Antonio's strange sadness comes from business worries, but the play unfolds it as a sort of love melancholy over Bassanio, and perhaps something deeper, since Shakespeare, like Burton, believed in mysterious and unassuagable grief:

> I am a tainted wether of the flock,
> Meetest for death; the weakest kind of fruit
> Drops earliest to the ground, and so let me.

One of the principal themes of *The Merchant of Venice* is the bond of flesh, miserable, vulnerable, loving human flesh that by marriage mirrors heaven, as opposed to alliance of gold, which is deceiving, subject to fortune, and good only when given.

Antonio, like Shylock, is in some way an outsider. He thinks the world 'A stage, where every man must play a part, And mine a sad one'. But the play is swept by tides of boisterous jollity. As a child, my favourite characters in it were Gratiano and Launcelot Gobbo; Shylock was too terrifying. Acted by Donald Wolfit he was as bad as Fagin, and far too terrible to be sad; his grief was just a crazy poetry. Still, it would be rash to maintain that Shakespeare does not intend the depths of his characters or the submerged currents of his plays. What one might perhaps say is that Shylock begins as a closely observed comic character, but he takes over, as characters will in any fiction that feeds on reality, and gets out of hand. The awe-inspiring result is the play we have, in which final reconciliation is not a final consolation.

Each of its first three scenes shows a new star part, and the first act taken as a whole reveals a world. The world is London with its attendant great houses, and its commercial reality at the core; it is not really Italy apart from a few strokes of colouring. Portia is weary as Antonio is: this is not a happy world except for lovers on its fringes. The luscious wording denotes a 'comic' world, but it also presages disaster, loss and squandering as surely as in *Richard II*. Shakespeare values money, his view of masques is unenthusiastic; here as in *Romeo* and *King John* and the verses of Thomas Combe, these revels have their sinister side. The sums of money are serious: three thousand ducats is what the Queen might spend; Shylock's best diamond is worth two thousand, but forty ducats is the normal price of a diamond.

The Prince of Morocco in the second act is attractive and sexually active, though we find out later that Portia loathes the idea of having to marry him, and perhaps we should assume so from the beginning. The English were slave-traders and racially self-satisfied; Morocco is another outsider. I think Shakespeare likes him, and he is worth examining as a foretaste of Othello. Launcelot Gobbo's scene with his father is based on the pleasing story of Will Summers, the jester to Henry VIII who died under Elizabeth, and his Shropshire uncle, which Robert Armin tells. Young Gobbo owes something to Launce in *The Two Gentlemen of Verona*, but fits more closely into the action and even into the deep pattern of this play. Under Elizabethan law no servant could leave his master without a testimonial on pain of a year's imprisonment. This clown's affectionate relationship with Jessica serves to redeem both of them. His intimacy is a clown's rather than a servant's; Shylock is too mean to keep a proper servant, so he employs this natural clown, but he is glad to be rid of him:

> Lock up my doors, and when you hear the drum,
> And the vile squealing of the wry-neck'd fife,
> Clamber not you up to the casements then . . .
> But stop my house's ears – I mean my casements;
> Let not the sound of shallow fopp'ry enter
> My sober house.

The scene is real enough, because masquers did parade the streets of London. The bagpipes in act 1 and act 4 are real too: 'If they hear the bagpipe then the bears are coming' is in the *Oxford English Dictionary* from a 1625 manuscript. Spenser calls them 'the solace of the rural bride', and they seem to have been particularly obnoxious in Lincolnshire and Lancashire. Shakespeare thought they were a joke, but Armin records village people dancing to them.

Lorenzo steals Jessica, and the Jew is mocked before the end of act 2, but it is at least implied that the Duke is on Shylock's side, if only because he has been robbed. The clouds darken over Antonio, and one feels at this point that the play must end in tragedy by mere process of natural sanction. But if this is a play rooted in natural justice, then it is harsh justice. The Prince of Arragon chooses the silver casket being obsessed with honour, and his reward is a fool's head. His only discernible sin is pride. Shakespeare will deal severely with the cult of honour in *Henry IV*.

The third act opens with the taunting of Shylock and his unanswerable retort. His prose is as fully characterized as his verse, and as brilliant, and as deadly serious. His rhetoric is so passionate and his argument so close to the bone that neither can be called hollow. As his passion increases through the play, so his style of speech shows more and more possibilities. This passionate, tragic rhetoric in prose is one of Shakespeare's most extraordinary inventions '. . . and no satisfaction, no revenge; nor no ill luck stirring but what lights o' my shoulders; no sighs but o' my breathing; no tears but o' my shedding! . . . Out upon her! Thou torturest me, Tubal. It was my turquoise; I had it of Leah when I was a bachelor; I would not have given it for a wilderness of monkeys.'

Portia and Bassanio speak their beautiful verses and hear pretty music about the deceiving nature of Fancy; brides and grooms come together (somewhat incredibly) until the thunderbolt from Venice scatters them. Antonio petitions Shylock in vain, Portia lays her plot, and Launcelot has a rather poor piece of clowning with Jessica and Lorenzo. He seems to have got a Moorish girl pregnant. This whole scene (act 3, scene v) is tasteless, dispiriting and rather meaningless, but it is certainly by Shakespeare. Launcelot Gobbo is too perky to be earthy; perhaps the scene has an Italian model. It has even been suggested that Shylock owes something to the Pantaloon character of the Commedia dell'arte.

Act 4 is a trial scene of studied eloquence, exciting in the climax and the

The Shakespeare coat of arms.

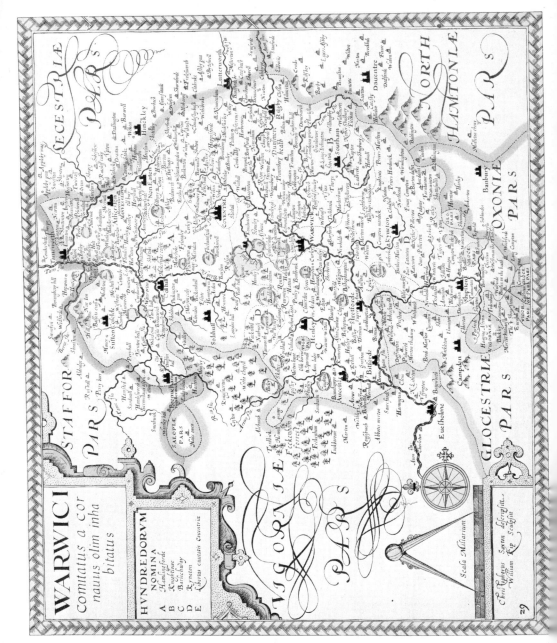

Shakespeare's Warwickshire: Saxton's map of 1576.

Frontispiece to Annalia Dubrensia, *'(being a collection of verses by various writers) Upon the yeerely celebration of Mr. R. Dover's Olimpick Games upon Cotswold Hills', 1636. (See pages 28–9.)*

Two portraits of Shakespeare: (above) *the so-called Chandos portrait, by an unknown artist;* (opposite) *Martin Droeshout's engraving in the First Folio. (See pages 193–4.)*

Dro et hout : sculpsit London.

To the Reader.

This Figure, that thou here seeft put,
   It was for gentle Shakespeare cut;
Wherein the Grauer had a strife
   with Nature, to out-doo the life:
O, could he but haue drawne his wit
   As well in brasse, as he hath hit
Hisface; the Print would then surpasse
   All, that was euer writ in brasse.
But, since he cannot, Reader, looke
   Not on his Picture, but his Booke.

An Elizabethan masque: writers and musicians performing at Sir Henry Unton's wedding feast.

(Left) *Johannes de Witt's drawing of the interior of the Swan Theatre, 1596.*

(Below) *A detail from Claes Janzs Visscher's engraving of London showing the Globe Theatre, 1616.*

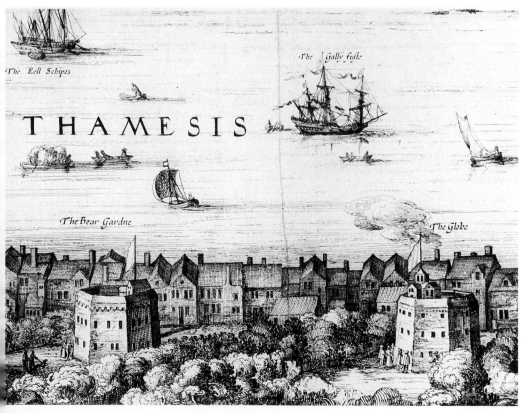

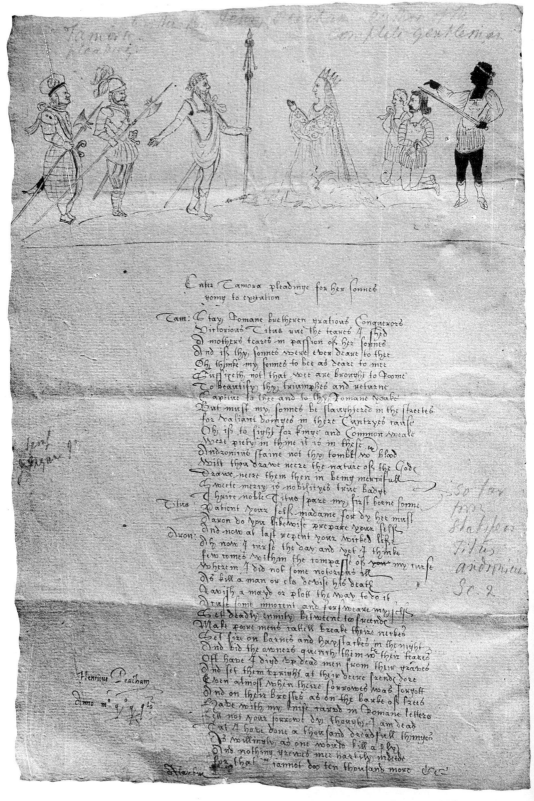

Henry Peacham's drawing of a performance of Titus Andronicus, *1594. (See page 55.)*

hould my performance perish.

Rom. Thou haft *Ventidius* that, without the which a
Souldier and his Sword graunts fcarce diftinction : thou
wilt write to *Anthony.*

Ven. Ile humbly fignifie what in his name,
That magicall word of Warre we haue effected,
How with his Banners,and his well paid ranks,
The nere-yet beaten Horfe of Parthia,
We haue iaded out o'th Field.

Rom. Where is he now?

Ven. He purpofeth to Athens, whither with what haft
The waight we muft conuay with's,will permit :
We fhall appeare before him. On there, paffe along.
                                              Exeunt.

Enter Agrippa at one doore, Enobarbus at another.

Agri. What art the Brothers parted?

Eno. They haue difpatcht with *Pompey*,he is gone,
The other three are Sealing. *Octauia* weepes
To part from Rome: *Cafar* is fad,and *Lepidus*
Since *Pompey's* feaft, as *Menas* faies,is troubled
With the Greene-Sickneffe.

Agri. 'Tis a Noble *Lepidus.*

Eno. A very fine one: oh,how he loues *Cafar.*

Agri. Nay but how deerely he adores *Mark Anthony.*

Eno. *Cafar*? why he's the Iupiter of men.

Ant. What's *Anthony*,the God of Iupiter?

Eno. Spake you of *Cafar*? How,the non-pareill?

Agri. Oh *Anthony*,oh thou Arabian Bird!

Eno. Would you praife *Cafar*,fay *Cafar*,go no further.

Agr. Indeed he plied them both with excellent praifes.

Eno. But he loues *Cafar* beft,yet he loues *Anthony* :
Hoo Hearts,Tongues,Figure,
Scribes,Bards,Poets,cannot
Thinke fpeake, caft, write,fing,number: hoo,
His loue to *Anthony.* But as for *Cafar*,
Kneele downe,kneele downe,and wonder.

Agri. Both he loues.

Eno. They are his Shards,and he their Beetle,fo:
This is to horfe: Adieu,Noble *Agrippa.*

Agri. Good Fortune worthy Souldier,and farewell.

Enter Cafar,Anthony,Lepidus,and Octauia.

Antho. No further Sir.

Cafar. You take from me a great part of my felfe:
Vfe me well in't. Sifter,proue fuch a wife
As my thoughts make thee,and as my fartheft Band
Shall paffe on thy approofe: moft Noble *Anthony*,
Let not the peece of Vertue which is fet
Betwixt vs,as the Cyment of our loue
To keepe it builded,be the Ramme to batter
The Fortreffe of it:for better might we
Haue lou'd without this meane,if on both parts
This be not cherifht.

Ant. Make me not offended,in your diftruft.

Cafar. I haue faid.

Ant. You fhall not finde,
Though you be therein curious,the leſt caufe
For what you feeme to feare,fo the Gods keepe you,
And make the hearts of Romaines ferue your ends :
We will heere part.

Cafar. Farewell my deereft Sifter,fare thee well,
The Elements be kind to thee,and make
Thy fpirits all of comfort : fare thee well.

Octa. My Noble Brother.

Anth. The Aprill's in her eyes, it is Loues fpring,
And thefe the fhowers to bring it on : be cheerfull.

Octa. Sir,looke well to my Husbands houfe : and

Cafar. What *Octauia*?

Octa. Ile tell you in your eare.

Ant. Her tongue will not obey her heart,nor can
Her heart informe her tougue.
The Swannes downe feather
That ftands vpon the Swell at the full Tide :
And neither way inclines.

Eno. Will *Cafar* weepe?

Agr. He ha's a cloud in's face.

Eno. He were the worfe for that were he a Horfe,fo is
he being a man.

Agri. Why *Enobarbus* :
When *Anthony* found *Iulius Cafar* dead,
He cried almoft to roaring : And he wept,
When at Phillippi he found *Brutus* flaine.

Eno. That yeare indeed,he was trobled with a rume,
What willingly he did confound,he wail'd,
Beleeu't till I weepe too.

Cafar. No fweet *Octauia*,
You fhall heare from me ftill : the time fhall not
Out-go my thinking on you.

Ant. Come Sir,come,
Ile wraftle with you in my ftrength of loue,
Looke heere I haue you,thus I let fou go,
And giue you to the Gods.

Cafar. Adieu,be happy.

Lep. Let all the number of the Starres giue light
To thy faire way.

Cafar. Farewell,farewell.   *Kiffes Octauia.*

Ant. Farewell.   *Trumpets found.*   *Exeunt.*

Enter Cleopatra,Charmian,Iras,and Alexas.

Cleo. Where is the Fellow?

Alex. Halfe afeard to come.

Cleo. Go too,go too : Con e hither Sir.
                    Enter the Meffenger as before.

Alex. Good Maieftie: *Herod* of Iury dare not looke
vpon you,but when you are well pleaf'd.

Cleo. That *Herods* head,Ile haue : but how? When
Anthony is gone,through whom I might commaund it:
Come thou neere.

Mef. Moft gratious Maieftie.

Cleo. Did'ft thou behold *Octauia*?

Mef. I dread Queene.

Cleo. Where?

Mef. Madam in Rome,I lookt her in the face: and
faw her led betweene her Brother,and *Marke Anthony.*

Cleo. Is fhe as tall as me?

Mef. She is not Madam.

Cleo. Didft heare her fpeake?
Is fhe fhrill tongu'd or low?

Mef. Madam,I heard her fpeake,fhe is low voic'd.

Cleo. That's not fo good : he cannot like her long.

Char. Like her? Oh *Ifis* :'tis impoffible.

Cleo. I thinke fo *Charmian*:dull of tongue, & dwarfifh
What Maieftie is in her gate,remember
If ere thou look'ft on Maieftie.

Mef. She creepes:her motion,& her ftation are as one.
She fhewes a body,rather then a life,
A Statue,then a Breather.

Cleo. Is this certaine?

Mef. Or I haue no obferuance.

Cha. Three in Egypt cannot make better note.

Cleo. He's very knowing,I do perceiu't,
There's nothing in her yet.

The

A page from the First Folio showing a scene from Antony and Cleopatra *marked for correction by he proofreader.*

The Workes of William Shakespeare,

containing all his Comedies, Histories, and Tragedies: Truely set forth, according to their first ORIGINALL.

The Names of the Principall Actors in all these Playes.

William Shakespeare.	Samuel Gilburne.
Richard Burbadge.	Robert Armin.
John Hemmings.	William Ostler.
Augustine Phillips.	Nathan Field.
William Kempt.	John Underwood.
Thomas Poope.	Nicholas Tooley.
George Bryan.	William Ecclestone.
Henry Condell.	Joseph Taylor.
William Slye.	Robert Benfield.
Richard Cowly.	Robert Goughe.
John Lowine.	Richard Robinson.
Samuell Crosse.	Iohn Shancke.
Alexander Cooke.	Iohn Rice.

(Left) *The list from the First Folio naming the leading actors in Shakespeare's company, the Lord Chamberlain's Men.*

(Below) *Two of the 'principall actors': Richard Tarlton and Robert Armin.*

Kemps nine daies vvonder.

Performed in a daunce from
London to Norwich.

Containing the pleasure, paines and kinde entertainment
of *William Kemp* betweene *London* and that Citty
in his late Morrice.

Wherein is somewhat set downe worth note; to reprooue
the slaunders spred of him: many things merry,
nothing hurtfull.

Written by himselfe to satisfie his friends.

LONDON
Printed by *E. A.* for *Nicholas Ling*, and are to be
solde at his shop at the west doore of Saint
Paules Church. 1600.

Title-page from Kemps Nine Daies Wonder. *The comic actor Will Kemp, a member of the*
Chamberlain's Men from 1594–9, morris-danced his way from London to Norwich in 1600.

Richard Burbage.

William Sly.

Michael Drayton.

Ben Jonson.

(Above) *Henry Wriothesley,*
3rd Earl of Southampton,
1603.

Queen Elizabeth I.

The monument in Titchfield Church, Hampshire, to the 1st Countess of Southampton and to the 1st and 2nd Earls. The kneeling figure on the side of the tomb (facing left) is the 3rd Earl.

The tomb of Alice, Countess of Derby. (See Appendix 1.)

The wall-monument to Shakespeare in Holy Trinity, Stratford-upon-Avon.

interplay of persons and tones. It is Shylock's downfall and the last we hear of him. He is crushed almost to silence under an avalanche of penalties and icy, contemptuous phrases. His part is a diminuendo; after his confidence and rage he is caught, then cornered, then baited, then crushed. Moments of silence are often significant in Shakespeare, and Shylock's exit is one of them. The idiotic intrigue about the rings that follows is like the noise of a cocktail party when the subject is changed after the silence following the news of cancer.

Shakespeare's effort to overcome this problem gives us in the fifth act one of his most magical firework displays. At the end of act 3, scene ii, Bassanio's lyric stanza was a mere twirl, but act 5 is deeply lyrical. Even the succession of classical images that begins it is not pedantic or too rhetorical; the images are a genuine communication and mutual play between the lovers, and are woven into the texture of the play:

> In such a night
> Stood Dido with a willow in her hand
> Upon the wild sea-banks, and waft her love
> To come again to Carthage.

All the instances are tragic, but tragedy is going to be turned into comedy, by Portia (and by resigned Antonio), by 'a good deed in a naughty world'. Heavenly music and real music combine to charm, and Launcelot runs about imitating a hunting horn, his innocence renewed. The earthly music, a hymn to Diana, is lost: we have only Jessica's response. 'I am never merry when I hear sweet music', but Lorenzo makes a little speech which is a minor version of Berowne's praises of love in *Love's Labour*, and of Theseus on imagination in the *Dream*. The intrigue plays itself out pleasantly, and the play is over. It is assumed (act 5, scene i, line 292) that Shylock will die rich, and somehow still is rich. The language of act 5 is true to Shakespeare's normal habits: the sonnet style gets mocked (line 242) and so does cutler's poetry on a knife-blade, though Shakespeare likes that better because of its simple, proverbial wisdom: 'Love me, and leave me not' on a gold wedding ring. Love, mercy and the harmony of the universe itself are victorious: 'The moon sleeps with Endymion, And would not be awak'd.' That is from Marlowe's translation of Ovid: 'the moon sleeps with Endymion every night.'

But the memory of Shylock is not abolished. The injustice of the society he complained of is radical, and his speech on slaves and slavery (act 4, scene i, line 89) is unanswerable. Comedy has distilled itself into no more than an enchanted atmosphere, the more enchanted the less credible, and hardly extending beyond one social class, one to which Shakespeare did not belong. Shylock is remembered when the beautiful music and the closing lines are forgotten, and I fear that he makes nonsense of the music of the spheres;

You have among you many a purchas'd slave,
Which, like your asses and your dogs and mules,
You use in abject and in slavish parts,
Because you bought them; shall I say to you
'Let them be free, marry them to your heirs –
Why sweat they under burdens? – let their beds
Be made as soft as yours. . . .'

It is possible there were few slaves in England, but Shakespeare had thought about the subject, had he not? Shylock oversteps the boundaries of his play; and in the next two plays – but in a different way – the same thing occurs with Falstaff. In that case we know that the comical villain was and still is so extremely popular that his going beyond all limits was a success. The plays come near to sinking under him, but he makes them the successes they are. It was an actors' theatre. If there was any director it was the author in co-operation with his fellow actors – that is, the principal actors, though the travelling actors in *Hamlet* suggest that the chief actor, who would be Burbage, had some authority. As the English verse theatre became more and more popular, Shakespeare concentrated on Burbage's parts and two or three other principal parts, all played by the sharers in the company. The only exception is that the young boys from the *Dream* seem to be growing up, and more taxing women's parts begin to increase.

In the course of the two *Henry IV* plays, Henry V grows up and passes numerous initiation tests. His fat friend Falstaff and other such companions are not entered for the same race, and Henry outgrows them, but Falstaff and his like are so captivating that one is sad to see Henry V outsoar and abjure them. They are low-life comics in a new sense, because they are neither peasants nor buffoons, but a kind of riff-raff with pretensions; they have a better social basis for wit than poor Launce or Gobbo, and they are more woven into the action and the pattern of the plays than any previous clown. Falstaff is socially above the status of a clown, which sets Shakespeare free to create the funniest of all his comic characters, and one of the most moving. He owes a little to the Bastard in *King John*.
    Auden thought Falstaff inhabited a kind of paradise of bohemian charity, in which one never grew up, but he is not at all innocent, and the Prince has always been going to reject him in the end. The Prince is a bit of a cold fish, but he is the only one of all these kings who, through his adventurous boyhood, really knows the English people. One observes that Shakespeare, since he wrote the play, must have known the world he talks about. Travelling taught him a great deal (he complains in the *Merchant* how they always mend the roads in summer but never in winter when they disintegrate) but Southwark taught him more. His Boar's Head is in East

170

Cheap, but he moved south of the river about this time, which may have brought back memories.

The theme of civil war has turned by a different emphasis to that of rebellion, and the sufferings of war and of the people are also transmuted. It is not entirely Falstaff who brings about that alteration: it is also the Prince who is already being groomed for his central part in *Henry V*. Shakespeare is as swift as ever to learn from his sources, but he has considerable freedom to adapt, since the events of these plays are as long ago to him as the Napoleonic wars are to us. Shakespeare might just have known a very old man whose grandfather fought at Agincourt. The recent loss of the last English territory in France had silhouetted that age against a darkness.

The Queen's Men had an old play registered for printing in 1594 and printed in 1598 called *The Famous Victories of Henry V*, which appeared in a shortened form, and in prose printed as verse. The clown's part in it was played by Richard Tarlton, who died in 1588; he also played the Lord Chief Justice. In Shakespeare's *Henry IV, Part 1* the low characters are much funnier, but there are fewer obscenities. Falstaff was originally called Oldcastle, as he is in the *Famous Victories*, but Sir John Oldcastle was a real historical character, and not only a Protestant martyr out of Foxe's *Book of Martyrs* (1563) but a cherished ancestor of Cobham, the Lord Chamberlain. Born in 1378, he was hanged as a heretic in 1417: the reverberations of the scandal lasted fifty years or more.

Falstaff is a name rather gleefully adapted from Fastolfe in *Henry VI, Part 1*, a cowardly knight. 'I have a whole school of tongues in this belly of mine; and not a tongue of them all speaks any other word but my name. . . . My womb, my womb, my womb undoes me.' He is too fat and too impotent to do any real harm, but he is a rogue all the same. Unfortunately, Fastolfe in real life had been a Lollard and therefore he was yet another Protestant hero, but at least he was not an ancestor of the Lord Chamberlain. In Thomas Fuller's *History of the Worthies of England* (1662) the thunder was still rumbling: 'Now as I am glad that Sir John Oldcastle is put out, so I am sorry that Sir John Fastolfe is put in.' Dr Richard James, Librarian to the antiquarian Sir Robert Cotton, who founded the great collection used by Camden, Bacon and others, said similar things in a letter of 1625, naming Shakespeare. The Catholics were on the side of the theatre; Father Robert Persons the Jesuit wrote of Oldcastle in 1604 as 'a ruffian knight as all England knoweth, and commonly brought in by comedians on their stages'.

Lord Cobham died in 1597, and since he is likelier than his son to have made a fuss, being more influential and notably humourless (Essex's friends called him Lord Fool), his death helps us to date the play. As Lord Chamberlain, Cobham senior was the greatest Court official; the Master of the Revels was his subordinate officer, and together they claimed huge powers over the London theatres, not precisely defined until the Licensing

Act of 1737. Harvey and Russell, Oldcastle's friends in the original *Henry IV, Part 1*, became Bardolph and Peto, probably to avoid offence to Sir William Harvey and Lord Bedford, though all these original names have left traces here and there in our text. Such wholesale name-changing sounds as if a grand remonstrance had come from the Privy Council (Cobham was a member), or through the Master of the Revels.

The Queen does not seem to have cared twopence; in fact she is said to have enjoyed the joke, and commissioned a play about Sir John in love that had to be written in a fortnight: *The Merry Wives of Windsor*. But Shakespeare had to apologize publicly: he did so in the Epilogue to *Part 2*. 'If you be not too much cloy'd with fat meat, our humble author will continue the story, with Sir John in it, and make you merry with fair Katharine of France; where, for anything I know, Falstaff shall die of a sweat, unless already a be kill'd with your hard opinions; for Oldcastle died a martyr and this is not the man.'

As the London theatres became more successful, the machinery of repression became more rather than less active, and at the same time a younger generation of writers soon to be barking at Shakespeare's heels, the generation of Marston and Ben Jonson, shifted the momentum of fashionable playmaking towards the satiric, and provoked worse troubles for themselves than Shakespeare ever encountered. The plays that Shakespeare wrote during those years are sometimes seen as the expression of some inward disturbance of his soul, and yet whatever we concretely know of him, including his behaviour over the Oldcastle affair, suggests that he was extremely good-humoured and high-spirited. His deepest anger speaks for many, not for himself, and it is always on the same subjects. He loved England and the English with the same passion as John of Gaunt. Falstaff goes deeper in him than Hamlet; humour is more instinctive and enters more profoundly into his nature than the elaboration of a tragedy.

Henry IV begins with the sad King intending a Crusade.

> No more the thirsty entrance of this soil
> Shall daub her lips with her own children's blood;
> No more shall trenching war channel her fields,
> Nor bruise her flow'rets with the armed hoofs
> Of hostile paces. . . .
> Forthwith a power of English shall we levy,
> Whose arms were moulded in their mothers' womb
> To chase these pagans in those holy fields
> Over whose acres walk'd those blessed feet
> Which fourteen hundred years ago were nail'd
> For our advantage on the bitter cross.

But the first bad news comes at the end of this monologue: it is the beginning of rebellion by Owen Glendower, and Hotspur's quarrel with the King. From at least the time of the *Merchant*, where Shylock forced him to it, Shakespeare has thought seriously about act structure. Again, in the three scenes of act 1 of *Henry IV, Part 1* we have a fresh star part in each: the King, Falstaff with the Prince, and Hotspur. Falstaff's language is warm, abundant and various, more fantastical than the Prince's comic prose: but one requires the other, since it is essential to Falstaff that there are as many jokes about him as by him, and that as God is good in himself and the cause of goodness in us, Falstaff is humorous in himself and the cause of humour in others.

He is absurd and we tolerate his intolerable flavour only because we laugh at him. He is also gallant in a way, and sad below the surface from his first to his last appearance. 'The old tavern at Eastcheap' is an inheritance from *The Famous Victories of Henry V*, but it is Falstaff who brings it to life, and the same sadness and delightfulness invests the entire social world in which Falstaff operates. He is a life-enhancer about whom moral points are scarcely worth making, because he gives more to life than ever he gets out of it. He really is as he says as melancholy as a castrated tomcat 'or a lugg'd bear . . . or the drone of a Lincolnshire bagpipe', but he heaves with laughter about it, and so do we. This scene must have been swiftly written, as Gadshill is both a name and a place-name: in the *Famous Victories* it was a nickname, the place being a notorious danger spot on the Dover Road.

Hotspur's first speech is a virtuoso performance like Mercutio's and Romeo's, about a courtier on a gory battlefield, 'perfumed like a milliner'. Hotspur is the Prince's missing half, and when the Prince overcomes him he will somehow take over his poetry and better it, and yet Hotspur while he lives is more memorable in tone or style, even if he has less of the opportunities that situation offers the Prince in poetry. In fact he is Mercutio to the Prince's Romeo, the Prince being usually overshadowed until near the end of *Henry IV, Part 2* by the presence of Falstaff. Hotspur has faults of character, of course, but the moral balance of the play, although it is perfectly in control and almost boringly orthodox, seems to matter less because Falstaff makes it irrelevant. And yet it controls him too: he has been doomed from his remotest sources in the fifteenth century. He is the Vice of a morality play ensnaring youth, and the clown of a farce like Peele's *Old Wives' Tale*, a traditional figure in the theatre long before Shakespeare breathed life into him. Almost the most amazing thing about these plays is that Falstaff does not in fact wreck them but is part of them: their moral balance takes a beating from him, but failure is what makes him and his friends so moving.

The second act opens in the inn yard at Rochester at four in the morning with the carriers setting out for London. For accuracy of social observation, for humour and anarchic prose poetry, it ranks with the sheep-shearing feast in *The Winter's Tale*, among the best outlines that Shakespeare ever wrote, yet it is made of nothing, and taken separately the jokes are not much either. Cumulatively it relishes a world, 'Charles' wain is over the new chimney . . . poor jade is wrung in the withers out of all cess . . . Peas and beans are as dank here as a dog . . . the most villainous house in all London road for fleas'. The elaborate practical joke of the ambush which follows would lack zest without this setting in a life and a society that many writers did their best to describe in these ten years, without achieving so piquant and economic a delineation. 'Ah, whoreson cater-pillars! bacon-fed knaves! They hate us youth/Down with them; fleece them.' After many re-readings one can still crow quietly over *Henry IV*; in the theatre it is always over too soon.

The third scene shows Hotspur in prose, furious and reckless, commenting on a letter, and in verse with his wife Kate, whom he treats with a conscious bluffness that Henry V will use later on his French Kate. This scene is a rather brief interlude before we reach the Boar's Head, with Francis the drawer and an intrusion of the Sheriff whom the Prince addresses in verse. The practical joke is concluded, the buffoonery is nearly over and the robbed carriers are repaid with interest. 'There let him sleep till day. I'll to the court in the morning. We must all to the wars.'

The third act opens with entertainment of a different kind: Hotspur and Glendower meet at Bangor, where Glendower's daughter speaks only Welsh, and sings a Welsh song. The English lines about magical music and the meaning of the lovesong are in the purest golden style, but both Glendower and Hotspur have speeches earlier in the same scene of a more exotic kind. The triple division of England between the rebels is made more thrilling by its context of goats and earthquakes and sandy-bottomed Severn. Hotspur gives the scene an electric and in the end a sexual tension.

> And those musicians that shall play to you
> Hang in the air a thousand leagues from hence. . . .

At Westminster the King chides his son, this being the first time they have met in the play. In a sense its entire plot is only a knot to draw its many threads together. The father and son scene is perhaps too long, but no doubt the audience expected solemnity, and so far they had been offered very little of that, because Hotspur is so witty and full of fire that he mocks away solemnity. Now the Prince undertakes to wash away his shames with Hotspur's blood, and orders are issued for the war. In the third scene of the act we return to Falstaff, but the Prince is distinctly brisker with him, and although he calls him 'my sweet beef' all he will offer from his restored position at court is 'I have procured thee, Jack, a charge of foot.' He moves into blank verse as he sets out for the war.

Act 4 leads up to the battle and act 5 enacts it. We see the Prince's friends through the eyes of a messenger to doomed Hotspur:

> All furnish'd, all in arms;
> All plum'd like estridges, that with the wind
> Bated like eagles having lately bath'd;
> Glittering in golden coats, like images;
> As full of spirit as the month of May
> And gorgeous as the sun at midsummer;
> Wanton as youthful goats, wild as young bulls.
> I saw young Harry with his beaver on,
> His cushes on his thighs, gallantly arm'd,
> Rise from the ground like feathered Mercury,
> And vaulted with such ease into his seat
> As if an angel dropp'd down from the clouds
> To turn and wind a fiery Pegasus,
> And witch the world with noble horsemanship.

Shakespeare is talking about animal spirits, heat of blood, and in terms of a tournament. The description is energetic, and it describes what of course the stage is unable to show; the constant shifting of metaphor is part of the energy, it does not really say what the Prince looked like, but it draws on the listener to imagine and depict him.

The Queen held tournaments at Whitsun, and a poetry of chivalry existed. George Peele wrote Lord Northumberland a splendid poem of the kind called 'Honour of the Garter' when he was made a Knight of the Garter in 1593, for which he was paid three pounds by that economic nobleman. Peele has a vision of knights by moonlight at Windsor, 'water'd by that renowned river Thames', led by Renown on a flying horse dressed in falcon's feathers:

> And lo, a wonder to my senses all,
> For through the melting air perfum'd with sweets
> I might discern a troop of Horsemen ride
> Armed cap de pe with shield and shivering lance,
> As in a flash or calm transparent brook
> We see the glistering fishes scour along.
> Caesar himself was there, I saw him ride
> Triumphing in his three and twenty wounds. . . .

It is worth the deviation of a moment or two to observe in what ways and to what degree Shakespeare was the greatest poet of his time. I am fond of George Peele, but he does not stand comparison, yet one can see how this kind of poetry as well as other kinds has watered the roots of the play.

Hotspur gets so excited by the Prince's description that he comes close to melodrama, but before that can be consummated, Shakespeare backtracks to Falstaff on the march near Coventry, making for Sutton Coldfield and Shrewsbury by more or less the route of what is now the Telford motorway. The Prince was sent a day earlier through Gloucestershire, by Oxford and Moreton in the Marsh, but he turns up in this scene; Shakespeare has forgotten about Gloucestershire. Falstaff has allowed the likelier soldiers to buy themselves out, and has a ragged troop left over, 'slaves as ragged as Lazarus in the painted cloth . . . a hundred and fifty tattered Prodigals lately come from swine-keeping. . . . I'll not march through Coventry with them, that's flat.' The corrupt pressing and buying-out process was much used by Elizabethan captains and much complained about. When one thinks of the Armada muster one should remember Falstaff and his Dad's Army. (Indeed it is a pity that Shakespeare did not live to write about the Home Guard of 1940, which was a very Shakespearean organization.) The placing of this scene between two of Hotspur's is an explicit and deliberate criticism of the honour code of war. Falstaff's men, who are vivider in his words than if we saw them, are 'food for powder, food for powder; they'll fill a pit as well as better' so that the heroic blank verses of the nobility have a hollower ring than usual. Shakespeare's problem is to combine these elements.

The King himself opens act 5. 'How bloodily the sun begins to peer Above yon bulky hill!' The motto of this act might be a line of Ralegh's: 'only we die in earnest, that's no jest.' The Prince 'to save the blood on either side' offers a duel with Hotspur, but the moment the highminded nobles and the King are offstage, he is left alone with Falstaff. Conversation is friendly but has a chilly touch. 'Say thy prayers, and farewell.' 'I would 'twere bed-time, Hal, and all well.' 'Why, thou owest God a death.' Falstaff's wish is that of the English soldiers before Agincourt; the brief words are very carefully calculated. His monologue against honour will be echoed when Henry V is wandering round the English camp on that night. There is no doubt where Shakespeare's root feelings lay. Hotspur and Prince Henry are permitted their chivalrous daring and self-sacrifice, but that is (and is meant to be) pathetically youthful, only a shade less idiotic than the high spirits of Mercutio and Tybalt. The truth of politics and war lies with the King, who sends out friends disguised as kings to be killed instead of himself.

Falstaff is terrified of course. 'God keep lead out of me! I need no more weight than mine own bowels. I have led my ragamuffins where they are well pepper'd; there's not three of my hundred and fifty left alive, and they are for the town's end, to beg during life.' One needs to consider the meaning of the London streetname Cripplegate, and the sixteenth-century old soldiers who begged at St Paul's. 'I like not such grinning honour as Sir Walter hath.'

The values of battle having been undermined by realism, they are now overturned by comedy. Hotspur dies seeing his own folly; the Prince treats him with a certain cool mockery, but then courtesy also, and says an affectionate mocking goodbye to Falstaff, who is pretending to be dead. As soon as he is out of the way Falstaff steals Hotspur's corpse, which he pretends he killed, and the Prince connives at the lie 'if it will do thee good'. The battle and the play are over in a page or two more of blank verse by noblemen. And yet Shakespeare had a strong feeling for the poetry of war, at least of single combat. He distanced it with symbolism until it became a kind of metaphor (act 1, scene iii, line 101):

> Three times they breath'd, and three times did they drink,
> Upon agreement, of swift Severn's flood;
> Who then, affrighted with their bloody looks,
> Ran fearfully among the trembling reeds
> And hid his crisp head in the hollow bank. . . .

Henry IV, Part 2 has Rumour for an introduction 'painted full of tongues' to explain a rather complicated bit of plot. The costume is oddly reminiscent of the fantastical gown in which Prince Hal submitted himself to his father, described by Holinshed: 'a gown of blue satin, full of small eyelet holes, at every hole the needle hanging by a silk thread with which it was sewed. About his arm he wore a hound's collar full of SS of gold. . . .' Shakespeare had ignored that famous and unexplained costume, but perhaps it worked in his imagination. 'Painted full of tongues' is even stranger than Peele's Renown on the flying horse dressed to the heels in falcon feathers.

The first act opens with messengers from the battle of Shrewsbury reaching Northumberland, where the Earl receives them raging:

> . . . let one spirit of the first-born Cain
> Reign in all bosoms, that, each heart being set
> On bloody courses, the rude scene may end
> And darkness be the burier of the dead!

It is a relief to turn to Falstaff, who has acquired a page and got back to London. His scene with the Lord Chief Justice is little more than self-definition, being as he says witty in himself and a cause of wit in others. He shows himself up in about a hundred ways in as many sentences as an appalling old reprobate. The third scene of the act brings in a conspiring archbishop who rails with venom against the common people: 'And now thou wouldst eat thy dead vomit up, And howl'st to find it.' It ought not to need underlining that these are not Shakespeare's views, being put in the mouth of a scheming prelate.

Act 2 opens with two comic officers called Fang and Snare come to arrest Falstaff for debt at the suit of the Hostess of the Boar's Head. The Lord Chief Justice quells the resulting riot. The star of this scene is the Hostess, a match for Falstaff and in a way his female equivalent, a younger and more strident version of Juliet's Nurse. She loves the old villain and that is the point of her, as he wheedles his way out of trouble. She is called Mistress Quickly and her friend is Doll Tearsheet. The last scene of the act is a long one at the Boar's Head, which introduces Pistol. Like the other comic scenes in this play, it is unhurried and unbuttoned, a kind of hopeless wonderland. Falstaff is supposed to be in York with soldiers, but he dallies. The Prince is worried about his father, but he seems to be sinking back into low life. They are summoned as the act ends. 'Now comes in the sweetest morsel of the night, and we must hence, and leave it unpick'd.'

The last few lines of act 2 are as moving as a death-scene, and in their way they are one, because the darkness is closing in around Falstaff, and the Prince's hints to Poins about reforming himself are going to come true. Act 3 opens with the King's monologue to Sleep, one of those virtuoso pieces that seems to exist for its own sake until one examines how precisely it does its work in the play. The King's night is in contrast to Falstaff's, and his son must enter into it. The ship-boy in this monologue gives just the touch of reality that the play needs at this point: one thinks of ships far out at sea in storms, whose purpose is to guard England and the King. The boy is an extraordinary symbol of innocent sleep.

> Wilt thou upon the high and giddy mast
> Seal up the ship-boy's eyes, and rock his brains
> In cradle of the rude imperious surge,
> And in the visitation of the winds,
> Who take the ruffian billows by the top,
> Curling their monstrous heads, and hanging them
> With deafing clamour in the slippery clouds,
> That with the hurly death itself awakes?
> Canst thou, O partial sleep, give thy repose
> To the wet sea-boy in an hour so rude. . . .

The King broods in London over politics, but Sir John Falstaff is wandering about all over England pressing men to fight rebels. He was sent to York, but he has got himself to Gloucestershire. Even Shakespeare can scarcely have done this by carelessness; he refers to the place in detail. Various kinds of confusion may have occurred, but when literary critical prejudice is applied to topography, confusion is worse confounded. A question about the price of bullocks at Stamford fair has been used by scholars to argue that Falstaff really was on the way to York, but Stamfords abound, and the likeliest one to interest a Winchcombe farmer is Stamford Bridge in Worcestershire, where the Teme runs down to meet the Severn, an important point on one of the most important droving routes for Welsh cattle. It was worth going round to avoid a hill, and the King himself did so, returning from Wales by way of Basingstoke, but Falstaff is in Gloucestershire because Shakespeare knows the places and the people he mentions, and the Gloucestershire interlude is a pivot to the moods of the play. It is Falstaff's happy climax, his last holiday even though he claims to be in a hurry; yet it begins the machinery of his downfall, which might easily have happened more sordidly but is carefully set against the expectations of Justice Shallow.

Shallow is placed at Winchcombe, where in real life Robert Dover of the Cotswold Olympics was at some time a lawyer, and close to Strensham, where the magnificent tombs of Thomas Russell's family still survive. The local colour is painted unusually thick: Master Dommelton comes from Dumbleton near Broadway, Will Squele is a cotsole (Cotswold) man, Woncot is Woodmancote near Dursley, three miles from the Hill, which is by Winchcombe, Barston is Barcheston, ten miles from Stratford, John Doit of Staffordshire is from not far away, and the Visor family and the Perkes (Perkis) family really lived where Shakespeare puts them. The hade land (act 5, scene i) is the last strip of a field where the plough turns, which is therefore not ploughed until later: this is still true. The red wheat Shallow has sown there is a Gloucestershire variety of late wheat, called Red Lammas.

These Gloucestershire scenes have a real social density; even Falstaff is given a boyhood, as page to the Duke of Norfolk, which Oldcastle was in real life. Shakespeare has made his point about the pressed men in *Part 1*; now we shall see them on the stage, drawn with amusement and affection from real life. Shallow is unlikely to be a personal portrait, but he probably is a private joke as well as a type. He was a Cotswold justice from Shakespeare's years in the wool trade maybe: he is nothing like a Lucy, though he inherits the *Luce/louse* joke (old jokes are best), and nothing at all like the ghastly Gardiner.

Every word of the Gloucester scenes is gold dust. Enter Justice Shallow and Justice Silence, with Mouldy, Shadow, Wart, Feeble, Bullcalf. For the gentry, this is a world of cousins and nephews and bonds of ancient acquaintance, which is how Falstaff enters it. It is also decayed and ridiculous, and the old men's memories are lies. 'Jesu, Jesu, the mad days that I have spent! and to see how many of my old acquaintance are dead!' These remarks toll like bells through the rest of the play. 'Certain, 'tis certain; very sure, very sure. Death as the Psalmist saith, is certain to all; all shall die. How a good yoke of bullocks at Stamford fair?' Ecclesiasticus remarks (38, 24–5), 'How can he get wisdom that holdeth the plough ... and his talk is but of the breeding of bullocks?' Perhaps that text had stimulated Shakespeare, but it scarcely represents his view, and I would rather see the market prices as contrast to the theme of old age, and as part of the rural setting.

A 'score of good ewes may be worth ten pounds', not a low price though we are far from London. In *The Winter's Tale* eleven sheep yield a tod of wool, and 'every tod yields a pound and odd shilling', so a score would yield about two pounds a year. A shepherd who owned his own grazing would make above ten pounds, but anyone with expenses would make less. This scene has several streams of humour of different kinds running through it and several of sadness. The more intelligent soldiers buy their way out; they are all sweet and pathetic without being to the least degree idealized: they are much more real than the characters in a pastoral, and more moving. Falstaff is merciless about Shallow, and by reducing him brings him down to the same pathetic level at which we love him.

The successful impact of this play and of this scene is not a matter of structure. The looseness of structure that attaches to comic scenes (though this scene has a skeleton) has somehow set Shakespeare free to a brilliance which is as it were unbuttoned and impromptu. The whole thing is conversation, yet its undercurrent of implicit poetry is very strong. One proceeds with reluctance to the battle of Gaultree in Yorkshire in act 4, though it has splendid tournament verse:

> Their neighing coursers daring of the spur,
> Their armed staves in charge, their beavers down,
> Their eyes of fire sparkling through sights of steel,
> And the loud trumpet blowing them together. . . .

But anxiety is more allayed and imagination satisfied by the prospect of peace: 'Let them have pay, and part.'

> My lord, our army is dispers'd already.
> Like youthful steers unyok'd, they take their courses
> East, west, north, south; or like a school broke up,
> Each hurries towards his home and sporting-place.

Prince John is as cold and tricky as his father, and wins by stratagem. Old Falstaff arrives late and takes a prisoner by funnier and more sympathetic guile: Lancaster treats him with disdain and has his prisoner executed. 'Good faith, this same young sober-blooded boy doth not love me; nor a man cannot make him laugh. . . .' Another shadow has fallen over Falstaff's future. The end of act 4 sees the final quarrel of the King with his son, and their final reconciliation, when the Prince has been caught trying on the crown. There is to be no more civil war: an irony the audience will understand as one. The crown is like pinching and scalding armour on a hot day, the sleep of death has divorced 'So many English kings' from it. The Prince fears it and accepts it, and the King dies happy.

Shallow is about his business in act 5. It would be the same at any time for two hundred years afterwards, and the dinner he orders recalls the love of food and drink in James Woodford's eighteenth-century *Diary of a Country Parson*: 'Some pigeons, Davy, a couple of short-legg'd hens, a joint of mutton, and any pretty little tiny kickshaws, tell William cook. . . . A friend i' th'court is better than a penny in purse. . . . Come, come, come, off with your boots.' In London Henry V is King and takes on majesty of language and of sentiment:

> Brothers, you mix your sadness with some fear.
> This is the English, not the Turkish court;
> Not Amurath an Amurath succeeds,
> But Harry Harry. Yet be sad, good brothers. . . .

He is reconciled to the Chief Justice, as the chronicles record that he was, and proclaims the change in himself with an eloquence that retains its rooted Englishness. As Warwick said of him in the previous act, 'The Prince but studies his companions Like a strange tongue, wherein, to gain the language, 'Tis needful that the most immodest word Be look'd upon and learnt. . . .' He speaks better English than other Kings now, because it is more downright and direct, as well as having courtly eloquence and pregnant meanings. What his verse lacks is those whispers of poetry his melancholy father had, and the mysterious glimmerings of Glendower's verses. His language is a character study and a social placing. He is as moral as the Bible and as powerful in utterance, but for the rest of this play he is cut off from Falstaffian language. He belongs now to a list of kings. Shallow and Falstaff sit in an orchard, but news of the succession brings them rushing to London. Quickly and Tearsheet are arrested in a tiny comic vignette that remains unresolved. We know that the Beadle was played by John Sincklo, or Sinclair, who specialized in funny thin men. The rejection of Falstaff in the King's terrible speech as he comes from his coronation is the climax of the play. It has been calculated from the beginning of *Henry IV, Part 1*. The new king intends his former friends 'Shall all be very well provided for', though now they go to prison. In the same way, he saw that the victims of his highway robbery were repaid. The point is not underlined and carries little conviction, but Shakespeare like the King had no alternative.

In 1595 Drayton published an epic poem called *The First Four Books of the Civil Wars between the Two Houses of Lancaster and York*. It is not his best work, but it has some passages in common with Shakespeare's plays, and it may have been an influence, since they were friends, and Drayton even at his worst always has a drowsy charm. The livelier and crazier language of Pistol comes straight out of the mouth of the Braggart in Eliot's *Ortho-epia Gallica*, an unlikely sounding source which scholars did not notice until 1953, having underestimated Shakespeare's studiousness and his magpie curiosity about different kinds of language. The nightingale in *Romeo and Juliet* comes from the same book. Eliot was a Warwickshire man two years younger than Shakespeare, who set up as a French teacher in London in 1589 after roaming the continent for ten years. He was keen on Rabelais, and was a friend of Greene the pamphleteer.

About 1596 Shakespeare moved south of the river to Southwark, where his company now worked. In 1597 he bought the greatest town house in Stratford, New Place, of which only the foundations survive. It had been grand enough in 1540 to be noticed by Leland the antiquary as 'a pretty house of brick and timber', but it had gone downhill since then. The Cloptons had built it, but tenant succeeded tenant. In 1549 it was left 'in great ruin and decay and unrepaired' by Thomas Bentley, a former President of the College of Physicians. In 1563 it was sold to William Bott of Snitterfield, who sat for a year on the Stratford Council but got thrown out for saying there was not an honest man in it. Bott was more than once accused of the blackest villainy, including the murder of his own daughter with rat poison; if she died childless, the son-in-law's estates came to Bott. This surprising crime never came to court, and I think the details are so bizarre as to be incredible: they tell us more about what kind of thing people believed than about what happened, but New Place does not sound like a happy house at the time.

Bott sold New Place in 1565 to William Underhill, clerk of the assizes at Warwick, who left it within weeks to his son and heir, another William. This man sold it to Shakespeare by a deed dated 4 May 1597 on formal payment of £60: we do not know the real price. In July Underhill was poisoned by his own adolescent son Fulke, at Fillangley near Coventry; the boy was hanged at Warwick in 1599. The Underhill estate was forfeited, then regranted to Fulke's younger brother Hercules when he came of age in 1602. Shakespeare had to arrange confirmation of the sale of New Place with Hercules, with a formal fee of one-quarter of its annual value. Apart from the College, the old priests' house, which was Crown property but leased to Thomas Combe in 1596, Shakespeare had the biggest rambling old house in the town, though in other ways not the most desirable; but Shakespeare was a romantic as well as a practical man. The Underhills had Cotswold interests, and the Gloucestershire scenes in *Henry IV* may derive from his househunting negotiations. They certainly express a longing to get back to his roots.

By January of 1598, Shakespeare was trying to buy land. Abraham Sturley, an agent of Sir Thomas Lucy, wrote then to Richard Quiney, on a visit to London: '. . . I pray God send you comfortably home. This is one special remembrance of your father's [Adrian's] motion: it seemeth by him that our countryman Mr. Shaxsper is willing to disburse some money upon some odd yardland [thirty-acre field] or other at Shottery or near about us.' He wants to interest Shakespeare in 'the matter of our tithes. . . . If obtained would advance him indeed, and would do us much good.' The price of corn was high that year, and maltsters who stored it were resented. Deputations had gone to Thomas Lucy, Fulke Greville and elsewhere. On 4 February an enquiry into the chief holders of corn and malt within Stratford revealed that Sturley held 12½ quarters or 100 bushels for Sir T.

Lucy, and Mr Dixon another 16 quarters or 128 bushels for the same gentleman; W. Shakespeare had 10 quarters or 80 bushels, making him third for quantity in the Chapel Street Ward of Stratford – not a huge, but not a negligible amount. In that year his name was printed on his plays for the first time, and Francis Meres wrote about him as the supreme English poet. He was famous even in Cotswold villages. Sir Charles Percy at Dumbleton in Gloucestershire wrote in a letter that 'if I stay here long in this fashion, at my return I think you will find me so dull that I shall be taken for Justice Silence or Justice Shallow.' The *Henry IV* plays entered into popular imagination as soon as they were performed, and Falstaff and Shallow became household words.

· 7 ·

Greatness

Shakespeare had now entered a phase of undeniable and recognized mastery, but neither in 1598 nor at any other time did he proceed smoothly from success to success. That is not just because London life was so disturbed at the end of Elizabeth's reign. No play was quite like the last, and his wrestle with form and construction, and even with tragic and comic conception, continued vigorously. Even so, I am unable to account for *Much Ado About Nothing*, nor is it quite great. It has serious admirers, and bits of it give genuine pleasure, mostly the low comedy and the lyrical verse, but I find it the least memorable of Shakespeare's plays. It has a deep pattern that suggests maturity and even greatness; it may even represent the birth pangs of a new conception of comic pattern or form. Scholars complain of its whimsical or throwaway title. I suspect Shakespeare wrote it hurriedly in the disturbed time of the removal of the Theatre to build the Globe.

Most of this play is in prose, a sharpened version of the witty exchanges of Lyly's boy actors, to represent a world where women equalled and outwitted men, an idealized theatrical Italy. Shakespeare had been working this vein on and off for years, but I cannot help feeling that in *Much Ado About Nothing* some of the prose is on autopilot. The tone for long stretches is an unvaried rapid bird-twitter of verbal sparring that gives one a headache; the characters are not sufficiently characterized by difference of language; and the whole performance is too artificial for my own taste, though it is too clever to be cloying. Dogberry continues the Gloucestershire type of humour, though Aubrey records that his original in real life came from Long Grendon in Oxfordshire, on Shakespeare's Edgehill route to London. A strange confirmation of his reality came to light in a letter of Burghley to Walsingham written in August 1586 at the time of the Babington plot. John Payne Collier, a librarian to the Duke of Devonshire who became a notorious Shakespeare forger, printed it in 1844, but it was later verified by A. L. Rowse, who quoted it from State Papers in his *England of Elizabeth* (1950). It is genuine enough: England was full of Dogberrys, it appears.

Sir, as I came from London homeward in my coach, I saw at every town's end the number of ten or twelve standing with long staves, and until I came to Enfield I thought no other of them but that they had stayed for avoiding of the rain, or to drink at some alehouse, for so they did stand under pentices [projecting upper parts] at alehouses. But at Enfield finding a dozen in a plump, when there was no rain, I bethought myself that they were appointed as watchmen, for the apprehending of such as are missing. And thereupon I called some of them to me apart, and asked them wherefore they stood there. And one of them answered, 'To take three young men'. And demanding how they should know the persons, one answered with these words. 'Marry my lord, by intelligence of their favour.' 'What mean you by that?' quoth I. 'Marry,' said they, 'one of the parties hath a hooked nose.' 'And have you' quoth I 'no other mark?' 'No' saith they. And then I asked who appointed them. And they answered one Banks, a head constable, whom I willed to be sent to me. 'Surely Sir, whosoever hath the charge from you hath used the matter negligently. For these watchmen stand so openly in plumps as no suspected person will come near them; and if they be no better instructed but to find three persons by one of them having a hooked nose, they may miss thereof.'

All the same, they did catch the three men at Harrow, not very far away.

This play was a great success in its day. It was one of those Leonard Digges picked out for special mention. The Digges family are interesting friends of Shakespeare; Thomas Russell married Leonard's mother as a widow and brought her to Alderminster, south of Stratford, in 1603, but Shakespeare then already knew the distinguished scientist Thomas Digges, since he took the names Rosencrantz and Guildenstern in *Hamlet* from a Danish painting in Digges's possession. Digges is named as Master of the Works at Dover on a map in the British Museum; he was also an astronomer, a mathematician, and a student of war.

The Corpus (Oxford) manuscript about poets that first records the poaching rumour about Shakespeare, and that of his dying a papist, shows great interest in the Digges family. The eldest son Sir Dudley (1583–1639) lived to be Master of the Rolls and settled in Kent, where he left £20 a year for a running match between a young man and maiden of Faversham and a young man and maiden of Chilham, to be held annually on 19 May, St Dunstan's Day. Leonard (1588–1635), by contrast retired in 1619 to University College, Oxford, where for the rest of his life he shared rooms with Philip Washington; they died within a day of each other. Leonard became a close friend of John Davies of Quinton, and through him of James Mabbe, a fellow of Magdalen and a Spanish expert. Mabbe, like Leonard Digges, wrote complimentary verses for the Shakespeare Folio of 1623.

Leonard wrote a shorter and a longer version, of which the longer and more interesting appeared posthumously, with the 1640 edition of Shakespeare's poems.

> ... Let but Beatrice
> And Benedick be seen, lo, in a trice,
> The cockpit, galleries, boxes, all are full
> To hear Malvolio, that cross-gartered gull. ...

He is writing from memory and confusing *Much Ado* with *Twelfth Night*. He must have seen both, probably in his late teens, but he has no text. It is odd how closely interwoven this circle of Shakespeare's younger friends and admirers is. Endymion Porter was one of the Porters of Aston sub Edge and Mickelton, and it was he who got the King's costume for Robert Dover for the Cotswold Olympics; Thomas Russell was Endymion's cousin's godfather and his friend. John Davies was at Magdalen with Thomas and Edward Bushell of Marston, whom Shakespeare knew and trusted. They were all the minor gentry of the Cotswolds; it was in that lake that Shakespeare swam.

Everything is mocked in *Much Ado*, even blank verse and music. 'Is it not strange that sheeps' guts should hale souls out of men's bodies?' The musical lyrics are enchanting all the same, and offer hints and feelings that the audience will follow better than the characters can. The play is a tangle of deceits and symbols of deceit, even the garden:

> ... say that thou overheard'st us
> And bid her steal into the pleached bower,
> Where honeysuckles, ripened by the sun,
> Forbid the sun to enter. ...
> The pleasant'st angling is to see the fish
> Cut with her golden oars the silver stream,
> And greedily devour the treacherous bait.

This particular scene (act 3, scene i) ends with a ten-line sonnet. But the verse in the play is only a variation where one is much needed. Dogberry and his partner Verges do the same service more effectively. In the climax of the play, the resolution of its intrigues in the last act, Dogberry has his part, but the mixture is that of oil and water: he is almost too stupid to be very funny by now, and one cannot believe in a world that combines all these elements. The mourning for Hero is pretty enough, though of course she is not dead but is reconciled with her unbelieving husband, who remarries her before he knows who she is: this is arranged by a friar. When the villain is captured we are told, 'Think not on him till to-morrow'; everybody dances and that is the end.

Much Ado's principal source was Belleforest's 1582 translation of Italian stories by Matteo Bandello, one of Shakespeare's commonest source-books. The play seems to refer to a night law of 1595. Dogberry's watch is like Falstaff's muster, and Hugh Oatcake and George Seacoal add to the pleasing repertory of names. 'But manhood is melted into curtsies, valour into compliment, and men are only turn'd into tongue': the honour system of the young sparks is attacked and proved inadequate in new ways. In the second scene of act 5 we are treated to a snatch of a ballad over thirty years old, like the bits and pieces of ballad in *Henry IV*. The musical culture of the educated 1590s coexisted with a rougher popular music. Shakespeare expresses scorn for ballad-makers but shows affection for old songs, for which he has an ear and a memory.

Just possibly the play was commissioned and so was its style. The courtly wit in conversation was a real vogue, particularly among women, and ended by infecting even the pulpit. The references (act 3, scene iii) to 'that Deformed' and 'Pharaoh's soldiers in the reechy painting', and 'god Bel's priests in the old church-window', and 'shaven Hercules in the smirch'd worm-eaten tapestry, where his codpiece seems as massy as his club', conjure up a first audience to whom these allusions were familiar. If that is really true, then the commissioner might be Southampton, who loved *Love's Labour's Lost*, or some friend of his who owned the reechy painting and the worm-eaten tapestry.

Much Ado is neatly dated by the fact that Meres, writing in 1598, had never seen it, but Will Kemp, who left the company in 1599, acted in it. Kemp had already danced his way to Norwich and now proposed to dance his way to Rome. He was a robust fellow, and a one-man band, who had a continental reputation by 1589, when Thomas Nashe dedicated *An Almond for a Parrot* to him (with reference to 'that merry man Rablays', who stands behind so much Elizabethan literary humour, for better or for worse). Kemp could move between companies as he chose: the great serious actors needed a reliable supporting company and a supply of plays, but as a famous clown Kemp was independent. Ben Jonson in *Antipodes* (printed in 1640) complained of Kemp's impromptu conversations with the audience: Elizabethan clowning was evidently as anarchic as Elizabethan printing. This is why Shakespeare so often isolates his clowns' scenes from any scene which carries on the plot. He seems content, though in *Hamlet* he has stern words to say on the subject.

Robert Armin succeeded Kemp as clown to the Chamberlain's Men, and scholars see a distinction between him as a more intellectual and Kemp as a more rumbustious kind of clown. I doubt whether anyone would have noticed this if we had not known of the succession. They were both writers, both wits and both acrobats, good at physical clowning. The theatre altered as taste and patronage altered, but I do not think the change from Kemp to Armin represents a crucial moment.

> Since Robin Hood, maid Marian
> And Little John were gone a,
> The hobby horse was quite forgot
> Whence Kempe did dance alone a:
> He did labour after the tabor
> For to dance: then into France
> He took pains to skip it,
> In hopes of gains he will trip it
> On the toe.

THOMAS WEELKES
Ayeres or Phantasticke Spirites for Three Voices, 1608

There is no doubt about Kemp's high-spirited performances. High spirits breathe from every page of his *Nine Daies Wonder* (1600), which is funnier than most fiction. 'O Kemp, dear Master Kemp, you are even as welcome as, as, as, and so stammering he began to study for a fit comparison, and I thank him at last he fitted me: for saith he, thou art even as welcome, as the Queen's best greyhound.' Shakespeare's comic prose owes something to the liveliness of Kemp's.

Shakespeare himself was still an actor, of course. In 1598 he played in Ben Jonson's *Every Man in his Humour*, which incidentally refers to *Henry IV*. In Jonson's 1616 Folio Shakespeare is named first among 'The principal comedians' in the play. It was Shakespeare, so Rowe tells us, who first noticed Jonson's talent, got this play accepted, and secured him for the Chamberlain's Men. Jonson had two views of Shakespeare: one envious and slightly sour, as his habit was, the other of admiring worship, which in the end came to overwhelm him. He was seven or eight years younger than Shakespeare. He went to school at Westminster under Camden, was apprenticed to a builder, served as a soldier, married at twenty-one, and broke his apprenticeship to become an actor; in 1597 he was working under Henslowe. His earliest plays have not survived, except for *The Case is Altered*. In 1597 he was in trouble over the satire *The Isle of Dogs*, and in 1599 he went to prison and was branded on the thumb after murdering a fellow actor called Gabriel Spencer in a duel; Jonson claimed his sword was ten inches shorter.

Every Man in his Humour was a dramatic enactment of the consequences of dominant passions, a little pedantic in the execution. All the same, its theme and scheme were of particular interest to Shakespeare, and had an influence on his own treatment of his sources. He had been conscious of this sort of interplay since Ben Jonson had been a schoolboy. Corporal Nym in *Henry V* is always talking about humours; he may be a joke at Jonson's expense, but not a very malicious joke.

Jonson's play observes unity of time, and may have been the first of his plays to do so. It takes just one long summer's day. He was already a master of complexity and climax. In *The Case is Altered*, which he adapted from Plautus, but in a quite different way from Shakespeare's *Comedy of Errors*, Jonson's climax is a stage full of characters at cross-purposes, with all the strands of his plot coming together into one elegant if jejunely worded solution. For better or for worse, that is a comment on his reading of Latin drama. In *Every Man in his Humour*, Jonson uses time quite differently from Shakespeare or anyone else in the English theatre. And he is more urban: where Shakespeare's plots move from the town to the country, Jonson's moves from the country to the town, the centre of his interest. He dislikes Shakespeare's sudden conversions and rebirths, and mistrusts the twilight zones of his comedies and their element of lyrical magic. Later in life Jonson broke away from linear plots, which in comedy at least Shakespeare never adopted. All the same, the interaction between them is deeper and more multiple than appears at first sight, and Latin comedy stands behind them both.

It is more important, if the theatrical gossip recorded by Rowe is true, that Shakespeare rescued Jonson from Henslowe, and that they became (which is certain) close friends. It used to be imagined that London writers in those days met at a tavern called the Mermaid, which is where Ben Jonson when he became famous held court among lesser poets. In every London generation there have been such places, and there is no reason to distrust the tradition. It is a curious thought, though not one to put weight on, that if Shakespeare late in his life and Jonson made too much noise in their tavern, the baby they would have woken up was the infant Milton, who was born a few houses away.

James Burbage had not concluded his negotiations for renewing the lease of the Theatre when he died in January 1597; he had agreed to pay the ground landlord Giles Allen £24 instead of £14 a year, and to let the building itself revert to Allen in the end, though not in five years as Allen wanted. Burbage had then spent £600 on the old monks' refectory of Blackfriars, which stood within the city limits but came under the Crown, not under the Mayor and council of London. He spent more fitting that up as a theatre, but local protests prevented its use. The lease of the Theatre ran out in April and went unrenewed. In July, after *The Isle of Dogs* scandal, the Privy Council ordered the Shoreditch and south bank theatres to be pulled down, including the Curtain and the Theatre by name. This order was not executed, but a satirist wrote in 1598: 'One like the unfrequented Theatre/Walks in dark silence, and vast solitude.' Giles Allen used to come to the George Inn, Shoreditch, four times a year to receive his quarterly rents, and in autumn of 1598 Cuthbert Burbage, as his father's heir, agreed there to exorbitant terms for a new lease; even so, Allen refused to accept Richard Burbage as security for his brother, so the negotiations fell through, and Allen made a plan 'to pull down the same, and to convert the wood and timber thereof to some better use'. This was the last straw.

Allen spent Christmas in the country. After dark on 28 December Cuthbert and Richard Burbage, with a friend called William Smith from Waltham Cross, who had a financial interest in their enterprises, a carpenter (builder) called Peter Street, and about a dozen workmen, came and dismantled the Theatre to the ground. Mrs Burbage, the widow of James, was there to watch them do it. By a clause of the old lease it was perfectly legal. Giles Allen accused them of riotous assembly, 'unlawful and offensive weapons as namely swords, daggers, bills, axes and suchlike ... very riotous, outrageous and forcible manner' and illegal destruction, 'not only then and there forcibly and riotously resisting your subjects, servants and farmers, but also then and there pulling, breaking, and throwing down the said Theatre in very outrageous, riotous and violent sort, to the great disturbance and terrifying ... of divers others of your Majesty's loving subjects there inhabiting'. The Burbages took the spoils of these ruins across the river in boats, and there they used them to build the Globe, close by the Rose and the Bearpit, on the south side of Maiden Lane (now Park Street) to the west of Dead Man's Place. Allen sued for £800 damages, but he lost his case. He even sued for forty shillings for the trampling of his grass.

In the inventory of the goods of Sir Thomas Brend, whose son Nicholas leased the site of the Globe, it was described as 'newly built' on 16 May 1599, and 'occupied by William Shakespeare and others'. Shakespeare was now a person of substance both at Stratford and in London. When Richard Quiney came to London in October 1598 and stayed till February, in a laborious and successful attempt to negotiate tax relief for Stratford-upon-Avon, one of his first moves, on 25 October, was to borrow £30 from Shakespeare:

> Loving Countryman: I am bold of you as of a friend, craving your help with £30, upon Mr. Bushell's and my security or Mr. Mytton's with me. Mr. Roswell is not come to London as yet, and I have especial cause. You shall friend me much in helping me out of all the debts I owe in London, I thank God, and much quiet my mind, which would not be indebted.... You shall neither lose credit nor money by me, the Lord willing. ... I will hold my time and content your friend, and if we bargain farther, you shall be the paymaster yourself. ... I fear I shall not be back this night from the Court. Haste! The Lord be with you and with us all. Amen. From the Bell in Carter Lane. ...

Mr Bushell is Edward or Thomas Bushell of Broad Marston near Stratford, allies by marriage both of the Grevilles and of the Quineys. He became a gentleman usher to the Earl of Essex. Richard Mytton was a gentleman servant to Sir Edward Greville. The network of trust is based on local loyalty and old acquaintance and alliance. A younger Quiney called Thomas married Shakespeare's daughter Judith. The father, Adrian, was sent to the Marshalsea prison in London with other friends of the Shakespeares by Sir Thomas Lucy (the second) as High Sheriff in 1601, when Sir Edward Greville sued the Corporation in Stratford for riot in a quarrel over Bankcroft, the riverside meadows. Old Quiney was killed in 1602 by accident by his own servant, as bailiff of Stratford trying to put down a riot by Greville's servants.

The Quiney family can therefore appeal to an old Stratford friend for money in a Stratford cause, and yet rely through a network of relationship on the Greville household as security. It was surely through the same kind of network that the trouble between Sir Edward Greville and the Corporation was smoothed over for the time being in the autumn of 1598. It would be nice to know more about Shakespeare's relationship with Richard Mytton, and anything at all about Mr Roswell. A younger Thomas Bushell (1594–1674), whom Shakespeare must have known for twenty years or so, is the subject of one of the strangest of Aubrey's *Brief Lives*. He was a music-loving, grotto-loving bachelor obsessed with death, a servant of Francis Bacon and an operator of silver mines in Wales, and 'the greatest arts-master to run into debt (perhaps) in the world'. Charles I's Queen gave him an Egyptian mummy which he installed at Enstone in Oxfordshire, in a grotto among marvellous waterworks, 'but I believe long before this time the dampness of the place has spoiled it with mouldiness.'

It seems clear from other letters that Quiney got his money at once. Meanwhile, his father wrote to him about early November: 'If you bargain with Wm. Sha. or receive money there, bring your money home that you may; and see how knit stockings be sold. There is great buying of them at Evesham.' His brother's man and 'Edward Wheat' had bought £20 worth there, 'wherefore I think you may do good, if you have money'. Abraham Sturley wrote on 4 November in reply to a letter of 25 October received on the 31st. He noted that trouble with the lord of the manor, Sir Edward Greville, was over for the time being, and Quiney would concentrate on tax relief, 'and that our countryman Mr. Wm. Shak. would procure us money, which I shall like of as I shall hear when, and where, and how; and I pray let not go that occasion. . . .'

In January of 1599 the Stratford town accounts record a load of stone for ten pence bought from Shakespeare, probably for bridge repairs, the stone being very probably left over from repairs to New Place or the demolition of some ruinous shed or wall. Stone in the Cotswold area has always been more expensive to buy than profitable to sell, and people keep useful heaps of it lying about in case of need. In Stratford, this would have been even more true, as the local stone is neither abundant nor wonderful. So it was another friendly act, to sell the stone for ten pence. Richard Quiney may have arranged it.

In London, Shakespeare's literary reputation was still growing as more people began to read his famous works. Allusions to *Venus and Adonis* and *The Rape of Lucrece* are too numerous to catalogue: one will stand for all. The poet and antiquary John Weever wrote Shakespeare a blushing sonnet in his Epigrams in *The Oldest Cut and Newest Fashion* (1599), about Rose-cheek'd Adonis, Fair fire-hot Venus, Lucrece, Proud lust-stung Tarquin, and 'Romeo, Richard, more whose names I know not . . .'. In the same year, William Jaggard published *The Passionate Pilgrim by William Shakespeare*, a miscellany of twenty poems most of which were not by him, and all of which were probably filched in one way or another from their authors or from the owner or owners of the manuscript collection they reproduce. It was a tribute of a kind, I suppose. In the third (1612) edition, Jaggard added two quite long poems from Thomas Heywood's *Britain's Troy*. Heywood, in a note of protest in his *Apology for Actors* in the same year, went out of his way to treat Shakespeare with the utmost courtesy and warmth. '. . . I must acknowledge my lines not worthy his patronage, under whom he hath published them, so the author I know much offended with Mr. Jaggard that (altogether unknown to him) presumed to make so bold with his name.'

I take the Shakespeare of this period to be the youngish intelligent face of Martin Droeshout's engraving in the First Folio of 1623. Portraits of Shakespeare include forgeries of numerous kinds and widely different dates. The Chandos portrait in the National Gallery is convincing at first glance; it was once owned by Sir William Davenant, then by Betterton, then Mrs Barry, all theatrical characters, and its provenance from Joseph Taylor the actor, who was Shakespeare's colleague, and its having been painted by Burbage, depend on the evidence of Oldys, another Restoration actor. That is not to be relied on, because Davenant was absurdly inventive; the portrait differs a little from the Stratford monument and the Droeshout engraving.

This latter is probably genuine. Droeshout, who was fifteen when Shakespeare died, worked from some kind of sketch of a much younger man than the Stratford monument shows. Ben Jonson wrote that he caught the likeness precisely, and Shakespeare's friends who supervised the Folio must have thought the same. The Shakespeare it commemorates is in his thirties; he was thirty-five in 1599, but I estimate the date of the lost original sketch at about 1601, which leaves fifteen years for the difference between the Droeshout image and the monument. Their similarity and degree of difference confirm the authenticity of both.

None of the other pictures have any authority at all. They must be judged by their likeness or unlikeness to Droeshout and the monument. The Felton portrait is close, but based on a late state of the engraving. The Janssen portrait may be the right date, but it portrays someone else. Only the Chandos portrait cannot be quite dismissed. Droeshout shows a successful young Londoner, the monument a retired Stratford poet, but the Chandos portrait is like a Snitterfield man. The chestnut beard might be thought to confirm the hair colour we are told the Stratford monument had at its restoration (after eighteenth-century whitewashing) in 1861, which may or may not have been its original colouring, and which is certainly not visible today.

The first production of Shakespeare's or anyone's at the Globe which we can date exactly is *Julius Caesar*, which Thomas Platter of Basle saw there on 21 September 1599. The Globe was now the most magnificent theatre London had ever seen, but it was thatched with straw and stood among tenements and poor houses. The performance began, announced by trumpets from the roof and the unfurling of a banner, at about two in the afternoon. Platter noticed with amazement that two or three plays were performed in different places in London on every afternoon of the week: 'then the best actors have the most audiences.' He calls them all 'comedies', but he included in that category 'the tragedy of Julius Caesar', which is the one he saw. At the end 'they danced according to their custom perfectly beautifully, two dressed in men's and two in women's clothes.' Another traveller a few months later praised the theatre 'in the ancient Roman manner' and the fact that everyone could see, but otherwise noticed only the heads of 'some Counts and Noblemen' stuck up on the spikes of London Bridge on the way home.

All the same, to judge by its date of composition the opening play at the Globe was *Henry V*. Falstaff and his friends had made *Henry IV* immensely popular and famous. People quoted Shakespeare in everyday conversation: 'I set thy lips abroach, from whence doth flow Naught but pure Juliet and Romeo' (John Marston in 1598). They referred to him in intimate letters: 'All the news I can send you that I think will make you merry is that I read in a letter from London that Sir John Falstaff is by his Mistress Dame Pintpot made father of a goodly miller's thumb, a boy that's all head and very little body; but this is a secret' (Lady Southampton in 1599). *Henry V* was the expected climax. Shakespeare does replay the Falstaff theme, though he transmutes it, but from its first moment this play belongs to the Muse of fire: it gives full play to the heroic poetry he had spent years perfecting. Henry V was both Shakespeare's hero and the nation's: the play's mood is that England may never see such days again. An empire meant an empire in France, an extended kingdom, and England would never have one again.

The past is purified, mythified and made innocent in *Henry V*. Not just the figure of Henry with his Falstaffian past and his devotion to more convincing ideals than personal honour, but the poetry, the texture of words and the victorious momentum of the play have given a simple but powerful kind of inspiration to English people at strange moments and in difficult places down to the present generation. Shakespeare's role as national poet of the English people should not be thought to detract from his greatness in the least degree, though it does detract from his impartiality as historian, a quality to which he had no pretension. Yet he was never merely a propagandist, either for England or for the Elizabethan age. The first impartial historians of modern times were Camden and de Thou; their careers were not untroubled, nor was the publication of their works free of obstacles.

This play is dated by a reference to the Earl of Essex in Ireland between March and September of 1599. It was mentioned in the Stationers' Register of May 1600, and printed in that year, not very well. On 4 August it was noted in the Register that *As You Like It*, *Henry V*, *Every Man in his Humour* and *Much Ado About Nothing* were 'to be stayed'. They all belonged to the Chamberlain's Men, and the last two were later properly registered and well printed in quarto: *As You Like It* has no quarto, *Henry V* a bad one, but a transfer of rights was duly registered in August. The company was beginning to protect its literary property, apparently for the first time. The quarto text cut the play from three hours to two, and cut away eleven parts, so it may be a touring version. The King of Scotland, later James I of England, was furious at the mockery of a Scotsman, and although he saw the play in December 1605, the Folio publication cuts out a lot of its profanity. The text contains faint but definite traces of a part for Falstaff (e.g. act 5, scene i), which Shakespeare removed, almost certainly for writer's reasons, not from anyone's pressure. Henslowe paid £10 on 15 October 1599 for the *Life of Oldcastle*, which is later than *Henry V*, and reflects Falstaff's immense popularity.

The style of the first stinging lines of the play had distracted attention from the unique device of such a chorus. The Prologue sets a tone, as well as furthering the action and pointing with exalted modesty to its unique greatness of theme. The dented helmet of Henry V was in the Abbey and Shakespeare had seen it; no doubt in 1599 other helmets of the same generation were well known. The references to the theatre itself are almost equally striking and thrilling. But the play then begins slowly, with a mildly farcical pair of bishops discussing the state of the realm and the King's new character, which they heavily underline. All the same, Shakespeare has lavished lines of great beauty and humorous subtlety on these silly fellows. When they address the King, which they do with uncorseted prolixity, they parody the elderly world he means to escape, and at the same time they set out plainly his legal position, since this is not to be a wild escapade, but a legitimate war.

Later in the play the right of the King's quarrel with France is questioned, but we must know at least that it was arguable, and that the King himself may believe in it. What fires him all the same is neither ambition, though he shows that, nor the legal argument, but the Ambassador's insult with the Dauphin's present of tennis balls. (Tennis was not only a courtly but a popular game played everywhere since the days of Henry VIII, so Shakespeare and his audience did not think of it as specially royal.) The King's speech is a sizzling and unforgettable piece of rhetoric:

> For that I have laid by my majesty
> And plodded like a man for working-days;
> But I will rise there with so full a glory
> That I will dazzle all the eyes of France,
> Yea, strike the Dauphin blind to look on us.
> And tell the pleasant Prince this mock of his
> Hath turn'd his balls to gun-stones, and his soul
> Shall stand sore charged for the wasteful vengeance
> That shall fly with them; for many a thousand widows
> Shall this his mock mock out of their dear husbands;
> Mock mothers from their sons, mock castles down;
> And some are yet ungotten and unborn
> That shall have cause to curse the Dauphin's scorn.
> But this lies all within the will of God,
> To whom I do appeal. . . .

Now that the wheels are in motion, the first act closes at once. 'Now all the youth of England are on fire. . . .' The chorus announces the second act at Southampton in the same high terms. It opens all the same with Falstaff's comic and quarrelsome friends; I take Nym to be Ben Jonson. 'I dare not fight; but I will wink and hold out mine iron. It is a simple one; but what though? It will toast cheese, and it will endure cold as another man's sword will . . .', '. . . and Pistol's cock is up, And flashing fire will follow.' Apart from the relief of pure comedy, the point of this scene is that Falstaff is dying. His death is lapped in comic language slowly transmuted to a lyric sadness, a distilled essence of Falstaff. We never see him, but the ominous notes are clearly sounded. 'By my troth, he'll yield the crow a pudding one of these days: the King has kill'd his heart.' In the second scene of this act, the King deals with traitors who plotted to assassinate him: a more terrible version and bloodier re-enactment of his rejection of Falstaff. Assassination plots, real or imaginary, were common enough under Elizabeth, and Shakespeare draws on popular horror of this appalling crime. There was no way of dealing with an inadequate monarch in those days except by assassination, and learned churchmen in England and overseas discussed whether any conditions existed that might justify regicide. But Elizabeth was greatly loved: 'to have ruled with your loves' was her proudest boast, and she was now an elderly woman.

The audience's sympathy with the King would have been unhesitating. Roman Catholics are not mentioned, but they will certainly have come to mind. Seen in these terms, the King's speeches are very powerful. The conspirators confess and repent as Elizabethans were expected to do and commonly did. Their terrible and sad deaths are the prelude to the innocent death of Falstaff, the saddest scene Shakespeare ever wrote, in which even the poor jokes add to the sadness. The account is in vernacular prose, connected mostly by 'and' and 'then', faltering towards its devastating climax. It ends with the added sadness of the parting of soldiers not likely to come home. Shakespeare has not deserted his old themes and loyalties.

The last scene of the act is the last thing that must happen before battle commences: the English embassy to France, with Exeter speaking for the King about the horrors of the war. It is as if France herself were a living creature that must suffer, and in fact the destruction and restoration of the order of nature in France is a powerful sub-theme of the play that takes over in the end from the Muse of fire.

The chorus to the third act describes the royal fleet at Southampton, and the siege of Harfleur, punctuated by the first cannonfire.

The Globe owned a real cannon. The fleet is an astonishing tour de force, which may be based on a painting of the fleet of Henry VIII sailing to the Field of the Cloth of Gold; but it is also based on observation:

> Play with your fancies; and in them behold
> Upon the hempen tackle ship-boys climbing;
> Hear the shrill whistle which doth order give
> To sounds confus'd; behold the threaden sails,
> Borne with th'invisible and creeping wind,
> Draw the huge bottoms through the furrowed sea,
> Breasting the lofty surge. O, do but think
> You stand upon the rivage and behold
> A city on th' inconstant billows dancing;
> For so appears this fleet majestical,
> Holding due course to Harfleur. Follow, follow!
> Grapple your minds to sternage of this navy
> And leave your England as dead midnight still. . . .
>   . . . and the nimble gunner
> With linstock now the devilish cannon touches,
> And down goes all before them. Still be kind,
> And eke out our performance with your mind.

It will be seen that in this play Shakespeare constantly seeks to go beyond the bounds of plays, and perhaps the bounds of poetry, but in doing so he is intensely dramatic. No one else has used a description in the theatre with such energy: by demanding more of the dramatic context of his play he has transformed it. The business of battles in the theatre was always a problem that had to be got round, usually with skilful and original variations, since the theatre cannot really show the clash of armies, but in

Henry V Shakespeare transcends it remarkably and very originally. I do not believe he could have done so earlier in life, because he could not then have commanded the force and energy of this poetry.

Fine as the chorus is, the King's rhetorical poetry goes beyond it, as Shakespeare shows in this act by setting them side by side. King Henry's battle speech before Harfleur is yet another unexpected tour de force. The basis of Henry's eloquence is often to be found in Holinshed or Hall, and in some form in *The Famous Victories of Henry V*, but Shakespeare has transfigured it in this case as in others. He has made the English army almost more heroic than the King, and given them, or at least the gentry, an equally noble ancestry with his own:

> And you, good yeomen,
> Whose limbs were made in England, show us here
> The mettle of your pasture; let us swear
> That you are worth your breeding – which I doubt not. . . .

But Shakespeare has not given up his habit of mocking upper-class noble sentiments with farce, and we descend at once to the disgraceful and farcical hangers-on of Falstaff – that is Nym, Bardolph, Pistol and the Boy, who has a fine satiric monologue about the others. Comic Welsh, Irish and Scottish captains follow, characters I particularly treasure. We see all too little of them, yet they are memorably etched, and keep one's mind off the serious side of the battle, which must be secondary to the climax of Agincourt. The King reinforces one's natural distaste for throat-slitting by warning Harfleur in awful terms of the consequences of a city being taken by force; Harfleur luckily surrenders: Shakespeare is idealizing.

We move to a charming scene in French with the Princess Katharine trying to learn English, then to the grandiloquent and defiant Court of France, with a splendid list of French titles, almost all from Holinshed's list of the dead at Agincourt. Scene vi is an interesting overlap of Pistol with the comic Welshmen, and the Welshmen (who are valiant soldiers) with the King: the threads of the army are beginning to be drawn together. Bardolph is due to be hanged for robbing a church, and Henry approves the sentence.

The French herald Montjoy arrives to warn him of disaster 'and tell him, for conclusion, he hath betrayed his followers, whose condemnation is pronounc'd'. All these scenes are shot through with ironies of contrast. The King's reply to Montjoy is in several moods and tones: until now he has been a king in a puppet play, though noble enough, but the disaster that looms is real, and his humbler confidence is more humanly attractive. All the same, he takes a phrase of more old-fashioned defiance from Holinshed: 'We shall your tawny ground with your red blood . . .'. Suddenly this is the eve of Agincourt, and the act ends with the brilliant portrait of the French lords on the eve of battle: a prose scene of negligent aristocratic boasting and betting and mocking; it rings eerily hollow.

Taken separately those seven scenes were a ragbag, leading us from Southampton to Agincourt in one act, but they work together. The chorus to the fourth act introduces the English army before battle, the most serious theme of the play. Shakespeare has to get the French lords out of the way before he can broach it. If they were moved to the beginning of act 4, which is perhaps where he first intended them to go, they would spoil his balance. Usually the scene following a chorus and opening an act has been in contrast to the chorus, but as the play progresses the relationship of chorus to scene becomes subtler. Ben Jonson missed the point of all this when he criticized the chorus as a mere device for wafting us through time and space. The chorus here is thrilling in his language and just as evocative as usual, and here as before what he describes looks like what is about to be enacted:

> The royal captain of this ruin'd band
> Walking from watch to watch, from tent to tent,
> Let him cry, 'Praise and glory on his head!'
> For forth he goes and visits all his host;
> Bids them good morrow with a modest smile,
> And calls them brothers, friends, and countrymen.
> Upon his royal face there is no note
> How dread an army hath enrounded him. . . .
> That every wretch, pining and pale before,
> Beholding him, plucks comfort from his looks. . . .

But this is not what Shakespeare has in store, or it is and is not. Henry is magnificent: he is holy with his brothers, sweet with old Sir Thomas Erpingham, who gives him comfort rather than the reverse, a foil to Pistol, pleased with Fluellen. But he comes among his men on even terms in disguise, and their despair and courage are more convincing: they strike a truer note than his pious optimism and wit and courage. What he says about the humanity of kings may perhaps come from Montaigne, but what Williams and Bates say about the war has a simple honesty that comes from experience of life. The King answers them, of course, but they are unanswerable. 'I am afeard there are few die well that die in a battle.' As I conceive this scene, the King draws a certain moral strength from their conversation, but they draw little from him, their minds are already made up. 'I do not desire he should answer for me, and yet I determine to fight lustily for him.'

The entire chivalrous backcloth of this play was necessary to make this one scene possible. These are the first English peasants Shakespeare has ever portrayed without comic or affectionate contempt: they are perfectly real, they speak precisely their own language, which is powerfully plain; its touch of poetry is mostly Biblical. The King concludes in verse with famous and self-pitying lines that humble him and make one sorry for him. He feels his guilt and his father's, and he prays for pardon: that is as much as he can do. We are the audience, so we are God, and we forgive him.

'The sun doth gild our armour: up, my lords!' The French go to battle boasting worse than ever; the sad, still look of the English line is reported to them. The King makes his wonderful speech to Westmoreland, part of which is versified Holinshed: an underestimated writer from whom Shakespeare has learned tricks he will soon use in adapting Plutarch for *Julius Caesar*. This speech has also some touches of Hall's *Chronicle*, but as it progresses it takes wing. The last and best part of it is Shakespeare's own; it was the pious part that was Holinshed's. I find the recitation of titles here mysteriously moving, perhaps because they are nearly all place-names that taken together speak for England, and the repeated play on Crispin/Crispian, with the veterans showing their scars year after year and claiming brotherhood of the King, unbearably so.

> He that outlives this day, and comes safe home,
> Will stand a tip-toe when this day is nam'd,
> And rouse him at the name of Crispian.
> He that shall live this day, and see old age,
> Will yearly on the vigil feast his neighbours
> And say 'To-morrow is Saint Crispian'.
> Then will he strip his sleeve and show his scars,
> And say 'These wounds I had on Crispin's day'.
> Old men forget: yet all shall be forgot,
> But he'll remember, with advantages,
> What feats he did that day. Then shall our names,
> Familiar in his mouth as household words –
> Harry the King, Bedford and Exeter,
> Warwick and Talbot, Salisbury and Gloucester –
> Be in their flowing cups freshly rememb'red.
> This story shall the good man teach his son. . . .

This is immortality of a very desirable kind, and happy the son whose father taught him such a story. If ever anyone deserves for their name to become a household word in his country, that man was Shakespeare.

The battle is built up in suspense: the urgency of messages, the French herald at the last moment, the King's mounting rage. But the only scene of fighting is the idiot Pistol taking Falstaff's old part, with a French prisoner and the Boy to do translation. The French lords appear in horror and disarray; Henry hears of the deaths of friends; the Welsh captains, still between comic and serious, record events: the French have murdered the boys with the English luggage, 'wherefore the King most worthily hath caus'd every soldier to cut his prisoner's throat', though in fact he had done so already, as a safety precaution when the French reformed for an attack.

And yet he is still threatening to do so at a later stage: I am unable to sort this out, but Empson has discussed it with his usual acumen. Quite suddenly the French herald reappears to beg the bodies of the dead, and the battle is over:

> For many of our princes – woe the while! –
> Lie drown'd and soak'd in mercenary blood;
> So do our vulgar drench their peasant limbs
> In blood of princes. . . .

One knows what Shakespeare feels about the feudal upper class better from this scornfully written sentence, spoken by a foreigner of course, than from many other passages in his plays. *Henry V* ends quietly and beautifully, unwinding from triumph into comedy, with the Duke of Burgundy's fine speech about the French countryside, which sounds just like England except for the one word 'vineyards', and the royal marriage, which is in purely comic tradition though without low characters. The chorus concludes with a sonnet tying the play to the next reign, in which France is called 'best garden of the world', and quite right too. The Boy is presumably murdered, and Pistol is dishonoured; he goes home to live as a thief and a pimp. The chorus to act 5 records Henry's refusal to have 'His bruised helmet and his bended sword' carried before him through London, and makes an elaborate and gratuitous compliment to the Earl of Essex, by way of Julius Caesar:

> As, by a lower but loving likelihood,
> Were now the General of our gracious Empress –
> As in good time he may – from Ireland coming,
> Bringing rebellion broached on his sword,
> How many would the peaceful city quit
> To welcome him!

It was not to be. Essex felt he was badly treated in Ireland and had enemies at home, as indeed he was and had. He returned without permission, burst in on the Queen, who was half dressed and wigless, and fell at once into dire disgrace. Unable to bear this, he broke into idiotic and almost unsupported rebellion, with Lord Southampton as one of his handful of lieutenants. Essex had been drawn into a trap; he was beheaded and Southampton went to the Tower. At the time of *Henry V* that lay in the future, but it would happen quite soon. Shakespeare had evidently backed a popular hero, whom he may well have preferred to the Cecil family, but his hero lacked staying power.

There are several traces in *Henry V* of the imminence of *Julius Caesar*, which must have been begun almost before *Henry V* was finished. Platter of Basle reckoned it had about fifteen actors, though the list of characters calls for nearer thirty: but Platter may not have counted servants and minor characters, and parts were probably doubled. This play is Shakespeare's first to be firmly based on Plutarch, whose Roman lives are much fuller and more informative than his Greek ones, though he wrote in Greek. Shakespeare used Sir Thomas North's English version of Amyot's French version, including its few mistakes. (I have discussed in Appendix 7 the Earl of Derby's copy of this book.)

Plutarch was almost but not quite a great writer. By hindsight the greatest of his achievements may be his contribution to Shakespeare, in moral and historical analysis as well as in narrative history and the portrayal of character, which last with all its consequences was his principal aim. It is the Plutarchian bone-structure that makes *Julius Caesar* more austere than other plays. It contrasts strongly with *Henry V*, and all the more so with the comedies that followed. There were other Caesar plays in Italian, Latin and French, including an Oxford *Caesar's Revenge*. The ghost is Elizabethan, but Shakespeare makes little of that, much more of music. He compresses time to six days and two battles into one. The play was not printed until 1623, but it was popular, as we know from Digges and others.

Julius Caesar is quite short (2477 lines) and moves swiftly. It is not really about Caesar so much as Caesar's revenge, but the towering Caesar dominates it more effectively than the more psychologically interesting Brutus, about whom there inevitably hangs a shadow of negativeness because he is the person to whom a succession of things happen. The real Brutus was tougher and more sinister, just as the real Welsh archers of Agincourt were tougher and deadlier figures than Bates and Williams in *Henry V*. *Julius Caesar* is almost but not quite a revenge tragedy, and almost but not quite a history play. Once again Shakespeare has produced a new form of play, not only a new play, and having produced it he will desert it, though Hamlet owes something to Brutus, just as Cassius on Caesar, 'such a thing as I myself', owes something to Henry V on the King, 'in his nakedness he appears but a man'. The anti-populism in *Julius Caesar* reflects classical sources rather than Shakespeare's views, but he is interested by the Roman mob.

In act 1, scene i, the Tribunes are like the Mayor's officers putting down theatres and festivals: 'What dost thou with thy best apparel on?' One notices that the cobbler easily holds his own with these incisive boobies. The Admiral's Men had a play in two parts called 'Caesar' and 'Pompey' in 1594 and 1595, and the fuss about Pompey in this scene is a raising of the hat to that way of looking at Caesar. In the second scene Caesar and Antony are merry, as the cobbler was, but the audience knows what the soothsayer means about the Ides of March, and what will come of Brutus and Cassius left alone on the stage. Caesar absent, and Caesar carped at, still dominates the stage:

Why, man, he doth bestride the narrow world
Like a Colossus, and we petty men
Walk under his huge legs, and peep about
To find ourselves dishonourable graves.
Men at some time are masters of their fates:
The fault, dear Brutus, is not in our stars,
But in ourselves, that we are underlings.

Add the talk of honour and of the common good, and you have something that strikingly resembles the kind of conversation the Earl of Essex
must have been having. But Cassius is by no means Shakespeare's hero.
The play is about a conspiracy to murder, and about envy and its consequences. Brutus is dangerously in love with honour, always an ambivalent
virtue to Shakespeare.

Till then, my noble friend, chew upon this:
Brutus had rather be a villager
Than to repute himself a son of Rome
Under these hard conditions as this time
Is like to lay upon us.

The conditions are those of living under an emperor; what Brutus is unable
to accept is monarchy. Cassius 'loves no plays ... hears no music ...
smiles in such a sort As if he mock'd himself ...'. Shakespeare is thrilled
with the physical detail he has found in Plutarch, which brings all these
Romans to life as no English biography until Boswell's *Johnson* brought
people to life. He even adds some sharp detail of his own: Cicero's 'such
ferret and such fiery eyes', for instance – an interesting view of Cicero.
Shakespeare seems to have known enough about him to be shocked by his
intrigues; or is he the model of someone like Bacon? To convey the flavour
of conspiracy, the conspirators lapse into evil prose in this scene; they
return to more epigrammatic verse only as it closes. The stiff verse of much
of the play, with its overtone or subtone of Latin, seems to have made
Shakespeare uneasy. The thunder and lightning and signs and portents of
the night derive from Marlowe's *Lucan*: they can still make one shiver in
an old-fashioned way, and Shakespeare's new version of Marlovian verse is
a brilliant contrivance, but one cannot write an entire play like that.

Act 2 finds Brutus meditating in the early hours of morning. 'I cannot by
the progress of the stars Give guess how near to day....' The morning is the
Ides of March, conspiracy has come to action, and only the slave Lucius
sleeps. Portia, wife to Brutus, intervenes in vain; her part is too noble to
have much human meaning but she certainly adds to the tension by
foreseeing evil: 'for here have been Some six or seven, who did hide their
faces Even from darkness.' She is a balance to Caesar's wife Calpurnia, who
has more signs and portents. The warnings and auguries intensify: ancient
literature is full of them.

The third act is Caesar's murder and its first results: they hinge on Antony, since the conspirators have virtually no policy. Antony is formidable in grief, in cunning and in rage:

> And Caesar's spirit, ranging for revenge,
> With Até by his side come hot from hell,
> Shall in these confines with a monarch's voice
> Cry 'Havoc!' and let slip the dogs of war,
> That this foul deed shall smell above the earth
> With carrion men, groaning for burial.

This is inherited or recycled rant, which the subject of the play attracted from English theatrical tradition. The dogs of war last figured in the prologue to *Henry V*, and we have seen all too much of *Até* in this biography. But in the second scene of the act speeches are made to the people; there Antony is formidable in eloquence. Brutus speaks a brilliant imitation of formal Latin prose, as finely chiselled as the plot of *The Rape of Lucrece*, but it could scarcely be less effective as popular oratory: it is frigidly cold. Still, the plebs applaud him until Mark Antony speaks his famous speech, which I take to be the turning point of the entire play, and its greatest, most demanding performance. The plebs go wild about it, and their riotous interventions give Antony a necessary chance to get his breath: he speaks in snatches of thirty and thirty-five lines. The act closes with the light relief of the death of Cinna the poet, torn to pieces by clowns for his bad verses, a scene as comical as it is horrifying: one can feel the breath of the mob. (The story is in Plutarch.)

In the fourth act Antony and Octavius distance themselves from their ally Lepidus, whom they use like the ass to bear a load, 'and turn him off, Like to the empty ass, to shake his ears, And graze in commons'. Brutus and Cassius quarrel more seriously. Shakespeare picks with glee on a philosopher in Plutarch who quotes Homer, transformed by Thomas North into a preposterous jingle. Shakespeare makes him a poet reciting his own verses, sententious and bad enough, but not as horrible as North's. Now the shadows begin to close in: Portia has 'swallow'd fire' and died, the battle of Philippi is imminent, a hundred senators are dead.

An early version of the news of Portia's death survives alongside the later one: it was an absurdly cold and inhumanly noble little scene, where the later one makes Brutus a gentler, sadder character. Brutus ends the act with a scene of lyrical drowsiness and music (Lucius is asleep again) and a brief appearance of Caesar's ghost which Brutus treats with agnostic curiosity, as Hamlet does his father's. The last act is Philippi and the suicide of Brutus: 'Caesar, thou art reveng'd, Even with the sword that kill'd thee.'

The first part of *Julius Caesar* is conceived and executed with fullness and organically, but the end of the play is perfunctory. I do not think Shakespeare had lost interest in the plot, though he was probably bored with the problems of dramatic battles, but the play appears to have been finished hastily. One must never underestimate the great pressure under which Shakespeare worked. It must have been both a stimulus and a nightmare for a poet to write so often against time. Ralegh's poems and writings were almost all composed in the infinite, melancholy leisure of the Tower: where else would one settle down to write a history of the world and an endlessly long love poem to the Queen? Jonson worked in the theatre, but in comparison with Shakespeare's his work is meagre.

My favourite character in the last part of *Julius Caesar* is the freed Parthian Pindarus, who is bound to kill Cassius on demand and does so. He speaks only ten lines or so, but Shakespeare likes him, and it shows:

> Far from this country Pindarus shall run,
> Where never Roman shall take note of him.

Let us hope, as I am certain Shakespeare hoped, that he got safely home to his desert. They look for him later in the play but no one finds him. The play ends with a last taste of Antony's eloquence, like a roll of drums.

As You Like It is much harder to date. It was noted 'to be stayed' in the Stationers' Register for 1600. It alludes to *Hero and Leander*, published in 1598, and seems too perfect for an earlier date. Robert Armin, known as Tutch from the comedy of *Two Maids at More-clacke*, seems to have played Touchstone. All this indicates 1599, but the date is not a secure one. Shakespeare uses Lodge's *Rosalynde* (1590), a prose romance of great merit, and of course Lyly; his act 2, scene i, is like the act 2, scene i of Greene's *Orlando Furioso*. Music is an essential element of the play, and so are its formal and bold devices. The plot is light and fantastic, with an elegant knot or cat's cradle of simple feelings: it is love, not wit, that carries the comedy, 'Obscured in the circle of this forest' (act 5, scene iv). Yet Lodge's romance has an element of realism injected into it by Shakespeare, which dramatic enactment needed. The Forest of Arden is not a painless place and not everything ends well there. Arden stands for the Ardennes, but Shakespeare will have been pleased by the coincidence of names with Warwickshire.

Thomas Lodge was an interesting man, an exquisite writer who went to sea to avoid the plague of 1592, and reappeared in London as a doctor to write his *Treatise of the Plague* in 1603. His advice was: 'Briefly, to live in repose of spirit, in all joy, pleasure, sport and contemplation amongst a man's friends, comforteth heart and vital spirits, and is in this time more requisite than any other things.' He wrote a defence of poetry and the arts as early as about 1580, *An Alarum against Usurers* (1584), *Robert Duke of Normandy* (1591), *Margarite of America* (1596) and *Rosalynde* (1590, with nine editions before 1614), and numerous other works. His lyrics are scattered through his romances, and are charming: 'Love in his bosom like a bee doth suck his sweet', so he will whip love with roses and bind him with roses. His lyrics melt like snowflakes in the hand. 'And so sing I, with down a down, a down a.'

> A blithe and bonny country lass,
> Heigh ho, the bonny lass,
> Sat sighing on the tender grass,
> And weeping said, Will none come woo me?
> A smicker boy, a lither swain,
> Heigh ho, a smicker swain,
> That in his love was wanton fair,
> With smiling looks came straight unto her. . . .

We are clearly not too far from the world of Shakespeare's *A Lover's Complaint*. All Lodge's poems are love poems: Shakespeare both admires and mocks him. The forest life in the play has deeper roots, because in English the forest is a perpetual golden age, being the world of Robin Hood, so that when courtiers play at golden ages among the trees, reality takes over. The myth of Shakespeare the deerstealer probably arose from *As You Like It*, because the Robin Hood-like mythology of deerstealers was ready and waiting to receive him. The myths have withered now; perhaps they died in that extraordinary forced migration of deer described by Thomas Peacock in his essay 'The Last Day of Windsor Forest'.

As You Like It was revived at Wilton in 1603, but later it was neglected: it was not highflown enough for the courtly pastorals of Charles I or biting enough for the Court of Charles II. Its gentleness and fragile fragrance and its deliberately old-fashioned quality have appealed to me all my life, in spite of a number of unlikely productions: it has, as it were, nothing to declare but its poetry.

> *Rosalind* . . . I'll go find a shadow, and sigh till he come.
>
> *Olivia*   . . . pray you, if you know,
>   Where in the purlieus of this forest stands
>   A sheep-cote fenc'd about with olive trees?
> *Celia* West of this place, down in the neighbour bottom.
>   The rank of osiers by the murmuring stream
>   Left on your right hand brings you to the place.
>   But at this hour the house doth keep itself. . . .

Yet *As You Like It* is by no means cloying. Both at home and in the forest Shakespeare assembles a world of most varied social elements; I think it was the clashes of their language and the morals of their different behaviour that inspired him to write the play. We know from the theatrical tradition which Oldys passed on to the Restoration theatre that Shakespeare played Adam, the faithful elderly servant. If so, he gave

himself some very good lines. The Arden edition of the play has a
particularly good introduction and commentary by Agnes Latham (1975),
who makes the point that Shakespeare apparently went beyond Lodge to
the *Tale of Gamelyn*, a poem that sometimes occurs in manuscripts of
Chaucer's Canterbury Tales, and gives Orlando his essentially English
tone. I accept this to be true, but he would have to have read it in a manuscript, because it is not in the blackletter Chaucer editions of his time. The
thought of Shakespeare burrowing in Chaucer manuscripts for unregarded
poems is attractive, and certainly not impossible. It looks to me as if he was
shown the poem by an editor who rejected it; perhaps he was asked his
opinion. But here alas I am building conjecture on conjecture, as I undertook not to do. What we do know is that Shakespeare has drawn his
characters more crisply than Lodge, and has added satiric Jaques (who
confirms a date in 1599 when satire was the rage) and the clown
Touchstone.

The play begins in prose, with Orlando the ill-treated younger brother
complaining to Adam. When his elder brother Oliver attacks him he puts a
wrestling lock on him: 'you have train'd me like a peasant, obscuring and
hiding from me all gentlemanlike qualities. The spirit of my father grows
strong in me, and I will no longer endure it.' A professional wrestler is set to
provoke and kill him at a challenge match, but Orlando wins and goes into
exile in the forest with Adam, where they are bound to meet the old Duke,
also exiled, 'and a many merry men with him; and there they live like the
old Robin Hood of England . . . and fleet the time carelessly, as they did in
the golden world.' Rosalind, who loves him, and Celia her cousin,
daughters of the old Duke and the new, dress as boys and run away too to
the same Forest of Arden. This plot is almost too absurd to write down, but
it runs along fast and charmingly. At his wrestling match Orlando recalls
Henry V: 'You mean to mock me after; you should not have mock'd me
before'.

> Now go we in content
> To liberty, and not to banishment.

Act 2 is in Arden. The Duke beautifully and sententiously declares his
happiness. Freezing cold is more acceptable than courtly flattery, there are
tongues in trees, books in brooks, sermons in stones, and good in everything. Jaques reads nature more bitterly, he grieves over a wounded deer,
and watches it weeping.

> . . . and the big round tears
> Cours'd one another down his innocent nose
> In piteous chase; and thus the hairy fool,
> Much marked of the melancholy Jaques,
> Stood on th' extremest verge of the swift brook,
> Augmenting it with tears.

Orlando has a moving scene with the old servant, who is eighty years old (act 2, scene iii) but insists on following him. This old man is so real that one wonders whether he was based on an individual; but his poetry, the delicacy of his language and of his mind, are purely Shakespearean. He sounds like an old country servant, not like some great nobleman's retainer. His purity and sweetness of nature are Shakespeare's strongest statement yet about English country people. He very slightly recalls Sir Thomas Erpingham who died at Agincourt, but his language has the same Biblical overtones as that of Williams and Bates.

Rosalind and Celia as boys have Touchstone for attendant: they encounter woodlanders called Corin and Silvius and a sub-theme of love intrigue begins. They buy a respectable little cottage. A nobleman sings an Arcadian lyric to Jaques, who satirizes it; Adam collapses, and Orlando interrupts the old Duke's forest banquet to have him entertained. They exchange some affecting verses about the basis of kindness and of society, which are intellectually central (if anything is) to the play. Jaques discourses traditionally, but with a pepper of Mercutian sharpness in the verse, on the seven ages of man. All these tours de force of poetry are strung together more or less anyhow, so that taken together they express the life of the forest and the centre of the play. The lyrics are briskly melancholy but extremely beautiful. The whole second act is a study in the true and good in human society, the links of mercy, of religion, of love and of blood. Adam's heroic faithfulness is only the extreme case.

The third act is love-intrigue and humour, and the forest encounters of the characters. A woodland girl called Phebe (boy as girl) falls for Rosalind (boy as girl as boy) and suddenly quotes Marlowe:

> Dead shepherd, now I find thy saw of might:
> 'Who ever lov'd that lov'd not at first sight?'

The country people, being Arcadians, are permitted blank verse, and the language of this scene (act 3, scene v) is finely balanced, with a counterpoint between metre and vernacular rhythm. It is fresher and livelier, therefore, than later pastoral poetry, being genuinely dramatic even at its mildest. The subterfuges and confusions make one dizzy on the page, but in the theatre they are transparent and entertaining. It is important to notice that Shakespeare's love comedies involve numerous illusions. 'The stage', wrote Bacon, 'is ever more beholding to love than the life of man. For as to the stage, love is ever matter of comedies and now and then of tragedies; but in life it doth much mischief. . . .' Elsewhere he sourly remarks, 'But it is not good to stay too long in the theatre.'

As act 4 opens, Jaques dissects melancholy, including his own, and is mocked for it by Rosalind. But Orlando enters with blank verse and Jaques, who speaks it elsewhere, retires from the fray. The huntsmen sing a song, and Orlando's brother comes in search of him, meets a lion, and is rescued by Orlando; this converts the brother and makes Rosalind declare herself in love:

> 'Twas I; but 'tis not I. I do not shame
> To tell you what I was, since my conversion
> So sweetly tastes, being the thing I am.

Act 5 gives Touchstone and Audrey a scene with a delightful rustic called William. All the pairs of lovers will come together in a brisk series of revelations, a Mozartian dance with changes of partner and returns, as the last of the comic juices are squeezed from the orange. Pages sing the prettiest of lyrics, 'It was a lover and his lass'. Hymen descends from heaven to end the action ceremoniously. Jaques is still satirical. Throughout the play, he is the character who does not fit, and who keeps the conversation from cloying. His defence of satire (act 2, scene vii) is effective, and places Shakespeare squarely on the side of the new satiric vogue of writers like Marston and Jonson, and against the suppression of satiric writings that took place in 1599, with the burning of books by the Bishop of London. Jaques exists only to be satiric: on the plot he has no effect at all.

> ... give me leave
> To speak my mind, and I will through and through
> Cleanse the foul body of th' infected world. ...

But Jaques is not Shakespeare, nor is he the hero of the play: Shakespeare's heart is in Adam. Rosalind is the star part, with Orlando as conventional hero. At this time Lyly was being revived for resurrected boys' companies, so *As You Like It* was Shakespeare's counterblast. In his set-piece on the ages of man, Jaques was simply moralizing the new banner of the Globe: *Totus mundus agit histrionem* – All the world's a stage. As for the conversion at the end, it may or may not be relevant that in March 1599 the Duc de Joyeuse retired from the world and became a Capuchin: at least one should remember that such things did happen.

The Merry Wives of Windsor offers plentiful internal evidence that it was written in a furious hurry: the Restoration theatre tradition recorded by John Dennis in 1702 and Rowe in 1709 was that the Queen had demanded a play about Falstaff in love, and Shakespeare wrote it in a fortnight. In the 1840s James Halliwell-Phillipps possessed a Commonwealth manuscript of the *Merry Wives*, which, if it were rediscovered, might throw some light, but I have not traced it. Some of the play's minor confusions suggest that it may have been meant to be set in Gloucestershire and was then moved to Windsor. The Garter Feast on 23 April would be a likely occasion, and Lord Hunsdon's installation as a Knight of the Garter offers a tempting moment, since we have evidence of his extraordinary magnificence on that occasion; he borrowed £2000 immediately after it, twice as much as Falstaff got out of Shallow. But Hunsdon's Garter was in 1597, and 1600 is much likelier. The play was registered in mid-January 1602 and printed that year as played 'divers times before her Majesty and elsewhere', but it was unknown to Meres in 1598, later than Jonson's *Everyman in his Humour* (1598), and of course later than *Henry IV*. It seems to come just before *Hamlet*, which affects the quarto text of the *Merry Wives*.

Shallow and Silence were famous now, and Shallow as much as Falstaff was what the Queen expected. We have a letter making jokes about Shallow and Silence written by a gentleman from Dumbleton. Falstaff hiding in the laundry basket comes from Richard Tarlton's *Newes out of Purgatorie* (1590), which I take to be by Robert Armin. The joke about 'garmombles' seems to me as funny as it is unintelligible; it is said to refer to a German duke; I suspect it may have been a very old joke indeed. The play is extremely funny altogether, and there is no sense in dwelling on confusions of detail, systematic puns or any other scholarly problem, least of all the identities of people it might be modelled on. Enough has been said about luces and louses and Lucys; jokes like that are meant to run very swiftly. This is a play to take lightheartedly; it is Queen Elizabeth's gift to the theatre, and Shakespeare's to her.

Mine Host talks like Pistol, and Sir Hugh Evans the Welsh parson is Fluellen out of *Henry V*. Falstaff has stolen Shallow's deer and Evans wants to reconcile them, and to marry Shallow's cousin Slender to Anne Page. Nym, Bardolph and Pistol invade this peaceful small-town scene like marauding sharks. I cannot think why the prose should be so funny, but it sparkles and crackles along.

> You Banbury cheese!
> Ay, it is no matter.
> How now, Mephisophilus!
> Ay, it is no matter.
> Slice, I say! pauca, pauca! slice! That's my humour.

It scarcely matters who says what. Slender is sadly upset by it all. He wants his book of Songs and Sonnets or his book of riddles to go wooing with. The prose is crammed with short, sensuous phrases, about dinner, lechery, a glover's paring-knife, a shower that sings in the wind, 'bowl'd to death with turnips', 'piss my tallow', and of course parody. 'I will knog his urinals about his knave's costard when I have goot opportunities for the ork'; 'by gar, he shall not have a stone to throw at his dog'; 'By gar, de herring is no dead so as I vill kill him'; 'like a many of these lisping hawthorn-buds'; 'Like sir Actæon he, with Ringwood at thy heels'; 'Well, I will smite his noddles'; 'I'll no pullet-sperm in my brewage'; 'Old, cold, wither'd, and of intolerable entrails.' It is simply impossible to run through all the examples.

The plot of the *Merry Wives* is well enough known to need no repetition here. It is a series of attempts at seduction by Falstaff which end in disaster, because the wives of Windsor are teasing their jealous husbands but defending their own honour. In the final night scene lovers are married off, idiots fooled, and Falstaff punished by choirboys dressed as fairies, led by the Welshman. 'Am I ridden with a Welsh goat too? . . . 'Tis time I were chok'd with a piece of toasted cheese.' 'Seese is not good to give putter; your belly is all putter.' '"Seese" and "putter"! Have I liv'd to stand at the taunt of one that makes fritters of English? This is enough to be the decay of lust and late-walking through the realm.'

This is an unexpectedly moral play in the end. Falstaff's punishment is only like 'rough music', with which village communities used to protect themselves against adultery until living memory in England. At the very end everyone is reconciled and invited home, 'And laugh this sport o'er by a country fire'. A serious point is made against forced marriages and their consequences of 'A thousand irreligious cursed hours'. *The Merry Wives of Windsor* is deliberately set in country tradition, from the greyhound 'outrun in Cotsall' to Herne's Oak in Windsor forest, which was felled under George III and replanted in the wrong place. No one saw Herne's ghost again until Queen Victoria had a new oak put in the traditional place. He sounds like a cross between the dangerous ghost of a murdered, probably a hanged man, and the wild or magic midnight hunt of the dead, which goes back to Odin. But no written record of Herne or his oak goes further back than Shakespeare.

The Windsor setting is careful; even the surnames appear to be real Windsor names, though that may be coincidence. The fairy verses about Windsor embody real superstitions, but they are meant to be lighthearted and fantastical: superstitious, simple people were a minority in a London theatre. The references to the Garter Chapel however are very vague: I doubt whether Mistress Quickly as the Fairy Queen would have been acceptable if a serious compliment to the Knights of the Garter were intended. This is a comedy to be heard after dinner and, to judge by the torchlight dancing, indoors.

In the first scene of act 3, Evans sings a snatch of Marlowe's poem 'Come live with me, and be my love'. He intermingles with it a phrase from a metrical version of Psalm 137, 'When as I sat in Pabylon': he says the music makes him melancholy and we note that the rivers are in common. The prayer-book and psalms are parodied elsewhere: by Pistol early in the play, 'He hears with ears,' and by Pistol again about high and low, rich and poor (act 2, scene i, line 101). These jokes are not very subversive, but familiar and jolly. The Bible was so closely present to Shakespeare and his audience that they must have used and adapted it both seriously (the resurrection of the dismembered in *Henry V*) and in jokes, by mere instinct, without giving a thought to the matter.

211

If there is a little more such mockery in the *Merry Wives*, that is because it was written fast and, as it were, impromptu, without self-censorship or public censorship. Our text seems to derive immediately from an early acting copy; the Master of the Revels would have removed Brook if he got the chance because the Cobham family was sensitive about his name. Jacobean editors cut out profanities: people were fined for swearing in the household of the Prince of Wales. *The Merry Wives of Windsor* gives off a strong whiff of a world of disrespect and hilarity that was on its last legs when Shakespeare wrote the play. It is the other side of the coin of the paranoia and paralysis historians observe at the end of the Queen's reign. He sets it far in the past, when Eton was a small, isolated chapel in the fields. The reference to that is curious, and makes one wonder whether Eton boys rather than Windsor Chapel choirboys may not have played in the *Merry Wives*. It would add something to the joke of Abraham Slender finding himself married to 'a great lubberly boy' in Eton chapel.

From 1598 to 1601 a sharply contested literary war broke out between satiric poets, particularly Marston, Jonson and Dekker. Apart from what Shakespeare says about satire through Jaques, and about the misfortunes of players in *Hamlet*, he appears to be little concerned. It was a war between *jeunes féroces* and he was now an elder statesman. Had he died of plague in 1603, or been hanged after the Essex rebellion, he would still be the greatest English poet of all time.

Some of the plays in the war of poets were extremely lively, and Shakespeare certainly knew all about them. The Globe was involved in the crossfire.

1598 Marston: *The Scourge of Villanie* (satires)
              Histriomastix (St Paul's boys)

1599 Jonson: *Every Man out of his Humour* (Globe)
              The Case is Altered (Blackfriars boys)

1600   *Cynthia's Revels* (Blackfriars boys)

1601 Anon: *Jack Drum's Entertainment* (St Paul's boys)
              Marston and Dekker rumoured to be planning a counter-attack
              (Globe)

     Jonson: *The Poetaster* (Blackfriars boys)

     Dekker: *Satiromastix* (Globe, and then St Paul's boys)

1603 Jonson: *Sejanus* (at the Globe, with Shakespeare as an actor)

1605 Marston: *The Malcontent* dedicated to Jonson.

1605 Jonson,
       Chapman
       and Marston: *Eastward Hoe* (leading to imprisonment)

John Marston was an odd fish. He was a young lawyer who took to
literature in an ambitious way, rather as John Donne did, and ended as a
Hampshire seaside vicar. His tomb in the Temple had the inscription
Oblivioni sacrum, meaning that his soul was immortal and his body
forgotten. He was quarrelsome, freakish and something of an ass, but not
without talent or humour of a black kind. He bargained with Henslowe as a
patron, but knew he could fall back upon the Globe. His family had mutual
friends with Shakespeare through his Warwickshire connection, so it is
interesting to observe that some of his dramatic verse is based on
Shakespeare too. Some of the borrowing is quite shameless, including
titles and characters: Touchstone in *Eastward Hoe*, for instance. Some is
subtler or more vulgar.

> ... Night like a masque is entered heaven's great hall,
> With thousand torches ushering the way:
> To *Risus* will we consecrate this eve. ...
> > *(The Insatiate Countess)*

> Thou mother of chaste dew, night's modest lamp,
> Thou by whose faint shine the blushing lovers
> Join glowing cheeks, and mix their trembling lips
> In vows well kissed, rise all as full of splendour
> As my breast is of joy! You genital,
> You fruitful, well mixed heats, O bless the sheets. ...
> > *(The Fawne)*

> ... Hurl'd down by wrath and lust of impious king,
> So that where holy Flamins wont to sing
> Sweet hymns to heaven, there the daw and crow,
> The ill-voiced raven and still chattering pye,
> Where statues and Jove's acts were lively limned
> Boys with black coals draw the veiled parts of nature
> And lecherous actions of imagined lust;
> Where tombs and beauteous urns of well dead men
> Stood in assured rest, the shepherd now
> Unloads his belly. ...
> > *(Sophonisba)*

Shakespeare's reputation, and that of Kemp and Burbage at this time, is
neatly reflected in three plays of uncertain hand performed at St John's

213

College, Cambridge: *The Pilgrimage to Parnassus*, and the two sequels, parts one and two of *The Return from Parnassus*, satires on literature and academic life, but gentler and more amusing in a donnish way than what was going on in London. Poetical young men had Shakespeare mania, their conversation was 'pure Shakespeare and shreds of poetry', 'Oh sweet Mr. Shakespeare! I'll have his picture in my study at the court.' These are not great plays, but charming and innocent home-made entertainments by talented boys. One of the plays has a joke the audience would have understood about Chester or Cheshire, which has suggested to editors an author's name. The conjecture has never been verified because no such name has been found on the books of the college, though that would not quite rule it out. It remains curious that *Love's Martyr* by Robert Chester (1566–1640) was printed by Edward Blount in 1601 with an appendix of poems by Marston, Chapman, Jonson, *'Vatum Chorus'*, *'Ignoto'*, and William Shakespeare. The full title is *Love's Martyr, or Rosalin's Complaint, allegorically shadowing the Truth of Love in the Constant Fate of the Phoenix and the Turtle*. The poems of the appendix form an interlinked series with an underlying narrative.

The book was dedicated to Sir John Salusbury, an ancestor of Dr Johnson's Mrs Thrale. This tough old villain was notorious for running a riotous Wrexham election, and the publication looks like an attempt to establish him as sensitive and civilized. He was married in 1586 to Ursula, bastard daughter of Lord Derby, he was squire to the Queen in 1595 and he was knighted in 1601, in which year Jane, the eldest of his ten children, was fourteen. Shakespeare's piece – 'The Phoenix and the Turtle' – appears to be about a childless marriage, which raises problems of date, but it is based on the Phoenix and Turtle part of Chester's long poem, and the poet who follows Shakespeare corrects him about the posterity of the marriage, so that Shakespeare's mistake is deliberate: he has chosen to write about the intensity of love itself alone, and his poem has an exact place, like a scene in a scenario. Similarly, Jonson's signed poem is about a man not impotent who spares his wife sex:

> We do not remember here
> Such spirits as are only continent
> Because their lust is spent.

'Twas not their infirmity, says Shakespeare, it was married chastity. His poem is so purely powerful that he shows himself in it a mystic of earthly love. It is the most breathtaking of all his poems, and I have heard old critics, devoted to poetry of many kinds all their lives, agree on it as the greatest poem in the English language. It is metrically thrilling, extremely original and intellectually and emotionally powerful. It uniquely combines an extreme of passion with an extreme of tranquillity. The

214

invocation of the birds, which I think owes more to Ovid than to Skelton, is as strange as it is satisfying. Shakespeare's 'The Phoenix and the Turtle' is profoundly refreshing, and it sits among its handful of lesser poems like a phoenix in a privet hedge, but it must be restored to its context if one is to understand it fully.

Thomas Salusbury, Sir John's elder brother, was executed after the Babington plot in September 1586; John inherited, and married in three months. In Robert Chester's poem the turtle grieves for 'my turtle that is dead' and the phoenix offers to share that sorrow and take the turtle for a true love: the phoenix then enjoins purity of thought:

> For we must waste together in that fire
> That will not burn but by true love's desire.

They fling themselves into the flames, hoping a new creature will be born from their ashes. In Chester's Conclusion, 'Another princely phoenix upright stood.' I must say firmly that I see no reason at all why the whole poem should be dated back to 1586. 'My turtle that is dead' is a mate not a brother, and poor Thomas Salusbury would not possibly be commemorated in such terms so soon after his nasty execution. The common-sense view is that Shakespeare's contribution was commissioned by Salusbury through Chester, shortly before it was printed, as Jonson's and Marston's verses certainly were, with the consequence that this extraordinary poem was written about the same time as *Hamlet*. Chester's poem, as well as Shakespeare's, is about love, and about a traditional story: it is not about the Salusbury marriage.

> Lovers are like the leaves with winter shooken,
> Brittle like glass, that with one fall is broken.
> O fond corrupted age, when birds shall show
> The world their duty. . . .

Salusbury and Chester shared a passion for anagrams and mystical devices. The female phoenix mating with a male turtle is an innovation. Greek turtles are female, real ones attempt both roles as many birds do. The Salusburies were a formidably learned and poetic family. John's stepfather knew Greek, Latin, French, Italian and Spanish, and Lord Herbert of Cherbury was sent as a boy of nine to learn Welsh in his house. Poems were presented at Christmas in Welsh and Latin, and masques to which friends contributed were common in the household. Sir John died in 1612; it is almost certain that some manuscript verses once in his family that congratulate Heminges and Condell on Shakespeare's First Folio (1623) are by his son Henry, who lived until 1634. Hugh Holland, whose sonnet on Shakespeare was printed in the 1623 Folio, was another Denbighshire man, and apparently a Salusbury cousin. The same

Salusbury manuscript has a Ben Jonson poem in it that was printed with 'The Phoenix and the Turtle'.

The Earl of Essex's downfall came of failing to deal with Tyrone in 1599 in Ireland; he was defeated in diplomacy. He returned to England at the end of September, and within hours of bursting in on the Queen at Nonesuch he was in deep disgrace. The Queen waited a day, found no movement in his favour, and committed him to Lord Egerton's custody at York House. Sir John Harington attempted intercession, but she gripped him by the girdle and shook him. 'By God's Son,' she said, 'I am no Queen! That man is above me! Who gave him command to come here so soon?' She discussed Essex with Bacon, to whom Essex had been a generous friend; he was thrilled by the intrigue and seized the opportunity to begin to change sides. 'Essex!' she said. 'Whensoever I send Essex back again into Ireland, I will marry you. Claim it of me.' Robert Cecil was 'merely passive and not active in this action': Essex had dug his own trap and would now fall into it. Ralegh urged Cecil to be active because Cecil's 'malice is fixed, and will not evaporate by any of your mild courses', but Cecil was wiser in his generation than the sons of light. At the end of November the case of Essex came before the Star Chamber. Nothing resulted from that, but he was dangerously ill and isolated; then he recovered.

Mountjoy was sent to Ireland as Lord Deputy; he promised Essex that if the King of Scotland would act he would lead an Irish army into England. In the spring, Southampton crossed over to Ireland with a letter from Essex to Mountjoy begging him to fulfil this promise, but Mountjoy had changed his mind. Bacon advised the Queen against a public trial, because Essex was too popular in England, so he was tried and admonished privately by a special court at York House in June, kneeling before it, then permitted to stand, then to sit; Bacon was one of the prosecutors. Essex was threatened with the Tower and a gigantic fine, but was sent home again in the end to his house beside the Temple to await the Queen's pleasure. He pretended abject worship of her, but spoilt the effect by writing about a valuable monopoly of sweet wines that he feared to lose. Far worse, she was told that he ranted in private, 'Her conditions are as crooked as her carcase.'

Early in 1601 he begged the King of Scotland to act, and the King agreed to send an ambassador. Essex's friends filled the city with rumours of treason and catastrophe. On the Saturday morning of 7 February he was summoned again by the Privy Council: he refused to go. At this last moment Sir Gelly Merrick and other friends got the Chamberlain's Men to put on Shakespeare's *Richard II* at the Globe in the afternoon to put people in mind of abdication. The players were reluctant because the play was old, but he paid them twenty shillings and they did perform it. Essex's rebellion exploded on the Sunday with the feeblest of splutters. 'Saw, saw, saw! Tray, tray!' shouted Sir Christopher Blount, but no one moved to support him. Essex was blockaded in Essex House and artillery was brought up. Nearly a hundred persons were arrested; Essex and Southampton were tried on 19 February and went to the Tower. There Essex collapsed as a human being; he was executed on the 25th, but Southampton survived in prison to be released to popular acclaim in 1603, when the King of Scotland became James I.

The players sent Augustine Philips as representative to answer the Privy Council about the production of *Richard II*, but they were not punished, and any cloud they were under soon passed over. In May, this Council took action against the Curtain, and Shakespeare's company was lucky to escape. We have new evidence of the careful attention that Shakespeare's audience gave to any hint of treason that his plays might suggest, however unintentionally. I have discussed in Appendix 2 the manuscript notebook recently bought at Sotheby's by the British Library, which quotes some lines spoken in *Henry IV* about an insinuating usurper, with the word 'Queen' substituted for 'King'. The meaning of those plays for their audiences and the effect of their performance in their own day were more disturbing than we realize. Politically, Essex never stood a chance, I suppose, but if he had returned from Ireland in triumph things might have ended otherwise. Shakespeare after all had already compared him to *Julius Caesar*. The Queen's fears were real and the crisis was serious.

It was during this crisis that Shakespeare wrote *Hamlet*. It was registered in July 1602, and printed in a short, corrupt version in 1603 'as acted . . . in London, Cambridge, Oxford and elsewhere'. The scene with the players suggests the conditions of about 1601. *Hamlet* was unknown to Meres in 1598; Gabriel Harvey wrote a marginal note in his copy of the 1598 edition of Chaucer that mentions *Hamlet*, but the note is not datable. The play echoes *Julius Caesar* and alludes to its performance (act 3, scene ii, lines 102–3) in 1599. A reference in *Hamlet* to 'The late innovation', which means insurrection, which sent the actors out on the roads (act 2, scene ii, line 330), sounds extremely like the Earl of Essex. Still, it is just possible to give 'innovation' its modern meaning, and make it refer to the boy actors. I would prefer to do so, since I do not accept that *Hamlet* owes anything to great events except its sombre tonality, and maybe not even that. Hamlet himself is more like undecided Brutus than dithering, hysterical Essex.

The theme of the play was old, and the first dramatic treatment may have been by Kyd. Lodge wrote in *Wits Miserie* (1596) of 'the ghost which cried so miserably at the Theatre like an oyster wife, *Hamlet revenge!*' Tucca in Marston's *Histriomastix* says 'My name's *Hamlet Revenge*.' The ultimate source, if one is to go back so far, is Orestes or Oedipus, but Shakespeare knew nothing about the Oedipus complex, which makes him an innocent witness to it, if one chooses to find it in the play. In my own opinion what one finds is more interesting. Shakespeare has taken a worn-out, well-known, ranting Senecan tragedy and asked himself what would happen if Hamlet were real, how would he think and behave? It is famously a one-man tragedy, one vast part meant for a great actor. I am unable to see it as confused or over-written, though it is certainly (in the second quarto and the Folio) extremely long; it may have been intended in this full and flowing version for a university audience. The reader interested in the myth of *Hamlet* in itself should look at John Wain's fine poem 'Feng', which is adapted from the *Historia Danica* of Saxo Grammaticus, a twelfth-century repository of earlier Norse stories.

The ghost's entry is brilliantly set: in the darkness and silence one can hear every footfall of the verse, making the most trivial phrases memorable. Shakespeare was a fine natural storyteller among other things, particularly of ghost stories. It is the awe and horror of the watchers that make the ghost real, the ghost itself being simply a frowning old man in armour, whom Shakespeare is supposed to have acted. Perhaps it was dimly seen or strangely lighted, but description gives it powerful presence and majesty. The apparition is connected with war: the entire play in fact has an epic setting little noticed by producers; apart from the ghost it begins and ends with Fortinbras. Shakespeare had friends who knew Elsinore, and something about that or another castle had worked in his imagination. It is not impossible he visited Southampton in the Tower. The castle in *Hamlet* is more than a setting, almost a character in the play, and the ghost belongs to it. The repetition of the omens before Caesar's death is meant to be blood-chilling, and an improvement on *Julius Caesar*:

> The graves stood tenantless, and the sheeted dead
> Did squeak and gibber in the Roman streets;
> As, stars with trains of fire, and dews of blood,
> Disasters in the sun; and the moist star
> Upon whose influence Neptune's empire stands
> Was sick almost to doomsday with eclipse. . . .

From this full-blooded pagan vision (look what the power of context has done to the word 'moist') Shakespeare moves to defiance, to ritual like a litany, to respect, then to superstition about cock-crow, and finally to his extraordinary few lines about Christmas, when 'No fairy takes, nor witch hath power to charm, So hallowed and so gracious is the time.' They are just as superstitious as what preceded them, but a tinge of Christianity has transmuted them. Morning breaks in its grey mantle. Taken just as poetry, this scene can hold its own with any other that Shakespeare ever wrote. Taken as drama, it is his best opening scene so far, though the opening of *The Merry Wives of Windsor* runs it close. As a poet he is already perfect, he is everything he can be, but as a theatrical writer he never ceases to learn or to experiment.

The King in scene ii is stiffly king-like, but that is because Shakespeare does not intend us to like him, and yet the whole play might be rewritten in the style of Kyd as this King's tragedy, with Hamlet as a minor character like Laertes. But Hamlet compels attention, by his appearance in contrast with Court dress, and by his philosophic obsession with 'is' and 'seems'. Shakespeare has just been reading Montaigne, and the play shows it clearly. He is eloquent in a new, moral tone of eloquence. This is a play beyond the reach of boy actors. Even the incomparable Ophelia seems beyond them, though a boy must have played her. Had he played Anne Page and the Portia in *Julius Caesar*, and Celia perhaps (who was not very tall) or a singing page in *As You Like It*?

Hamlet's first monologue splits the scene. His horrified voice broaches the theme of longing for suicide, but most of the speech is about the grossness of his mother's swift remarriage; it colours what Shakespeare can already do in the way of monologue with satiric bitterness like that of Jaques, which is much less obscure and more powerful than young Marston's Juvenalian ranting. As an attempt to integrate a satiric character among verse of great lyrical beauty, Hamlet is a rerun of *As You Like It*, with the satirist as main character.

The third scene of the play presents Laertes and Ophelia. Critics have suggested that Hamlet's true problem is sexual guilt, and that Ophelia is no better than she ought to be. Not in this scene: Laertes advises her overprudently, she replies with mild but spirited mockery, and then Polonius appears to advise Laertes still more overprudently. Several noblemen wrote advice of this kind for their sons and dependants, so one has no need to look for an individual of whom Polonius may be a parody. He is certainly nothing like Lord Burghley, who in his letters seems a charming old man and nobody's fool. But there is nothing that some scholar, somewhere, will not be found to believe about the plays of Shakespeare, and *Hamlet* is more afflicted than most.

The King drinks to the sound of trumpets and of cannons. Hamlet is on the battlements waiting for the ghost, but while he waits he makes a speech against Danish drunkenness, which was indeed notorious and survives in amazing anecdotes. When Christian of Denmark visited England under James I he failed to survive dinner, his daughter the Queen of England passed out on the dance floor, three ladies were too drunk to appear in a masque, someone was sick, and another lady spilt custard all over the King. All the same I think it is English drunkenness Hamlet was really talking about.

The ghost suddenly breaks in on this speech. Hamlet addresses it in such terms that he is uncommitted to believing in any particular origin or nature of such an apparition. Brutus and Hamlet are more sophisticated than the haunted kings of the history plays: by suspending belief about its nature, Shakespeare has made this apparition immeasurably more real. The ghost is not heaven-sent, it sighs for revenge and causes tragedy. It impersonates the ethics of a blood-feud in an intimate family setting, transforming obligation into a dense knot of contradictions; the same thing happened in Agamemnon's family. In Norse sagas as in Greek epics, a woman, guilty or innocent, always starts the machinery of tragedy.

Hamlet's eloquence is majestic, but the ghost's shorter lines and its silences are more so. Its state of purgatory is deeply rooted in medieval superstition rather than in Catholic dogma, and it is obvious enough that the underworld of such thoughts and imaginations was in common between Shakespeare and his audience: it takes longer than a generation to extinguish fires like those; they may burn on for hundreds of years after the dogma is gone which once supported them. The ghost's awful story of its afterlife in purgatory is still a kind of ghost story to make the flesh creep: 'I could a tale unfold whose lightest word Would harrow up thy soul. . . .' Pagan and Catholic images intermingle: 'And duller shouldst thou be than the fat weed That roots itself in ease on Lethe wharf. . . .' Some of this is original: the 'juice of cursed hebona' for instance is somewhere between henbane and black ebony, throne wood of the god of Sleep, or the dark yewtree. The horrifying effects of the poison, which we are given in lurid detail, must also have more sources than one.

It is an important condition of what follows that Hamlet's split feelings about his mother and his stepfather, which extend into feelings about all sexuality, have their origins in the ghost's divided feelings. The ghost now becomes his private secret and obsession, hence his somewhat brittle mockery of it to his friends. His longing is to lay it to rest, but its demands are of course implacable, since they arise from intimate and pagan reality: there is no Christianity or forgiveness about the ghost.

The second act with its claustrophobia must surely have recalled the Court. It opens on Polonius sending a spy to watch his son in Paris, and misinterpreting Hamlet's horror with Ophelia as 'the very ecstasy of love'. The King and Queen employ Rosencrantz and Guildenstern in a similar way to work on Hamlet. The old booby Polonius makes his comic–tedious revelation to the King in a pedantic version of courtly language. No writer of the age was sharper than Shakespeare at catching a tone so precisely, and his range of experience of tones was wider than a modern writer's.

Frances Yates has commented interestingly on the rhyme Polonius reports that Hamlet sent Ophelia: 'Doubt that the sun doth move . . . But never doubt I love.' It represents an archaic view of the universe which she associates with neo-platonism. Nothing could be likelier than that, because Giordano Bruno's kind of philosophy has left many traces in Shakespeare's poetry. Yates attaches to Bruno the hint of universal doubt in 'Doubt truth to be a liar'; and yet in the context of the play her explanation seems too high-flown. These are conventional, therefore naturally archaic love-verses, deliberately pitched at a low level of poetry; I do not believe they can really embody Shakespeare's deep thoughts about the universe, though they are almost bound to allude to a way of thinking that was common in his circle.

Polonius and the King agree to hide behind the arras to spy on Hamlet and Ophelia, but meanwhile Polonius confronts Hamlet, only to be mocked, and Rosencrantz and Guildenstern fare little better. Hamlet's satiric prose in this scene (act 2, scene ii) has a sour–sweet epigrammatic quality and a laconic rhetoric. 'Oh God, I could be bounded in a nutshell and count myself a king of infinite space, were it not that I have bad dreams.' He controls the conversation as firmly as Socrates in a dialogue, speaking clearly to the audience but in riddles to the other actors. As a philosopher, he is perfect master of the language of renaissance philosophers, and makes more than Biblically vivid the nature of man and the problem of seeming and being, but he is a layman's not a professional's philosopher: that indeed is his strength.

From philosophy he proceeds to a tart discussion of actors. The players who have come to Elsinore are 'the tragedians of the city'. The set characters he expects are the King, the adventurous knight, the lover, the humorous (quirky or type-cast or eccentric) man, the clown and the lady; they suggest something nearly as simple as a mummers' play, but it will be in blank verse. They are on the road in Lent, with trumpets to announce their arrival. Polonius on the varieties and subvarieties of plays is not to be taken very seriously, except for their range: 'Seneca cannot be too heavy nor Plautus too light.'

Hamlet knows and loves these satirizing actors: 'We'll e'en to't like French falconers, fly at anything we see.' The parodies that follow, of speeches based on the *Aeneid*, are funny enough, and close to self-parody, because with tactful revision they could be made to sound like real Shakespeare, though I take it they are directed against Kyd and Peele:

> Hath now this dread and black complexion smear'd
> With heraldry more dismal; head to foot
> Now is he total gules, horridly trick'd
> With blood of fathers, mothers, daughters, sons,
> Bak'd and impasted with the parching streets. . . .
>   . . . For, lo! his sword,
> Which was declining on the milky head
> Of reverend Priam, seem'd i' th' air to stick.

This kind of verse, set in a scene of castigating prose, is a mockery of the status and condition of verse. But the dramatic point is that the bad verse moves Hamlet, and breeds in him the idea of a play to catch the conscience of the King. The actors are 'the abstract and brief chronicles of the time' because they seem to touch on his father's tragedy, as *Richard II* seemed to touch on something. Several elements in this long scene look like detachable pieces, but they are not: least of all Hamlet's final verse monologue, his rousing of himself to action. The device of a play within a play to expose a murderer, which Hamlet says he has heard of, was not unique: Heywood refers to it in his *Apology for Actors*, and Massinger uses it. But Shakespeare's actors are of particular interest. They speak for a tradition that embraces Termagant and Herod in the Mysteries. The mirror held up to nature, which outlaws monstrosities, goes back to Cicero and Aristotle, though I do not see Shakespeare as taking that ideal very literally. Hamlet's speech against overacting rings truer.

Act 3 sets the scene for Hamlet observed, but what we hear is his famous, impressively personal and well-argued monologue on suicide. 'To be or not to be' echoes Marlowe's old scholastic joke in *Faustus* about the *On* and the *Me On*, being and non-being in Platonic philosophy. When he notices Ophelia he speaks harshly to her, clearly because the horror of his father's fate and mother's marriage has embittered him against women and disabled him from love (he is himself about to commit murder, and unlikely to survive it). She sweetly laments his madness, but of course she knows no reason for it. The King decides to act first, and to have Hamlet murdered in England; the actors and their play upset him badly enough to confirm this decision. Drama has consequences.

The play begins with a dumb-show of the murder, and a very short prologue that Hamlet derides: 'Is this a prologue, or the posy of a ring?' It is metrically very close to 'The Phoenix and the Turtle', and to Shakespeare's gravestone inscription, and to 'Fear no more the heat o' th' sun': also to the couplet on Alexander Aspinall's gift of gloves. But the lines are lame, the extra syllable worsens them, and the rhymes are jejune. The King asks Hamlet as Cecil or Queen Elizabeth might ask, 'Have you heard the argument? Is there no offence in't?' The amount of byplay among spectators at the play is suggestive of alarming liveliness among Court audiences. Hamlet becomes distinctly obscene with Ophelia.

When the play is broken off, Hamlet is sent for to the Queen; at the end of the scene he is close to a conventional revenge murderer, a villain out of Kyd: 'Now could I drink hot blood. . . .' But he repents within a sentence, the natural bond still holds. Polonius will hide in the Queen's room. The King has his monologue of remorse without repentance; Hamlet comes within an ace of killing him there and then, but will not do him the benefit of killing him at prayer. In his mother's room he thinks the King is behind the arras and does kill, but the victim is only Polonius. He then reproaches his mother with furious passion; the ghost appears but she cannot see it. He leaves her in despair, which she might well feel after such an excoriating outburst. In the entire play this scene is the height of his passion and the beginning of action. He must leave for England, but he is in no doubt of outwitting the plotters of that episode. Why such an episode at all? It is in order to have him out of the way while Ophelia goes mad and kills herself for scorned love.

The early scenes of act 4 are occupied with the consequence of Polonius' murder. Hamlet pretending madness is extremely funny on this subject and wholly cold-blooded. He meets Fortinbras going to war in Poland, and Shakespeare recapitulates in ten lines his rage about colonial war, more scornfully I think than ever before:

> This is th' imposthume of much wealth and peace,
> That inward breaks, and shows no cause without
> Why the man dies.

I doubt whether the images and patterns of images that can be traced in particular plays tell us much about Shakespeare personally, but there is plenty of gruesome detail of physical corruption in this one, which emerges with such force it may well have been brewing for years or suppressed for years. It is a horror both medical and sexual. Yet he treats Ophelia so gently that I do not believe the sexual repugnance in *Hamlet* lies as deep as the physical repugnance, of which the obvious source is the plague. That had attacked Stratford as well as London, and no sensibility could be unaffected by it. The actors' passions shamed Hamlet to action, and the stupid war spurs him to bloodshed. Of his worst crime, which is Ophelia's suicide, he remains unconscious. It will unleash a double vengeance, in which Laertes and Hamlet must both murder and both die. But the drama is not just a complicated machine: in more ways than one it is Shakespeare's fullest play.

Ophelia's mad ballad is utterly unexpected and memorably effective. It has several meanings and moves us in several ways at once. The point is perhaps worth making that Shakespeare's ballad plays – those which use traditional poetry or deeply turn on it – overlap comedy and the darkest tragedy. They occur about the middle of his career, and my impression is that the sad underlying momentum of ballad music intensifies until *King Lear*. This play itself, like *Lear*, is a folk story, hence its density of plot and motive.

> He is dead and gone, lady,
> He is dead and gone;
> At his head a grass-green turf,
> At his heels a stone.

Hamlet's madness was unreal, hers is real: he was sexually taunting, she is in despair, and the despair unlocks a stream of sexual innuendo. Hamlet toys with suicide, she commits it. He behaved worse and worse to her scene by scene, she dealt with him coolly until she snapped. He murdered her father, 'She speaks much of her father,' both their fathers are murdered. What she conveys is love, purely and intensely. Hamlet is self-obsessed, she is not; the satirist is not satirized, her expression is lyrical, though it is allusive. Her last word is death; her double grief for her father and his murderer mirrors Hamlet's for his father and betraying mother, but Ophelia is innocent and Hamlet is not.

With the return of Laertes, and the escape and return of Hamlet, the climax of the play becomes inevitable. It takes the form of another device turned back on its deviser. Its most memorable scenes are the graveyard and the duel. The idea of a gravedigging clown and a dead clown in a graveyard echoes a story of Robert Armin's about a Scottish royal jester and his conversation in a graveyard and prophecy of his own death, which promptly took place. It also continues the ballad theme, which fixes this play to the earth; and it allows Hamlet more satiric moralizing, and sets his dramatic confrontation with Laertes. Hamlet's satire has many sources, including Montaigne and apparently Erasmus (Ossa like a wart), but the momentum of it is single, his motive power is disgust. The priest's refusal to sing a requiem for a suicide is horrifying to us, but normal in Shakespeare's day and until yesterday. It is intended as only one more element in the sadness of Ophelia's death. The emotions in the play are by now so tense and its ironies so complex that the fifth act plays far better and more movingly than it reads – in the Folio edition Hamlet's final utterance is 'O, O, O, O.' All the same, the last act resembles the rest of the play in being, as George II remarked with disapproval, full of quotations.

The duel scene is odder to us than it was to its first audience. Duelling matches were highly organized and extremely popular, their audiences knew the fine points, as it were. Sword displays took place in theatres as an alternative to plays, and one must think of an audience that might attend both. Swordsmen were led in procession through London with music like actors arriving in a country town, or like the travelling circuses of fifty years ago. The duel in *Romeo and Juliet* was real and deadly; this one pretended to be a match with buttoned foils; both kinds were common. The courtier Osric is a small bonus, a character straight from life, whom neither Hamlet nor Shakespeare can abide. The tone is cool, but the audience knows this is going to end badly. Laertes has his revenge and dies, the Queen drinks the poison the King meant for Hamlet, and she dies. Hamlet's last living act is to kill the King, his last conversation is to leave good order in the state. But what one remembers for ever are his few personal words to his only friend. They are about his own honour. Fortinbras and his army usefully remove the dead bodies before the jig.

> If thou didst ever hold me in thy heart,
> Absent thee from felicity awhile,
> And in this harsh world draw thy breath in pain,
> To tell my story.

Throughout his career in London, even when his art seems to overleap limits, Shakespeare thinks of himself as a Stratford man. In April 1601,

Thomas Whittington died at Shottery. He was an old shepherd to the Hathaway family. By his will he left 'Unto the poor people of Stratford forty shillings that is in the hand of Anne Shaxspere, wife unto Mr. William Shaxspere, and is due debt unto me, being paid to mine executor by the said William Shaxspere or his assigns, according to the true meaning of this my will.' It looks as if he banked it with her, there being of course no banks. If it were borrowed money one would expect interest to be paid; if it were wages then Shakespeare alone would be mentioned.

This represents a social bond we are very glad to know about. Anne Shakespeare left as little trace in records as most women of her class and time. It is all the more pleasing to know that she was on friendly terms with an old shepherd of her father's family. He had probably told her long ago what his small sum of money was for. He lived at Hewland with her father until he died in 1581, then with the widow until she died in 1599. Edgar Fripp records the names of eight shepherds living in Stratford. One called Cox, who lived opposite Shakespeare's father in Henley Street, left money when he died in 1600 to the widow and children of Thomas Hathaway, another of Anne Shakespeare's family. His worldly wealth was £73, but Thomas Wittington's was only £50. He was just well enough off to leave money to the poor. It is hard not to think of Adam or of Corin in *As You Like It*:

> Sir, I am a true labourer: I earn that I eat, get that I wear; owe no man hate, envy no man's happiness; glad of other men's good, content with my harm; and the greatest of my pride is to see my ewes graze and my lambs suck.

On 8 September in that same year, John Shakespeare was buried. He was forty-four years married and probably close to seventy years old. He may have been even older, because he was bailiff in 1568, and must have been well over thirty to hold that office. Shakespeare inherited his father's Henley Street houses, where his mother lived on for seven more years, nearly to the day, with her daughter Joan Hart, the poet's only surviving sister, who was now thirty-two. She was married rather late to William Hart the hatter; her eldest son was only a year old, but she bore three more children, the youngest a son born in 1608, a fortnight after his grandmother's death, when Joan was thirty-nine.

In the year of their father's death, Shakespeare's brother Gilbert was thirty-three, Richard was twenty-seven and Edmund, who became an actor, was twenty-one. Shakespeare himself was thirty-seven, famous, comparatively wealthy and apparently at the height of his powers. Yet, for whatever reason, his work was soon to enter a disconcerting phase.

His economic performance was smoother than his literary production. In 1602 he bought 107 acres of arable land from William and John Combe, the contract being dated 1 May, 'for three hundred and twenty pounds of current English money to them in hand'. This also gave him rights of common pasture in the parish. Gilbert Shakespeare signed for his brother. In the same year Shakespeare's rights to New Place were confirmed. Two orchards appear in this document which were not mentioned before, probably through oversight. In September he bought a cottage with a quarter of an acre's garden opposite his house. No one knows what he used it for, but in his will he left it to his daughter Susanna, his eldest child who in 1602 was nineteen. Its purchase was part of the process of establishing himself at Stratford as if he had never left. In the last years of Elizabeth he was not liking London, and neither was anybody else. One must remember that had things gone wrong at the succession to the old Queen, his career there might suddenly have been finished. And yet the Queen could be merry: 'We are frolic at Court,' wrote the Earl of Worcester in 1602. Irish music was in fashion, and there were country dances in the Privy Chamber.

Transition

The last of the twelve nights of Christmas is 6 January, the feast of the Epiphany of Christ and the increase of light. In medieval tradition and in Elizabethan practice, this was the last night of the authority of the Lord of Misrule, an anarchic Master of the Revels with a dark side to him, whose title was sometimes usurped by a real person until the party was over. In Lyly's *Endimion* (1591), someone says, 'Love is a lord of misrule, and keepeth Christmas in my corps.' Shakespeare's *Twelfth Night; or, What You Will*, is a comedy with a dark side to it. The subtitle, *What You Will*, was either pre-empted or stolen by John Marston for a play in which he worked the phrase to death, performed quite early in 1601, before Jonson's *The Poetaster*, which came late in the spring of that year. Shakespeare's play was certainly written by February 1602, when it was performed at a Middle Temple feast, though it was not necessarily new at that time. The lawyer and diarist John Manningham recorded the occasion in a miscellaneous notebook, which also contains the joke about King Richard and William the Conqueror (Burbage and Shakespeare).

Manningham understood what the title means I think, because he began by writing 'At our feast we had a play called Mid . . .', then crossed out the 'Mid' (*A Midsummer-Night's Dream*) and wrote 'Twelve Night or What You Will. Much like the Comedy of Errors or *Nenechmi* [sic] in Plautus, but most like and near to that in Italian called *Inganni*', with details of the Malvolio intrigue, which he thought 'a good practice'. I do not like John Manningham, but he was evidently keen on Shakespeare. Scholars have sensibly pointed out that his note must represent discussion by the experts, but I do not see why discussion should not have followed immediately on performance. You did not have to be a professional scholar of dramatic history in the 1600s to be familiar with Plautus and Italian comedy: students owned books of that kind, and their pouncing on a borrowed plot is one reason why Shakespeare uses multiple sources to cover his tracks.

Leslie Hotson wanted *Twelfth Night* to be the Court play for Twelfth Night in 1601, in honour of Virginio Orsino the Duke of Bracciano, a small duchy in western Italy north of Rome. The Duke wrote home to his wife that he was entertained with 'a mixed comedy with pieces of music and dances'. We have a memorandum of Lord Hunsdon's about it:

> To confer with my Lord Admiral and the Master of the Revels for taking order generally with the players to make choice of play that shall be best furnished with rich apparel, have great variety and change of music and dances, and of a subject that may be most pleasing to her Majesty.

The Chamberlain's Men performed and were paid, but Orsino's visit was unexpected until Christmas Day, and even Shakespeare would not have written such a perfect play so swiftly, nor would Orsino necessarily be best pleased with a character named after him. Anyway, *Twelfth Night* alludes to Dekker's *Satiromastix*, which was an answer to Jonson's *Poetaster*. So the Twelfth Night Court play of 1601 cannot have been Shakespeare's *Twelfth Night*. He wrote it later in the year, and Orsino's name came in useful. Shakespeare was notably careless about names. Hunsdon's note has a different interest, because it gives such a vivid impression of the conditions under which Shakespeare worked. His note is not so very different from the way the Queen's wishes might be expressed today: she was certainly not asking for *Hamlet*, and perhaps not Shakespeare at all.

The original for *Twelfth Night* was *Gli Ingannati – The Deceived –* which was played at Siena in 1531 and printed in Venice in 1537. Its prologue refers to 'your lots on Twelfth Night', and its induction was called 'La Notte di Beffana', which is Italian for Twelfth Night. This word is properly *befana* or *befania*, a corruption of the Greek word *epiphania*. It means not only the day but also the old crone, a female Father Christmas, who personifies the day and brings presents to children. In Italy and Greece presents are still given for Epiphany rather than at Christmas. But the spelling *beffana* is interesting because it suggests *beffa*, a humiliating practical joke, precisely like the trick played on Malvolio. If Shakespeare read *Gli Ingannati* or at least its prologue in Italian, he would very likely have had to look up *befana* or *beffana* in a dictionary and found *beffa* next to it.

Shakespeare also used Barnaby Rich's 'Apolonius and Silla', from *Riche his Farewell to Militarie Profession* (1581), which was an adaptation of Belleforest and Matteo Bandello, source of so many of his stories. He had taken an important hint from this same story by Rich in *Romeo and Juliet*, where Phaeton is a waggoner with a whip (act 3, scene ii). Rich was Shakespeare's older contemporary; he wrote strongly worded books about the inadequacy of the English army and the ill-treatment of soldiers. He may easily be the B.R. who wrote a brilliantly lively translation of the first two books of Herodotus (1584). He certainly wrote a rhetorical dialogue set in ancient Athens, called the *Second Tome of the Travels of Don Simonides*, published in that year, which C. S. Lewis found 'extremely funny, though I am not sure whether this was intended'.

The literary culture available to Shakespeare was a richer mixture than one imagines, and no generation of scholars has failed to find new traces of it in his work. All the same, he is less knowing and less salacious than Italian comedy, including *Gli Ingannati*, and here as elsewhere he probably saw his original through filters and adaptations, even if he was acquainted with its first form. It is a curious thought that Belleforest's adaptation of Bandello was called *Histoires Tragiques*. Shakespeare saw the *Menaechmi* of Plautus through the filter of his own *Comedy of Errors*, which he now reworked into something rich and strange. The theme of a heroine disguised as a boy taking messages to the lover she lost (boy playing girl dressed as boy, etc.) is an old favourite on which he can always discover new variations: the fact that he takes one from Rich should not diminish one's instinctive and verifiable feeling that this is part of his stock-in-trade.

The play has an inner circle who could be called courtly characters, and an outer circle of antique hangers-on like Belch, the sad surrogate Falstaff, and Aguecheek, like Shallow's cousin Slender. The extreme outsider is Feste, a clown who must travel the roads: he will be put out of doors at the end, and his final ballad has a shattering sadness. I am sure Armin played Feste, because his influence can be felt in the whole conception of the character. A fragment of Tom o' Bedlam's song, the real traditional song of mad beggars, recorded before Shakespeare's time and long after it, casts a cruel light on the fate of naturals cast out (see Appendix 9). The most impressive production of this play I ever saw (by Michael Gearin-Tosh) seemed to me to be *Twelfth Night* through Feste's eyes. The players moved through a perspective of two long lines of receding maypoles, the front ones I think coming right out into the audience, but focused on a nothingness.

The action of the play is a continuous current passing through all the persons, so that they do constitute one world, but one in which the central, courtly characters are observed from the decaying edges. It is a bit of luck that Roy Fuller as a schoolboy once played Fabian, the crucial intermediary between high and low, and has recently recorded some very perceptive notes on the play from Fabian's point of view. 'More or less unplumbable depth in a minor character', he writes, 'is typical of the play, which, as has often been noted, is of haunting freshness and charm.' He is particularly strong on that ambiguity of relationships in which Shakespeare delighted and this play delights.

Some critics have exaggerated the gaiety of the play, some its dark side, and some both. Some have seen the devices of deception and delusion as an extension of Hamlet's problem about being and seeming. Frank Kermode called it 'a comedy of identity, set on the borders of wonder and madness', a verdict that sounds more interesting than it really is. Auden thought it a farewell to comedy. 'Shakespeare was in no mood for comedy, but in a mood of puritanical aversion to all those pleasing illusions which men cherish and by which they lead their lives.' I have long hesitated over this view, but I do not really think any part of it is defensible. The word 'mood' is wrong for a start, and the word 'puritanical' is too vague, and the illusions in *Twelfth Night* are not the props of normal life. But typically of Auden, the grain of truth in his criticism is of huge importance compared to the husks of verbiage. I had thought of treating this play in the previous chapter, since it has a claim to be set beside *Hamlet*, but it is transitional as well. The transition I mean did not lead Shakespeare to write *Twelfth Night*, but was partly the consequence of having written it, or of the experience of writing it. One must take into account that Shakespeare was now extremely tired.

Act 1 plunges into events. Orsino's opening words are so beautiful that they often pass unexamined, but they convey delight, courtly pleasure and artifice, surfeit and 'a dying fall'. What does he mean about love? Presumably that love has a boundless appetite which is surfeited at once by whatever it loves and has to move on. 'O spirit of love, how quick and fresh art thou!' This is not a very innocent duke. He is in love with Olivia, but Olivia is going to lament a dead brother for seven years:

> The element itself, till seven years' heat,
> Shall not behold her face at ample view;
> But like a cloistress she will veiled walk,
> And water once a day her chamber round
> With eye-offending brine. . . .

In the second scene shipwrecked Viola has lost a brother too, and longs to be a servant to Olivia. The third introduces another contrasting vignette and a third star part: Sir Toby Belch, Olivia's uncle, with her servant Maria. Belch has introduced Aguecheek as a suitor who has 3000 ducats a year, plays the viol, 'speaks three or four languages word for word without book, and hath all the good gifts of nature'. He turns out to be a fool, but a voluble one; he and Belch set one another off better than any of Falstaff's friends set him off.

In the fourth scene of the act, Viola is dressed as a boy in the Duke's service and the Duke sends him as an emissary to Olivia, but the Duke fancies Viola's girlish looks and Viola is in love with the Duke. In the last scene of the act Feste has to talk himself out of disgrace with Olivia, who falls at once in love with Viola. Feste had wandered off somewhere; he is threatened with dismissal. Malvolio the steward is noticeably nasty about him, but his impertinent wit brings him back to Olivia's favour. 'O, you are sick of self-love, Malvolio, and taste with a distemper'd appetite.' Malvolio is not the only character in this first act to be very crisply characterized; this is done not only by a person's habit of speech (Belch and Aguecheek) but equally by what is said to them and about them: Malvolio on Viola as a boy for instance. 'Not yet old enough for a man, nor young enough for a boy: as a squash is before 'tis a peascod, or a codling before 'tis almost an apple; 'tis with him in standing water, between boy and man. He is very well-favour'd, and he speaks very shrewishly; one would think his mother's milk were scarce out of him.'

Act 1 of *Twelfth Night* presents the lightest and sunniest of comedy worlds. Act 2 crowds confusion on confusion. Viola's twin brother Sebastian was rescued by a sea captain called Antonio who is besotted with him. Viola meanwhile sinks deeper into her intrigue: 'Poor lady, she were better love a dream' (a line that would have pleased Freud), 'Disguise, I see thou art a wickedness. . . . O Time, thou must untangle this, not I.' Belch and the clown and Aguecheek sit up drinking and singing; Belch is a timeless old drunk, and time hardly exists for any of his friends. They make too much noise, they sing catches, Belch burbles fragments, Maria the maid fails to quell them and the sneering Malvolio fails worse. The topers are depicted with loving care in successive stages of drunkenness, but their sadness is apparent. They are not really young or fit enough for the enchanting melody of 'O Mistress Mine', they are failures in love as in drink, without worldly hope.

Scene iv shows Viola with the Duke and more music: the Duke wants a song from Feste, who is 'about the house' and sang it last night: what he sings is 'Come away, come away, death' – a very different song from 'Mistress mine', which he sang for Sir Toby Belch. The Duke pays him and he wanders away again, leaving the Duke and Viola to a dialogue about love, and how women 'are as true of heart as we'.

> And what's her history?
> A blank, my lord. She never told her love,
> But let concealment, like a worm i' th' bud,
> Feed on her damask cheek. She pin'd in thought;
> And with a green and yellow melancholy
> She sat like Patience on a monument,
> Smiling at grief. Was this not love indeed?

Scene v, in vigorous contrast, broaches the plot against Malvolio. Olivia's servant Fabian takes part, because Malvolio got him into trouble with Olivia 'about a bear-baiting here'. Maria likes old Belch and hates Malvolio as much as anyone. They watch him and mock him, and hook him with the bait of a letter. The act ends with the intrigue in full swing. There is still not a cloud in the sky that could not easily be dissolved.

The third act gives Viola a scene with Feste, at the end of which she praises the profession of fool. She encounters Toby and Andrew, then Olivia and Maria: she and Olivia are then left alone for more frustrating talk of love. The business of a numerous household is foreign to us of course, but to Shakespeare Olivia's household is normal. She rules it, but it can hardly be ruled, and Feste is ungovernable. So far he has done nothing but make jokes and sing songs, but he has established that he has a life of his own, and in his songs deep springs of feeling.

Now Aguecheek is jealous of Viola's success with Olivia and he tries to challenge her. Malvolio makes a fool of himself, as the letter told him to do. Sebastian takes money from Antonio, who is *persona non grata* in the city. The clouds are beginning to appear. Olivia thinks Malvolio really has gone mad, and his tormentors take over. 'Come, we'll have him in a dark room and bound.' Toby challenges Viola on Aguecheek's behalf, telling each of them how formidable the other is. All the same, the duel is beginning when Antonio breaks it up. He is then arrested, and appeals to Viola as Sebastian. She fails to recognize him but realizes her twin brother may be alive.

Act 4 is more of the same. Aguecheek hits Sebastian in mistake for Viola, so Sebastian beats him and draws his sword on Toby. Olivia parts them and Sebastian willingly takes over Viola's place in her affections.

> What relish is in this? How runs the stream?
> Or I am mad, or else this is a dream.
> Let fancy still my sense in Lethe steep;
> If it be thus to dream, still let me sleep!

Feste dresses up as Sir Topas the Curate to mock Malvolio; extremely funny as this scene is, the impression of cruelty is not absent. Malvolio is in despair, and the mockery continues rather long. Yet I doubt if Shakespeare was clearly conscious of what he was creating until it was finished, though when Feste says he is 'Like to the old Vice' of the Morality Plays, some touch of the sinister must certainly be intended. Sebastian by contrast is fully and perfectly in love; his expressive wonder is one of the most dramatic moments in all Shakespeare, it is exactly what one does feel at such a moment, though in his case the unexplained mistaken identity increases the sensation.

> This is the air; that is the glorious sun;
> This pearl she gave me, I do feel't and see't. . . .

Sebastian and Olivia marry. The Duke encounters Feste, and Antonio is brought to him, accused of his part in a war at sea. His defence is that 'A witchcraft drew me hither: That most ingrateful boy there by your side. . . .' Before his case is decided, Olivia arrives. The Duke reproaches her for cruelty in a speech that alludes to the Greek romance called the *Ethiopica*, which had existed in English since 1569. That is a formidably long and floridly ornamental tale, but romantic it undoubtedly is, and Shakespeare enjoyed it much more than we do. When the intrigues and punishments are played out, all Feste has to say is 'And thus the whirligig of time brings in his revenges,' and all Malvolio has to say is 'I'll be reveng'd on the whole pack of you.' The play ends with 'When that I was and a little tiny boy'. Setting aside its sadness and its refrain, what it expresses is proverbial wisdom: 'a foolish thing was but a toy, by swaggering could I never thrive, tosspots still had drunken heads . . . a great while ago this world began.' The song is satiric, but its sadness is unmistakable. Feste lives now in a house by the church, maybe therefore an almshouse, 'when I came unto my beds' may mean he is an old man. At least he is not dismissed to walk the roads.

Like so many of Shakespeare's plays, *Twelfth Night* has stray lines of startling beauty which one is unable to unlearn, even when one has forgotten where they come from. They sometimes offer insights into a whole lost world:

> . . . it is old and plain;
> The spinsters and the knitters in the sun,
> And the free maids that weave their thread with bones,
> Do use to chant it. . . .

> Carry his water to th' wise woman.

> I think we do know the sweet Roman hand.

> let thy tongue tang with arguments of state. . . .

> Whom the blind waves and surges have devour'd.

Is the collapse of poor old Toby Belch a replay of the rejection of Falstaff? Not quite, because Belch is greedy, cunning (he plotted the Malvolio intrigue before he brought in Fabian), and violent, as well as innocently hopeless. Aguecheek was just born to fail, his vices are superficial and hilariously funny, and one thinks 'poor old Aguecheek' just as much before he opens his mouth as when he bleeds. The weakness in all this is the character of Sebastian, who takes on a woman for life at ten seconds' notice, and beats up the ruffian knight and his nephew. I would not want my daughter to marry him, but of course he is no more intended to stand examination than the plot of which he is a figment. Maria is an improvement on Tearsheet, I think. But I cannot help connecting the punishment of Belch and Aguecheek, let alone Malvolio, with a sinister streak of cruelty, nor can I help connecting the cruelty with the sadness, which echoes Falstaff in a minor key. I suspect that the solution lies in Robert Armin's *Nest of Ninnies*, which certainly has a cruel streak as well as an intense sadness; he must have been writing his memoirs of fools and naturals at just this time.

Troilus and Cressida uses Chaucer, Lydgate and Chapman's *Iliad*. Shakespeare has often referred to the same myth or fiction in other plays. This was printed in 1609, 'as it was acted by the King's Majesty's servants at the Globe', and then again in the same year with that claim cancelled, and an Epistle praising Shakespeare's comedies:

> Eternal reader, you have here a new play, never staled with the Stage, never clapper-clawed [cf. act 4, scene iv] with the palms of the vulgar, and yet passing full of the palm comical. . . . refuse not, nor like this the less, for not being sullied with the smoky breath of the multitude.

We are told at this period by a foreign observer that the English were smoking everywhere, most of all in the theatre. But I do not for a moment think Shakespeare wrote this Epistle. All the same, it raises questions about the play, which is certainly experimental and may have been privately commissioned. Literary echoes and allusions date it rather securely to about 1602; it may represent some kind of riposte to Chapman.

It looks to me as if Shakespeare was asked for an *Iliad* play, and responded (as in *Hamlet*) with one that showed what such people might be like outside their static fictional frames. His Pandarus and his Thersites might in principle be one and the same actor. Troilus on his own has wonderful love poetry, but everybody else except Hector is utterly unchivalrous. Satire dismantles honour. The play was long disregarded or called a 'problem play'. Its modern productions, which have been brilliant and more and more frequent, began I believe with its revival by Nevill Coghill. I find it thrilling; it plays even better than it reads, but I am still unable to expound it because there is so much torsion in the plot that its momentum is unpredictable and its effect by no means single. In the Folio it was printed between *Henry VIII* and *Coriolanus* as a tragedy, but the page numbering shows it should have followed *Romeo*. There was trouble about the right to reprint it. It may have been commissioned for the satiric young gentlemen of the Inns of Court; it mocks heroes, it mocks marriage and it mocks manipulators.

The first scene has fourteen (and a half) lines of unrhymed sonnet. Pandarus talks in prose but Troilus talks in verse, as happens at times in the *Merry Wives* and in *Twelfth Night*. Shakespeare is still preoccupied with how to manage confrontation between characters of quite different kinds, but his solutions in *Troilus and Cressida* are more radical than ever before. The problem may be special to poets in the theatre. The nearest he ever came to a play wholly concerned with everyday life was *The Merry Wives of Windsor*, but even that had its lyrical aspect: it was not quite the 'bourgeois comedy' some critics have called it. A poet in the theatre needs emotions of an intensity or characters exalted enough to justify verse expression, yet if he is to express the world he must have low life as well, playing one off against the other, and in the Elizabethan theatre some comic element, and to Shakespeare's mind some musical element, are indispensable.

All this was easiest managed in English history plays, Shakespeare's first great successes, and in lyrical comedies. He had written only four formal tragedies before *Troilus*, two of them Roman (the early *Titus Andronicus*, and *Julius Caesar*), and *Romeo* and *Hamlet*, but *Hamlet* had created a demand for more satiric, philosophizing plays, and more tragedy. He trod carefully on this difficult ground. *Troilus* is the least obvious of plays and the most ambivalent; it is irreducibly multiple.

The prologue sets the story of the Greeks. 'Sixty and nine that wore Their crownets regal' sailing to the Trojan war; he names the gates of Troy from Caxton and Lydgate, 'Beginning in the middle', as Horace advises, and 'thence away To what may be digested in a play.' As poetry, the prologue's speech is not intended as seriously as that of the chorus in *Henry V*. Troilus knows the armies are 'Fools on both sides' and so does Shakespeare; all that Troilus wants is Cressida.

We see her in the second scene where the warriors are described, Hector in verse and Ajax, 'valiant as the lion, churlish as the bear, slow as the elephant', in prose. In quite a long prose exchange, Pandarus recommends Troilus in vain. The heroes' return from battle he describes sportively, like a return from hunting or a game of football – 'that, that, look you that; there's a fellow!' – but the common soldiers are dismissed as 'Asses, fools, dolts! chaff and bran, chaff and bran! porridge after meat'. The metaphor in the *Iliad* about Ajax being as stubborn as a donkey beaten out of crops is basic to the description of his character in battle, but not mentioned. Cressida is pert: 'And I'll spring up in his tears an 'twere a nettle against may.' She scorns her uncle Pandarus, but confesses alone to a secret attraction to Troilus.

> Yet hold I off. Women are angels, wooing:
> Things won are done; joy's soul lies in the doing.
> Men prize the thing ungain'd. . . .

The Greeks in scene iii have more dignity; they fling around grand orthodox words. At this formal council of war Ulysses shines, his worldly wisdom will prove objectively true throughout the play, but one does not like him better for it. He praises hierarchy, 'The primogenity and due of birth, Prerogative of age, crowns, sceptres, laurels . . .'. Without it 'appetite, an universal wolf', would end by self-cannibalism. Shakespeare recurs to this in *Lear* (act 4, scene ii) and something similar happens in the Thomas More play, where 'man like ravenous fishes Would feed on one another'. The doctrine is traditional and widespread; it is not personal to Shakespeare, indeed it occurs in the *Iliad*.

Ulysses turns his eloquence on Achilles, whose behaviour he mocks. If the interruptions are removed, he speaks 132 lines, the longest block being 62. We have had no such display of rhetoric since Mark Antony. But it has no obvious effect. Aeneas enters as a Trojan herald with lighter and more spirited lines, issuing a challenge from Hector in tournament terms:

'Trumpet, blow loud, Send thy brass voice through all these lazy tents. . . .'
Ulysses then plots with Nestor what is to be done. This third scene is
written in decent but not glittering verse; it seems to me far too long, but it
fed an appetite for rhetoric we have lost, and another scene is soon to come
which balances it.

The second act opens with relieving mockery in prose between antiheroic Thersites and the bear Ajax. Achilles and Patroclus join in, also in
prose. The next scene is in verse, a council of war at Troy in which Priam
presides but the formal speech is by Troilus, and in a more sparkling vein
than the leaden rhetoric of Ulysses, who to my mind recalls a senior
politician as seen by Siegfried Sassoon. Troilus talks not about hierarchy
but about honour, and about loyalty. Cassandra breaks in on this conclave
raving prophecies and Hector remarks with some truth that Troilus and
Paris have spoken 'not much Unlike young men, whom Aristotle thought
Unfit to hear moral philosophy' – the anachronism about Aristotle probably mattered no more to the audience than it does to me, except as a joke.

Hector appeals instead to the law of nature and property 'To curb those
raging appetites that are Most disobedient . . .'. The moral philosophies of
both these councils are flawlessly orthodox, yet the confrontation they
lead to is disastrous and tragic. The point is not that they are rant and cant,
but that Shakespeare is deliberately ironic about the results of elderly
wisdom. Thersites voices his mockery and bitterness clearly enough in the
next scene, and no one in the audience has any doubt about the tragedy to
come. He quibbles with Achilles much as Feste proves that everyone else
is a fool in *Twelfth Night*; Agamemnon arrives to scold Achilles in verse
but makes no progress and relapses into prose with Ajax. Ulysses comes
too, and they set about flattering Ajax in surprising terms that parody the
Gospel:

> Praise him that gat thee, she that gave thee suck;
> Fam'd be thy tutor, and thy parts of nature
> Thrice-fam'd beyond, beyond all erudition;
> But he that disciplin'd thine arms to fight –
> Let Mars divide eternity in twain
> And give him half. . . .

The third act begins with music. In the course of verbal sparring
Pandarus sings Paris and Helen a lyric about love with obscene innuendo.
It is quite unlike normal Shakespeare, in fact it is a comic song with no
touch of poetry, the kind of thing Dekker or Marston might write, only
better executed and extremely well devised for its context in the play:

> . . . The shaft confounds,
> Not that it wounds,
> But tickles still the sore.
> These lovers cry, O ho, they die!

> Yet that which seems the wound to kill
> Doth turn O ho! to ha! ha! he!
> So dying love lives still.

The whole scene is in prose, and the corrosive acid of parody has entered into its composition. In the next scene Pandarus comes on Troilus moping for Cressida: one scene affects the reading of the next.

> I stalk about her door
> Like a strange soul upon the Stygian banks
> Staying for waftage. O, be thou my Charon,
> And give me swift transportance to these fields
> Where I may wallow in the lily beds. . . .

The love scene that follows is in cool prose that moves later into impassioned verse, with antiphonal, contrasting sonnet-like speeches about how their names might become proverbial for truth and for falsity, as of course they did. In the very next scene Calchas, a Trojan traitor, demands that Agamemnon should exchange the prisoner Antenor for his daughter Cressida; Agamemnon agrees. The Greeks work on Achilles by making him envious of Ajax. Ulysses has a speech of seventy-five lines scarcely interrupted: his speeches are evidently part of his character, the wise Privy Councillor who can manipulate men and has only reasons of state in his heart. Patroclus is ashamed:

> Sweet, rouse yourself; and the weak wanton Cupid
> Shall from your neck unloose his amorous fold,
> And, like a dew-drop from the lion's mane,
> Be shook to airy air.

At the end of this scene Achilles complains that his mind is 'troubled, like a fountain stirr'd; And I myself see not the bottom of it'. 'Would the fountain of your mind were clear again,' remarks Thersites, 'that I might water an ass at it. I had rather be a tick in a sheep than such a valiant ignorance.'

Three acts are over. In the fourth, Diomedes has brought Antenor home to Troy. Troilus and Cressida are still happy. What is said is perhaps central to Shakespeare's feeling about his play:

> O Cressida! but that the busy day,
> Wak'd by the lark, hath rous'd the ribald crows,
> And dreaming night will hide our joys no longer,
> I would not from thee.

Aeneas takes her to be handed over to the Greeks. Troilus consents somewhat too easily one might think; Cressida rages. Their parting is the most moving scene in the play. In the fifth scene Ajax appears in arms to challenge Hector, ridiculous in valorous, exaggerated verse:

> Thou, trumpet, there's my purse.
> Now crack thy lungs and split thy brazen pipe;
> Blow, villain, till thy sphered bias cheek
> Out-swell the colic of puff'd Aquilon.
> Come, stretch thy chest, and let thy eyes spout blood. . . .

The Greeks greet Cressida with kisses; she seems pleased. Then the preliminaries of the duel begin; but that turns out bloodless, because Hector says Ajax is his first cousin. The two armies now intermingle in a truce, with extreme courtesy and some unexpected encounters. They behave in fact like old-fashioned European officers, a point well brought out by the 1985 Stratford production, which set the play in a kind of ruined battlefront hotel in about 1870. The verse rings brazenly, though a sharp-eared critic might observe a touch of the parody *Aeneid* verse from *Hamlet*: 'When thou hast hung thy advanced sword i' th' air, Not letting it decline on the declined . . .'. But these words are Nestor's and Nestor dodders. All the same, the play is as much Shakespeare's revenge on heroic verse as it is on heroic values. Among all the foolery and mobility, Achilles is ominous, measuring Hector as it were for his coffin.

The fifth act simply continues the fourth. Achilles opens it:

> I'll heat his blood with Greekish wine to-night,
> Which with my scimitar I'll cool to-morrow.

The wine, of course, is Elizabethan Greek wine, perhaps malmsey from Monemvasia, and the scimitar is intended to conjure up a sixteenth-century Greek weapon, maybe from some illustrated book. Shakespeare gives scimitars to Morocco in the *Merchant* and to Aaron in *Titus*. The outbursts of Thersites spatter the heroes like heavy rain: Patroclus is a masculine whore, Agamemnon has not so much brain as earwax, Thersites would sooner be a toad or a leper than be Menelaus, Diomedes is a false-hearted rogue. That turns out true, because he seduces Cressida. Troilus sees it and suffers: 'The bonds of heaven are slipp'd, dissolv'd, and loos'd.' The war has only to begin again for the climax of the tragedy to take place, and war recommences in the next scene. The setting out is fraught and the battle far more hectic than usual, with numerous brief encounters and more hide and seek about it than most stage battles. Patroclus dies, and Achilles avenges him on Hector with an unchivalrous device amounting really to treachery. Troilus survives. The brief speeches in these scenes are powerful: in the last few pages of the last act Shakespeare suddenly extends his powers.

The Epilogue is spoken by Pandarus, sour and mocking and more than a little disgusting, on the subject of the whorehouses of Southwark; the final couplet about venereal disease. Did Armin make this very funny? The aftertaste of the play is unpleasant, and the final battle rather horrifying than in any sense noble. It is not easy to sum up this play, or to come to a well-founded verdict. It fascinated my own generation as very young men, and continues to attract as well as to puzzle and in some ways repel. Not much is left holy by it, except by implication its opposites such as fidelity and virtue. Cressida is a medieval fiction based originally on the Chryseis of the *Iliad*, in which poem Troilus is already dead. He is supposed to have been sacrificed by Achilles on the altar of Apollo. The disparity of the medieval story and the classical Homeric setting is one of the elements of incoherence in the play, yet most of its elements exist as hints in the *Iliad*, and Shakespeare builds powerful and bitter ironies on this very disparity. There is no doubt that it works extremely well in the theatre.

All's Well That Ends Well has little great verse in it, and among its characters Shakespeare likes only two, Lafeu and Helena. It offers no real problem of construction or momentum, but I take it to be a relatively light play, flung together in a hurry. The Folio prints it first, very likely (to judge from the chattiness or vagueness of stage directions) from Shakespeare's manuscript. It appears to me earlier than *Measure for Measure*, later than certain plays of 1600 and 1601 to which it alludes, and therefore about 1602, but I would not be surprised to be proved wrong. G. K. Hunter in his Arden edition suggests a tentative date of 1603–4. The difference matters very little, so long as we have the series in the right order, as I hope we have.

Half of the play is in prose and of that half about eighteen per cent is in rhyme, which recalls *Twelfth Night*. I am reluctant to connect this or any play to the famous puzzle of *Love's Labour Won*, a title recorded by Meres in 1598, now presumed lost if it ever existed. I also doubt whether this is a later revision of an early play. The problem of the names Viola and Violenta seems to tie it close to *Twelfth Night*. It is possible to see Parolles as related to Pandarus in *Troilus*, but that may be going too far.

The story comes from the *Decameron* of Boccaccio through William Painter's collection of translations, *Palace of Pleasure* (1566–75). Shakespeare has used more than one episode, and he has tightened the links in the story to give it a continuous moral momentum. Critics complain about a lack of coherence all the same. Some console themselves by identifying folk-themes or ancient story patterns: the despised person who attains happiness by curing the King's sickness, and the wife who performs impossible tasks and claims a reward. Shakespeare had a strong feeling for patterns of this kind, just as Boccaccio had, but their abstract form does not determine the structure of the play that emerges. Its characters are too real for playing-card roles; they are severely criticized (I think Shakespeare dislikes Bertram and his weakness as much as I do), and they alter. Realism alters the balance of the folktale, satire eats away at conventional values, nothing is as simple on the stage as a narrative on the page, because by saying one thing a character may inspire us to think another, reversing our perception and our moralizing from what seems to be presented. It is this skill of Shakespeare's that makes the plays of these transitional years so hard to expound.

Bertram's father has died and he is summoned to Court. The King is dying, though Helena's father, who was a great physician, might have cured him. She loves Bertram, but

> 'Twere all one
> That I should love a bright particular star
> And think to wed it, he is so above me.
> In his bright radiance and collateral light
> Must I be comforted, not in his sphere.

The scene is crowded; we meet the good old Countess, the coarse-minded and cynical Parolles, and the 'old lord' Lafeu, but the star part is Helena's and this play is hers. She has an interesting trick of bursting into passionate and intellectual verse monologue in the middle of a prose conversation with ghastly Parolles. The first act sways between the Court and the country house, where the clown quotes Rabelais (act 1, scene iii) and sings comic verses like the song Pandarus sang. His repertory includes some subtle playing with scripture (act 4, scene v). The Countess discovers Helena's love for Bertram and encourages her to go to Paris to heal the King.

> Now I see
> The myst'ry of your loneliness, and find
> Your salt tears' head.

In the second act Bertram is desperate to go off to the wars but has to stay in Paris being too young, 'Creaking my shoes on the plain masonry'. Lafeu introduces Helena to the King, whom she cures, and claims Bertram for reward. The couplets in which she addresses the King about his cure are spell-like, as if the cure were magical, though they are only about the passing of time – three ways of saying two days must pass:

> Ere twice the horses of the sun shall bring
> Their fiery torcher his diurnal ring,
> Ere twice in murk and occidental damp
> Moist Hesperus hath quench'd her sleepy lamp,
> Or four and twenty times the pilot's glass
> Hath told the thievish minutes how they pass. . . .

Maybe this skill is not essentially different from that of the parody love-verses to Rosalind in *As You Like It*, but Shakespeare does the trick spiritedly, and better than anyone else. I do not think he intends 'great' poetry in this play, but he does intend great variety of linguistic texture, and some pointed lines that verse makes memorable. As for the plot, Shakespeare turns the old patterns inside out: the match of Bertram and Helena is disastrous from the beginning: 'I'll to the Tuscan wars, and never bed her.' She follows him of course: having first got him she must now win him. Bertram is a hero only in a military sense; the play has only a heroine. Her impossible tasks are set by him: to get the ring from his finger and to bear him a child.

> And is it I
> That drive thee from the sportive court, where thou
> Wast shot at with fair eyes, to be the mark
> Of smoky muskets? O you leaden messengers,
> That ride upon the violent speed of fire,
> Fly with false aim; move the still pierced air,
> That sings with piercing; do not touch my lord.

Helena goes to Italy dressed as a pilgrim while Bertram is proving himself as a soldier. Parolles is his Pandarus, and Helena takes another girl's place to get his ring and his child, and makes him accept a ring she had from the King. Parolles is exposed as a coward, a liar and a betrayer: his undoing is memorably funny and disgraceful, but the point is quietly made that Bertram is just as bad in his way. Parolles being down can be honest. 'Simply the thing I am Shall make me live. . . . Rust, sword; cool, blushes; and, Parolles, live Safest in shame. Being fool'd, by fool'ry thrive.' He is almost Pistol almost moralized.

In the last act everyone meets again at the country house. Having lost Helena, Bertram begins to love her, and after some difficult moments she saves him from the King's fury, appearing first disguised this time as a jeweller to give evidence about the ring. The moment of recognition and reconciliation and virtual resurrection works like magic, as it always does in Shakespeare's late comedies.

Shakespeare's plays, like the tragedies of Euripides, are none the worse for their simple elements and their sense almost of pantomime: the *Alcestis* offers an especially interesting comparison. Parolles ends up as fool to Lafeu, and 'The King's a beggar, now the play is done.' The wholly immoral notion that nothing matters because it was all right in the end dissolves in good temper and lightheartedness, natural bonds are restored, and virtue, peace and pleasure look as if they might last for ever. It is no use frowning over this play: Shakespeare is beginning to recover himself. His comedies after *Twelfth Night* always depend on an almighty king or duke to award the final verdict on the characters. In *Twelfth Night* the comic world was all but out of control. But one of the most important paradoxes of his career is that the formally romantic comedies of his later period, with their popular, almost pantomime patterns, are more and more deeply moving, more nourishing to the soul than the glamour of the *Dream* and the wit and humour and spirits and poetry of *Love's Labour's Lost*.

All's Well is written with freshness, salt and dash. It is a tolerant play: 'Though you are a fool and a knave, you shall eat,' says Lafeu to Parolles. It is not 'a bountiful answer that fits all questions . . . like a barber's chair, that fits all buttocks – the pin buttock, the quatch buttock, the brawn buttock, or any buttock'. It does not show us humanity humanely or very fully. The love that fuels it and the reconciliation that concludes it are not enough to overwhelm the busy intrigues: for better and worse that must be put down to Boccaccio. The play therefore falls short of greatness, yet it is not without brilliance, and I nourish an affection for it, more than for most of the minor comedies.

Measure for Measure is another matter: it might well be called a great play. It intermingles tragic or at least serious and moral themes with comic material: Coleridge, who is often wrong but always acute, thought its comedy disgusting and its tragedy horrible, and even Walter Pater, who saw that its morality might be Shakespeare's own, felt the play should have been a tragedy. Professor Raleigh provided the important insight that if people asked for a comedy while Shakespeare was writing his great tragedies, what they got was *Measure for Measure* or *Troilus and Cressida*. But the dates, so far as we know them, do not seem to fit that proposal, at least if it were taken literally.

In 1603 the Queen died and the plague revisited London. James I came to the throne, the Chamberlain's Men became the King's Men, though they had to take in an actor called Lawrence Fletcher, who was 'comedian to his Majesty' in Scotland and came south with him. In July the King was rowed up the Thames to his coronation for fear of the plague, and crowned behind shut doors, to the great disappointment of his people. The pageant, designed with lavish symbolism and pedantry run riot by Jonson and Dekker, was put off until March 1604, when Shakespeare, who now had the status of a Groom of the Chamber to the King, presumably attended the King from the Tower to Westminster. We have the record of an issue of four and a half yards of scarlet-red cloth for his livery by the Master of the Wardrobe, Sir George Home, though he may not have had to march. The pageant had elaborate arches, speeches and heaven knows what else, but Dekker and Jonson both record that many of their devices had to be abandoned because of the unbearable noise, the uncontrollable crowds and the King's impatience. James hated these occasions because he was genuinely frightened of crowds, quite unlike Elizabeth, who loved them: Armin describes his terror as the people pressed up against a door to see him.

In August that year Shakespeare was named with nine others to wait on the Spanish Ambassador, the Constable of Castile, while he was in London for a peace conference. On 26 December 'Measure for Measure, by Shaxberd' was played before the King. He is named in the records as author, not just an actor. It was one of eleven plays that Christmas. Southampton was out of prison and in favour. At some time James I is supposed to have written a friendly personal letter to Shakespeare, which the Duke of Buckingham (1648–1721) said had been in Davenant's hands, but no such letter survives. If it had been in any other hands one might more securely believe in its reality.

Measure for Measure was not written to flatter the King's mercy and justice. The story comes from Cinthio's *Hecatommithi* (hundred tales), via George Whetstone's play *Promos and Cassandra* (1578). Of all Shakespeare's Italian sources, Cinthio is the most rewarding to someone with an afternoon to spare, because the extraordinary formal structure of Cinthio's tales has such a simple and obvious influence on Shakespeare. He wrote about unlikely or ill-assorted couples, a subject that goes back at least to Theocritus. Shakespeare had an eye for such sources: they are not to be thought of as part of his casual reading, he sought them out. Cinthio is an enjoyable writer of short stories, though the later ones smell of the lamp. Shakespeare used him again for *Othello*, where the bones of his structure supply the radical conflict of the play.

Measure for Measure as Shakespeare wrote it has some contemporary resonance. Whores have been a theme of his for some time: this play remembers the pulling down of houses of ill fame in time of plague in 1603. The association of whoredom and physical corruption, gliding disease, in his plays since *Hamlet*, appears to me to be rooted in the plague rather than in venereal disease, but no doubt as a Londoner he was closely acquainted with the ravages of both. By 1604 he had left the south bank and was lodging with a Huguenot hatmaker called Christopher Mountjoy, at the corner of Silver Street and Mugwell (Monkwell) Street, near St Olave's in Cripplegate; he had known the Mountjoys at least since 1602. I have wondered whether Shakespeare's interest in herbal and Paracelsian – that is, unorthodox – medicine, which in those years was associated with Huguenots, may not have been a strand in his relationship with the Mountjoy family. John Hall, who married Shakespeare's daughter Susanna in 1607, was a Paracelsian, as we shall see. By 1604 Hall may have already settled in Stratford.

Act 1 sets the scene. The play shows traces of revision, but no one can determine whether the 1604 version is first or final: I think first. The simple constable Elbow is like Dogberry, the spying Duke like Henry V and VIII, and Claudio's sister Isabella is like Helena. At several points *Measure for Measure* condenses and improves on the language of *All's Well*. The Duke leaves Vienna with Angelo in charge: 'Spirits are not finely touch'd But to fine issues' and virtue must be outgoing. 'Mortality and mercy in Vienna Live in thy tongue and heart.'

The second scene swiftly shows us social problems. Lucio, a coarse gentleman, hears from Mistress Overdone ('I have purchas'd as many diseases under her roof as . . .') that Claudio is arrested for getting a girl pregnant, and due to be beheaded: Angelo has unleashed penalties 'Which have, like unscour'd armour, hung by th' wall'. The pimp Pompey tells her all 'houses of resort' in the suburbs are to be pulled down. These two are comic and pathetic characters. 'I'll be your tapster still. Courage, there will be pity taken on you; you that have worn your eyes almost out in the service, you will be considered.' Claudio moralizes to Lucio on his own fate: 'Our natures do pursue, Like rats that ravin down their proper bane, A thirsty evil; and when we drink we die.' Claudio is secretly married to the girl he got pregnant, unable to be so publicly because of delicate negotiations about a dowry, and sends a message to his sister, who is just about to enter a convent: the nuns are charming. Meanwhile the Duke returns disguised as a friar to watch the progress of reform. His speech about 'liberty plucks justice by the nose; The baby beats the nurse, and quite athwart Goes all decorum' recalls Ulysses on hierarchy in *Troilus*, and, just as in *Troilus*, the action of the play will comment on it.

In the second act Angelo judges, harshly and against good advice, as eloquently as Ulysses, but with a line of argument that intuitively we reject for its cold severity. Claudio's sentence is confirmed. Elbow the constable brings in Pompey and the foolish Froth, but they run rings round him, tire out Angelo until he leaves, and in the end get let off. They are ordinary minor comic figures, a little too funny to be real, but with some sharp touches of reality. 'He, sir, sitting, as I say, in a lower chair, sir: 'twas in the Bunch of Grapes, where, indeed, you have a delight to sit, have you not?' 'I have so; because it is an open room, and good for winter.'

Now Isabella pleads with Angelo for mercy in almost Portia's words in the *Merchant*, but more briefly and in dramatic terms more effectively. She adds arguments of her own, not original ones but striking by the electric power of the verse:

> Merciful Heaven,
> Thou rather, with thy sharp and sulphurous bolt,
> Splits the unwedgeable and gnarled oak
> Than the soft myrtle. But man, proud man,
> Dress'd in a little brief authority,
> Most ignorant of what he's most assur'd,
> His glassy essence, like an angry ape,
> Plays such fantastic tricks before high heaven
> As makes the angels weep; who, with our spleens,
> Would all themselves laugh mortal.

This famous little speech is central to the play and to the problems critics have about it. Shakespeare perfectly understands that we can laugh where the angels weep. Perhaps *Measure for Measure* should not be called a tragedy or a comedy but just a social Morality. Shakespeare is on Isabella's side, and so are the audience. It is the fact of her being a woman that gives her verses an added tang. She offers Angelo 'prayers from preserved souls,

From fasting maids, whose minds are dedicate To nothing temporal'. (There are more nuns in Shakespeare than one thinks, and more crows, and more gunshots.) Angelo discovers that he wants her body, and offers the bargain of her body for her brother's life, which of course she refuses. This last scene of the act is so sharply and powerfully worded as to be made psychologically credible and painfully real.

In the third act the Duke visits the prison and preaches to Claudio a sermon on death which one remembers: 'Be absolute for death; either death or life Shall thereby be the sweeter.' Isabella visits her brother and tells her tale, but he answers with a chilling meditation not on the acceptance but the horror of death: 'To lie in cold obstruction, and to rot'. It has been too often anthologized to be transcribed here. It subtly transmutes the Duke's sermon into something much more terrifying; the two must be taken together. The Duke in disguise restores Claudio to virtue and comforts Isabella with the beginnings of an intrigue, which introduces Mariana, engaged once to Angelo but abandoned because her brother died and her prospect of a dowry died with him. The Duke then encounters Elbow and Pompey, Lucio, who refuses to bail Pompey and slanders the Duke, and Overdone, against whom Lucio has informed. These little scenes are saved from appearing as the jejune string of moral examples they really are only by comic brio. The Duke concludes the act with iambic tetrameter couplets, a curiously misplaced exercise. Brave men have dismissed them as an interpolation; I am almost sure Shakespeare wrote them. 'To draw with idle spiders' strings Most ponderous and substantial things!' sounds like him, and so does the neatly knotted riddle at the end. The Duke in the third act has been superhuman.

Act 4 opens with a song sung by a boy: 'Take, O, take those lips away'. We have a setting of it by John Wilson, Oxford Professor of Music from 1656 to 1661, who was eighteen in 1603 and may have worked for Shakespeare. The words of the song are said to be adapted from a Latin poem, but I fear they are not. The Latin is medieval and in the only version I have seen unmetrical. It says 'Spread girl thy rosy cheeks, tinted with pink of Tyrian vermilion, give lips, coral lips; give gentle kisses like a dove, part of the sap of the loving soul,' or to be more precise, in R. Noble's version (1923), 'of the mindless soul' (*amentis* for *amantis*). A later bit of this idiotic lyric was used by Fletcher to the same metre and music as Shakespeare's song. The only reason for discussing the matter is that should it be true that Shakespeare did know the Latin and use it, then he probably got it from an appendix to the Paris edition of Petronius (1587), which it is pleasing to think that he might have read. Fletcher's stanza does certainly come from the Latin, which goes on to speak of snowy breasts and wounding nipples, also of a cinnamon-flavoured bosom and delights on all sides. That is enough about that.

Shakespeare's song is a sad one about faithlessness. The scene forwards the intrigue, which makes use of a garden 'circummur'd with brick', with a vineyard on the west and a wooden gate to it. Isabella hands over the big vineyard key and the small garden key so that Marina can keep the midnight assignment. A lot of secret things go on in Shakespearean gardens and orchards, as in shrubberies in Jane Austen's day. In this case we are dealing with a 'garden-house' (act 5, scene i). The Puritan play-hating writer Philip Stubbes attacked these in his *Anatomie of Abuses* (1583). 'Then to these gardens they repair when they list, with a basket and a boy, where they meeting with their sweethearts receive their wished desires.' He also had a passion against hats without hatbands.

The machinery of the play begins to move swiftly: scene ii begins, 'Come hither, sirrah. Can you cut off a man's head?' Pompey is appointed assistant to Abhorson the executioner, but they are meant to kill Barnardine instead, a convicted felon. Barnardine has been drinking, feels unfit to die, and refuses to do so: luckily a pirate dies in prison so they can use his head for Claudio's. Angelo has had the girl but wants Claudio killed anyway. The grotesquer persons are curiously enjoyable, and one likes them, even horrifying Abhorson. I knew a public hangman once who made conversation much like his. The act closes in swirls and eddies of intrigue, as the Duke, undisguised, re-enters Vienna to the sound of trumpets.

The fifth act is no more than one scene of 536 lines, and the subtleties of the solution are quicker to read than to describe. Only Lucio is punished. He is condemned to be married to his whore, then whipped and then hanged. This is not meant seriously: it is just a hearty Elizabethan joke. In the end he is forgiven his other crimes; only the marriage to the whore is carried out. 'Marrying a punk, my lord, is pressing to death, whipping, and hanging.' 'Slandering a prince deserves it.' One is not wrong to see a cruel streak here and there in the play: whipping and the rack are elements in it, and the threat of execution in prison is rather real. The Duke's and Claudio's dialogue on death is uncomfortably powerful. This play is about London, in spite of its exotic elements, or at least London is more present to it than to any other play of Shakespeare's.

From this moment Shakespeare turned to tragedy and dropped comedy until his last years. Such a conversion is not to be explained only by public taste or by private patronage or by Burbage's demands as an actor. It was a decision. One can well understand his approaching his great themes by a slow and careful spiralling towards them; it is the ceasing to write comedy, and the return to comedy only in another, more stylized form, that requires explanation. The Armin characters in his recent works had been somewhat similar, almost as if Armin wrote them for himself. I think the increase of parody of styles and of plots in *Troilus* marks a self-critical as well as a satiric period. One must assume that any writer who was so constantly wrestling with the forms he used, and who wore out form after form to the bone, must have been dissatisfied with his own work.

It does look in these plays I have called 'transitional' as if Shakespeare were dissatisfied, not just with himself but with the inner form and meaning of comedy. His affronted moral sense had eaten into its edges. As for poetry, he seems to have been able to summon that out of the air whenever he chose to do so, for a set-piece like the lament for Hector in *Troilus* or the death dialogue in *Measure for Measure*. Now he wished to take a subject that might fully extend or display his powers as a poet, not only in set-pieces but again and again, as in *Romeo* and in *Hamlet*. In *Othello*, he knew exactly what he was demanding of himself. Cinthio's story was a perfect framework.

All the same, the break is not perhaps so clean as I have suggested. The Account of the Office of the Revels for the first of November 1604 to the end of October 1605 records *Othello* (*The Moor of Venice*) on All Saints' day (Hallamas Day) 1604, *The Merry Wives of Windsor* on the following Sunday, *Measure for Measure* on St Stephen's Night, the play of *Errors* on 28 December (Innocents Night), *Love's Labour's Lost*, *Henry V* and *The Merchant of Venice* in the new year. It is therefore not possible to show from this evidence whether *Othello* or *Measure for Measure* was written first.

It is fairly clear that they were written within a year of each other, though it might be counterproductive to try to write two plays at once. What dictates the priority of *Measure for Measure* is that this possible order fits better into the scheme of development that we discern in Shakespeare. This is just a matter of common sense, a dangerous but not a negligible weapon in Shakespeare studies. How far in advance of a Court performance did Shakespeare write his plays? A new king made it possible to revive old plays, as the record shows. It is possible and I think likely that Shakespeare was already at work on *Othello* before the Queen died, or was already committed to it. If so, his first play written specifically for the new reign of the King of Scotland in London was *Macbeth*.

The Revels Office account used to be thought a forgery, but it was recently proved beyond question to be genuine by several conclusive tests. We have records of other performances around this time too. During the plague the company got thirty shillings at Bath, twenty at Shrewsbury, forty at Coventry, twenty-five and eightpence at Ipswich, fifteen at Maldon and twenty at Oxford. The Chamber Account, when the Court was at Wilton keeping clear of London, records a payment to 'John Hemyngs one of his Majesty's players', on 2 December 1603, 'for the pains and expenses of himself and the rest of the company in coming from Mortlake in the county of Surrey unto the Court aforesaid, and there presenting before his Majesty one play'. William Cory, the Eton schoolmaster–poet (who had to resign for the usual reasons), was told at Wilton in August 1865 by Lord Pembroke's mother, Lady Herbert, that 'we have a letter never printed from Lady Pembroke to her son, telling him to bring James I from Salisbury to see *As You Like It*, "we have the man Shakespeare with us"; she wanted to cajole the King in Ralegh's behalf, – he came'. No one else has ever seen this letter, but there is no reason to doubt that it existed. The King did in fact visit Salisbury.

The Chamber Accounts for 1603–4 record payments to John Hemynges for plays at Hampton Court, four just after Christmas, two on New Year's Day and one on Candlemas Day, and another at Whitehall on the 19th, perhaps Shrove Tuesday. We learn from a courtier's letter that 'On New Year's night we had a play of Robin good-fellow,' which confirms the fact that Puck was not a proper name. A fuller letter from Sir Walter Cope of Cope's Castle, later rechristened Holland Park, to Robert Cecil refers to a private performance of particular interest in 1604.

> I have sent and been all this morning hunting for players, jugglers, and such kind of creatures, but find them hard to find, wherefore leaving notes for them to seek me, Burbage is come, and says there is no new play that the Queen hath not seen, but they have revived an old one, called *Love's Labour's Lost*, which for wit and mirth he says will please her exceedingly. And this is appointed to be played tomorrow night at my Lord of Southampton's, unless you send a writ to remove the *corpus cum causa* to your house in Strand. Burbage is my messenger, ready attending your pleasure.

We know from yet another courtier's letter that Southampton entertained the Queen, the Duke of Holst, and the Court at his house with 'revels' on 13 and 14 January 1605. 'It seems we shall have Christmas all the year.'

Cinthio's stories are a catalogue of unlikely or ill-suited couples. *Othello* pivots on a devilish device successfully used to destroy a man we pitied and admired, until he reaches the point of nauseating us; all the same we grieve for him. The heroine is almost too purely pathetic, but warm and alive like all Shakespeare's girls. Othello as a man has just enough faults to be played on: he is jealous and passionate, with a certain suppressed violence about him that can be observed in habits of speech. But he is an attractive and romantic, even a magnetic figure; we feel this as much as Desdemona does. Her name, I suppose, is Greek – *dysdaimona*, unfortunate; the origin of Othello's is unknown, but it might be based on *Ottoman*, for he is a Moor from the Turkish Mediterranean, where the power of Venice was still formidable, and the English were now successfully trading. But Shakespeare's travels are imaginary. As he grows older they become more vivid: now it is Cyprus, one day it will be the Caribbean, always it is imaginary. He has a power to take us where he had never been.

The first act is set in Venice, and its climax is Iago's plot. As a boy I used to feel Iago was impossible, like Marlowe's Jew of Malta, too wicked to be credible; I knew nothing about sexual jealousy or ambition, and lacked the self-knowledge to understand envy. As an adult I find Iago painfully real, and this sets me free to observe how Shakespeare sees his suffering as he saw Aaron's in *Titus Andronicus. Othello* is a play about terrifying adult male passions, small wonder that innocent Desdemona is swallowed up in it; I wish I did not think it was so real.

The first scene reveals Iago's thwarted ambition. Cassio, 'Forsooth, a great arithmetician', has been preferred as Othello's deputy. One should not think of Ralegh's mathematician Matthew Roydon, or his 'bookish theoric', but rather of the Digges family. A mathematician was already in those days a master of fortification, and might have many practical skills. Iago's outburst against intellectuals is a typical soldier's grouse, but it lacks substance in Shakespeare's eyes:

> Why, there's no remedy; 'tis the curse of service:
> Preferment goes by letter and affection,
> Not by the old gradation, where each second
> Stood heir to the first.

Iago's character and motive are very clearly drawn; nothing that happens later should drive them out of one's head. He is deliberately, almost professionally treacherous: 'I am not what I am.' This kind of Machiavellian Italian fascinated the Elizabethans. Thomas More hated Machiavelli, Thomas Cromwell loved him. Shakespeare's generation tried to explain the appalling phenomenon of the rise of such men, since Thomas Cromwell had a large spiritual progeny. They run riot in the kind of 'Jacobean tragedy' that Webster wrote (Webster was by this time already writing), and they existed and flourished in the real world. Iago's conversation is as salted with sex and satire as anyone's: in him we have for the first time the satirist and derider as principal villain. For that reason I count this as the last transitional play as well as the first of a series of great tragedies.

Iago's racialism is devastating; it contains an element of sexual disgust. 'Even now, now, very now, an old black ram Is tupping your white ewe'; '. . . your daughter and the Moor are now making the beast with two backs'; 'To the gross clasps of a lascivious Moor'. Othello appears in the second scene: his formidable dignity, a dramatic version of natural authority, appears at once in his casually eloquent and controlled syntax and pride of speech, his first sentence being twelve sinewy lines long, 'I fetch my life and being From men of royal siege. . . .' The wonderful line with which he stops a brawl and which Eliot admired as pure poetry is functional, ironic and more or less proverbial; it occurs in more than one form: 'Keep up your bright swords, for the dew will rust them.'

The third scene is the Duke's Court, which is as busy with great events as a King's in an English history play: messenger arrives on the heels of messenger. 'The Turkish preparation makes for Rhodes . . .'; '. . . and now they do restem Their backward course, bearing with frank appearance Their purposes towards Cyprus.' Desdemona's father drags Othello before the Duke. His speech in defence is modest, fluent and powerful. Between his and her father's we feel we know the girl before she appears. Othello's account of his wooing has a slight but thrilling tinge of the exotic. It is a tour de force of persuasion and of poetry, a wonderful vignette of love. His conversation is like the *Mappa Mundi* in Hereford Cathedral, 'of antres vast and deserts idle, Rough quarries, rocks, and hills whose heads touch heaven . . . Cannibals . . . men whose heads Do grow beneath their shoulders'. His life has been a romance of 'disastrous chances', war, slavery, escape and wanderings.

Shakespeare has probably been reading Ralegh's *Discoverie of Guiana* (1596). The headless belly-headed men may arise from rumours about Inca sculptures, but they might as easily reflect the coloured drawing of a Pictish prince based on the Virginian pioneer settler John White's Red Indians, naked with a face tattooed on his torso. It was coloured by Jacques le Moyne de Morgues, a Huguenot refugee who died in London in 1588, servant to Ralegh and the most brilliant flower painter in Europe. His way of looking and his combination of unrestrained vividness in depiction with an almost Chinese sense of natural rhythm have a lot in common with Shakespeare; their ideals are similar and it is just possible that they knew each other. His life had been as adventurous as Othello's. But in this speech the point is that Othello speaks like a character in a romance; Desdemona has fallen in love with a character out of a romance: 'This is the only witchcraft I have us'd.' The marriage is recognized, Othello is sent to Cyprus, and Desdemona is allowed to follow next day. Iago is given charge of her, and cold-bloodedly lays the foundations of his plot.

The second act opens in Cyprus. Iago will end each of its three scenes with a monologue, which, as at the end of act 1, follows on a conversation with his accomplice Roderigo, with whom also he began the play. But the opening scene of the second act is the officers of Cyprus looking out to sea, doing the work which a chorus did in *Henry V*. The storm is terrific: Shakespeare never bettered it, certainly never in so few words. The Turkish fleet is scattered and wrecked like the Spanish Armada, a memory less than twenty years old, and as easy to recall as if one spoke of barbed wire in the late 1930s. This storm is necessary to the plot, because it brings Cassio and then Iago and Desdemona ashore before Othello. There follow ninety lines of quibbling satiric exchange between Iago and Desdemona, and of Cassio's increasing familiarity with her. Iago is obscene and, as Desdemona remarks of his wit, 'These are old fond paradoxes to make fools laugh i' th' alehouse.' The exchange is both vile on Iago's part and defenceless on hers; the effect is tense. Othello arrives at last with his higher style.

> If it were now to die,
> 'Twere now to be most happy; for I fear
> My soul hath her content so absolute
> That not another comfort like to this
> Succeeds in unknown fate.

They are really both helpless victims of an intrigue which the audience knows and must watch work itself out, but of which the lovers have no suspicion. In this earlier part of the play, Iago has far more to say and do than either of them. He is eaten up with lust as well as envy, 'the thought whereof Doth like a poisonous mineral gnaw my inwards . . .'. His verse, when he speaks in verse, is dense and pointed, never easy and never soaring, but as effective as a pistol shot.

Othello proclaims a celebration, at which Iago gets Cassio drunk. They discuss English drinking habits, a normal subject for satire which occurs in *Hamlet* and in numerous prose writers and coarse-witted pamphleteers. Iago sings a blunt soldier's song and a Scottish ballad about drunken quarrels, prudently substituting King Stephen for King Harry, and Yorkshire dialect for Scottish. The first substitution would have been crucially important under the old Queen, and both under James I. The fight Iago fuelled takes place with Shakespeare's usual expert observation of drunks, Cassio seems to have wounded an officer badly, the alarm bell rings, Othello descends like a thundercloud, and Cassio is disgraced. Iago continues his machinations.

The third act begins with the intrigue of the handkerchief. Cassio approaches first musicians, then a clown, then a lady to secure Desdemona's intercession; Iago offers to help. Cassio speaks with her while Othello is out on business, and she promises to help, but Othello returns and sees him leaving: 'Ha, I like not that.' She pleads for Cassio with indiscreet warmth; Iago then plays on Othello until he is on fire with jealous suspicion. Set down coldly, Iago's devices seem too obvious to fool a child, but the psychological processes of this act are terribly real, subtler for example than those of *Hamlet*. Othello's language (act 3, scene iii) takes on the quality of Iago's. Iago does not tempt like a devil, he deceives like a person; both Cassio and Othello praise him for honesty, they rely on him. I do not think Shakespeare likes Othello's extreme possessiveness about his wife any more than his suspicion of her:

> O curse of marriage,
> That we can call these delicate creatures ours,
> And not their appetites! I had rather be a toad,
> And live upon the vapour of a dungeon,
> Than keep a corner in the thing I love
> For others' uses.

Emilia, Iago's wife, steals the handkerchief which he leaves in Cassio's lodgings. As Iago watches Othello begin to change and to suffer, he has a moment almost of compassion: 'not poppy, nor mandragora, Nor all the drowsy syrups of the world, Shall ever medicine thee to that sweet sleep . . .'. They are Iago's best brief flight of poetry, and introduce the passionate poetry of loss that Othello speaks as he suffers, which is a match for Hamlet in pathos and in disgust. All the same, I doubt whether Iago's mandragora lines are just a musical transition; Shakespeare was himself so compassionate in a 'post-Christian' way that if a devil out of hell in one of his plays secured the damnation of a soul, the devil in Shakespeare would express some compassion for the soul it had damned.

Othello at his saddest still shows his weakness: the hollowness of war is seen in his lines by a very proud man to whom nothing else but war has mattered. And yet who would not feel such a hollowness if love was going badly? Othello is tortured, and scarcely accountable for his words or moods. His shame extends to his black face. It is essential to Othello that he is a black man. His passions are a deep and variable sea; there is something deliberately exotic about them, as there is about the handker-chief the Egyptian gave his mother as a piece of love-magic.

> A sibyl that had numb'red in the world
> The sun to course two hundred compasses
> In her prophetic fury sew'd the work;
> The worms were hallowed that did breed the silk;
> And it was dy'd in mummy which the skilful
> Conserv'd of maidens' hearts.

The fourth act is Desdemona's decline. As it opens, Iago is working on Othello, who reaches fever pitch. He breaks into prose, speaks in frag-ments, falls to the ground. When he recovers, Iago has other tricks to play on him: he is fertile in devices. Othello is now frantic and calling for poison. 'Do it not with poison; strangle her in her bed, even the bed she hath contaminated.' He slaps her face in public and she weeps.

A letter recalls Othello to Venice, leaving Cassio in command of Cyprus: 'You are welcome, sir, to Cyprus. – Goats and monkeys!' Alone with Desdemona, Othello mutters crazily, then breaks down in self-pity turn-ing to rage. The poetry involves us deeply in the passion. So it does in *Hamlet*, but here the verse is more personal and the passion more terrible. No such use of nervous and powerfully ranging verse to express an intimate psychological process can be found in an earlier play of Shakespeare's than this one. The syntax is strong and straightforward, the rhetoric informal and real, breaking on an 'O, O'. The similes and symbols of disgust are ordinary enough, it is the rhythm of passionate speech that makes them unique:

> O ay, as summer flies are in the shambles,
> That quicken even with blowing.

> Heaven stops the nose at it, and the moon winks;
> The bawdy wind, that kisses all it meets,
> Is hush'd within the hollow mine of earth
> And will not hear it.

Iago now plans to kill Cassio, so that his plot with Othello can mature. Desdemona laments as it were her own death with the willow song, before her servant sees her to the bed where she is going to die:

> My mother had a maid call'd Barbary:
> She was in love; and he she lov'd prov'd mad,
> And did forsake her. She had a song of 'willow',
> An old thing 'twas, but it express'd her fortune,
> And she died singing it. That song to-night
> Will not go from my mind. . . .

The ballad was an old one with music of its own, but the refrain was from a song by John Heywood, collected by John Redford with an interlude called 'Wit and Science' about 1541. The earliest manuscript of the ballad music is about 1615, but Shakespeare's musician seems to have adapted it, since his words require a slightly different tune.

In the fifth act action comes at once but suspense continues. The plot to murder Cassio misfires, leaving both Roderigo and Cassio wounded. Othello thinks Iago attacked Cassio as a loyal friend to avenge his honour; he rushes off to kill his wife. Iago kills Roderigo to keep him quiet, and Cassio thinks Iago has rescued him.

The second scene is the slow death-scene, as full of love, fear and innocence as it is of death. It is Shakespeare's oldest theme, the destruction of an innocent girl, and of her destroyer. Iago's other schemes are scarcely credible, they are like a bad detective story, and the audience must have them constantly explained in detail, because Iago is a perfect actor and his machinations would otherwise (as in a detective story) be unplumbed until the last chapter. But this scene is all too real, most real where the words are scantiest.

Iago's wife Emilia was Desdemona's servant. She is the vital witness to the handkerchief, she is loyal to her dead mistress, and so the plot unravels. Iago kills her:

> *Emilia*   What did thy song bode, lady?
> Hark, canst thou hear me? I will play the swan,
> And die in music. Willow, willow, willow. –
> Moor, she was chaste; she lov'd thee, cruel Moor;
> So come my soul to bliss, as I speak true;
> So speaking as I think, alas, I die.

> *Othello*   I have another weapon in this chamber;
> It was a sword of Spain, the ice-brook's temper. . . .

Whip me, ye devils,
From the possession of this heavenly sight.
Blow me about in winds, roast me in sulphur,
Wash me in steep-down gulfs of liquid fire.

He recovers himself and speaks coolly before he seeks his own death. He calls himself honourable as murderers go, speaks of his service to the state, of his loving not wisely but too well, of his own tears. Still speaking with this forced coolness he kills himself. Iago's fate is to be tortured to death; Othello admires his silence.

There is not much comfort at the end of *Othello*. If it were filmed it should end in the torture-chamber. It must have been a labour of Hercules to write it; Rowse notices that verbal idiosyncrasy increases in it. The plague broods over it like 'the raven o'er the infected house, Boding to all'. It is as if Shylock had a play big enough to contain him; it has no hero. The most terrible thing about it is Othello's consciousness.

· 9 ·

Tragedy

King James doubled the £10 a time payable for Court performances, and more than doubled the number of them. The theatre was at the height of its fashion: the young Oliver Cromwell acted at Cambridge, and peers wrote plays 'for the common players'. But so far as I can determine, in 1605 Shakespeare wrote nothing. He was busy enough as an actor no doubt, and he cannot have been other than exhausted. He was forty, with eleven years to live. Early in 1605 Ben Jonson went to prison as one of the authors of *Eastward Hoe* for the mocking line 'Ah ken the man weel; he's one of ma thirty-pund knights.' Yet Jonson was used as a writer of Court masques, an art form neglected today though it attracted great poets and greater designers. Still, Shakespeare was the King's servant and Jonson was not; it may be that the King had too much respect for his astounding moral and theatrical greatness to employ him for ornamental and ceremonial pleasure. Jonson was, as M. C. Bradbrook puts it, silken and bland at Court, but mercilessly satirical about courtiers in the theatre. Shakespeare had more restraint and a more formidable integrity.

It is interesting to observe the questions debated publicly before Elizabeth and before James by the university of Oxford; they are some index of the mood of the times. In 1566 they included whether a private person has the right to take arms against a prince, even an unjust prince. In 1592 Oxford argued whether a judge should go against his own conscience in following the law, and whether dissimulation might be permissible in time of religious persecution. For James I the university debated whether imagination can produce real effects, and whether babes imbibe the morals of nurses from their nurses' milk. Holinshed, in his *History and Description of Scotland*, points out that this was a Scottish preoccupation. On 27 August 1605, the King was entertained at Oxford with three weird sisters, *Tres Sibyllae*, written in Latin by Matthew Gwynne. His interest in witchcraft and demonology was famous of course. It was soon to wane in the crisper intellectual climate of the south, but in 1605 the dankness of his northern theology still clung to him. Shakespeare was planning *Macbeth*.

The play had not matured before 5 November. The Gunpowder Plot discovered on that day was the brainchild of crazy and despairing papists. There was more violence than policy about it, but its result was a closing of the ranks, a public horror and relief, with a sense of gratitude and loyalty to the King that the Privy Council might have prayed for in vain. I have no space to analyse the tragedy of personalities even briefly, but the Warwickshire connection was strong, and the London tavern the conspirators frequented was one that Shakespeare knew well.

The result of the plot in Warwickshire was devastating. The confiscation of estates brought in new landlords and extinguished old tenancies, which led to a wave of enclosures and much misery among country people perfectly innocent of the plot, and finally to a local peasant revolution. *Macbeth* reflects the aftermath of the Gunpowder Plot. Its reference to 'equivocation' is usually pinned to the trial of Father Henry Garnet, which took place on 28 March 1606, where the prosecution made strong points about that doctrine.

'Equivocation' means the right and duty to keep a secret, without telling a direct lie, by giving an answer that has two meanings and letting the questioner deceive himself. The point is that direct lies were thought to be wrong, even if one was (so to speak) a member of the resistance being tortured by the Gestapo. Some secrets absolutely must be kept: for example, the priest must keep the secrets of the confessional. Henry Garnet was a Jesuit, an innocent and a good man. The prosecution were determined to implicate him in the Gunpowder Plot, of which he disapproved. It was of course easy for them to make hay of his defence by showing to the court that he held a doctrine which released him from the normal obligation to give a plain honest true-hearted answer to an important question. Equivocation sounds like an over-clever, quibbling kind of lie, and the word Jesuitical has had a bad meaning in English ever since. What is strange from our point of view is that people minded so much about telling lies to their torturers. Equivocation was a scrupulous stratagem: nowadays one would just tell a good hearty lie and hope for the best. The old Catholic theology could not abide the genuine conflict of rights; it preferred to smooth over contradictions and refine paradoxes into infinite subtlety.

But the somewhat metaphysical question of equivocation fascinated the Jacobeans. Marston has it in his play *Sophonisba*, registered on 17 March, eleven days before Father Garnet's trial. It may well be implicit in the Oxford debate about dissimulating one's religion. I do not think the trial is a secure criterion for dating *Macbeth*, but there are others, all pointing to 1606. *Macbeth* may have had a Court performance at Hampton Court in August before James I and the King of Denmark. The play is brief and pungent, though whether it was shortened for the Court or more likely written for it is not absolutely certain; I think it was written for the King, because it introduces his ancestors (admittedly imaginary ones), but even more so because it raises the question of Scottish earls.

The Scots lords and followers of James I roused resentment, as Ben Jonson's comment in *Eastward Hoe* and his fate indicate. Even to this day, long after the union of the two kingdoms, Debrett records that English noblemen of every rank take precedence over Scottish noblemen of equivalent rank, even in Scotland. There must have been some ferocious campaigning about that: recognition of the Scottish peerage by English peers was an important issue. Shakespeare goes out of his way to underline the hoary antiquity of Scottish nobility; in fact he makes the first creation of earls in Scotland the historical point of the play. The part played by the pre-Norman English Court in *Macbeth* reinforces this message. So does the importance given to Seward, Earl of Northumberland. *Macbeth* had a strong dynastic and political resonance. We may feel otherwise, which is why critics fail to notice the earls, but we must make an effort of historical imagination about the Court of James I in 1606.

From *Hamlet* onwards, the success of evil and the damage it does have increased. In *Macbeth* Holinshed is compressed and darkened. The Admiral's Men had a play about King Malcolm in 1602, and tough old comic Kemp had written in his *Nine Daies Wonder* in 1600 of 'a penny poet whose first making was Macdoe or Macdobeth or Macsomewhat'. Shakespeare's Hecate comes from Ovid, whom he adapts as no one else can: even his witches have to be classicized. It seems to have escaped notice that Shakespeare has also been reading Anthony Copley's *Fig for Fortune*, a long poem about suicides, not at all without merit.

No doubt he was drawn to it when he considered Othello's suicide, or even Hamlet's, since that play dwells on suicides; I suspect he remembered it in Macbeth's most famous speech. Copley also wrote the lines 'Give me the man that with undaunted spirit Dares give occasion for a tragedy'. The Elizabethans and Jacobeans were fascinated by the subject; an engraving of the suicide of Seneca stood at the head of his widely read works. They died by it too. A former bursar of Balliol killed himself on Ralegh's last expedition when Ralegh blamed him for its failure. The case of Sir Richard Grenville, who would rather 'fall into the hands of God than into the hands of Spain', was famous. Copley was once a student at the English College in Rome, which trained priests for the English mission. He attracted some pleasing invective from the Jesuit Robert Persons (another ex-bursar of Balliol by the way), who remembered him there as a 'wanton boy' going up into the pulpit to preach with a rose in his mouth. If Shakespeare could be indebted to Marston's *Sophonisba* in this play, as editors propose, a touch of Copley is equally likely.

It is part of a biographer's task to observe how Shakespeare put his plays together, but not to usurp the function of a full commentary and exhaustive discussion of every play. In *Macbeth* Shakespeare draws on more than one episode in Holinshed, he seems to have known George Buchanan's *History of Scotland* (1582) in Latin, and if Kemp was really referring to a play, he may have known that. A trace, a touch, a metaphor, may come from anywhere, consciously or unconsciously. Shakespeare makes the banners of Norway flout the sky 'And fan our people cold'. In *Sophonisba* Marston, in some of the best few lines he ever wrote, has this:

> . . . three hundred sail
> Upon whose tops the Roman eagles stretch'd
> Their large spread wings, which fann'd the evening air:
> To us cold breath, for well we might discern
> Rome swam to Carthage.

The porter's allusion to the gates of hell is meant vaguely to recall the Mystery Plays of the Harrowing of Hell which so many people still remembered, but without expressing any elaborately coded meaning: Macduff is not Christ, Shakespeare has simply darkened the scene where he seemed to lighten it, just as he did with Pompey and Abhorson in the prison in *Measure for Measure*, and the gravedigging scene in *Hamlet*. It was ordinary for him to echo his own early work: in this play mostly *Richard III* and *The Rape of Lucrece*. With a theme like *Macbeth*'s it is not surprising to find echoes of Seneca, but I doubt they were deliberate.

The play is about the growth and consequences of evil, and the violent disruption of natural order. Not every question a jury might ask is settled with certainty: the evil works in us; it plays in our imaginations, only its consequences are certain. *Othello* narrows gradually from the entire Levant to one dark room; *Macbeth* opens out at the end on to history, a nation and a world, but both plays have the same tightening climax. The text, alas, is somewhat rotten; it was not printed until 1623. In some places it shows traces of having been censored for profanity, though no one knows when. But *Macbeth* is gripping from the first line to the last, and its poetry is sharply memorable.

The first scene is a brief introduction to the witches. They seem to hover and to disappear in smoke. They certainly seize on the imagination and set a tone. One knows immediately that the story is going to be wicked and enthralling and end badly. One accepts the witches at this headlong encounter, though they would be less acceptable if they were introduced with careful philosophy, like the ghost in *Hamlet*. This first scene is little more than an induction or dumb show, but its effect is comparable to that of the Prologue of *Henry V*.

The play proper begins as it ends, with bloody and primitive war. The kerns and gallowglasses of the Western Isles are meant to recall the contemporary Irish, kerns being light-armed but greatly feared infantry, and gallowglasses old-fashioned cavalry armed with axes, but at this time Scots infantry serving in Ireland. There was of course a Macdonald in

Shakespeare's day; their title of Lord of the Isles is now a title of the Prince of Wales, though the clan chief is still Lord Macdonald. Romantic excitement over Scotland, an unviolated region until 1745, is already to be felt in *Macbeth*: Macbeth's 'brandish'd steel . . . smok'd with bloody execution', he 'ne'er shook hands, nor bade farewell to him, Till he unseam'd him from the nave to th' chaps'. This seems to me to be quite as shocking as the witches, but it confirms my view that the stray line 'I'll make say of thee' which the Prince says to Falstaff in Sir Edward Dering's manuscript of *Henry IV* is a chance survival of genuine Shakespeare. To 'make say' is to slit a buck's belly to test its fatness. Macbeth and Banquo were 'As cannons overcharg'd with double cracks'; Shakespeare cannot resist the noise of gunfire, anachronistic or not.

The third scene brings the witches to earth. They have their comic side, but the comedy is grotesque and a little disgusting. Shakespeare connects them with sailors' stories. James I really believed that witches had raised a storm at sea against him at the time of his marriage. Their verses are like the chanting of spells; the metre is traditional for that purpose and survives to this day in children's rhymes associated with magic. In the prophecies to Macbeth and Banquo, we have the kernel of the play. In Macbeth they fall on corrupt soil and excited imagination, in Banquo on cool virtue.

By the end of the act Macbeth has had his first promotion, his wife's ambition is kindled, Duncan, King of Scotland, is her guest and his murder is planned. She is a figure of pure evil, she will suffer remorse but no contrition, and she will die by suicide. Morally, psychologically and linguistically, Macbeth and his wife were conceived together, as foils to one another. She is a distillation from the history plays, but Shakespeare has not presented so wicked a woman since *Titus Andronicus*, and perhaps never so demanding a part to be played by a boy. The high quality of acting in the company he wrote for must have increased to make these later tragedies possible, and the comedies that followed them. The boys' parts after about 1605 become more and more ambitious, culminating I think in *The Winter's Tale*.

Duncan's approach to the castle has the eerie quality of a pastoral interlude before the storm bursts, like the one in the *Oedipus* of Sophocles:

> This castle hath a pleasant seat; the air
> Nimbly and sweetly recommends itself
> Unto our gentle senses.
>   This guest of summer,
> The temple-haunting martlet, does approve
> By his lov'd mansionry that the heaven's breath
> Smells wooingly here; no jutty, frieze,
> Buttress, nor coign of vantage, but this bird
> Hath made his pendent bed and procreant cradle.

Where they most breed and haunt, I have observ'd
The air is delicate.

The second act is the unforgettable murder. As it opens the moon is
down, we have passed midnight. 'A heavy summons lies like lead upon
me,' says Banquo. He prays to God to restrain 'the cursed thoughts that
nature Gives way to in repose!': he dreamed last night about the three
Weird Sisters. Macbeth has a fit of horror at a dagger hanging in the air, 'and
wither'd murder, Alarum'd by his sentinel, the wolf, Whose howl's his
watch, thus with his stealthy pace, With Tarquin's ravishing strides,
towards his design Moves like a ghost.' His wife is horrified and horrifying:
'I heard the owl scream and the crickets cry.' She is more practical, more
deadly, so that Macbeth's remorse and guilt get little sympathy. He must
wash, he must take in the daggers 'and smear The sleepy grooms with
blood'. She will do it for him. The knocking at the gate interrupts them, as
knocking interrupted Othello. They go to wash. The porter is a satirist,
almost a clown, but his slowness increases tension and his grim jokes add
to horror. The scene turns on contrast between guilty knowledge and
the casual innocent life of a great house, but the thread of horror is
continuous:

Our chimneys were blown down; and, as they say,
Lamentings heard i' the 'air, strange screams of death . . .
. . . the obscure bird
Clamour'd the livelong night. Some say the earth
Was feverous and did shake. . . .

When the news of Duncan's death breaks, it explodes like a second
murder. Macbeth acts out a part well enough, but the words he speaks in it
are truer than he knows. 'Had I but died an hour before this chance. . . . The
wine of life is drawn. . . .' When he speaks of the corpse, his words run away
with him even more wildly:

Here lay Duncan,
His silver skin lac'd with his golden blood;
And his gash'd stabs look'd like a breach in nature. . . .

The King's children fly off like a flock of birds, and the act ends in omens of
the unnatural: an owl kills a hawk, horses run mad. One must realize that
people really believed in such omens. I remember being told as a child that
when Edward VIII walked behind his father's coffin, the cross dropped off
the crown that stood on it. When John Aubrey 'was a freshman at Oxford,
1642, I was wont to go to Christ Church, to see King Charles I at supper;
where I heard him say, "That as he was hawking in Scotland, he rode into
the quarry, and found the covey of partridges falling upon the hawk."
When I came to my chamber, I told this story to my tutor; said he, *that
covey was London.*'

In the third act Macbeth has Banquo murdered and sees his ghost; resistance begins to be organized. Banquo, of course, knows how Macbeth has fulfilled the witches' prophecies, and hopes their prophecy for his own children may come true. Poetry in this act flickers here and there like low flames, but without the blaze of set-pieces. The action is very dramatic and Shakespeare extends his powers of language only to sharpen it. The first exception to this is the moment of sick brooding before Banquo's death. It is only a moment:

> Light thickens, and the crow
> Makes wing to th' rooky wood;
> Good things of day begin to droop and drowse,
> Whiles night's black agents to their prey do rouse.

The second exception is Hecate's speech to the witches (act 3, scene v) which is certainly a set-piece almost detachable from the play. 'Come away, come away', the 'song within' called for in the stage directions, comes from Thomas Middleton's *The Witch* (1610), and is not Shakespeare's. Hecate is off to capture 'a vap'rous drop profound' from the corner of the moon, and use it to delude Macbeth to his downfall. She does not really need to do that, since his downfall is bound to occur, but she personifies the delusions by which evil operates, and it may be that without her inter- ference and the promptings of the witches Macbeth might have seemed enigmatic or too normal. The witches in *Macbeth* are like the gods in the *Iliad*; nothing happens through them that might not have happened without them, but they are a dramatic way of expressing what does happen. One must assume that evil was thought to be diabolic, but Shakespeare throws more light on its consequences than on its nature in *Macbeth*. Here he means to concentrate on guilt, on horror and on remorse, as if the last stage of *Othello* had been infinitely extended. In this sense Hecate and her witches suit his moral purpose.

The rest of the play is Macbeth's downfall. Act 4 opens with the memorable *cuisine* of the witches, expressed in the precise form of traditional magical instructions that goes back to ancient Greek and Egyptian magic. 'Liver of blaspheming Jew . . . Nose of Turk, and Tartar's lips . . .'. The witches are not nice, but Shakespeare is just fooling about. I am not sure what he had against Tartars, whom he perhaps drags in for alliteration and exotic quality. 'Finger of birth-strangled babe Ditch- deliver'd by a drab' is not only disgusting and 'unchristened', as scholars point out; it is also pitiful, and casts a gruesome light on Shakespeare's England, which after all was continuous with Hardy's. The entire list consists of the most repulsive things he can think of. He does not really find blasphemy repulsive, but the human liver and the dismembered nose and lips and finger.

The stage directions call for a song entitled 'Black Spirits'. Like the earlier witch song, it comes from Middleton's *The Witch* and was interpolated into Shakespeare's play by actors. *Macbeth* did harm by its success, and witches multiplied in the theatre. When Sir William Davenant revived it he put in a ballet of witches on broomsticks in mid-air. Shakespeare gives his witches just enough to do but no more. No one else until Milton could have written Hecate's speech about the drop on the corner of the moon, nor could Shakespeare have written anything so silly as the songs in Middleton's *The Witch*. The songs were ones the actors already knew; they could also see that Middleton used *Macbeth*. The revival of the play when the two songs were added was probably the one in 1611 that the physician and astrologer Simon Forman saw on 20 April. Forman thought Banquo and Macbeth were riding when they met 'three women fairies or Numphs', but he knew the play was set 'in the days of Edward the Confessor' and he liked the prodigies. He noticed that 'mackdove slewe mackbet', and that Lady Macbeth went sleepwalking 'and confessed all, and the doctor noted her words'. But his accounts are confused: in *The Winter's Tale* he forgot that Hermione survived, and in *Cymbeline* he failed to notice the Queen.

Macbeth addresses the witches in formal terms, stressing the overthrow of nature, 'though the treasure Of nature's germens tumble all together, Even till destruction sicken . . .'. The word *germen* suggests Lucretius on the mingled pain and pleasure of sexual love (4, 1073–1120): but had Shakespeare read that? *The Oxford English Dictionary* records it in no earlier English writer, nor is it a French word. In *Lear* (act 3, scene ii) he speaks of the *germens* of which man is made, so he thinks *germen* and *semen* mean the same, which once against suggests Lucretius. In *The Winter's Tale* (act 4, scene iv) he calls them seeds. I suppose the likeliest immediate source is some learned man philosophizing in Latin in his own age, but until such a writer can be identified, Lucretius remains a possibility: he would have appealed to the poet of the Sonnets. But perhaps an even likelier source is Paracelsian medical theory, which we shall meet again.

Macbeth is teased with riddling visions and deluded into false security except for the disturbing vision of Banquo's successive offspring, the eighth of whom carries a glass sphere in which Macbeth sees many more, 'and some I see That twofold balls and treble sceptres carry': the progeny of James I. Macbeth has now become a typical tyrant in a tragedy; his next move is to murder Macduff's wife and children.

Now Malcolm and Macduff in the Court of England discuss tyranny and virtuous kingship; Malcolm tests Macduff and finds him sound. The King of England is described in the exercise of his hereditary and miraculous power of curing the disease called the King's Evil by his touch. This power was part of the definition of an English sovereign down to Queen Anne, the last for a long time to rule by right of blood, who cured Samuel Johnson of the King's Evil in his childhood. It sets legitimacy and sanctity here in contrast with tyranny, usurpation and evil. News comes of the latest murders, and an army marches into Scotland. But the point of this scene (act 4, scene iii) is its humanity: the restoration of nature. It is essential to the play that Malcolm and Macduff should be simple, good, valorous, and nothing more, which is why they are a little dull.

The fifth act contains extraordinary poetry: first of all Lady Macbeth's delusions and blood-washing, poetry in prose. This a guilty, imaginary vision, more real as Shakespeare surely feels than the folkloristic witches. Macbeth's friends desert him; he is crazy with defiant rage. He wants his wife cured of guilt by medicine; when the Doctor fails to do that Macbeth rounds on him. Yet in the few lines where he begs for it we do feel the suffering that is in evil:

> Macbeth   Cure her of that.
> Canst thou not minister to a mind diseas'd,
> Pluck from the memory a rooted sorrow,
> Raze out the written troubles of the brain,
> And with some sweet oblivious antidote
> Cleanse the stuff'd bosom of that perilous stuff
> Which weighs upon the heart?
> Doctor   Therein the patient
> Must minister to himself.
>
> Macbeth   What rhubarb, senna, or what purgative drug,
> Would scour these English hence?

Macbeth's greatest lines are at his wife's death. It is part of Shakespeare's power with characters that Macbeth's words seem to come from so deep within him, to break out from so deep a level in him that scholars disagree about the thought behind the thought. Yet he communicates immediately with everyone in the theatre. His despair is first hinted in his words at the discovery of Duncan's death; this is its full expression in verse which is energetic as language but emotionally very weary. The end follows swiftly. Macbeth is like a bear tied to a stake (act 5, scene vii): he fights and dies, refusing suicide and eager for violence to the last breath. Malcolm is acclaimed King of Scotland:

> My Thanes and kinsmen,
> Henceforth be Earls, the first that ever Scotland
> In such an honour nam'd.

It is only in this last speech that we learn that Lady Macbeth died by suicide, but Shakespeare knew it when he wrote Macbeth's greatest lines.

About the time Shakespeare wrote *Macbeth*, religious persecution intensified in the aftermath of 5 November 1605; it was not just a search for

Gunpowder Plotters but for anyone disaffected in religion and lacking that all-important social bond, as it was thought to be, of the communion service. The church warden and the sidesmen of Holy Trinity Stratford drew up a list at Easter 1606 which they put before the Vicar in May, naming twenty-one persons for failing to receive the Sacrament. The law imposed an annual fine of £20 rising to £60 for this offence. At least seven of these twenty-one were Catholic or had some Catholic connection. Margaret Reynolds and her husband had harboured a fugitive Jesuit in Henley Street, and Mr Reynolds paid a fine every month for not attending the parish church. Sybil Cawdrey had a Jesuit son. The Sadlers asked for time to clear their consciences. Susanna Shakespeare was one of those named. She and the Sadlers stayed away from the Vicar's court in spite of being summoned. When she did appear her case was dismissed. It is possible she did take the sacrament; ten of the others are known to have done so. On 5 June 1607 she was married in the same church to John Hall, a strong Protestant and a most interesting man.

Hall was an unorthodox doctor, almost certainly trained by one of the Paracelsian schools of medicine in France or Switzerland. He lacked an English medical doctor's degree, but he was famous, devoted, intelligent and successful. He owned a fine house close to Shakespeare's in Stratford, and some land at Evesham, which was probably chosen for its fertility to grow medicinal plants. He got his BA at Queen's, Cambridge, in 1594 and his MA in 1597. It is a reasonable guess that he was in Stratford for some years before his marriage. Paracelsian medicine was associated with Huguenots; one of its chief proponents was Sir Theodore Mayerne, an immigrant who became physician to James I. Its unorthodoxy extended to religious and social questions; the fascinating but complicated history of the Paracelsian movement has been luminously analysed by Hugh Trevor-Roper (1985).

Paracelsus wrote (among other things) on industrial diseases, on surgery and on syphilis. He had been a miner and a military surgeon. Born in Switzerland in 1493, he died in Vienna in 1541. He disliked intellectual stuffiness, lectured in the vernacular, which in his case was the thickest kind of Swiss German, and despised the official textbooks of medicine. There was more than a streak of craziness and phoney mysticism in him, but that was not passed on to John Hall. John Hall was a Cambridge contemporary (or nearly so) of William Harvey, a greater man than any Paracelsian, who established the circulation of the blood. In an age when doctors killed more patients than they cured, a state of things which I understand continued to be average down to 1900, John Hall was remarkable. We can say so because we have a record of his cures, which are fundamentally chemical.

When he died in 1635 he left manuscript notebooks, one of which was translated from Latin and published by his colleague Dr James Cooke in

1657 as *Select Observations on English Bodies*. It contained 178 cases, and is now in the British Library, but the rest of Hall's papers, including another notebook, have been lost. The medical authorities quoted include Quercitanus (Du Chesne) the Paracelsian master, and the medieval John of Gaddesden. The English bodies include the poet Drayton, Hall's own wife and daughter, Mrs John Davies of Quinton, various Rainsfords, Quineys, Sturleys, Greens and Combs, the Earl and Countess of Northampton and the Bishop of Worcester. He was an efficient herbalist, and too busy to hold local office for long, or to accept a knighthood from Charles I. He travelled to see patients at Worcester, at Ludlow and elsewhere. His father before him was a physician who died in 1607, six months after his son's marriage, leaving his son his medical books, but others on astronomy, astrology and alchemy to a friend, with instructions to teach his son if he should ever show interest in those subjects. This generation gap is of great interest; I think it is clear that Shakespeare belonged intellectually on the younger man's side of it, while Simon Forman, for example, who among other things was a lecherous half-crazed old fellow and a backstreet fortune-teller, belonged on the father's side. Anyone curious about alchemists and astrologers of that age should read the diaries of Dr John Dee. They are not very long but they contain numerous surprises.

It is possible that Hall was an important influence on Shakespeare from the time of *Hamlet*. The French doctor in the *Merry Wives* might have been his joke; Caius of Cambridge died in the 1570s, but Shakespeare may have picked his name quite carelessly as he did Oldcastle's. Certainly Cerimon in *Pericles* is the model of a Paracelsian doctor. The connection of Hall with Huguenots is interesting too. Schoenbaum sensibly suggested that Shakespeare may have been introduced into that circle by Jacqueline Field, the Stratford printer's wife, but he may equally have met them through Hall, or Hall through them, before Hall came to Stratford. At any rate, these persistent French connections are worth watching. John Hall's daughter Elizabeth (1608–70) married a barrister called Thomas Nash, son of Anthony Nash of Welcombe, a friend of Shakespeare, but they were childless. When Dr Hall died in 1647, he left Susanna Hall £50 in his will. Elizabeth was remarried in 1649, just a month before her mother's death, to John Barnard of Abington, a small, dull, pleasant manor between Northampton and Cambridge. Charles II made him a baronet in 1661, so Shakespeare's granddaughter died a titled lady.

Most of Hall's recorded cures were by vomits and purges, some by inhaling, by nourishing potions or by eye-drops. To cure Mrs Beats of Ludlow of asthma he used conserve of red roses, Raisins of the sun stoned, Sugar-candy, Oil of vitriol and Sulphur, then the fumes of Frankincense, Mastic, Juniper, Storax and Terebinth, and for a long time afterwards a drink distilled from Coltsfoot, ground-ivy, mullein, speedwell, elicampany, knapwood, scabious, hysoop, herb trinity, great figwort, both kinds of maidenhair, harehound, the cordial flowers, roots of oris, angelica, soapwart and water-betony. He also included guaianum which was Fugger Brothers monopoly; attacking its use for the cure of syphilis had got Paracelsus into severe trouble. When Hall's wife got the cholic he injected her anally with a pint of heated sherry: 'This presently brought forth a great deal of Wind, and freed her from all Pain. . . . With one of these clysters I delivered the Earl of Northampton. . . .'

He tried to restore a young woman with a feverish cough by building up her strength with the best boiled veal, chicken, frogs, snails and river-crabs. 'She sucked women's milk, nourished with cool and moistening diet, as lettuce. A year after this she died.' He attempted to cure melancholy. Here his most interesting case was the aged Bishop of Worcester, whose son had committed suicide out of guilt after hounding a Catholic priest to his death. 'Mr. Drayton an excellent poet, labouring of Tertian was cured by the following: the Emetic infusion, Syrup of violets a spoonful, mix them. This given wrought very well both upwards and downwards.' He left no notes about Shakespeare, or none were published. Vain treatments were not usually recorded unless in contrast to a later treatment that worked; these notes are the monuments of his successes, and Shakespeare may well have died in his hands. Yet the plays contain many traces of poetic versions of such a doctor.

Shakespeare's principal residence was New Place, but lodging in London, with the Huguenot lady's hatter Christopher Mountjoy, was going to land him in a difficult position as witness in a law case: he tactfully wriggled out of it. The case was Belott versus Mountjoy, in which Shakespeare was examined in May of 1612 about events in 1604. Stephen Belott was Mountjoy's apprentice, who was encouraged by Shakespeare to marry his master's daughter Mary on 10 November of that year. A servant remembered that Mountjoy got Shakespeare to persuade Belott to marry Mary, presumably for the usual reasons. Apprentice and master then quarrelled about the payment of a dowry. Belott claimed he was promised £60 on marriage and £200 to be left by will, but received only £10 and some 'household stuff'. He feared to do just as badly out of Mountjoy's will, so he brought his case in 1612.

Shakespeare said he had known them both 'about ten years or so', that is since about 1602, two years before the marriage. He agreed there had been a dowry promised, but 'of goods and money' is struck out of the record, and Shakespeare claimed not to remember the amount. He remembered nothing about £200 by will, nor did he remember what goods Belott was given on marriage. The court referred the dispute to the overseers and elders of the French church in London, who awarded Belott twenty nobles, that is between £6 and £7. The documents in this case are rather numerous, but they contribute less than John Hall's *Select Observations of English Bodies* to what we know of Shakespeare and his background in these years. Still, they do tell us he had some influence with the young, and that he was on the side of marriage and on the side of women. And he took trouble not to be used against either side by the other. The court was the Court of Requests, and all the papers (first noticed in 1909) are in the Public Record Office. The contrast between the casual events of Shakespeare's everyday life and the intense series of his plays is at first sight disconcerting, but it is what we ought to expect.

Shakespeare had reached the age when friends begin to die. Old Mr Pope the actor had not continued with the company when it became the King's Men; he died not long afterwards. In May of 1605 the actor Augustine Phillips died, leaving 'to my fellow William Shakespeare a thirty shillings piece in gold', with similar legacies to other actors, clothes and musical instruments to apprentices, twenty shillings to the preacher at his funeral, and a silver bowl worth £5 to each of his executors. He died at Mortlake, which is where the actors were sent for to go to Wilton to the King. He had been an actor in the 1580s or earlier; the *Robert Phillippe mummer* who was buried in Shoreditch in 1559 may well have been of the same family.

Phillips was senior enough to represent the company at the Essex enquiry about the playing of *Richard II*. He appears to have married Edward Alleyn's 'sister Phillipes'; they had four daughters and one son, 'Austyn Phillipps, son of Austen, a player', who died at the age of three. He was a devout member of the Church of England and on good terms with his fellow actors. Payne Collier thought that at the end of his life he specialized in comedy; it is clearer that he specialized in music. Phillips's *Jig of the Slippers*, entered in the Stationers' Register in 1595, may be his. But in 1603 he acted in Jonson's *Sejanus*, and so did Shakespeare. That was a work of rigid neo-classicism, an uncompromisingly learned tragedy that Marston was still sneering at in 1606. It was not a popular success and what was worse, Jonson was summoned by the Privy Council to answer accusations of treason and popery in it. The truth surely is that when the company accepted a play (and they were always at their wits' end for new ones) everybody acted in it. It is only a freak of chance that in a few cases we have actors' names. Throughout Shakespeare's life, his fellow actors are a silent stage army, at least as important as his fellow writers. Just one thread connects them with Stratford and his family.

Shakespeare's brother Edmund was an actor who was twenty in 1600 and probably in London by the late 1590s, though we know nothing at all about his career, which cannot have been very glamorous. There are other cases of acting as a family business; not only that of Austen Phillips, but for example William Sly, perhaps a Warwickshire man, who died in August 1608. John Sly was a player to Henry VIII, and Thomas Sly played pipe and tabor for William Kemp all the way from London to Norwich. Edmund Shakespeare is not known to have married, but he had a bastard son who died in August 1607 and was buried at St Giles without Cripplegate. Edmund died that same December; he was buried at St Mary Overy, now Southwark Cathedral, 'with a forenoon knell of the great bell' and a ceremoniousness that cost his brother twenty shillings. In that winter the Thames was frozen solid.

The year was hard everywhere, but worst in the Midlands. Inside Stratford life went on normally enough: in 1605 Mr Aspinall was made to remove his pigstyes from the wall of the church. But profits were falling, men were out of work, prices were high and grain very short. For all these ills enclosures of common land were made the scapegoat. They were worse hated in smooth Fielden than in shaggy Arden, though in all Warwickshire 'something of the sweetly reasonable attitude of pastoral and woodland communities', as Joan Thirsk calls it, infected the agricultural areas as well.

Northamptonshire enclosures (27,000 acres in 1578) were the highest. In 1607 a crowd of five thousand assembled in that region. There were outbreaks in five villages between Rugby, Kettering and Market Harborough. Gallows were erected at Leicester on 6 June, but the people tore them down on the 8th. Open trouble lasted more than another week. This was the beginning of the people called Diggers, fillers of ditches and levellers of walls on common land, who smouldered on in spite of hangings and government commissions until the King was beheaded in 1649 and Diggers and Levellers were extinguished by Cromwell. In 1607 the Diggers of Warwickshire addressed the people of all England in a brave and pathetic letter.

It was in this period, when the outbreak was brewing, that Shakespeare wrote *King Lear*. He uses the old chronicle play, *The True Chronicle History of King Lear*, registered in May 1594 and again in May 1605, and only then first printed. Shakespeare's *Lear* was registered in November 1607, 'as it was played before the King's Majesty at Whitehall on St. Stephen's night at Christmas last', so he wrote it in 1606, soon after *Macbeth*. The clue to its terrifying emotional impact is Tom o' Bedlam's ballad, which runs through *Lear* like a thread, and which Feste had already quoted in *Twelfth Night*. Robert Graves suggested many years ago that this real mad beggar's ballad, which exists in earlier and later versions but in one perfect version from just this time, may have been adapted by Shakespeare himself. I believe this is right: the classic version is in several ways unlike a ballad; it is certainly an adaptation by a great poet, and the poet of *King Lear* is the likeliest. Can it have been played at the end, as Feste's song is played? I have printed this remarkable ballad in Appendix 9.

No one now need have the slightest doubt that Shakespeare has left us two distinct versions of *King Lear*, of which the second is an able and most interesting version of the first. The Folio version (1623) revises the quarto version (1608); both are available in the Oxford *Shakespeare* of 1986. I have not treated them separately, because although I had already been convinced by Steven Urkowitz (*Shakespeare's Revision of Lear*, 1980) and by others that Shakespeare had most effectively cut and sharpened his play in revision, I had never read the two texts separately and completely until this biography was in its final stages. The implications of the two versions are of great technical and theatrical, but of less biographical interest. Specialized readers must refer to the learned literature which continues to appear. The essential point that one version is a revision of the other was noticed by Harley Granville-Barker in 1927.

Much lies behind Lear: he extends backwards into folklore as well as literature. In John Clare's boyhood the old women of his village still knew Lear's story. His passion is like the passion of an old Irish weather god or the King of Summer, and like Christ's passion in a Mystery Play that moves from taunting to suffering. Shakespeare utterly transforms the older play, with its jollity and its happy ending, and its origins in Geoffrey of Monmouth. Cordelia's death is Shakespeare's invention. The battles interest him little, so he all but collapses two into one. The plot exists for the sake of its mad and anguished scenes, the climax of a special poetry of madness and of black, sharp phrases, that Shakespeare has perfected until here he gives it full rein. The end of the play just crumbles away like surf, as the plots of late Euripides often do: this plot is a machine that has served its purpose, and the problems of King Lear have no solution.

Lear recalls Othello in folly and in rage, but he commits no murder. As a character he is more innocent than Hamlet or Romeo or Troilus, his madness is real, and his passion winnows him. Cordelia has the same sweetness as other tragic heroines since Juliet, but seen through Lear's agonized brain she is more moving than they are. Lear and Gloucester share the character of Oedipus, but I believe that Lear's passion is more widely and deeply rooted in nature than the self-lacerating passion of Oedipus, to whom ultimately Gloucester may owe his blindness. Or do they both owe it to some blind, wandering old man, begging and singing about his fate? There have always been blind, wandering old men until modern times.

Shakespeare took Lear's faults seriously. Unkindness to a daughter and the King's unnatural will were serious matters to him. But Lear's situation is proverbial: he is the King who had three daughters, tempest-tossed by the consequences of not having a son, and he is the man who gave away his wealth and suffered that ingratitude which Shakespeare always treats with special bitterness. This is proverbial vision, projected by the self-defence of old people in villages. The value Shakespeare attaches to loyalty, kindness, gratitude and relationship reflects the ordinary values of small communities: Snitterfield as opposed to Cripplegate.

There are other aspects of King Lear: the irony of wild weather that expresses his wildness yet is less unkind, less unnatural, than ingratitude;

the fool assuming folly in contrast with the real Fool, King as fool and fool as sane man; the rewards of honesty, the devastation of royalty. Indeed the poetry of the play is inexhaustibly full, and all its paradoxes and thunderclaps are generated by its plot, by Shakespeare's eye for what he can use in a plot, and by his boldness in adaptation. He takes from anywhere. 'I'll go to bed at noon' is a flower from Gerard's *Herball*; 'Ripeness is all' comes from the same source, from a flower that turns to thistledown and 'The ripeness is all'. But Shakespeare is not always so gentle: *King Lear* subjects ideas of what is natural to deadly contrast and analysis. I do not believe that the play is about purgation or 'redemption', whatever that is taken to mean. Shakespeare's intimate values may be those of a Christian village, but his intellect is savage, searching and sceptical; he is not sure in this play that nature can be restored, or that it reasserts itself.

The first act sets up the plot, but it is full of hints and rumblings. It opens in satiric, educated prose between Gloucester and Kent and Gloucester's bastard son Edmund. Lear divides his kingdom. 'Meantime we shall express our darker purposes . . .': which of his daughters loves him most? Goneril and Regan offer flatteries. 'What shall Cordelia speak? Love, and be silent.' This division with the map is bound to be disastrous; it recalls the conference dividing Britain between the rebels in *Henry IV*. Shakespeare knows about divisions and about differences: 'The vines of France and milk of Burgundy'. Were these legendary or widely known? He means the cattle that graze on the edge of Burgundy, on the foothills of the Alps. The quarrel that follows is catastrophic, and all its ironies will come home to roost. Venal Burgundy will reject Cordelia disgraced, but the King of France will take her happily.

The second scene shows Gloucester's castle and reveals the bastard Edmund plotting against Edgar, his legitimate brother, and poisoning his father's mind with a false letter. Gloucester rages about eclipses in the sun and moon that portend evil. 'Love cools, friendship falls off, brothers divide; in cities, mutinies; in countries, discord; in palaces, treason; and the bond crack'd 'twixt son and father. . . . We have seen the best of our time: Machinations, hollowness, treachery, and all ruinous disorders, follow us disquietly to our graves.' Edmund derides these views: 'an admirable evasion of whoremaster man, to lay his goatish disposition on the charge of a star!' Edgar enters. 'Pat! He comes like the catastrophe of the old comedy,' as Edmund remarks, and Edmund poisons and manipulates his mind too: he is a grossly motivated and instantly effective Iago.

In the third scene Goneril takes a firm line with her father, but in the fourth Kent in disguise joins Lear as a servant, and when Goneril's steward Oswald provokes the old man to strike him, Kent sees him off. The Fool tells Lear what a fool he is. Lear threatens him with whipping – a threat and a reality constantly verified in Armin's lives of fools, I regret to say.

'Truth's a dog must to kennel'. This Fool is more like one of Armin's *Nest of Ninnies* than any other in Shakespeare; he is probably intended as a natural, a sharp-witted halfwit. Lear calls him boy, so Armin is not playing the part: he really is a boy.

Goneril provokes Lear to fury, and he leaves with his followers, cursing her. The Fool loves him and goes with him. (He calls him Nuncle Lear as if he belongs to him.) Goneril forewarns Regan, and Lear sends Gloucester. The Fool comforts the King, but the act ends ominously:

> O, let me not be mad, not mad, sweet heaven!
> Keep me in temper; I would not be mad!

Some of the most frightening and effective lines in the first act are already disjointed fragments: 'Who is it that can tell me who I am?'; 'Lear's shadow'; 'So, out went the candle, and we were left darkling.' In the second act real madness and false madness multiply, and the great storm begins. Even Edmund in his trick against Edgar in the first scene says, 'Here stood he in the dark, his sharp sword out, Mumbling of wicked charms, conjuring the moon. . . .' From now on Edgar is on the run; his disguise will be poor Tom, so we shall have Lear, Fool and Poor Tom together. Still, loyalty has a part to play. Kent assaults Oswald the steward verbally and physically, referring to Goneril as 'Vanity the puppet'. 'Thou whoreson zed! thou unnecessary letter! My lord, if you will give me leave, I will tread this unbolted villain into mortar, and daub the wall of the jakes with him.' Kent is now as furious as Lear and as bizarre as the Fool, or nearly so: 'Smoile you my speeches, as I were a fool?' ('Smoile' is a touch of assumed servant's dialect for smile.) 'What, are thou mad, old fellow?' He gets put in the stocks, though Gloucester protests. A little later in time, an actor was put in the stocks for performing a play on a Sunday for a bishop in his own house; it was an intolerable indignity.

Edgar escapes to the woods, 'My face I'll grime with filth, Blanket my loins, elf all my hairs in knots, And with presented nakedness outface The winds and persecutions of the sky.' He knows of Bedlam beggars in the country who prick themselves with pins and splinters and sprigs of rosemary. (One of Armin's fools was beaten with rosemary by actors until he bled.) They go about 'low farms, Poor pelting villages, sheep-cotes, and mills' with curses and prayers, demanding charity: 'Poor Turlygod! poor Tom!' Meanwhile Lear and his Fool find Kent in the stocks. 'Winter's not gone yet,' says the Fool, 'If the wild geese fly that way.' Kent is freed when the Fool has had his mockery of him, based like his rhymes on proverbial wisdom. Lear rages and pleads with Regan: 'on my knees I beg.' He is not yet mad, except in the extremity of his raging curses; what is enacted is his loss of grip on events, his transformation into a victim.

Lear's madness is Shakespeare's invention, but it is of course central to the conception of this play. It may have been sparked off by the senility of

271

Brian Annesley, a gentleman pensioner of the old Queen, whose two wicked daughters tried to have him declared mad in order to have his estate, while his good youngest daughter Cordell pleaded with Cecil that he deserved better than 'at his last gasp to be recorded and registered a Lunatic'. In 1608 Cordell married Sir William Harvey, Southampton's mother's widower. Shakespeare certainly knew them, and certainly knew Bedlam, which he must have often passed between house and theatre.

But Lear leads an orchestra of madness: Shakespeare's experiment is with poetry and prose in a particular relation, one moving swiftly into the other; the core of this poetry lies in the language of madness. It is the trio or quartet of mad prose that produces the pure substance and deepest element of this play's language. It has a vivid intensity and a powerful context. This amazing language begins differently for every character, the Fool's in his natural condition, Edgar's in the imitation of a mad beggar, Lear's in rage. Some observations of madness in the play are taken from Samuel Harsnett's *Egregious Popish Impostures* (1603), which, like Reginald Scot's on *The Discoverie of Witchcraft* (1584), is an investigation of imposture. Among those Harsnett attacked was Robert Debdale of Shottery, a neighbour of the Hathaways, who carried about with him relics of the martyred priest Thomas Cottam, brother of that John Cottam who taught at Stratford from 1579 to 1582. Shakespeare's own views are hard to come at, but he speaks of relics without scorn in *Julius Caesar*. The most potent influence on his mind, even in *Lear*, is Montaigne. I do not see *Lear* as a clinical study in madness; I think the madness exists for the sake of the extraordinary interplay of language that it unleashes. Madness is so terrible it is almost holy: what is stricken by God is abominable, therefore suffering, therefore taboo, and under God's special protection, sacred, awe-inspiring. The same pattern exists in Greek (Oedipus) and in real life in Islamic attitudes to madness. Tom o' Bedlam's song has the lines

> I know more than Apollo
> For oft when he lies sleeping
> I see the stars at bloody wars
> In the wounded welkin weeping.
> Therefore I sing
> Any food any clothing.
> Fear not, fear not,
> Poor Tom will injure nothing.

The same song has a line about 'Sweet whips ding-dong'. The place of punishment and self-punishment in *Lear* opens new perspectives into the play. Lear's curses are intended to punish; they are cosmic, calling on the forces of nature, but just as impotent as the raging of the weather, which sounds like the wrath of God but is not. Kent in the stocks is not humiliated because his mind is sane. The Fool, who disappears in the end for Lear to play fool to himself, lives most fearfully and closest to the ground, yet he gets through his awful life, just as Feste does. As Lear suffers, he both punishes and is punished; the beginning of the storm is audible as he speaks:

> I will have such revenges on you both
> That all the world shall – I will do such things –
> What they are yet I know not: but they shall be
> The terrors of the earth. You think I'll weep.
> No, I'll not weep.
> I have full cause of weeping: but this heart
> Shall break into a hundred thousand flaws
> Or ere I'll weep. O Fool, I shall go Mad!

In the third act we are on the Cotswold heath that Gloucester has already characterized: '. . . the night comes on, and the high winds Do sorely ruffle; for many miles about There's scarce a bush.' Shakespeare knew such places, and the vagrants who wandered there. The act opens with a piece of business necessary to the plot, in which Kent meets a gentleman and sends a message to Cordelia; Shakespeare takes the opportunity to have the King's plight described before we see him, and the foul weather well established. In the next scene Lear rages in verse as if he himself were a force of nature. The Fool comments in prose; his riddles are very bitter. Kent finds them both wandering, and exchanges views with Lear in powerful verse about the wrath of heaven and the fear of it. Then he leads them to a hovel as the Fool sings Feste's song, ending in a prophecy of the ills of England. This is a series of sour jests and paradoxes, but as a theme or sub-theme it has great importance.

As the Fool enters, Lear groans over the English poor:

> Poor naked wretches, wheresoe'er you are,
> That bide the pelting of this pitiless storm,
> How shall your houseless heads and unfed sides,
> Your loop'd and window'd raggedness, defend you
> From seasons such as these? O, I have ta'en
> Too little care of this! Take physic, pomp;
> Expose thyself to feel what wretches feel,
> That thou mayst shake the superflux to them,
> And show the heavens more just.

The mad scene that follows expresses terror, pity and black calamity. There are strands in it of satiric morality and of proverbial feeling, as well as of real madness in which Pillicock and the act of darkness, sexual guilt, play their part. Lear goes mad almost deliberately and satirically. We have real madness brilliantly counterfeited (the youth), the natural with his upside-down sanity (the boy), and satiric rage (the old man). The strain of satire in madness was a trick of Hamlet's, a ramming into one person of Touchstone and Jaques.

Gloucester intrudes on this, but he understands nothing. He recognizes neither Kent nor his own son. Meanwhile Edmund is promoted in his place and he becomes a hunted man. Gloucester and Kent bring Lear and Poor Tom and the Fool to a farmhouse, where Tom and Lear exchange mad imaginations of hellfire, where Nero is an angler in the Lake of Darkness. Scholars make a fuss over this, but Edith Sitwell was right to point to a 'bottomless' lake in Greece that Nero tried to plumb. Shakespeare does not need to have read about it in Pausanias: it was proverbially famous and occurs even in traditional Jewish commentaries on the Psalms. But its principal meaning here is Stygian, and related to the 'act of darkness'. It was the punishment of Nero for plumbing the unplumbable earthly lake.

The phrase about Nero is like many in these scenes, lucid on the surface but a bit surreal, and yet magically concentrated. If there is any touchstone of 'pure poetry' in Shakespeare, it could be found in these fragments of mad prose. The antiphonal, cumulative talk of the three madmen is complex and terribly effective. The mock trial is an old device, but here it has a particular reality: Lear is a mad king imagining he is a king. Kent, Gloucester and the Fool take him away to Dover, and Edgar as Poor Tom ends the scene with a monologue of couplets, a heavy formal closure of this part of the play. The last scene of the act is Gloucester caught and blinded in a scene of grotesque horror, and discovering the truth about Edmund and Edgar: 'Go thrust him out at gates and let him smell His way to Dover.'

The fourth act brings Lear to Cordelia. First, Edgar as Tom meets his blinded father, to whom Shakespeare gives lines of resigned goodness and absolute despair: 'As flies to wanton boys are we to th' gods – They kill us for their sport. . . . Here, take this purse, thou whom the heavens' plagues Have humbled to all strokes.' Gloucester is Oedipus out of Seneca, who asked to be led to a cliff-edge by his daughter. Goneril like a worse Lady Macbeth despises her husband for 'cowish terror' and takes up with Edmund. Even this scene of reproach and intrigue has wonderful lines in it: 'France spreads his banners in our noiseless land. . . .' Kent reaches the French camp at Dover, hears news of Cordelia's grief, and tells of the King's shame at 'his own unkindness'. Lear is in the town and Cordelia searches for him:

> . . . he was met even now
> As mad as the vex'd sea, singing aloud,
> Crown'd with rank fumiter and furrow weeds. . . .
> Search every acre in the high-grown fields. . . .

The Doctor knows how to cure him by giving him repose. He has 'many simples operative, whose power Will close the eye of anguish . . .'. Cordelia prays to the blessed secrets and unknown powers in the earth to spring up at her tears. Now Regan plots to take Edmund from Goneril and to have Gloucester murdered. Blind, he comes to Dover cliffs and makes his thrilling speech about them: no topographical passage in all Shakespeare's works is quite so evocative, from the crows and choughs in mid-air far below to the murmuring surge 'That on th' unnumb'red idle pebbles chafes'. Shakespeare's company had acted in Dover more than once.

Gloucester jumps, or thinks he does, but Edgar saves him by a cliff, finds him as a peasant (with another accent), and having described the cliff downward describes it upward: a tour de force of imaginary description. They observe Lear 'fantastically dressed with weeds', madly muttering, first in prose then verse; sex is on his mind: 'The wren goes to't, and the small gilded fly Does lecher in my sight. . . . Down from the waist they are centaurs, though women all above . . . But to the girdle do the gods inherit, Beneath is all the fiends'. . . .' Lear and Gloucester recognize and pity one another, and men come to bring Lear to Cordelia but he escapes. 'Why, this would make a man a man of salt, To use his eyes for garden water-pots, Ay, and laying Autumn's dust.' Edgar defends his father from Oswald and kills him, and finds in his papers a plot of Goneril's to kill her husband. Cordelia finds her father at last, dressed again and sleeping; she wakes him with music and a kiss:

> You do me wrong to take me out o' th' grave.
> Thou art a soul in bliss; but I am bound
> Upon a wheel of fire, that mine own tears
> Do scald like molten lead.
>
> I am a very foolish fond old man. . . .
>
> I fear I am not in my perfect mind. . . .

It should be noticed that even at this point, except for Gloucester's tragedy, *Lear* might have ended happily with the wicked punished or dead, Lear restored and Cordelia triumphant. Shakespeare would not accept that unserious resolution. Act 5 begins with preparations for battle. Edgar in disguise again reveals Goneril's plot to her husband; Edmund having pretended love to both sisters makes a monologue of Machiavellian wickedness: these intrigues are unmemorable and almost too swift to follow. In the quickly moving succession of scenes the fact that 'Men must endure Their going hence, even as their coming hither' is true in more senses than one. Lear and Cordelia are captured, perfectly and sweetly reconciled, almost like lovers. The wicked victors quarrel, Edmund accused issues a challenge that Edgar answers, this time as a knight. His disguises, like those of Odysseus in the *Odyssey* and Dede Korkut in the central Asian epic, *Dede Korkut*, have gradually ascended the social scale. Goneril and Regan murder each other, and as dying Edmund remarks, 'I was contracted to them both'. All three now marry in an instant. Gloucester's 'great heart bursts'. Edmund has had Cordelia hanged and Lear now enters (rescued) holding her in his arms, a scene that recalls, however moving it may be, the textually corrupt finale of Euripides' *Phoenissae*.

No one has seen the Fool since the Heath; now Lear, in his pitiful last speeches, cries out 'And my poor fool is hang'd!' as if he could no longer tell one from the other. The Fool was all he had; so was Cordelia. He recognizes her death and dies as he does so. Meanwhile the idiotic nobleman Albany is arranging the state: Shakespeare's contempt for the nobility in this play, apart from Gloucester as a victim, Kent dressed as a servant and Edgar dressed as anything, is absolute. His views are vehement: 'O, I have ta'en Too little care of this. . . . So distribution should undo excess, And each man have enough. . . . handy-dandy, which is the justice, which is the thief? . . . Strip thy own back!' The play ends in awe of Lear's sufferings. Kent will follow him to death. Edgar has the last words: they offer no solution, no comfort at all, but they express what Shakespeare offers to his audience:

> The weight of this sad time we must obey;
> Speak what we feel, not what we ought to say.
> The oldest hath borne most; we that are young
> Shall never see so much nor live so long.

It has been claimed, and increasingly accepted over the last ten years or so, that *King Lear* was revised by Shakespeare himself. If that is true of *Lear*, it may be so of many plays; sometimes the two versions can be reconstituted with near certainty. But between quarto (1608) and Folio (1623) publication both may be defective. In the case of *Lear*, the quarto lacks a hundred lines of the Folio and the Folio lacks three hundred of the quarto. What is worse, no two of the twelve known copies of the first quarto are exactly the same as each other, so running corrections as well as running errors seem to be the rule. It is important to have it in mind that Shakespeare did sometimes revise quite radically, he did sometimes work with the printers, he did care for the fate of his plays, though he was seldom or never in complete personal control of what survived.

There are several places here and there among Shakespeare's plays where it is clear enough that a muddle or a difficulty was cleared up in production, producing a revised text. In the quarto text of *A Midsummer-Night's Dream*, Theseus reads out a list of entertainments, commenting on each one, but in the Folio Lysander reads the list while Theseus only comments. In act 4 of *Richard II* the flinging down of half a dozen gloves in challenge like the playing of a hand at cards must have seemed absurd, particularly when they were all picked up. The Folio text at least reduces the number of these gloves. Those texts of Shakespeare that contain cuts also contain purely literary revisions, so it is reasonable to assume

Shakespeare himself altered his work long after its first presentation in the theatre.

There were no producers; it was an actors' theatre, with an author dealing directly with the actors. Additions, cuts and revisions may have been made in more ways than one, particularly in revivals or provincial productions when the writer was absent. Armin's ability to produce good pastiche blank verse in his *Valiant Welshman* suggests that the ability to do so was not as uncommon as it would be today. The acid test of genuine Shakespeare must remain the test of quality. In *King Lear* the King's prose turns to verse rather easily, but the verses are quite often longer and rougher than the formal iambic style of certain speeches. I am sure this is deliberate. Lear carries the genius of the prose and verse fragments through into more formal verse towards the end of the play, which is still loose enough to recall and is meant to recall his madness. His final lines are calculated with metrical perfection, set against a silence and characterized as the words of a dying man. Lear was cured by herbs, sleep and music (as Lady Macbeth could not be) though his rage and almost his madness can revisit him. These are extreme cases of curable and incurable melancholy. Lear has the weakness and pathos of an old man cured of such a disease: Gloucester's last words are spoken for both of them.

I take *Antony and Cleopatra* to come soon after *King Lear*. The variation of theme or colour from *Macbeth* to *Lear* and *Lear* to *Antony and Cleopatra* is obviously deliberate; in the choice of source material each supplies what the last lacked, but in smaller ways, in what was demanded of the actors, and in the awe-inspiring powers that Shakespeare exercised at this time, in his early forties, they are intimately linked. But it is foolish to claim absolute certainty, and several dates will have to be discussed together.

In May 1608 *Pericles, Prince of Tyre* and *Antony and Cleopatra* were registered together. *Pericles* owes something in the character and method of Cerimon to the Doctor in *Lear*, but I do not think they were written in swift succession, and I put *Pericles* after *Timon of Athens*, which ends a series of plays from Plutarch. *Pericles* marks a return to romance and revival and resurrection, and therefore belongs to the next chapter. *Coriolanus* was written before Jonson's *Epicene* (1609) and recalls the enclosure riots of summer 1607, so it can reasonably be put in late 1607 or 1608. *Timon* could be just before or just after *Coriolanus*, but it has to be after *Antony and Cleopatra*, because it was in writing *Antony* that Shakespeare came across the obscure story of Timon. I take *Timon* to be the end of the series and the last tragedy that Shakespeare ever wrote, because one can see in it why he might abandon tragedy, how its vein was exhausted for him, but one cannot see that in *Coriolanus*. *Timon* is a tragedy not of its hero but of the city of Athens. It goes beyond *Coriolanus*.

Lear is the fullest of the tragedies but *Antony and Cleopatra* is the most exalted, in the great sweep of its verse and a sense of nobility and of immortality attendant on love. Those who think Shakespeare rearranged his sonnets as a sequence about this time might well point to *Antony and Cleopatra* to confirm how his mind was moving. His *Antony and Cleopatra* is solidly based on Plutarch's account of the subject in his life of Antony, where the roots of the play's thrilling contradictions of character are already easy to observe. Plutarch was comparing Antony to Demetrius Poliorcetes, 'two persons who have abundantly justified the words of Plato, that great natures produce great vices as well as great virtues. Both alike were amorous and intemperate, war-like and munificent, sumptuous and overbearing.' But in the interest of his hero, Plutarch is prepared to treat the young Caesar Augustus harshly. His sources are mostly Greek, not Latin, even for his Roman subjects, and he is by no means always on the side of the big battalions. This play reveals both Plutarch and Shakespeare at their best.

The monument scenes at the end of the play, which dramatize Cleopatra's decision to die rather than to be led in triumph through Rome, are based on a poem by Horace (*Odes*, 1, 37) added to Plutarch's version. Readers in search of historical truth should consult the standard commentary on Horace by Nisbet and Hubbard, but they must not expect analysis of that kind from Shakespeare; indeed they must allow that he misinterpreted even what he knew. The story of Antony and Cleopatra is one of those rare cases in which the truth is as dramatic as Shakespeare's fiction, but the truth was not available to him. Plutarch's Antony does not really perish by his vices, but by his evil genius the Egyptian Queen. Plutarch's Demetrius eats and drinks himself to death, but his Antony 'had been of all men the most illustrious and powerful, and in the end had fallen not ignobly, a Roman by a Roman overcome'. Cleopatra crowns his tomb with garlands and kisses, and dies 'as became the descendant of so many kings'.

Other English writers had handled the same material, including Chaucer and Gower. Samuel Daniel, who so often ran neck and neck with Shakespeare, issued a *Cleopatra* in 1594, revised it in 1599, and rewrote it in 1607, perhaps under the influence of Shakespeare, in a more dramatic, less static and descriptive version. A few faint echoes show that Shakespeare was conscious of it as poetry, but not as a dramatic composition. From that point of view it is negligible. Barnabe Barnes in *The divils charter* (February 1607) treats Cleopatra's serpents with particular gusto, but the effect is that of farcical melodrama. They are 'Fed fat and plump with proud Egyptian slime Of seven-mouth'd Nilus but now turned lean. . . . What now proud worms? How tastes you prince's blood?' Some scholars have found traces of Chapman in the lines about 'a cloud that's dragonish' and elsewhere, but these are insubstantial. The image of a cloud and a fading pageant probably come from a sermon, as the Arden editors point out.

278

The only striking similarity I have to add to this list is in some verses written for a private ceremony, probably the engagement of Lady Derby's daughter to Lord Chandos in 1607, which was precisely the likely year of *Antony and Cleopatra* (registered in May 1608). Shakespeare did not attend this country ceremony, but a masque by his friend Marston was performed at it. I will discuss these verses in Appendix 1, but their most relevant line to this play is 'Compounded all of fire and air'. 'Fire and air' are hinted at earlier in the scene (act 5, scene ii), where Cleopatra threatens 'I shall show the cinders of my spirits Through th' ashes of my chance.' Similar images of the four elements occur in other plays, in *Henry V* of a horse, for instance. But Cleopatra's dying words have a particular and beautiful resonance in their context: she is stepping off the edge of the world. In a way she is like the Medea of Euripides. I assume she was acted by a boy with special qualities.

That boy's name might well be William Ostler, whose career was sufficiently distinguished for John Davies of Hereford to call him the Roscius of our times, after the most famous of ancient actors, in a poem published in *The Scourge of Folly* in 1611. In 1601 William Ostler was a boy among the Children of the Queen's Chapel, acting in Ben Jonson's *Poetaster*, but in 1604 he was a member of the King's Men. By 1610 he was 'principal comedian' in Jonson's *Alchemist* and in 1611 he married. His days for acting women's parts cover the years of Lady Macbeth, Desdemona, the virtuoso young man's part of Edgar in *Lear* and, if his voice was still right for it, Cleopatra. There are distinct similarities in what is demanded of Edgar and of Cleopatra. The part of all these I think him least likely to have played is Lady Macbeth, who I suppose to have been acted by an older boy. These conjectures are not undiluted moonshine, because there must have been roughly such a boy, and William Ostler was roughly the right age. Shakespeare cut his plays according to the cloth of his actors.

Montaigne, the Bible and Philemon Holland's translation of Pliny all contribute to the earthy texture of the play. But Shakespeare's setting is astonishingly and vividly modern. Enobarbus the satiric soldier is his own creation, and his personal tragedy is centrally important because it stands for many. When I first read *Antony and Cleopatra* as a schoolboy, Enobarbus and then Eros and Charmian were the characters who interested me most. It is only in performance that Cleopatra comes to life, but modern performances are often too lavish. This is a play of short successive scenes in contrasting stage areas; it is one vast and single poem with a rhythm and energy all of its own. It makes sense of a remark of Sir Stephen Spender's, that Shakespeare's metrical unit is the entire play. The characters are foils to one another: Antony is worm-eaten with love and therefore his brilliance is clouded with moodiness, but there is no madness and not much soul-searching; the womanly outweighs the manly verse.

279

The first scene sets the tone. Demetrius and Philo are Greek names, as I am sure Shakespeare knew, but they stand well for Antony's followers, dismayed by 'this dotage of our general's', 'a tawny front', 'a gipsy's lust'. Cleopatra appears at once, twisting him round her little finger. It was Agatha Christie who cleverly pointed out that there is a touch of the Dark Lady of the Sonnets about Cleopatra. The verse is superbly controlled under the pressure of her personal habit of speech, which is in all her moods unlike anyone else's in the play. Antony's eloquence is more obvious: it has a hollow, baroque quality, but in the course of the action truth will fill it. 'There's beggary in love that can be reckon'd'; 'Let Rome in Tiber melt, and the wide arch Of the rang'd empire fall!' as it is bound to do if love is supreme. Yet Rome will survive in other hands; it will be more durable than such a hero as Antony; he will break himself against it. The second scene carries the same message in another mode. Enobarbus and the Queen's women are fooling together when a soothsayer whom they treat as a joke makes some ominous prophecies. Politics flood in on Antony: 'These strong Egyptian fetters I must break, Or lose myself in dotage.' We know how that will end. Enobarbus in prose points it out to him, but Antony orders departure.

In the third scene Cleopatra plays Antony like a fish. In Rome the prig Caesar expresses his contempt:

> Let's grant it is not
> Amiss to tumble on the bed of Ptolemy,
> To give a kingdom for a mirth, to sit
> And keep the turn of tippling with a slave,
> To reel the streets at noon, and stand the buffet
> With knaves that smell of sweat.

Caesar's contempt extends to the people: 'This common body, Like to a vagabond flag upon the stream Goes to and back, lackeying the varying tide, To rot itself with motion'. Shakespeare does not put such sentiments into the mouths of his favourite characters or ours. But Caesar's praise of Antony for toughness as a soldier is both horrifying and curiously beautiful. It is an extreme of pastoral realism. 'Yea, like the stag when snow the pasture sheets, The barks of trees thou brows'd.' Even 'The stale of horses and the gilded puddle Which beasts would cough at' has a certain pastoral attractiveness as well as repulsiveness. North's Plutarch says 'to drink puddle water, and to eat wild fruits and roots . . . as they passed the Alps they did eat the barks of trees'. Shakespeare's stag 'when snow the pasture sheets' and his gilded puddle are his own experience of life.

The fifth and last scene of the act is a portrait of Cleopatra left alone with her women, more desperately and more dramatically in love than earlier Shakespeare heroines. The second act introduces Pompey. Its language is syntactically sinewy and highly spiced: '. . . all the charms of love, Salt Cleopatra, soften thy wan'd lip . . .'; 'Keep his brain fuming. Epicurean cooks Sharpen with cloyless sauce his appetite. . . .' But Pompey's good moment has passed, because Antony is now in Rome. The movements of world power throughout the play are like tidal flows of the sea, with the sea's inevitability. The second scene is Rome, with Enobarbus in full-blooded verse. The meeting of great men is tense and lively, perhaps because more stands or falls by it than by any analogous meeting in the English history plays. Here Shakespeare has had his political analysis done for him by Plutarch, who has a more powerful grasp of events than the English chroniclers of dynastic wars. Enobarbus makes a satiric interruption in prose, for which he cheerfully accepts reproof: 'That truth should be silent I had almost forgot.' 'You wrong this presence; therefore speak no more.' 'Go to, then – your considerate stone!'

Antony agrees to marry Octavia. But before the scene ends Enobarbus tells the joys of Egypt to Agrippa and Mecaenas; they are not unenthusiastic, and once again one can see that the sirens will draw Antony back to Alexandria. Enobarbus ends with the extraordinary set-piece of his praise of Cleopatra, static at first, then more and more motionable. It is simply embroidered from the heavier, oversweet prose of North's Plutarch, an adaptation that shows as great technical skill as anything in this magnificent play. One should consider the closeness and unlikeness of the verse and prose together, word by word. The attendant ladies in Cleopatra's ship are more fully imagined and more erotic in Shakespeare than in Plutarch, the transition being I think in the idea of mermaids, which we owe to North and Amyot, not to the Greek text of Plutarch. To the Elizabethans, the ancient world was a wonderland of uninhibited passions, untasted luxuries, and mighty destinies. Above all, it was unchristian. Marlowe's Dido has an influence here.

From this moment (act 2, scene ii) it is clear that Cleopatra is victoriously attractive. It was a stroke of Shakespeare's to introduce the description at this point, when we already knew her. In advance, it must have led to anticlimax; as things are, it sharpens the sadness of Antony's Roman mistake. We see him now for a moment with Octavia, then with the ominous soothsayer, who steers him home to Egypt. 'And though I make this marriage for my peace, I' th' East my pleasure lies.' One ten-line scene of the bustle of departure, and we are back there ahead of him, with Cleopatra in a black mood. She wants music, 'food Of us that trade in love', she wants billiards, she wants a fishing rod. The news of Antony's marriage excites her to an extreme of rage. Within one scene she runs through six or seven moods (act 2, scene v).

Meanwhile Caesar and Antony patch an uneasy peace with Pompey; once again Enobarbus ends the scene (in prose) with a fellow soldier. 'He will to his Egyptian dish again; then shall the sighs of Octavia blow the fire up in Caesar. . . .' The celebration banquet begins with servants' conversation and with music: it is a comic scene of increasing drunkenness with a sinister subplot ending in wild revelry. It is a miniature play in itself, brilliantly constructed and memorably funny. The song to Bacchus apparently conveys a popular view of the more cheerful odes of Horace, or possibly of the *Carmina Burana*, but it may owe more to the vintage invocation in Virgil's second *Georgic* (4–8):

> Come, strip with me my god, come drench all o'er
> Thy limbs in must of wine, and drink at every pore!
>
> (*trans.* JOHN DRYDEN)

'With thy grapes our hair be crown'd' is probably meant literally: 'Plumpy Bacchus with pink eyne' is certainly more Elizabethan than Roman.

So far the play might be a comedy. The banquet scene was set among Romans, not in Alexandria, where revels are only described. But this banquet has Roman undercurrents of treachery and of comic ignorance of Egypt. Shakespeare was fascinated by Egypt, which was not outside Elizabethan knowledge. The evidence for that is not just the alligator in *Romeo* and Hamlet's willingness to eat one, or the Sibyl's handkerchief in *Othello*: there are twelve columns of Egyptian granite in Chipping Campden church, and Cardinal Wolsey's tomb is Egyptian stone. It was confiscated at his fall by Henry VIII and kept at Windsor until the time of George III, who sent it to the crypt of St Paul's, where Nelson lies buried in it, perhaps as victor of the battle of the Nile.

Another reason for setting this banquet among Romans is probably the strain it would have put on the boy playing Cleopatra. His changes of mood already demand a virtuoso actor, as much so or more than the part of Edgar in *Lear*. Cleopatra moves from one tour de force to another, but we remember her as beautiful, not drunk. The banquet scene is satirical. It closes the second act; in the third the play dives towards tragedy.

It is in Caesar's words that we hear Antony is back with Cleopatra:

> Cleopatra and himself in chairs of gold
> Were publicly enthron'd; at the feet sat
> Caesarion, whom they call my father's son,
> And all the unlawful issue that their lust
> Since then hath made between them. Unto her
> He gave the stablishment of Egypt; made her
> Of lower Syria, Cyprus, Lydia,
> Absolute queen.
>
> His sons he there proclaim'd the kings of kings. . . .

The same magnificent and meaningless event, taken from the same sentences of Plutarch, inspired a wonderful poem by Kavafis with a different nuance. Two of his poems – 'The God leaves Antony' and

'Alexandrian Kings' – coincide with scenes in this play; they are among his masterpieces, and perhaps because they are based on Plutarch and not on *Antony and Cleopatra* they are fit to mention in the same breath as Shakespeare's scenes. I know of almost no other later poet of whom that could be said. Shakespeare's treatment is of course completely subservient to a dramatic purpose:

> He hath given his empire
> Up to a whore, who now are levying
> The kings o' th' earth for war. . . .

The next scene carries us with the usual vigorous swiftness to Actium, where even an Elizabethan schoolboy would know that Antony was defeated. Enobarbus grumbles, Cleopatra dominates, Antony makes his fatal decision to fight at sea. The battle is a swift succession of scenes: armies march this way and that and there 'is heard the noise of a sea-fight'. Can it have been the noise of cannon? Enobarbus and a horrified friend report the catastrophe.

Actium is all over in less than fifty lines, and we are back in Alexandria. Antony's fury and shame are the beginning of his nobility; Cleopatra can only beg for pardon, but for her that is another new mood. We flicker between Caesar's camp and Cleopatra's palace, as if this were a sharply cut film rather than a stage play. Antony turns wild in his rage, has a servant whipped, and fiercely berates Cleopatra. She wins him round, and there has been a sexual excitement in their quarrels and moods, as there is in their whole relationship; the flight from Actium was part of it:

> I will be treble-sinew'd, hearted, breath'd,
> And fight maliciously. For when mine hours
> Were nice and lucky, men did ransom lives
> Of me for jests; but now I'll set my teeth,
> And send to darkness all that stop me. Come,
> Let's have one other gaudy night. Call to me
> All my sad captains. . . .
> . . . and tonight I'll force
> The wine peep through their scars. . . .

It is at this moment that Enobarbus decides to desert Antony; the fourth act sees them both dead. We see both sides as before, then the strange scene of Kavafis's 'The God leaves Antony', the mysterious music. ''Tis the god Hercules, whom Antony lov'd, Now leaves him.' Antony goes to his last battle like a young gallant; when he hears that Enobarbus has deserted he sends 'his chests and treasure' after him. Enobarbus sees his sin at once, and repents as bitterly as Judas. I used to suppose he died by suicide, but I think he dies of pure grief, as Gloucester dies in *Lear*.

Antony wins a day's battle: he has his brilliant and victorious moment with the Queen. On the second day she betrays him:

> Swallows have built
> In Cleopatra's sails their nests. The augurers
> Say they know not, they cannot tell; look grimly,
> And dare not speak their knowledge. . . .

In the wording of this play, the mere poetry, Shakespeare shows great powers and close attention. He could write a line like 'O sun, thy uprise shall I see no more' without difficulty, just as Sophocles could write such delusively simple-looking lines that one always remembers. But the verbs in Antony's despairing speech give it extraordinary strength (act 4, scene xii). In one sentence we get 'spaniel'd . . . gave . . . discandy . . . melt . . . barked . . . hovertopped'. He has used the word 'discandy' effectively before in this play (act 3, scene xiii), but in the whole of English literature it has never been recorded again. 'Spaniel'd' is as good. The printers of the Folio misread it by the omission of one stroke as 'pannelled' but 'spannel'd' (spaniel'd) is certain to be right. It occurs in the same sense in Copley's *Fig for Fortune*; Shakespeare had hoarded the usage. In Antony's approach to suicide, wild exalted language and very simple language alternate as his mood does; the first makes the second more moving, like an intervention of reality: 'there is left us Ourselves to end ourselves'; 'Unarm, Eros; the long day's task is done, And we must sleep.'

This is a love tragedy, but it is also a triumph of love. Shakespeare feels that more strongly than Plutarch did, though Plutarch was not an unromantic man:

> Where souls do couch on flowers, we'll hand in hand,
> And with our sprightly port make the ghosts gaze.
> Dido and her Æneas shall want troops,
> And all the haunt be ours. . . .
> . . . I will be
> A bridegroom in my death, and run into 't
> As to a lover's bed.

Cleopatra at the very end purely, simply and physically loves him as he does her. Her lamentation of him and her suicide in the fifth act, in which the plot by no means slackens pace, are more masterly than anything else in the play. They are one of the high points of Shakespeare's poetry, though it may be the arching construction of the whole play that makes them so. Two small matters are worth noticing all the same. One is the dramatic effectiveness of Cleopatra's scene with the clown, which is chilling as well as funny, and makes her humanly brave, as well as setting her dying grandeur in thrilling relief. The other is her motive. She scorns the Romans and adores her dead Antony. She is not deceived by Caesar, and will not be part of his triumph. She wants to die, to be with Antony; she will not live to be Caesar's victim. Both are true. Charmian is morally higher, as Eros is higher than Antony, but the hero and heroine are the famous lovers, and the subject of this play is their love, and the world they lost for it. We are not in love with either of them but we can see how someone else could be.

Cleopatra's horror of the mob (act 5, scene ii) reflects I believe Shakespeare's horror of public executions and the crowds they attracted. The year 1607 was that of the Diggers and Levellers in Warwickshire. It was certainly a year of hanging, but Shakespeare is thinking of London. Modern critics say Shakespeare has been misread to make the British Empire like the splendid Roman Empire; my own view of Shakespeare is rather that ghastly Rome stands for ghastly London.

Coriolanus, another Roman play based on Plutarch, raises in an acute form the question of Shakespeare's attitude to the people and to mobs. In these plays it has a Roman or Plutarchian colouring which does not necessarily include England. Antony and Cleopatra delight to mingle with the common people; Caesar despises them for it, but Shakespeare rather likes them for it. In *Coriolanus* there is some influence of William Camden, but only by way of antipopulist rhetoric. The conflict is very boldly stated from the beginning. 'Let us kill him, and we'll have corn at our own price'; 'We are accounted poor citizens, the patricians good. What authority surfeits on would relieve us.' Plutarch begins the list of grievances not with hunger but with usury. Shakespeare is thinking of the poverty and distress in the country.

Jonson's *Epicene* in 1609 borrows a phrase from *Coriolanus*, so it was probably written in 1608. It is a long, full work, swift and terse, with no songs but only military and triumphal music. It analyses Rome in formal terms, but lacks the anecdotal detail, the warmth and truth to life of *Antony and Cleopatra*, because Plutarch lacks them. He could attain them only in the modern Roman lives where his sources were full; his Coriolanus is only a foil to his Alcibiades, a much more interesting figure:

> The origin of all lay in his unsociable, supercilious, and self-willed disposition, which in all cases is offensive to most people; and when combined with a passion for distinction passes into absolute savageness and mercilessness. Men decline to ask favours of the people, professing not to need any honours from them: and then are indignant if they do not obtain them. . . . Such are the faulty parts of his character, which in all other respects was a noble one.

One is not meant to be convinced by Menenius and his fable of the parts of the body. The source of that is Camden translating John of Salisbury, rather than Plutarch or Livy. If 'The senators of Rome are this good belly,' Shakespeare knows that his audience will view their claim to central usefulness in the state with some cynicism. When Caius Marcius makes his contemptuous entrance, one is certainly not supposed to like him. The people are clearly enough characterized to bring home the message of his speech to English listeners, but that does not mean they like it or feel justly rebuked.

The verse is supple, strong and sarcastic:

> ... you are no surer, no,
> Than is the coal of fire upon the ice
> Or hailstone in the sun. ...
> They'll sit by th' fire and presume to know
> What's done i' th' Capitol, who's like to rise,
> Who thrives and who declines; side factions, and give out
> Conjectural marriages, making parties strong,
> And feebling such as stand not in their liking
> Below their cobbled shoes.

War with the Volsces interrupts all this. Marcius' bloodthirsty mother reinforces the lesson of his awfulness and of the tradition in which he was reared. The ladies are pleased with the revolting story of a little boy tearing a butterfly to pieces: at war now he vilely abuses his men and wins the battle more or less on his own. He had an enemy rival in Aufidius, but their encounter is inconclusive. The language of the officers is a special sort of upper-class speech which Shakespeare has gradually elaborated for such people, full of brief noble sentiment, tight-lipped Spartan phrases and suppressed rant. When the war is won, Marcius is given his title Coriolanus, but Aufidius is left dangerously alive and smouldering.

The second act is alleviated by touches of humour, and its verse is elegant, but the plot marches onwards along its road to doom. Coriolanus refuses to beg the consulship from the Roman people, but he is deemed by the Senate to have fulfilled this formal obligation. The people mutiny, while Aufidius in act 3 is at Antium giving promise of trouble. Coriolanus gives his view of the 'mutable, rack-scented' people more clearly than ever: 'You speak o' th' people As if you were a god, to punish, not A man of their infirmity.' He is justly accused of treason, and after some tumultuous scenes, which from a dramatic point of view are very well managed, he goes into exile, giving the crowd a final verbal lashing as he does so.

It will be evident that I think *Coriolanus* a lesser play than *Antony and Cleopatra*. It is also a transitional play, a deliberate contrast and a new experiment. It comes closer than any other to being about politics as we now understand them, but these are political events so distant in Shakespeare's eyes as to be fabulous. *Coriolanus* touches on realities, as all of Shakespeare does, but it is not a scenario for the future, only the tragic downfall of one man. It is the Volsces not the Romans who eventually kill him. Shakespeare is near the end of the series of his tragedies. Perhaps he is at the end of his tether as a tragic poet. The last two, *Coriolanus* and *Timon of Athens*, are violent, cruel plays. They are the dark side of Plutarch, and of the ancient world, which makes early Stuart London seem all but homely by comparison. The absence of Christianity is marked.

The fourth act brings Coriolanus to Antium, where he contrives to break in on Aufidius at dinner. This is the liveliest and best scene in the play (act 4, scene v), and it has the most of those flashes of flinty poetry that briefly illuminate scene after scene. The old enemies meet as chivalrous host and guest, bound as closely to one another as two knights after a tournament. They are innocently homosexual. This extraordinary relationship is convincing enough in its way, but unreal at the same time. It goes back to Chaucer and beyond:

> Let me twine
> Mine arms about that body, where against
> My grained ash an hundred times hath broke
> And scarr'd the moon with splinters; here I clip
> The anvil of my sword, and do contest
> As hotly and as nobly with thy love
> As ever in ambitious strength I did
> Contend against thy valour. Know thou first,
> I lov'd the maid I married; never man
> Sigh'd truer breath; but that I see thee here,
> Thou noble thing, more dances my rapt heart
> Than when I first my wedded mistress saw
> Bestride my threshold. Why, thou Mars, I tell thee. . . .

So Aufidius and Marcius go off to war against Rome. 'But when they shall see, sir, his crest up again and the man in blood, they will out of their burrows, like conies after rain, and revel all with him.' Aufidius is nettled by the new friend's success, and muses analytically over him, and more obscurely over the nature of power, at the end of act 4. This is not a lucid speech, but it has more ring of real feeling than most monologues. If it were more perfect it would be less effective as drama.

In act 5 Coriolanus spares Rome for his mother's sake after a long scene of intercession, too formally rhetorical for my own taste, the final speech being more than fifty lines long. Aufidius has hoped this might happen and plots his downfall, accusing him of treason to the Volsces. 'Kill, kill, kill, kill, kill him!' they all shout, and Coriolanus dies. 'Let him be regarded As the most noble corse that ever herald Did follow to his urn', 'Trail your steel pikes.'

Has Shakespeare so exhausted his warmth in the great tragedies that he is left cold? Is it the moral machinery of his fictions that is breaking up, as it seemed to do in the earlier plays I have called transitional? This play has its champions. It is not negligible, and at every rereading I have always found new facets that held me enthralled. The pressure it puts on language and on the rhythms of verse is fascinating. But the next play, the last tragedy, is the strangest of all: *Timon of Athens*. It is possible that Shakespeare left it unfinished when he abandoned Plutarch for ever.

It may be that the company pressed Shakespeare too hard for another Plutarch play, and that this one was not only unfinished but never acted. It was printed in the Folio to fill a gap, while a dispute over the rights to *Troilus and Cressida* was being concluded. If that had not happened, it is open to us to conjecture that it might never have been printed at all, though I am reluctant to take that view, because I like *Timon*. Still, as it stands the verse is often irregular, the construction is ramshackle, and some of the characterization surprising. *Timon of Athens* has been attacked with the usual all-purpose weapon of a theory (theories) of divided authorship. Such theories throw no light on real problems; they contradict one another, and they fasten on details which other works of Shakespeare furnish sufficient analogies to defend. *Timon* is difficult to date, but I think it shows consciousness of *Volpone* (1606), and must come close after *Coriolanus*. The story is clearly told and the end excellent. It is the tragedy not of Timon but of Athens. Timon himself is transformed from rage to sanctity, like Oedipus at Colonus. But some minor characters are unreal, and the early acts are not convincing and not fully embodied. Possibly it represents yet another attempt at a completely new *kind* of play: one can judge the intentions of an artist only where his work is completely successful, and not always then, but *Timon* is not.

Was it meant to be a play like one of those moral dialogues of Erasmus that the sixteenth century thought so lively, or like the ancient dialogues of Lucian? Lucian had been translated into French by 1582; and a Timon play of that decade seems to have been based on him. Shakespeare could have seen Lucian whether in Latin or in French; the Latin version was by Erasmus. But some details of his play suggest the Italian version by Boiardo (1494), which is already halfway to being dramatized. About the year 1600, the wills of students dying in Oxford were proved at the Chancellor's Court and the inventories of their possessions give details of their books, among which Italian comedies and tragedies occur: Italian was becoming a usual influence in England. Can anyone have shown Shakespeare a Greek text of Lucian? He was hungry for literature of every kind, and for the classics even when they turned to dust in his mouth. Where did he get the peculiar curse 'mayest thou split open', *diarrageies*, which occurs in the first two lines of *The Birds* of Aristophanes?

The noise and bustle of Timon's house are mentioned in Seneca's letters. Here the poet, the painter, the jeweller and the merchant are Timon's clients; the poet is the most interesting, since the sententious story he tells is the story of this play. His views of the nature of poetry are also of some interest, since they show a clear appreciation of what I take to be Shakespeare's own attitude, in spite of the poet's affectation:

> Our poesy is as a gum which oozes
> From whence 'tis nourished; the fire i' th' flint
> Shows not till it be struck: our gentle flame
> Provokes itself, and like the current flies
> Each bound it chafes.

Timon is generous. He rescues a friend from prison, gives a dowry to bring lovers together, buys from all and sundry. His foil is the satiric philosopher Apemantus, who derides the world and the clients. Music and a banquet follow, and then a masque, but before the end of act 1, scene ii, Timon is bankrupt, as his steward realizes. The masque consisted of Amazons, introduced by Cupid, a typical early Stuart extravaganza. *'And to show their loves each single out an Amazon, and all dance, men with women, a lofty strain or two to the hautboys, and cease.'* The exchange of presents, the light verse of Apemantus' grace before meals, and the masque after dinner faintly recall Marston's ceremonies for Lady Derby's daughter in 1607. Similarly, the curses in act 4 outMarston Marston, and show his influence on an elder and far greater poet. I do not think of these connections as hard enough evidence to alter the date of *Timon of Athens*, putting it before *Cymbeline*, but I am a little inclined to see the 1607 ceremony as a *terminus post quem* for this play.

In the second act Timon's false friends desert him. Apemantus reappears, this time with a Fool belonging to a lady. It seems that 'natural' fools were more often harboured by women than by men. In Shakespeare's plays they often frequent women. Lady Arundel, the first English subject to be painted by Rubens (in 1620), has a Fool, a dwarf, and a dog. The conversation between Timon and his steward, in which he hears the worst (act 2, scene ii), is dramatic and contains brilliant verse. 'To Lacedaemon did my land extend' and 'You tell me true' convey his shock pungently; the eloquence is the Steward's:

> ... when our vaults have wept
> With drunken spilth of wine, when every room
> Hath blaz'd with lights and bray'd with minstrelsy,
> I have retir'd me to a wasteful cock
> And set mine eyes at flow.
>   Prithee no more.

In the third act Timon begins to be isolated and enraged. Alcibiades is banished, for pleading to the Senate for mercy to an old soldier, for his violent rioting and 'factions': he will turn against Athens as Coriolanus does against Rome. The act ends with Timon's famous banquet of tepid water and the revelation of his rage. The guests declare him mad. 'One day he gives us diamonds, next day stones.'

Timon's devastating formal cursing of Athens opens the fourth act. As an all-inclusive political invective I do not see how it could be bettered, as a human utterance it is terrifying, and as poetry magnificent and formidable. The inclusiveness curiously resembles that of genuine ancient curses of which I suppose Shakespeare knew nothing. Plutarch offers only a faint hint of them, and Lucian nothing. He adjures women to be incontinent, slaves and fools to take over government, servants to steal – 'Maid, to thy master's bed' – sons of sixteen to beat out their father's brains with his own crutches.

> Piety and fear,
> Religion to the gods, peace, justice, truth,
> Domestic awe, night-rest, and neighbourhood,
> Instruction, manners, mysteries, and trades,
> Degrees, observances, customs and laws,
> Decline to your confounding contraries
> And let confusion live. Plagues incident to men,
> Your potent and infectious fevers heap
> On Athens, ripe for stroke. Thou cold sciatica,
> Cripple our senators, that their limbs may halt
> As lamely as their manners. Lust and liberty,
> Creep in the minds and marrows of our youth,
> That 'gainst the stream of virtue they may strive
> And drown themselves in riot. Itches, blains,
> Sow all th' Athenian bosoms, and their crop
> Be general leprosy! Breath infect breath,
> That their society, as their friendship, may
> Be merely poison! . . .
> Timon will to the woods, where he shall find
> Th' unkindest beast more kinder than mankind.

The Steward follows him almost as Adam followed Orlando in *As You Like It*. Timon has another long, embittered monologue, while he digs for roots and finds buried gold. Alcibiades passes by – 'Follow thy drum; With man's blood paint the ground, gules, gules' – with two whores; Timon begs them to spread venereal disease, and Alcibiades to be merciless against Athens. They leave him to a further bitter monologue addressed to earth:

> Whose womb unmeasurable and infinite breast
> Teems and feeds all; whose self-same mettle,
> Whereof thy proud child, arrogant man, is puff'd,
> Engenders the black toad and adder blue,
> The gilded newt and eyeless venom'd worm,
> With all th' abhorred births below crisp heaven
> Whereon Hyperion's quick'ning fire doth shine. . . .

His next visitor is Apemantus; they exchange insults of withering rage and great verbal beauty. In a curious echo of *Antony and Cleopatra* the phrases 'page thy heels' and 'Candied with ice' occur within three lines of one another. After chewing some roots they reach friendlier terms and break into prose, but they quarrel again soon enough: 'Beast!' 'Slave!' 'Toad!' 'Rogue, rogue, rogue!' Apemantus leaves and bandits approach; Timon expounds the cosmic system as thievery and gives them gold. Last comes the Steward, but the Steward is driven away, though kindly. This succession of episodes is oddly reminiscent of the earlier comedies of Aristophanes, which I am compelled to wonder whether Shakespeare knew in some form. *Timon of Athens* is classicized, perhaps over-classicized; it is very distant from a medieval Morality Play, though it is also distant from Aristophanes.

In the final act (act division being more cursory than usual in *Timon*) the hero encounters painter, poet and senators, as Alcibiades threatens Athens. He offers the Athenians a tree to hang themselves:

> Why, I was writing of my epitaph;
> It will be seen to-morrow. My long sickness
> Of health and living now begins to mend,
> And nothing brings me all things. . . .

> Timon hath made his everlasting mansion
> Upon the beached verge of the salt flood,
> Who once a day with his embossed froth
> The turbulent surge shall cover.

An illiterate soldier takes a wax impression of the writing on his tomb, to bring it to Alcibiades (act 5, scene iii), who 'hath in every figure skill'. Wax impressions of ancient coins existed, and of course seals; ancient inscriptions were collected, but where does Shakespeare get the idea of taking wax impressions of them? The verses turn out to be a malediction in awkward couplets, based on Plutarch. They are probably intended to sound like a translation, and so they do. Athens surrenders but Alcibiades is merciful. This recurrence of a simplistic, antirealist and skeletal structure at the very end of the play suggests that the episodic scheme and the disinterest in realistic motive were deliberately adopted. The setting is more than formal all the same. It shows a varied, interrelated world of many social levels.

Why else the Fool whose only joke is about venereal disease? Why else the illiterate soldier? It may be that in *Timon of Athens* we have a masterly sketch never fully executed. We know from the second, revised version of *Lear* that Shakespeare would tighten up motivation in revising, but in this case perhaps that opportunity or need never arose. I doubt the 'freedom' of the verse, which may well have been exaggerated in transmission, and which is often easy to restore to Shakespeare's normal perfection. But this is a one-man play, or nearly so, as *Coriolanus* was, though its world has social density of a different kind. Its conservatism is moral, the curses called down on Athens are moral as well as physical, and come uncomfortably close to Britain in the late 1980s as older people see it. Timon despises the middle and upper class characters: the only good people are the Steward, the soldier and maybe the bandits.

Timon of Athens is in several ways clearly connected with *King Lear*; it might have been written after *Lear* was revised, or in reaction to the labour of that revision. The cursing of Athens in Timon (act 4, scene i) has a submerged or forgotten connection with the great plague of Athens described in Greek by Thucydides and in Latin by Lucretius, but Shakespeare is obviously talking about Elizabethan and Stuart London, where the 'plague' has been rampant. To connect that so closely with the severest of moral condemnations of the city was a bold as well as a terrifying step for him to take. Timon the tragic satirist is the climax of a long series of satiric characters, from the melancholy Jaques onwards, and with him the vein withers. Timon calls down Shakespeare's curse on London, a curse that had been fulfilled.

It is suggestive, at least, that John Marston seems to have written nothing new for the theatre after 1607; one must assume he was drifting towards his later decision to take holy orders in the Church of England. *Timon* is a very full statement of the theme of nature denatured. The only sense in which nature is restored or thought redeemable in it is the lonely grave on the shore of the salt sea. In another way, when Alcibiades spares the Athenians, Timon's rage is over and normal relations are briefly reasserted, but Shakespeare puts little emphasis on that; his emphasis is on Timon, who is like an angry saint or an angry prophet, terrifying to the end. In this, of course, he goes further than Lear, and Shakespeare reaches an impasse.

The influence of sermons on Shakespeare is not to be discounted, though it must remain speculative. This sentence on death, for example, is like an echo of several of the late tragedies: 'If it were but a sleep no man would fear it at all; for who feareth to take his rest when the night approacheth?' It comes from a sermon by Henry Smith, printed in 1614, but probably preached in London at St Clement Dane's in the late 1580s. On 9 September 1608 Shakespeare's mother was buried at Stratford. From that time onwards Shakespeare wrote the series of his late comedies, with their sense of liberation and resolution, their quasi-divine interventions and their continual hints of resurrection. In June 1607 his daughter Susanna had married John Hall; his granddaughter Elizabeth was born in February. In the December of 1607 his brother Edmund had died and so a few months before had Edmund's bastard child. These events taken together are a watershed between generations, and a watershed of Shakespeare's life.

In the period of his mature tragedies, and perhaps earlier and later as well, he had taken to spending time in Oxford. The obvious attraction of

the place for him apart from the architecture and the convenience of a
halfway house between Stratford and London was the Bodleian Library,
which opened in early November of 1602. Entry cost a shilling and scholars
from all over the world were very soon visiting and using it. But its books
were accumulating for years before it formally opened, and even before
that Oxford was full of books; as a society, it was the kind that books
always create. That is why it is impossible to rule out Shakespeare's access
to sources that might seem beyond his personal scholarly attainment. We
know that he came often to Oxford from an anecdote of John Aubrey's, one
of the few pieces of more or less scurrilous gossip about Shakespeare that
modern writers tend to take seriously, since it suits their world view.

The minor dramatic poet Sir William Davenant, who was born probably
on the last day of February in 1606, at the Tavern in Cornmarket, Oxford,
later called the Crown, liked it to be believed that he was Shakespeare's
bastard son, though neither his poetry nor his face would suggest it. His
real father, John Davenant, was 'a very grave and discreet citizen', Mayor of
Oxford in 1621; his mother was 'a very beautiful woman, and of very good
wit, and of conversation extremely agreeable'. The eldest son Robert
became a fellow of St John's, a bishop's chaplain, and then a vicar. William
was second son; the third became an attorney. Two daughters married a
fellow of Corpus Christi and a canon of Hereford. All that was in the future,
within Aubrey's memory, but it indicates social status, and the sort of
person Shakespeare would meet if he stayed with the Davenants, as he
undoubtedly did, if not in the Tavern then in the Cross, now the Golden
Cross, which shared its courtyard. The Golden Cross had a prettily
decorated Elizabethan painted chamber, with the motto 'Fear God above
all thing', which does not sound right for the scene of a seduction.

> Mr. William Shakespeare was wont to go into Warwickshire once a year,
> and did commonly in his journey lie in this house in Oxford, where he
> was exceedingly respected. (I have heard parson Robert say that Mr. W.
> Shakespeare has given him a hundred kisses.) Now Sir William would
> sometimes, when he was pleasant over a glass of wine with his intimate
> friends, e.g. Sam Butler (author of *Hudibras*), etc. – say, that it seemed to
> him that he wrote with the very spirit that Shakespeare [wrote], and
> seemed contented enough to be thought his son: he would tell them the
> story as above, in which way his mother had a very light report.

Aubrey is shocked by Davenant, whom he knew well. He knew which
girl gave Davenant the pox, knew his schooling, his schemes and scrapes,
saw his plays, and went to his funeral. But his story is about Davenant, not
about Shakespeare. The only confirmation, or more likely the origin of it,
lies in an old joke about 'Goodman Diggle', printed by John Taylor the
waterman poet in *Wit and Mirth* (1629). This joke was later told of
Davenant and Shakespeare by the antiquary Thomas Hearne, who was

Bodley's Librarian, in his diary for 1709: 'Mr. Shakespear was his God-father and gave him his name. (In all probability he got him.)' The fuller version was told by Pope at dinner late in his life. It was that Davenant as a little boy of seven or eight was extremely fond of Shakespeare and went flying home from school to see him. 'An old townsman' asked him where he was running and he said to see his godfather. 'There's a good boy,' said the old man, 'but have a care that you don't take God's name in vain.' This sour old man sounds to me like one of the Puritan fellows of colleges who hated actors, perhaps a fellow of Corpus. The joke I take to be proverbial. The myth of Shakespeare's affair has so many weak links as to be incredible, but he probably really was Davenant's godfather, and Davenant certainly admired him extremely.

I might have neglected this bit of gossip altogether, except that it fixes Shakespeare in a place and a social world that are of interest for his life, and shows him as a loving, domesticated man: 'I have heard parson Robert say that Mr. W. Shakespeare has given him a hundred kisses.' Shakespeare's contempt for whores is obvious in the Sonnets, as it is in *Timon of Athens*, where his brother's plight may well have strengthened his feelings. The only other shred of gossip about his sex life is the story about King Richard and William the Conqueror, which I would judge to be untrue. He was a faithful man, or at least a man who greatly valued faithfulness. 'The Phoenix and the Turtle' is about sublimated, sexless or sexually repressed love; so are the sonnets to Southampton. One may well ask whether the late comedies are not the unexpected result of his faithfulness in love, the unsought reward of his temperament and of his life. But nothing is perfectly simple.

Resurrection
and Restoration

From 1607, Robert Johnson, who was about twenty-four, wrote music for Shakespeare's plays. He was a lutanist like his father, indentured two years after his father died to the Lord Chamberlain from 1596 to 1603, and lutanist to the King in 1604. In 1611 he moved to Prince Henry's household. He is known to have worked on *Cymbeline*, *The Winter's Tale* and *The Tempest*, for Webster on *The Duchess of Malfi*, for Beaumont and Fletcher, and for Ben Jonson on his masques at Court. His father before him was a Court musician, John Johnson, who flourished from 1579 to 1594. His widow had a grant of land from the Queen in 1595. John Johnson wrote a number of 'dumps', and played an important part in developing the lute duet. It seems likely to me that Robert and the exploiting of his young talent were a powerful influence on Shakespeare's final phase as a dramatist. He had always been addicted to romances, which were the staple reading matter of the day, but I do not think he was as close to Beaumont and Fletcher as critics have said. For him the main attraction of pastoral settings was their erotic and their musical possibilities. The new generation of younger dramatic poets, with exceptions we have seen, to which one might add Thomas Middleton, left him untouched, but music was as necessary to him as it was to the Court. It gave him more than he gave it, including the inspiration of his lyrics.

It must have been of importance to Shakespeare that in 1608 the Children of the Revels, who used the roofed 'private' theatre at Blackfriars, and the Children of St Paul's, both active companies in the early years of James I, were dissolved, and the King's Servants took over the Blackfriars theatre. The new possibilities for productions of a different kind hardly need to be spelled out, but *Pericles* was performed by 'His Majesty's Servants at the Globe', which continued in use until it was burned down during a performance of *Henry VIII*. Beaumont and Fletcher, who had already written for the Children's Company, continued to write for the Blackfriars theatre under the King's Servants in sweetly sonorous but slightly dull and vapid verses. Shakespeare's late works do not really suggest that they were written to be played in a room with a roof, by artificial light, with special acoustics that were new to him: Court performances after all had always been indoors. But some influence of the new conditions does seem to flit across his pages and if nothing else, a new covered theatre that could be used in foul weather must have brought an increase of profits to the company. The same may be said of the collapse of the Children's companies, though whether the professional stage gained more by the extinction of their competition than it lost by the withering away of a seed-ground for young actors is hard to guess.

Pericles, Prince of Tyre used to be thought of, by Dryden among others, as Shakespeare's first play, perhaps because of its deliberate simplicity and innocence, and the charming archaism suggested by ancient Gower as introducer of the acts. But there is little doubt about its date. It was registered for printing in May 1608 by Blount, and published as a quarto by Thomas Gosson in 1609, 'as performed by H.M. Servants at the Globe, by William Shakespeare'. The Venetian Ambassador Zorzi Ginstinian saw it performed before the late November of 1608, and George Wilkins published his prose version of the romance in that same year, 'Being the true history of the play of Pericles, as it was lately presented by the worthy and ancient Poet John Gower'.

Shakespeare's affection for John Gower is charming, and he may well have played that part himself, since he played old men's parts. He knew Gower's tomb at Southwark, with the head resting on a pile of his works: *Vox Clamantis, Speculum Meditantis* and *Confessio Amantis* – The Voice of One Crying, The Mirror of Meditation and The Lover's Confession: the source of Pericles. They were in Latin, French and English: Stowe had never seen a copy of *Speculum Meditantis*, though he thought one existed in Kent. The tomb has been over-restored; in Shakespeare's day it would have looked older than it does now, though it still is a most moving monument to an old poet. There are other versions of the story, and Wilkins seems to have felt Shakespeare had stolen his, but Gower is the key. The earliest version of all is *Apollonius, King of Tyre*, a Latin romance written under the Roman Empire, still very readable. The element of mystery, and the mysterious beauty of symbolism, go back to the ancient world, where mystery religions were already intertwined with the origins of romantic narrative. The sea that washed over Timon's grave takes on a deeper meaning in *Pericles*.

Ben Jonson, with his recurrent lack of delicacy, called it in 1631 'some mouldy tale', and although it was often reprinted it entered the Folio collection of Shakespeare's plays only in the second issue of the third edition in 1664. At every rereading it has grown in my estimation, and I still find it among the most moving of all Shakespeare's plays. The simplicity of its means rivals that of *Timon*, and its pure, direct reliance on poetry never ceases to astonish. Shakespeare has taken a dive backwards from fashion, but one is not surprised that the play was very popular, or that it leads on to his final period, like that of Beethoven's late quartets. His poetry at the heart of dramatic construction 'like the current flies Each bound it chafes'. He not only loves Gower, but takes evident delight in the moralizing, prosing element of the old man.

I do not find Gower to have been an important influence on anyone else at this time, though Stowe revered him. Personally I have always found him enjoyable, though not in enormous doses. He is like a lesser and more bookish Chaucer. But I believe that *Pericles* embodies more clearly than any other play some of the everlasting purposes of poetry, which Shakespeare had intuitively grasped from the Latin literature he read as a schoolboy. The recovery of Pericles and the meaning of the storm are a reversal of *King Lear*, but Cerimon is prefigured in *Lear*'s Doctor, 'The worth that learned charity aye wears'. Cerimon is very like Shakespeare's son-in-law John Hall, and I think of Marina as an echo of Shakespeare's daughter Judith.

Ben Jonson in this year was composing his *Masque of Queens* performed at Court in February 1609, with a fairified and jejune version of the witches from *Macbeth*, minor poetry in bad taste. It was not the art of the Court masque that gave Shakespeare *Pericles*, but a profound sense of realities. As a biographer I am forced to note, though I put little weight on the conjecture, that in the woodcut of Gower on the title-page of the prose version by Wilkins we may just possibly have a representation of Shakespeare as he appeared on the stage. It should also be recorded that the text of the play shows some influence of the obscure dramatic poet John Day (c.1574–1640), not sufficient to make a case for him as co-author or original author, but an undoubted influence in a few phrases confined to a few scenes, hardly more substantial in fact than that of Antony Copley's *Fig for Fortune* a few years earlier.

All the same, Day and Wilkins both worked on *The Travails of the Three English Brothers* (1607), which has Fame as a Chorus very like Gower. Day wrote mostly for the Children of the Revels, and four of the six plays of his that have survived were printed between 1606 and 1608; Shakespeare is certain to have been conscious of him. We know little about him beyond the fact that he stabbed a fellow actor to death in 1599, and was hated by Ben Jonson. He liked apparently tragic plots that turned out happily. He was a light-hearted, stylish writer, much influenced by prose romances, and 'life begot in death' was one of his themes.

Pericles was revived for a French ambassador 'in the King's great chamber' at Whitehall in 1619 when Shakespeare was dead. 'After two acts, the players ceased till the French all refreshed them with sweetmeats brought on china voiders, and wine and ale in bottles. After, the players begun anew.' The interest of this is the placing of an interval, exactly where the play best admits of one. Act 3 begins with Gower on night, and an elaborate dumb-show. No evil except for the enigmatic tale of incest much affects the play until the fourth act; the first two have a certain deliberate innocence. Gower speaks in the metre of the real Gower, quoting Latin (good things are the better for age) and speaking with greater formality in the first two acts. He warms up as we get used to him, or as Shakespeare gets used to writing him, but the touch of parody persists. So Act 3 begins 'Now sleepyslacked hath the rout; No din but snores the house about . . .'; while in the introduction to the whole play Gower rises from his ashes 'To sing a song that old was sung . . . at festivals, On ember-eves and holy-ales; And lords and ladies in their lives Have read it for restoratives. The purchase is to make men glorious. . . .'

Robert Greene in his *Vision* in the late 1590s had described Gower's appearance in an attempted pastiche of the old poet's verse style, in a scene in which moral Gower's ghost scolded him and amorous Chaucer's comforted him. Greene's pastiche is much less effective than Shakespeare's, but Shakespeare's choice of Gower may well be an amused reflection on Greene's *Vision*. Gower's verse style did influence what C. S. Lewis calls the 'Drab Age' poets whose 'grand function was to build a firm metrical highway out of the late medieval swamp'. Shakespeare has got long ago to dry land, and writes his Gower lines from that point of vantage, but Greene is still floundering. Gower is a far better poet than C. S. Lewis realized, better, I think, than anyone but Shakespeare has ever realized, unless we count Greene. Christopher Ricks, in his *Force of Poetry* (1985), is the first critic to see him as Shakespeare did.

Pericles is a suitor for the King of Antioch's daughter; he must answer a riddle and win her, or else die. The answer is the King's incest with his daughter. Pericles sees this and hints at it; the King is murderously angry but prefers trickery. Pericles decides on flight. He loved the girl at first, but now he feels revulsion:

> You are a fair viol, and your sense the strings;
> Who, finger'd to make man his lawful music,
> Would draw heaven down, and all the gods, to hearken;
> But, being play'd upon before your time,
> Hell only danceth at so harsh a chime.

The King sends a murderer after Pericles, whom we see at home in Tyre, in melancholy monologue. Like Antonio in *The Merchant of Venice* he is unable to master or understand his own melancholy, which at least in his case the audience perfectly understands. His honest courtier Helicanus advises patience and is told the truth; he then advises foreign travel.

The murderer is relieved to find Pericles gone to Tarsus, where the King and Queen are brooding over a local famine, which Pericles brings grain to relieve. The simple bones of the story so far are set in verse which by Shakespeare's standards is of an ordinary eloquence, and there is no other attempt to disguise the clear, romantic narrative, or to excuse its lack of realism, except that the people are real.

Before act 2 Gower, who sweetly takes any blame for this archaic simplicity, explains that news of the murderer drives Pericles on from Tarsus and he suffers shipwreck: 'Till fortune, tir'd with doing bad, Threw him ashore, to give him glad.' Pilch and Patch-breech and the Master, three fishermen out of Plautus or out of a fishermen's pastoral, with some touches of John Day about their phrasing, find Pericles wandering on the shore, 'A man whom both the waters and the wind In that vast tennis-court hath made the ball For them to play upon . . .'; 'Come, thou shalt go home, and we'll have flesh for holidays, fish for fasting days, and moreo'er puddings and flapjacks, and thou shalt be welcome.' The next day good King Simonides of Pentapolis is holding a tournament for his daughter Thaisa's suitors on her birthday and, lo and behold, the fishermen fish up some rusty armour that Pericles had inherited from his father, which they give him when he asks for it.

Each of the Knights has an emblem and a motto. Pericles has 'a wither'd branch, that's only green at top', but it is Pericles who wins the wreath. Simonides thinks him 'but a country gentleman', but the Princess loves him. Pericles thinks the King is like his father, who 'Had princes sit like stars about his throne, And he the sun, for them to reverence', while his own status is that of a mere glow-worm, 'The which hath fire in darkness, none in light' – another emblem. He describes himself as a gentleman educated 'in arts and arms' and 'looking for adventures in the world'. The Knights dance in armour to cheer him up. Strangeness and freshness are the point of this dance, as that of the Amazons in *Timon*: here again, men and women dance together. Meanwhile, news reaches Tyre that the King of Antioch and his daughter were riding in a chariot when 'A fire from heaven came and shrivell'd up Their bodies, even to loathing; for they so stunk. . . .' Helicanus decides to wait twelve months for Pericles to come home before accepting the throne of Tyre for himself. At Pentapolis, Simonides tells the Knights that his daughter has now decided to 'wear Diana's livery' for twelve months before marrying, and this gets rid of the Knights, but the truth is that she intends to marry Pericles, and he approves. Among other accomplishments, Pericles turns out to be a fine musician, and a brief series of tests prove him brave, honourable and chaste:

> It pleaseth me so well that I will see you wed;
> And then, with what haste you can, get you to bed.

That is the end of the act. Gower opens the next by reporting that 'Hymen hath brought the bride to bed, Where, by the loss of maidenhead A babe is moulded.' Pericles leaves with his wife to be King of Tyre, first in dumb-show then in Gower's spirited narrative. They run into a storm in which their ship dives up and down like a duck. As the first scene opens, the child, a daughter, is born in the storm: 'a more blusterous birth had never babe.' The Queen has died and the sailors, rough and superstitious but brave and not unkindly men, insist she must be thrown overboard. Pericles addresses her in one of the most obviously and at the same time subtly beautiful speeches in Shakespeare's works. One suddenly sees that this is the beginning of the centre of his story, which he takes deadly seriously, however blurred he may leave the outer edges. It corresponds to the curse in *Timon* and the storm in *Lear*:

> A terrible childbed hast thou had, my dear;
> No light, no fire. Th' unfriendly elements
> Forgot thee utterly; nor have I time
> To give thee hallow'd to thy grave, but straight
> Must cast thee, scarcely coffin'd, in the ooze;
> Where, for a monument upon thy bones,
> And aye-remaining lamps, the belching whale
> And humming water must o'erwhelm thy corpse,
> Lying with simple shells. O Lychorida,
> Bid Nestor bring me spices, ink and paper. . . .

The entire speech is fourteen lines, but with it Shakespeare has broken open a vein of poetry that he follows. The second scene of act 3 introduces Cerimon at Ephesus and his 'secret art' of 'blest infusions That dwell in vegetives, in metals, stones . . .'. Here the Queen's coffin is washed up with a letter in rhyming verse from Pericles. Cerimon has 'heard of an Egyptian That had nine hours lien dead' and was brought back to life. With music and mysterious applications he achieves the Queen's return to life, something close to the heart of romance as of Christianity, a bodily resurrection of the dead. The words of this scene are not many, but they are as thrilling as its enactment. Meanwhile Pericles names his child Marina and leaves her to be nursed at Tarsus; he departs grieving. In Ephesus his Queen becomes a nun.

Gower introduces act 4 with a charming tale of Marina's education, and a new dramatic development; the Queen of Tarsus envies her and hires a murderer, because she overshadows the Queen's own daughter Philoten:

> Be't when she weav'd the sleided silk
> With fingers long, small, white as milk;
> Or when she would with sharp needle wound
> The cambric, which she made more sound
> By hurting it; or when to th' lute
> She sung, and made the night-bird mute,
> That still records with moan. . . .

They find Marina sad by the seashore, picking flowers for her nurse's grave, remembering her mother and the storm. The murder misfires but she is carried off by 'the great pirate Valdes' and taken to Mytilene to a brothel. This involves a comic low-life scene: 'I warrant you, mistress, thunder shall not so awake the beds of eels as my giving out her beauty stir up the lewdly inclined.' At Tarsus they pretend Marina is dead and build her a monument. Gower appears before it (act 4, scene iv) to explain Pericles returning to find her, with a dumb-show of his passionate sorrow. Gower reads us Marina's epitaph, how the sea will for ever 'Make raging battery upon shores of flint'. But Marina in her brothel converts all the customers, so the Pandar, the Bawd and their servant are desperate. 'She's able to freeze the god Priapus, and undo a whole generation.' She escapes to a decent house where she seems to live by arts:

> She sings like one immortal, and she dances
> As goddess-like to her admired lays;
> Deep clerks she dumbs; and with her needle composes
> Nature's own shape of bud, bird, branch, or berry,
> That even her art sisters the natural roses. . . .

There is no English Elizabethan art more expressive of innocence and intense beauty than women's work: nor is there any pure hero in Shakespeare in the sense that Marina is a pure heroine.

Gower introducing act 5 brings Pericles mad with sorrow to Mytilene in a ship draped in black. In other versions he rages, but Shakespeare makes him dumb with grief. Marina is found with her fellow maids in 'The leafy shelter that abuts against The island's side'. She cures him by singing, but the words of the song are unrecorded. They recognize each other at last; Pericles hears heavenly music and then sleeps. Diana appears to him in a vision and summons him to her temple in Ephesus. There, of course, he rediscovers his wife, who is High Priestess. Gower intervenes again (act 5, scene ii):

> In feather'd briefness sails are fill'd,
> And wishes fall out as they're will'd.

The scene of final resolution sustains the level of the curing of Pericles and the revival of his Queen. Cerimon gives the explanations. To him Pericles says 'Reverend sir, The gods can have no mortal officer More like a god than you.' The Queen hears that her father has died ('Heavens make a star of him!'), so she and Pericles go to reign in Pentapolis, leaving Marina and her host to reign in Tyre. Gower moralizes in an Epilogue, but its emphasis is heavier than the play's has been. Indeed, he is a foil to the play, as well as an excuse for its simplicity and romance quality. One may well consider what difference a Gower-like chorus by, let us say, Plutarch would have made to *Timon of Athens*. The differences are very instructive.

* * *

301

In 1609, plague closed the theatres yet again. With or (as I believe) without Shakespeare's direct co-operation, the Sonnets were registered on 20 May by Thomas Thorpe as 'a Booke called Shakespeares *sonnettes*'. Edward Alleyn bought a copy for fivepence on 19 June. Few copies survive, and only twelve of the Sonnets circulated in manuscripts that survive. The first reprint (1640) has an interest of its own, and so have the tributes that were printed with it, but it was bowdlerized to conceal homosexuality, and was incomplete and disarranged. Shakespeare's arrangement was never quite understood since his own day until Katherine Duncan-Jones published her article, 'Was the 1609 *Shakespeare's Sonnets* really unauthorized?' in the *Review of English Studies* in 1983. Malone had noticed in the eighteenth century that Daniel's sonnets were Shakespeare's model, but not the implication of so studied an arrangement that Shakespeare must have been as it were his own editor. What Thomas Thorpe plundered in fact was not a miscellaneous mass of poems but a precisely designed book. It was not reprinted in the poet's lifetime, and no echo of its publication has come down to us beyond Alleyn's diary and those of the manuscript miscellanies containing stray Shakespeare sonnets which derive from the printed text, as most of them (though not all) certainly do. The first authentic reprint was in 1711, from a copy of the original edition that belonged to Congreve.

It is possible that Shakespeare's being out of London was a precondition for the publication of his Sonnets. Thomas Thorpe had an interest in Shakespeare's circle all the same, and if no one else objected, it is hard to conceive that the poet was other than glad to see them launched on their voyage to immortal fame. Thorpe had published Marlowe posthumously, but also plays and masques by Jonson, Chapman and Marston, including a beautiful *Sejanus* (1605), with Jonson's elaborate notes. One must take into account that the famous 'Mr. W.H.' may be a deliberate subterfuge intended to keep the public guessing, as indeed it has done. The dedication is the one thin piece of evidence we have that Shakespeare himself had nothing to do with the publication of his Sonnets, or that he wished to appear to have nothing to do with it. We were not meant to know more.

His name was valuable. In January of the same year *Troilus and Cressida* was registered and printed as 'Written by William Shakespeare', and 'acted by the King's Majesty's servants at the Globe'. It had been registered before by another printer in 1603, but stopped until 'he hath gotten sufficient authority for it'. Now it was reissued twice in one year, with the second issue scrapping the reference to performance and claiming in a facetious, anonymous preface that it was 'a new play, never staled with the stage', and that 'the grand possessors' would not have been willing to see it printed. The inference is clear that this was a stolen or a private manuscript. In 1612, Jaggard reprinted his *Passionate Pilgrim* with two long poems of Thomas Heywood's which he stole without acknowledgement.

Heywood protested in his *Apology for Actors* in the same year: 'But as I must acknowledge my lines not worthy his patronage, under whom he hath published them, so the author I know much offended with Mr. Jaggard, that (altogether unknown to him) presumed to make bold with his name.' A reissue has survived in a single copy in the Bodleian Library, with a new title-page that leaves out the name of Shakespeare, so it seems that the poet could, when he chose, make an effective protest.

The troubles of success began to dog Shakespeare. Since August 1608 he had been one of the seven 'housekeepers' of the Blackfriars theatre, with the two Burbages, the otherwise unknown Thomas Evans, Heminges, Condell and Sly. Each of them paid £5 14s 4d a year towards a rent of £40. But Sly died in the same month, so Shakespeare's share became one of six. Twenty years after his death the Blackfriars shares had become nearly twice as valuable as the Globe shares, but that may not have been so in 1609. In 1636 a sixth share at Blackfriars would have been worth £120, and a sixth at the Globe £66 13s 4d.

As a tithe-holder at Stratford, Shakespeare petitioned the Lord Chancellor Lord Ellesmere, probably early in 1609. The tithe fields owed a rent of £27 13s 4d a year to the Barker family, but this had to be gathered from forty-three people. Shakespeare had about an eighth, which cost him £5 a year. The Combes were supposed to pay the same for the other half of the bit of land he held; Thomas Greene, his cousin, had a right of succession to the Combe holding, which was due to be his in 1613. But the Combes were refusing to pay their share of rent, many others had made no agreement about how much they ought to pay, and Lord Carewe of Clopton was trying to persuade everyone to refuse to pay anything.

Shakespeare, Thomas Greene and Richard Lane petitioned for a settlement, their petition being a mighty complex document, directed chiefly against Lord Carewe. The business seems to have ended happily, at least with William Combe, who agreed to pay what he thought was acceptable: £5 for his half, and 6s 8d for other bits and pieces. This affair brings theatrical and agricultural investment into an interesting contrast, and it underlines the complexity of landholding and tenancy arrangements. In 1610 Shakespeare confirmed his title to the 107 acres and common pasture rights he had bought from the Combes in 1602 for £320, and to twenty acres of pasture, which came either in place of the common rights or in addition. This new agreement cost him £100.

Beaumont and Fletcher's *Philaster* was their first successful play, a heavy-handed imitation of Shakespeare's style, including that of *Cymbeline*. John Davies mentioned *Philaster* in a book registered in October 1610, Simon Forman saw *Cymbeline* at the Globe in summer of 1611, and in several ways *Cymbeline* elaborates and improves on *Pericles*. But something that happened outside the playhouse confirms a date in 1610 for its first production. On 4 June of that year Prince Henry, who was born in 1594 and became Duke of Cornwall in 1603 at his father's accession, was created Prince of Wales on reaching the age of sixteen. *Cymbeline* is about two princes in Wales, and I am certain that it was intended to allude to Prince Henry and Prince Charles, and that its first audience would have understood it to do so. The landing at Milford Haven is another obvious dynastic tribute.

The Court of the Prince of Wales and his patronage were of great importance between 1610 and his early death in 1612. That glittering and short-lived glory has attracted historians, but the particular connection with Shakespeare seems to have gone unnoticed. It is not impossible that the Prince as a patron may have drawn Shakespeare into his series of romance comedies, though I doubt that. One would expect both royal and princely taste to be more closely expressed in the Court masques.

Cymbeline is deliberately naive in construction, without the excuse of ancient Gower. Its plot is an amalgam of different bits of Holinshed, the *Decameron*, scraps of minor poets, and old Shakespearean themes and devices. It contains a strange, original stage machine involving the funniest stage direction in Shakespeare: '*Jupiter descends in thunder and lightning, sitting upon an eagle. He throws a thunderbolt. The Ghosts fall on their knees.*' Doctor Johnson is also at his funniest about this play:

> To remark the folly of the fiction, the absurdity of the conduct, the confusion of the names, and manners of different times, and the impossibility of the events in any system of life, were to waste criticism upon unresisting imbecility, upon faults too evident for detection, and too gross for aggravation.

Even Professor Raleigh in 1907 wrote 'For many years Shakespeare took upon himself the burden of the human race, and struggled in thought under the oppression of sorrows not his own. That he turned at last to happier scenes, and wrote the Romances, is evidence, it may be said, that his grip on the hard facts of life was loosened by fatigue, and that he sought refreshment in irresponsible play.' Some scholars have asserted on absolutely no evidence that Shakespeare's plot was invented for him by an older and sillier dramatist. But the basis of sound criticism of *Cymbeline* is that he sought out his materials deliberately and that they released fresh energies in him as a poet. A. L. Rowse sees the point, though he thinks it 'a tired man's play'. That impression arises from its minor confusions; it was probably printed at the end of the Folio from a scribal copy, imperfect in itself and never corrected for use as a 'prompt book' in the theatre. Rowse writes, 'It must be admitted that the master pulled it off, with all his old virtuosity drawing an improbable number of threads together at the end.'

Crazy old Simon Forman died in September 1611, so he never saw *Cymbeline* in print, and his record of it derives from performance, but he followed the wild interweavings of the plot better than was usual with him.

> ... and in the end how he came with the Romans into England and was taken prisoner and after revealed to Imogen, Who had turned herself into man's apparrel and fled to meet her love at Milford Haven, and chanced to fall on the cave in the woods where her two brothers were and how by eating a sleeping Dram they thought she had been dead and layed her in the woods and the body of Cloten by her in her love's apparrel that he left behind him and how she was found by Lucius etc.

One has known undergraduates write less knowledgeable accounts of Shakespeare plays, even the ones with simple, quasilinear plots. Johnson, in his powerful *Preface*, the best piece of Shakespeare criticism ever written, I suppose, suggests, 'The plots are so loosely formed, that a very slight consideration may improve them, and so carelessly pursued, that he seems not always fully to comprehend his own design.' That is because the plot of plays like *Cymbeline* is a light construction intended to carry something more important, as the plot of *Pericles* does. But it is deliberately and very ingeniously constructed all the same. It looks naive but it is not simple, and in this it reflects a recurrent taste of Shakespeare's in poetry, which permits verse like 'Fear no more the heat o' the sun'.

Cymbeline owes his name to Cunobelinus of Camelodunum (Colchester) who died in old age between AD 40 and 53, a King who had sought the alliance of Augustus and recognized his supremacy. The expansion of his power and the aggressive intrigues of his sons provoked the Roman invasion of Britain, but the old man died before that dire event took place. Shakespeare will have known something, though probably not much, about this since his schooldays. To the British it remained a romantic and fascinating story, though the nineteenth-century classical scholar Mommsen, in his *Provinces of the Roman Empire*, confined it more or less to a couple of footnotes, and it is hard now to see *Cymbeline* through any eyes but Shakespeare's.

The explanation of past history he offers in his opening scene recalls *All's Well* or *Pericles* rather than Tacitus or Suetonius; it is only the names that have a thrilling and familiar ring. The young man Posthumus, exiled for winning the affections of Cymbeline's daughter, is the son of Sicilius, 'who did join his honour Against the Romans with Cassibelan', and whose two other sons 'Died with their swords in hand'. Cymbeline also had two sons, but they were stolen from the nursery twenty years ago. As Posthumus leaves, he gives the Princess Imogen a ring and a bracelet to keep for ever. She spurns the reproaches of her furious father:

> *Cymbeline*   What, art thou mad?
> *Imogen*   Almost, Sir: Heaven restore me! Would I were
> A neat-herd's daughter, and my Leonatus
> Our neighbour shepherd's son!

Cymbeline	Nay, let her languish
	A drop of blood a day, and, being aged,
	Die of this folly.

Cymbeline wants to match Imogen with the Queen's son, his own stepson Cloten, who is a clot: boastful, cowardly and profoundly ungentlemanly, despised by courtiers. But Imogen is as witty and extreme in wit as Mercutio, loving and charming, a more courtly if less magical Marina. Cloten's name recalls Philoten in *Pericles*.

In Rome an assortment of foreigners discuss Posthumus in prose. When Posthumus arrives, the sneering Italian Iachimo forces him to a bet that Imogen will be proved unfaithful. In England the Queen gathers poisonous flowers but the doctor deceives her (act 1, scene v): they 'Will stupefy and dull the sense awhile . . . To be more fresh, reviving'. The Queen gives this drug as a sovereign remedy to Pisanio, the servant and friend of Posthumus and Imogen.

Iachimo turns up in England, tries a frontal attack on Imogen's virtue which fails, and gets himself hidden in a chest in her bedroom where he steals her tokens (act 2, scene ii). The device is an old one, the scene a little like *The Rape of Lucrece*, but warmer. Drowsiness comes slowly. 'The crickets sing, and man's o'er-labour'd sense Repairs itself by rest,' as they do in Gower's description of the wedding night in *Pericles*, when:

> The cat, with eyne of burning coal,
> Now couches fore the mouse's hole;
> And crickets sing at the oven's mouth,
> Aye the blither for their drouth.

Iachimo on Imogen asleep is both erotic and repulsive, though in *Philaster* Beaumont and Fletcher steal from his speech without intending Shakespeare's double effect. Indeed, they stumble into a mouth-licking gruesomeness, where the speech in Shakespeare shows delicacy through a haze of lechery. 'Tell me gentle boy,' asks Philaster,

> Is she not parallelless? Is not her breath
> Sweet as Arabian winds when fruits are ripe?
> Are not her breasts two liquid Ivory balls?
> Is she not all a lasting Mine of joy?

In Shakespeare's version Imogen has a mole on her breast 'cinque-spotted, like the crimson drops I' th' bottom of a cowslip'. I dwell on this difference because the coarseness and worldly success of the imitation helps to set Shakespeare in the context of the 1600s, and because I wish to drive a last nail into the coffin of the old opinion that Beaumont and Fletcher were the fresh, original poets whose style refreshed the failing powers of old

Shakespeare. At no time of life would he have written that ludicrous line about liquid ivory balls. His metaphors are active where theirs are indulgent:

> How dearly they do't! 'Tis her breathing that
> Perfumes the chamber thus. The flame o' th' taper
> Bows toward her and would under-peep her lids
> To see th' enclosed lights. . . .

The idiotic Cloten hires music outside Imogen's window. The song is 'Hark, hark, the lark', and Robert Johnson's music for it has survived in a Bodleian manuscript. Johnson leaves out the two lines 'His steeds to water at those springs On chalic'd flow'rs that lies', probably in order to avoid the hissing of the letter 's'. It is a strange thought that by 1610 musicians had become too exquisite for Shakespeare. His own musical taste extended to the robust, but it embraced perfection, and he was content to have his verses set by a fine musician who cut them in order to do so.

'I have assail'd her with musics, but she vouchsafes no notice,' says Cloten to his mother. To the musicians he says, 'it is a vice in her ears which horse hairs and calves' guts, nor the voice of unpaved eunuch to boot, can never amend.' Roman messages threaten war, but in Rome Iachimo proves to Posthumus that he has been in Imogen's bedroom (act 2, scene iv). The young man rages in a long, horrified monologue of fifty-three lines, like Claudio in *Much Ado* (act 4, scene i): Shakespeare is still capable of satirical frenzy.

The third act prepares for war. Pisanio gets a letter from Posthumus telling him to murder Imogen. An intelligent reader could now work out the rest of the plot, but the question to ask is how Shakespeare will arrange it. He still has surprises in store: the lines and scenes that raise *Cymbeline* above the earlier comedies it so far resembles are still to come. Imogen and Pisanio are summoned to meet Posthumus at Milford Haven. Her innocent enthusiasm is exciting even to the mere reader.

In act 3, scene iii we are in the mountains at last, at the cave of Belarius and his two sons. This is said to be Hoyle's Mouth near Tenby, though I have been unable to discover why. Shakespeare's company played once in north Devon; did they sail across from Tenby? Belarius is the old courtier and we see him teaching his sons natural religion, 'how t' adore the heavens'. 'Hail, heaven!' 'Hail, heaven!' 'Now for our mountain sport.' They are a more vigorous version of the Forest of Arden, an image of that great Jacobean project, the golden age recovered.

The whole of this scene transposes the poetry of the play to an innocently heroic level which is Imogen's natural atmosphere. Pisanio and Imogen are close by the cave when Pisanio shows her the letter commanding murder. It must be underlined that in spite of unlikeliness her reaction to this betrayal is as humanly convincing as her lover's was to his. They then decide on disguise and prudent observation, so she dresses as a boy. Cloten catches Pisanio at Court and dresses as Posthumus to set out to find Imogen: 'Meet thee at Milford Haven! I forgot to ask him one thing; I'll remember 't anon. Even there, thou villain Posthumus, will I kill thee.... With that suit upon my back will I ravish her; first kill him.... foot her home again.... I'll be merry in my revenge.' This is pantomime wickedness and no more frightening than a children's film with 'Look out behind you.' The 'I forgot ...' indicates Shakespeare's view of his own plot clearly enough. Meanwhile Imogen as a boy discovers the cave, like Goldilocks and the bears. Belarius and his sons surprise her: 'Behold divineness No elder than a boy!'; '... Great men, That had a court no bigger than this cave ... Could not out-peer these twain.'

In act 4 the awful Cloten reaches Wales. The brothers leave Imogen in their cave and she takes the drug the Queen has given Pisanio. Belarius, observing the boys, remarks not for the first time that their royal nature shows itself; the boys observe Imogen's singing and her cookery. It is all charming and a joke. Cloten arrives, attacks one of the boys, and is killed, and the boy re-enters with his head (Cloten had threatened to stick theirs on London bridge): 'I have sent Cloten's clotpoll down the stream....' But Imogen now seems equally dead, so they lay her by the grave of their nurse, whom they think of as their mother. Beheaded Cloten is still dressed as Posthumus. The scene is an amazing conjunction of the bizarre, the comic and the extremely beautiful. Its climax is apparently the recitation of 'Fear no more', but not so. Imogen wakes with dead Cloten, and Lucius the Roman with his captains and soothsayer comes upon her, collapsed over what she took for the dead body of Posthumus, which they help her to bury.

Belarius tries in vain to keep his sons away from battle, 'to be still hot summer's tanlings and The shrinking slaves of winter' but they override him, and all three with noble and patriotic sentiments set out for war. Act 5 begins the war and ends it. Posthumus changes disguises and sides, Iachimo is publicly shamed, then Posthumus, Belarius and his sons rescue Cymbeline, and Posthumus gives a fiery account of the three strangers to a British lord (act 5, scene iii) in vigorously complex language. He then surrenders to the British in despair as a Roman. The resolution of all this comes to him as a sleeping prisoner in a vision, with Jupiter descending on an eagle lowered with strings as its climax.

This pleasing operatic moment gives delight and hurts not, like the climax of Handel's *Semele*. It can never have been awe-inspiring; it must always have been jolly. Thereby it furnishes a clue to how we are meant to take all the dramatic thrills and spills of the play. The archaic solemnity of Jupiter's language is a pastiche written with relish, like Gower's speeches in *Pericles*, but not a parody. The actors must keep straight faces, though the audience may smile:

He came in thunder; his celestial breath
Was sulphurous to smell; the holy eagle
Stoop'd, as to foot us. His ascension is
More sweet than our blest fields. His royal bird
Prunes the immortal wing, and cloys his beak,
As when his god is pleas'd.

When the eagle has gone, and these words are said, one almost begins to believe in it. But the mysterious book, the riddling oracle, and the comic gaolers are less convincing and for better as well as worse *Cymbeline* comes at this stage very close to a pantomime. The final explanations and reconciliations re-establish it as romantic dynastic drama. Posthumus knocks Imogen down as a pert page, but she recovers consciousness as if rising from the dead. This most preposterous of scenes, with its multiple overlapping and counter-moving explanations, Shakespeare takes perfectly seriously: 'Hang there like fruit, my soul, Till the tree die!' The climax is too complicated to recount: it is a symphony of dramatic hammer-blows of joy and peace, something that Shakespeare has never before attempted on such a scale. What one remembers most from this play is a sprinkling of phrases and images: Britain 'In a great pool a swan's nest', and the ruddock 'With charitable bill', and above all the character of Imogen, the atmosphere she carries with her.

In the summer of 1610, a touring party of the King's players was on the road again, though one may doubt whether Shakespeare was part of it. His interest centred more and more on Stratford. The places they played are instructive, though, and raise questions nonetheless fascinating for remaining unanswered. Did they do *Lear* at Dover? Was it *Henry IV* they did at Shrewsbury? They played at Oxford too, though perhaps not in term, since the arrangement was made with the Mayor, not with the university. They played also at Stafford and at Sudbury. These recorded productions were not, of course, the only ones; we know them because a few local records happen to survive here and there, listing the money paid to players. At Dover and Oxford and at Stafford they got ten shillings 'for a gratuity', in addition to entry money I think, though Chambers thinks 'gratuity' at Dover means the performance was not permitted. Whatever it does mean, at Sudbury they got only five shillings, which was worth about half a crown in 1590. One does not like to think that they made no further profit at all.

Simon Forman saw *The Winter's Tale* at the Globe in May 1611. It must have been new in May, since the dance of satyrs apparently derived from Jonson's Court masque *Oberon*, played on New Year's Day, and *The Winter's Tale* was performed at Court on 5 November. It was a more magical, less complex *Cymbeline*, increasing every strength of that play, but still not without a supply of fresh romantic incidents. At the end of act

3 it splits into two parts with Time as a chorus. The pastoral romance *Pandosto* by Greene, on which the play is based, has 'The Triumph of Time' as its subtitle. Shakespeare's title means an old story told for winter entertainment, a romantic old tale, but he also takes names from Sidney's *Arcadia*, and Autolycus from Ovid, where he appears as a thief and an illusionist. (Shakespeare corrects the wrong spelling of Autolycus by Marston in *The Countess of Derby's Entertainment* (1607).) It is curious that the soothsayer Philammon in *Cymbeline* is named after the twin brother of Ovid's Autolycus (*Metamorphoses* 11, 314–17). The statue coming alive in *The Winter's Tale* is Ovidian too, and so is the rape of Proserpine.

Shakespeare's view of the classics was not as tough and salty as Greene's. It is Shakespeare alone who returns Hermione to life and reconciles the King. He cuts out Greene's interest in incest, and makes the process of jealousy swifter, less lingering and smouldering. But he builds on Greene, particularly on certain words such as *Affection* and *Rigour*. Greene wrote *Pandosto* in a sweetly chiming prose style with much sententious charm, but less vigour and no sharpness:

> Devising thus with himself, he drew nigh to the place where Fawnia was keeping her sheep, who casting her eye aside and seeing such a mannerly shepherd, perfectly limbed and coming with so good a pace, she began to forget Dorastus and to favour this pretty shepherd, whom she thought she might both love and obtain. But as she was in these thoughts, she perceived then it was the young prince Dorastus. . . .

Still, this even-paced narrative is not to be underestimated: Shakespeare constantly borrowed phrases from it.

The principal event of the play really occurred in fourteenth-century Bohemia, where it generated popular ballads. The story probably came to England with the followers of Anne of Bohemia, who married Richard II in 1382. At the time Shakespeare selected it, the Princess Elizabeth was about to marry Frederick, the Elector Palatine, when she reached the age of sixteen in 1612. It has been suggested that *Cymbeline* and *The Winter's Tale* were both readapted for the winter of 1612 to 1613 for the celebrations interrupted by her brother Prince Henry's death. But the imperial prophecies in *Cymbeline* have their explanation in Henry's creation Prince of Wales, and *The Winter's Tale* was first performed when Elizabeth was fifteen. The only connection I can find in it to the Court celebrations of 1613 is a curious vogue for reanimated statues, which appear in Campion's *Lords' Masque*, and Beaumont's Gray's Inn masque.

Princess Elizabeth went away to Heidelberg. Her husband lost the Upper Palatinate in 1623, and died in exile in 1632; her brother Charles I of England was not powerful enough to enforce any claims of hers. She was first brought to London when she was twelve in 1608, and saw *The*

Winter's Tale in November of 1611 when she was fifteen; who knows whether she thought it was directed specially to her? I greatly doubt whether it really was, since it was not designed as a Court play. But it was played again at Court at the end of October 1612, when the marriage festivities were in full swing. The wedding was on 14 February 1613. On 20 May that year, John Heminges was paid for fourteen Court productions, at least six of them Shakespeare plays, including *The Winter's Tale* yet again.

The Winter's Tale was licensed by Sir George Buck, who became Master of the Revels in August 1610, though he was doing the work of that office for some time earlier. This fact although boring in itself has a crumb of interest, because the later Master Sir Henry Herbert granted a licence without fee in May 1623 for 'an old play called Winter's Tale formerly allowed of by Sir George Bucke . . . though the allowed book was missing'. This confirms that the precise text of any play as permitted was supposed to be the text printed, though in fact it might have perished or been altered in revivals. There appears to have been no quarto publication, so this play had to wait for the 1623 Folio edition. It had become a more important consideration to protect plays owned by the King's Servants from piracy than to present them to the public in printed form.

The play opens on diplomacy in Sicily with Bohemians, and an exchange of royal visits: 'we cannot with such magnificence, in so rare – I know not what to say. We will give you sleepy drinks, that your senses, unintelligent of our insufficiency, may. . . .' King Polixenes of Bohemia has been visiting Leontes of Sicily and his wife Hermione for nine months: 'Nine changes of the wat'ry star hath been The shepherd's note since we have left our throne. . . .' These words were perhaps meant to open the play, but the prose scene was added as a necessary introduction. Hermione treats her husband's friend with warm and intimate kindness. Polixenes and Leontes increase the attention we are already paying to innocence and to close relationship:

> We were as twinn'd lambs that did frisk i' th' sun
> And bleat the one at th' other. What we chang'd
> Was innocence for innocence; we knew not
> The doctrine of ill-doing. . . .

Leontes is stricken, without serious reason and with no suggestive Iago, by a fit of jealousy, convinced that his wife and friend are lovers. 'I have tremor cordis on me; my heart dances. . . .' His verse is as disturbed as his emotions. He takes up his child and speaks wildly to him. This play is about nature and growth, children, and the renewal of life, but its first act looks like another *Othello*. As a drama of human passions it is extremely strong and painful. It is possible that I have been dazzled by good productions, but from this point of view I feel it almost the strongest, the most disturbing and in the end the most satisfying of Shakespeare's plays. It moves swiftly into the opening tragedy, step by step, but the contrast of innocent charm is so well sustained that one can scarcely credit what one sees. Leontes is one of Shakespeare's most terrible creations, because there is no reason for his behaviour; it is self-generated and comes over him like a fever. As it masters him, he suffers worse. Both as poetry and as psychology his speeches are a tour de force.

The decent old courtier Camillo is ordered to poison Polixenes; he betrays the plot and helps him to escape. This single scene with its short introduction is an act. In the second Hermione and her ladies are playing with the young Prince. He will tell them a story: 'A sad tale's best for winter. I have one Of sprites and goblins. . . . There was a man . . . Dwelt by a churchyard – I will tell it softly; Yond crickets shall not hear it.' At this moment the King enters. He hears of the escape, has the boy taken from the Queen, and the Queen sent to prison. His courtier Antigonus reprimands him. Leontes has sent to Delphos (a common confusion of the island of Delos and Delphi, a mountain site wrongly thought in Western Europe to be undiscovered) to hear the truth from Apollo. Meanwhile Paulina, one of the Queen's ladies, goes to the prison to fetch Hermione's newborn baby meaning to move the King's heart with it. This is a catastrophic failure: the King is sleepless, furious, and by now nearly mad. He commands Antigonus to burn the child, then makes him swear to take it to some desert place and there abandon it.

In act 3 the messengers, who bear the Plutarchian names Cleomenes and Dion, report from Delphos. Shakespeare's account of it is touched with a sense of its reality, which is more than antiquarian romance. It could well derive from Plutarch, but Virgil (*Aeneid* 3, 91–2) at least added something and may have supplied everything. Venetian and even English sailors knew Delos, and Lord Arundel, whom Shakespeare knew, was soon to begin plundering there. Arundel made his first continental journey in 1613, to convey the Princess Elizabeth to Heidelberg, with Inigo Jones as one of his attendants.

> The climate's delicate, the air most sweet,
> Fertile the isle, the temple much surpassing
> The common praise it bears.
>   I shall report,
> For most it caught me, the celestial habits –
> Methinks I so should term them – and the reverence
> Of the grave wearers. O, the sacrifice!
> How ceremonious, solemn, and unearthly,
> It was i' th' off'ring!
>   But of all, the burst
> And the ear-deaf'ning voice o' th' oracle,
> Kin to Jove's thunder, so surpris'd my sense
> That I was nothing.

The antiquarian description is a splendidly fresh attempt to bring the thing to life, and an interesting improvement on the Jupiter in *Cymbeline*, and on Cymbeline's phrase 'And smoke the temple with our sacrifices', which conveys a murky excitement of a different kind. Leontes now formally charges his Queen, who speaks in her own defence like a Greek tragic heroine (except for the line 'The Emperor of Russia was my father'). The sealed oracle arrives at last and is opened. Leontes rejects it, the little Prince dies of horror, the Queen faints and Leontes repents. But Paulina tells him of the Queen Hermione's death: he vows to weep away his life.

Antigonus reaches 'The deserts of Bohemia' with the baby. He is comforted by a dream that names the child Perdita, but is then punished by being eaten by a bear. This remarkable event is observed by a shepherd, who will raise Perdita, and his boy or clown, two of the funniest comic intruders in all Shakespeare. The clown, on the subject of the ship (which wrecks) and the bear eating the nobleman, gets better every time one reads or hears him. We are at the end of act 3, but the heart of the play is not the sin of Leontes; it will be his repentance and the restoration by the natural and religious sanction of innocent life.

> *Clown*   I'll go see if the bear be gone from the gentleman, and how much he hath eaten. They are never curst but when they are hungry. If there be any of him left, I'll bury it.
> *Shepherd*   That's a good deed.

The beautiful resolution of the play in the last two acts opens with the comic senility of Time as chorus, excusing the gap in the action of sixteen years. Polixenes' son Florizel has fallen in love with the Shepherd's daughter, the secret Princess Perdita. Polixenes, with Camillo now his servant, plans to investigate this situation in disguise. The vagabond Autolycus, a disreputable cast-off servant, a stealer of sheets left to dry on hedges, cheats the Shepherd's lad out of his money, singing invigorating and wicked lyrics before and after. As a pastoral this play is closer to Brecht than to Virgil; that is not without parallel on the Elizabethan stage. Shakespeare has worked all his life at perfecting his particular mixture of real and fantastical, the poetry and the humdrumness and comedy of country life, of which this play offers the extreme form. We see the rustics from many points of view at once, not least their own. Shakespeare loves them, and everything about them, even while he is laughing at them.

Florizel, Perdita and all the rest meet at a sheep-shearing feast of 843 lines (act 4, scene iv) which concludes the act. It is an extraordinary amalgam of jollity and events, and in the theatre perhaps the most exhilarating scene that even Shakespeare ever wrote. It is as swift as it is high-spirited, punctuated with dances, including the dance of the twelve satyrs left over from a Court masque, and some amazing flower-poetry and Ovidian poetry. 'Apprehend Nothing but jollity,' says Florizel:

> The gods themselves,
> Humbling their deities to love, have taken
> The shapes of beasts upon them: Jupiter
> Became a bull and bellow'd; the green Neptune
> A ram and bleated; and the fire-rob'd god,
> Golden Apollo, a poor humble swain,   `
> As I seem now. Their transformations
> Were never for a piece of beauty rarer. . . .

The Shepherd is homelier, but more convincing. His memory of his dead wife's behaviour gives a ground of reality that sets off everything to follow:

> Fie, daughter! When my old wife liv'd, upon
> This day she was both pantler, butler, cook,
> Both dame and servant, welcom'd all; serv'd all;
> Would sing her song and dance her turn; now here
> At upper end o' th' table, now i' th' middle;
> On his shoulder, and his; her face o' fire
> With labour, and the thing she took to quench it
> She would to each one sip.

Perdita argues with disguised Polixenes, preferring simple flowers that are close to nature above hybrids and streaked, bastard garden flowers. This passage is emblematic, but at the same time its particularity of flowers and precision of season make it extremely vivid and earthy. From those she moves into her famous praises of the flowers of spring, almost too famous to quote but never too familiar to look as fresh as the day they were written, and in their context distinctly erotic. She wants to strew them over Florizel: 'What, like a corpse?' 'No; like a bank for love to lie and play on.' As I have said, the vividness of Shakespeare's daffodils, and of his rather scanty but vivid range of flowers throughout his life, curiously parallels the work of Jacques le Moyne de Morgues as a painter; the same mixture of delighted freedom, emblematic formality and precise observation underlies them both. Shepherds and shepherdesses dance, the old discuss the young, Autolycus makes his riotous entrance and exit:

> Master, there is three carters, three shepherds, three neat-herds, three swineherds, that have made themselves all men of hair; they call themselves Saltiers, and they have a dance which the wenches say is a gallimaufry of gambols. . . . One three of them, by their own report, sir, hath danc'd before the King. . . .

As a mixture of tones all in some sense but all in different senses pastoral, this scene is as carefully contrived as the mad scene in *Lear*. Its music is closer to popular than usual, and pastoral only with a difference:

314

the character of Autolycus may owe a lot to the songs he adapts. The flowers here rework and outdo the flower language in *Hamlet*, the old Shepherd is allowed blank verse because it suits his dignity, but clowns make their presence felt at every level: poor simple Mopsa contrasts with the Shepherd's lad, both contrast with Autolycus. Florizel proposes, the Shepherd agrees, and suddenly Polixenes reveals himself, like the thunderstorm in Beethoven's Pastoral Symphony. Camillo advises the young couple to flee to Leontes in Sicily, while he works on Polixenes:

> A course more promising
> Than a wild dedication of yourselves
> To unpath'd waters, undream'd shores. . . .

They exchange clothes with Autolycus in order to get away. Autolycus then entangles the Shepherd and his lad in a new intrigue of his own, so that everyone can meet again in the last act. It is a short act, and most of it is spent in the usual explanations running counter to the truth until they are all combed out smoothly, most of which we hear reported in prose: 'Such a deal of wonder is broken out within this hour that ballad-makers cannot be able to express it.' The old Shepherd stands by 'like a weather-bitten conduit of many kings' reigns'. He and his son are elevated to the rank of gentlemen, which they carry off with wonderfully comic dignity. The most extraordinary moment in the entire play is that in which Paulina unveils Hermione's statue (by Giulio Romano!) and it comes to life. The scene at its climax is nearly silent.

This ought, when one states it so baldly, to be the ludicrous extremity of romance, but nothing in all Shakespeare works better in the theatre. Hermione speaks just a few words to Perdita. Only Perdita can distract her from her long and wordless embrace with Leontes. If the same actor plays Hermione in the first half of the play and Perdita in the second, that would be part of the reason, but it is also true that where no words are adequate Shakespeare uses none. To have contrived such a climax after the explanations and other resolutions are over was a theatrical masterstroke.

My only reason for treating *Henry VIII* next, where it breaks the continuity of the comedies, is that *The Tempest* was conceived as a final statement, while *Henry VIII* was an exceptional commission, so I prefer to leave *The Tempest* its dignity of the final position.

The production of Shakespeare's last plays clusters around the great London events of 1612–13. The demand for entertainment created by the royal marriage put an enormous strain on the King's Servants. The marriage contract was signed in May 1612, and by 10 February 1613 the arrangement of mock battles and fireworks on the Thames had already cost £6000, that is, the equivalent of two or three noblemen's entire estates, a figure that today would run into millions. The Inns of Court alone had spent more than £4000 on two masques. It was evidently under these circumstances that Shakespeare wrote a history play, for the first time since *Henry V* in 1599. *Henry VIII* stands alone in many ways, and it also poses an interesting historical problem. Under Elizabeth, the subject would have been dangerous and Shakespeare's treatment of it impossible. The interesting question is whose point of view does it represent? It adapts its historical sources very freely, and deals boldly with royal and noble characters. It looks like a suggested or a commissioned play, but commissioned by whom? The likeliest answer is the Earl of Arundel.

When Elizabeth came to the throne there was only one duke left alive: Norfolk, whom she beheaded in 1572, because he was mentioned as a possible suitor for the Queen of Scots. Thomas Howard, Earl of Arundel (b.1585), was his grandson. The sons of Dukes of Norfolk were normally Earls of Surrey, but our Thomas Howard's father, Philip, had inherited the title of Arundel through his mother. It made him and Thomas in turn the premier earls of England, but the dukedom died with the beheaded grandfather; Philip died in the Tower in 1595 as a Catholic martyr.

Thomas Howard, Earl of Arundel, was eighteen when James I came to the throne. He became an extremely rich man, and created the first great English collection of classical antiquities; outside the royal family he was the greatest patron of his day. It was he who paid for the magnificent monument of the poet Henry Howard, Earl of Surrey, which is at Framlingham. Late-built monuments like this seem to begin with James I's to Mary Queen of Scots in Westminster Abbey. Surrey was executed in 1548; his father escaped the same fate by twenty-four hours, because of the opportune death of Henry VIII. The Earl of Arundel's obsession was the restoration of the rights and titles of his family. He did achieve the hereditary office of Earl Marshal, which gave him a measure of control over all precedence, heraldry and nobility, but the ultimate prize was the dukedom, which eluded him. There being at the time no dukes, earls began to assume ducal coronets; Robert Cecil was the first, but today it has become normal practice. The view of politics and personalities taken in Shakespeare's *Henry VIII* seems to represent the hindsight of Lord Arundel, and his ancestors are singled out for respect in the play.

It should also be noted that Arundel's dead grandfather's brother, the Earl of Northampton (1540–1614), was still alive and powerful. The two brothers were sons of the Earl of Surrey buried at Framlingham. Surrey was a legendary figure whose amorous adventures attracted Nashe and Drayton; his beautiful poems were first published in 1557, ten years after his death, and I have the impression that they were an important influence on Shakespeare. The Earls of Suffolk and of Nottingham were Arundel's cousins; in 1606 he married the Earl of Shrewsbury's daughter, making the Earls of Pembroke and of Kent his brothers-in-law. He danced in Jonson's masque *Hymenaei* for the new Earl of Essex's marriage to his cousin, and seems to have belonged to the Court of Prince Henry. Clarendon calls him later in time 'the Image, and Representative of the Primitive Nobility, and Native Gravity of the Nobles, when they had been most Venerable'. He appears to have looked like a rich and sober Venetian businessman.

Shakespeare's *Henry VIII* was written about the same time as *The Tempest*, and certainly before June 1613, very likely before the royal marriage. It may have been written soon after May 1612, at the time of Henry More's Virginia expedition. It prophesies that James I was to found 'New Nations'. His strategy of one Protestant and one Catholic royal marriage to keep the peace in Europe meant that history had to be rewritten, and yet neither Henry nor Anne Boleyn might be blamed. Modern history soon interfered to alter the picture yet again, but *Henry VIII* is the play of a moment, Shakespeare's most political and most dated play. It seems to have had the title or subtitle *All Is True*. The heroine is Queen Katharine of Aragon.

It was first printed in the Folio, but the manuscript seems to have been lost in June 1613 in the fire at the Globe, and the play to have been reconstructed from the memories of actors. That would explain metrical anomalies which Tennyson attributed to Fletcher as a co-author, since they echo his characteristic faults. But they are not difficult to clean away, being mostly caused, as so often happens in Shakespeare's plays as we have them, by the substitution of more ceremonious titles than those he used. The actors cared more than he did for the proper naming of lords.

The prologue opens, 'I come no more to make you laugh.' This is not to be 'a merry bawdy play', 'A noise of targets', but a story of how soon 'mightiness meets misery'. The Epilogue takes up the same theme. Trumpets woke those who came to sleep; the City was not abused; only good women would have liked this play, 'For such a one we show'd 'em'. Dr Johnson thought Jonson supplied these bits; they are mechanical enough for him, but good enough for Shakespeare. If any other poet than Shakespeare worked on *Henry VIII*, then he did so in revision of the reconstructed text after the fire. One must not underestimate the creative powers of actors to supply pastiche. Robert Armin's imitation of *Cymbeline* in *The Valiant Welshmen* is a sufficient example to establish the level at which they would do it.

Henry VIII opens with Norfolk's thrilling description of royal festivities at the Field of the Cloth of Gold: masques, dwarfish pages like 'cherubins, all gilt', men like diamond mines 'made Britain India', such tournaments 'That Bevis was believ'd'. This introduces Buckingham's quarrel with Wolsey; by the end of scene i Buckingham goes to the Tower. The King judges this in scene ii, with an interesting analysis of the fate of the poor and the effect of taxes from Norfolk, who speaks in strong terms. The King abuses Wolsey with the solid country image of hacking a tree until 'The air will drink the sap'.

I feel forced to interject that in historical fact things were otherwise: the poor of the suburban village where I was born, Ruislip in Middlesex, appealed successfully to Wolsey against the enclosure of their fields for sheep-farming, which he forbade, for fear they should be turned out of their cottages 'and the praise of God be lost'.

By the end of act 1 Henry, at a masked party given by Wolsey, has fallen for Anne Boleyn (called Bullen in the play). The whole act is spirited; by this time of life Shakespeare knows enough about upper-class entertainments, and about the European diplomacy of his own day, to mirror both with elegance and conviction.

Act 2 gives Buckingham his speech as a doomed nobleman:

> Go with me like good angels to my end;
> And as the long divorce of steel falls on me
> Make of your prayers one sweet sacrifice,
> And lift my soul to heaven.

But there is something formal about it: he is only a symbol, a nobleman rises only to fall. Many suppressed thoughts Shakespeare must have kept to himself under Elizabeth peep into the open in this play. Anne Bullen has a scene with an old lady of admirable earthiness in which she disclaims royal ambition. The old lady tells her she would suffer crowning if the truth were told: 'I myself Would for Carnarvonshire. . . .' Anne speaks decently enough, but the old lady sets the tone in which the audience is thinking.

The third act shows Katharine as distressed heroine with the sad music of *Orpheus with his lute*. Shakespeare gives her fine speeches not in the chronicles, but there is something a little cold about these royal intrigues of which we know the outcome; he does not feel free enough to create character and detail as he did in his real tragedies. She is:

> Shipwreck'd upon a kingdom, where no pity,
> No friends, no hope; no kindred weep for me;
> Almost no grave allow'd me. Like the lily,
> That once was mistress of the field, and flourish'd,
> I'll hang my head and perish.

So far the play is a waterfall of lamentations: first Buckingham, now the Queen, and in the same act Wolsey, whose last speeches are the most powerful in the play. In them one pities not him personally but the whole process of inevitable falls and tragedies that Tudor monarchy engendered, yet one does pity and admire him also for his freedom and dignity in expressing that.

We are now at the same point as we were at the opening of act 4 of *The Winter's Tale*. How can Shakespeare so enliven his last two acts as to produce a triumph? He begins with a coronation. Then Katharine hears of Wolsey's death and achievements, including Christ Church at Oxford, and sees a vision of spirits in white indicating heaven. Her dying speeches express kindness to the King. So the fourth act has returned, in spite of the coronation, to the solemn pavane of the third. In the fifth Henry tests the bishops made famous by their roles in the Reformation: 'He has strangled his language in his tears.' Elizabeth is born. The King overrides his Council to save his good Bishop from the machinations of his enemies. The play ends in the child Elizabeth's baptism, with one of Shakespeare's best crowd scenes. It is the crowd and the porter in my view that redeem and in its last moments enliven the play. The last scene of all is a beautiful and solemn prophecy by a saintly bishop of the future glories of England under Elizabeth and James.

Henry VIII is difficult to discuss because its bones are well articulated, but some of its treatments are perfunctory, so that it descends at times towards the condition of a pageant, yet it is carefully written, and if its scenes led better into and out of one another it would be a wonderful play. It may be that my personal affection for it is disproportionate; Katharine is moving, the attempt to portray sanctity is at least a fascinating failure, maybe even a success. Wolsey is the sketch of a mighty portrait, Anne is the beginnings of another, but the subject was too dangerous, and the same may be said of Henry. He is too lightly touched to dominate the play, and the attempt to make him a good king founders on the wish to show him warts and all. Butts, the good doctor, attracts one's interest for a second, but not much is made of him. The infant Elizabeth is no substitute for Marina or Perdita, though no doubt the early audience supplied feelings of their own, as people will to this day to films about the monarchy.

Shakespeare's was not the first play on its royal subject; Thomas Cromwell and Wolsey were treated as early as 1602, and Thomas More apparently earlier. In 1605 Heywood brought events down to Queen Elizabeth's coronation and the foundation of the Royal Exchange – a curious climax. In the same year Henry VIII was a character in a play by Samuel Rowley entitled *When you see me, You know me*. It is a strange irony that of Shakespeare's *Henry VIII* one should most vividly remember the audience, the crowd scene at the royal baptism, 'the youths that thunder at a playhouse and fight for bitten apples'. But to make the climax a baptism fits Shakespeare's mood after *Cymbeline*. He took the coronation as the prelude to such another tragedy as Buckingham's and Wolsey's and the Queen's. Anne's coronation was not a climax on which he could pause since he knew what became of her.

In his last plays the references to voyages and the sea increased. In 1609 John Donne was interested in a post with the new Virginia Company. Southampton had money in that, and so did many of Shakespeare's London acquaintance. The first expedition was disastrously mismanaged, and a new company, to which Donne preached an amazing sermon on 13 November 1622, had to be formed:

> It shall redeem many a wretch from the Laws of death, from the hands of the Executioner, upon whom, perchance a small fault, or perchance a first fault, or perchance a fault heartily and sincerely repented, perchance no fault, but malice, had otherwise cast a present and ignominious death. It shall sweep your streets, and wash your doors, from idle persons, and the children of idle persons, and employ them: and truly, if the whole country were but such a *Bridewell*, to force idle persons to work, it had a good use. But it is already, not only a *Spleen*, to drain the ill humours of the body, but a *Liver*, to breed good blood, already the employment breeds good Mariners. . . .

That is Donne, not Shakespeare, and 1622, not 1611 or 1612, but it is worth bearing in mind when one considers *The Tempest*.

There is a sense in which this play is pure fiction: the first and only attempt that Shakespeare ever made to make up a plot out of his head. But it uses conventions and hints from Italian popular comedy. The storm in Virgil's *Aeneid* is an influence, and so is Florio's translation of Montaigne, which appeared in 1603. The play was triggered off by the wreck of the *Sea Adventure* off Bermuda in July 1609, reported in England in 1610. One of the most brilliant of Leslie Hotson's contributions to Shakespeare studies is his demonstration of how Shakespeare knew about that. Thomas Russell had married Anne Digges, the rich widow of Thomas Digges (1545–95), the astronomer, mathematician and military and civil engineer, making Sir Dudley Digges (1583–1639) and Leonard (1588–1635) his sons-in-law. Shakespeare's friend Heminges was a witness at the marriage. Russell tried to buy Clopton House, selling his Chipping Campden estate in order to do so, but the sale fell through, and he settled at Alderminster near Stratford. Thomas Russell was five years younger than Shakespeare. Dudley did not move to Warwickshire, but he was knighted in 1607, MP from 1610, and in the end Master of the Rolls. He invested heavily in the Virginia Company, and the *Sea Adventure* was their flagship.

Dudley Digges and a certain William Strachey contributed some complimentary verses to Jonson's *Volpone* and *Sejanus*, and this same Strachey got the job of 'secretary in Virginia' that Donne wanted. The two first published accounts of the wreck of the *Sea Adventure* were Jourdan's *Discovery of the Bermudas* and an official account of the state of the colony, but this official version was largely based on a letter to a lady by William Strachey. The letter was not printed until 1625; it is an awe-inspiring thought that it might, had things gone otherwise, have been a letter from John Donne, but there is no doubt at all that Shakespeare drew on it in writing *The Tempest*.

Two months after Strachey's letter reached England, and two weeks after the official report was registered at Stationers' Hall, Sir Dudley Digges was at Alderminster, where he signed a financial document on 22 November 1610. Digges was mad on sea journeys. He helped to send his London fellow parishioner Hudson to his death, and to found the Northwest Passage Company; in all his marine enterprises William Leveson, one of the trustees of the Globe in 1599, and an old neighbour of the Digges family in Philip Lane, was a sharer. We know from the younger brother Leonard's verses about Shakespeare that the poet wrote his plays very swiftly. *The Tempest* may well have been his example, though in 1611 Leonard Digges was twenty-three, and he is thought to have gone to Spain in that year.

It is hard to weigh the influence of Italian comedy, which was traditionally a matter of plots from a repertory of typical situations improvised together by actors of well-known traditional characters: the actors had worked together a long time and knew their routines, and a new narrative was easily accommodated. Verse of course could easily be improvised; the improvised cross-talk between audience and actors at the Zakynthos carnival in living memory was in faultless verse, and Zakynthos (Zante) was once steeped in Italian influence. From as much of Italian popular comedy as has been recorded in writing and can be studied, one discerns only elements and characters that had caught Shakespeare's eye – the magic island and the monster, for example – but the influence of humour and tone, hard as those are to discuss objectively, appear to me even more pervasive in *The Tempest* than has been said. And yet these are the merest sparks that set his imagination alight, the merest hints. They are not a repertory of his devices, and his verse is incomparably more powerful, his dramatic sense more highly charged.

The Tempest is his last play, and most of its means are simple, but if someone called it his greatest and most memorable work, I would be tempted not to disagree. What makes it so is its elements and then its conclusion, its abdication of magical powers and perfect manipulations, and the freedom of Ariel. Without natural religious magic, as I call it, Shakespeare had found the representation of the world and our life by dramatic art as comedy more and more intolerable. He had never attempted it without the suggestion of magic or an all-powerful good monarch since *Twelfth Night*. In *The Tempest* he yet again invented a completely new kind of play, but it was meant to be the last. I greatly doubt whether he had a hand in *The Two Noble Kinsmen* beyond the merest sketch, though his influence is in all the plays of Beaumont and Fletcher.

For many years I resisted the view that in *The Tempest* he says his goodbye to poetry. There seemed to be some fragments of evidence pointing in other directions; he bought property in London later; the burning of the Globe might have meant more. I hate the sentimental eagerness of old critics to see lines in his plays as the expression of his life.

But poetry always is the expression of one's life, and of the world, at some remove or other. No one is more delighted than I am to find the flowers of his rustic youth growing in Ovid or in Gerard's *Herball*, or his patriotic sentiments in the dustiest chronicles, but because the dates coincide I am bound to acknowledge that in *King John* he remembers his own son's death, and that at the end of *The Tempest* he means these to be the last words he will ever write: he is Prospero and he abdicates, but he believes something in him is Ariel who is set free.

Frank Kermode calls *The Tempest* 'a pastoral drama . . . concerned with the opposition of Nature and Art . . . Prospero's Art and Caliban's Nature. Caliban is the core of the play.' If this is true, it constitutes an interesting link with *The Winter's Tale* and with *Cymbeline*. No doubt if one takes the word 'pastoral' in the broad sense Kermode gives it, his analysis is rather exact, and it has the strength of giving Caliban his due at last. Caliban is both delightful and intriguing; he is the limit to Prospero's moral power, and wicked as he may be, Shakespeare likes him as he never liked Cloten. He embodies Shakespeare's thoughts and some of Montaigne's about colonialism. The similarity of his name to Cannibal is not by chance, but in general I think Kermode in his able introduction to the Arden edition paints him too damningly.

I do not think Shakespeare knew or cared much about 'nature divorced from grace, or the senses without the mind'. Thank God he was not a theologian, certainly not a Puritan Christian one. Indeed, the powerful belief in great creating (and restoring) nature in his last plays is remarkable for its absence of Christian dogma. As for ungraced nature, in one of his last Christian utterances, 'Why, all the souls that were, were forfeit once' (*Measure for Measure*, act 2, scene ii). But there is no doubt that some of the moralizing, as well as some of the physical details of William Strachey's letter and the two pamphlets, lingered in Shakespeare's mind when he came to write. Montaigne's essay 'Of Cannibals' is of greater importance than any of this.

I give Montaigne more weight in Shakespeare's mind than Kermode does; it fits the view of happy nature and corrupting civilization in all his late plays, but this is dramatic art, and Shakespeare is Shakespeare, so both views are present, Montaigne's and its opposite. As for 'art' and 'Nature' and 'Pastoral', the art contrasted with nature in *The Tempest* is itself the intuition and the perception of nature; the only Christian prayers are Caliban's 'I'll seek for grace' and Prospero's call for mercy in the Epilogue.

The tempest in *The Tempest*, with its realistic commotion and its undertones of providential magic, started to blow in *Pericles*, and in a sense it had revived in *The Winter's Tale*, the bear that ate Antigonus being its terrestrial form. In *The Tempest* it seems at first as terrible, and more real, with thunder noises and wet sailors and the splitting of the ship. In Miranda's description the shipwreck is still dramatic, but words are calmer than enactment, and the eyes of compassion are the first hint of human divinity. Prospero transforms the tempest into silence and providential beauty. His own sad story 'In the dark backward and abysm of time' intertwines with it. Ariel, in his report, makes it magical. In his lyrics it becomes masque-like, the vision of a pantomime transformation scene.

But there is much more to this long scene. It not only reveals an entire romantic story in detail, made painless in the telling and effectively dramatic by interchanges of person, but it reveals Prospero at his full height, the relationships and power structure of the island, and the quality of the characters, Miranda, Ariel, Caliban and the Prince. Prospero, the ruined King, was too much devoted to liberal arts and the 'secret studies' that in Elizabethan England so often accompanied them. His wicked brother Antonio grew powerful like the ivy that destroys a tree (a metaphor for old age in Latin poetry, but here a typically Shakespearean transformation of politics to intimate relationship). 'Me, poor man – my library Was dukedom large enough': Prospero suffered his own emblematic storm of 'winds, whose pity, sighing back again, Did us but loving wrong'. Prospero's lines are fine and dignified, but the best and most lyrical poetry enters with Ariel.

Prospero himself is now touched with inhuman magic, and his account of the witch Sycorax, who sounds like a *sucubus*, and of the 'freckl'd whelp, hag-born' is as memorable as it is fantastical. Caliban outdoes him, even so. After this crescendo come Ariel's famous lyrics and the poetic diminuendo of Ferdinand and Miranda, beginning to fall in love. Shakespeare never wrote a better first act.

> *Caliban*   I must eat my dinner.
> This island's mine, by Sycorax my mother,
> Which thou tak'st from me. When thou camest first,
> Thou strok'st me and made much of me, wouldst give me
> Water with berries in't, and teach me how
> To name the bigger light, and how the less,
> That burn by day and night; and then I lov'd thee,
> And show'd thee all the qualities o' th' isle,
> The fresh springs, brine-pits, barren place and fertile.
> Curs'd be I that did so!

Caliban's sin, according to Prospero, was seeking 'to violate The honour of my child'.

> O ho, O ho! Would't had been done.
> Thou didst prevent me; I had peopl'd else
> This isle with Calibans.

I do not think Shakespeare would have given Caliban this amusing and sympathetic answer if he viewed him with moral horror. On the other hand, Caliban is not transformable into a civilized man. But he is equally not intended for a negro, or a Red Indian, or a slave; he is just a monster poor fellow, and an amiable one. He is capable of bad behaviour, but it is warm-blooded, where Prospero's fault is cruelty and the exercise of power. That is why he abdicates in the end, to become a gentle human king who has learned from his own and others' sufferings to be compassionate.

Caliban is an enjoyable curser, another sympathetic characteristic:

> You taught me language, and my profit on't
> Is, I know how to curse.

He provokes Prospero and Miranda to such bad temper that he seems to compel them into his own image. It would appear therefore that colonial corruption of manners is mutual. This observation appears in numerous letters about Virginia and the events there, written just a few years before Donne's sermon in 1622, just a year after his appointment as Dean of St Paul's. One should not be surprised to find it implicit in Shakespeare's *Tempest*. Some pointed and relevant letters have survived among the papers of Sir N. Rich.

In the second act we encounter the wrecked courtiers and their various imported attitudes to the island: 'I think he will carry this island home in his pocket, and give it his son for an apple.' 'And, sowing the kernels of it in the sea, bring forth more islands.' 'Ay.' Antonio the usurper mourns his son Ferdinand as dead; the others discuss the ideal commonwealth. As a philosopher, Shakespeare belongs to the light cavalry, but he is sharp and clear enough to be the cause of philosophy in others. In the second scene Caliban meets the unvirtuous comic sailors, whom he loves for their bottle of drink, and celebrates his freedom as their servant in a song: ''Ban, 'Ban, Ca – Caliban, Has a new master – Get a new man.' His catalogue of natural resources is even better and far earthier than before. One might maintain, though Shakespeare was surely not quite conscious of the fact, that of all Shakespeare's male characters Caliban alone is genuinely and by birth a great poet.

In the first scene of the third act Ferdinand and Miranda are deeply in love, but Prospero must delay the climax. The Prince as an enforced labourer and the Princess brought up in a cave without human acquaintance beyond her father make a charming couple. The suggestions of mildly incestuous affection should not be over-stressed, but they are present, as they might be in any folktale where relationships are familial. Meanwhile Ariel taunts the sailors to beat each other, and Caliban gleefully invents ways for them to murder Prospero:

> Remember
> First to possess his books; for without them
> He's but a sot, as I am, nor hath not
> One spirit to command; they all do hate him
> As rootedly as I. Burn but his books.

Ariel sees and mocks and reports all. Caliban is oddly innocent: just after his wickedest bit of plotting, Shakespeare gives him the perfect lines that begin 'Be not afeared. The isle is full of noises, Sounds and sweet airs, that give delight, and hurt not. Sometimes a thousand twangling instruments. . . .' Ariel threatens the wicked in severe terms:

> whose wraths to guard you from –
> Which here, in this most desolate isle, else falls
> Upon your heads – is nothing but heart's sorrow,
> And a clear life ensuing.

The third act has been a Morality Mystery: by the end of it, guilt and remorse are at work in the wicked King, who intends suicide, and in the two conspirators, who remain defiant. In the fourth act Ferdinand has passed his test and Prospero grants Miranda to him. Ariel is to 'bring the rabble' while Prospero presents an injunction to chastity and then a masque to the young lovers. In this play Shakespeare develops very fully his recent technique of the long scene planned like music, as if it were an act, and this act does in fact consist of one long scene; so does act 5. The resolution and conclusion of the play begin here with the masque: 'Some vanity of mine art; it is my promise, And they expect it from me.'

The masque begins in some ways more stiffly than the masque in *A Midsummer-Night's Dream*; its stiffness is neo-classical, but it enters deeply into the texture of *The Tempest*, and I think determines the quality of its conclusion. Iris addresses Ceres as goddess of 'creating Nature', but typically Shakespeare has roughened and sharpened the pastoral element with rustic and even technical words: 'Thy banks with pioned and twilled brims' are dykes fortified with branches; 'To make cold nymphs chaste crowns' is more traditional, but not overpretty. The dialogue of formal verses is beautiful, and expressive of refreshment and natural fertility, but it is the last lines of the masque, those that introduce human dancers, that take one's breath way:

> You sun-burnt sicklemen, of August weary,
> Come hither from the furrow, and be merry;
> Make holiday; your rye-straw hats put on,
> And these fresh nymphs encounter every one
> In country footing.

I think it is these lines, with their faint undertone of the end of a season, that suggest to Shakespeare the miraculous words of Prospero that conclude the masque and begin to conclude the play: from now on, it is really a monologue by Prospero punctuated by events and shows and acts of power, and ending in his abdication and the lyrical release of Ariel:

> You do look, my son, in a mov'd sort,
> As if you were dismay'd; be cheerful, sir.

Our revels now are ended. These our actors,
As I foretold you, were all spirits, and
Are melted into air, into thin air;
And, like the baseless fabric of this vision,
The cloud-capp'd towers, the gorgeous palaces,
The solemn temples, the great globe itself,
Yea, all which it inherit, shall dissolve,
And, like this insubstantial pageant faded,
Leave not a rack behind. We are such stuff
As dreams are made on; and our little life
Is rounded with a sleep.

Prospero must now achieve his own peace; Caliban and the drunks must be punished, though hardly worse than Falstaff in the *Merry Wives*; and meanwhile the audience needs comedy and diversity. The fifth act completes the cycle of punishments and restorations and reconciliation. It is perhaps all that is left of Christianity to Shakespeare: the forgiveness of sins and the resurrection of the dead. Prospero's speech of conjuration and of power ends in his abdication and the sound of solemn music. Its first sentence is of eighteen lines, strongly articulated with ebbs and flows and counter-currents of rhythm. One more sentence of abjuration ends it in eight. He then addresses the enchanted courtiers, first 'Holy Gonzalo, honourable man' with whom he weeps, then the others in turn. Ariel sings and dresses him as King.

The marriage of Ferdinand and Miranda is introduced as a wish of his brother the usurper, who believes his son Ferdinand and Prospero's daughter Miranda are both dead. If they should live, 'I wish Myself were mudded in that oozy bed Where my son lies.' Can Shakespeare have been thinking somewhere below the surface of his mind of Hamnet? Do the restored daughters and very close relationships of these plays allude subconsciously to Judith? She was now twenty-seven, and remained unmarried until she was thirty-two. The happy lovers are revealed as if in a vision, quietly playing chess together. The explanations that are introduced into this act are so magical as not to rob it of its transforming and mysterious quality, or of its climax. Caliban gets called 'this demi-devil . . . this thing of darkness' ('I shall be pinch'd to death'), but his only punishment is to tidy up the cave, and one must assume he inherits the island: 'I'll be wise hereafter, And seek for grace.' As for Ariel, 'to the elements Be free, and fare thou well!'

This is the most fantastical and visionary of Shakespeare's plays, stuffed full of shows and transformations and epiphanies of spirits, which we must take seriously, suspending disbelief however we may smile at the shows or catch one another's eyes here and there. Caliban is the most real part of the fiction, but he is also a figure of fantasy and of comedy, to whom human values do not quite apply in their usual direct way. He is Falstaff fantasized, and we love him for his childishness and because he is rejected. Prospero has personal problems: his restoration is the purging of his bitterness, the withering away of his power, and his resurrection not as a king (Ariel dresses him only in a hat and sword, not a crown and robes) but as a human being. When he gets home, 'Every third thought shall be my grave.'

The audience, by their applause, must release him from 'this bare island', which is the stage. His project was to give pleasure. His epilogue is in the metre of the inscription on Shakespeare's gravestone.

> Now I want
> Spirits to enforce, art to enchant;
> And my ending is despair
> Unless I be reliev'd by prayer,
> Which pierces so that it assaults
> Mercy itself, and frees all faults.
> As you from crimes would pardon'd be,
> Let your indulgence set me free.

· 11 ·

The End of a Life

We are able to follow Shakespeare a long way into his silence. A life does not end with a dramatic exit from the stage, or the perfect conclusion of a comedy or of a tragedy. We know that he retired to Stratford, but also that he had unfinished business in London. He was still a sharer in the company, and still at least in principle an actor. On 16 February 1613, 'Much expectation was made of a stage play to be acted in the Great Hall by the King's Players, where many hundred of people stood attending the same; but it lapsed contrary, for greater pleasures were preparing.' A masque was performed instead. The play that was postponed was either *The Tempest*, one of the plays performed later and paid £60 for in May, with an extra £20 from the King, or perhaps, as I suspect, *Henry VIII*. On 29 June that year, the Globe theatre burned to the ground. Sir Henry Wotton describes the catastrophe with disinterested cheerfulness, and two jejune ballads were written about it, one of which I have recorded in Appendix 10.

> Now, to let matters of state sleep, I will entertain you at the present with what has happened this week at the Bank's side. The King's Players had a new play, called *All Is True*, representing some principal pieces of the reign of Henry VIII, which was set forth with many extraordinary circumstances of pomp and majesty, even to the matting of the stage; the Knights of the Order with their Georges and garters, the Guards with their embroidered coats, and the like: sufficient in truth within a while to make greatness very familiar, if not ridiculous. Now, King Henry making a masque at the Cardinal Wolsey's house, and certain chambers being shot off at his entry, some of the paper, or other stuff, wherewith one of them was stopped, did light on the thatch, where being thought at first but an idle smoke, and their eyes more attentive to the show, it kindled inwardly, and ran round like a train, consuming within less than an hour the whole house to the very grounds. This was the fatal period of that virtuous fabric, wherein yet nothing did perish but wood and straw, and a few forsaken cloaks; only one man has his breeches set

on fire, that would perhaps have broiled him, if he had not by the benefit of a provident wit put it out with bottle ale.

Thomas Larkins, writing on the last day of June, records that 'the fire catched and fastened upon the thatch of the house, and there burned so furiously as it consumed the whole house, and all in less than two hours, the people having enough to do to save themselves.'

To Shakespeare it was a disaster, and the end of something. The sharers had to pay £50 or £60 each for the rebuilding, and we know that some years later Heminges and Condell, the editors of the Folio Shakespeare, held all the shares. Shakespeare's heirs show no record in their papers so far discovered of any transaction involving shares in the company, so it looks as if Shakespeare sold up his interest before his death, just as Marston had sold his share of the Blackfriars theatre and 'the apparel, properties, and play-books of the Children of the Queen's Revels' before 1610, probably by 1608. Naturally the company continued in existence, acting at Court and at Oxford, where this time the Vice-Chancellor paid them, and elsewhere.

Shakespeare was so famous that it is no longer worth collecting every reference to him: in 1607 and 1608, his *Hamlet* and *Richard II* were being played in ships at sea, 'which I [the captain] permit to keep my people from idleness and unlawful games, or sleep'. But after the excitements of 1613, he never wrote another play. On 4 February 1614, his brother Richard was buried at Stratford, but that does not seem to be the straw that broke his back. More likely it was the burning of the theatre. It is possible that when he wrote *The Tempest* he intended to retire, or it was in his mind to do so. That is my own view of what happened. But on 10 March 1613, at the beginning of the spring of the year that saw the Globe burn in early summer, he bought a house in London, at Blackfriars, near Puddle Wharf, from Henry Walker, 'citizen and minstrel', for £140. After his many changes of rented London rooms he came to rest in the Gatehouse of a medieval priory.

This was a carefully negotiated transaction, with trustees, a payment of £80, a mortgage of £60 to Mr Walker, and a complicated record of tenancy and ownership. John Heminges was a trustee; the house was rented to John Robinson, and left in 1616 to Susanna Hall and her male heirs, or failing her to Judith. Scholars now suppose that his theatrical income was something more than £200 a year, except in plague years, though Sir Sidney Lee reckoned it was £700. It is hard to see quite why he bought this London property, unless to live in it, and in that case it suits a London income of about £200. The letting of it fits the suspicion that he left London when the Globe was gone, but its physical position suggests that his principal interest had already been turned to the Blackfriars theatre, for which *The Tempest*, with its music and amazing devices, might well have been written. He was not driven out of business by the new theatrical style, the development of which was enfeebled by his absence, but he was close to fifty, and he was surely exhausted. We know that he was still working that spring, because at the end of March he made his heraldic emblem and motto for the Earl of Rutland. It was in June that silence fell.

People were still overwhelmed by Shakespeare's early poems, and of course by the plays:

> Whence needy new-composers borrow more
> Than Terence doth from Plautus and Menander

as Thomas Freeman wrote in 1614. At Stratford his life can be traced only through local business, through the affairs of his friends and the fortunes of his family. There is nothing abnormal except at the end. In 1611 his name was added in the margin of a list of seventy-one names, including John Hall's, of those who gave money 'towards the charge of prosecuting the Bill in parliament for the better Repair of the highways', which came before Parliament in April and June 1614. Alas it failed, and that so far as I know was Shakespeare's only intervention in national politics. He was a user of highroads, and a lifelong sufferer from their condition. It would be fair to call the highways a matter of local as well as national interest.

In July 1614, yet another great fire broke out in Stratford. Old John Combe died the next day, leaving Shakespeare £5 and the parish his expensive monument. In the Christmas accounts of the Chamberlain of Stratford for 1614, twenty pence was paid 'for one quart of sack and one quart of claret wine given to a preacher at the New Place'. That was a normal courtesy, and no doubt he was a normal preacher. Whether the fact that Shakespeare put him up at New Place indicates his own status as a gentleman, the size and status of his house or the theological views of his family, we are unable to determine. In any small town or big village today there are certain houses and people who might expect, let us say, to give lunch to a visiting preacher: who they would be depends on a number of social factors, including those I have mentioned. The claret and the sack for the preacher at New Place mean that Shakespeare would be expected to give a party for the man, much as people still do; it would mean he was considered socially sound by the parish. Much the same kind of local goodwill in Stratford would result from his supporting the highways repair bill in Parliament.

Enclosures of common land were very much more controversial, and in the case of the Welcombe enclosure one ambiguous phrase in the record throws weight on the question of Shakespeare's attitude to landowners who were his neighbours and to the dispossessed. In the particulars of 'ancient freeholders in the fields of Oldstratford and Welcombe', he is listed in September 1614 with '4 yard land, no common nor ground beyond Gospel bush, no ground in Sandfield, nor none in Slow hill field beyond Bishopton, nor none in the enclosure beyond Bishopton'. In October he entered into an agreement with William Replingham of 'Great Harborowe' in the same county that he and his heirs and also Thomas Greene (his cousin) should be indemnified for any loss of tithe value in their fields 'by reason of any enclosure or decay of tillage there meant and intended'. The damages were to be assessed by 'four indifferent persons'. This sort of negotiated agreement was the normal preliminary to the enclosing of land held in common.

This Replingham was the lawyer and agent acting for a cousin of his own, Arthur Mannering (or Mainwaring), who was Steward to the Lord Chancellor, Lord Ellesmere. Their local ally was William Combe, the nephew of old John Combe, who had just died in July. Young William acquired his landholdings from Sir Henry Rainsford and Lord Carew of Clopton at the age of twenty-eight. When old John died, most of his land went to Thomas Combe, and that lay in a different part of Stratford. (Here I follow Chambers.) William was a new force in local affairs.

The enclosure was a rationalization and regrouping of scattered strips of land among open fields into bigger, enclosed fields, with a conversion of use from ploughland to sheep pasture or of common grazing to enclosed cultivation. It would throw men out of work and might raise the price of grain, but in the long run it would favour agricultural improvement within the new enclosures, because the new, big fields would each come under one man's control. Enclosure has often been made a scapegoat by social historians, as well as by the old peasants, for more complicated evils; it certainly was so by those who suffered from it in the seventeenth century. Like everything else to do with farming from that day to this, it raised issues much more complicated, and frequently more socially damaging, than they looked. The early Stuart poor were very poor indeed. They were often starving, and a frightening proportion of them were wandering the roads. Their world at its worst was that of Lear on the heath.

Thomas Greene worked as town clerk for the town of Stratford, and we have his detailed journal of events. His task was to oppose this enclosure on behalf of Stratford. In November, 'At my cousin Shakespeare coming yesterday to town I went to see him how he did. He told me that they assured him they meant to enclose no further than to Gospel bush . . . and that they mean in April to survey the land, and then to give satisfaction and not before, and he and Mr. Hall say they think there will be nothing done at all.' So far, Shakespeare's attitude seems quite clear. He has agreed with Replingham, taking measures to defend his own interest and his cousin's against a threat he scarcely fears. It is possible he might have profited personally from enclosure, but he is not pressing for that. He was wrong about the survey.

10 Dec. that the survey there was past, and I came from Wilson to look [up] Mr. Replingham at the Bear and at New Place, but missed him, and . . . he was not to be spoken with.

23 Dec. Letters written one to Mr. Mannering another to Mr. Shakespeare with almost all the company's hands to either: I also writ of myself to my cousin Shakespeare the copies of all our oaths . . . also a note of the inconveniences would grow by the Enclosure.

11 Jan. 1615. At night Mr. Replingham supped with me. . . . he assured me before Mr. Barnes that I should be well dealt withall, confessing former promises . . . and his agreement for me with my cousin Shakespeare.

Sept. W. Shakespeare's telling J. Greene that [he?] was not able to bear the enclosing of Welcombe.

The last ill-written and ambiguous sentence of these hasty notes may mean either that Shakespeare could not bear it, or that Shakespeare told John (brother of Thomas) that Thomas could not bear (or could not bar) it. The first interpretation seems to me much the most likely; I can see no other which would make it worth Thomas Greene's while to record the sentence. This interpretation has the further merit of fitting the order of events. Shakespeare and John Hall had tried to calm Thomas Greene. The council approached Mr Combe, but uselessly; in December Mr Mannering began to lay out his scheme on the ground, and by doing so provoked a flurry of activity; the council wrote to Mannering, to Shakespeare, to Mr Archer of Tamworth, who owned Bishopton, and to Sir Francis Smith, who owned land at Welcombe. They begged Mannering to remember the fire that had just devastated their town, and warned him that enclosure would bring down the curses of the seven hundred almspeople of Stratford on his head. They may perhaps have written the same to Shakespeare, but I greatly doubt it; he was approached as being among their allies, one who might help prevent the evil.

Combe's men built their hedgemound and their ditch to a length of nearly three hundred yards. In January 1615 Greene advised William Walford and William Chandler to buy a Welcombe lease. Having done so, they could claim rights of common, and three days later, on 9 January, they began filling in Mr Combe's new ditch. A crowd gathered. William Combe came on his horse, and had his men, one of whom was called Stephen Sly, fling Walford and Chandler to the ground, while he 'sat laughing on his horseback and said they were good football players'. Combe called the corporation 'puritan knaves', a term of abuse so general as to have little specific meaning, and tricksters. He offered Greene £10 to buy himself a horse if he agreed to suggest a truce to the council, but Greene refused. Next day the women and children came out from Stratford and from

Bishopton, and filled in the entire ditch. On 28 March at Warwick assizes the court heard the petition of Stratford, and declared the enclosure to be illegal unless good cause for it could be shown in open assizes. Stratford had won.

Mannering and Replingham withdrew, but young Combe was not pacified. He threatened and he cursed, he beat the smallholders, imprisoned them and impounded their sheep and their swine. He bought up whatever houses and whatever land he could, until Welcombe was a deserted village. In the late winter of 1616 the Chief Justice of the King's Bench, who was Sir Edward Coke, told Mr Combe to 'set his heart at rest; he should neither enclose, nor lay down any arable, nor plough any ancient greensward.' In April of that year, William Combe gave up in despair, which Greene noted in his diary, but in June he offered new proposals to his 'very loving friends and kind neighbours' to enclose a smaller area on newly negotiated terms. There was another court order against him in 1617, but he brought a counter-action. Finally, in 1619, a petition of Stratford to the Privy Council produced a letter to William Combe from the Master of the Rolls, which commanded him to plough the land as it had been ploughed in the past, and to replace the greensward until such time as a further order might be made by an assize judge. By that time, of course, Shakespeare was dead. He left his sword to Thomas Combe, but nothing to William.

This dispute is worth the attention given to it for a number of reasons, above all the implacable and successful resistance of the women and children, which surely turned the tide, but also for a number of details that illuminate life, and Shakespeare's life. Thomas Greene for example was not just a cousin; in 1609 he was living in Shakespeare's house and expecting to spend another year there. His daughter Elizabeth was born at New Place in 1612; then he moved into St Mary's House 'in a young orchard', and made it 'pretty, neat, gentlemanlike'. He was a Treasurer of the Middle Temple.

Shakespeare was drawn into the affair firstly in self-defence, and secondly by relationship. Mannering and Replingham were too sharp for him, but he foresaw their failure, which when it came to a court decision they swiftly admitted. One sees the grim mood of the citizens of Stratford, and one all but hears the resentful voices of the poor, and of all those families who sent out women and children. Some of the points at issue are mentioned almost by chance. Mr Combe is willing in June of 1616 to allow 'the better sort' of Stratford people, not just everybody, to dig for sand on his ground. The importance of this activity for building is clear enough from the old Guild Pits that used to mark the northern boundary of Stratford-upon-Avon, surviving today in the more polite name of Guild Street.

In another sense Thomas Greene was the hero. One can watch him masterminding the defence from the beginning. He was an able lawyer, and a mediocre poet as well, who in 1605 wrote a complimentary sonnet to Drayton of doughy heaviness, and Latin verses on the fear of death a few days before the birth of his son Thomas, baptized at the end of December 1614: *Estque cinis subito qui modo civis erat.* – 'And the human is suddenly humus.' His Latin was pretentious but not good. He was born in Warwick in a mercer's family, and educated at Staples Inn and the Middle Temple, where he became a bencher, Reader and then Treasurer. He resigned as Clerk and Steward of Stratford when Shakespeare died, and moved to Bristol, dying there or in London in 1640. His career was not extraordinary, but the life of the country depends on such careers. The success of Stratford at law against William Combe on so many occasions and at so many levels must owe more than a little to him. He was a useful cousin to have.

Thomas Greene apparently looked up to Shakespeare. Aubrey says of the playwright, 'He was wont to go to his native Country once a year. I think I have been told that he left two or three hundred pounds per annum there or thereabouts: to a sister.' But as time went by, he was reputed richer. John Ward, Vicar of Stratford in 1662, says, 'I have heard that Mr. Shakespeare was a natural wit, without any art at all; he frequented the plays all his younger time, but in his elder days lived at Stratford: and supplied the stage with two plays every year, and for that had an allowance so large, that he spent at the Rate of a thousand pounds a year, as I have heard.' However exaggerated that may be, it gives the impression that Shakespeare made in Stratford.

Even the family portraits and the scale of Shakespeare's houses suggest some degree of grandeur, and the story of his mulberry tree a garden of some scale. His friends among the old Stratford families seem to have been kept lifelong, though one does wonder what happened between him and Richard Field, the publisher of his early poems and those of Thomas Combe. They appear to have lost contact, though that may be an illusion, because after the early 1590s Shakespeare was probably never again in complete control of his publications. The company seem to have printed his plays, and Thorpe printed the Sonnets.

Shakespeare had the reputation of being extremely funny, which he is bound to have been, and of being gentle, a natural gentleman in his dealings even in London. That is not surprising either; in all the anecdotes about him, some too obviously mythical to repeat here, his gentleness and wit are apparent. In his encounters with Ben Jonson, he is less cumbrous, at times gleefully ironic, and always seems to win. There are numerous stories of his drinking both in London and in the country, but they are nearly all connected with his poetry or the general reputation of poets. The reputation is justified, in my experience of them, so I credit it of Shakespeare, up to a point at least. It is a relief to observe, since his everyday friends for most of his life must have been in the theatre, where we know how greatly and uniquely he was esteemed, that his country friends and his London friends overlapped, at Clifford Chambers and at Hall had a London house until he died, and that Shakespeare's grand-daughter Elizabeth Hall visited London at the age of sixteen.

Even in the mythology which accumulated for two hundred years after his death, there are glimpses of Shakespeare that may be real. The tradition of the alehouse at Wincot near Stratford may not be right, but one may believe of it 'that 'twas often resorted to by Shakespeare for the sake of diverting himself with a fool who belong'd to a neighbouring mill', even though the story was recorded in 1780. The same writer, Edward Capell (1713–81), an inspector of plays for the Lord Chamberlain, speaks of an old traditional story of a very old Stratford man 'of weak intellects, and yet related to Shakespeare', who remembered that he had seen him brought on to the stage on another man's back. That would be as Adam in *As You Like It*.

William Oldys (1696–1761), the first full-scale English biographer with his *Life of Sir Walter Raleigh* (1736), made notes about Shakespeare, in which he tells this story of Shakespeare's younger brother, in a slightly different but more detailed and convincing version. John Jordan (1746–1809), a wheelwright who became a self-educated antiquarian, knew of Shakespeare's father's wool dealing, which only very recent research has confirmed, so it is curious that he records that 'The large barns, built with bricks still standing in the Guild-pits, by the side of the Birmingham road, have always been thought to have been built by him' (the poet). I find it easier to believe in this than in the rumours of Shakespeare's corre-spondence with James I, which derive from Davenant, but who knows?

One of the few recorded quarrels that disturbed these years was with the Lane family. Master Nicholas Lane of Bridge Town, beyond the Avon, was a farmer and a moneylender of the poet's father's generation, who sat on a commission with Thomas Lucy and sent an armed horseman to Tilbury in Armada year. He was a violent fellow, fined for nearly murdering a man with a crabtree cudgel in 1592, and dead by 1595. In his stone effigy at Alveston he looks as uncompromisingly ferocious in death as he ever can have been in life. He fought a long suit with John Shakespeare to recover a loan he made to the poet's uncle Henry.

John Lane, brother to Nicholas, was a Catholic. John Lane, son of Nicholas, got himself sued for riot, and for libelling the Vicar and the aldermen, and reported by the churchwardens for drunkenness. The Vicar was unpopular, but John Hall the doctor was his supporter and a church-warden, who gave the church a pulpit. This John Lane was sued for slander of Susanna Hall in July 1613 in the church court at Worcester Cathedral, which regulated most cases of bad behaviour short of theft or murder.

'About five weeks past the defendant [Lane] reported that the plaintiff [Susanna Shakespeare, now Susanna Hall] had the running of the reins and had been naught with Ralph Smith at John Palmer.' Robert Whatcott, one of the witnesses of Shakespeare's will, appeared for Susanna. John Lane failed to appear, so a fortnight later he was excommunicated. 'The running of the reins' means venereal disease; the slander was therefore serious, though Lane, who was only twenty-three years old, may well have been drunk. Ralph Smith was thirty-five and Susanna was thirty. The dispute is insignificant really; what is interesting is the relationships that took the strain of it without breaking.

Ralph Smith was the son of a winemerchant and a nephew of Hamnet Sadler, therefore certainly a family friend. Susanna was a respectable wife and mother, her daughter Elizabeth being five years old. John Lane's sister Margaret was married to John Greene, the brother of Thomas Greene. In the same month of July John's uncle Richard Lane made Thomas Greene and John Hall the trustees of property that he settled on his son and daughter. I am inclined to see this as evidence of a deliberate strengthening of links between the families, a patching up of the trouble John Lane had caused. Later in time, John Lane's first cousin Thomas, the son of Anthony Nash of Welcombe, married Elizabeth Hall in April 1626 when she was eighteen and he was thirty-three.

John Lane himself led the local protests in 1619 against the appointment of a Puritan vicar, which was favoured by the churchwardens, such as the Hathaways, Anne's brothers, and John Hall. The churchwardens were a force in the town. You could be reported to the local church court for 'loitering forth of church at sermon time', 'sleeping in the belfry, with a hat on, upon the Sabbath', 'wearing a hat in Church', 'late coming to Church', and so on. They acted in the case of a row between Alice Parker and Goody Bromley, 'an ill-look woman' with the evil eye. She had threatened the wife of Adrian Holder 'to overlook her and hern', and shouted, 'Aroint thee witch,' and 'get her home or a would brush the motes forth of her dirty gown.'

John Shakespeare had sued a Matthew Bromley for debt, and a certain Thomas Woodward was 'admonished in court several times to desist' from keeping company with Matthew's grandson William, who was an excommunicated man. The case is rare and unexplained. It was not possible to live in Stratford without knowing such people and seeing such scenes, but John Hall must have known better than most, being a small-town doctor. The tradition that he lived at Hall's Croft until Shakespeare's death is very feeble, being not much more than a hundred years old, though the house that survives does feel like a doctor's house. He died in 1635 and Susanna was buried beside him in 1649. Thomas Nash had died in 1647, but Elizabeth was remarried a month before her mother's death, at the age of forty-one, to John Bernard, later Sir John, of Abington in Northamptonshire, a widower of her own age. Her portrait with Thomas Nash still hangs in their house in Stratford.

The Queen stopped at New Place in 1643 during the Civil War, and King's officers were billeted there, but no one quite knows whether or how well Susanna could write. The note made by a cavalier officer in a copy of Henri Estienne's *Marvellous Discourse upon the Life of Katherine de Medicis*, that he got it from Susanna Hall when he was staying at New Place, suggests by date that she had Shakespeare's books. We know that she could sign her name, but when James Cook bought John Hall's manuscript casebooks 'intended for the press' from her in 1644, which he later published as *Select Observations upon English Bodies*, she appears not to have recognized her husband's handwriting.

James Cook was a doctor in attendance on parliamentary troops, who were by that time guarding the bridge over the Avon. Hall had left his books to his son-in-law Thomas Nash, and his manuscripts to 'burn them or do with them what you please', but it appears that they lingered on in the house, as is the way of books and papers in big houses. Some of them were looted by a certain Baldwin Brooks, later bailiff of Stratford, in pursuit of a debt the law had allowed, in 1637. The last hope of survival of Shakespeare's personal papers and manuscript writings seems to have died with Lady Bernard in 1670. By that date, if they survived they would probably have been treasured.

Susanna Hall's English epitaph makes her sound like a good vicar's or doctor's wife, as she was, and very like Shakespeare's ideal women:

> Witty above her sex, but that's not all,
> Wise to Salvation was good Mistress Hall:
> Something of Shakespeare was in that, but this
> Wholly of Him with whom she's now in bliss.
> Then, passenger, hast ne'er a tear
> To weep with her that wept with all?
> That wept, yet set herself to cheer
> Them up with comforts cordial,
> Her love shall live, her mercy spread,
> When thou hast ne'er a tear to shed.

On 10 February 1616 Thomas Quiney married Judith Shakespeare. He was the son of Shakespeare's old friend Richard, but Richard had died in 1602, leaving a widow and nine young children. The eldest of them did well enough, married a Sadler, prospered as a London grocer, and invested in Virginia. Thomas was a winemerchant, nearly twenty-seven years old, and Judith was just thirty-two; there were four years and a few days between them. They seem to have married hurriedly, since the ceremony was in Lent without the usual permission from the Bishop; they then neglected two summonses to the court at Worcester, and in March

Thomas was excommunicated, and perhaps Judith was too, though that punishment was not as permanent or as grave as it sounds. Walter Nixon, who summoned them, was summoned himself later before the Star Chamber, for bribery and forgery in the same Bishop's court of Worcester. But there was worse. At the time of the wedding a girl called Margaret Wheeler was heavily pregnant, and Margaret named Thomas Quiney as the father of her child. In mid-March her child was still-born and she died in childbed; they were buried together.

Anyone could get into trouble over sex. Judith Sadler, the daughter of Hamnet and Judith, was supposed to have had a child by William Smith. She fled from Stratford, and 'did upon her knees swear that the said William Smith did not ever at any time have any carnal knowledge of her body, and did acknowledge that she had done him great wrong in raising such a fame, and did there with tears protest that she was heartily sorry that she had done him that injury, and that one Gardiner was the true father of the child.' This was read out in court in the church. A case that comes closer to Margaret Wheeler's is that of Daniel Baker, bailiff in 1603. He got Anne Ward pregnant, she named him and said he was willing to marry her; she was made to go through a ritual of penance but he was not.

The Wheelers were a low-life family. In 1624 Richard Wheeler was in the local church court for calling a woman who said he was a rogue 'whore and sowlike whore and divers other filthy speeches'. Elizabeth Wheeler, summoned to the same court, swore 'God's wounds' as the old Queen might have done, but this was a more repressive age. She also cried out, 'a plague of God on you all; a fart of one's arse for you.'

When Margaret Wheeler died in childbirth the case came to the church court, brought by Mr Greene. Thomas Quiney appeared in court on Tuesday, 26 March 1616. On the 25th Shakespeare had signed a revised form of will, in a weak hand, if (as I think) the signatures are his own, and the will was not signed for him by a lawyer. The faint suspicion remains that Thomas and Judith hurried their wedding because Thomas was determined to be married before the affair with Margaret became public, either because he feared being forced to marry her, or because he knew the Shakespeares would have refused him as a husband for Judith. As it was, Shakespeare did rewrite his will, to try to protect Judith from an untrustworthy man. I believe it killed him, because in a month he was dead.

Yet they were passionately in love. Their first child was born in November, though he died as a baby of six months, the next in February 1618, and the third in August 1619. All three were boys. The parents stayed together forty-six years, until Judith died in February 1662 at the age of seventy-eight. Thomas Quiney did turn out untrustworthy all the same, unfaithful sexually, a heavy drinker, and financially so incapable that trustees were appointed for his wife and children. The offence with Margaret Wheeler was punished by a sentence of public penance in a white sheet at Morning Prayer on three successive Sundays, but he swiftly had that commuted (or was it Shakespeare who arranged it?) to appearing before the minister in the privacy of Bishopton chapel in his ordinary dress, and paying five shillings to the poor. The wineshop he kept was called the Cage; it stood at the corner of High Street and Bridge Street. He was fined later for allowing disorderly drinking there.

Was Judith Shakespeare swept off her feet at thirty-two? Why had she not married before? What kind of father was Shakespeare to her? She was a twin who had lost her twin; they are sad, very affectionate children. Is she at all reflected in those wonderful girls in the late plays? Are any other family relationships reflected in their insistent patterns? We cannot say. But we do know how much Shakespeare cared about the betrayal or the corruption of innocence and beauty. It was his lifelong theme, almost as much so as faithfulness in love. Judith remains to me the greatest enigma in his life, and the key to emotions that we cannot quite unlock. It is improbable that he ever got over Hamnet's death, and highly probable that he loved Judith twice as much as a result, and cherished and protected her. I say this only from the ordinary experience of life. The same experience dictates that such an intense paternal love does not always lead to happiness. I strongly suspect that if anything was wrong at all with the poet's domestic life, it was not too little love but too much.

His constant comings and goings between London and Stratford point to a lifelong feeling for home and for his wife. If it were otherwise, he could have bought a house elsewhere. He had simply arrived at the social position in Stratford his father might have foreseen for him in his prosperous years, only by other means, and perhaps to a degree that was beyond expectation. The anchor of his moral and his physical view of the world was in Stratford. Intellectually he had soared into another atmosphere, which was French or Italian or international. He knew the big world, he had seen the Court, he had been one of the King's Servants named to attend on the Spanish Ambassadors to make the first peace with Spain since the Armada.

But it was not so singular then as it might seem to be today for someone retired to a country town to have had those experiences. His experience had included sufferings which he recorded in detail, both in a sonnet (66) and in Hamlet (act 3, scene i), in terms which are both general and searching (cf. sonnets 29–30). In all this experience, Stratford remained central. He had not at a practical level deserted his wife, and inwardly he seems to have loved her. I do not understand how he could have got through his life in the way that he did without her. When he worked so hard, it was her nest he was building. When he was morally, intellectually and imaginatively exhausted, what else is there that could have sustained him? In his soarings and swoopings in love with love, let alone in love with poetry, he reserved to the private part of his mind the private part of his life, the solid reality of his wife and family at Stratford.

So we arrive at the second-best bed. Shakespeare's lawyer was Francis Collins of Warwick, who was lawyer to the Combe family as well. His was a normal, Protestant form of will, but of some length and complexity, and revised at the time it was signed. The hand is unidentified, but I suppose it could be his own. It is apparently not that of Collins, as used to be thought. We know so little about Shakespeare's own hand, having nothing to go on but a few signatures, and some of those uncertain, that only negative conclusions about written documents attributed to his hand are possible: there are things one can be sure he did not write, but none that one can be sure he did, on the basis of his very few undoubtedly genuine signatures. He makes his will 'in perfect health and memory God be praised', commending his soul into the hands of God 'and my body to the Earth whereof it is made'.

He crosses out 'son in law' and leaves directly to Judith £150, the hundred for her dowry and the fifty if she surrenders any claim to a cottage in Chapel Lane which he was leaving to Susanna. This hundred is already generous, but Judith gets another hundred and fifty if her husband settles the same sum on her. Otherwise she gets the interest, and the children get the main sum of money when she dies. He leaves his sister Joan £20 and all his clothes: she had three living sons of sixteen, eleven and eight years old, and her husband was alive. She is allowed to live in the Henley Street house, for a nominal rent of a shilling a year, and in fact she did so until she died in 1646 at the age of seventy-seven. Her three sons get £5 each. He leaves his plate to little Elizabeth Hall. In the earlier version it was going to Judith, but now she gets only 'my broad silver and gilt bowl'. He leaves £10 to the poor of Stratford, where £2 was normal.

Thomas Combe gets his sword, Thomas Russell gets £5 as executor, Collins gets £13 6s 8d, which is an even number of ten marks, a traditional sum like guineas. Richard Burbage, John Heminges and Henry Condell, the last survivors of the Chamberlain's Men, and the oldest members of the company, get a mark each to buy a mourning ring, but they are named after Hamnet Sadler, William Reynolds, Anthony Nash and his brother John, who get the same. Richard Tyler is crossed out and Hamnet Sadler substituted. William Walker gets twenty shillings as a godson.

William Reynolds was thirty-one and newly married to Frances de Bois, who came from London. They married at Clifford Chambers in August 1615; his parents had been Catholics and harboured Jesuits. The Nash brothers are from Welcombe; Anthony Nash had just taken over the Bear in Bridge Street from Thomas Barber, who died within a few days of his wife in August 1615. (Both Barber's two wives were Catholics, but he was three and nearly four times bailiff, and a pillar of support to Thomas Greene in the town's affairs.) Anthony Nash died in 1622, leaving the Bear to his son Thomas, who in 1616 was nearly twenty-four; it was he who married Shakespeare's granddaughter Elizabeth. There is no obvious reason why Richard Tyler was crossed out, except to accommodate Hamnet Sadler without altering the calculations. He was certainly alive; a few years later he was a church warden attacking the Vicar about the poor state of the fabric of the church. William Walker was the son of a successful local tradesman with some suggestion of a Snitterfield connection; the boy was baptized on 16 October 1608, so he was only seven years old.

Shakespeare is very careful to mark not only association and kinship but the degree of it. His sword would have gone to his son; it was a gift with meaning. The £5 to nephews is an extremely handsome tip, but the money to the poor is lavish, and the money for Judith is a lot. Susanna gets his Stratford property, 'all my barns, stables, orchards, gardens, lands', and so on, and also the Blackfriars house 'near the Wardrobe', that is, near the offices of the Master of the Revels.

Shakespeare adds between lines, 'Item I give unto my wife my second best bed with the furniture'. Much crazy speculation has been raised on this small foundation. It is true that most wills provided for widows and this does not, but the reason is obvious. John Hall and Susanna were to move into New Place and look after Anne Shakespeare as they were uniquely fitted to do. The 'second best' bed was William and Anne's old marriage bed. The grander New Place bed in the best bedroom must go to John Hall and Susanna, but William remembered at the last moment to reserve his wife's bed, in which by now she no doubt habitually slept, for her own. The rest of his 'goods, plate, jewels and household stuff' he left to John Hall, on whom he could rely.

Anne Shakespeare died seven years after her husband, on 6 August 1623, at the age of sixty-seven, just before the First Folio of the plays was published. It is likely that her Latin verse epitaph was composed by John Hall in his wife's name. In English it would read like this:

> Mother who gave me breasts and milk and life,
> for all of it I pay you with a stone:
> would a good angel move this stone away
> then Christ's body your image would come out.
> My prayer is vain, come quickly Christ, may she
> shut here in this tomb rise up and seek heaven.

The compression of some parts of the Latin and the conventional facility of other parts suggest that Susanna told John Hall what she wanted him to say. John Hall died in 1635, fighting an outbreak of the plague in Stratford. Susanna lived on in her house until 1649.

The last happy month that we can trace in William Shakespeare's life is the August of 1615, when his friend Anthony Nash took over the Bear in Bridge Street, and when he attended the wedding of William Reynolds. I am not sure why that was held in Clifford Chambers, which in those days was an idyllic place, but the likeliest reason is that Frances de Bois was staying with the Rainsfords. Since it was August, no doubt Drayton was staying there too, as his habit was. But I do not believe the late story about Shakespeare dying of a fever caught carousing with Drayton and Ben Jonson, certainly not that the carouse was in London and that he rode home with the fever on him. He was exhausted and upset. The burning of the Globe was the beginning of the end, though he lived to see it rebuilt. He was less able to stand a shock than he had been. His sister Joan's husband William Hart the haberdasher and hatter suddenly died, and was buried on 17 April 1616. The 23rd was Shakespeare's fifty-second birthday and he died on that day.

As a tithe-holder and therefore a lay rector, he had the right to be buried at the east end of Holy Trinity church; the right was exercised. He wanted to be left there undisturbed: that was his last personal wish. But he feared for the future and his fear was justified, because another of the family stones was defaced to commemorate a later vicar; it was restored only in modern times, for the sake of the Shakespeare connection. Shakespeare knew just what his own stone ought to be like. Its inscription may be the last four lines of verse that he ever wrote – a conversation with gravediggers:

> *Good friend for Jesus sake forbear*
> *To dig the dust enclosed here:*
> *Blest be the man that spares these stones,*
> *And curst be he that moves my bones.*

He left no money for any other monument, but one was built on the church wall by his friends. Its Latin verses are in a widespread renaissance tradition on which Sidney and Shakespeare both drew, but they are not by him, and nor are the English tributary verses. Those are not disgraceful, but not good enough to be attributable to any particular poet. The Latin says 'Nestor for wisdom, Socrates for genius, Virgil for poetry: the earth covers him, the people grieve for him, heaven has him.' The English verses are these:

> Stay passenger, why goes thou by so fast?
> Read if thou canst, whom envious Death hath plac'd
> Within this monument: Shakespeare: with whom
> Quick Nature died: whose name doth deck this tomb
> Far more than cost: sith all that he hath writ
> Leaves living art but Page to serve his wit.

These couplets are not different in style from a number of verse offerings to Shakespeare. They are probably not by Hall, certainly not by anyone as good as Jonson or even Drayton. The phrase 'Read if thou canst' is unusual, and strangely recalls the illiterate soldier in *Timon*. At this time, medieval frescoes were being obliterated by written texts. My own suspicion is that the couplets were composed by someone like Leonard Digges. If that is true, then probably his stepfather Thomas Russell, Shakespeare's friend and executor, was paying for the monument. Anyone who has visited Strensham church near Tewkesbury will know that the Russells favoured sepulchral monuments of great beauty. 'Quick Nature died' sounds to me like young Digges; he wrote two long poems in tribute to Shakespeare, both of them decent enough, and of interest enough, to make one pause over him.

The bust of Shakespeare on his monument is impressive rather than beautiful, though it has its beauty. No one has ever despised it except academic intellectuals, who seek in vain in Shakespeare for their own characteristic features. The face is solid and formidable; it is an old countryman's face, with more dignity than glamour. The bust has been more than once restored, including a whitewashing in the neo-classic period suggested by Johnson's friend and Shakespeare's great editor Edmond Malone, whose work to this day underlies all the poet's biographies. There will always be new biographies, because he is a subject of never-ending interest, but there is only one authentic head of Shakespeare. The colouring seems convincing to me; it is copied from other such monuments. He looks as a real poet would look who had worked hard all his life, and known a world outside poetry: one who had roots somewhere like Warwickshire. The huge dome of the head confirms the suggestion of the Droeshout engraving. This image is an older, heavier man, who might in foggy weather have trouble with his breathing.

A note made in 1653 records that Shakespeare's monument in Stratford church was made by Gerard Johnson, which is probably true. The firm was Dutch; it had been in London since 1567 and was now, since 1611, in its second generation. They did a lot of work in the Midlands; at Stratford they built John Combe's stone monument, but they worked also in terracotta. Southampton and Rutland employed them, but their tombs and memorials are also to be found in quite small country churches.

Shakespeare's design is a skull, his father's coat of arms with the falcon crest, and two cherubs for labour and rest. Labour has a spade, Rest has a skull and a torch turned down. His own pose is like the historian John Stowe's on his monument in St Andrew Undershaft in London. Shakespeare sits writing and ready to speak, in a classic niche between a fine pair of Corinthian columns. His quill pen used to be made of stucco, but now the Rector brings him real swan's feathers. Perhaps they come from the swan sanctuary between the Stratford Hilton and the river.

APPENDIX 1

A Private Commission

I have pursued a personal interest in the private commissions Shakespeare may have undertaken for their literary as well as their social interest, because more even than the theatre, with its largely nameless audience, they show poetry in a precise social context to which it must adapt. Shakespeare's own inscribed gravestone is an example, and the very different inscription on his wall monument shows by contrast how intimately and directly he could speak in poetry. So I ought not to have been surprised when this interest led me, by way of a private masque written by Shakespeare's younger friend John Marston, to the discovery of some unpublished verses which I find it impossible not to attribute to Shakespeare. They are comparatively minor verses for a social occasion. Before dealing with them, it will be better to say a little more about his private commissions. It is possible that one should add to these the verses on Mr Aspinall's present of gloves (see page 31), and the epitaph on the Stanley tomb at Tong, which I have discussed in Appendix 7.

Until recently the only evidence that Shakespeare ever worked on private commissions from the aristocracy was the stray fact of an entry in an account book at Belvoir Castle for 1613. 'Item 31 Martii to Mr. Shakespeare in gold about my Lord's impreso 44s. To Richard Burbadge for painting and making it in gold 44s.' An *impreso* is an emblem with a motto precisely like the ones Shakespeare invents for *Pericles* (act 2, scene ii) and it seems likely that the Earl of Rutland, who was Southampton's friend and fellow-prisoner in the Tower until 1603, had thought of Shakespeare because of this scene and that Shakespeare brought in Burbage as a painter.

The 1613 royal tournament at Belvoir does not sound like a success. 'The day', wrote Sir Henry Wotton to a friend, 'fell out wet, to the disgrace of many fine plumes. . . . The rest were contented with bare *imprese*, whereof some were so dark that their meaning is not yet understood. . . .' Lord Pembroke presented 'a small, exceeding white pearl, and the words *solo candore valeo*'. Lord Montgomery had 'a sun casting a glance on the side of a pillar, and the beams reflecting with the motto *splendente refulget*'. To judge from the examples in *Pericles*, Shakespeare's will have been better.

Pericles presented 'A wither'd branch, that's only green at top' with the motto *'In hac spe vivo'* – In this hope I live. These *imprese* (*impreso* is a wrong form) are not the same as the heraldic devices on shields, since Pericles has no shield: they are handed to the Princess by each knight's attendant, but Pericles has no attendant. The audience is not shown the *imprese*, which is why the Princess describes them to her father.

Shakespeare undertook another private commission in 1607, which has been overlooked. It is not only a unique pleasure to present unknown verses by Shakespeare in print for the first time, but also a little alarming, because modern attempts to attribute little-known or unknown works to his authorship have often misfired. The 1607 poems have been neglected; the manuscript has an excellent provenance, but it appears that the verses had seldom been read since soon after 1607 until December 1986. In itself the signature 'W.S.' may mean anything or nothing, but the case for the signature of these poems is very much stronger. Most of the marginal works attributed to Shakespeare are simply not good enough to be written by him; these verses are minor work, but a few of them are certainly good enough, and the whole series seems to have been written by a single author. Without the signature one would suspect some close disciple of Shakespeare, if one hardly dared to suggest the poet himself, but given the signature little or no doubt remains.

I should add here that having discovered these verses through the manuscript I assumed they were unknown, because they are not in the standard list by Chambers of the known and suspected forgeries of J. P. Collier, but Collier did in fact print them in his *New Particulars* (1836). Even A. H. Tricomi, commenting on Collier as a forger of Marston in the *Huntington Library Quarterly* (Vol. 43, 79–80), neglects this manuscript leaf. The new Oxford Shakespeare editors report Collier's publication and note its absence from the list of his Shakespeare forgeries, but have not looked at the manuscript, which is quite genuine with the possible exception of part of the signature. Collier had not noticed that the signature was in the hand of Marston. He may have messed about with the signature, but he did not forge it all. Collier is rather annoyed that 'the signature is different' (p. 62). His interpretation is that the verses indicate 'a species of lottery', 'in which hearts were hung as fruit on an artificial tree'.

J. O. Halliwell attacked Collier in a privately circulated pamphlet of twenty-five copies in 1853, *Observations on the Shakespearian Forgeries at Bridgewater House*, listing the documents he thought were forged, but without mentioning these verses. The forgeries were all supposed to have been found in 'unopened bundles' of documents, which is certainly not true of Marston's masque. Halliwell produced in facsimile a letter purporting to carry Southampton's initials. It is apparent that the 'S' of that 'H.S.', which must be due to Collier, is utterly unlike Marston's curious 'S' at the foot of the new verses. Collier in his publication of the verses does not recognize the signature to be in Marston's hand. Controversy apparently passed them by, concentrating on what purported to be official documents, and on freaks of forgery such as a letter from the poet Daniel suggesting Shakespeare for the post of Master of the Revels. Mere poetry was ignored.

The scene is a formal ceremony of present-giving at a country house, a ritualized, almost a masque-like performance of a familiar action, enacted between close friends and members of a family with an audience of the same kind. This is a ceremony of friends and neighbours, an extended family and kinship group, to celebrate a most important binding link: an engagement to be married. There are fourteen present-givers, a number deliberately chosen, I suppose, to represent the fourteen lines of a sonnet. The presents are similar, so perhaps one person paid for them all; certainly one person arranged the entire ceremony from the time when the presents were commissioned, as soon as the marriage was arranged. That is the person who employed Shakespeare; and I take it to be Alice, the dowager Countess of Derby. The engagement is that of her eldest daughter, Anne, to Lord Chandos.

There is not more than one small textual problem in these poems. Scholars will need to consult the manuscript for themselves, and no doubt it will be published in facsimile. I have chosen to reproduce it in modern spelling for ordinary readers, though specialized scholars will undoubtedly pore over its original spelling and punctuation. There is no reason to think the manuscript is autograph: it was intended to be a clean copy for use at the Earl of Huntingdon's house at Ashby-de-la-Zouch in Leicestershire. I do not suppose that the signature was added until it arrived there, certainly not by the copyist. But one or two strange spellings do suggest Shakespeare's Warwickshire accent, not unlike a modern Staffordshire accent, unless we are to think a local copyist altered these spellings. The same possibility occurs here and there in his dramatic works. Here he calls Lady Compton *Lady Coumpton* and spells coloured *coulored*. An amethyst is an *amatist*, a spelling used earlier by alchemists, but also by Sidney in his *Arcadia*; from 1596 or so, and certainly from 1611 (the date of the authorized Bible) onwards, it would have been ignorant and old-fashioned.

The occasion of the masque and the present-giving is the same because both involve the same people. Lady Derby had planned her visit to Ashby the previous winter, but she was stopped by snow, as Marston says in his *Entertainment* for the end of July 1607:

> For scarce her Chariot cut the easy earth
> And journied on, when winter with cold breath
> Crosseth her way. Her borrowed hair doth shine
> With Glittering Icicles all crystalline,

> Her brows were periwigg'd with softer snow,
> Her russet mantle fring'd with Ice below
> Sat stiffly on her back. . . .

I am not sure why her hair is borrowed, unless as a goddess, and one hopes that the rest of the picture is exaggerated. The seventeenth century thought of Ashby as a long way north: Charles Cotton wrote in similar terms to Sir Aston Cockayne, and 1607 was the year of 'a great frost' long remembered. It was also the year of the execution of the Derbyshire witches at Bakewell. In late July, Lady Derby was greeted with music at 'the Park corner', again as she entered the park 'treble cornets reported to one another', and suddenly she came to 'an Antique gate' where she was entertained with Marston's verse. The Earl of Huntingdon, Chief Forester of Leicester forest, was 'the high silvan that commands these woods', and his wife, who was Alice Derby's daughter, was 'his bright Nymph fairer than the Queen of floods'. The learned entertainment continued indoors, with music and singing, Shakespearean fairy talk, and the presentation of 'a very curious and rich waistcoat'.

Some plumes 'of Carnation and white' for knights seem to derive from Jonson's *Hymenaei* (1606), and may well have been the same plumes that he used at Court, since two of the dancers are the same. The most learned bit of Marston's masque is a list of the obscure Latin names of the sons of Mercury, which he took from the *Mythologia* of Natalis Cornes. It is fascinating to observe that Shakespeare was better informed than Marston, since the masque gives 'Auctolius' as one of them. Perhaps it was this queer list that stirred Shakespeare to look up Ovid's *Metamorphoses*, which gives Autolycus, son of Mercury, power over thievery. Autolycus was an Arcadian, and therefore doubly suitable for his role in *The Winter's Tale*.

THE ARGUMENT

In the course of reading the necessary and vast material for a life of Shakespeare, I became interested in a possible influence on him of a younger and lesser poet, the satirist John Marston, and in Shakespeare's obvious influence on him. It is a pleasing thought that the first person to notice this connection was Rupert Brooke, and that, had he lived, he might well have found what I have found. I was also particularly curious about masques and private performances of every kind, which are marginal and yet important in the history of the public theatre, particularly under the Stuarts. I therefore consulted Arnold Davenport's *Poems of John Marston* (1961), which he completed just before his early and sudden death at the age of forty-eight in 1958. Davenport's main interest was in satirists, but in editing Marston he had to deal with *The Entertainment of the Dowager*

Countess of Derby, written by Marston and performed in late July or early August 1607 for the engagement of her eldest daughter, Anne, to Lord Chandos. Here, as often elsewhere, I follow Davenport's suggestions, which are well argued in his introduction.

The only full manuscript of the masque that survives is in the Huntington Library in California (E.L.34.B.9), to the Director of which I am very grateful for permission to publish this text. A manuscript of part of the masque is in the British Library (Sloane 848), dated by its copyist 1607, August, but that is hasty and useless. Marston refers in a letter to having copies hastily made. The Huntington manuscript was once in the collection of the Bridgewater family, and presumably of the first Lord Bridgewater, John, the son of Thomas Egerton, Lord Brackley, who was Lord Chancellor and the second husband of Alice Derby. To the Huntington–Bridgewater manuscript of the masque was attached a stray leaf, which survived with it and is still with it. Davenport used the stray leaf as a key to unlock the secrets of the masque, because it consists of a series of short poems, often no more than four lines each, recited by ladies, whose names are given, at some sort of ceremonial present-giving to the bride. The presents were emblematic, and the poems are like riddles: all the presents seem to be jewels or such things, but it is sometimes hard, now that we have only the words, to guess what they were.

The stray leaf is headed 'Ashridge Library', in what looks to me like an early nineteenth-century hand, with the catalogue note F–4–3. Ashridge was an Egerton house in Hertfordshire which passed to Lord Brownlow in the nineteenth century. This estate survives, in the hands of the National Trust, as some fine woods on the edge of the Chilterns near Ivenhoe Beacon, not far from Tring and Mentmore. John Egerton, the first Lord Bridgewater, settled there sixteen miles from his father's and Alice Derby's house at Harefield. The old Ashridge was a house in which Queen Elizabeth had lived as a young woman, but it was replaced in 1808 by a new building in extravagantly 'Elizabethan' style, just about the time that Marston's *Entertainment* first attracted attention.

H. J. Todd printed some extracts from that in 1801 in the fifth volume of his *Works of Milton*, and the same extracts were reprinted by J. Nichols in his Progresses of James I in 1828. As an Egerton manuscript, our stray leaf and Marston's masque formed part of the Bridgewater collection, and must have belonged to that library since August 1607, since Thomas Egerton was (as I have said) Alice Derby's second husband. The papers of her daughters and granddaughters, who took other titles, would not survive in this collection. The whole library was sold to Mr Huntington in 1917 through Sir Montague Barlow of Sotheby's without an auction. The sale was to meet death duties, sales by auction being hazardous at the time. The library as sold included an early *Hamlet*, a 1600 quarto of *Titus Andronicus*, and a copy of Milton's *Comus* belonging to one of the boys who acted in it, which was later unfortunately sold off as a duplicate. The manuscripts from Ashridge had been moved to Bridgewater House in London, presumably by the Duke of Sutherland, who inherited as nephew from the last Duke of Bridgewater in the early nineteenth century. They were probably moved at the time of the rebuilding of Ashridge.

I should make one further point here. John Payne Collier, a famous forger of Shakespearean documents, had access to the Bridgewater papers in the 1830s and 1840s. I did not know that he ever saw this stray leaf, but he handled Marston's masque, and used its title-page for his purposes. He did pounce on genuine documents as well as giving publicity to those he invented. I assume that these few poems were beyond his capacity and too subtle for him. After some uncertainty, I dismiss the possibility that Collier wrote or interfered with these poems. It remains doubtful whether he touched the signature.

Sir Edward Dering's manuscript of Shakespeare's *Henry IV*, edited by J. O. Halliwell-Phillipps in 1845, contained not a stray leaf but 'a slip of paper' that recorded the names of country-house actors in *The Spanish Curate*, perhaps as early as 1619, the year in which Sir Edward was knighted (1845 edition, p. xiv). One of these actors is called Mr Donne. It is not impossible, indeed given the company it might seem likely, that this was John Donne the poet, but the poet became Dean of St Paul's in 1621, so the performance of *The Spanish Curate* would have to have been in 1620, or very soon before or after that year. The Dering manuscript itself, which is an adapted *Henry IV, Parts 1* and *2*, is equally hard or still harder to date. It appears to have been made by a genuine poet, since it contains at least one excellent joke at Falstaff's expense that occurs in no other text: 'I'll take say of ye', which means drawing the knife along a deer's belly to see how fat he is. The other actors in the *Curate*, apart from Dering, were Sir T. Wotton, Sir Warham St Leger, Robert Heywood, Thomas Slender, Mr Donne and Mr Kemp. The same slip of paper carries a second, slightly different list for the same characters: F. Manouch, John Carlile, Jack of the Buttery, and George Perd are the new names, making ten instead of nine. These lists offer an analogy to our ceremony.

The new Shakespeare poems are a family manuscript commemorating a family occasion. Arnold Davenport was interested only in the occasion and in the names, which are certainly fascinating. The more important present-givers are an interrelated family group from the higher aristocracy, the grandest of all being the first named, the widow of Ferdinando Strange, Earl of Derby, who is said to have died by poisoning after an attempt to involve him in an intrigue against Queen Elizabeth, which he spurned. His sad story was pieced together by Christopher Devlin in *Hamlet's Divinity* (1963). Alice Derby was patroness to Spenser and to Milton, and now it seems to Shakespeare as well. She is buried in Harefield Church in

Middlesex in one of the most beautiful tombs in England, a few miles across the fields from where I was born. The daughter who became Anne Chandos later married Lord Castlehaven, a sadistic sexual pervert who was publicly executed in his wife's and Lady Derby's lifetime: that catastrophe is the background to Milton's *Comus*. The little ceremony of the present-giving was not the prelude to a happy life.

The poetry on the stray leaf is in Elizabethan 'secretary' hand. It is not a particularly easy example, but with the possible exception of one word it can be read. The names opposite each few lines are in italic and therefore very much easier. My own suspicion, which is not meant to be insulting, is that Arnold Davenport saw that it was not Marston, who wrote an elaborate, rather beautiful italic hand, and never seriously examined it. The names and the verses are probably written by the same person; it would be common practice at this period to use both types of writing in a variety of combinations.

When I had begun to decipher the poems I thought it just possible that they might really be by Shakespeare: those I first read were at least good enough not absolutely to rule him out, though they are only minor verses for a private occasion, much the kind of verse that occurs in love-notes in his comedies. He does use the same verse form for that sort of purpose. Marston uses it in his dedication to Lady Derby, but much less well, as one would expect. I think Marston is imitating these verses.

It was the signature that altered everything. I had gone to Mr R. E. Alton of St Edmund Hall in Oxford to have the handwriting examined and properly deciphered; I knew that the hand was not Shakespeare's, and not the famous 'Hand D' of *Sir Thomas More* which has been attributed to Shakespeare, but that still left a wide-open field, and there were lines I was unable to read. Mr Alton is not responsible for my conclusions, but without his help I would have been lost. The signature is very odd. Davenport records it as 'W:SR:', which suggests Shakespeare among other possibilities. In fact someone has played with the signature, writing first 'W:Sʰ:' and then changing that without erasure to 'W:Sℛ:', suggesting both (certainly) 'R' and (perhaps) 'K'. In a manuscript of this date, when William Shakespeare was a famous and much-imitated poet, 'W.Sh[K]R' is certainly meant to mean Shakespeare.

There is no question of forgery, because the signature, though nothing else on the stray sheet, is in the hand of John Marston. It is clear from the little poems that they are not Marston's own work, but he was there, and he knew Shakespeare, and when he signs this copy with the poet's initials I think we must believe him. His hand in the odd signature is immediately recognizable by his peculiar 'S', and the 'W' is his 'W'. I am sure this text would have been recognized as Shakespeare's long ago if anyone had bothered to read it in modern times, or at least at any time since Greg's facsimile publication of Marston's hand. Lady Hunsdon's 'O be not proud, though. . . .' oddly recalls a sonnet by Donne, a member of the Egerton household from 1597 to 1602. The same Donne sonnet echoes a Shakespeare sonnet. Lady Berkeley's 'fire and air' recalls *Antony and Cleopatra* at just the time when Shakespeare had been writing it, and a number of other lines recall his work in other ways. The poems are uneven, though some are very good, but I do not wish to make them out to be more important than they are. It is conceivable that some of the ladies wrote their own verses.

They do in small ways alter our view of Shakespeare, because here he is playful, and reveals a frontier of verse with life and of his own comedies with life. That may be thought to throw some light on the sonnets. Then one is interested in his accepting a private commission, and in his never bothering to print these verses. His other undoubted private commission was his riddling emblem for the Earl of Rutland mentioned above. These verses in their way are also emblematic. Shakespeare's early friend Thomas Combe translated an emblem book from the French, and Daniel translated emblem verses from the Italian.

The poetry of emblem books veers between the two opposite poles of originality, which leads towards the amazing conceits of 'metaphysical' verse in the later seventeenth century (though much earlier abroad), and convention, a solid basis of familiar symbolism which permits a descant on a scarcely stated theme. An example of the second of the two tendencies is to be found in a sonnet on a portrait of Queen Elizabeth at Hampton Court, preserved in W. Hutton's guide to that palace (1897) and reprinted as the first poem in John Holloway's *Oxford Book of Local Verse* (1987). Its symbols or emblems are the swallow, the weeping stag, and the tree or love-tree. The same polarity and the same familiar emblems are to be found in these new poems and elsewhere in the works of Shakespeare.

The persons and the occasion are suggestive. It looks as if Shakespeare himself was not present. Did he not bother or was he not asked? Did Marston get him the job, or did he (more likely) get it for Marston? His obvious point of contact was with Lady Hunsdon, whose husband had been his employer in the Chamberlain's Men. But this group of people may add slightly to the case often made in the past, that Shakespeare as a young man worked for Lord Strange's Men. In that case Ferdinando's widow had probably followed his fortunes. For her, unhappy lady, this stray page of writing has an unexpected meaning after so long. It makes her beyond question the most interesting patroness in the entire history of English literature: Spenser, Shakespeare, Milton. You cannot do better than that.

The Poems

(Huntington Ms. E.L.34.B.9)

LADY DERBY

As this is endless, endless be your joy,
Value the wish, but not the wisher's toy;
And for one blessing past God send you seven
And in the end the endless joys of heaven.
Till then let this be all your cross,
To have [?share] discomfort of your loss.

LADY HUNTINGDON

Alas, your fortune should be better,
Still must your servant be your debtor:
Sure nothing equals your desert
Except your servant's faithful heart.

LADY HUNSDON

O be not proud, though wise and fair,
Beauty's but earth, wit is but air,
As you be virtuous be not cruel,
Accept good will more than a jewel.

LADY BERKELEY

Witty, pretty, virtuous and fair,
Compounded all of fire and air,
Sweet, measure not my thought and me
By golden fruit from fruitless tree.

LADY STANHOPE

O Philomela fair and wise,
What means your friend to tyrannize
And make you still complain of wrong?
Henceforth his praise shall be your song,
Which none but you can sing so well,
When none his true love shall excel.

LADY COMPTON

What may be said of you and yours?
You are his joy, yours he procures:
He doth your virtue much adore,
You reverence his as much or more:
Draw where you list, for in this tree
Your fortunes cannot bettered be.

LADY FIELDING

Fie, let it never make you sad
Whether your Chance be good or bad:
If your love give but half his heart,
The devil take the other part.

MRS GRESLEY

The fruit that is so early gotten
In the eating may prove rotten,
If your love's heart do prove untrue
The fault is theirs that chose for you.

MRS PACKINGTON

In love assured, he is he
That sends this poor pale heart to thee:
As e'er you hope to be regarded,
Pray that his faith may be rewarded.

MRS K. FISCHER

Who saith thou art not fair and wise,
This paper tells him that he lies:
The worst thing that I know by thee
Is that (I fear) thou lov'st not me.

MRS SACHEVERELL

Although this heart false coloured be,
Sweet fair one, think not so of me,
For he that this your token sends
Was ever true to all his friends.

MRS M. FISCHER

Good Lord, how courteous I am grown
To give so many hearts away,
But those that I gave lost mine own:
If I had twenty none should stay.

MRS DANVERS

All evil fortune hast thou mist,
Great is the virtue of th' Amatist
If (Amatist) thou mayest say,
Then blest is such a wedding day.

MRS EGERTON

What luck had you to stay so long:
Fortune (not I) hath done you wrong,
The hearts are gone without recall,
Would I had power to please you all.

W.Sh[K]R.

THE PRESENT-GIVERS AND THEIR PRESENTS

The present-givers are all women or girls, and they are all neighbours or close relations of the Earl and Countess of Huntingdon of Ashby-de-la-Zouch on the border of Leicestershire and Derbyshire. This Countess was the bride's younger sister, but she had been married for six years. The ladies give their presents and recite their verses in order of precedence, Lady Derby first. The archives of the borough of Leicester record a payment for the entertainment of the Countess of Derby and the Earl of Huntingdon on 27 July 1607. The Queen's Players got 30 shillings. The hire of two horses for the Mayor and his sergeant, 'to ride on into the forest' to meet the Earl and the two Countesses hunting, was disallowed by the town council.

No members of the Brydges family, to which Lord Chandos belonged, were present, or if they were there then they were silent. There are several hints in the poems that this was a goodbye ceremony performed principally by the women of the bride's family. But Lord Chandos is a significant figure. He was born Grey Brydges in 1579 and inherited his title in 1602, aged twenty-three. His father was a close friend and supporter of the Earl of Essex, and lucky to keep his head on his shoulders after Essex's rebellion. The new Lord Chandos lived at Sudeley Castle and was called 'King of the Cotswolds'. He had a bitter family quarrel over the inheritance with his cousin Elizabeth, and it was thought he should marry her to settle it, but he refused. A few years after his marriage he was closely associated with Lord Herbert of Cherbury. He died suddenly in 1621. John Donne's friend the Countess of Bedford thought Chandos was poisoned by spa water.

Alice Derby was a daughter of Sir John Spencer of Althorpe. Her first husband, Ferdinando, Earl of Derby, died in 1594. Her second was Thomas Egerton, Lord Brackley, a Privy Councillor and Lord Chancellor (1603), whom she married in 1600. She gives a ring. The second word of her last line is hard to read, as there has been an erasure. The alternative reading would be 'share'. Whether the discomfort is loss of virginity or loss of one's old family I am not sure. It can scarcely be the loss of the ring, because that would apply to her husband's, not her mother's present, in life as in Shakespearean comedy.

The second lady is Elizabeth, Countess of Huntingdon, an Egerton by birth, younger sister of the bride. The ceremony takes place in her husband's family house at Ashby-de-la-Zouch. Her gift is perhaps a jewel in the shape of a heart.

It is curious that Spenser's *Prothalamion*, which he wrote in autumn 1596 for the double marriage of two daughters of the Earl of Worcester from Essex House, has a connection with the Huntingdon family. The fifth Earl of Worcester, formerly Lord Herbert, was married in 1571 to Elizabeth Hastings, fourth daughter of the second Earl of Huntingdon, who was therefore the mother of both brides. It is not uncommon by any means to discover that Elizabethan noble families are related by marriage, nor is it surprising that Spenser had lived at Essex House before, when it belonged to the Earl of Leicester, but the celebration of noble weddings by professional poets is not very common, and it is reasonable to suppose that a poem by Spenser published in 1597 was still remembered in 1607. The Huntingdon–Ellesmere manuscript is a text for enacting the kind of elaborate ceremony that Spenser's *Prothalamion* describes in symbolic terms. It is also fair to remark that the two bridegrooms of the *Prothalamion* were no great catch, and one of the brides was by no means young. The explanation for this may be that the Earl of Worcester was a Catholic. He was the direct ancestor of the Dukes of Beaufort, to whom he transmitted the blood of the Plantagenets and the royal arms of England, but that of course was through the male line.

The third lady is Alice's sister Elizabeth, who is married to George Carey, the second Lord Hunsdon, who after a brief interval inherited from his father the office of Lord Chamberlain to Queen Elizabeth. His father had been the Queen's first cousin. Lady Hunsdon is Lady Huntingdon's and the bride's aunt, but only Lady Huntingdon's mother takes precedence before her in her own house; Lady Hunsdon is not a Countess. Her present is a jewel but not an emblem.

The fourth lady is Lady Berkeley (Berckly). She is Lady Hunsdon's daughter, another Elizabeth, and therefore a first cousin of Lady Huntingdon and of the bride. She is married to Sir Thomas, the son of Henry, Lord Berkeley. Sir Thomas (1575–1611) did not live long enough to succeed his father, but this lady's son did so. As a boy of thirteen he was married off by his parents to a girl of nine. Elizabeth Berkeley's present is apparently a gilded or a golden apple.

The fifth present-giver is Catherine, who is married to Sir Philip Stanhope, later Lord Stanhope and finally Earl of Chesterfield. She is the Earl of Huntingdon's sister and by birth a Hastings, and therefore the bride's sister's sister-in-law. Her present seems to be a nightingale; once again I assume a piece of jewellery. The reference to tyranny is to Ovid's story about Philomela, and the complaining of wrong may mean no more than musical lamentation.

There is some uncertainty about Lady Compton, the sixth lady in the ceremony. The likeliest candidate is Elizabeth, the daughter of a Lord Mayor of London, Sir John Spencer, who came from Suffolk and was unrelated to the Spencers of Althorpe. This lively girl had been stolen from her home in London in 1598, hidden in a baker's basket, by William, the second Lord Compton, later first Earl of Northampton. When his mean and aged father-in-law the Mayor died at last in 1610, William is said to have gone crazy for a time at the thought of all the money he had inherited. His father, Henry, the first Lord Compton, had been married to Frances, a sister of the fourth Earl of Huntingdon, which means Elizabeth Compton's mother-in-law had been the present Lady Huntingdon's great-aunt. But when Frances died, Henry Compton had married Alice Derby's sister Anne, making his son Alice's sister's stepson. William Compton and his stolen bride called their son, who grew up to be the cavalier Earl of Northampton (1601–43), Spencer Compton, but the Mayor remained obdurately furious. Queen Elizabeth is said to have calmed him down. He died leaving between half and three-quarters of a million pounds, not a penny of it to charity. Lady Compton's present is in the shape of a tree.

The seventh is Susan, Lady Fielding, married to Sir William, later Earl of Denbigh. She was a sister of the Duke of Buckingham. The Fieldings lived close to Ashby-de-la-Zouch. Her gift might be a divided heart.

Arnold Davenport connected Mrs Gresley with Susan Ferrers, who married George, son of Sir Thomas Gresley of Drakelow, just across the border in Derbyshire; Castle Gresley is even closer to Ashby-de-la-Zouch, and the eighth lady, like the seventh, is quite probably a neighbour. In 1610 the miscellany at the end of the *History and Gazetteer of Derbyshire* (Glover and Noble 1829) records a violent election quarrel and 'great affray' between Sir George Griesley and Sir Philip Stanhope. Is her present in the shape of fruit or of a heart?

Packington is even closer, just to the south of Ashby-de-la-Zouch. Davenport thought the lady may be a sister of Sir John Packington of Westwood in Worcestershire, a Privy Councillor, but the village of Packington is closer. Her present is the poor, pale heart. It seems possible that the ceremony has taken a fresh turn, and that the last seven presents, or some of them, come from the bridegroom's family. In that case, the 'early gotten' fruit of Mrs Gresley might be a strawberry, and the message might be his.

The two Mrs Fischers (Fishers) defeated Arnold Davenport. Mrs R. Fischer was born Elizabeth Tyringham and her mother was a Throckmorton. Robert Fischer lived at Packington, or Great Packington, Warwickshire; in 1607 he was twenty-eight. His father was a knight (1604) and Robert was knighted in 1609. He succeeded his father in 1619 and became a baronet in 1622. He served as Sheriff of Warwickshire. Mrs W. Fischer was probably married to Robert's younger brother, but Robert is recorded at Balliol (aged nineteen) though W. Fischer is not, so the relationship might be more remote.

The first Mrs Fischer speaks of 'this paper', and her present may be a portrait, probably a miniature, of the bride, or else it might be a mirror, in which case why the paper? Do they present their emblems and verses like the knights at the tournament in *Pericles*? The two Fischers are tenth and twelfth. The second of them seems to refer to playing cards.

The eleventh lady, Mrs Sacheverell, is Elizabeth, married to Jacinth Sacheverell of Morley in Derbyshire, not far away. Her father was Sir

Richard Harpur and her uncle Sir John of Swerkston in Derbyshire (north of Ashby), to whom Marston refers in a letter about his masque. He is writing to Sir George Clifton, apologizing for not having sent a copy:

> First with my own hand I wrote one copy; for all the rest which I had caused to be transcribed were given and stolen from me at my Lord Spencer's. Then with all sudden care I gave my copy unto a scrivener to write out, who is now upon it and will instantly have ended it.

Lord Spencer is Alice Derby's brother Robert, the first Lord Spencer of Althorpe. Sir Gervase was probably one of the knights in the masque. I have considered and rejected the idea that the masque itself was at Ashby House, as its manuscript says it was, but the ceremony of presents was at Althorpe, Lord Spencer's house in Northamptonshire, because that is too far south to favour the Gresley, Packington, Drakelow and Swerkston neighbours so well, or the recorded visit of Alice Derby to the Huntingdons. Marston must have gone south with her to her family house at Althorpe, where naturally the Spencer family will have wanted copies of the masque done at Ashby. The present-givers, like the masquers, were at Ashby: Alice Derby's visit to her daughter's house was combined with a family ceremony for her other daughter's engagement, which was performed chiefly by those women of her family who could be mustered there. Mrs Sacheverell gives an enamelled heart. Once again it is sent by Chandos.

The thirteenth lady is perhaps one of the Danvers family of Dauntsey in Wiltshire, one of whom became the Earl of Danby. Davenport prefers the wife of a Middle Temple man from Culworth in Leicestershire. George Herbert's mother, Magdalen, who died in 1627, married Sir John Danvers, and George Herbert himself met and married Jane Danvers at Dauntsey in 1629. She was one of the daughters of Charles Danvers of Brynton. They seem a likelier family than the Leicestershire lawyer's, but this is quite a humble lady, far down the list. She brings or gives an amethyst. The spelling 'amatist' may imply a Latin pun about love based on a similar pun in Virgil.

The last lady is an Egerton, and Davenport's clever idea that she is a small girl is surely right. The first and last poems are particularly outspoken. She would be a tiny granddaughter of Alice Derby. Alice's second daughter Frances married her half-brother Sir John Egerton early in 1602, so this would be a little Egerton girl aged four or five. Double marriages of that kind were intended to secure succession to property. If Mrs Egerton is a child, perhaps she gives nothing, or the empty basket. The point about 'stay so long' is that Anne Chandos was at least twenty-six. She was a Stanley, not an Egerton, eldest daughter of the Earl of Derby. The marriage, arranged no doubt with some difficulty due to her father's death, finally took place early in 1608.

APPENDIX 2

A Shakespeare Notebook

A British Library manuscript bought at Sotheby's in December 1986 contains about fifty-eight lines of scraps of verse from *Henry IV, Part 1*, from the first two scenes of the third act. The lines seem to be remembered (largely misremembered) from a performance, and chosen for striking metaphor or simply for political doctrine: 'His presence must be like a Robe pontifical not seen but when 'tis wondered at', and so on. The quarto edition of *Henry IV, Part 1* was available in 1598, so that this inaccurate and partial record of the text may well be earlier. The play was first performed in 1597. It is clearly earlier than the Queen's death, since instead of 'King' the writer notes 'he must pluck allegiance from men's hearts even in the presence of the Queen.' The reference is to Bolingbroke as a successful usurper, and brings the Essex and Southampton circle forcibly to mind. It is a practical example of Shakespeare's dramatic poetry inspiring or feeding seditious thoughts. The handwriting has not been identified but it looks like a courtier's.

This notebook is unorthodox in more ways than one. Its principal contents are some lengthy notes in bad Latin, in the same hand but less maturely written, on theological matters. On the question whether angels served God before man was created, he notes, 'I believe this, but I deny that Adam was the first Man, and I say it cannot be proved that God or Angels existed before Man.' This sort of freedom of thought recalls the enquiry into Ralegh and his circle held at Cerne Abbas in 1594. The point about pre-Adamite man is made by Thomas Nashe in *Pierce Pennilesse his Supplication to the Divell* (1592): 'Hence Atheists triumph and rejoice, and talk as profanely of the Bible as of Bevis of Hampton. I hear say there be Mathematicians abroad, that will prove men before *Adam*, and they are harboured in high places, who will maintain it to the death, that there are no devils.' In *Christs Teares over Jerusalem* (1593) he writes, 'He establisheth reason as his God. . . . Straightly he will examine him where he was, what he did, before he created Heaven and Earth; how it is possible he should have his being before all beginnings.' The Jesuit Robert Persons in his attack on Ralegh in 1592, spoke of his private school of atheism in which 'a certain necromantic Astronomer is master', meaning, I take it, the mathematician Thomas Harriot, a member of Ralegh's household, whom Nashe also intends.

359

It should therefore come as no surprise that a later hand than the writer's adds to the title of the theological discussion in our manuscript, which was 'On God', the annotation: 'Notes on a lecture by Thomas Harriot (As I believe)'. This same or another later hand adds a further explanation: 'Notes on Sorbonne discussions. Paris 1594'. That was the year of the expulsion of the Jesuits from the Sorbonne when Henry IV had become a Catholic, and also the year of the Cerne Abbas enquiry, in which Harriot is named. The Sotheby's sale catalogue notices an apparent reference to Doctor John Dee the alchemist, in a discussion of spirits: 'a Ghost, as these English here call it. D.D. says that they often appear headless.' A crystal ball is also mentioned. A marginal note against the horror of remorse says, 'Remember D. Williams.' The phrase *Angli isti*, 'these English here', might be thought to confirm Paris as the place where the discussion or lecture took place, though we have no other record of it, but the writer's Latin is not good enough to ensure that he knew the correct usage of *isti*. The reference to Sorbonne discussions in 1594 remains slightly puzzling, but the information is too specific to be doubted.

This notebook is a missing link. It connects freethinking in religion with a hint of interest in treason, and a sympathizer with Thomas Harriot and Ralegh (therefore also with Thomas Kyd and Christopher Marlowe) with Shakespeare's audience. I do not think the political meaning of the Shakespeare notes is mistakable: they are the observations of a courtier: 'he must pluck allegiance from men's hearts even in the presence of the Queen.' Whether the writer of these notes wrote them as an observer or intended to play the part he described might be a question that circumstances would decide. His beginnings of a commonplace book or his stray notes on two scenes of a play do cast light on the sharp political consciousness of Shakespeare's audiences, and so on the episode of the revival of *Richard II* on the eve of Essex's rebellion. I do not believe it is a coincidence that the writer kept the Shakespeare and the theology in the same secret notebook. When he wrote or copied the Shakespeare into one end of it, the other end already contained the dangerous record of his unorthodoxy in religion.

APPENDIX 3

The Passionate Pilgrim

This careless anthology was printed in its first form in 1599 without having been registered at the Stationers' Company: had it been registered it would presumably have been stopped. It was boldly attributed on its title-page to W. Shakespeare and it does contain some of his work. The publisher, William Jaggard, was a villain. In 1619 he printed ten quarto editions of plays, eight of them written by Shakespeare, but some of them falsely dated to 1600, some to 1608. They are linked by the watermark of their paper and by their title-pages. In May 1619 the Lord Chamberlain wrote to the Stationers' Company forbidding the printing of plays belonging to the King's Men 'without some of their consents'. The letter no doubt caused Jaggard to panic, and to pretend his new editions were old ones. Yet it was Jaggard's partner and son Isaak Jaggard who issued the First Folio edition of Shakespeare's plays in 1623, soon after his father's death. The old man had been alive when it was being printed. The Jaggards were probably used because of the scale and difficulty of the Folio. It is surely relevant that in 1621 they had produced Ralegh's *History of the World*.

The Passionate Pilgrim had a second title-page halfway through: *Sonnets to Sundry Notes of Music*. A second edition survives only in fragmentary form. The third, in 1612, had the subtitle, 'Certain Amorous Sonnets, between Venus and Adonis, newly corrected and augmented, By W. Shakespeare'. A furious reference by Thomas Heywood to the theft of nine poems from his *Troia Britannica* (1609), which was also printed by Jaggard, but now reappeared under Shakespeare's name in the 1612 *Passionate Pilgrim*, suggests that Shakespeare might take action against Jaggard; the book reappeared without Shakespeare's name on it, so we must assume that he did so.

Given such a history, the authors of individual poems in *The Passionate Pilgrim* are not always easy to identify. It begins with sonnet 138, 'When my love swears . . .', sonnet 144, 'Two loves I have . . .', and a sonnet from *Love's Labour's Lost* (act 4, scene iii). Then follows the first of four sonnets scattered here and there in the anthology about Venus and Adonis. The last of the four had already appeared in Griffin's *Fidessa* in 1596. All four seem to have been written in competition in the same form and on the same theme; they do not read like one poet's four variations on a theme. On the other hand, the last two sonnets of Shakespeare's 1609 collection are similarly related but both apparently written by Shakespeare. The second of the four Venus and Adonis sonnets draws consciously on Ovid's 'Salmacis' in the *Metamorphoses*, as Marlowe drew on Salmacis for Leander. It reads like a response to Marlowe. I am inclined to date all three of the first three sonnets to an early stage in the composition of *Venus and Adonis*, and to suspect that Shakespeare wrote 'Scarce had the sun dried up the dewy morn . . .' but not the others. Masefield suspected that Shakespeare wrote all three, though not Griffin's. It is not incredible.

After the first Adonis sonnet comes another from *Love's Labour's Lost* (act 4, scene ii). There follow three stanzas in the metre of *Venus and Adonis*, complaining about a fickle girl. Anyone might have written them; they are a song or a dramatic fragment of a lost, long poem like *A Lover's Complaint*. J. P. Collier printed some similar stanzas from a commonplace book at Hamburg, signed 'W.S.'. They could all easily come from Shakespeare's wastepaper basket when he was a young man. The next poem is a sonnet by Richard Barnfield, printed in his *Poems in divers humors* in 1598. Then a two-stanza song in *Venus and Adonis* stanzas, not good enough for Shakespeare in my opinion. The lyric 'crabbed age and youth . . .' appeared with four added stanzas in Thomas Deloney's *Garland of Goodwill* (1631). As a song and as a poem it works better as it is. Several poets and musicians could have written it; so could Shakespeare. But did he write songs that he never used in plays? Of course he could have done, but did he? It seems to me more likely than not that he did.

The next two poems are sets of stanzas as before, which might be very early wastepaper-basket verses by the great man. The *Sonnets to sundry notes of Music* follow. The first song, 'It was a lording's daughter', is not Shakespeare, though I like the end of it:

> Then, lullaby, the learned man hath got the lady gay:
> For now my song is ended.

The next one is a song from *Love's Labour* (act 4, scene iii) with two lines missing. (Even one of the *Venus and Adonis* sonnets has a line missing, supplied in an inferior version later in the century.) *Englands Helicon*, a miscellany of Elizabethan verse published in 1600, printed the same song and named Shakespeare as the author. Since it also printed the next ('My flocks feed not . . .'), but without any name but 'Ignoto', it remains anonymous. So does the next, which is a long string of *Venus and Adonis* stanzas of which other versions exist in manuscript. The anthology closes with Marlowe's 'Come live with me, and be my love', which appeared in a fuller and better state in *Englands Helicon* as 'The Passionate Shepherd to his Love', and finally 'As it fell upon a day . . .', a fine poem by Barnfield about the nightingale. This poem, unlike the others, is better here than in the shorter version in *Englands Helicon*. It contains some of my favourite lines in Elizabethan poetry:

King Pandion he is dead,
All thy friends are lapped in lead,
All thy fellow birds do sing,
Careless of thy sorrowing.

APPENDIX 4

Edmund Ironside

It was only in the last stages of writing this book that I became convinced by the forcible arguments of Eric Sams that Shakespeare might just have written *Edmund Ironside* in 1588. If he did, he was in London then, and consulting historical records on a scale no earlier dramatic writer in English had ever done. This would be his first play, banned presumably in 1589 and apparently once revived after his death, but not printed, and its projected second part never written. I reject almost none of the implications of *Edmund Ironside*'s being by Shakespeare: indeed they would fit perfectly into the skeleton of this biography and enliven it at a point where it needs enlivening. But I fell at the last ditch: the writer sounds like Shakespeare, knows what he knows, speaks as he speaks and lacks what he lacks; he is Shakespeare's twin as it were, but in the end I did not quite believe he was good enough. The comic villain Twist is not funny enough, and I thought the cruelty too cruel and the banality too banal. I understand my judgement here is purely that of a poet, and subjective, but I am unable to abandon it. If Shakespeare did not write this play, he undoubtedly knew it or others like it. Since its manuscript is written on law-ruled paper of a kind only lawyers used, and since the play uses William Lambarde's *Archaionomia* (1568) for the laws of Canute, one thinks of the Inns of Court. It is only a matter of time before someone says Bacon wrote it. But Shakespeare possessed *Archaionomia*: his copy is in the Folger Library.

There is little doubt about its date: it comes after the bombshell of Marlowe's *Tamburlaine* in 1587, which was imitated within a year by Greene (*Alphonsus*), Lodge (*The Wounds of Civill War*), Peele (*The Battle of Alcazar*) and Kyd (*The Spanish Tragedy*), and then by Shakespeare (*Henry VI*). Lodge's *Civill War* is Roman, so *Edmund Ironside* becomes the first English historical play of the type associated with Shakespeare. It comes before the episcopal wrath of 1589, when the Archbishop of Canterbury was appointed a censor by the Privy Council; he would surely have banned it, or censored it. Its fate pointed Shakespeare to the safer pagan territory of *Titus Andronicus*: we owe his Roman plays and his use of Plutarch partly to the Marprelate controversy. Sams thinks *Edmund Ironside* uses Plutarch, but it quotes some Latin, suggesting an intermediate source. Shakespeare may have played in it as a young actor: it is at least tempting to wonder if 'ye shakerag' (line 1261) is a private joke. I doubt if the chorus in act 3, scene iii is Shakespeare:

> He flies to Worcester, Edward follows him.
> The way is long and I am waxen faint.
> I fain would have you understand the truth
> and see the battles acted on the stage
> but that their length would be too tedious. . . .

The virtuoso bits of verse (cf. lines 31ff. and 2024ff). seem to me most interesting in the history of dramatic verse development, but not Shakespeare's; others may judge otherwise:

> How pleasant are these speeches to my ears
> *Aeolian* music to my dancing heart
> Ambrosian dainties to my starved maw
> Sweet-passing *Nectar* to my thirsty throat
> rare *cullises* to my sick-glutted mid. . . .

A *cullis* is an invalid broth and the text is *mid* (belly) not mind. Of course, anyone who claims something is the very earliest Shakespeare may reasonably maintain that its being bad is no argument against its authorship, providing enough connections of language can be established without subjective judgements. Dr Sams makes a strong case on many such grounds. But my impression is that Shakespeare was too intelligent and too humorous to let these lines pass. They are the sort of thing he parodied, and the sort of poetry an Elizabethan computer would have turned out, of whom there were many: 'Gravy to glide through my sick-glutted gut', or should it be 'Gilded gravy grieves my sick-glutted gut?'

Appendix 5

Hand D in Sir Thomas More

This handwriting occurs in some ill-organized revisions by several hands of a play severely treated by the censors, that is by the office of the Master of the Revels. Its identification as that of Shakespeare himself was necessarily based on the few signatures which are the most we have for certain of his writing. If the text of his will is in his own hand and not in a clerk's, that would alter the matter, but it is not certain that even the signatures to that are his autograph. Clerks did sign things for people, odd as it seems to us. If those two signatures are really his, as is very probable, then he was an ill man when he signed. That is very probable too.

Hand D was singled out as Shakespeare's by Sir E. Maunde Thompson, who was perhaps no better at Elizabethan than he was at ancient palaeography. Still, he was better than I am at both, and great men have agreed with him. Some scholars still do. My objections to his view are based firstly on physical examination. The 'W' of Hand D and its double 'l' are possible, but I do not think that he is right, and I have some doubts even about the 'W'. I am not convinced that the 'S' of Surrey is Shakespeare's 'S'. Elizabethan hands often are hard to identify, and Shakespeare's signature being so small and peculiar a sample of his writing, and anyway so variable, I would be reluctant to press my doubts and would be compelled to remain merely not quite convinced, were it not that *Sir Thomas More* is (in my view) such piffle. The verse is banal, the metrical control by no means masterly, and the sentiments of More less Shakespearean than scholars brought up in the great days of Empire used to believe.

No doubt we all see Shakespeare to some extent in our own image. My own opinion is that in spite of all its scientific and geographic expansion and the excitement of its theatre and its music, and the irrepressible vivacity of life that characterizes that age, it was also a time of deep and intolerable misery, which Shakespeare felt, and would not have betrayed. Of course he believed, and would have to make More believe, that loyalty to the Crown was best, rioting barbarous and civil war odious, but not in such naive terms. R. W. Chambers has discussed the ideas in More and compared them with Shakespeare's known ideas, but I do not agree with all of his discussion. He is convincing about Shakespeare's 'passionate advocacy of authority' being combined with 'confidence in the generosity of the common people', but he argues unsafely from Ulysses in *Troilus and*

366

Cressida, and from the feeble touches of humour in the More play. It is not his view of Shakespeare that I find distasteful, but his view of More, whom I see in this play as somewhat wooden.

It is extremely unlikely that Shakespeare would undertake part of the doomed revision of a botched play of multiple authorship in 1593 or 1594, when he was already famous. He cannot be proved ever to have done such a thing, but certainly not after he was an established writer. Yet that is the date suggested. Early in this century it was of course quite common to entertain the idea of multiple authorship in Shakespeare's own work, but the vogue is now over. One of the principal motives of the 1923 publication 'Shakespeare's Hand in the Play of Sir T. More', by Pollard, Greg, Maunde Thompson, Dover Wilson and R. W. Chambers, which revived and amplified the argument of Maunde Thompson's essay on 'Shakespeare's Handwriting' (1916), was to bring the pretension that Oxford or Derby or Bacon was the true author of Shakespeare's works 'crashing to the ground', by producing dramatic poetry in his own handwriting. The manuscript is British Library Harleian 7368: it was on show in 1986 in the King's Library, attributed to Shakespeare. Maunde Thompson had been Director and Principal Librarian of the British Museum, but the claim was first made by the liberal Roman Catholic controversialist Richard Simpson in *Notes and Queries* for July 1871. The first facsimile of the manuscript appeared only in 1910, and the play was properly edited for the Malone Society by W. W. Greg in 1911. As that wise man remarked, 'The question is one of stylistic evidence, and each reader will have to judge for himself.'

Greg identified one of the writers as Thomas Dekker and later, when Farmer produced a facsimile of a dramatic manuscript by Anthony Munday, observed at once that Munday had written most of *More*, acting partly it seems as a scribe. The Munday manuscript was bound in a leaf of the same medieval manuscript as the Thomas More play. The Munday manuscript was dated in another hand December 1596, when Munday (1560–1633) was thirty-six and Dekker in his early twenties. If December 1596 is a date of purchase and covers both books, then Dekker would be very young to be working on *Thomas More*, unless, of course, both plays are later than we think.

About most of these arguments I remain open to persuasion, but I cannot quite accept that the quality of Hand D's contribution to *Sir Thomas More* is good enough for Shakespeare after his earliest history plays. The likeness of the handwriting is undeniable, but likeness is not infrequent, and on so narrow a basis as Shakespeare's signatures it is not a demonstration of identity. My archivist friend Francis Edwards calls Hand D 'Elizabethan typewriter'. We should not be surprised to discover or rediscover old plays or contemporary plays taking a roughly similar line to his: *Edmund Ironside* (see Appendix 4) is one example, perhaps the most striking, but there are others. Shakespeare is knowable if at all by the texture of his verse, by his dramatic constructions and by the odd beauty or reality of his characters. His wisdom is a light that comes and goes, often from unexpected corners of his plays. Shakespeare is extremely funny. His poetry throws off sparks like the sparks of wit. *Sir Thomas More*, even Hand D in it, fails all these tests. I have the impression that few scholars are now sure it is genuine, but that is a lesser argument. On the other hand, I must admit to changing my mind more than once about its literary merit.

APPENDIX 6

Hoby, the Cecils and Richard II

When *Richard II* was new, Robert Cecil saw a private performance of it. Sir Edward Hoby wrote to him from a house in Canon Row, Westminster, on 7 December 1595:

> Sir, finding that you were not conveniently to be at London tomorrow night, I am bold to send to know whether Tuesday [9 December] may be any more in your grace to visit poor Canon Row, where as late as it shll please you a gate for your supper shall be open: and King Richard present himself to your view. Pardon my boldness that ever love to be honoured with your presence, neither do I importune more than your occasions may willingly assent unto; in the meantime and ever resting at your command, Ed. Hoby.

Hoby and Robert Cecil were both at Trinity College, Oxford, together, a college addicted to drama from its foundation, though on a lesser scale than Christ Church with its two tragedies and two comedies every Christmas from 1554. A letter survives from the Privy Council to the Master of the Revels on a loan of costumes to 'the new College in Oxford', including those for three kings, two dukes, a queen, a prince, 'six plumes or more if you can', six masquers and four torch bearers, for 'a learned Tragedy'. I owe these details to J. R. Elliott's article in *Oxoniensia* (1985). They represent a small beginning, but Trinity was active in staging plays throughout the century.

It was not chance that Cecil and Hoby were at Trinity together, since they were first cousins. Lord Burghley as a young man married the sister of a friend at St John's, Cambridge, not at all a powerful alliance, but she soon died and his second marriage was more careful: he married one of the three cleverest sisters in England, so that Edward Hoby, Robert Cecil and Francis Bacon were first cousins. Burghley's son by his first wife, Thomas, came to no particular good. Edward Hoby inherited a palatial house at Bisham on the Thames where the splendid family monuments have survived, including that of his mother, who died very old and had been obsessed with grand funerals, on which subject she used to pester Garter King of Arms. Edward married Lord Hunsdon's daughter in 1582; the marriage was unhappy and only his bastard Peregrine carried on the family. But his Hunsdon connection confirms the strong suspicion that his letter to Robert Cecil refers to

369

Shakespeare's *Richard II* acted by the Chamberlain's Men, including of
course Shakespeare himself. Since this is the only case where we know
about this kind of private, swiftly commissioned performance, and since
the people concerned are of some interest, I thought it worthwhile to dwell
a little on these details. Lord Burghley was a meritocrat, but his son
naturally grander; Hoby was bluer-blooded and married to the Queen's
cousin. He translated a Spanish book on the theory and practice of war,
reported to Elizabeth on Armada preparations in 1588, and sailed on the
Cadiz expedition in 1598. In 1607 he acquired the monopoly of wool-
buying in Warwickshire and Staffordshire. He also wrote some anti-papist
pamphlets, including one called 'A Countersnarl for Ishmael Rabshacheh a
Cecropidan Lycaonite'. The Hoby tombs at Bisham are of striking beauty,
particularly the obelisk with the Hunsdon swans.

William Cecil's Marriages

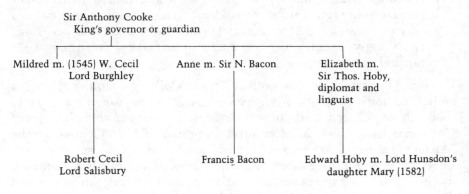

Sir Anthony Cooke
King's governor or guardian

Mildred m. (1545) W. Cecil   Anne m. Sir N. Bacon   Elizabeth m.
Lord Burghley   Sir Thos. Hoby,
                                                             diplomat and
                                                             linguist

Robert Cecil   Francis Bacon   Edward Hoby m. Lord Hunsdon's
Lord Salisbury   daughter Mary (1582)

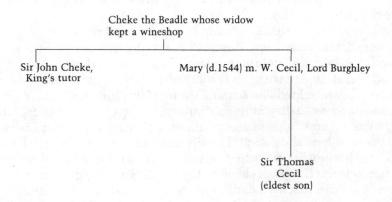

Cheke the Beadle whose widow
kept a wineshop

Sir John Cheke,   Mary (d.1544) m. W. Cecil, Lord Burghley
King's tutor

Sir Thomas
Cecil
(eldest son)

APPENDIX 7

The Derby Copy of North's Plutarch

The copy of the first edition of Sir Thomas North's translation of Plutarch's *Lives*, which belonged to Ferdinando, the fifth Earl of Derby, who may have been Shakespeare's patron, has a most interesting pedigree. William Chaderton, the Bishop of Chester and former President of Queen's College, Cambridge, gave it to Ferdinando's father Henry, the fourth Earl, probably about the time of its publication. Ferdinando's widow Alice, Countess of Derby, later gave it to someone called William, and the booksellers Pickering & Chatto, who recently handled the book, have conjectured that the William concerned might be Shakespeare (Catalogue 658). Shakespeare must have known the first edition of North's Plutarch, since he used it for *Titus Andronicus*, printed in 1594, but it may have been the second (1595) edition that so heavily influenced his later Roman plays.

After this mysterious William, who I think was very likely a member of Alice's family, the book reappears in the hands of Edward Stanley in 1611. Even if one disregards the possible or probable connection of Lady Derby and her husband with Shakespeare and discounts Shakespeare's supposed lost years in Lancashire, as I think one should, there remains the coincidence that the epitaphs in Tong church for Sir Thomas Stanley (d.1576), younger brother of the fourth Earl, first owner of this book, and of his son Edward Stanley, who died in 1632, are recorded by William Dugdale and another (manuscript) source to be by Shakespeare, and their tomb was built in Shakespeare's lifetime. A poet's verses might be used or adapted when he was dead, as in fact George Herbert's were, but a tomb and an epitaph might certainly be commissioned in one's lifetime, particularly by a son who built his father's monument at some expense, and wished to be buried with him. I accept the probability that Edward Stanley really did commission an epitaph by Shakespeare.

All the same, I do not believe that the William to whom Alice Derby gave this book, and who passed it on to Edward Stanley, was Shakespeare. Ferdinando died in 1594, and his brother William became Earl of Derby. Alice Derby quarrelled with him about money and possessions, and so he may not be the William we are looking for, but the field remains open, and the likelihood that a book possessed by two Earls of Derby, given away by Lady Derby and ending up in less than a generation in the hands of a Derby cousin, had never left the family, has a pressing claim to be accepted. Still, it remains possible, though unlikely, that Lady Derby did give this very book to Shakespeare, who would certainly have liked it, and who did use a copy so regularly that one must assume he owned one from about 1595. In that case (permitting conjecture to be built upon conjecture) one would have to consider the handwriting of the ownership inscriptions more closely. The one that could be Shakespeare's has been torn but it was italic. His generation used both italic and 'secretary hand' alternately or in various combinations. But at this stage of conjecture the possibility has become distinctly thin.

The book in question was sold in 1985 to the Shakespeare Memorial Trust, but the Pickering & Chatto catalogue is still the standard, and is likely to remain the classic exposition of the case. I am most grateful to Christopher Edwards for help about this matter. I do not think that two probabilities make a certainty, or that two cobwebs make a rope, but it must be said that Ferdinando's patronage and the Countess of Derby's entertainment at Ashby in 1607, and the tomb at Tong do to some degree confirm one another, and confirm Shakespeare's connection with this family.

The epitaphs on the Stanley tomb at Tong, which are still to be seen there, though the tomb has been moved from the north side of the chancel to the east end of the south aisle, were recorded and attributed to Shakespeare by Dugdale in his *Visitation of Shropshire* (1664) and in an earlier manuscript. E. K. Chambers discusses them quite fully (vol. 1, pp. 551ff.). Sir Edward's at least is obviously commissioned and not amateur verse, and oddly close to the style of Shakespeare. The tomb was built in the early seventeenth century to commemorate Sir Edward Stanley (1562–1603), his father Sir Thomas who died in 1576, and mother (d.1586) and his various children, living and dead. The likely date of it is about 1612.

On Sir Edward

Not monumental stones preserves our Fame,
Nor sky-aspiring Pyramids our name;
The memory of him for whom this stands
Shall outlive marble and defacers' hands:
When all to Time's consumption shall be given,
Standly for whom this stands shall stand in Heaven.

On Sir Thomas

Ask who lies here but do not weep,
He is not dead, he doth but sleep.
This stony Register is for his bones,
His fame is more perpetual than these stones,
And his own goodness with himself being gone
Shall live when Earthly monument is none.

APPENDIX 8

Paracelsus and Shakespeare

The argument I have suggested about an influence of medical theory on Shakespeare's view of the world, extending into ideas of resurrection, is advanced by some similarities in the writings of Sir Thomas Browne, whose statement of intimate belief appeared as *Religio Medici* (1642). In Section 48, on the physical indications of resurrection from the dead, his first example is the emergence of creation from chaos, and 'separation of that confused mass into its species'. He speaks of Adam's fertility and 'the magic of that sperm', of 'the artificial resurrection and revivification of Mercury', and the fact that plants can be revived and made to flourish from their ashes: 'to a sensible Artist the forms are not perished'. My attention was drawn to the parallel with Shakespeare's last comedies by a remark of Coleridge, who thought it a crazy notion picked up by Shakespeare from Paracelsus.

But there is more. In the second paragraph of the first chapter of his *Garden of Cyrus* (1658), Thomas Browne points to an explanation that pleased him of a difficulty of the story of creation in Genesis. He thought Paradise was planted on the third day of creation: that the earth in fact was created full of seeds, which then began to grow. 'Gardens were before gardeners, and but some hours after the earth.' This makes gardens older than medicine or botany. 'For though Physic may plead high, from that medical act of God, in casting so deep a sleep upon our first Parent; and Chirurgery find its whole art, in that one passage concerning the Rib of *Adam*, yet there is no rivalry with garden contrivance and herbery.' The 'medical act of God' in sending Adam to sleep is very like the medical acts of Cerimon in *Pericles*, of the doctor who cures Lear, and of other dramatic devices in which Shakespeare in the last phase of his work in the theatre delights.

I take it that the interlinked family of ideas about creation, restoration and medicine that Shakespeare and Sir Thomas Browne have in common was not alchemical, though the ideas extended into chemistry and so into alchemy; they were not precisely theological ideas but rather a theory of nature, and perhaps coloured as much by Jewish as by Christian discussion of Genesis. Thomas Browne is interested in pagan parallels to Genesis, but Shakespeare is not, at least in this context. His theory of nature is outside the framework of Genesis; it is rooted in the arguments of an interpreter,

373

not in the text itself. 'Great creating nature' has priority over medicine, over astrology, and over human systems of thought. I think this indicates Paracelsus.

There is another even stranger piece of medical background to late Shakespeare. The parts of a disease, 'beginning, increase, full state and decline', were very commonly, almost proverbially likened to those of a play. This was how comedy was thought to imitate life. The intoxicating and erudite T. W. Baldwin, in Chapter 15 of his *Shakespeare's Five Act Structure*, gathers examples including Erasmus, Quintilian and the Winchester master Christopher Johnson (1565). Lear's disease and restoration, and the purging of Leontes and resurrection of Hermione in *The Winter's Tale* seem to mirror the division, or rather the progression of the disease, as if the play were a fever chart, a case history.

APPENDIX 9

Tom o' Bedlam's Song

This song was treated by Robert Graves in *The English Ballad* (1927) as 'Loving Mad Tom' (p. 102). It was first printed in Giles Earle's *Song Book* (1615) but Graves printed a version selected from numerous variants. He later devoted a separate short book to the subject, which I have read many times and used to possess, but the Bodleian Library has no copy and I have not found one anywhere. In it, Graves suggests Shakespeare as the original author, and *King Lear* as the occasion, observing that there were earlier versions as well as later ones. The argument is to be found in an enlarged version of the 1927 essay, first in his *Common Asphodel* (1949) and again in his *Crowning Privilege* (1955), with plentiful versions of the text.

> From the hag and hungry goblin
> That into rags would rend ye,
>> The spirits that stand
>> By the naked man
> In the book of Moons, defend ye,
> That of your five sound senses
> You never be forsaken,
>> Nor wander from
>> Yourselves with Tom
> Abroad to beg your bacon.
>
> When I short have shorn my sow's face
> And swigged my horny barrel,
>> In an oaken inn
>> I pound my skin
> As a suit of gilt apparel.
> While I sing, 'Any food, any feeding,
> Feeding, drink, or clothing?
>> Come, dame or maid,
>> Be not afraid,
> Poor Tom will injure nothing.'

Of thirty bare years have I
Twice twenty been enraged,
    And of forty been
    Three times fifteen
In durance soundly caged,
On the lordly lofts of Bedlam,
With stubble soft and dainty,
    Brave bracelets strong,
    Sweet whips, ding-dong,
With wholesome hunger plenty.

The Moon's my constant mistress
And the lonely owl my marrow.
    The flaming drake
    And the nightcrow make
Me music to my sorrow.
I slept not since the Conquest,
Till then I never waked,
    Till the roguish fay
    Of love where I lay
Me found and stript me naked.

I know more than Apollo,
For oft, when he lies sleeping,
    I see the stars
    At bloody wars
And the wounded welkin weeping,
The moon embrace her shepherd,
And the queen of love her warrior,
    While the first doth horn
    The star of the morn,
And the next the heavenly farrier.

The gipsies Snap and Pedro
Are none of Tom's comradoes;
    The punk I scorn
    And the cutpurse sworn,
And the roaring-boys' bravadoes;
The meek, the white, the gentle
Me handle, touch, and spare not,
    But those that cross
    Tom Rhinoceros
Do what the panther dare not.

With an host of furious fancies,
Whereof I am commander,
    With a burning spear
    And a horse of air
To the wilderness I wander;
By a knight of ghosts and shadows
I summoned am to tourney
    Ten leagues beyond
    The wide world's end –
Methinks it is no journey.

I'll bark against the dogstar,
And crow away the morning;
    I'll chase the moon
    Till it be noon,
And I'll make her leave her horning.
But I will find bonny Maud, merry mad Maud,
I'll seek whate'er betides her,
    And I will love
    Beneath or above
That dirty earth that hides her.

APPENDIX 10

Fire at the Globe

The ballad on the Globe fire that survives was printed in 1816. Peter Beal republished the manuscript version from the collection of John Hopkinson (1610–80), now in the Yorkshire County Archives at Bradford, in the *Times Literary Supplement*, 20 June 1986. There were two ballads registered for printing, but no printed copy of either has survived. The Bradford manuscript was written down by 1641, but it contains some obvious errors which I have corrected. I have also modernized its spelling.

> Now sit thee down Melpomene
> Wrapt in a sea-coal robe,
> And tell the doleful tragedy
> That late was play'd at Globe,
> For no man that can sing and say
> Was scarred on St Peter's day.
> Oh sorrow, pitiful sorrow,
> And yet all this is true.
>
> All you that please to understand,
> Come listen to my story,
> To see death with his raking brand
> Mongst such an auditory,
> Regarding neither Cardinal's might
> Nor rugged face of Henry the Eight.
> Oh sorrow . . .
>
> This fearful fire began above,
> A wonder strange and true,
> And to the stage-house did remove
> As round as tailor's clew,
> And burned down both bean and snag
> And did not spare the silken flag.
> Oh sorrow . . .
>
> Out run the Knights, out run the Lords,
> And there was great ado:
> Some lost their hats and some their swords,
> Then out ran Burbage too:

The reprobates, though drunk on Monday,
Pray'd for the fool and Henry Condy.
Oh sorrow . . .

The periwigs and drumheads fry
Like to a butter firkin,
A woeful burning did betide
To many a good buff jerkin,
Then with swoll'n eyes like drunken Fleming
Distressed stood old stuttering Heming.
Oh sorrow . . .

No shower his rain did there down force
In all that sunshine weather,
To save that great-renowned house,
Nor thee O alehouse neither:
Had it begun below sans doubt
Their wives for fear had piss'd it out.
Oh sorrow . . .

Be warned you stage strutters all,
Lest you again be catched,
And such another burning fall
On them whose house is thatched:
Forbear your whoring breeding biles,
And lay up that expense for tales.
Oh sorrow . . .

Go draw you a petition,
And do you not abhor it,
And get with low submission
A licence to beg for it,
In churches sans churchwardens' checks
In Surrey and in Middlesex.
Oh sorrow, pitiful sorrow
And yet all this is true.

Peter Beal gives very full information about what is known of the fire, though by the time this book is printed more still may be known, since archaeologists began work on the site in March 1987. The second Globe was shut down by the Puritans in 1642, and destroyed to build tenement houses in 1644 by Sir Matthew Brand. Beal notes that Henry Bluett, in a letter to his uncle five days after the burning in 1613, says that the play was a new one that had not been acted more than two or three times before.

APPENDIX 11

Shakespeare's Biographers and Critics

There are numerous jokes and legends about Shakespeare that began to circulate in his lifetime or soon after, and persons of antiquarian, scholarly or romantic curiosity began to visit Stratford when at least the end of his life was still within living memory. One particularly vigorous branch of traditional gossip was transmitted through William Davenant and other theatrical people to the theatre of the Restoration, and so to Dryden and to Pope. Dryden knew also through John Hales of Eton (1584–1656) the Stuart Court opinion of Shakespeare. Another was associated with Ben Jonson. The entire subject has been fully treated by Samuel Schoenbaum in *Shakespeare's Lives*, a very amusing and very thorough study, and by F. E. Halliday in his *Cult of Shakespeare*, an equally surprising and delightful book. All that I wish to do here is to underline a few conclusions that are important to biographers.

First of all, there is no reason whatsoever to suspect that anyone but Shakespeare wrote the plays and poems. He is named as a writer of plays in the records of Court expenses, and named as a poet by John Marston in the manuscript of Lady Derby's ceremony (see Appendix 1). He published poems under his own name, his fellow actors knew him as a writer, and Ben Jonson recognized him as a great writer. Contrary theories depend to various degrees on snobbery, perversity and the mania for decoding which is so often combined with touches of megalomaniac self-importance. Since I believe this to be the sober truth, I hope I may say it without offence. The Bacon theory was dreamed up by a dotty lady visitor and by a cuckoo vicar of Barton on the Heath. Shakespeare's education, if it was the normal one for his time and class, was adequate to make him a poet or a great poet; he learned to be a dramatist in the theatre.

I have not retailed all the jokes and Jonson encounters, because the tradition of such stories is so often unreliable, but any interested reader may find them in the reference books I have listed. But I do take seriously the information available to John Aubrey. He understood Shakespeare's supreme importance, as one may see from the circle of laurel he drew beside his notes, and he spoke to old William Beeston the actor, the son of Christopher Beeston who belonged to the Chamberlain's Men in 1598, and acted with Shakespeare in Jonson's *Every Man in his Humour*. Christopher Beeston built the Phoenix, his own theatre, in the year following

Shakespeare's death, and died himself in 1638, but William lived on until 1682. The Beestons lived in Shoreditch, where they were Shakespeare's neighbours. It was old William Beeston who told Aubrey that 'he understood Latin pretty well: for he had been in his younger years a schoolmaster in the country.' This last item could be hearsay. He also remarked that Shakespeare was 'the more to be admired [because] he was not a company keeper: lived in Shoreditch, wouldn't be debauched, and if invited to, writ he was in pain.'

Schoenbaum has dealt with the more extravagant foliage of Shakespeare mythology, which he has severely lopped. The growth of criticism and scholarship begins with the First Folio, and the work of Shakespeare's friends and fellows Heminges and Condell. His reputation was rather precisely described by Leonard Digges, his executor's stepson and obviously his fan and friend, in 1623 in the Folio and at greater length in the poems of 1640. The Folio included tributes by Ben Jonson, by Hugh Holland the traveller, a poet of Jonson's circle and almost certainly of Shakespeare's, and 'I.M.', almost certainly James Mabbe of Magdalen College, Oxford, friend of Digges and therefore at least an admiring acquaintance of Shakespeare's. Digges was living at University College while Mabbe was at Magdalen. Both were devoted to Spanish literature. Balliol College library has a copy of the *Rimas* of Lope de Vega in which Digges writes to a friend on the fly-leaf, referring to 'Mr. Mab', and comparing the poems to Shakespeare's Sonnets. Hugh Holland was devoted to music as well as to poetry; Camden thought highly of him. He is discussed by Guiney in her *Recusant Poets*. Another Welshman, probably Sir Henry Salisbury, who also knew Holland, wrote another verse tribute addressed to Heminges and Condell, but it is not very good and remained unpublished until modern times. Milton's famous sonnet first appeared in the 1632 Folio: in 1623 he was only fifteen. The incisive prose opinion in *Theatrum Poetarum* (1675), by Milton's nephew Edward Phillips, sounds to me, as it did to Malone and Warton, as if Milton composed it.

... such a Maker, that though some others may perhaps pretend to a more exact *Decorum* and *oeconomie*, especially in Tragedy, never any express't a more lofty and Tragic heighth; never any represented nature more purely to the life, and where the polishments of Art are most wanting, as probably his learning was not extraordinary, he pleaseth with a certain wild and native Elegance; and in all his Writings hath an unvulgar style, as well in his *Venus and Adonis*, his *Rape of Lucrece* and other various poems as in his Dramatics.

The tone of this criticism and of Milton's verse allusions to Shakespeare really derives I think from Ben Jonson, and it persisted into the eighteenth century. Only Lady Newcastle (*Sociable Letters*, 1664, letter 123) took a line of her own, praising him mostly for his precise characterization, even of women. The first serious attempt at a biography came with Rowe's edition in 1709, though today it has only antiquarian value. The growth of biography both as an art and as a branch of historical science is oddly bound up with Shakespeare, its most difficult subject. William Oldys the antiquary (1696–1761) attempted Ralegh, but the first great success in the area of English literary biography was reserved for the life of Dryden by Dr Johnson's friend Edmond Malone, the Irish barrister. It was Malone who guided Boswell's steps towards his *Life of Samuel Johnson*, and Boswell's son who produced the vast unfinished heap of Malone's Shakespeare material in 1821 after Malone's death. Early Victorian science in many of its branches concentrated on the accumulation and the classification of huge collections, on which later conclusions have been based.

That is certainly true of the Shakespeare industry. Many of the most interesting and sensitive emendations of the text used once to be made by poets, like Dr Johnson and Alexander Pope, though no poet is an infallible textual critic. Housman made an excellent emendation in the Sonnets, and more recent poets have had important critical insights, but since W. Greg's contributions to the bibliographical and typographical aspect of Shakespeare scholarship, textual scholarship has become a forest unsafe for amateurs. The same thing became true of the scientific aspect of Shakespeare biography soon after Malone. It is the archive-readers who slowly and steadily accumulate the telling truths. The process is by no means over, as the careers of A. L. Rowse and of L. Hotson demonstrate. The most uncontrollable mass of material was unearthed by J. O. Halliwell-Phillipps (1820–89), not only in books and in an impossibly huge edition, but in a snowstorm of privately printed pamphlets, not all of which are now easy to find. His biography in the *Dictionary of National Biography* makes alarming and fascinating reading. My impression of those of his works I have read has been that not all of his scholarship has been distilled into the later scholarly literature. There are crumbs and tatters of evidence for this and that in the life of Shakespeare that lurk forgotten in the pages of Halliwell-Phillipps, as they do in those of his less reliable contemporary J. P. Collier (1789–1883).

And yet an attempt must sometimes be made to digest both the old and the new material between the covers of one book, and having laid the ascertainable facts side by side in chronological order, to see what they suggest. In this century, the notoriously unpromising dryness of the documentary truths about Shakespeare and the increasing specialization of criticism have determined that the plays and the life are usually treated separately, even within one book. Yet the whole point of writing a biography of Shakespeare at all is to try to relate his life to his writings and his writings to his life. I have not discovered an older biography better than Sidney Lee's, for all its faults, or a modern one better than Rowse's, though Masefield's pithy and brilliant *William Shakespeare* (1911) deserves honourable mention. It was a paperback by F. E. Halliday that first convinced me many years ago that the life might still cast light on the works. Research into the life of Shakespeare is inevitably research at the same time into the history of such researches. I have been astounded to discover the enormous quantity and very high quality of the work done on him in the last forty years. Some of this work gets lost: Orwell's essay on Tolstoy's view of *Lear* is not read as much as it deserves, nor are the Shakespeare essays of Yeats. In every direction it appears that substantial progress can still be made, but the ramification of these studies has now gone so far that it has become difficult for one person to master all the material. All that a writer like myself who is not a professional Shakespearean can hope to do is to offer a fresh, partial point of view, prolegomena, a few new or unregarded crumbs for the general pile, a first step for someone younger who may just be starting. Even from the textual point of view, neither the great Cambridge edition of the 1860s nor the Oxford edition of the 1980s is perfect.

It is impossible to rob Shakespeare of his mystery. But at the moment most serious scholars of his life seem to think him rather elusive than mysterious. Schoenbaum's gentle ironies have been expended on the withering away of nonsense, but what we do securely know about Shakespeare, and it is much more than one might imagine, may make a less strong impression. Schoenbaum is a writer of admirable lucidity and extraordinary scholarly acumen: he has cleared away a wilderness. But it would be a great pity if his inevitably negative influence on conjecture were to check conjectures that might usefully be tested, or to lead younger scholars to suppose whatever is knowable is now known, all evidence having been sifted. The chaos of a hundred years ago would be preferable to that. Shakespeare's mystery is in his works, not in his biography. The aspiring biographer should begin by reading and rereading (and seeing) the works many times over, and then settle down to picking off small, identifiable problems of the life, one by one, like Malone and Halliwell-Phillipps and E. K. Chambers.

In observing the behaviour and ideals of earlier critics and scholars I have been forced to examine my own. Why write about him? If he is not to me the radiant rational genius that Pope loved, the romantic or the national poet of later centuries, the Elizabethan hero or the poet of eternal England that he once was, why write about him? Because he is the most enjoyable and greatest poet I have ever read, and the most interesting, because he can do more in poetry with a little finger than I can in a lifetime, because of his exhilarating unevenness, and exemplary mixture of concentration and carelessness, his images, his phrases, his characters and his dramatic contradictions. One is curious about the original background of such a man, and as one becomes older one gets curious about the effect of his poetry on his life. Sidney Lee was originally named Solomon, his first

Shakespeare essay was about Shylock, and he had an obituary in the *Jewish Chronicle*. For all I know to the contrary, he may be a remote cousin of mine. It is possible to see his motive in adopting Shakespeare and Queen Victoria for his subjects as an outsider's identification with the core of Englishness. I feel myself to be formally, though not really, an outsider. I do not think the Shakespeare I cultivate is wholly in my own image. Something close to worship of Shakespeare and a profound curiosity about him arise from the qualities of his poetry and from his own nature: that is all one can say.

Bibliography

STANDARD BOOKS

Aubrey, J., *Miscellanies* (1857)
  Brief Lives (ed. Barber, 1975)
Auden, W. H., *The Dyer's Hand* (1963)
Baldwin, T. W., *Shakespeare's Five Act Structure* (1963)
Barton, A., *Ben Jonson, Dramatist* (1984)
Bloom, J. H., *Shakespeare's Church* (1902)
Boas, F. S., *Shakespeare and his Predecessors* (1940 edition)
Bradbrook, M. C., *The School of Night* (1936)
  Shakespeare, the Poet in his World (1978)
Brinkworth, E. R. C., *New Light on the Life of Shakespeare* (1975)
Bush, D., *English Literature in the Earlier Seventeenth Century* (1966)
Chambers, E. K. *William Shakespeare: A Study of Facts and Problems* (1930)
  Sources for a Biography of William Shakespeare (1946)
Coghill, N., *Shakespeare's Professional Skills* (1964)
Devlin, C., *Life of Robert Southwell* (1956)
  Hamlet's Divinity (1963)
Eccles, M., *Shakespeare in Warwickshire* (1961)
Empson, W., *Essays on Shakespeare* (1986)
Freeman, R., *English Emblem Books* (1970)
Fripp, E. I., *Shakespeare's Stratford* (1928)
  Shakespeare Man and Artist (1938)
  (ed.) *Stratford Records* (various dates)
Greg, W., *Elizabethan and Jacobean Quartos* (1922–6)
Guiney, L. I. (ed.), *Recusant Poets* (1938)
Gurr, A., *Essays in Criticism* (1971)
Halliday, F. E., *Shakespeare* (1956; newly illustrated edition 1986)
  The Cult of Shakespeare (1957)
  The Life of Shakespeare (1961)
Halliwell-Phillipps, J. O., *Illustrations of the Life of Shakespeare* (1874)
  Outlines of the Life of Shakespeare (1887)
Hewins, A. (ed.), *The Dillen* (1981)

HMSO, *Shakespeare in the Public Records* (1985)

Holmes, M., *Shakespeare and his Players* (1972)

Honigmann, E. A. J., *Shakespeare: The Lost Years* (1985)

Hotson, L., *Shakespeare versus Shallow* (1931)
  I, William Shakespeare do appoint Thomas Russell (1937)

Johnson, Samuel, *The Plays of William Shakespeare* (1765)

Jones, E., *The Origins of Shakespeare* (1977)

Joseph, H., *John Hall* (1976)

Latham, M. W., *The Elizabethan Fairies* (1930)

Lea, K. M., *Italian Popular Comedy* (1962)

Lee, Sir Sidney, *A Life of William Shakespeare* (1898; revised edition 1915)

Lewis, C. S., *English Literature in the Sixteenth Century Excluding Drama* (1954)

Long, J. H., *Shakespeare's Use of Music (Histories and Tragedies)* (1971)

Muir, K., and Schoenbaum, S. (eds), *New Companion to Shakespeare Studies* (1971)

Nichol Smith, D., *Shakespeare Criticism* (1932)

Noble, R., *Shakespeare's Use of Song* (1923)

Parry, G., *The Golden Age Restor'd: The Culture of the Stuart Court* (1981)

Pollard, A. W., *et al.*, *Shakespeare's Hand in Sir Thomas More* (1923)

Raleigh, W., *Shakespeare* (1907)

Ralli, A., *History of Shakespeare Criticism* (1932)

Rowse, A. L., *The England of Elizabeth* (1950)
  William Shakespeare: A Biography (1963)
  The Elizabethan Renaissance (1971–2)
  Shakespeare the Man (1973 and 1988)
  Simon Forman (1974)
  Prefaces to Shakespeare's Plays (1981)

Russell, J., *Shakespeare's Country* (1942)

Saintsbury, G., *History of Elizabethan Literature* (1887)

Sams, E. (ed.), *Shakespeare's Edmund Ironside* (1986)

Schoenbaum, S., *Shakespeare's Lives* (1970)
  William Shakespeare: A Documentary Life (1975)
  William Shakespeare: A Compact Documentary Life (1977)
  Shakespeare and Others (1984)

Selden, J., *Table Talk* (1927)

Sternfeld, F. W., *Music in Shakespeare's Tragedies* (1967)

Trevor Davies, R., *Four Centuries of Witch Beliefs* (1947)

Trevor-Roper, H., *Renaissance Essays* (1985)

Tucker Brooke, C. F. (ed.), *The Shakespeare Apocrypha* (1908)
  Shakespeare of Stratford (1926)

Urkowitz, S., *Shakespeare's Revision of Lear* (1980)

Wilson, F. P., *The Plague in Shakespeare's London* (1927)

Yates, F., *Occult Philosophy in the Elizabethan Age* (1979)
  Collected Essays, vol. 2: Renaissance and Reform (1983)
Young, W., *History of Dulwich College* (1889)

The Oxford *Complete Works of Shakespeare* (1986–7) appeared too late for me to consult its essential volume of textual notes. The introduction to its *Textual Companion* (1988) is a full and balanced survey of Shakespeare studies.

Keene, D., *Cheapside Before the Great Fire* (1985), and Scouloudi, I., *Returns of Strangers in the Metropolis* (1985), were publicly noticed too recently for me to consult them as I would have wished. I would also have wished to use David Wills, *Shakespeare's Clown* (1987), on Armin in multiple clown scenes, Alan Young's *Tudor and Jacobean Tournaments* (1987) and Roland Wymer's *Suicide and Despair in the Jacobean Drama* (1986).

GENERAL REFERENCE

The Arden Shakespeare
The London Shakespeare
Bartlett, J., *A Complete Concordance to Shakespeare* (1966)
Bullough, G. (ed.), *Narrative and Dramatic Sources of Shakespeare* (8 vols, 1957–65)
Chambers, E. K. (ed.), *Shakespeare Allusion Book* (1932)
Ditchfield, P. H., *Shakespeare's England* (1917)
Views of the Past (British Library Exhibition Catalogue, 1987)
Shakespeare Survey (annual since 1948)
Cambridge Bibliography of English Literature (1940)
The Dictionary of National Biography
The New Grove Dictionary of Music (1980)
Victoria County History of Warwickshire

Index

compiled by the author

Picture Acknowledgements

The publishers wish to thank all private owners, museums, galleries and other institutions for permission to reproduce the illustrations, as follows:

The Shakespeare coat of arms, page 1, from a painting by F. Booth, Herald Painter at the College of Arms, under the direction of J. P. Brooke-Little, CVO, Norroy and Ulster King of Arms. British Library: 2, 3, 10 below right. Reproduced by permission of the Marquess of Bath, Longleat House, Warminster, Wiltshire: 8. In the collection of the Duke of Buccleuch, Boughton House, Northamptonshire: 13 above. Reproduced by permission of the Governors of Dulwich Picture Gallery: 12 above left, above right, below left. Reproduced by permission of the Folger Shakespeare Library: 9. Fotomas Index: 7 below, 10 above left, below left, 11. A. F. Kersting: 14, 15, 16. The Methuen Collection, Corsham Court, Chippenham, Wiltshire: 13 below. The National Portrait Gallery, London: 4, 5, 6, 12 below right. Endpapers: Allegorical map of Warwickshire from Michael Drayton's *Polyolbion*, 1612, British Library. The publishers have endeavoured to acknowledge all known persons and collections holding copyright or reproduction rights for the illustrations in this book.

The family trees (pages xi–xiii) are based on those in E. K. Chambers' *William Shakespeare* (1930).